SOUTHWEST FRANCE

the collected traveler

MUSEE MAILLOL
FONDATION DINA VIERNY
59-61 rue de Grenelle 75007 PARIS
TARIF REDUIT

Also in the series by Barrie Kerper

CENTRAL ITALY
The Collected Traveler

PARIS
The Collected Traveler

PROVENCE
The Collected Traveler

MOROCCO
The Collected Traveler

VENICE
The Collected Traveler

NORTHERN SPAIN
The Collected Traveler

SOUTHWEST
FRANCE

the collected traveler

Selected by Barrie Kerper
New York

First Edition

Library of Congress Cataloging-in-Publication Data is available upon request

ISBN 1-4000-5004–9

Design by Lynne Amft

Cover photos: Digital Vision/Getty Images (Roussillon), Michael Storrings/PhotoDisc/Getty Images (fleur-de-lis pattern)

Because many of the essays that appear in this book were originally published some years ago, prices, hours, and contact information may have changed, and Fodor's cannot accept responsibility for facts that are outdated or for inadvertent errors or omissions. So always confirm information when it matters, especially if you're making a detour to visit a specific place.

Special Sales

Titles in the Collected Traveler series, as well as all other Fodor's Travel Publications, are available at special discounts for bulk purchases for sales promotions or premiums. For more information, contact your local bookseller or write to Special Markets, Fodor's Travel Publications, 1745 Broadway, New York, NY 10019. Inquiries for Canada should be directed to your local Canadian bookseller or sent to Random House of Canada, Ltd., Marketing Department, 2775 Matheson Boulevard East, Mississauga, Ontario L4W 4P7. Inquiries from the United Kingdom should be sent to Fodor's Travel Publications, 20 Vauxhall Bridge Road, London SW1V 2SA, England.

PRINTED IN THE UNITED STATES OF AMERICA

10 9 8 7 6 5 4 3 2 1

dedication

*Once again, for my mother, Phyllis, who always
believed my boxes of files held something of
value, and in loving memory of my father, Peter,
who considered visiting Paris and the landing
beaches of Normandy two of life's requirements
but never had the opportunity to visit France's
southwest.*

*And for Pierre Tomasi, geologist and a former
mayor of Rodez, and his lovely wife, Catharine,
whose knowledge of and passion for the southwest is unsurpassed.*

acknowledgments

I have been most fortunate that such a dedicated team of people has worked on producing the books in this series, both at the Crown Publishing Group, where the books were first launched, and at Fodor's Travel Publications, where a new team of publishing professionals has enthusiastically embraced the books. I remain indebted to Lynne Amft, Shaye Areheart, Amy Boorstein, Becky Cabaza, Whitney Cookman, Joan DeMayo, Jill Flaxman, Bette Graber, Teryn Johnson, Doug Jones, Mark McCauslin, Derek McNally, Philip Patrick, Tim Roethgen, Andrea Rosen, and Max Werner: Thank you for the first six books! Early thanks to my new team at Fodor's, including Chuck Bloodgood, Kathy Burke, Karen Cure, Denise DeGennaro, Ensley Eikenburg, Paul Eisenberg, Jane Glennon, Fabrizio LaRocca, Linda Schmidt, Robert Shields, and Liri Sofia: I am still pinching myself that I am now working with the best folks in the travel-book publishing business! Special thanks are due to Bonnie Ammer and Alison Gross, also in the Fodor's family, who were the first two colleagues with whom I shared my idea for this series nine years ago. I am most appreciative of the assistance of three hardworking interns, Emily Korn, Mai Bui-Duy, and Wing Mai Sang, who willingly researched and verified hundreds of facts and figures, and approached every assignment with zeal. Everyone at the Maison de la France office in New York has been helpful, kind, and enthusiastic on every occasion that I've visited or called, but special thanks must go to Marion Fourestier and Jana Kravitz, who introduced me to a number of southwest enthusiasts on both sides of the Atlantic, notably the vivacious Elfie Majoie of DMI Tours, who came through at the last minute with a number of photographs featured in this book. Sincere thanks also to Jim Falkner at Air France, and to Kimberly Beer, who researched and wrote some of the practical-information entries even though she has a consuming, full-time job in subsidiary rights. I sincerely thank each of the individual writers, agents, and permissions representatives for various publishers and periodicals without whose cooperation and understanding there would be nothing to publish. My heartfelt thanks go to Luc and Lorraine Paillard, and Pierre and Catharine Tomasi, for their hospitality and *les repas délicieux* from their respective kitchens in Gourdon and Rodez. My friend and colleague Amy Myer deserves particular thanks for agreeing to join me and my then three-year-old daughter for a week's driving trip to various corners of the southwest—I wish she had not departed before I was stuck in the Toulouse parking garage, but I sure am glad she was there for the hike up Quéribus. I am deeply grateful to Chip Gibson, my wonderful boss who is without doubt one of the world's legendary leaders. Finally, thanks to my husband, Jeffrey, and our daughter, Alyssa, who still asks to return to the southwest even though she was sick three times on the flight from Paris to Bordeaux.

contents

Le Petit Train de Rocamadour

★ **GRATUIT** ★

Imprimerie Gramatoise - 05 65 33 12 56

№ 015276

The Dordogne and the Lot

Corners of the Midi-Pyrenees

Languedoc-Roussillon

Flavors and Tables of the Southwest

Good Things, Favorite Places

Introduction

"A traveller without knowledge is a bird without wings."
—Sa'dì, *Gulistan* (1258)

Some years ago my husband and I fulfilled a dream we'd had since we first met: we put all our belongings in storage and traveled around the countries bordering the Mediterranean Sea for a year. In preparation for this journey, I did what I always do in advance of a trip, which is to consult my home archives, a library of books and periodicals. I have been an obsessive clipper since I was very young, and by the time I was preparing for this extended journey, I had amassed an enormous number of articles from periodicals on various countries of the world. After a year of reading and organizing all this material, I then created a package of articles and notes for each destination and mailed them ahead to friends we'd be staying with as well as appropriate American Express offices—although we had no schedule to speak of, we knew we would spend no less than six weeks in each place.

My husband wasted no time informing me that my research efforts were perhaps a bit over the top. He shares my passion for travel (my mother-in-law told me that when he was little, he would announce to the family exactly how many months, weeks, days, hours, minutes, and seconds were left before the annual summer vacation) but not necessarily for clipping. (He has accused me of being too much like the anal-retentive fisherman from an old

Saturday Night Live skit, the one where the guy neatly puts his bait, extra line, snacks, hand towels, and so on into individual sandwich bags. In my defense, I'm not *quite* that bad, although I *am* guilty of trying to improve upon pocket organizers, and I do have a wooden rack for drying rinsed plastic bags in my kitchen.

While we were traveling that year, we would occasionally meet other Americans, and I was continually amazed at how ill-prepared some of them were. Information, in so many different forms, is in such abundance in the twenty-first century that it was nearly inconceivable to me that people had not taken advantage of the resources available to them. Some people we met didn't even seem to be having a very good time; they appeared to be ignorant of various customs and observances and were generally unimpressed with their experience because they had missed the significance of what they were seeing and doing. Therefore I was surprised again when some of these same people—and they were of varying ages with varying wallet sizes—were genuinely interested in my little packages of notes and articles. Some people even offered to *pay* me for them, and I began to think that my collected research would perhaps appeal to other travelers. I also realized that even the most well-intentioned people could be overwhelmed by the details of organizing a trip or may not have the time to put it all together. Later friends and colleagues told me they really appreciated the packages I prepared for them, and somewhere along the line I was being referred to as a "modern day hunter-gatherer," a sort of "one-stop information source." Each book in the *Collected Traveler* series provides resources and information to travelers—people I define as inquisitive, individualistic, and indefatigable in their eagerness to explore—or informs them of where they may look further to find it.

While there is much to be said for a freewheeling approach to travel—I am not an advocate of sticking to rigid schedules—I do believe that, as with most things in life, what you get out of a trip is equal only to what you put into it. James Pope-Hennessy, in his wonderful book *Aspects of Provence,* notes that "if one is to get best value out of places visited, some skeletal knowledge of their history is necessary. . . . Sight-seeing is by no means the only object of a journey, but it is as unintelligent as it is lazy not to equip ourselves to understand the sights we see." Distinguished military historian Stephen Ambrose, before his passing in 2002, reminded us in his last work, *To America,* that "it is through history that we learn who we are and how we got that way, why and how we changed, why the good sometimes prevailed and sometimes did not." He also noted that "the last five letters of the word 'history' tell us that it is an account of the past that is about people and what they did, which is what makes it the most fascinating of subjects." I feel that learning about a place is part of the excitement of travel, and I wouldn't dream of venturing anywhere without first poring over a mountain of maps, books, and periodicals. I include cookbooks in my reading (some cookbooks reveal much historical detail as well as prepare you for the food and drink you will most likely encounter), and before I leave I also like to watch movies that have something to do with where I'm going. Additionally, I buy a blank journal and fill it with all sorts of notes, reminders, and entire passages from books I'm not bringing along. In other words, I completely immerse myself in my destination before I leave. It's the most enjoyable homework assignment I could ever give myself.

Every destination, new or familiar, merits some attention. I don't endorse the extreme—spending all your time in a hotel room reading books—but it most definitely pays to know something about your destination before you go. Even if you've previously traveled to the southwestern corner of France for pleasure, you still have to do some planning to get there; and if you've traveled there before on business, you still have to keep up with what's happening in the cities and towns where you meet clients. So the way I see it, you might as well read and learn a little more. The reward for your efforts is that you'll acquire a deeper understanding and appreciation of the place and the people who live there, and not surprisingly, you'll have more fun.

"Every land has its own special rhythm, and unless the traveler takes the time to learn the rhythm, he or she will remain an outsider there always."
—Juliette De Baircli Levy, English writer, b. 1937

Occasionally I meet people who are more interested in how many countries I've been to than in those I might know well or particularly like. If *well-traveled* is defined only by the number of places I've been, then I suppose I'm not. But I feel I *really know* and have *really seen* the places I've visited, which is how *I* define *well-traveled*. I travel to see how people live in other parts of the world—not to check countries off a list—and doing that requires immediately adapting to the local pace and rhythm and (hopefully) sticking around for more than a few days. Certainly any place you decide is worthy of your time and effort is worthy of more than a day, but you don't always need an indefinite period of time to immerse yourself in the local culture or establish a routine that allows you to get to know the merchants and residents of your adopted neighborhood. Alain de Botton, in *The Art of Travel*, notes that John Ruskin, from an early age, "was unusually alive to the smallest features of the visual world." Ruskin was apparently distressed by how seldom people noticed the small details of everyday life. "He deplored the blindness and haste of modern tourists, especially those who prided themselves on covering Europe in a week by train (a service first offered by Thomas Cook in 1862): 'No changing of place at a hundred miles an hour will make us one whit stronger, happier, or wiser. There was always more in the world than men could see, walked they ever so slowly; they will see it no better for going fast. The really precious things are thought and sight, not pace.'"

One of the fastest ways to adjust to daily life in France, wherever you are, is to abandon whatever schedule you observe at home and eat when the French eat. Mealtimes in France are generally well established, with some variation as one travels from north to south. (Due to the warmer climate in the South, notably in the summer months, people start their day a bit earlier, take a longer *sieste*, and eat dinner later.) You need to be sure to buy provisions for a picnic or find a place to eat by one o'clock, because the restaurants will be full (or the day's specials completely finished) and the shops closed. Likewise, dinner is not typically served at six—an hour that is entirely too early for anyone in a Mediterranean country to contemplate eating a meal. Yvonne Lenard, in her delightful book *The Magic of Provence,* expresses this well in writing that residents and visitors alike must learn inflexible rules: "Everything will close down at noon sharp, except food stores, which *may* remain open a little longer: shops, post office, gas stations, garages, city hall, banks will shut tight, since their employees shall be going home for *déjeuner.* And *déjeuner,* as practiced in France, holds nothing in common with what we Americans know as lunch. Some places will re-open around two, or two-thirty, or three, some not until four, and others not at all. So, all errands should be completed before closing time, and if you have plans for the afternoon, or guests over for dinner, get going before it is too late. Besides, nobody wants to miss out on the best part of the morning in town: the hours devoted to food shopping." To avoid feeling like you've arrived at a restaurant at altogether the wrong time, simply keep in mind that most cafés are open by six in the morning and that their typical assortment of croissants and rolls is usually gone by ten o'clock. Breakfast at inns and hotels, in my experience, typically begins at eight. Lunch is served fairly strictly beginning at noon and ending at two and is still considered the main meal of the day. Dinner is usually served beginning as early as seven-thirty, but the majority of the locals will not sit down to dinner until at least eight and usually later. If you're starving and you arrive promptly at seven-thirty, you'll probably find the staff still scurrying about, and you'll probably be the first customer of the evening. Adjust your schedule, and you'll be on French time, doing things when the French do them, eliminating possible disappointment and frustration.

I personally prefer this Mediterranean timetable—I grew up in a family that ate dinner later—and I believe that a big meal in the middle of the day, in combination with an evening stroll, is healthier than one at the end of the day. I find nowadays that when my husband and I receive an invitation for dinner and it's for an hour before eight P.M., I am crestfallen, and the date looms ahead like a dreaded task. I would also add here that it is rewarding to rise rather early. It may be difficult to convince vacation travelers who like to sleep late to roll out of bed a bit earlier, but if you sleep in every day, you will most definitely miss much of the local rhythm. By ten A.M. in France—and in any Mediterranean country—much has already happened, and besides, you can always look forward to a delicious afternoon nap.

About fifteen years ago the former Paris bureau chief for *The New York Times,* John Vinocur, wrote a piece for the travel section entitled "Discovering the Hidden Paris." In it he noted that the French have a word, *dépaysement,* which he translated into English as "the feeling of not being assaulted by the familiarity of things, a change in surroundings where there is no immediate point of reference." He went on to quote a French journalist who once said that "Americans don't travel to be *dépaysés,* but to find a home away from home." This is unfortunate but too often true. These tourists can travel all around the world if they desire, but their unwillingness to adapt ensures they will never really leave home. I am of like mind with Paul Bowles, who noted in *Their Heads Are Green, Their Hands Are Blue,* "Each time I go to a place I have not seen before, I hope it will be as different as possible from the places I already know. I assume it is natural for a traveler to seek diversity, and that it is the human element which makes him most aware of difference. If people and their manner of living were alike everywhere, there would not be much point in moving from one place to another."

Similar to the *dépaysés*-phobic are those who endorse "adventure travel," words that make me cringe, as they seem to imply that unless one partakes of kayaking, mountain climbing, biking, rock climbing, or some other physical endeavor, a travel experience is somehow invalid or unadventurous. *All* travel is an adventure, and unless "adventure travel" allows for plenty of time to adapt to the local rhythm, the so-called adventure is really a physically strenuous—if memorable—outdoor achievement. Occasionally I hear a description of a biking excursion, for example, in which the participants spent the majority of each day in the same way: making biking the priority instead of working biking into the local cadence of daily life. When I ask if they joined the locals for a morning *café au lait* or an evening *apéro* (short for *apéritif*), shopped at the outdoor *marché*, went to a local *fête* or *foire,* or people-watched in the *place,* the answer is invariably no. They may have had an amazing bike trip, but they did not get to know France—one has to get off the bike a bit more often for that—and if a biking experience alone is what they were seeking, they certainly didn't need to fly to France: there are plenty of challenging and beautiful places to bike in the United States.

I believe that *every* place in the world offers *something* of interest. In her magnificent book *Black Lamb and Grey Falcon,* Rebecca West recounts how in the 1930s she passed through Skopje, in what was then Yugoslavia (and is now the Republic of Macedonia), by train twice, without stopping, because friends had told her the town wasn't worth visiting. A third time through she did stop, and she met two wonderful people who became lasting friends. She wrote, "Now, when I go through a town of which I know nothing, a town which appears to be a waste land of uniform streets wholly without quality, I look on it in wonder and hope, since it may hold a Mehmed, a Militsa." I too have been richly rewarded by pausing in places (Skopje included) that first appeared quite limited. While it's true the world is more accessible today—and therefore feels smaller—I do not believe it is more homogenous. Those who think France isn't exotic enough for their taste are simply mistaken. Perhaps it's been a while since they were there; perhaps they've never been at all. Things *are* different in France, as Freda White noted in her wonderful book *Ways of Aquitaine:* "France remains entirely herself, no matter how manners alter, and that is why travel in France is an adventure. The British traveller having crossed the narrow strait of the Channel, finds himself further abroad than if he had crossed the Atlantic. He notices instantly the outward signs of *la Civilisation française,* a mode of manners and customs taught uniformly to every French child."

"Travel is fatal to prejudice, bigotry, and narrow-mindedness."
—Mark Twain

"The world is a book, and those who do not travel read only a page."

—Saint Augustine

I am assuming if you've read this far that something has compelled you to pick up this book and that you feel travel is an essential part of life. I would add to Mark Twain's quote above one by Benjamin Disraeli (1804–81): "Travel teaches toleration." People who travel with an open mind and are receptive to the ways of others cannot help but return with more tolerance for people and situations at home, at work, and in their cities and communities. James Ferguson, a nineteenth-century Scottish architect, observed this perfectly when he wrote, "Travel is more than a visitor seeing sights; it is the profound changing—the deep and permanent changing—of that visitor's perspective of the world, and of his own place in it." I find that travel also ensures I will not be quite the same person I was before I left. After a trip I typically have a lot of renewed energy and bring new perspectives to my job. At home I ask myself how I can incorporate attributes or traits I observed while traveling into my own life and share them with my husband and daughter. I also find that I am eager to explore my own hometown more fully (when was the last time you visited your local historical society, or the best-known tourist site in your part of the country?), and in appreciation of the great kindnesses shown to me by people from other nations, I always go out of my way to help tourists who are visiting New York City—Americans or foreigners—by giving directions, explaining the subway, or sharing the name of a favorite museum or a place to eat.

The anthologies in the *Collected Traveler* series offer a record of people's achievements and shortcomings. It may be a lofty goal to expect that they might also offer an opportunity for us to measure our own deeds and flaws as Americans, so we can realize that, despite cultural differences between us and our hosts in *any* country, we have much more in common than not. It is a sincere goal, however, and one that I hope readers and travelers will embrace. Bruce Northam, author of a wonderful little book, *Globetrotter Dogma,* perhaps puts it best of all: "Remember, we are all one. Find out for yourself what a miraculous world we live in, contrary to media portrayals . . . as the global village shrinks, we become increasingly aware of our interdependence. Because we all play a part, however small, in the interlocking of cultures, our new objectives should include having firsthand interactions with the staggering beauty and diversity of our planet."

About This Series

The *Collected Traveler* editions are not guidebooks in the traditional sense. But they *are* books that guide readers to other sources: each edition is really the first book you should turn to when planning a trip. If you think of the individual volumes as a sort of planning package, you've got the right idea. If you enjoy acquiring knowledge about where you're going—whether you plan a trip independently or with a like-minded tour organization—this series is for you. If you're looking for a guide that simply informs you of exact prices, hours, and highlights, you probably won't be interested in the depth this book offers. (That is not meant to offend, merely to say you've got the wrong book.)

A few words about me may also help you determine if this series is for you. I travel somewhat frugally, not out of necessity but more because I choose to. I respect money and its value, and I'm not convinced that if I spent $600 a night on a hotel room, for example, it would represent a good value or I would have a better trip. I've been to some of the world's finest hotels, mostly to visit friends who were staying there or to have a drink in the hotel bar. With a few notable exceptions, the majority of these places seem to me all alike, conforming to a code of sameness and predictability. Nothing about them is particularly French, Moroccan, Italian, Spanish, or Turkish—you could be *anywhere*. The cheapest of the cheap accommodations don't represent good value, either. I look for places to stay that are usually old, possibly historic, and that have lots of charm and character. I do not mind if my room is small; I do not necessarily need a television, telephone, or hair dryer; and I most definitely do not care for an American-style buffet breakfast, which is hardly what the locals eat. I also prefer to make my own plans, send my own letters and faxes, place my own telephone calls, and make my own transportation arrangements. Not because I think I can do it better than a professional agent (whose expertise I admire) but because I enjoy it and learn a lot in the process. Finally, lest you think I do not appreciate elegance, allow me to state that I do indeed enjoy many of life's little luxuries, when I perceive them to be of good value to me.

This series promotes the desirability of staying longer within a smaller area. Susan Allen Toth, in one of her many wonderful books, *England as You Like It,* subscribes to the "thumbprint theory of travel": spend at least a week in one spot no larger than a thumbprint covers on a large-scale map of England. Excursions are encouraged, she explains, as long as they're no more than an hour's drive away. As I have discovered in my own travels, a week spent in one place, even in a spot no bigger than my thumbprint, is rarely long enough to see and enjoy it all. *The Collected Traveler* focuses on one corner of the world, the countries bordering the Mediterranean Sea. I find the Mediterranean endlessly fascinating: the sea itself is the world's largest, the region is one of the world's ancient crossroads, and as it stretches from Asia to the Atlantic, it is one of the most culturally diverse regions on the planet. As Paul Theroux has noted in his excellent book *The Pillars of Hercules,* "The Mediterranean, this simple almost tideless sea, the size of thirty Lake Superiors, had everything: prosperity, poverty, tourism, terrorism, several wars in progress, ethnic strife, fascists, pollution, drift nets, private islands owned by billionaires, Gypsies, seventeen countries, fifty languages, oil drilling platforms, sponge fishermen, religious fanatics, drug smuggling, fine art, and warfare. It had Christians, Muslims, Jews; it had the Druzes, who are a strange farrago of all three religions; it had heathens, Zoroastrians and Copts and Baha'is." Diversity aside, the great explorers in the service of Spain and Portugal departed from Mediterranean ports to discover much of the rest of the world, as

Carlos Fuentes has noted in *his* excellent book, *The Buried Mirror:* "The facts remained that the Mare Nostrum, the Mediterranean, had been to all effects and purposes an Islamic lake for nearly eight hundred years, and that European expansion was severely hindered by such mastery. To find a way out, a way around, a way toward the Orient became a European obsession. It began in the Venetian republic, with Marco Polo's opening of overland trade routes to China. But soon the rise of a new Muslim power, the Ottoman Empire, once more threatened the Mediterranean; the Ottomans captured Greece and the Balkans and forced Europe and its rising merchant class to look elsewhere." And look elsewhere they did: Prince Henry of Portugal, who became known as Henry the Navigator, arranged the sailing expeditions to Madeira, the Azores, Senegal. In 1488 the Portuguese went on to discover the Cape of Good Hope, and ten years later under Vasco da Gama they added India to these ports of call. "This sea," writes Lisa Lovatt-Smith in *Mediterranean Living,* "whose shores have hosted the main currents in civilization, creates its own homogenous culture, endlessly absorbing newcomers and their ideas . . . and is the one I consider my own." I too consider the sea my own, even though I live thousands of miles away from it.

With the exception of my *Morocco* edition, this series focuses on individual cities and regions rather than entire countries, as readers who are not new to *The Collected Traveler* already know. I do not plan to compile a book on all of France, for example, since each corner of France is a member of two communities, European and Mediterranean. I have tried to reflect this wider world sense of community throughout this edition on Southwestern France; especially in *The Kiosk—Points of View.* When I first contemplated this edition, I knew I would have to take a broad, inclusive approach rather than a strictly geographic one. When the French refer to Southwestern France, they are usually talking about a region encompassing the Dordogne, Bordeaux, and Aquitaine, the Lot Valley,

Montauban, Toulouse, possibly Gascony, Albi, the Cévennes, and Roquefort. The Pays Basque (the French Basque region) is usually considered separately, as is Languedoc-Roussillon, though both occupy parts of Southwestern France. But as so few North Americans have a clear idea of the Pays Basque and as many have never heard of Languedoc-Roussillon, it feels right to include these regions in this book—I will never publish individual editions on these areas and will not include them in any future editions on France. This seeming confusion over boundaries is vexing to nearly everyone, as readers will discover when they select guidebooks to use for visiting the Southwest—each guidebook defines the region differently. Some include the regions to the north and northeast of Bordeaux—Poitou-Charentes and the Limousin; some include parts of the Auvergne while others exclude everything east of Toulouse. The confusion partly lies in distinguishing between the twenty-two French regions and the much smaller *départements,* of which there are ninety-five. I can't resist sharing cookbook author Paula Wolfert's comments on the definition of the Southwest: "To my surprise I have found that food commentators disagree about just which areas are encompassed by the term 'South-West France.' I've seen texts that ignore the Ariège portion of the Pyrenees, that omit every part of Languedoc, and that delineate Gascony as a special and separate culinary zone. Certainly each province has its own specialties, but there is a land the French call Sud-Ouest, which can be gastronomically defined. As drawn on the accompanying map [in the book], it is the land of preserved meats—confits—a preparation that unified such diverse regions as the Basque country, the Béarn, the Quercy, the Gers, and the western portions of the Languedoc." Freda White, in *Ways of Aquitaine,* notes that after the 1789 French Revolution, "the new governments wanted to wipe out the memory of the old feudal overlordships. They ordained new administrative boundaries, usually representing the courses of the rivers after which they are named. Thus Poitou became Vienne; Berri, Cher; Saintonge, Charente. This was logical, but as every woman knows, logic in life is not reasonable. The modern *départements* are often convenient neither for economics nor for administration." The conclusion I draw from all of this is that it's silly to attempt to stick to formal boundaries, especially in this age of a borderless Europe. So though this particular thumbprint is a bit bigger than I traditionally promote, you can manageably see it in one trip (though it would be ideal if you allowed about three weeks).

Each section of this book features a selection of articles from various periodicals and an annotated bibliography relevant to its theme. The articles and books were chosen from my own files and home library, which I've maintained for over two decades. (I often feel I am the living embodiment of a comment that Samuel Johnson made in 1775, that "a man will turn over half a library to make one book.") The selected writings reflect the culture, politics, history, current social issues, religion, cuisine, and arts of the people you'll be visiting. They also represent the observations and opinions of a wide variety of novelists, travel writers, and journalists. These writers are typically authorities on the Southwest, or all of France, or both; they either live there (as permanent or part-time residents) or visit there often for business or pleasure. I'm very discriminating in seeking opinions and recommendations, and I'm not interested in the remarks of unobservant wanderers. Likewise, I don't ask someone who doesn't read much what he or she thinks of a particular book, and I don't ask someone who neither cooks nor travels for a restaurant recommendation. I am not implying that first-time visitors to France have nothing noteworthy or interesting to share— they very often do and are often very keen observers; conversely, frequent travelers are very often jaded and apt to miss the finer details that make Southwestern France the exceptional place it is. I am interested in the opinions of people who want to *know* this part of France, not just *see* it.

I've included numerous older articles (even though some of the specific information regarding prices, hours, and the like is no longer accurate) because they were particularly well written, thought provoking, or unique in some way, and because the authors' views stand as a valuable record of a certain time in history. Often, even with the passage of many years, you may share the same emotions and opinions of the writer, and equally as often, *plus ça change, plus c'est la même chose.*

A word about the food and restaurant section, *Flavors and Tables of the Southwest:* I have great respect for restaurant reviewers, and though their work may seem glamorous—it sometimes is—it is also very hard. It's an all-consuming, full-time job, and that is why I urge you to consult the very good food and restaurant guides I recommend in the bibliography, cookbooks included. Restaurant (and hotel) reviewers are, for the most part, professionals who have dined in hundreds of eating establishments (and spent hundreds of nights in hotels). They are far more capable of assessing the qualities and flaws of a place than I am—I have eaten in only a few dozen places and stayed at fewer hotels and can therefore tell you only about my limited experience—and they are probably more capable than your in-laws, who perhaps were somewhere in the Southwest for a week and never took a meal outside of their hotel and maybe never left Bordeaux. I don't always agree with every opinion of a reviewer, but I am far more inclined to defer to their opinion than to the opinion of someone who is unfamiliar with French food in general and the cuisine of the Southwest in particular, for example, or of someone who doesn't dine out frequently enough to recognize what good restaurants have in common. My files are bulging with restaurant reviews, and I could have included many, many more articles; but it would be too repetitive and ultimately beside the point. I have selected a few articles that give you a feel for eating out in this varied part of France, alert you to some things to look for in selecting a truly worthwhile place versus a mediocre one, and highlight some dishes that are not commonplace in America.

The annotated bibliography for each section is one of the most important features of this book, and they represent my own favorite aspect of this series. One reason I do not include excerpts from books in my editions is that I am not convinced an excerpt will always lead a reader to the book in question, and I think good books deserve to be read in their entirety. Art critic John Russell wrote an essay in 1962 entitled "Pleasure in Reading," in which he stated, "Not for us today's selections, readers, digests, and anthologizings: only the Complete Edition will do." Years later in 1986 he noted in the foreword to *John Pope-Hennessy: A Bibliography* that "bibliographies make dull reading, some people say, but I have never found them so. They remind us, they prompt us, and they correct us. They double and treble as history, as biography, and as a freshet of surprises. They reveal the public self, the private self, and the buried self of the person commemorated. How should we not enjoy them, and be grateful to the devoted student who has done the compiling?" When I pick up a nonfiction book, I always turn first to the bibliography, as it is there that I learn something about the author who has done the compiling as well as about other notable books I know I will want to read.

When I read about travel in the days before transatlantic flights, I always marvel at the number of steamer trunks and the amount of baggage people were accustomed to taking. If it had been me traveling then, however, my bags would have been filled with books, not clothes. Although I travel light and seldom check bags, I have been known to fill an entire suitcase with books, secure in the knowledge that I would have them all with me for the duration of my trip. Each bibliography in this book features the titles I feel are the best ones available and the most worth your time. *Best* is certainly subjective; readers will simply have to trust me that I have been extremely thorough in deciding which books to recommend. (I have read them all, by the way, and own them all, with the exception of a very few I borrowed.) If some of the lists seem long, they are, but the more I read, the more I realize there is to know, and there are an awful lot of really good books out there! I'm not suggesting you read them *all*, but I do hope you will not be content with just one. I have identified some books as *de rigueur*, meaning that I consider them required reading; but I sincerely believe that *all* the books I've mentioned are important, helpful, well written, or all three. I keep up with book publishing, but there are surely some books I've not seen, so if some of your favorites aren't included here, please write and tell me about them.

I have not hesitated to list out-of-print titles because some very excellent books are declared out of print (and deserve to be returned to print!) and because many, many out-of-print books can be found through individuals who specialize in out-of-print books, booksellers, libraries, and online searches. I believe the companion reading you bring along on your trip should be related in some way to where you're going. Therefore the books listed in *Good Things, Favorite Places* are mostly novels that feature characters or settings in Southwestern France or aspects of France and the French.

Readers familiar with my other books may notice the absence of a section featuring personalities in this edition. The reason is simply that I was unable to put together an assortment of articles that I felt was truly representative of the Southwest. Note, too, that books on French art and architecture styles, local artists, gardens, and museum catalogs are highlighted in *Good Things, Favorite Places*.

Together the articles collected and books cited will lead you on and off the beaten path, and present a reality check of sorts. Will you learn of some nontouristy things to see and do? Yes. Will you also learn more about the better-known aspects of Southwestern France? Yes. Bordeaux and its vineyards, foie gras, the Pyrenees, the beaches of coastal Languedoc-Roussillon, open air *marchés,* prehistoric caves, Armagnac, the Three Musketeers, Biarritz, the cafés on the Place du Capitole in Toulouse, medieval architecture, a glass of Corbière, and a lazy day on the Lot are all equally representative of the region. Seeing them *all* is what makes for a memorable visit, and no one, by the way, should make you feel guilty for wanting to see some famous sites. They have become famous for a reason: they are really something to see, the Bordeaux vineyards, Carcassone, Rocamadour, and the beach at Biarritz included. Canon number eighty-four in Bruce Northam's *Globetrotter Dogma* is "The Good Old Days Are Now": he wisely reminds us that destinations are not ruined even though they may have been more "real" many years ago. "'Tis a haughty condescension to insist that because a place has changed or lost its innocence it's not worth visiting; change requalifies a destination. Your first time is your first time; virgin turf simply is. The moment you commit to a trip, there begins the search for adventure."

You will have no trouble finding a multitude of other travel books offering plenty of noncontroversial viewpoints. This is my attempt at presenting a more balanced picture. Ultimately it is a compendium of the information that I wish I'd had between two covers years ago. I admit it isn't the perfect book; for that, I envision a waterproof jacket and pockets inside the front and back covers, pages and pages of accompanying maps, lots of blank pages for notes, a bookmark, mileage and size conversion charts . . . in other words, something so encyclopedic, in both weight and size, that positively no one, my editor assures me, would want to read it! I think I envisioned such a large volume because I believe that to really get to know a place, to truly understand it in a nonsuperficial way, one must either live there or travel there again and again. It seems to me that it can take nothing short of a lifetime of studying and traveling to grasp France. I do not pretend to have completely grasped it now, many trips later; nor do I pretend to have completely grasped the other Mediterranean destinations that are featured in *The Collected Traveler;* but I am trying to get closer to it by continuously reading, collecting, and traveling. And I presume readers like you are, too. All of this said, I am exceedingly happy with *The Collected Traveler,* and I believe it will prove helpful in heightening your anticipation of your upcoming journey, your enjoyment of it while it's happening, and your remembrance of it once you're back home.

It is not difficult to convey how very beautiful, wonderful, and unique Southwestern France is; Bordeaux and the Dordogne especially are discussed in a multitude of books, as are Toulouse and Carcassone, and North Americans are finally beginning to discover Languedoc-Roussillon. But the region's real draw is more subtle, and I hope after reading this edition, and traveling there, you will discover why many people refer to parts of the Southwest as *la France profonde.* In a piece he penned a few years ago for *FranceGuide,* the impressive annual magazine published by Maison de la France, writer David Downie wrote, "As I slalomed from village to gift-wrapped village down fancy-ribbon roads, I rounded a bend high above the Dordogne River where the regions of Aquitaine, Midi-Pyrenees and Limousin meet. Suddenly a flock of white geese appeared on the cliff edge, honking and lifting their wings at the twilit, turreted silhouette of Belcastel château. That lovely sight, for one fleeting moment, seemed to sum up the secret of Southwestern France—a conspiracy of natural beauty and man-made wonders, surely orchestrated by masters of *l'art de vivre.*" *Bon voyage* and *bonne route!*

Practical Information

"In French, les toilettes *means both the room (the* cabinet*) and the toilet itself. It's the same for men and for women. It's a curious word and difficult to get used to, because it's in the plural, even if you're in an apartment where there is clearly just one such fixture. You can also say 'W.C.,' but* les toilettes *is the best, and good under all circumstances (a passepartout). You* cannot *use* les chiottes. *No foreigner can, and a Frenchman is very careful about when he uses it."*
—Polly Platt, *Savoir Flair! 211 Tips for Enjoying France and the French*

A–Z Practical Information

Ac

Ac is a shortening of the Latin ending *acum,* which was affixed to a name to indicate "place of" or "villa of." This I learned from Ann Barry, in her memoir *At Home in France* (see the *Dordogne and the Lot* bibliography for more on this wonderful book), who in turn learned from her neighbor, Charles. According to the knowledgeable Charles, *ac* "appeared when names started to be written down in Latin, usually in lists of parishes or in monastic charters. The earliest records are from the ninth century, but probably that is only the tail end of a process of writing down names in Roman Gaul that goes back to the era just after Caesar's conquest (about 50 B.C.). The form *acum* or *iacum* was applied to both personal names and to existing Celtic places. Thus Pauliac or Tauriac suggest the villas of Paulus or Taurus. Carennac, on the other hand, suggests 'the place of the quarried stone,' based on a possible Celtic root *carenna.*" Charles postulated that the place names of the old Haut-Quercy region may be among the least affected by historical change in all of France. Neither the Visigoths (in the Garonne Valley) nor the Francs (north of the Vézère) contributed much settlement to the area, and so antique forms of place names are more common there.

Accommodations

Unless you are traveling for an extended period of time throughout the Southwest or throughout France, I don't recommend showing up without a reservation. There is a certain appeal to traveling without them, and I am sympathetic to it, but to those who prefer to travel without the restriction of reservations, I would recommend at least reserving for the first night or two of your journey. I say this because you may underestimate how tired you'll be upon arrival, and the last thing you'll want to do is search for a place to stay. Having a known base from which to embark on your spontaneous itinerary is welcome indeed. And during the summer months, and especially August, when nearly all Europeans are *en vacances,* it is never advisable to arrive without a reservation, not even at a mountain hut in the Pyrenees. In the off-season reservations are not essential in many parts of the Southwest, and I have traveled here without making advance reservations for every night of my trip, with success. But no matter when you plan to travel, keep in mind that many of the most wonderful lodgings are quite small, with only a few rooms, and they can fill up fast even during the so-named shoulder seasons, fall and spring. Be aware, too, that during the winter months, some places are closed entirely, and many *patrons* take their own vacation in the month of November. If you do arrive in any town of Southwestern France without a room, the local tourist office staff can assist you in finding accommodations. Some tourist boards also house an office of Loisirs Accueils, a nationwide reservations service. Loisirs Accueils agents offer information on hotels, *gîtes,* B&Bs, and campgrounds, from more than fifty agencies throughout France. The French tourist offices in North America and in France have contact information for each Loisirs Accueils office, but as these agencies seem to me to be most useful for spontaneous travelers who show up in person, I do not provide the phone numbers or addresses here. (Note that a fee is charged for the services of Loisirs Acceuils; the general e-mail address is loisirs.accueil@ wanadoo.fr.).

The Southwest features an abundance of all types of accommodations, from budget to *luxe,* so travelers seeking one level of comfort or a combination will have a great number of options. These options are, for me, one of the great joys of traveling in France and elsewhere around the Mediterranean. Here in North America, of course, we have some wonderful and wonderfully expensive places to stay, as well as a growing number of bed-and-breakfast establishments. We also have an overabundance, in my opinion, of inexpensive, characterless places (and that are therefore overpriced for what they are). I refer to these as "plastic places," where all the furnishings are plastic, acrylic, or—my favorite—"wood product." Sometimes a continental breakfast is included in the price, which typically consists of a previously frozen bagel or something resembling a muffin and dreadful coffee with nondairy creamer. Breakfast served at the Libertel chain in France includes croissants, baguettes, sliced meats, an assortment of cheeses, jams, butter, cereals, an assortment of yogurts, and fresh-brewed coffee with real milk. You don't have to be French to recognize that the croissants and baguettes are not of top quality, but they are real, and you can always count on the coffee being good. What we *don't* have in North America (or at least in the States) that France *does* is a great number of moderately priced, simple, but well-cared-for places that are usually quite charming and that often offer a very good—if not excellent—meal or two in the bargain. By moderately priced, I mean in a range of $80 to $150 a night; though I have over the years stayed in places in France that were between $25 and $60 a night that were rather exceptional in terms of the furnishings in the rooms (quality pieces, sometimes antiques), and the quality of the breakfast; even if it was only a *tartine*—that classic French breakfast of a sliced baguette slathered with butter— and coffee, the baguettes were delivered from the corner bakery, and the coffee, as I've noted, was always good, served in an individual pot with a pitcher of warm milk. All of this is to say that to sleep in France, and especially in parts of Languedoc-Roussillon, Gascony, and the Basque Country, your wallet doesn't have to be opened wide; accommodations can be extremely affordable, even for budget travelers. Additionally, the variety of lodgings in France allows you to become more familiar with the different accommodations networks and to experience a variety of lodgings in one trip. I sometimes plan my itinerary around a special inn or hotel where I want to stay, feeling it is nearly equal in importance to the particular village or historic site I am keen on visiting.

Keep in mind that though France's star rating system for lodging establishments is rather more reliable than those in Italy and Spain, for example—which award stars based on the number and range of amenities available rather than charm or quality of hospitality—it would be a mistake to depend solely on stars: the only amenity standing between a three-star place and one awarded four stars may be a swimming pool, a bigger bathtub, a hair dryer, or a ceiling fan. You may even, in your research and travels, discover places that are not classified and therefore have no rating. A zero rating means either that the tourist office has deemed not to award the establishment even one star or that the owners of the lodging have not requested to be reviewed. I have stayed in a number of places with no rating throughout France and they were all perfectly fine and clean, some even quite deserving of at least one or two stars. The regional tourist offices in France publish hotel and accommodation brochures but they rarely offer any subjective descriptions of the place. One of these booklets in particular is a bit more useful than others: *Languedoc Roussillon Méditerranée: Camping, Hôtels et Résidences, Villages de Vacances, Agences Immobilières*. The guide includes a page of practical information about travel in the region, a distance chart, phone numbers for regional airports, a list of eight specialty brochures to request and a great Web site (www.sunfrance.com) for discovering the region. Far better than all of this is to ignore the stars and read a thorough description of a place so you know exactly what you're paying for.

All of France's rated lodgings are graded from one to four stars (and, as noted above, no stars, as well as another category, four-star luxury). Stars indicate the availability of facilities, mostly, and there is often little or no difference between a two- and a three-star establishment, but a hotel with two stars must have an elevator (unless it's on one level) and a telephone in every room, and at least 40 percent of the rooms must have their own bathrooms, while a lodging with three stars must provide a room-service breakfast, and 80 percent of the rooms must have baths. Only four-star inns are required to have a restaurant, and all of the rooms must have attached bathrooms. Generally speaking, most one-star establishments are simple accommodations and usually shared bathroom facilities. Two- and three-star establishments can be bed-and-breakfast or regular hotel accommodations, usually with a private bath. Four-star and luxury hotels represent the highest standards of service and can be quite luxurious or slightly less so. Here are the types of accommodations you'll find in the Southwest:

Auberges are country inns, usually modestly priced and usually representing a good value. The word *auberge* can be a little misleading, however, as some *auberges* are decidedly not at all modest but quite luxurious. Accommodations noted as *relais, logis,* and *hostellerie* are in the same category as *auberge*.

Auberges de jeunesse (youth hostels) are one of the most popular choices for those seeking budget accommodations (and if it's been a while since your salad days, keep in mind that hostels are not just for the under-thirty crowd). Younger budget travelers need no convincing that hosteling is the way to go, but older budget travelers should bear in mind that some hostels do offer individual rooms, reserved mostly for couples or small families. Do compare costs, as sometimes hostel rates are the same as those for a room in a real (albeit inexpensive) hotel, where you can reserve in advance and comfortably keep your luggage (when hosteling, you must pack up your luggage every day, and you can't make a reservation.) Additionally, most hostels have an eleven P.M. curfew. Petty theft—of the T-shirts-stolen-off-the-clothesline variety—seems to be more prevalent than it once was, so it would be wise to sleep and shower with your money belt close at hand. There are no age limits or advance bookings, but many hostels require membership in Hostelling International, whose national headquarters are located at 733 Fifteenth Street N.W., Suite 840, Washington, D.C. 20005; 202-783-6161; fax: -6171; www.hiayh.org. Hours are 8:00 A.M.–5:00 P.M. Eastern Standard Time, with customer service staff available until 6:00 P.M. An HI membership card is free for anyone up to his or her eighteenth birthdate. Annual fees are $25 for anyone over eighteen and $15 for those fifty-five and over. HI staff can give you addresses and phone numbers for the council affiliates nearest you.

Camping (known simply as *camping* or sometimes *campings municipaux*) can be a viable option for those who have a car and preferably a lot of time, and there are plenty of campgrounds in both the cities and small towns of the Southwest. The thing to understand about the European conception of camping is that it is about as opposite from the American conception as possible. Europeans do not go camping to seek a wilderness experience, and European campgrounds are designed without much privacy in mind. Campgrounds in France are rated just as hotels are, receiving from one to four stars. Three- and four-star sites offer amenities ranging from hot water showers, facilities for washing clothes and dishes, electrical outlets, cafés, and flush toilets to tiled bathrooms with heat, tennis courts, swimming pools, cafés, bars, restaurants, telephones, televisions, and grocery stores. It's camping at its most civilized. Sites awarded one and two stars will always have flush toilets but not always hot water; still, a number of these lesser campgrounds offer stunning scenery. For complete information about camping in France, you should inquire at the Maison de la France office nearest you in North America.

It's been my experience that at municipal campgrounds during the off-season, no one ever comes around to collect fees. The campgrounds are still open and there is running water, but the thinking seems to be that it just isn't worth it to collect money from so few campers. (This will not be true at privately run campgrounds.) Outside the larger towns and cities you may see signs for *camping à la ferme,* which is camping on a farm. Typically such sites offer few facilities, but the setting is usually beautiful and quiet and often comes with a home-cooked meal or two. Off-site camping is *interdit* (prohibited) in Languedoc-Roussillon (and I believe across the Southwest as well) due to the very great and real danger of fire. If you plan to camp for even a few nights, I recommend that you join Family Campers and RV'ers (FCRV). Annual membership (valid for one year from the time you join) is $25. The FCRV is a member of the Fédération Internationale de Camping et de Caravanning (FICC) and is the only organization in America authorized to issue the International Camping Carnet for camping in Europe. Only FCRV members are eligible to purchase the carnet—you cannot purchase it separately—and the fee is $10. The carnet is like a camping passport and provides entry into the many privately owned, members-only campsites. It offers campers priority status and occasionally discounts. An additional benefit is that instead of keeping your passport overnight—which hotels and campgrounds are often required to do—the campground staff keep your carnet, allowing you to hold on to your passport. One FICC membership is good for the entire family: parents and all children under the age of eighteen. To receive an application and information, contact the FCRV at 4804 Transit Road, Building 2, Depew, N.Y. 14043; 800-245-9755; phone/fax: 716-668-6242; www.fcrv.org.

Chambres d'hôtes or *maisons d'hôtes* (bed and breakfast) accommodations in France may be simple or rather fancy and are offered in private homes or small inns. Many *chambres d'hôtes* are members of the Gîtes de France network (see page 27), but their membership is not always obvious, as some owners do not display their Gîtes logo. *Chambres d'hôtes* were once viewed as rather quirky accommodations existing solely as a way for farmers and other country people to earn extra money. But in the late 1980s the bed-and-breakfast tradition was suddenly all the rage, and many French (and a number of foreigners) were eager to buy and renovate properties into rustic-yet-elegant accommodations. Rates are generally not expensive, usually the equivalent of a one- to three-star hotel, and you often get to spend time with your hosts (and practice your French) and enjoy delicious home-cooked meals (often prepared with raw ingredients straight from the *potager*—kitchen garden—or the henhouse). Also, B&B accommodations are often great for families—Southwestern hosts enjoy fussing over children, and many places offer suites or large rooms complete with a kitchenette. B&B hosts also like to share their suggestions for local restaurants, cafés, hikes, shops, and sites to see, so you'll feel like you're an insider faster than you might if you were staying at a hotel.

Château accommodations are also an option, as both privately owned châteaus and *châteaux-hôtels* accept guests in France. At a private château you are a guest in someone's home, an experience akin to staying at a bed-and-breakfast establishment. Some privately owned châteaus don't welcome overnight guests but do offer private tours. Some sources of information include *Chateaux & Hotels de France*, *Relais & Châteaux* and *Châteaux & Country*

Internet Resource (www.chateauxandcountry.com), a Web site—in both French and English—that is a complete château resource featuring castles available for accommodation, special events, and tours. Profiles of each château include color photos, its history, location, and practical details.

Foyers and *residences* are both simple options for budget travelers and are classified with usually one star or none. Local tourist offices also have listings.

Gîtes de France accommodations are available as either bed-and-breakfast lodgings or as weekly or monthly rentals. The word *gîte* means "abode" or "lodging," and Gîtes de France is a network of typically inexpensive accommodations in private homes. When I've stayed at a *gîte* as a bed-and-breakfast guest, the family or individual host was very welcoming and my room was simple but nice and immaculately clean. Breakfast may be served with the whole family around a large table and café au lait presented in large bowls (which I hardly ever see in Paris anymore) or completely separate from the household. In the simpler *gîte* lodgings towels tend to be small and thin, and sometimes there isn't soap, so remember to pack your own. If you are renting a *gîte*, ask if bed linens and towels are provided (they're often not), and if it's a chilly time of year, ask for a cost estimate to turn on the heat, which isn't included in the rental price. *Gîtes* are rated by a system of between one and four *epis* (wheat sheaves), depending upon the amenities each property provides. There are more than fifty thousand *gîtes* throughout France, and the Maison des Gîtes de France et du Tourisme Vert offers more than one hundred *gîte* guidebooks classified by region, department, or theme. These books are available at the main office in France at 59 rue St.-Lazare, 75439 Paris; 33.1/49.70.75.75; fax: .42.81.28.53 and at some bookstores in North America. Alternatively, inquire at one of the Maison de la France offices for assistance in obtaining them.

One *gîte* guide in particular that I think is worth seeking out is *Gîtes Bacchus*, which details about thirty bed-and-breakfasts and rentals located on vineyard properties. (To read of a wonderful experience at Château Bujan, a *gîte bacchus* in the Côtes de Bourg, see James Redmond, "Vintage Vacations: A Bordeaux Vineyard Welcomes Wine Enthusiasts," *FRANCE Magazine*, Winter 2000–01.) All the *gîtes* guides have color photos and maps and are in both French and English; a number of *gîte* properties are suited for families. You may browse the Gîtes de France Web site as well at www.gites-de-france.fr.

Home exchange might be an appealing option. I've read wildly enthusiastic reports from people who've swapped apartments or houses, and it's usually always an economical alternative. Here are some services to contact.

~*Homelink International* claims to be the world's largest home exchange organization, with more than twelve thousand members, more than twenty offices around the world, and three directories published each year. Contact information: Homelink, P.O. Box 47747, Tampa, Fla. 33647; 800-638-3841 or 813-975-9825; fax: -910-8144; www.homelink.org.

~Intervac—created from the words *international* and *vacation*—was founded in 1953 in Switzerland by a group of teachers who were looking for economical means to travel. After a few exchanges, they realized this was also a great way to cultivate international friendships and understanding. Intervac services are available in fifty countries, and the company publishes three directories a year with more than twelve thousand listings. Contact information: Box 12066, S-291, 12 Kristianstad, Sweden (world headquarters); 30 Corte San Fernando, Tiburon, Calif. 94920 (U.S. address); 800-756-HOME; www.intervacus.com.

~Seniors Home Exchange is limited to members over age fifty. Contact information: www.seniorshomeexchange.com.

~Trading Homes International was founded in 1991 and was a founding member, with thirteen other exchange companies, of the International Home Exchange Association. Its staff believes home exchange is "a way to give people a whole new perspective on what travel can really be like when you vacation as a local and not as a tourist." Contact information: P.O. Box 787, Hermosa Beach, Calif. 90254; 800-877-TRADE; fax: 310-798-3865; www.trading-homes.com.

~HomeExchange.com (www.homeexchange.com) is a Web-only home exchange company. Based in Santa Barbara and founded in 1996, it features more than two thousand listings, and through the Web site's discussion board you can read about others' experiences.

Hotels are where most of us stay when we travel, but you should know that the word *hôtel* in French has a number of meanings besides an establishment that provides lodgings. It refers also to a private, aristocratic mansion (known as a *hôtel particulier*); a city hall (*hôtel de ville;* every French town of any size has one); a hospital (*hôtel-Dieu*); a general post office (*hôtel des postes*); an auction house (*hôtel des ventes*); and a home for wounded (*invalide*) war veterans (the most famous being the Hôtel des Invalides in Paris). Recommendations for hotels (the lodging kind) from general guidebooks are usually reliable, but books exclusively about hotels are even better. As with guidebooks, the right hotel book for you is the one whose author shares a certain sensibility or philosophy with you. In the same way that you put your trust in the author of a guidebook, you put that same faith in the author of a hotel guide. Once you've selected the book you like, then trust the author's recommendations, and make your decisions. I have never understood those people who, after they've made a reservation, seek some sort of validation for their choice—by searching the Internet, for example—for other travelers' comments and opinions. I find this to serve no good purpose and to be a poor use of time, and it makes me wonder why those people consulted the hotel books in the first place. Remember: *you don't know the people writing reviews on the Internet, and you have no idea if the same things that are important to you are important to them.* Authors of hotel guides carefully share their standards with you and explain the criteria they use in rating accommodations. I believe—because I read a lot of travel guidebooks and hotel guides—that most of the time authors are clear about what they look for and expect in hotel establishments, and though you might not always agree, you may at least understand how they arrived at their conclusions.

Hotel chains are not generally my cup of tea, either here in the United States or abroad. But some individual properties within a chain can be surprisingly unique, and sometimes an itinerary doesn't lend itself to perfection; there may be a day that requires many hours in the car (or the bus or train) and one has to stop for the night in a city or town that is merely a resting spot en route to somewhere else. Though I try to avoid traveling a great distance in one day, it is occasionally unavoidable, and I am grateful that there are a number of French hotel chains one can count on to be clean, serviceable, and just off the highway. These chains are also good to know about if you are traveling by car in the high season, you did not make advance reservations, and you are having trouble finding a place to stay. (One advantage to chain hotels is that they are usually big, with lots of rooms.) Formule 1, Première Classe, and Nuit d'Hôtel are all budget establishments. (Formule 1 is owned by the Accor chain, which also owns Motel 6 and Red Roof Inns in North America, as well as more upscale hotels such as Etap, Ibis, Mercure, Novotel, and Sofitel.) Just like Motel 6, these budget lodgings are functional, basic, and clean and are located on major highways and roads on the outskirts of towns and cities in France. Rooms are typically small, and bathrooms and showers can sometimes be down the hall, but if you haven't reserved in advance, they may be your only choice. Not every chain has air conditioning in all rooms, and be prepared for some front desks that are staffed only in the morning and early evening—at other times of day guests "check in" by using a computer terminal and a credit card. To research locations in the Southwest or to make reservations, visit the Accor Web site at www.accor.com; or Nuit d'Hôtel's at www.envergure.fr/nuitdhotelfr.html; or the site for Première Classe at www.premiereclasse.fr.

Monasteries and convents are a singular (and budget) accommodation choice. I have not seen a book exclusively devoted to monastery lodgings in France, but the French tourist offices in North America can provide interested readers with information on lodgings of this sort. (It is not required to be Christian to stay at a monastery, by the way.) You should know that staying at a convent is not the same as staying in a hotel, and you should not expect great comfort or a lot of amenities. (Few monasteries have a television or a private telephone, for example.) Rather, what you will find are simple, immaculately clean quarters, solitude, possibly a meal or two (though you need to eat when the resident monks or nuns eat), not much English spoken (a great opportunity to practice your French!), a possible curfew, possible single-sex accommodations (some convents admit only men, others only women)—and a wholly unique and untouristy experience.

Pension is another word for simple, good value accommodations, often including meals. Typically, a *pension* is in the same category as an *auberge, logis,* or *hostellerie.*

Renting an apartment or villa might be a suitable choice depending on how long you'll be in the area and the number of people you're traveling with. While I very much like staying in inns and hotels, I also like renting because it can be a quick way to feel a part of the local routine—you have daily chores to accomplish just like everyone else (except that I would hardly call going to pick up provisions at the local *marché* a chore). Though your tasks are mixed in with lots of little pleasures, sight-seeing, and trips, you often avoid the too-much-to-do rut. What to eat suddenly looms as the most important question of the day, the same question that all the local families are trying to answer.

General accommodation notes to keep in mind: ~Ask for a reservation confirmation in writing. Though I may place an initial telephone call to an inn or hotel, I prefer that the final communication be by fax or hard copy of an e-mail. This allows for any language errors to be corrected and serves as an official document. While a hard copy alone does not guarantee something won't go wrong, producing one can certainly help at check-in. If you arrive at your lodging and the staff cannot honor your reservation, be polite but firm in asking for a better room elsewhere in the hotel (at the same price) or a comparable room at another lodging. (You could also push the envelope here and ask that they pay for your first night, this being their mistake and an inconvenience to you. The hotel is obligated to find you comparable alternative lodgings—not to pay for your night someplace else—but I figure this is part of a bargaining process in arriving at a solution.) You should also ask them to pay for your transportation to the other location (should this be the result), which the staff should not hesitate to do. ~When you first arrive at your hotel, ask to see your room first. This is a common practice in Europe, and it is understood that if a room is not to your liking, you may request a different one. This is also your opportunity to ask for a room upgrade; if the hotel is not fully booked (and it rarely will be during low season), you may end up with a significantly nicer room at the same rate. It never hurts to ask. ~Speaking of fully booked: if you've been told that you can't get a room, call again between four and six P.M. and double-check. This is the time of day when many establishments cancel the reservations of guests who haven't shown up. ~If a hotel you choose also has a reservations office in the United States, call both numbers. It is entirely possible that you will be quoted different rates. Also, some of the more expensive hotels offer a rate that must be prepaid in full, in advance of your trip, in U.S. dollars, but that is lower than the local rack rate. ~No matter what type of lodging you choose, *always* inquire if there is a lower rate. Reservationists—and even the owners of small inns—always hope the rate they quote will be accepted, and if you don't ask about other possibilities, they will not volunteer any. In addition, ask if there are corporate rates; special rates for seniors, students, or government and military employees; weekend rates (this usually applies only to city hotels, as business travelers will have checked out by Friday); and even special prices for newlyweds.

Hotels and inns large and small all want to fill their rooms, and if you'll be staying four nights (sometimes three) or longer, you may also be able to negotiate a better rate. Most important, ask for how long the rate you're quoted is available and how many rooms at that price are left. In smaller places especially, a day can mean the difference between securing a reservation or losing it.

~Breakfast is rarely a good value taken at a hotel, especially in France where a typical French breakfast consists of a coffee drink and a croissant or roll. Save some money—and get the same thing, often better—and join the locals at the corner café. Many hotels these days, having recognized they can earn a bit of a markup on breakfast, will automatically add the cost of breakfast to your bill (saying that breakfast is included in the price)—unless you state in advance that you will not be taking breakfast at the hotel. I am in the habit of mentioning this both at the time I make the reservation and again when I check in. Occasionally, I have had to fight for the charge to be removed from my bill. (I once had a most *formidable* hotelier tell me that I had to pay for breakfast whether I ate it or not, and that *all* hotels in France had the same policy!) It is no doubt disappointing to hotel owners when their guests do not take breakfast, but the breakfast offered is a marked-up commodity that guests should have the option of choosing or not, as they wish. I should mention that I don't *always* opt for breakfast outside of the hotel. When traveling with young children, it is sometimes simply faster and less complicated to have breakfast in the same building, especially if I'm getting an early start on the day.

Aérospatiale and the Airbus

Following in the tradition of legendary pilots like Antoine de Saint-Exupéry (the author not only of *Le Petit Prince,* which continues to sell about 300,000 copies a year in France and about half that in the States, but also of *Wind, Sand, and Stars, Night Flight,* and *Flight to Arras*), Toulouse is headquarters of Airbus (which now shares the aircraft production world market with Boeing in Seattle) and Aérospatiale Matra. Since 1917 generations of planes have been designed, built, tested, and sold on what was the site of Aéropostale, and in 1999 a new company was formed in Europe: the European Aeronautic, Defense, and Space Company (EADS), which brought together Aérospatiale Matra, Germany's DaimlerChrysler, and Spain's CASA. This union created the largest aerospace company in Europe and the third largest worldwide. Visitors to Toulouse have the opportunity to visit Aérospatiale. Ninety-minute guided tours are offered by Taxiway, a company specializing in industrial tourism. Taxiway brochures are available at the Toulouse/Blagnac airport and at the tourist office. Tours are in English, German, Spanish, and Italian, and there are two different tours, one *visite Airbus* and the other *visite Concorde.* For information and reservations, contact Taxiway at 10 avenue Guynemer, 31770 Colomiers, France; 33.05.61.18.06.01; fax: 05.62.74.08.68; e-mail: reservation@ taxiway.fr; www.taxiway.fr.

Airfares and Airlines

We all know that not everyone pays the same price for seats on an airplane. One reason is that seats do not hold the same value at all times of the year, month, or even day of the week. The best way therefore to get the best deal that accommodates your needs is to check a variety of sources and be flexible. Flexibility is, and has always been, the key to low-cost travel, and you should be prepared to slightly alter the dates of your proposed trip to take advantage of airline seats that hold less value.

If you think all the best deals are to be found on the Internet, you're mistaken: airlines, consolidators, and other discounters offer plenty of good fares over the telephone and through advertisements. Many people have cornered me over the years and asked for my "secret" to finding a cheap airfare. The answer is that there is no secret, only diligent research. Price isn't the only factor in planning a trip, and if a supposedly cheap fare is offered only at times that are inconvenient for me, then it isn't cheap at all, it's outside the realm of possibility and therefore worthless. If there is a secret to finding the best fare, it is this: on any day of the week, the lowest fares can be found *equally* among Web sites, wholesalers, airlines, charters, tour operators, travel agents, and sky auctions. No Web site, not even Orbitz, can claim to offer all choices for all travelers, and you don't know who's offering what until you inquire.

Air France. I like flying a country's own airline whenever possible, and France's official airline is Air France, founded in 1933. Although Air France fares are usually among the highest available, its off-season fares are among the lowest, and it offers some unbeatable packages and deals throughout the year. Air France in the twenty-first century is poised to dominate the regional industry as Europe's third-largest carrier. The airline recently underwent major changes in routing and now uses the more popular system of hub connections rather than its former system of point-to-point routes. In fact, Paris's Charles de Gaulle 2 hub ranks as the main connection through Europe. (France's other major hubs are Lyons, Marseilles, Clermont-Ferrand, and Bordeaux.) Air France's main gateways from North America include New York (John F. Kennedy and Newark airports), Atlanta, Boston, Chicago, Cincinnati, Houston, Los Angeles, Miami, Philadelphia, San Francisco, Washington D.C., Montreal, Ottawa, and Toronto. Air France's main North American office is at 120 West 56th Street, New York, N.Y. 10019, and its toll-free number is 800-2-FRANCE (in Canada, dial 800-667-2747). Like other airlines, Air France offers specially priced Internet-only fares that are discounted from promotional fares, and it's worth it to browse the site periodically (www.airfrance. com) to check on airfare specials as well as packages. In fairness, over the years I have heard a few complaints about Air France's service from family members and friends; perhaps you have, too. After not flying Air France for many years, I decided to give the airline a try when I was beginning work on this book, and I can honestly report that I was particularly impressed with the airline. My flight plan took me from New York to Paris, Paris to Bordeaux, Toulouse to Paris, and Paris to New York. I learned from the reservations agent that the good fare I received essentially covered only the transatlantic legs of the journey; but I found that for in-country flights Air France rewards passenger loyalty by charging practically nothing for them. Pricing aside, the entire flying experience was enjoyable (except for the Paris-Bordeaux leg, when my three-year-old daughter threw up three times; still, the flight attendants could not have been more helpful; I can't say the same for the prim, polka-dot-bowtied businessman sitting next to me, but *tant pis*). Air France provides an entire line of engaging little activity packages for kids called Planète Bleue, and surprisingly, even the special meal I had ordered in advance was remarkably good. I encourage you to consider what Air France is offering at the time you are making your flight plans.

Charter flights. Reputable charter flights should not be approached with trepidation. I've had three good experiences on them—one to Paris—and encourage you to investigate them. The limitations are that most charters offer only coach class, and they tend to be completely full—in fact, a charter operator is legally allowed to cancel a flight up to ten days before departure if it doesn't fill enough seats. Although I did not experience any problems on my charter flights, delays are common, and (as with consolidators) passengers have no recourse. But operators who organize charter flights are required to place passengers' payments for the flight in an escrow account, so if the flight is canceled or if the operator doesn't abide by its agreement, you receive a refund. A publication called *Jax Fax Travel Marketing Magazine* lists more than five thousand scheduled charter flights to more than one hundred destinations worldwide. Previously available only to industry folks, the general public can now subscribe. A single issue can be purchased for about $5 as well as a one- or two-year subscription. Contact Jax Fax at 48 Wellington Road, Milford, Conn. 06460; 800-9JAXFAX or 203-301-0255; fax: -0250; www.jaxfax.com.

Airports and Getting To and Fro

The two major airports in the Southwest are to be found in Bordeaux (Merignac) and Toulouse (Blagnac). Other, smaller airports that have connecting flights to Paris and other French cities include Agen, Bergerac, Biarritz, Carcassonne, Castres, Lourdes, Montpellier, Nîmes, Pau, Périgueux, and Tarbes. A good book to consult for all your options is *Airport Transit Guide: How to Get from the Airport to the City Worldwide* (Ron Salk, editor-in-chief, Salk International Travel Premiums, Sunset Beach, Calif.). This handy, pocket-sized paperback is indispensable for frequent business and pleasure travelers and an awfully great resource for everyone else. It has been published annually for twenty years and includes ground transportation information for 447 airports worldwide. As stated in its introduction, "In the air, others worry about getting you safely from point A to point B. But on the ground you're on your own. And unless you're returning home or being met by a welcoming committee, getting from the airport to point C may require information you don't have. That's what this book is for." This book is a little hard to find—I used to see it frequently in bookstores, but now I rarely do. I ordered mine from Magellan's mail-order catalog (800-962-4943), but you can also call Salk directly at 714-373-5224 or visit its Web site (www.airporttransitguide.com). The book also features a world time zones map at the back.

Alliance Française

With approximately one thousand chapters in 138 nations worldwide (including 137 chapters in forty-five states across the United States and in Puerto Rico), the aim of Alliance Française—the official cultural arm of France—is to promote awareness, understanding, and appreciation of the French language and culture. French grammar and conversation classes are offered at all levels, and class size is typically small. Members have access to a library of books, videos, compact disks, periodicals, and special events. I have enjoyed my experiences with the Alliance over the years very much, and if there is a chapter near you, I encourage you to enroll in a class before you leave—and after you return! Or consider enrolling at the Alliance in one of its affiliates in the Southwest in Brive, Toulouse, Montpellier, and Bordeaux. To locate U.S. chapters or to enroll in classes in France, contact the Alliance Française at Délégation Générale de l'Alliance Française, 1900 L Street N.W., Suite 314, Washington, D.C. 20036; 202-689-3000; fax: -3100; www.afusa. org. The Web site features a list of frequently asked questions, as well as the costs for classes and accommodation possibilities.

Appellation d'Origine Contrôlée (AOC)

Translated as "controlled place of origin," AOC is an important food and wine term informing consumers that, for example, the wine they're buying is exactly what it purports to be: that is, that Bordeaux or Corbières wines (and others, of course) are made only from grapes grown in those regions. Before the establishment of the AOC designation, vintners were often concerned more with quantity than quality, and blending was common—grapes from as far away as Algeria were blended with those closer to home, and the vintner was allowed to refer to it as Burgundy or Rhône Valley or whatever. Like the label "certified organic," an AOC designation is about much more than a place name, and readers interested in learning about its various rules and stipulations should consult an authoritative wine resource, such as any edition of *The Oxford Companion to Wine* (Oxford University Press) or *Larousse Wines and Vineyards of France* (Arcade Publishing, 1991). One of my most favorite books about French wine, *Alexis Lichine's Guide* to the *Wines and Vineyards of France* (Alfred A. Knopf, 4th ed., 1989), includes very good details about the AOC in its first chapter.

Bargaining

Bargaining, whether for goods or for services, is perhaps less applicable to this edition of *The Collected Traveler* than to others. I have not encountered very many situations in the Southwest where bargaining is readily acceptable, except at open-air (or covered) markets where individual vendors sell produce, fish, bread, cooking utensils, clothing, bric-a-brac, and so on. It certainly is not the usual way of conducting business, but because I believe that nearly every item or service is negotiable to some degree, I think it is worthwhile to be aware of the basics of bargaining and how rewarding it can be for both buyer and seller. Bargaining makes many North American visitors uncomfortable. The reasons they are uncomfortable, I've found, is that they have never taken the time to understand and appreciate the art of bargaining, and they have some of the most backward and wrong opinions, usually stemming from the idea that they're surely being taken to the cleaners. It's important to *appreciate* bargaining: it's fun, interesting, and revealing of national character. It isn't something you do in a hurry, and it's not an antagonistic game of Stratego: bargaining does incorporate strategy, but it isn't territory being conquered or battleships sunk; the goods or services are on offer, and you do not have to purchase them.

However, I caution you against placing too much emphasis on the deal itself. There are few absolutes in the art of bargaining—each merchant is different, and the particulars of each transaction are different, and you will not be awarded a medal at the end of your visit for driving a hard bargain, especially if you have accumulated things you don't really want. More important than any of my tips is that you do not lose sight of the fact that what you want is something that appeals to you in some special way. Does it really matter, at the end of the day, that you *might* have gotten it for 20 or 50 euros less? If you end up with a purchase that you love and every time you look at it or wear it you have a warm feeling about your trip to France, it definitely does not matter what you paid for it. There is a difference between savvy bargaining and obsessive bargaining, and I don't know about you, but when I'm on vacation, obsessing about mercantile matters is the equivalent of postponing joy.

Rather than repeat my well-practiced tips here, I refer readers to my previous editions, especially *Morocco*. However, two are worth mentioning again:
~Politeness goes a long way. Vendors appreciate being treated with respect, and they don't at all mind answering questions from interested browsers. Strike up a conversation while you're looking at the wares; ask about the vendor's family,

share pictures of yours, or ask for a recommendation of a good local restaurant. Establishing a rapport also shows that you are reasonable and are willing to make a purchase at the right (reasonable) price. And if you're interested in buying antiques—or making large purchases of any kind—it would be worthwhile to get a copy of the *Know Before You Go* brochure from the U.S. Customs Service. You can write for a free copy (1300 Pennsylvania Avenue N.W., Washington, D.C. 20229) or view it online at www.customs.ustreas.gov (click "Traveler Information," then "Know Before You Go"). Dull as it may sound, I found this document to be incredibly interesting. Of special interest here are details on what you must declare, duty-free exemption, $400 exemption, gifts, household effects, paying duty, sending goods to the United States, freight shipments, duty-free shops, and cultural artifacts and cultural property.

Bastides

A *bastide,* according to Ina Caro in her wonderful book *The Road from the Past,* "was a military outpost built in sparsely populated areas, in which the rectangular grid pattern used by the Romans to facilitate the movement of troops and equipment was copied by both French and English kings." Readers who have visited Provence may recognize the word *bastide,* but there the word refers only to a private, grand estate—usually on relatively flat land and not at all fortified—and does not have the same history as a *bastide* in the Southwest. Though the French and the English built approximately 260 *bastides* in the Southwest around the end of the thirteenth century, *bastides* are, in fact, Roman in origin. You will not have any trouble finding *bastides* to visit and may even plan a *bastide* route, visiting a number of them in a single day. A few of the most popular are Monpazier, Monflanquin (referred to by many guidebooks as "perfect" because it is in the shape of a perfect rectangle), Sauveterre-de-Rouergue, Castelnau-de-Montmiral, Auvillar (with its spectacular circular market), and Villefranche de Rouergue. It's noteworthy that in the Middle Ages, freedom often meant relief from taxation, and a number of *bastides* were built by peasants who had been granted freedom from taxes and seignorial duties, which is why some *bastides* are named Villefranche (free city) or Villeneuve (new city). Many *bastides* are perfectly preserved, and visitors who frequent more than one will notice that they are typically built around a central marketplace framed by arcaded houses. Houses are of identical size, and the square grid of *rues* fan out from the central marketplace.

Biking

It's not surprising that the country that hosts the Tour de France (one hundred years old in 2003) welcomes cyclists of all abilities. Biking opportunities are not in short supply in Southwestern France, both for those who prefer the challenging heights of the Pyrenees and for those whose taste runs to flatter, gentler routes. You'll find information about local biking routes in some guidebooks, and the French tourist offices in North America and abroad have details also.

Cycling enthusiasts should inquire directly with the airline they're flying with about rules and regulations for carrying on bicycles. If you plan on renting a bike once you arrive, you'll find plenty of outlets that arrange for daily or weekly rentals. (Some guidebooks list specific names and contact information.) Be prepared to put down a deposit, however, which of course you do not get back if the bike is stolen or damaged. Keep in mind that bikes are rarely welcome on local buses but are occasionally allowed on buses that travel between cities. Cyclists are permitted to bring their bikes on some trains—you should check the SNCF timetables before showing up at the *gare* (station). A bicycle symbol appears on the timetables at the bottom indicating precisely which trains allow bikes. Two helpful vocabulary words are *vélo* (touring bike) and *vélo tout-terrain* (VTT, mountain bike). And if you'd like to be in France during the Tour de France, information about the legendary race and details of the route may be found online at the Tour's official site, www.letour.fr. Readers who might want to actually bike parts of the Tour route should search the archives of *The New York Times* either online or at the library for "Watching the Tour Over Handlebars" (Laurence Zuckerman, February 9, 2003). Zuckerman signed up with a company in Bloomington, Indiana, called VéloSport Vacations, headed up by Chris Gutowsky, who you might remember appeared in *Breaking Away* (one of my all-time favorite movies). He rode about fifty miles a day and had the opportunity to tackle several famous Tour ascents, including the Hautacam and the Col du Tourmalet. Zuckerman's piece is filled with good advice, including the observation that "it is possible to pack up your bike, rent a car and follow the Tour on your own. But hotels fill up quickly after the race route is announced in October, and the headaches involved in doing it yourself can be enormous. Indeed, the logistics of simply getting to ride along part of the route the day of the race, watch the finish and return to a hotel are the most challenging." Zuckerman also provides the names and contact information for five Tour de France operators as well as two bicycle shops that organize their own trips.

La Bise
A kiss, from the verb *baiser,* although the verb for "to kiss" is *embrasser.* Actually, *le bisou* is a social kiss, as opposed to *le baiser,* which is a much more passionate kiss—and in fact refers to much more—between lovers. In general the French kiss upon greeting each other, and they kiss again when saying farewell. The established practice is to kiss first the left cheek and then the right. In Provence and in other parts of the South in general, you may notice that many people kiss *three* times, always beginning with the left cheek. Men, too, if they are friends, sometimes kiss, though it is more common for them to shake hands enthusiastically, with an embrace or a pat on the back.

The Black Death
The plague was a significant and horrific undercurrent to life in France beginning in 1347, the year the French and English signed a truce in the Hundred Years' War. Ships from Genoa were being unloaded at Marseilles, and in addition to their cargo was an intruder from Crimea, unknown in Europe since the seventh century: the plague. The year 1348, in fact, was known as "the year of annihilation," as quoted in *Histoire de France* (Hachette) by Georges Duby. At the beginning of that fateful year, the Black Death was in Avignon and then reached Bordeaux at the beginning of the summer. From there, English ships carried it to England and Normandy. It reached Paris by August. Within the context of the Hundred Years' War, the plague was the reason for the truce of 1347 as neither France nor England had the money or the men to continue the fighting. A decimation of the population led to a lack of manpower, which led to an increase in wages and prices. Nobles thus levied more taxes or started petty wars to subsidize their lack of income. But with only a diminished population paying taxes, and a continuation of war, poverty increased, and the plague stepped in again as it tended to strike the poor rather than the rich, who were better fed and better able to escape. In a wider context, Europe became "an immense charnel" according to Duby. "The identity of the world, of order and of Divine will was forever shattered."

Bookstores
Like the French (and most Europeans in general), I prefer to buy whatever goods and services I need from specialists. One-stop shopping is a nice idea in theory, but it has not been very appealing to me, as convenience seems its only virtue. Therefore I buy fish from a fishmonger, flowers from a florist, cheese from a cheese shop, and so on. And when I'm looking for travel books, I prefer to shop at travel bookstores or independent bookstores with strong travel sections. The staff in these

stores are nearly always well traveled, well read, very helpful, and knowledgeable. An aspect I don't like about nationwide chain stores is that travel guides tend to be shelved separately from travel writing and related history books, implying that guidebooks are all a traveler may need or want. Stores specializing in travel take a wider view, understanding that travel incorporates many different dimensions.

Additionally, I must mention my two favorite mail-order book catalogs: *A Common Reader* and *Bas Bleu*. *A Common Reader* is issued monthly, while *Bas Bleu* comes out five times a year. Both offer an excellent selection of travel writing, biographies, history, cookbooks, and general fiction and nonfiction books for adults, as well as selected books for children. *ACR*'s selection is more extensive, but this does not make *Bas Bleu*'s offerings any less appealing. James Mustich Jr. is the man behind the *ACR* venture, and his reviews are of the sort that wander here and there and make you want to read every single book in the catalog. (His writing has been an inspiration to me for the annotated bibliographies in *The Collected Traveler*.) To add your name to these catalog mailing lists, contact *A Common Reader*. Contact information: 141 Tompkins Avenue, Pleasantville, N.Y. 10570; 800-832-7323; fax: 914-747-0778; www.commonreader.com. *Bas Bleu* contact information: P.O. Box 93326, Atlanta, Ga. 30377; 800-433-1155; fax: 404-577-6626; www.basbleu.com.

Bouchon

Readers already familiar with French will recognize the word *bouchon* (stopper, cork, float of a fishing line, and wisp of straw), perhaps especially as it appears in *tire-bouchon* (corkscrew). But *bouchon* also refers to the Quai des Chartrons and its side streets in Bordeaux, as these were the headquarters of the so-called *aristocratie du bouchon,* aristocracy of the cork.

Buses

Certainly within the city and town centers of the Southwest—even Bordeaux and Toulouse—it is seldom necessary to ride a bus, as most of what visitors will want to see and do is concentrated in a rather small area and you can usually walk from neighborhood to neighborhood without public transport. Also, I am very fond of the train, and I probably would never voluntarily choose the bus unless it were my only option.

C

Canal du Midi

Also known as the Canal des Deux Mers, as it was conceived as a way to connect the Atlantic with the Mediterranean, the canal is perhaps the most famous waterway in the Southwest (see the article featured in *Corners of the Midi-Pyrenees*). A slow and dreamy cruise on the canal is one of the ultimate stress-reducers. Motoring along at a gentle speed of about eight kilometers per hour forces one to unwind. If you are planning to either pilot a boat yourself or hire a captain, remember that locks are open from 9:00 to 6:00, with a one-hour break for lunch, usually from 12:30 or 1:00 to 1:30 or 2:00. A few companies to contact include:

Barging in France, S.A.R.L., Port de Plaisance, 21170, Saint Jean de Losne, France; 33.3/80.29.13.81 / fax: 80.29.04.67; www.barginginfrance.com. Barging in France operates under the name h2olidays, the sister company of H20, waterways specialists since 1987 (h2olidays branched out on its own in July 2001). Travelers may choose from houseboats for rent (self-drive), bed-and-breakfast barges (barges for charter only based on cruises for two, four, or six nights), or hotel barge cruises (the ultimate in luxury, usually for one week in length).

France Passion Plaisance, Boîte Postal 63, 71160 Digoin, France; 33.3/85.53.76.70; fax: 85.53.75.71; www.france-passion-plaisance.fr. In the Southwest, this company offers a short cruise (Toulouse–Le Segala–Toulouse, 28 locks, 19 hours); one-week cruise (Toulouse–Castelnaudary–Toulouse, 32 locks, 26 hours); and a two-week trip (Toulouse–Argens–Toulouse, 130 locks, 62 hours). Additionally, there are cruises from Agde and from Carcassone.

Locaboat Plaisance, Boîte Postal 150, 89303 Joigny Cedex, France; 33.3/86.91.72.72; fax: 86.62.42.41; www.locaboat.com. Founded in 1977, Locaboat pioneered the *pénichette,* and has been designing and building *pénichettes* in France for over twenty years. When I last checked, Locaboat offered what it refers to as "out and back" cruises in Gascony and the Lot and Garonne, and "one-way" trips, from Castelnaudary to Carcassone, for example.

Car Rental

Though one can get to and from the major cities and towns of Southwestern France—and even many of the smaller ones—by public transportation, it's a great convenience to have a car. Certainly if you are planning on visiting small villages in the Pyrenees or in the foothills, and the backroads of the Corbières, you will be glad to have a car, as there is little regular public transportation. Additionally, the Gorges du Tarn, the access roads into the Cévennes, and the Pont du Gard are best explored with a car. A car isn't necessary between individual cities and towns, but the flexibility a car allows is so appealing that I do recommend renting one for at least part of a journey in the Southwest. If you are renting a house or an apartment in the countryside, you will definitely need a car.

Driver's license. You don't need an international driver's license in France. Save the $10 fee for driving in less developed countries, where the absence of the license could open the door for bribery to cross a border. But if you will be living in France for a length of time and will have a car, getting the license is a good idea.

Leasing. In addition to renting options, consider leasing a car. I have leased a car on five occasions and anticipate leasing for many more—it is simply too good a value to pass up. Here are a few companies to consider. (I recommend them all, by the way; the reason you might choose one over another may have to do with availability of the vehicle you want.)

~*Auto France* offers what is known as the purchase/repurchase plan, in which you "buy" a car for a certain length of time, and then return it. The plan is a good deal because technically it operates more like a short-term lease, which makes the rental car exempt from European taxes. Auto France also offers the Peugeot plan, which allows you to pick up a brand-new Peugeot in one of more than thirty cities, and the rate—for trips of seventeen days or more—is VAT- and airport-tax-free. (You don't have to *keep* the car for seventeen days, but the price is the same if you drop it off earlier.) The rental price includes unlimited mileage, twenty-four-hour travel assistance, and all-risk auto insurance with full collision. There is free delivery and return of cars in major French cities and airports. You must be a permanent resident outside the EU and be visiting France for no more than 175 days within a twelve-month period. The brochure I last received featured eight different Peugeots, including wagons and minivans. Contact information: P.O. Box 760, 211 Shadyside Road, Ramsey, N.J. 07440; 800-572-9655; fax: 201-934-7501; www.auto-france.com.

~*Europe by Car* has been offering low-priced rentals and tax-free leases since 1954. It truly provides one of the best values around: in addition to its good overall rates (with special rates available for students, teachers, and faculty members), it offers a tax-free, factory-direct new car vacation plan. Contact information: 62 William Street, Seventh Floor, New York, N.Y. 10005; 800-223-1516 or 212-581-3040; www.europebycar.com.

~*Kemwel* is another company that offers a Peugeot short-term leasing program (which it refers to as the best-kept "secret" in the business) as well as regular car rentals, chauffeur-driven cars, car-pass vouchers, and motor-home rentals, all at competitive rates. Contact information: 39 Commercial Street, Portland, Me. 04102; 800-678-0678 or 877-820-0668 or 207-842-2285; fax: -2286; www.kemwel.com.

Parking garages. Ah, parking garages—along with keys and locks, they are not things for which I have a knack. I have less trouble with the *horodateur,* the machine into which you insert coins (or a credit card) that gives you a ticket, which you then display on your car windshield. There is another kind of *horodateur,* however, the kind inside parking garages. It gives you a ticket that you must insert into a stamping machine at the exit to the garage. In other words, the interior *horodateur* takes your money, but you can't get out of the garage unless the final machine gives you the green light. Lest you immediately conclude that parking garages in France are not worth the trouble, I do want to state that you will probably not ever have any problems. Unusual things happen to me that I'm sure never happen to other people. After many months of parking on the street and walking to a shopping mall near where I live, for example, I once decided to enter the mall's parking garage. I drove up to the ticket machine and pressed the button for my ticket. No ticket was issued. But inexplicably, the bar rose up, allowing me to drive through. As I did not have a ticket, however, I knew I would never be able to *leave* the garage, so I had to explain the situation to the manager, who appeared annoyed but could offer no explanation as to why the machine did not issue me a ticket. Anyway, if you find yourself parking in the underground garage in Toulouse, beneath the Place du Capitole—and you probably will, as it is the city's main parking garage and close to many hotels and historic sites—pay close attention to the system and try really hard not to be in the exit lane with cars behind you. I will spare you the entire story, but the nutshell version is that I was in this garage for *an hour and fifteen minutes* once because *I could not get out*. Even though I had dutifully paid my money, and it was the proper amount, the machine stated that there was an *erreur,* and I had to back up, with a line of cars behind me (this was in June, part of the reason why the garage was so crowded in the first place), and I had to get out of the car, find *le guichet* (window), ask the two men there what the problem was, only to be told that I had, in fact, done everything right, and *desolée,* they were sorry they could not explain it, but I should just go back and try again. Once more I got in line, by this time sweating profusely, and *voila!* the machine accepted my ticket, and I was free. I'm not alone in feeling this way—Ann Barry, in *At Home in France,* relates a similar but much less stressful experience she had in Avignon. After her time-consuming ordeal, she was wildly happy to drive out into the bright light of day, "my distrust in garage parking confirmed."

Roads and routes. Road maps and atlases employ coded route numbers for large and small roads: A for *autoroutes à péage,* or toll roads; RN for *route nationale,* the roads that were considered major before the autoroute network existed; and D for *départementale* roads, the smallest of the three. But most of the highway and road signs you'll see in France (and Europe in general) typically indicate cities or towns quite far away rather than road numbers. (Initially this threw me off. It reminded me of a sign I used to see years ago just outside Philadelphia for a restaurant at the New Jersey shore; the sign advertised that the restaurant was "minutes away" but was in fact two *hours* away.) Begin thinking in terms of *direction* rather than road number, and consult your map(s) often—you'll find that it's quite a sensible way of getting around, and it forces you to be better versed in geography.

Useful vocabulary: Faites le plein (Fill the tank; if you don't want to fill up the tank, request an amount in euros); *un bon* (gas station receipt); *convoi exceptionel* (the equivalent of vehicles carrying a wide load; I should let readers who will be driving know of an experience I had with a *convoi.* I was driving from Gourdon to Rocamadour at a speed that was definitely over the posted limit but not by much. Suddenly, I noticed that a *gendarme* was motioning to all the drivers ahead of me to pull over to the side of the road. I surmised that we were all being singled out for speeding, and I immediately began to rehearse the "I'm not from around here" routine that my friend Anne once employed—she was pulled over for speeding in Oregon once and, being from New Jersey, she simply said nothing more to the officer than "I'm not from around here" to every question he asked her, and finally, in exasperation, he gave up and waved her on. Happily, my situation was not the same; we were being pulled over to allow the *convoi exceptionel* to pass by.); *Vous n'avez pas la priorité* (You don't have the right of way, seen mostly at traffic circles, where you give way to traffic already in the circle coming from your left); *passage protégé* (indication, in a yellow diamond-shaped road sign on a main road, that you have the right of way over traffic on any minor side road; priority is always given to vehicles approaching from the right—*priorité a droite*—unless indicated otherwise); *cédez le passage* (yield to traffic); *rappel* (slow down, a reminder of the speed limit); *dépannage* (breakdown); *aire de repos* (rest area, sometimes with a view; note that on autoroutes there are toilet facilities every 20 kilometers or 12 miles); *Nous sommes sur la mauvaise route* (literally, We're on the bad route, or, I think we're lost); *a mi-chemin entre . . .* (halfway between . . .); *pneu* (tire, one of the more vexing French words, pronounced with the *p* sounded, as puh-NO); *Pouvez-vous la réparer aujourd'hui?* (Is it possible to fix it today?); and *service des urgences* (the emergency room of a hospital), a word you'll hopefully never need.

Carousels

First-time visitors to France may not think of carousels as an intrinsic part of its landscape, but as residents and those who have visited France before know, carousels are ubiquitous, appearing in nearly every city, town, and village. Carousels share room on my short list of sights that are uniquely and immediately identifiable as French. If you stumble upon a local *fête* or *foire*, a carousel will always be a part of the festivities. And though they are an utter joy and delight for children, young and old alike enjoy carousels. You may hear one long before you see it, and it is truly a spectacle not to be missed. If you have children in tow and they are as wild about carousels as my daughter, you positively *will not* be able to pass by without buying a ride, which costs about two euros. Though my daughter is not particularly discriminating when it comes to carousels, she has informed me that she thought those in Domme and Carcassonne were especially great. The word for a single ride is a *tour*, by the way, and most carousel operators sell packages of tickets for a reduced price.

Causses

Causses are limestone plateaux that are among the most distinctive features of the Southwest. Visitors will become familiar with the Causses de Gramat, Méjean, Noir, and du Comtal, among a number of others. Freda White, in *Three Rivers of*

France, notes that the rivers "have worn the lime right down to the ancient hard sea-bed. Once they are in the limestone country, the streams do not fall very rapidly; they are fairly near sea-level all the way. Their gorges are called '*couloirs*'—passages, or in the Tarn, 'canyons.'" The four Great *Causses* are the Sauveterre, Méjean, Noir and Larzac, and again according to White, towards their junction with the Lozère and Cévennes, the top of the *causses* is often higher than 3,000 feet. And there are people who are *causse*-addicts. "Nothing will do for them but the Great *Causses* with their silence, their solitude, their thin, high air and long empty vistas. For they are spiritual children of the desert; and the *causses* are desert country."

Chais

Chai refers to a building where wine is stored in barrels before it is bottled and laid in a *cave,* or cellar. It is a word you'll see often when reading about wine from Bordeaux and Gascony—I have never seen it used with regard to the wines of Languedoc-Roussillon. Some *chais* welcome visitors, and may sell you wine in a plastic barrel, filled up on the spot. I have never visited a *chai,* but my wonderful tour guide at Château Pichon Longueville in Pauillac recommended it, as well as a visit to a barrel maker, which I thought would be especially interesting. My guide believed that the tourist office staff in Bordeaux would have some suggestions for interested visitors.

Cheques-Cadeaux

This phrase for gift certificate or voucher may not be essential, but it certainly is useful if you would like to give a special gift to someone and don't know exactly what to select but do know that he or she will love a particular shop or service.

Children

France may not have the reputation that Italy and Spain do in extending a warm welcome to children, but in my experience the French have repeatedly been very kind to my daughter. I admit, however, that I have purposely set my expectations lower than I would elsewhere and have not tried to push my luck: while I know Alyssa would be made to feel welcome at the nicest restaurants in Italy, I have never taken her to anything more exalted than a Michelin one-star in France. Parents who keep this in mind will have nothing less than a positive experience in France.

A few months before Alyssa was born, I was feeling anxious that my life as a mother was going to drastically alter my ability to travel. My colleague and friend Bruce H. helped me snap out of this funk by pointing out that my husband and I would have to travel *differently* than we did before but would indeed still travel because we love it. As Bruce is both a parent and a world traveler, he advised us not to overthink the situation, because then we would find a million reasons *not to* travel. The way I see it, parents can either make the decision never to go anywhere—and thereby deprive both their children and themselves of a priceless experience—or plan an itinerary with kids in mind and take off on a new journey. I believe that children have as much to teach us as we do them, especially when traveling—their curiosity and imagination make even familiar destinations seem new. In an article entitled "How Foie Gras Was My Valley" (*Forbes FYI*, March 2002), Christopher Buckley reported that "the kids took one look at Beynac and let out a collective yesss. It's good for American children to confront antiquity that puts our own in perspective. The oldest houses in St. Augustine or Santa Fe seem pretty arriviste next to a 12th-century *bastide,* much less 17,000-year-old cave paintings." Also worth noting is a letter to the editor I read recently in the travel section of *The New York Times*. The writer stated she felt that the author of a previously published essay underestimated the impact of a five-year-old child's first trip to Europe. She emphasized that twenty years after *her* first trip to Italy, she became an art student, earned her master's degree in art history, and worked as a museum curator. My personal experiences in traveling with children have taught me that one should never underestimate how much children will absorb and retain, and what will inspire and enthuse them.

An observation you will be sure to make: in France—as in most other Mediterranean countries—young children stay up late at night, even at restaurants. Don't be surprised if it's ten or eleven o'clock and there are lots of kids running around, especially in Languedoc-Roussillon, closer to the coast. I've never seen the children looking unhappy or tired, and it seems to make sense in a part of the country with a tradition of an afternoon siesta.

Here are some general traveling-with-children tips that have worked for me that you may want to try:

Advance planning. If you really enjoy dining out in fine restaurants or hiking, it makes sense to plan a trip with other adults who also have children. This way two of the adults can have some time to themselves—perhaps for a day-long hike or a leisurely lunch at a nice restaurant—while the other two watch the kids. Taking turns throughout the trip ensures that the adults will feel they had some relaxing, kid-free time to pursue their rarely enjoyed interests as well as some quality time with the kids. Traveling with grandparents helps in this regard, too. ~Build excitement in advance of the trip by involving your children in the planning, showing them maps and books and talking about the things you'll see and do. ~For older kids, buy an inexpensive disposable camera and let them take their own pictures. ~For kids of all ages, buy a blank journal and help them create a record of the trip (the photos they take will go nicely in here).

At Your Destination. Wherever you arrive first in France—perhaps it will be Paris for a day—find a souvenir stand and buy one of those floaty pens—the kind where the Eiffel Tower floats back and forth—or some other kind of nifty pen so your kids can use it to write in their journals. ~When you arrive at an art museum, first buy some postcards. If you have more than one child, tell them that whoever finds the most paintings or works of art first will win a special prize. (You must decide this in advance; it could be *pain au chocolat, glace,* or a ride on a carousel—whatever your budget allows—but make sure it's something they will want to compete for.) If you have one child, tell him or her to find all the artworks—there is no race—to receive a special prize. ~Strollers are both a blessing and a curse when traveling: on the one hand, when your child needs to take a nap, he or she will fall asleep quite easily in the stroller; on the other, sometimes naptime is precisely when you've reached a spot where you are forced to wake him or her. You may want to consider changing course at some point in your trip. After a few days of leaving the hotel early in the morning and not returning until late in the evening, I decided to plan our days differently, making sure we left early in the morning with not too great a distance to go—so Alyssa could walk—and returning to the hotel in time for lunch and a siesta. In the midafternoon we would set out again, occasionally with but mostly without the stroller, making the days less physically exhausting for me and more fun for her. ~Fruit juices are sometimes unavailable in restaurants, but soda, unfortunately, almost always is. We do not keep soda in our home, so introducing Alyssa to soda has not exactly been what I consider welcome. But I feel that when traveling, a child who eats what he or she wants is a happy child, and I do not think it is productive to argue about food or drink in a restaurant. Parents all choose which battles they will wage with their children, and my own advice is that this shouldn't be one to choose.

Useful vocabulary: *une tasse* (a cup, usually a small one; you might think that you could simply say you want a small glass—*un petit verre*—but that phrase means a glass of brandy; *une tasse* is a useful word in restaurants when you want to indicate that you'd like a smaller cup for your child; *Servez-vous demi-portions pour les enfants?* (Do you serve half-portions for children? though usually there are choices for children printed on menus); and finally *palmier* (technically, palm tree) is the word for those festive, colorful bursts that look like they belong on wrapped gifts but are used to adorn certain ice cream dishes that are served at cafés and restaurants. Even if your French is pretty good, it is doubtful you would know this word, and if your child is on the verge of tears because his or her dish of ice cream *didn't* come with the pretty burst, you, too, will resort to asking the waiter what it's called.

Clothing

In general I pack light, and unless I have plans to be at fancy places, I pack double-duty items (stuff that can go from daytime to evening) in low-key colors that also mix and match so I can wear garments more than once. I also tend to bring items that aren't my favorites, figuring that if someone snatches my suitcase or rummages through my hotel room, at least I won't lose the things I love the most. Appearance counts for a lot with the French, and they—like other Europeans—tend to dress up a bit more than Americans. The French also remain conservative, especially in smaller towns, when it comes to visiting their religious houses of worship. You will earn respect and goodwill by refraining from wearing sleeveless shirts, and short skirts and shorts, no matter how hot it is. You may find this odd in a country where topless sunbathing is permitted on the beaches, but make no mistake about it: dressing inappropriately around town and in church is still frowned upon, even in bigger cities like Bordeaux and Toulouse.

While blue jeans are as popular in France as anywhere, I recommend reserving them for casual daytime wear and for only the most casual places at night (though it does make a difference if you dress them up by also wearing nice shoes, a blazer or a nice jacket, a button-down shirt, or a classic sweater or blouse). For men, suits and ties are necessary only at the finest restaurants and venues. Even at some one- and two-star Michelin establishments, diners wear *nice* clothes but not finery. Polo shirts and khakis are always appropriate during the day and at many bistros, cafés, clubs, and informal restaurants at night. The American obsession for color-coordinated jogging suits, complete with sneakers, is baffling to the French, who believe that jogging attire is worn *only* when engaging in that activity and is not a fashion statement.

Shoes. Although comfortable shoes are of the utmost importance, I never, ever bring sneakers—and I positively forbid my husband to bring them. *You* may never bring them again either once you realize that they scream "American," and as far as I'm concerned, there is little to gain in this world today by being identified as an American. (Alice Steinbach, in *Without Reservations: The Travels of an Independent Woman,* refers to this sneaker truth when she was at a bar in Paris and noticed a woman she thought was quintessentially French: "'I see you're American, too,' she said. I turned toward her, wondering how she had identified me as an American. She seemed to know what I was thinking, and glanced down at my feet. I followed her gaze. She was looking at my black leather Reeboks, which, we both knew, were not the sort of shoes any Frenchwoman over the age of thirty would ever wear.") I am partial to Arche and Mephisto walking shoes and sandals for men and women, but several other lines are available that are also stylish *and* comfortable. I recently discovered a unique shoe line just for women: "à propos . . . conversations." I loved the shoes right away when I read they were "influenced by European women whose fashion sense does not include white athletic shoes outside of sports." All the shoes—which are soft and flexible and easily fold down to handbag or briefcase size—are limited editions and sport such names as Liquid Lemons, Peacock Punch, Linen Sands, African Sun, and Khaki Krunch. More than a dozen styles are offered in two collections a year, and many styles are available two ways: with one solid center elastic band or two cross straps of elastic. "Like a scarf for your feet" is how they're trademarked. You can call 800-746-3724 for a catalog or view the styles online at www.conversationshoes.com.

Cooking Schools and Wine Courses

The best single source for cooking schools in France (and the entire world) is the *Shaw Guide to Cooking Schools: Cooking Schools, Courses, Vacations, Apprenticeships, and Wine Instruction Throughout the World* (ShawGuides, New York), updated annually. Both internationally famous programs and lesser-known classes are listed, and interested food lovers can also view updates to the guide at its Web site, www.shawguides.com. One of the better known programs in the Southwest is La Combe en Périgord, a cooking school in the Dordogne that offers one-week programs including hands-on classes, visits to markets, vineyards, flour millers, bakers, artisanal food producers, and dining in restaurants ranging from farmhouse cuisine to Michelin starred places. (See the article by Joyce Goldstein at the end of *Practical Information* for a more detailed description.)

Here are a few other good sources for cooking classes.

The International Kitchen, founded by Karen Herbst in 1994, specializes in more than forty unique cooking trips to France and Italy. A few Southwestern trips recently offered include "Week in the Heart of Bordeaux Wine Country"; "Bordeaux Cuisine at Château des Vigiers"; and "Cooking Journey in the Languedoc." Contact information: 55 East Monroe, Suite 2840, Chicago, Ill. 60603; 800-945-8606; fax: 312-803-1593; www.intl-kitchen.com.

Epiculinary, which offers twenty "distinctive cooking journeys" in Italy, France, and Spain, was founded by Catherine Merrill, a former travel agent specializing in European and culinary vacations. Its four Southwestern France trips include "Les Mimosas Cooking School"; "Classic French Cooking in Bordeaux"; "Truffles and Foie Gras"; "Château des Vigiers." Contact information: 321 East Washington Avenue, Lake Bluff, Ill. 60044; 888-380-9010 or 847-295-5363; fax: -5371; www.epiculinary.com.

L'Ecole des Chefs Relais Gourmands is perhaps the most appealing program I've ever heard about. I first profiled L'Ecole des Chefs in my *Paris* edition; you may recall that this unique program—which is not a traditional cooking school but an opportunity to work in restaurant kitchens—was founded by Annie Jacquet-Bentley, a Parisian now living in the United States. She created the program after she spent time studying with some French chefs and wanted to make the experience available to others. In the spring of 2001, however, the prestigious Relais & Châteaux hotel group acquired L'Ecole des Chefs, broadening the program to include nearly one hundred Relais Gourmand restaurants in seventeen countries. Classes are mostly in two- and three-star Michelin restaurants, and although they're for nonprofessionals, applications receive an extremely thorough review. A *stage* (stage, or length) is either two or five days, and apprentices may be asked to work for up to twelve hours at a time. There are five L'Ecole des Chefs participating restaurants in Southwestern France: Hôtel du Centenaire; Relais de la Poste; Château Cordeillan-Bages; Les Loges de l'Aubergade; and Les Pyrénées. To read about some first-hand L'Ecole experiences, see "How to Boil Four-Star Water" (Guy Trebay, *The New York Times,* September 4, 2002); "The College of Hard Cheese: Blood, Sweat, and Tuna" (Andy Birsh, *Forbes FYI,* November 2001); "How Great Paris Restaurants Do It" (*Saveur* no. 35, 1999); and "Gourmet Adventurism" (*Paris Notes,* March 1999). In Guy Trebay's *New York Times* article, which detailed his experience at the French Laundry in California, the author noted that September and October are the busiest months for classes, both in America and overseas—a point worth highlighting for interested participants. Personally, I think it is *une idée excellente* for a gift, and I wish some thoughtful person would give it to me! L'Ecole des Chefs internships are priced from about $1,100 to $1,400 for two days and from about $1,900 to $2,600 for five days. Contact information: 11 East 44th Street, Suite 707, New York, N.Y. 10017; 800-877-6464; www.ecoledeschefs.com.

Cuisine International, not to be confused with the International Kitchen, offers cooking courses in Italy, France, England, Portugal, and Brazil. Founded in 1987 by Judy Ebrey, the company (which is entirely family-run and -owned) hand-picks all of its schools. Its program in Southwestern France is based at the Domaine d'Esperance, the eighteenth-century country home of Countess J. L. de Montesquiou Fezensac, located in the heart of Bas-Armagnac, one and a half hours from Bordeaux. Since enrollment is kept to a maximum of nine, the classes are small and intimate, led by Chef Natalia Arizmendi, a *grand diplôme* of the Cordon Bleu. Contact information: P.O. Box 25228, Dallas, Tex. 75225; 214-373-1161; fax: -1162; www.cuisineinternational.com.

Les Liaisons Délicieuses, founded in 1994 by Patricia Ravenscroft, offers hands-on cooking classes with Michelin-starred chefs inside their restaurant kitchens as well as excursions to vineyards, markets, farms, museums, châteaus, and sites that bring French regional history and culture to life. During the year she lived in Paris with her family, Ravenscroft became the first nonprofessional American to work with Michelin-starred chefs in their restaurant kitchens. As the year progressed, the chefs, their families and friends became her friends, so her *carnet d'adresses* is substantial. Recently one of the trips offered to the Southwest was "A Winter Indulgence in Truffles and Foie Gras in the Dordogne." All Liaison trips are limited to eight to ten participants, and noncooks are also welcome—anyone who appreciates French food, wine, and culture will thrive on a Liaison journey. Contact information: 4710 30th Street N.W., Washington, D.C. 20008; 877-966-1810 or 202-966-1810; fax: -4091; www.cookfrance.com.

There are a great number of good resources for wine-tasting classes as well as information about vineyards and château visits. The list is so long, however, that I decided not to list them all here. Rather, the two sources below, which are the best-known organizations in the Southwest, also have an amazing amount of information on other wines and spirits—including Armagnac and Jurançon—throughout the region.

~La Maison du Vin, Conseil Interprofessionnel du Vin de Bordeaux (CIVB). This major organization is probably *the* one to know about for Bordeaux wines. La Maison du Vin is the headquarters for the CIVB, which represents all the region's wine-growers and shippers. When you arrive in Bordeaux, La Maison is a great place to visit to plan a vineyard itinerary, as it makes a wealth of information available to the general public, including a complimentary guide in French, German, and English featuring six hundred châteaus and a map of the Gironde vineyards. The CIVB's Bordeaux Wine School, established in 1989, offers courses in French, English, German, and Japanese. Students may enroll in two-hour introductory classes, wine weekend classes, or three-day intensive courses and learn how to start a wine cellar, match food and wine, and identify the aromas that define Bordeaux wines. Contact information: 1 cours du XXX Juillet, 33080 Bordeaux; 33.5/56.00.22.88; fax: .56.00.99.30; www.vins-bordeaux.fr.

~The Bordeaux Business School, founded in 1874, is the first business school to specialize in the wine sector at an international level. It offers a Wine MBA program that is taught exclusively in English and is open to only twenty participants per session. Wine MBA is no ordinary program: it is aimed at "executives working in the wine-related sectors, such as export managers, sales managers, marketing directors, estate managers, merchant house executives, buyers, oenologists. The participants, who will already have a Master's degree or equivalent, must also prove sound professional experience." The program begins each year in September and continues for thirteen months. Contact information: Isabelle Dartigues, Wine MBA Director, isabelle.dartigues@bordeaux-bs.edu; 33.5/56.84.22.29; fax: 33.6/10.34.22.17; www.winemba.com.

Course Libre *versus* Mise à Mort

These two terms differentiate two versions of a bullfight, the *course libre* being the French version and the *mise à mort* being the Spanish *corrida* version. Bullfights are held during spring and summer in Nîmes, across the Rhône in Arles, and in the Gers in Gascony, which remains the center of bullfighting in southern France. If you've never seen one, I encourage you to fit one into your itinerary. *Course libre* bulls are from the Camargue and are small with lots of particularly sharp horns. These black bulls are familiar with the ways of men (*les gardiens,* cowboys) well before they are brought into the arena. Spanish bulls, on the other hand, have no experience with men until they are face to face with the toreador in the *arène* (arena) and certainly have no familiarity with what men do in or outside of the arena. In the *course libre* the *razeteur* (bullfighter) must attempt to remove a knot of ribbons and/or flowers from between the bull's horns with the use of a razor comb. Unlike what happens in a *mise à mort,* the bull is not killed. The *course libre* is known in the Southwest as the *course landaise,* which takes its name from the Les Landes region of Gascony. Bulls were often run through the streets prior to a corrida, and daring villagers would run side by side with the bulls to the arena. This grew into a "sport" in its own right, similar to the famous running of the bulls in Pamplona, but in the nineteenth century laws were passed that confined this activity to an arena. The modern result is now referred to as *les course landaises.* According to Charles Neal in *Armagnac,* "Certain *écarteurs* [dodgers, or those who perform the passes] are legendary and still spoken of fondly (Coran, Suisse, Mazzantini, Meunier, Lalande, Forsans, the Gypsy brothers Ramunchito), while modern stars like Dusseau, Descazeaux, Laplace, Lalanne, Rachou, and Bergamo continue to improve upon the traditions set by their predecessors. . . . Corridas in Mont-de-Marsan, Dax, Bayonne, Aire, Eauze and Vic-Fezansac attract the top names in bullfighting every year," and have been staged as far west as Bayonne. The main bullfighting season runs from July to September. It pays to find out the dates of the scheduled *ferias* in advance of your trip—you run a great risk of not finding vacancies at any hotels in Nîmes before, during, or immediately after the bullfights. Ticket prices range from low to rather high, depending on whether you select *soleil* (sun), *ombre et soleil* (half shade and sun, meaning that as the sun moves across the sky, you'll be sitting in both shade and sun), or *ombre* (totally in the shade, and the most expensive) seats.

Cru

As wine is such a major part of life in the Southwest—not just in and around Bordeaux but in Corbières, Cahors, and Languedoc, too—it's helpful to know a few related words. Even if you don't drink wine, recognizing some French wine terms goes a long way toward understanding its cultlike following. *Cru* is among the most important to grasp, and it means "growth" or "vineyard." *Cru* is not a word bandied about much in Languedoc-Roussillon or in most other wine growing regions of France (Burgundy is an exception), but it's hugely significant in Bordeaux, and here's why.

In 1855 the Bordeaux Chamber of Commerce appointed the Bordeaux Brokers' Association—an official body attached to the Bordeaux Stock Exchange—to create the Classement des Grand Crus de la Gironde. According to Alexis Lichine—whose explanation of the classification in his *Guide to the Wines and Vineyards of France* is the best one I've ever read—Napoleon III was adamant about having a classification of Bordeaux wines completed in time for the 1855 Universal Exposition in Paris, where the best French wines would be on display for the rest of the world to see. In effect, the classification would list Bordeaux wines in order of their excellence "as demonstrated by the prices they had fetched over the years."

(Lists according to price had actually been in existence long before 1855: "By the end of the eighteenth century, the four wines that were later designated First Growths in 1855 were already recognized as the very best that Bordeaux had to offer and the prices paid for them were correspondingly high.") There was general agreement at the time that no one was better qualified than the brokers to rank the wines: as intermediaries between the *propriétaire* and the shipper, they were more familiar than anyone else with all the wines of commercial importance. But as Lichine explains, "this familiarity led to one inevitable and distorting limitation— wines which had little or no exposure in the Bordeaux marketplace received no attention, no matter what their quality. Therefore the great districts of today— Graves (except for Haut-Brion), which was classed along with the First Growths of the Médoc), Saint-Emilion, and Pomerol—were out of the running, because in 1855 they had no commercial or public recognition. The fact is that they were minor wines at the time. The brokers had no way of knowing that a century later Pétrus, Cheval-Blanc, and Ausone would all command prices equal to and often surpassing those of the First Growth Médocs." St.-Emilion and Pomerol were perceived to be on the "wrong" side of the river. Between Bordeaux and Libourne, the wine center for St.-Émilion and Pomerol, lie the Dordogne and Garonne Rivers, and until the early nineteenth century no bridge spanned the Dordogne, helping to create the belief that Libourne was a social backwater.

At the time the brokers got together to make the 1855 classification, there were only two notable wine regions: the Médoc for red wines and Sauternes-Barsac for sweet wines. (As Lichine notes, "Château Haut-Brion in Graves was an exception to the all-Médoc line-up because it was too well known and too well sold to be ignored by the brokers.") The brokers took into consideration the prestige of both the wine and the owner, as well as the quality of the soil and the exposure of the vineyard. (These last are regarded as remaining more or less constant from generation to generation regardless of who the owner is.) They ranked sixty-one wines as *crus classés* (classed growths), ranging from first to fifth. They also created a very short list of only four *premier crus* (first growths), which included Château Lafite, Château Latour, Château Margaux, and Château Haut-Brion. (According to *The Oxford Companion to Wine,* an authoritative source, Château Cheval Blanc and Château Ausone are sometimes regarded as *premier crus,* as is "the unclassified but generally acknowledged star of Pomerol, Château Pétrus.") The *premier crus* are the most prestigious and consistently excellent Bordeaux wines and are the ones you read about fetching enormous sums at auction (or even when purchased at a wine shop).

Now, if you're a newcomer to all this and feel that you have this one distinction clear, open up the nearest bottle of *vin de table* you have at hand, and keep reading. In 1867, a mere twelve years after the official classification, a gentleman named Charles Cocks, author of his own respected rating of Bordeaux wines, underscored the need for ongoing reassessment, writing that, as Lichine informs us, "like all human institutions, this one is subject to the laws of time and must, at certain times, be rejuvenated and kept abreast of progress." A major factor pointing to the need for reclassification is that though the quality of a vineyard's soil may remain the same, the owner may be forced to sell it or rent it out, or he may trade it for a better vineyard parcel elsewhere; such changes in ownership make updating constantly necessary. Another significant factor is the ability of the owner himself and the "effectiveness of his management as reflected in the know-how and dedication of his workers in the vineyards and the cellars . . . although the most conscientious grower in the world cannot overcome poor soils and unfavorable climate, he can have an influence—for the better—on all other aspects of the wine-making process." But no reclassification was done in 1867 or anytime soon thereafter.

The thread of the *cru* story doesn't pick up again until 1960, when the Syndicat des Crus Classés petitioned the INAO (Institut National des Appellations d'Origine) for an update of the 1855 classification. Either the 1855 classification had to be amended to reflect changes in production and market value, the Syndicat said, or else it should be left untouched and a completely new classification drawn up. The INAO responded that the rankings in the 1855 classification reflected quality at a given time in history and that it had no authority to change them. The INAO did establish guidelines for a new ranking, but these proved to be hotly debated, so much so that the INAO lost enthusiasm for the project. In the midst of all this debate, four prominent and "extremely able" wine brokers were delegated the task of performing a new classification. They created three categories of excellence, as opposed to the original five. The reaction to this development, too, was "explosive outrage," and the original classification stood.

Lichine himself was a member of the committee to amend the classification, and when he understood that progress would not be made, he created his own personal classification. (It appears on pages 72–75 of his *Guide to the Wines and Vineyards of France*.) In the course of preparing his rankings, he realized a most important truth that had not previously been emphasized: "Even in 1855 a wine ranked as a Second, Third, Fourth, or Fifth Growth was *not a second-, third-, fourth-, or fifth-rate wine*. This terminology has always been confusing. Actually, since only sixty-one among approximately three thousand vineyards in the Bordeaux area were considered worthy of being named Great Growths—whether first or fifth—as a group they comprise a majority of the world's finest red wines. To be second only after Lafite, Latour, Margaux, and Haut-Brion is vastly different from being second-rate. Moreover, it is only on average that the First are the best; in certain years others equal or even surpass them." Now we arrive at the year 1973, when an official reclassification finally took place. Somehow the Ministry of Agriculture allowed Château Mouton-Rothschild to be awarded the long-deserved accolade of first growth status, bringing the total number of *premier crus* to five. But the

Ministry went no further, and other châteaus that also deserve to be upgraded are still waiting. Whew.

Wines from several other Bordeaux wine areas are labeled *premier grand cru classé,* which makes them prestigious (and excellent) but not in that inner circle of five. Following *premier grand cru classé* are *grand cru classé* and *grand cru.* Just below all of *these* are the second growths, also referred to as "super seconds," which are also excellent and much valued. The super seconds are the best-performing wines ranked as second growths in the 1855 classification of the Médoc and Graves. To quote from *Oxford,* "There is no absolute agreement about which properties qualify as super seconds but Châteaux Pichon-Longueville-Lalande and more recently Pichon-Longueville (Baron) in Pauillac, Cos d'Estournel in St.-Estèphe, and Léoville-Las-Cases and Ducru-Beaucaillou in St.-Julien have all been nominated at one time or another." According to the editors of the *Oxford* tome, other strong candidates—though not second growths—include Châteaux Palmer in Margaux; Château La Mission-Haut-Brion and Domaine de Chevalier in Pessac-Léognan; and Châteaux Figeac and Canon in St.-Emilion. Joseph Wechsberg, in *Blue Trout and Black Truffles,* explains it this way: "Only the finest wines of the region, not more than ten per cent of the whole crop, are bottled and sold under the name of a château. The next best wine bears the name of certain districts and townships, such as Pauillac, St.-Julien, St.-Estèphe, Margaux, St.-Saveur, Cantenac. Wines that do not qualify for the district names may be called 'Médoc,' [provided] they come from the area bordered in the east by the Gironde and Garonne rivers and in the west by the Atlantic, contain at least ten degrees of alcohol, and are made from certain vines called Cabernet, Carmenère, Malbec, Merlot, and Petit Verdot. Médoc wines that do not fulfill these requirements may be sold only under the name 'Bordeaux Rouge' or 'Rouge Ordinaire.'" Finally, according to Jay McInerney in *Bacchus and Me,* there are the so-called *vins de garage,* boutique wines made in tiny quantities and selling for sky-high prices.

All of this is useful to know, and readers who are serious Bordeaux collectors and/or connoisseurs will consider this summary ridiculously elementary. But if you enjoy wine very much but are unable or unwilling to begin viewing it as an investment (I have not spent more than forty dollars on a bottle of wine in my life and probably never will), this knowledge of the rarefied world of *crus* is, frankly, not at all useful in actually *tasting* Bordeaux wines. The chances that the likes of us would ever be able to identify a *premier cru* and appreciate its depth and complexity over, say, a Bordeaux super second, are slim to none. But no matter. Learning about wine only increases one's understanding of the industry that first put Bordeaux on the map. And as Freda White has noted, "it is part of the experience of French travel to drink one of the famous vintages sometimes." I say that's what good wine bars are for—they allow us to try wines by the glass that we might never be able to afford by the bottle.

Cucagnan

Cucagnan is the name of a village in the Hautes-Corbières near Quéribus, one of the Cathar castles. I single it out here not only because it's picturesque—it was built in the form of an amphitheater, with lots of alleys and steep streets, and has been a protected site since 1969—or because it's so close to Quéribus—climbing to the top of this rocky peak remains one of my most distinctive memories of the Corbières, and even my three-year-old daughter was able to make the ascent—but because the village is host to regular performances of a philosophical short story in verse known as "The Vicar of Cucugnan's Sermon." The story was originally composed in Occitan by Achille Mir (1822–1901) but was later popularized by Alphonse Daudet, who produced a prose version of it in French. Mir reputedly gave the text its burlesque and moral qualities, and today performances are staged every day from April to October and on weekends in February, March, November, and December. I had been told that the show was particularly appealing to children, and while I agree that it is, it's no less enriching for adults—and plenty of French visitors attend, too. A paragraph from a tourist brochure captures the performance better than I'm able: "The audience is 'immersed' in the story and physically surrounded by powerfully graphic images. The voice of Henri Gougaud, a Carcassone writer, the scenery and the music combine to create a lively, colorful atmosphere which depicts poetically and humorously the prophetic journey of the vicar of Cucugnan."

Cultural Services of the French Embassy

The Cultural Services of the French Embassy is a strong resource in promoting Franco-American relations. The staff maintains an excellent Web site featuring up-to-date listings of French cultural events happening in the United States, related to visual arts, books, cinema, education, performing arts, music, people, television, and radio. The main office is located in New York at 972 Fifth Avenue, New York, N.Y. 10021; 212-439-1400; fax: -1455 and affiliate offices are found in nine other cities: Atlanta, Boston, Chicago, Houston, New Orleans, Los Angeles, Miami, San Francisco, and Washington.

Customs

There seems to be a lot of confusion over what items can and positively cannot be brought into the United States—on the part not only of travelers but of customs agents, too. The rules are not as confusing as they might seem, but sometimes neither customs staff nor travelers are up to date on them. Some examples of what's legal and what's not include: olive oil yes, but olives no (unless they're vacuum-packed); fruit jams and preserves yes, but fresh fruit no; hard cheeses yes, but soft, runny cheeses no; commercially canned meat yes (if the inspector can determine that the meat was cooked in the can after it was sealed), but fresh and dried meats and meat products no; nuts yes, but chestnuts and acorns no; coffee yes, but roasted beans only; dried spices yes, but not curry leaves; fresh and dried flowers yes, but not eucalyptus or any variety with roots. If you think all this is unnecessary bother, remember that it was quite likely a tourist who carried in the wormy fruit that brought the Mediterranean fruit fly to California in 1979. Fighting that pest has cost more than $100 million. For more details, call the U.S. Department of Agriculture's Animal and Plant Health Inspection Service at 301-734-8645 or visit its Web site (www.aphis.usda.gov; click "Travelers' Information"). If you call 866-SAFGUARD, you may listen to a recording of information for travelers.

D

D'Artagnan

D'Artagnan, of course, was the legendary fourth musketeer in Alexandre Dumas' novel *The Three Musketeers*. His real name was Charles de Batz, born in 1615 at the Château de Castelmore, near the town of Lupiac in Gascony. D'Artagnan is unquestionably the most celebrated hero of Gascony. As related by Charles Neal in *Armagnac: The Definitive Guide to France's Premier Brandy,* D'Artagnon "gained his fame not only by accomplishing numerous dangerous missions, but also for his humanitarian relations with those who served under him. He led troops during the Fronde War, the siege of Dunkerque and, in 1659, accompanied the royal convoy to St. Jean-de-Luz for the marriage of Louis XIV to the Princess of Spain." D'Artagnan is also the name of an absolutely first-rate company that is the leading purveyor of foie gras, sausages, smoked delicacies, and organic game and poultry in North America. Readers who truly want to immerse themselves in the cuisine and traditions of Southwestern France must, if you haven't already, get to know D'Artagnan. The company was founded in 1985 by Ariane Daguin, daughter of André Daguin, legendary chef-owner of the Hôtel de France in Auch, and George Faison, an American friend who met Ariane at Columbia University, where he was pursuing an M.B.A. At some point in his schooling, Faison decided banking was not the career for him, and in Ariane he met his future business partner (coincidentally, he also happens to be the brother of a Hollins University classmate of mine). The two of them pooled their resources and know-how to start D'Artagnan, the first purveyor of foie gras in the United States. The company today supplies a range of over three hundred specialty items to the world's top restaurants, hotels, retailers, cruise ships, and airlines. You may have seen D'Artagnan products—which include free range and organic meats and preservative-free charcuterie—in retail shops where you live, but if you haven't, familiarize yourself with all it offers by browsing its Web site (www.dartagnan.com). What a wonderful evening you could plan with recipes from one of the cookbooks recommended in the *Flavors and Tables of the Southwest* bibliography and quality products from D'Artagnan! Readers may also want to join D'Artagnan's Three Musketeers Club, a free membership service that entitles one to a monthly newsletter, recipe cards, and various special offers and events. Visitors to New York may rejoice in the D'Artagnan Restaurant and Rotisserie located on the east side of Manhattan. Both a restaurant and a take-out shop, you will find all the specialties of Gascony here, including a few of my favorites: French kisses (Armagnac-soaked prunes filled with foie gras) and croustade (a flaky, crusty apple dessert found throughout Gascony and Aquitaine). As an aside, readers may recall an article entitled "The Three Musketeers" that appeared in the December 2002 issue of *Gourmet*. This piece, by Patric Kuh, was a wonderful account of three female chefs from southern France, Anne-Sophie Pic, Ariane Daguin, and Hélène Darroze, all daughters of famous (male) chefs, who got together as the Nouvelles Mères Cuisinières to prepare an unforgettable feast. Leading gastronomes, journalists, chateau owners, and selected purveyors were invited to this "tip of the toque to their fathers." As Kuh noted, "Neither André Daguin nor Francis Pic, who died in 1992, had encouraged their daughters to pursue a career in cooking. But they had. When you're a cook's child, you get restaurants through the pores. You live by the tempo of a kitchen without being in one—the hour you play with your parent is between lunch and dinner, and the grazing good-night kiss that shouldn't wake you comes at midnight. These women had gone out into the world, into different fields of study, only to find that their passion lay, as it had for their fathers, at the professional stove." Contact information: 280 Wilson Avenue, Newark, N.J. 07105; 800-327-8246, extension 0; fax: 973-465-1870; D'Artagnan Restaurant and Rotisserie is located at 152 East 46th Street, New York, 10017; 212-687-0300.

Dates

Remember that, as in many other countries around the world, dates in France are written with the day first followed by the month and then the year, as in 9 September 1959. If you're having trouble adjusting, it may help to think of the elements of a date as units of measure—going from smallest (the individual day) to largest (the year). If you buy airline, bus, or train tickets in France, be absolutely certain you are purchasing them for the correct day you want to travel: the date will be printed in the order of day, month, year (and arrival and departure times will be given using the military clock, such as 1300 hours or 1500 hours).

E

Eating Out

Similar to other European countries, France offers a variety of eating and drinking establishments for residents and visitors. Though the features that distinguish a restaurant from a bar, for example, are usually clear, it's important to recognize the differences, and know what you should—or should not—expect from each place. As Sandra Gustafson reminds readers in *Cheap Eats in Spain,* "When ordering, remember where you are and stay within the limits of the chef's abilities. Do not expect gourmet fare in a self-service restaurant, and do not go to a proper restaurant and order only a small salad and glass of wine." What follows is a list of all the eating establishments you may encounter, and just as I recommend trying different types of accommodations, I also recommend trying different places at mealtimes:

Bar. A bar in France is not much different from a bar in any other European or Mediterranean country. A wide selection of alcoholic beverages are available, as well as sodas and a few other nonalcoholic choices, and some bars also serve light snacks and nibbles, such as olives or nuts. Even the smallest village in France will have at least one bar, or a café, usually frequented for the better part of a day by the local male population.

Bar à vin. This is a wine bar. Beer is sometimes also available, but a wine bar is probably not the best place to indulge in beer, for both price and choice.

Bistro or bistrot. The origins of the word *bistro* are obscure, according to *Larousse Gastronomique.* "It first appeared in the French language in 1884, and perhaps comes from the Russian word *bistro* (quick) which the Cossacks used to get quick service at a bar during the Russian occupation of Paris in 1815. There also appears to be a relationship with the word *bistreau,* which in the dialects of western France describes a cow-herd and, by extension, a jolly fellow—an apt description of an innkeeper. The most likely origin is doubtless an abbreviation of the word *bistrouille.*" Bistros in France today are typically small, informal neighborhood restaurants similar to taverns, offering home-cooked, inexpensive meals.

Café. First established in Constantinople in 1550, cafés originally served only coffee. Today a café in France offers a wide variety of coffee drinks as well as tea, hot chocolate, sodas, fruit juices like *citron pressé* (fresh-squeezed lemon juice served in a tall glass with a pitcher of water on the side), and alcoholic drinks. Light fare, such as sandwiches, salads, ice cream, croissants, and other pastries, are also typically available. A café typically has both counter and table service. A *café-tabac* is an establishment where you can also purchase stamps, cigarettes, postcards, lottery tickets, and *télécartes.*

Crêperie. Crêperies are usually small stands set up on city sidewalks (readers who've visited Paris may have a favorite they return to again and again; I used to swear by the one outside of Galeries Lafayette, and another near the Luxembourg Gardens), but they are not quite as prevalent in the South. But there are *crêperies* that are restaurants, and in fact I had a good little lunch at one in Sarlat. The entire menu is, as you might surmise, composed of crepes with fillings savory and sweet.

Ferme-auberge or *auberge à la ferme.* An *auberge* is an inn, while a *ferme-*

auberge is usually a modest inn in a rural setting that also serves inexpensive meals both for overnight guests and for those just passing through. *Fermes-auberges* are rarely mentioned in restaurant guides, and though they are considered firstly as places to spend the night, keep them in mind as good value restaurants, especially on a day when you might be driving a distance and need to stop for lunch. Much like the requirements for *agriturismo* properties in Italy, a *ferme-auberge* is supposed to by law grow a certain percentage of produce and/or raise poultry or livestock on its own property.

Restaurant. The French invented the word *restaurant* (from *restaurer,* to restore). According to *Larousse Gastronomique,* the word *restaurer* first appeared in the sixteenth century and meant, at first, "a food which restores" but was used more specifically for a rich, highly flavored soup thought capable of restoring lost strength. "The eighteenth-century gastronome Brillat-Savarin referred to chocolate, red meat and consommé as restaurants. From this sense, which survived until the nineteenth century, the word developed the meaning of 'an establishment specializing in the sale of restorative foods.'" Today a restaurant is either a large establishment with a chef, or a small one with an owner-manager who may do the cooking him- or herself. Though not universally formal, restaurants are definitely a step up from cafés and bistros. Three-star shrines offer outstanding food and service and ambience to match.

Le snack. One of my favorite incursions of English into the French language, *le snack* (pronounced as *snock*) is a snack bar set up in a beach town, park—anywhere, really, where someone might want a little something. I have seen everything from pizza, candy, and potato chips to ice cream, nuts, and sodas offered at *le snack* places. Truthfully, there's not really any reason to get excited about them, but if you're really starving and it's three o'clock in the afternoon, it'll do.

Tapas bar. Prevalent mostly in Toulouse, Languedoc-Roussillon, and the Pays Basque, a tapas bar—Spanish in origin—serves a variety of drinks as well as a full array of tapas, little hors d'oeuvres and nibbles that one can easily make a meal of or merely sample before a more substantial lunch or dinner. In larger cities in Spain, tapas bars are known for certain specialties or cooking styles, and it is the custom to bar-hop, spending enough time at each bar to sample a variety of tapas. Southwestern France doesn't have nearly the variety of tapas bars nor their specialties, but they are nonetheless wonderful places for hanging out. I love tapas bars, and outside Spain I like them best in Collioure. In Spain tapas bars have their own house brands of red and white wine and beer, but in France they make a wider range of wines, beers, and drinks available, though I always order what's local (and is therefore cheaper).

Here are some tips to keep in mind about eating in France.

Haute cuisine and Michelin stars. The October 1998 issue of *Wine Spectator* was devoted to Paris, and one section focused on restaurants, specifically fancy, three-star establishments. Should you want to experience Michelin-starred restaurants in the Southwest, at this writing the only three-star is presided over by chef Michel Bras in Auvergne. The *Wine Spectator* piece included a good summation and some of the best advice for Americans dining in France today. The writer stressed that Americans *are* welcome at the great restaurants of France—as long as they are few in number. "The maître d' at one three-star restaurant told me, 'When an American calls, I put him on the waiting list until I see how the reservations are balanced. The French don't like to eat in a dining room full of Americans, and neither do the Americans.'" This is worth remembering: assuming you do secure a reservation, it's a *bonne idée* (good idea) to reconfirm a few weeks in advance, and then again when you arrive. Betty Lou Phillips, author of *French by Design*, notes that tourists are often seated at the least desirable tables in a restaurant—near the kitchen, in a plant grove, or in a remote area far from the main dining room, where they are out of sight. "Service may be a further affront. Affable waiters who hover with friendly professionalism around the French can be less than welcoming toward strangers on holiday. Of course, some servers are cordial, helpful, and attentive even toward Americans who offend their sensibilities by sampling another's *pâté de foie gras, magret de canard* (breast of duck), or *crème brulée,* a habit the French think rather distasteful. (The American practice of sharing food or, less politely, spearing a morsel off someone else's plate is also a pet peeve of Letitia Baldridge, the well-known etiquette expert.)" Underlying all of this, Phillips adds, is a resentment against those not fluent in French, fed partly by the fear that foreigners will not fully appreciate the way cuisine expresses the culture of France and sets it apart from other European nations: "Some waiters can be overheard openly criticizing Americans for routinely leaving their knives and forks at all different angles rather than putting them together on the plate to show that they are finished. Not incidentally, the French also grudgingly claim Americans are unaware that in France servers are afforded a measure of respectability. Fortunately, most kitchens operate in happy worlds of their own, turning out dishes that help keep the French in everyone's good graces, thus avoiding leaving sensitive Americans simmering over various affronts." The *Wine Spectator* writer stated that this situation is unlikely to change drastically, since many of us are unlikely to return to a particular gastronomic temple, and it's presumed we don't know much about food, so we remain low on every restaurant's priority list. But the writer wisely reminded readers not to be intimidated: "Remember who's paying the bill."

To my mind, haute cuisine is not simply a dining experience: it's nothing less than an elaborate stage production of the highest caliber. True, it's very expensive, but properly executed, the experience is sublime and unforgettable and worth every euro. Ruth Reichl, editor of *Gourmet* and former restaurant critic for *The New York Times,* frequently reminded readers during her tenure at the *Times* to keep several points in mind when considering the price of fine dining in France: haute cuisine is extremely labor-intensive and typically requires enormously expensive ingredients; and you never have to wait for a table in France because you effectively "buy" a table for the afternoon or evening. Economically speaking, French restaurants are completely different from American ones, which concentrate on turning as many tables as possible during mealtimes; finally, prices on French menus include tax and tip, both of which add up to a hefty sum.

Prices. As in most other European countries, the price of food and drink is different depending on where you sit at a bar or a restaurant. If you opt for a table, remember that, as in other European countries, you can expect to remain at your table for as long as you like. A waiter may ask you to settle a bill if he or she is going off duty, but no one will come along and request that you leave: it simply isn't done. Note, however, that if you are in the center of Bordeaux, Toulouse, or Biarritz, you will reveal your ignorance if you complain about the tab. Remember, you are not paying upward of four or five dollars for a tiny cup of espresso; you are paying for the privilege of sitting at a table in surroundings that definitely aren't Kansas for as long as you want.

Menus. Don't let the words *prix fixe* or *plat du jour* necessarily turn you away from a potentially good meal. Just like the *menu turistico* in Italy and the *menú del día* in Spain, the *prix fixe* meal in France is often a good value, consisting of three preselected courses and nearly always including a carafe or half bottle of wine and coffee or tea. A *menu dégustation* or *menu gastronomique* (tasting menu) is offered at fine restaurants and also represents a good value, consisting of about six or seven small (and delicious) courses of which the chef is particularly proud.

Vegetarian dining. I highly recommend that you give up personal dietary restrictions (unless of course, they are health concerns) in favor of getting a taste of the culture you are experiencing. If you are served a dish particular to the region that contains meat, my opinion would be to defer to local custom and experience what it means to live in that region. But if you insist upon sticking to a vegetarian diet, don't be a pain in the neck at restaurants by asking five minutes' worth of pesky questions—almost all of which will have answers you won't like and that you could have predicted. Instead, get to know an organization called the Happy Cow's Global Guide to Vegetarian Restaurants and Health Food Stores, which offers information on vegetarian dining throughout the world. Visit its Web site, www.happycow.org, for resources specific to the Southwest. When I last checked, there were three listings in Toulouse: Bio Asis (21 rue des Amidoniers, featuring Indian, vegan, and organic foods as well as a salad bar); Saveur Bio (22 rue Maurice Fonvieille, offering a buffet and salad bar); and a health food store, Vert de Terre (17 rue Peyras), with organic produce as well as deli foods.

Useful vocabulary: *café complet* (a breakfast consisting typically of coffee or tea and a croissant or baguette; this is the standard breakfast served at *auberges,* small hotels, and B&B establishments, often with jam—*confiture*—and butter; occasionally a basket of different types of breads will be offered); *casse-croûte* (literally, "breaking the crust," an old word, now mostly out of use; it refers to a mid-morning snack, mostly for vineyard and farm workers who rise early and may consist of a baguette with local goat cheese, a light soup, or even a crepe or omelette); *entrée* (first course; other words for appetizers are *les hors d'oeuvres* and *les amuse-gueules;*); *premier plat* (second or main course); *la carte des vins* (wine list); *vin de la maison* or *vin ordinaire* (house wine); *Connaissez-vous un bon restaurant?* (Are you able to recommend a good restaurant?); *Je voudrais retenir une table, s'il vous plaît* . . . (I want to reserve a table, please) . . . *pour ce soir* (for tonight) . . . *pour demain soir* (for tomorrow evening) . . . *pour deux personnes* (for two people) . . . *à la terrasse* (outside); *Qu'est-ce que vous me recommandez?* (What do you recommend? the waiter's favorite question, which you could ask if you eat everything and are adventurous); *Avez-vous des plats sans viande?* (Do you have any dishes without meat?); *Pour commencer, apportez-nous* . . . (To begin, bring us . . .); *Je n'ai pas commandé ceci* (this is not what I ordered); *le pourboire* (tip); *une carafe de l'eau ordinaire* or *au robinet* (tap water; mineral water will sometimes automatically be brought to your table, but it isn't free, so if you don't want it, ask for tap water); *glaçons* (ice cubes); *qualité-prix* (good value); *sur place* (in the restaurant; useful at places that are take-out but that also have a few tables); *à emporter* (take-out). Finally, to show your appreciation for a fine meal, you can say *Merci beaucoup, le repas était très bien* (Thank you, it was a delicious meal).

Eleanor of Aquitaine

One of the towering personalities of the Southwest, Eleanor was born in 1122 to Guillaume X, duke of Aquitaine, and she was his only heir. In 1137, her considerable wealth—which included one of the largest domains in France—became part of the French Crown when she married Louis VII. The history and guidebooks say that Eleanor found Louis boring, and she reportedly was such a flirt while Louis was away on the Second Crusade that he annulled their marriage in 1152. In this same year, she married Henry Plantagenet, duke of Normandy and count of Anjou. Eleanor's dowry included territories in Poitou and the Limousin, and the Guyenne. In 1154, Henry became King Henry II of England, which meant that he and Eleanor held a fabulous fiefdom as vast chunks of French land (everything from Normandy, Brittany, and all the way to Spain) were now under the control of the English Crown. The rivalry between the French and English began, and the Hundred Years' War was sparked.

Eleanor, who was reportedly very pretty, was also very much ahead of her time as she proved to be smart, politically savvy, and cultured. When she backed her two rather misguided sons—Richard Coeur de Lion and Henry junior—in a rebellion against their father, Henry senior imprisoned her in England. Only after Henry's death, fifteen years later, was she able to return to Aquitaine. She has, deservedly, become a worthy role model for women of today. Eleanor, therefore, makes a good subject for a biography; though a number have been published, my favorite read about her is *The Book of Eleanor: A Novel of Eleanor of Aquitaine* (Pamela Kaufman, Crown, 2002, hardcover; Three Rivers Press, 2003, paperback). I tend not to prefer historical novels, but this one is an exception, and once begun I don't think you'll find it easy to put down—and it's not for women only: Eleanor's life was as dramatic, daring, and interesting as any man's of her time.

In 1204, Eleanor—who in the course of her life held the titles of countess of Poitou, duchess of Aquitaine, queen of France, and queen of England—died at the abbey of Fontevrault, eulogized as a queen "who surpassed almost all the queens of the world."

Europe and the European Union

France is a leading founder and member of the European Union (EU) as well as a staunch supporter of the conversion to a single currency, the euro. The euro, in fact, is significant not only economically but symbolically, as it is believed to prevent the EU member countries from finding reasons to go to war. The EU nations constitute the world's second-largest trading region with a single currency, after the United States.

On December 13, 2002, the EU officially added ten new members (the Greek portion of Cyprus, Czech Republic, Estonia, Hungary, Latvia, Lithuania, Malta, Poland, Slovakia, and Slovenia), creating, according to *The New York Times* of December 14, a "mega-Europe of 450 million people in twenty-five countries and an economy of more than nine trillion dollars, close to that of the United States." The new nations will formally join the EU in May 2004, and though the admittance of some did not come without some rather extensive negotiations and concessions, the more noteworthy footnote is an omission, that of Turkey. What Turkey and the United States hoped for was not immediate acceptance into the EU but the selection of a date to begin negotiations for Turkey's admission. Instead, the EU leaders agreed to meet in December 2004 to decide "whether the largely Muslim country of seventy million people was democratic enough and respectful enough of human rights to begin negotiations." Now, of course, twenty-five nations will have to agree on Turkey's fate rather than fifteen. Personally, I believe it is hard to ignore that there is a prejudice against Turkey, especially after the former French president, Valéry Giscard d'Estaing, remarked that Muslim Turkey was not a European country. This seems a grossly outdated and mean-spirited opinion, especially since, as noted in the *Times* article, "even before the decision on expansion, the first since Austria, Finland and Sweden joined in 1995, the union was engaged in an ambitious, open-ended experiment to redefine what it means to be a European. Both its believers and its skeptics say member nations are relinquishing sovereignty on a scale not seen since the Emperor Charlemagne tried to unify the continent 1,200 years ago." While I criticize the EU for its decision, I remain optimistic that its leaders will learn, before 2004, that Turkey is a moderate Islamic country with great potential as well as a loyal friend to its European neighbors and North America and justly deserves admission.

Maintaining the stability of the EU will not be an enviable task: by admitting these ten new members, most of them poor, former Communist countries, the average wealth per person is expected to fall by about 13 percent. Members must find ways to balance the interests of the rather wealthy nations against those of the poorer ones, and bridge the vast differences in their manufacturing, exports, imports, and residents' income.

F

Faire le Pont

This French expression is the equivalent of "long weekend" in English. When a holiday falls on a Thursday or a Tuesday, for example, the French like to *pont* (bridge) the holiday by also taking off on Friday and/or Monday. This is useful to keep in mind if there is a scheduled holiday during your trip, as stores and businesses may be closed for all or part of the time, hotel and restaurant reservations may be harder to secure, and the plumber you need to fix a major problem with the pipes at the *gîte* you've rented may be unavailable.

Festivals and Fairs

Joy Law, in her essential book *Dordogne,* notes that "the rhythm of daily life in Dordogne is governed as absolutely by the year's cycle today, both in the market towns and the countryside, as in the past and, although there has been a decline in religious observance, the nomenclature used by the church to denote its feast and saint's days persists. One will be told that the wheat must be sown by All Saints' Day and to beware of the three *terribles chevaliers*—St. George on 23 April, St. Mark on 25 April and St. Eutropius on 30 April—for these are the days when late frosts will ruin the harvest. (St. Eutropius was a first-century martyr who had reputedly evangelized the region.) The Feast of the Assumption of the Virgin on 15 August—the summer holiday equalled only in importance by Christmas—brings life in the department, as in the rest of France, to a complete standstill."

Fairs, *foires,* and *fêtes* are plentiful year round in the Southwest, and can be great fun to attend. When I first began working on this manuscript, I decided I would make a change and provide a complete list of all the major and local fairs and festivals in every town throughout the Southwest. I knew there would be many, so I assigned the task of compiling to one of my interns, Mai Bui-Dui, who diligently researched every fête and observance she could find, from the Atlantic to the Mediterranean and from the Pyrenees to the Massif Central. When she had finished only Aquitaine, and her typing ran to a great many pages, I realized I had made a mistake. I think it is unnecessary in my books to provide a definitive list of fairs and festivals—nearly all the smaller festivals are detailed in good guidebooks, and the Maison de la France offices have even more information and resources about them. What I do think worth repeating, however, are the major, national holidays as these will have some bearing on a visitor's trip *anywhere* in the Southwest. I have also selected a few local fêtes and celebrations that are unique to the region—some readers may be interested in attending one (or more), while others may prefer to avoid them. Keep in mind that hotel rooms and restaurant reservations are typically hard to come by at these popular times, so plan accordingly.

National holidays:

1 January
Easter Sunday
Easter Monday
1 May
8 May (Victory in Europe Day)
Ascension Day
Pentecost and the following Monday
14 July (Bastille Day)
15 August (Assumption)
1 November (All Saints' Day)
11 November (First World War Armistice)
Christmas Day

Selected Southwest celebrations:

Bordeaux Fête le Vin (Bordeaux Wine Festival). Begun in 1998 and continuing every other year, this hugely popular artistic and gastronomic event at the end of June pays homage to the beverage that gives the region its popularity. Jean-Michel Cazes, a well-known wine-grower in the area, succinctly sums up the festival: "Wine is a way of life. It encompasses culture, good food, and a festive atmosphere. The *Fête du Vin* is completely in keeping with these values."

La Félibrée—Fête Occitaine. The Félibrée is a major popular gathering in Périgueux celebrating Occitan language and culture. The day begins with an outdoor mass in Occitan, followed by a *taulado* (banquet). The afternoon is set aside for the Cour d'Amour (court of love), a show including music, dance, theater, poetry, and troubadour memories. Trades, such as clog- and basket-making, are demonstrated throughout the day.

Fête de la Transhumance (Shepherd's Festival). Transhumance (as explained in the entry below) marks the movement of flocks towards summer meadows. In Southwestern France it is celebrated in Laruns in the Vallée d'Ossau, and in

Lourdios in the Vallée d'Aspe. Transhumance usually occurs around the first Saturday in July, and there are traditional songs and dances, events, food, a mass, and blessing of the flocks.

Grande Semaine de Pélote Basque. The Basque Country has its own unique ball game, *pélote,* a sport that resembles a high-risk version of squash. Twenty different versions of *pélote* are known throughout the region, the most famous being *cesta punta,* played in a covered court called *jaï alaï.* During the second week of August *pélote* fever spreads like wildfire throughout villages in the Pays Basque.

La Grande Fénétra. This summer festival, held around the end of June and beginning of July, reflects pure *toulousain* spirit through traditional dance and music, performed on the essential *passo carriero,* a type of percussive instrument. A colorful folk parade winds through the main streets of Toulouse, finishing with a public dawn serenade in the heart of the old city.

Honneur à Notre Elu: this is a late springtime fete that I believe is only celebrated in Aquitaine. I happened to be in Domme once for the celebration, which is centered around a tall, pine pole decorated with red, white, and blue banners and ribbons. A sign at the top read *Honneur à Nos Elu,* and according to the Cadogan Guides authors, once the sign is erected in Domme, others go up in neighboring villages and towns. The signs may be different in other locales—*Honneur à Notre Mairie* or *au Patron* are common, and they may even display the names of newlyweds or a newborn baby. Whatever the signs say, they are referred to as *les mai,* or maypoles, and all the maypoles are erected for *la Plantation de Mai* festivities. "Once up, they are meant to rot away rather than ever be taken down. The Perigourdins apparently have been planting their maypoles ever since Gallo-Roman times, when a newly elected official would be honored with a similar pole crowned with a garland. Since the liberty trees put up during the Revolution, they have taken on an added republican virtue."

Floors

Repeat visitors to France will have already learned that the French do not count floors in a building in the same way we do in the States. What we call the ground or first floor is known as the *rez-de-chaussée* in France (sometimes abbreviated RC on elevator buttons). What we call the second floor is what the French call the first floor, or *premier étage.* Our third floor is the *deuxième étage,* our fourth is the *troisième étage,* and so on.

Food and Wines from France, Inc.

When looking for information on French food and wines, one of the best resources is SOPEXA, also known in the United States as Food and Wines from France. This particular branch of the government was created in 1964 by the French Ministry of Agriculture as the national marketing and promotion board for French food and beverage products. Now, more than thirty-five years later, SOPEXA is represented in thirty-three countries, employs about three hundred staff members, and generated the equivalent of approximately $103 million in 1997. SOPEXA's mission is two-fold: to build up the image and awareness of French food and beverage products with end consumers, and to help local retailers better market their French brands.

The SOPEXA Web site provides information on French wines, grapes, vintages, wine regions, and more, as well as other French food products such as preserves, jams, mustard, and cheese. There are also tips for matching wines with food as well as ideas for entertaining and recipes. SOPEXA offers a wine correspondence course booklet for $8. Contact information: 80 Maiden Lane, Suite 310, New York, N.Y. 10038; www.frenchwinesfood.com.

French Heritage Society

Formerly known as Friends of VMF—Vieilles Maisons Françaises, or Old French Houses—the French Heritage Society celebrated its twentieth anniversary in 2002 and proudly claims more than two thousand active members in fifteen U.S. chapters and the Paris chapter. Its mission is to fund-raise for both restoration projects and cultural exchanges in the United States and France. Early in 2002 FHS signed an accord with three other major preservation organizations in France and thus became the sole representative of these organizations for fund-raising in the United States: Les Vieilles Maisons Françaises, La Demeure Historique, and Le Comité des Parcs et Jardins. As part of its twentieth anniversary, they adopted the slogan "20 Years with 20 Grants" and set a fund-raising goal of $1 million to fund twenty new historic restoration projects, fourteen in France and six in the United States. In 1996 FHS sponsored the Château de Montréal in the Dordogne, which needed roof and window repairs and waterproofing on the terrace. This historic monument remained in the same family for 250 years and now is open to the public. Additionally, the Society's Grand Prix grant for 1999 was the Hôtel de Pierre in Toulouse, dating from 1535 and classified as a historic monument and the only stone building in a town whose monuments are mainly built in brick. The building's architect, Nicolas Bachelier, was also a student of Michelangelo.

The French Heritage Society strongly supports not only historical preservation efforts but Franco-American relations and thus established the Richard Morris Hunt Fellowship in 1990. The program promotes French and American architects in exchanging restoration and preservation techniques. In addition FHS sponsors educational programs: a one-week seminar on architecture and decorative arts in France; a three-week Student Experience Program; and Cultural Voyages, which grants members access to prestigious sites and often features hidden treasures, otherwise inaccessible to the public.

Events for members living in the United States include lectures, summer open houses, outdoor fairs, and tea time. FHS publishes a quarterly newsletter, *Au Courant*. On the cover of one of its brochures, FHS writes, "Architecture is a shared language." I encourage you to help preserve this unique language through your support of the French Heritage Society. Members receive a beautiful glossy copy of the architectural magazine *VMF,* as well as invitations to local chapter events and trips. The Web site is a great source of information on various projects, grants, and news. Contact information: 14 East 60th Street, Suite 605, New York, N.Y. 10022; 212-759-6846; fax: -9632; www.frenchheritagesociety.org.

The French Paradox

I always thought the so-called French paradox was a misnomer. There doesn't seem to be much that is paradoxical about a varied diet of fresh, seasonal food (even if it does include some animal fats), and alcohol in moderation, all in combination with regular exercise. Additionally, it is French tradition to sit down to a relaxed, leisurely meal at least once a day (twice a day in more rural parts of France), which I believe is healthful to digestion and spirit, and the French simply eat less than we do. The heaping platters and inches-thick pastrami sandwiches we're accustomed to are viewed as grossly excessive (and uniquely American) to the French. I usually *lose* weight when I'm in France, and you may, too, especially if you make lunch the biggest meal of your day and you walk a lot. Julia Child, in her monumental book *The Way to Cook* (Alfred A. Knopf, 1993), reminds us of another aspect of the French paradox that I feel is entirely overlooked in America but is taken to heart by the French: "*Fear of food, indulgences, and small helpings.* Because of media hype and woefully inadequate information, too many people nowadays are deathly afraid of their food, and what does fear of food do to the digestive system? I am sure that an unhappy or suspicious stomach, constricted and uneasy with worry, cannot digest properly. And if digestion is poor. The whole body politic suffers . . . *Final words.* The pleasures of the table—that lovely old-fashioned phrase—depict food as an art form, as a delightful part of civilized life. In spite of food fads, fitness programs, and health concerns, we must never lose sight of a beautifully conceived meal."

G

Greetings and Salutations

Just like the the Italians and the Spaniards, the French are very polite, which should be interpreted as meaning not that they are formal, just less casual than we are in North America. Men shake hands when greeting each other (women do, too, sometimes), and women usually always kiss each other on both cheeks. Men may also embrace and walk with their arms around each other's shoulders. When an introduction is made, a person is typically referred to not simply by his or her full name but as the son or daughter of someone. This is a way of emphasizing the family that the person comes from and is similar to the way one addresses mail in France: the family name is written in capital letters after the first name.

Gypsies

Gypsies, who prefer to be called Roma, are not as prevalent in the Southwest as elsewhere in France. The Roma do not, unfortunately, have a very good reputation. I myself have been aggressively surrounded by a pack of Gypsies in Nice, and all my pockets were thoroughly searched as well as every pouch on my backpack; friends and colleagues have reported similar encounters. The United Nations, in a report titled "Avoiding the Dependency Trap" dated January 16, 2003, found that the Roma in Hungary, Slovakia, Czech Republic, Romania, and Bulgaria often go hungry; one in six is "constantly starving"; and one in five families do not send their children to school because they lacked proper clothing. Only one-third of the Roma surveyed had completed high school or vocational school. The U.N. stated that "by measures ranging from literacy to infant mortality to basic nutrition, most of the region's Gypsies endure living conditions closer to those in sub-Saharan Africa than to Europe." It is the U.N.'s position that unless action is taken before these countries join the European Union, the Gypsies may become a permanent underclass. The U.N. also feels that if the Gypsies are marginalized, the cost of finding solutions will be higher and "will have few chances of success," which will only strengthen the hand of xenophobes and nationalists in those countries. Though the U.N. report placed some of the blame for the Roma's plight on their own communities, it also blamed the failed systems of education, labor, and economic and social development.

As recently as February 5, 2003, according to a report filed in *The New York Times,* a group of six hundred Gypsy organizations filed a $12 billion lawsuit against I.B.M., asserting that the computer company aided the Nazis in automating the Holocaust. Approximately 600,000 Gypsies, mainly from Central and Eastern Europe, are believed to have been killed by the Nazis and their allies during the Holocaust, and, according to the *Times* article, the Gypsies have long argued that they are the Holocaust's forgotten victims. If the suit is successful, it could bring payments to the few living Gypsy Holocaust survivors, as well as "finance health, social, and educational projects for the estimated 1.2 million survivors and their descendants in Europe." The Gypsies are apparently basing their lawsuit on information provided by Edwin Black, author of *I.B.M. and the Holocaust: The Strategic Alliance Between Nazi Germany and America's Most Powerful Corporation* (Crown, 2001). Readers familiar with Black's thoroughly researched but controversial book may recall his assertion, that before and during World War II, I.B.M. provided the punchcards and early computers that allowed the Nazis to organize the systematic extermination of the Jews and Gypsies of

Europe. A previous lawsuit was filed against I.B.M. shortly after the publication of Black's book by Jewish Holocaust survivors. It was dropped however, when it was feared that the suit might interfere with pending Holocaust settlements with Germany and Switzerland. A good book to read is *Bury Me Standing: The Gypsies and Their Journey* (Isabel Fonseca, Alfred A. Knopf, 1995) for a thoroughly fascinating and surprising account of Gypsy life.

H

Henri IV

In reviewing names of the Southwest to know, Henry IV is a noteworthy one. Being born in Pau does not alone make his life exceptional, but the fact that his father was Antoine de Bourbon (a Catholic) and his mother was Jeanne d'Albret (a Protestant) is; when he married Marguerite de Valois, sister of Henry II, in 1572, and later became King of Navarre, he led the Huguenots (French Protestants) in a number of battles against the French Roman Catholics. The most ugly Protestant-Catholic conflict in all of French history was the St. Bartholomew's Day Massacre in Paris. It was instigated by Catherine de' Medici, who became the widow of Henri II in 1559. De' Medici attempted to govern a very distracted country for her two royal sons while various factions (including Catholics and Huguenots) tried to gain control of the young monarchs for their own purposes. She tried for a time to play the two parties against each other, but in 1572, fearing the growing influence of the Huguenot Admiral de Cologny and taking advantage of a great party of Huguenots in Paris to celebrate the wedding of Henri IV, she orchestrated the massacre of thousands of Protestants. Henri IV himself escaped only because he changed his religion, and history has shown us that Henri was not a devout follower of either form of Christianity, as he officially changed his affiliation from Protestant to Catholicism and back again six times in his life.

Henri also initiated the Edict of Nantes in 1598, which, according to *A History of the Modern World* (Knopf, 2002), granted to every seigneur, or noble who was also a manorial lord, the right to hold Protestant services in his own household. The edict allowed Protestantism in towns where it was in fact the prevailing form of worship, but it barred it from Catholic episcopal towns and from a zone surrounding and including the city of Paris. The edict also gave Protestants their own means of defense, granting them about one hundred fortified towns to be held by Protestant garrisons under Protestant command. Significantly, "where in England the Catholic minority had no rights at all, and in Germany the religious question was settled only by cutting the country into small and hostile fragments, in France a compromise was effected, by which the Protestant minority had both individual and territorial rights. A considerable number of French statesmen, generals, and other important persons in the seventeenth century were Protestants." Henri IV is also famous for promising that all the families in his kingdom would have the financial means for "a chicken in every pot" (*un poule un pot*).

Hiking

With two *parcs nationals* (one in the Pyrenees and the other in the Cévennes) and four *parcs naturels régionals* (Landes de Gascogne, Causses du Quercy, Haut-Languedoc, and Perigord-Limousin), and the Grande Randonnée (GR) network of long- and short-distance footpaths, the Southwest is a veritable paradise for walkers. There are several different GR routes to consider: *grande randonnée* and *grande randonées de pays* (GRP) are loop trails where you begin and end at the same place and allow for a closer look at a single area over the course of a few days—these are essentially backcountry hikes with a *sac au dos* (backpack); *sentiers de petites randonnées* (PR) are day-hike trails, many of which are also circular routes. The longer-haul, more famous routes are the GR10, which traces the length of the Pyrenees from the Atlantic to the Mediterranean (how great would *that* be?, except you'd need two months off); the GR36, which links the Dordogne, Lot, and Tarn *départements;* the GR8, which runs the length of the Aquitaine coast; and the GR65, which shares some of the same Santiago de Compostela route across the Lot, Tarn-et-Garonne, Gers, and French Basque country.

The Fédération Française de Randonnée Pédestre (FFRP) maintains the GR trails and also publishes excellent topoguides for each route. You can find these guides in good bookstores throughout the Southwest or through the FFRP itself (14 rue Riquet, 75019 Paris; www.ffrp.asso.fr). The Web site has *un catalogue en ligne* where you can place an order to receive the full catalog. Two other FFRP route/map series are *promenade et randonnée* (primarily gentle walks that are an hour or a few hours in length) and *à pied en famille,* family hikes.

Friedrich Nietzsche once opined that "only those thoughts that come by walking have any value." I believe that whether one walks leisurely or hikes with a goal in mind, spending some time getting around via your own two feet makes you feel part of a place in a special way. While I would never plan a trip that had me out on hiking trails every day, setting aside some time for a ramble of any length is an especially good idea in Southwestern France, as daily life still centers so much on the land.

An important difference between hiking in the United States and in France (and in Europe and all around the Mediterranean basin) is that hiking is generally not a wilderness experience there, the way we know and expect it to be in North America. In Canada and the United States, wide open spaces and undeveloped land are of significant importance; but in countries like France, the land has been much more cultivated and lived on. Besides small villages and hamlets, transhumance— the seasonal migration of livestock, mostly sheep, and the people who tend them, from lowlands to higher pastures—also affects the land. Therefore, except in the wilder areas of the Pyrenees, what you walk on is well-worn route, not a leisurely hiking trail. The routes were obviously not created at random and often connect old paths that have existed for hundreds of years. There are very few places in Europe, now or ever, where you can backpack into a completely isolated area and not encounter roads, people, or towns. Conversely, there are few if any places in the United States where you can backpack and be assured of finding a place to sleep in a bed, plus a meal with wine or beer at the end of the day.

Horseback Riding

Guidebooks and the tourist offices, both here and abroad, offer information about horseback riding trips, lasting a few hours or a few days. Riding enthusiasts may enjoy reading "The Thrill of Liberté: Riding Without a Guide Through a Landscape Dotted with Castles in the Aude Region of Southern France" (David Nussbaum, *The New York Times,* May 5, 2002). Nussbaum, a rider from Massachusetts, details a five-day *randonnée en liberté* (unguided ride) that he took with his wife in the Aude region, about an hour south of Carcassonne in the middle of the Corbières. They worked with an American company called Equitours, and a French outfitter called La Ferme Équestre du Causse provided horses and equipment, arranged food and lodging, transported personal baggage, and assisted in emergencies. Contact information is provided in the article, which is worth searching the archives for I think; it issues an important caveat: "Only strong riders (and map readers) need apply."

Hundred Years' War

Not to reduce the importance of other historical events and venues in the Southwest, but the Hundred Years' War sits squarely at or near the top of any list. In addition to the politics and issues of sovereignty surrounding the war, the prominence of Bordeaux's wine trade was a significant (if little recorded in history books) factor, too, as Alexis Lichine outlined in his *Guide to the Wines and Vineyards of France:* "There was no communication barrier between London and far-off Bordeaux; the language of the English court at that time was French, and remained French up to the time of John of Gaunt, who was named Prince of Aquitaine in 1390. Thus, the Bordelais felt a closer kinship with their English rulers than they did with the equally remote French crown. The English allowed them to manage their own affairs, and where they intervened they usually came in on the side of the local burghers, granting them exemption from various sales taxes and trade restrictions that were required of other merchants from outside Bordeaux. By the middle of the fourteenth century, wine was Bordeaux's greatest export and the English were its best customers by far. Indeed, the English were quick to see that by helping the wine trade they would, in every sense, be helping themselves. . . . When the Hundred Years' War began, the burghers, quite happy under a regime so commercially beneficial to them, took the English side, fearing naturally that an end to English rule would mean an end to their privileges."

If it's been some time since you studied the war (or if you weren't really paying close attention when you did), it would be a good use of your trip preparation time to review it. The best resource for the nonacademic traveler I've ever seen is *A Brief History of the Hundred Years' War, 1337–1453,* a glossy twenty-page pamphlet referred to by the French as a *guide memento.* I found it—and a good selection of others in the same series—at the tourist office in Sarlat, one of the best tourist offices I've ever visited. Truthfully, I really wish all of the *guide memento* editions were available in North America. They provide thorough outlines of each subject, the text is laid out in an easy-to-read format, and each is filled with color reproductions of artworks pertaining to the era and topic. Quite simply, I think the series is excellent, and I urge interested readers to seek them out, either at the various tourist offices or in bookstores. More academic readers will naturally pursue other sources, but for the curious traveler seeking a good, overall introduction to the war, this *guide memento* can't be beat. (If I remember correctly, it was priced at about three to five euros.)

Lastly, to emphasize once again the importance of a little knowledge, Ina Caro, in *The Road from the Past,* shares an experience she had in the Dordogne: "Our guide turned out to be an unpleasant woman who still seemed angry at the English and their descendants for what had happened some six hundred years ago during the Hundred Years' War. Assuming I was English, she seemed to hold me personally responsible. In Beynac, do not make the mistake, as I have done on both my visits, of asking, in English-accented French, whether there is a tour of the castle given in English. At most places in France when you do this, the guides slow down, sometimes even enunciating individual words so that the average English-speaking tourist is able to understand the French, or throwing in a English word or two whenever they are able. The reverse was true at Beynac; the speed of the guide's rapid-fire French increased noticeably. On this second trip I made the additional mistake of letting the guide know I was an American. This appeared to increase her hostility, and my curiosity was piqued. While waiting for the group of French families taking the tour to gather on a castle battlement, I brought up the subject of American tourists and her feelings about them, and she said, 'At least the English know what the Hundred Years' War was about. American tourists aren't even interested.' Thinking about that for a moment, I concluded that her hostility was justified."

I

Immigration

Immigration has been at the forefront of Jean-Marie Le Pen's platform since he became a household political name in France, and it has also been a central issue on the agenda of the European Union nations. France is less xenophobic than it once was, and younger generations of French men and women do not have the same patronizing, colonial attitude that their parents and grandparents did. This was made abundantly clear during the 1998 World Cup soccer tournament in France. As Mort Rosenblum notes in *A Goose in Toulouse,* "A France that had gone into the tournament deeply divided over race and immigration policy was suddenly color-blind. Only blue, white, and red registered on the scale. The hero playmaker who scored two goals was Zinedine Zidane, born and raised in a nasty Marseille suburb, the son of an Algerian night watchman. No anti-immigrant bonehead wanted to send him back to North Africa, at least not before the 2002 games." I was in Provence during that year's World Cup, and I watched several matches at cafés crowded with French (and tourists) of every age and nearly every skin color. Their enthusiasm for Zidane, and *Les Bleus,* was infectious. But in mid-December of that same year, there were horrible riots in Toulouse, the result of the death of seventeen-year-old Habib Ould, found with a police bullet in him. Again to quote Rosenblum, "The story had the familiar buzz words evoking an underlying malaise that was troubling all of France: 'integration' and 'assimilation.' What they meant was that after centuries of absorbing new immigrant groups, Frenchmen of the old sort saw themselves faced with a people who prefer a different sort of Sunday lunch, which they would rather eat on Friday." After Toulouse there were incidents in other French cities, including Lyons, Lille, Paris, Strasbourg, Arles, and Grenoble. Something called the *vehicule flambé*—which I think you can figure out—was often employed. That this tragic chain of events originated in Toulouse, voted "the city where Frenchmen most prefer to live," made it a national *crise.* A few months after the Toulouse incident, Rosenblum was in Toulouse, and he stepped into a small stationery and newspaper shop. The owner was a woman "of a certain age" and "straight out of the manual: shopkeeper, mother, petit bourgeoise, who ruled her small domain." She explained to Rosenblum that she had heard about the trouble, but that afterward there were demonstrations in the streets, and that had made her afraid. " 'Mind you, it's not that I have anything against "les Arabes," but they come here and don't fit in with our way and yet expect everything for free from us.' 'Les Arabes,' in this context, has nothing to do with the Middle East. It is a semi-polite term—there are much worse—for North Africans from Algeria, Tunisia, or Morocco, three former French territories. Many of these 'immigrants' are second or third generation descendants of French citizens who as soldiers died defending France . . . The stationery store lady warmed to her theme. She was no racist, she assured me, as I paid for my papers and turned to leave. 'You just have to understand,' she concluded, *'ces gens-là . . .'* That translated to: those people. Everyone knows roughly who is included in that collective reference, but the connotations vary slightly as you move around France. In

Toulouse, it means olive-hued, Allah-fearing people who would rather eat lamb on a spit than duck or goose."

Though we have our own issues with immigration in North America, for the French and their European friends, it is a more complex problem to solve. The "melting pot" growth of the United States, and to a lesser degree in Canada, is something of a foreign concept to the French. But in addition to the uglier social aspects of discrimination and bigotry, Europe has a more pressing need to solve the problem: a sharp drop in the fertility rate. According to a 2002 report by the World Health Organization, as reported in the December 26, 2002, issue of *The New York Times,* in no western European country did the fertility rate reach 2.1, a marker that indicates an exact replenishment of the population. By contrast, the United States had a 2.0 rate, which demographers attribute to greater immigration. While this fertility trend was reported a few years ago, "its slow-building consequences are now coming into starker relief, as more West European countries acknowledge and take new steps to address the specter of sharply winnowed and less competitive work forces, surfeits of retirees and pension systems that will need to be cut back deeply." The shift is most drastic in Greece, Spain, Sweden, Germany, and Italy. (Italy also has the world's oldest population: the percentage of people sixty or older is 25, versus 16 percent in the United States.) The *Times* article noted that this low fertility rate is interwoven with an array of issues, one of which is immigration: "While many people would like to clamp down on the rising tide of new arrivals over the last decade, they may be forced to accept it, simply to fill jobs and maintain levels of productivity."

Institut National des Appellations d'Origine (INAO)

The INAO is *the* governing body of French wine. The organization was originally founded as the Comité National des Appellations d'Origine in 1935, by a group of French winemakers concerned about maintaining the standards of quality as defined by the *appellation d'origine contrôlée* (AOC; see entry above under A). The INAO essentially manages the AOC as it guarantees the standards established by the AOC, namely, the place of origin and quality of French wines.

Islam

With good reason of late, many North Americans are obsessing about Islam. I think that the obsession is overdue and is a positive step toward a better understanding and appreciation of one of our world's greatest and enduring religions. It may not be surprising to learn that Islam is the second religion of France—and not by a very wide margin—due to the number of French men and women who emigrated from her former Muslim colonies, but I suspect many Americans would be surprised to learn that Islam is now a major religion in the United States as well. Readers particularly interested in learning more about Islam may want to consult my *Morocco* edition, as I included a number of excellent books for further reading—most of these were, in fact, recommended to me by two professors of religion, one of whom is a good friend of mine now living and teaching in Cairo. I take credit, however, for two books in particular, *Islam: A Short History* (Modern Library, 2000) and *A History of God: The 4,000 Year Quest of Judaism, Christianity and Islam* (Alfred A. Knopf, 1993), both by Karen Armstrong. These books explore a number of themes central to Islam that I feel are essential; I'm not certain my scholar friends would also consider them so, but as parting thoughts, I would like to share two of them. One, which is so often overlooked and misunderstood in the West, is that the religion of Islam cannot be separated from society or politics. Western societies, especially the United States, have long believed in the separation of church and state. The thinkers of Europe's Enlightenment believed this separation freed religion from the inevitable corruption of affairs of state. But "in Islam," writes Armstrong, "Muslims have looked for God in history. Their sacred scripture, the Quran, gave them a historical mission. Their chief duty was to create a just community in which all members, even the most weak and vulnerable, were treated with absolute respect. The experience of building such a society and living in it would give them intimations of the divine, because they would be living in accordance with God's will. A Muslim had to redeem history, and that meant that state affairs were not a distraction from spirituality but the stuff of religion itself." Second, fundamentalism is not unique to Islam, and fundamentalists come in nearly every religious stripe (the word was first used by American Protestants, in fact), and it is a false stereotype to believe that Muslims are filled with hatred of the West. (It isn't difficult, however, to understand why some Muslims might be.) As Armstrong has noted, "On the eve of the second Christian millennium, the Crusaders massacred some thirty thousand Jews and Muslims in Jerusalem, turning the thriving Islamic holy city into a stinking charnel house." Until this time, the three religions of Abraham had coexisted relatively well in that great city for almost five hundred years. In our own times, Muslims worldwide admire the efficiency and technology of the West, as well as some of our democratic ideals. In fact, what many Muslims dream of is a balance between modernism and Islamic traditions. In her book *Islam*, Armstrong quotes Yusuf Abdallah al-Qaradawi, an al-Azhar graduate and director of the Centre for Sunnah and Sirah at the University of Qatar, as saying, "It is better for the West that Muslims should be religious, hold to their religion, and try to be moral." Armstrong herself writes, "Western people must become aware that it is in their interests too that Islam remain healthy and strong. The West has not been wholly responsible for the extreme forms of Islam, which have cultivated a violence that violates the most sacred canons of religion. But the West has certainly contributed to this development and, to assuage the fear and despair that lies at the root of all fundamentalist vision, should cultivate a more accurate appreciation of Islam in the third Christian millennium."

Jewish History in Southwestern France

With a community of about 600,000, France is home to the fourth-largest Jewish community in the world and the largest Jewish community in Europe. (But after Catholicism, Islam is the second-largest religion in France—and it is not a distant second.) Cities of the Southwest with historic Jewish communities include Narbonne, Perpignan, Bordeaux (its Grande Synagogue is the largest in France), Toulouse, Montpellier, Béziers, Lunel, Nîmes, Bayonne, Agen, Pezenas, and Pau. (Gurs, near Pau, is the site of one of France's largest concentration camps; approximately eight hundred Jews died there in 1940.)

As Americans have surely been reminded of lately, France has a delicate balance to maintain, not only among the citizens of her own country but with the United States as well. It's important to remember this balance—or imbalance, really—when France and the United States do not see eye to eye on international terrorism, Saddam Hussein, or the Israeli-Palestinian conflict. Still, it's hard to stomach that, in one month alone—April 2002—there were twenty-five acts of violence committed against French Jews, three of those in Toulouse, one in Montpellier, and one in Nîmes.

Some good books to consult for further information on sites, monuments, synagogues, cemeteries, and restaurants include Ben Frank's *A Travel Guide to Jewish Europe* (Ben Frank, Pelican Publishing, Gretna, La.), and *Complete Jewish Guide to France* (Toni Kamins, St. Martin's Press). For some excellent historical companion reading, two books stand out. *Your Name Is Renee: Ruth's Story as a Hidden Child* (Stacy Cretzmeyer, Biddle Publishing, Brunswick, Me., 1994) is the story of Ruth Kapp Hartz, a refugee. (This wonderful book was written by a college classmate of mine.) Ruth, only four years old in 1941, and her family were foreign Jews, originally from Germany, and as such were targeted to be expelled from the Unoccupied Zone. They had left Paris soon after the Nazis arrived in 1940, and their life since that time was one forced departure after another, moving from place to place in southern France, much of the time in hiding and several times nearly discovered. Ruth (alias Renee Caper) survived the war, and when it ended, she realized she was wrong about how the French population had acted during the Occupation. Because she was sheltered in the south, where she was treated kindly and protected by a number of citizens, she truly believed that 90 percent of the population had been involved in the Resistance. Upon her return to Paris in 1946, however, she was shocked and confused to confront anti-Semitism. In the afterword she offers some thoughts on how to account for this difference. I consider this work *de rigueur*, as well as *When Courage Was Stronger Than Fear: Remarkable Stories of*

Christians Who Saved Jews from the Holocaust (Peter Hellman, Marlowe & Co., Balliet & Fitzgerald, 1999; originally published as *Avenue of the Righteous,* Atheneum, 1980). When Hellman visited Yad Vashem, the National Holocaust Memorial in Jerusalem, he was especially struck by the simplicity of the Avenue of the Righteous. The avenue is really a path lined with carob—and more recently, olive—trees, and under each tree is a small plaque displaying the name of a Christian (and in some cases a Muslim) who saved one or more Jews from Nazi persecution. Hellman recognized that this simplicity was deceiving, that there was a dramatic story behind each and every one of these plaques. He decided that very day that he wanted to learn more about these remarkable people. In this book he profiles five documented cases of the Righteous, each representing a different country (France, Italy, Belgium, Holland, and Poland). His only criterion was that the Righteous person still be living and accessible, which obviously narrowed the field a bit. I include Hellman's work here both because it is inspiring and significant and because the chapter on Raoul Laporterie gives a very good account of life on both sides of the demarcation line. (Raoul owned a clothing business on the occupied side but lived on the Vichy side, making it possible to offer his services as a *passeur,* someone who could slip Jews and others across the border.) Recommending this wonderful book comes with a caution: avoid reading it on public transportation unless you don't mind others seeing your tears. Additionally, Maison de la France (the French Tourist Office) publishes two great brochures: *France for the Jewish Traveler* (authored by Toni Kamins and featuring four pages on Aquitaine, Midi-Pyrénées, and Languedoc-Roussillon as well as a good overall history and a page of useful Web sites), and *The Road to Jewish Heritage in the South of France* (which details the *carrières*—derived from the Provençal word *carreira,* for street) of Jewish communities in Provence and Languedoc.

L

Language

Everyone will tell you that it is essential to at least try to speak French when in France; this is true—the French warm to anyone who attempts to speak their beautiful language—but it is also true that the residents of *any* country love it when visitors try to speak their language. What people may not tell you is that French is still a nearly universal language. It has been my experience that *someone* always speaks French, even in such seemingly unlikely countries as Egypt, Portugal, Turkey, Greece, Spain (in San Sebastián, across the Pyrenees, and in Barcelona), Italy (the northwest corner), and Croatia. Spanish may be a very popular language in the States, but it won't serve you very well outside Mexico, Central and South America, Spain, and the Philippines.

You may notice that some French people in the Southwest speak the langue d'oc, or Occitan (see entry below). When I was on a tour in the caves of Roquefort Société (see "Roquefort: King of Cheeses"), a class of about eight boys and girls were also on the tour, with their teacher. I recognized that they were not speaking textbook French, and my host, Pierre Tomasi, confirmed that they were in fact speaking Occitan. Readers who visit the coastal and inland towns of Céret, Collioure, and Banyuls will notice that many of the residents speak Catalan, and some signage and menus appear in Catalan.

If you've studied Spanish or even Italian, you'll find that French is relatively easy to learn. Of course, the French I'm referring to is that spoken in Paris and the center of France, which is considered "standard" and is technically the French everyone learns in school.

As an aside, I would like to stress that it is never too early to begin teaching young children another language. Even my husband was pooh-poohing me when I would read to Alyssa in French, or teach her Spanish and Italian words. But she now knows more than a dozen words and phrases in French.

Lepanto

The Battle of Lepanto, in 1571, was a hugely significant conflict in Mediterranean—especially Spanish, Venetian, Greek, and Turkish—history. Though France was not directly involved in the battle, references to Lepanto are many in French history books, as well as by writers such as Fernand Braudel. The site of this naval battle lies near the entrance to the Gulf of Corinth, known at that time as the Gulf of Lepanto. The fleet that set out to fight the Turks was primarily Spanish, with strong papal and Venetian contingents. The Christians were victorious, reasserting Spanish supremacy in the Mediterranean, and the victory was celebrated with much fanfare in Europe. But as Sir Charles Petrie, in *Philip II of Spain* (1963), has noted, "The battle of Lepanto did not break the back of Ottoman naval power, it did not recover Cyprus, and it did not lead to the policing of the Mediterranean by Spain. Though a tactical victory of the first order, because of the dissolution of the [Holy] League strategically it left the Sultan the victor. But morally it was decisive, for by lifting the pall of terror which had shrouded eastern and central Europe since 1453, it blazoned throughout Christendom the startling fact that the Turk was no longer invincible. Hence onward to the battle of Zenta, in 1697, when Eugene, Prince of Savoy, drove in rout the army of Sultan Mustafa II into the river Theiss, and thereby finally exorcised the Turkish threat to Europe. Though there were to be many ups and downs, never was the full prestige of Suleyman the Magnificent to be revived. His reign marks the summit of Turkish power, and it was the day of Lepanto which broke the charm upon which it rested." More recently (2000), historian Bernard Lewis, in *A Middle East Mosaic,* notes that Lepanto made very little difference to the real balance of power in southeastern Europe and the Mediterranean. "The Turkish armies remained dominant on land; the Turkish fleets were swiftly rebuilt. When the sultan expressed concern about the cost, his grand vizier replied: 'The might of our empire is such that if we wished to equip the entire fleet with silver anchors, silken rigging and satin sails, we could do it.'"

An excellent account of Lepanto is found in *The Decisive Battles of the Western World and Their Influence Upon History,* volume 1, by J.F.C. Fuller (see page 155).

Lourdes

This Pyrenees village is believed to be the site where a fourteen-year-old girl named Bernadette Soubirous saw the Virgin Mary and discovered a miraculous spring in 1858. Since 1933, Bernadette has been honored with sainthood, and Lourdes attracts approximately six million visitors a year. I have never been there, but if making a pilgrimage to its spectacular basilica and grotto is what you desire, there are some useful publications available from the French tourist offices in North America detailing accommodations, guided tours, and transportation. While I think it's easy to sum up the commercialism that has grown up around Lourdes as crass and tacky, it's profoundly more difficult to dismiss the millions of quite sincere people who have traveled a considerable distance to visit one of the world's most popular Christian pilgrimage sites. As a result, if you do want to visit Lourdes, be mindful of the calendar: if you simply show up and it's a religious holiday, you may not find accommodations (though I've read that only Paris has more hotel rooms), and parking and driving around the area will be a nightmare.

Luggage

Of all the entries in *Practical Information,* this one may prove to be most valuable, as it includes information that may make the difference between a miserable or a hassle-free experience at the airport. December 31, 2002, was the deadline for America's 429 commercial airports to begin screening all passenger bags for explosives. (Many airports had already been doing this after September 11, but airports weren't officially required to do so until that December 31 date.) You may deduce from the installation of the new screening systems that lines will be longer, and patience required. But what will help *enormously* is to plan ahead and make sure you know what is and isn't permissible in both checked and carry-on luggage so that you do not make those long lines come to a complete stop, causing frustration for everyone. Though the screening systems are bound to be fine-tuned over time, you should be aware that they often produce false positives, setting off alarms for items such as chocolate, cheese, or sneakers packed close together. (The density of chocolate and cheese, and food items in general, resembles that of some explosives.) For packing tips and other advice, log on to www.tsatraveltips.us, maintained by the Transportation Security Administration (TSA). Just as important is to contact the airline you're flying and inquire about *any* item that might be cause for alarm, either by a screening machine or by a hand search, including jewelry, belt buckles, shoes, corkscrews, disposable razors, knitting needles, aerosol cans, safety pins, cigarette lighters, medical prescriptions, syringes, and photography equipment. Don't wait until you're at the airport to discover that you should have left an item at home. Consider, too, what you're wearing the day you fly—even if your luggage checks in okay, be courteous to others by not making everyone wait while you discard coins from your pocket, your watch, and that necklace.

Additionally, inquire about the permissible *sizes* of luggage, and the definitions of carry-on bags. What women define as their tote bag or purse may be open to scrutiny (a tote bag filled with clothes is usually considered not personal and therefore must be checked), though a large cosmetic case is typically considered small enough to be personal. A backpack is a carry-on personal item, but put it on wheels and it becomes checked luggage. Computer laptop cases can also be singled out for inspection: if anything is stashed in the bag besides papers, the computer, and writing utensils, it could be seen as a candidate for checked baggage. I actually welcome the limits on carry-on bags, as I have always been annoyed with people who try to sneak on more baggage than they should be carrying in the first place. Storage space on planes is limited, and less baggage means more on-time schedules and better passenger safety. I endorse the words of Antoine de Saint-Exupéry: "He who would travel happily must travel light."

Another important date the TSA established was December 19, 2002, when it began advising passengers not to employ locks on their luggage. This was recommended in case a passenger's luggage caused an alarm to go off, requiring the need for a hand search. To assuage some passengers' doubts about sending their luggage off on the conveyor belt without a lock, the TSA provides airports with disposable plastic locks to give to passengers who check bags. The idea is that if the plastic lock has to be removed for a hand search—which is sometimes conducted out of view of the passenger—another will be attached at the conclusion of the search. As a result, the TSA is now assuming some of the liability for luggage, which used to be solely the responsibility of the airlines. It would be wise, therefore, not to pack anything of value in your checked bags, since you don't know if your luggage will be searched and you may not witness the search while it's happening.

Still another concern for the TSA is *matching* luggage with passengers. If a passenger checks a bag and then for some reason does not board the plane, that's something to be suspicious about, and the unaccompanied bag must be removed from the plane.

Before the September 11 tragedy the biggest misunderstanding about carry-on luggage was the 22-inch bag, measuring precisely 9 by 14 by 22 inches and known as 45 linear inches to the airlines. Some airlines would (and still will) accept the 22-inch bag as legitimate carry-on luggage, while others did not (and still won't). I use and recommend the smaller 20-inch bag, even if I have to check it, simply because it is, in the end, more practical—it fits under airline seats neatly and will therefore fit almost anywhere else neatly. If you are sitting in the bulkhead seats, you will not be able to stash it under a seat, but because the bag is relatively lightweight, you can easily lift it up to store in an overhead bin.

I've read of a syndrome—really—called BSA (Baggage Separation Anxiety), which you may at first be inclined to laugh at; but as reports of lost luggage have escalated in the last few years, I'm not at all surprised that fear of losing luggage is now a syndrome. (All the more reason, I say, not to check bags, and *definitely* the reason to at least pack some essentials in a carry-on bag.) Essentials, by the way, don't add up to much: it's remarkable how little one truly "needs." Recently one of my bags did not turn up when I reached my destination, and the airline representative was honest enough to tell me that when flights are full, sometimes not all the bags are loaded onto the plane—intentionally (#&!). Distressing as this is, at least it explains part of the problem and is one more reason to keep essentials with you. ~Some airports and/or airlines have changed the cut-off times for passengers to check luggage, moving them up as much as thirty to forty-five minutes before departure—another reason to arrive at the airport early!

M

Maginot Line

I presume every reader knows of the Maginot Line, but in case you need a refresher, this line of French fortification was constructed along the German frontier between the years 1929 and 1936, under the direction of war minister André Maginot. Looking at a map of France, follow a route beginning near Geneva and paralleling the Swiss, German, Luxembourg, and Belgian borders, all the way to Dunkirk. The line, considered unbreachable, was constructed between the wars to deter a German offensive into France and consisted of semiunderground forts joined by underground passages. It was also protected by antitank defenses, and lighter fortifications continued the line to the sea. In 1940 German troops pierced the Belgian frontier line and outflanked the Maginot Line.

Markets

Outdoor markets are one of the great pleasures of France, and you'll find no shortage of them in the Southwest. Many of the smaller towns and villages host weekly or more frequent *marchés;* Toulouse has a large *marché* every Friday; and Bordeaux is perhaps especially dedicated to a thriving *marché* scene, with ten open-air markets, four organic markets, and five covered markets, at least one to visit every day of the week. Bordeaux even has its own "belly of Bordeaux" market, just as Paris had its Emile Zola–designated "belly of Paris" Les Halles *marché* (which has since closed and relocated to Rungis, near the Orly airport). The "belly of Bordeaux" is the *marché des Capucins,* known affectionately as the *Capus,* which had for more than three hundred years offered goods from all across France. In 1963 the wholesale portion of the *marché* was moved to the Brienne district of the city, bordering the main rail link, but the *Capus* continues serving the general public, with eighty stalls and a forty-million-franc facelift in 2001. In an article entitled "Au Printemps, Au Marché" (*The Sophisticated Traveler* edition of *The New York Times Magazine,* March 13, 1988), Patricia Wells noted that "France's market structure has changed little since the Middle Ages, when villages throughout the country established weekly marchés for the sale and barter of everything from livestock to clothing." She also added that "there are no markets as lively, as appealing, or as abundant as those in the sunny south." Hotelkeepers, concierges, and everyone in town know the market sched-ules; they're also available at local tourist offices and are featured in some guide-books, including Wells's *Food Lover's Guide to France* (Workman, 1987). Wells not only provides lists of daily and weekly markets but also food-related fairs, festivals, and shops—not to mention restaurants, cafés, and bars—in individual chapters on Languedoc; Gascogne, Toulouse and Quercy; the Dordogne; and Bordeaux and the Atlantic Coast. Even if you have no intention of purchasing anything, you should not miss walking around an outdoor (or indoor) market. Prices for food seem to be displayed and fixed in France, but at many flea mar-kets bargaining is the accepted method of doing business (merchants will tell you if it's not); therefore a visit to the market should not be an activity you try and do in a hurry. Take your time, remember to stop for something to eat or drink so your stomach (or companion) doesn't grumble, and enjoy searching for a unique souvenir or soaking up the atmosphere. *Marchés aux puces* (flea markets) nuts should definitely locate a copy of *Exploring the Flea Markets of France: A Companion Guide for Visitors and Collectors* (Sandy Price, Three Rivers Press, 1999). Additionally, a few Web sites may be of interest: www.antiquaires-sna.com, www.gazette-drouot.com, www.pagesbrocante.com, www.antiquites-en-france.com, and www.ma-brocante.com all feature directories of flea markets all over France. I found dozens of listings for places throughout the Southwest.

Dewey Markham Jr.

American Dewey Markham was mentioned in an article by Gene Bourg in the *Bordeaux et Aquitaine* section, and when I followed up on the reference, I learned that Markham is a name to know. Originally from New York, Markham earned a master's degree in cinema studies from New York University's School of the Arts, saw Paris for the first time in 1977, and was, like many of us, smitten with all things French, and decided to switch careers and become a chef. He enrolled in the no-nonsense program at the Culinary Institute of America (CIA) in Hyde Park, New

York, and stayed on for two more years helping to put together what is now the CIA's standard reference tome, *The New Professional Chef* (the more recent editions are published by John Wiley & Sons). Markham was then accepted as an editorial *stagière* (apprentice) at Anne Willan's Paris cooking school, La Varenne. He held various positions at La Varenne over the course of three years, and more important, met chefs and winemakers. In 1989, Markham's work permit expired, forcing him to return to New York. By this time, he had decided to become a wine importer, but while working at Sherry-Lehman, one of New York's top wine retailers, he wrote a book, *Wine Basics: A Quick and Easy Guide* (John Wiley & Sons, 1993). The money he earned from sales of this book helped him return to France, this time to Bordeaux, where he was determined to write a second book: *1855: A History of the Bordeaux Classification* (John Wiley & Sons, 1998) is the kind of masterpiece one dreams about creating, an accomplishment realized probably late in one's life. The book has been honored with numerous prestigious awards. More impressive is that a young American man who, only ten years before had no specialized knowledge of wine, let alone Bordeaux wines, or of its history, wrote the first book to reveal the actual story of the famous classification, one that stands among the classic Bordeaux reference works. A year before he completed this magnum opus, Markham married Catherine Goyon, who was at the time (I'm not certain she still is) the assistant director of marketing at Mouton-Rothschild. All of this is obviously of interest to readers and wine enthusiasts, but for visitors, the good news is that Markham arranges custom-designed tours to Bordeaux and the surrounding vineyards. As correspondent Stephen Meuse noted in an article about Markham in *The Boston Globe* (April 26, 2000), "Chateau doors open wide at his command, and he keeps busy providing guided tours in French or English that include access to winemaking facilities and tasting rooms that would be off-limits to ordinary mortals." Markham may be contacted via e-mail at dmarkham@ wanadoo.fr or the regular *poste* at 96 rue Laroche, 33000 Bordeaux, France; 33.5/56.52.13.51.

Money

The best way to travel is with a combination of local cash, American Express traveler's checks (other types are not universally accepted), and credit cards. If you have all three, you will *never* have a problem. (Note that you should not rely on wide acceptance of credit cards, especially in the countryside.) How you divide it up depends on how long you'll be traveling and on what day of the week you arrive. Banks, which of course offer the best exchange rate, aren't generally open on the weekends. If you arrive on a weekend and rely solely on your ATM card but encounter a problem, you can't fix it until Monday when the banks reopen. Overseas ATMs may limit the number of daily transactions you can make and place a ceiling on the total amount you can withdraw.

Jean Moulin

Moulin was France's most famous Resistance leader, and was accorded one of France's highest honors: a burial at the Panthéon in Paris in 1964, even though, as Patrick Marnham notes in his excellent book *Resistance and Betrayal: The Death and Life of the Greatest Hero of the French Resistance,* "A man's life can sometimes be defined by his death. In the case of Jean Moulin nobody knows when he died, or how or where. His body was never found." I am somewhat obsessed with the history of Vichy France, the Resistance, and the Nazi occupation of France, so when I learned Marnham's book was being published, I couldn't wait for its arrival. I was predisposed to find it fascinating, especially when I read the following endorsement by Alan Furst, a writer who has often woven wartime France into his novels: "If you are interested in France, the real France, or if you are interested in the Second World War, or if you are interested in courage, real courage, and how it can rise to meet the most severe test imaginable, then I believe you ought to make it your business to read Patrick Marnham's extraordinary book."

Marnham lived for twelve years in Paris and covered three French war crimes for the British and American press, so on the subject of a French Resistance leader he knows whereof he speaks (he is also not a novice at writing biographies, having penned one on Georges Simenon and another on Diego Rivera). He observes that "sources for the life of Jean Moulin are few and far between. He was a man with an obsessive habit of secrecy, as first noticed by his sister when he was an eighteen-year-old student in Montpellier. Whether for temperamental, personal or even political reasons, Moulin gave very little away, even to his closest friends. As far as he was concerned the entire world was on a "need to know" basis."

Noteworthy as Moulin's role as Resistance leader is, more pertinent to this book is that he is a son of the Southwest, born in Béziers, educated at Montpellier University, and nominated to Rodez in 1937 as prefect of the Aveyron. Visitors to Bordeaux should know also of the Centre Jean Moulin (located on the place Jean Moulin), a very good museum featuring collections devoted to World War II themes, the Resistance, and the Free French forces—there's also a reproduction of Moulin's clandestine office. Without giving away the complicated story of Moulin's fate and Marnham's conclusions, I do want to note that in Marnham's final notes, he informs us that in 1990 it was suggested that Moulin had not died in Gestapo custody but had been spirited away to Moscow in 1943 and swapped for some distinguished Nazi prisoner of war. Documentary evidence has also been published that Pierre Cot, Moulin's prewar mentor, had been listed as an anti-Gaullist informant by Soviet intelligence during the Second World War. In 1997, Gerard Chauvy, a historian from Lyons, published a book that cast serious doubt on the credibility of Raymond Aubrac, the communist resistance commander who was arrested at Caluire with Jean Moulin and who has always been one of the most important witnesses to Moulin's fate.

Movies

Plan a meal from one or more of the cookbooks mentioned in the *Flavors and Tables of the Southwest* bibliography, and invite some friends and family over for dinner and a movie. A favorite of mine is *Le Pays Bleu* (Blue Country), but you may find others appropriate to the Southwest or France in general by browsing us.imdb.com, the Web site of the Internet Movie Database). And while you're cooking, get in the mood by listening to some appropriate music: *C'est L'amour!* (RCA, 1996), *French Kiss* (movie soundtrack, Polygram, 1995), and *All the Best from France: 40 French Favorites* (Madacy Records, 1996). All are great choices that will have you ready to say *à votre santé!* (to your health/cheers!) when your guests arrive.

Museums and Monuments

Most state-run museums and monuments in France are closed on Tuesdays, while privately run museums are closed on Mondays, but always double-check before you set off, as this rule is not universal. Just as in the small towns of Italy and Spain, many churches, castles, and other sites in small French towns are kept locked, and you must find the caretaker and request the key. Caretakers will often volunteer to open the building and show you around; a small tip is appreciated and indeed expected. Sometimes the key is kept at the local government office or, more logically, at the bar. In the Southwest long lines are relatively rare, except perhaps at the height of summer in Rocamadour and Carcassonne.

An ongoing project of mine for this series is to compile a list of North American museums that hold notable collections of art, historical artifacts, documents, or other related *objets* that readers may view in advance of their Mediterranean trips (and hopefully continue their interest in when they return). It's all a part of immersing yourself, I believe, in your destination, and as the deadline approached for this edition, I found I was a long way from completing my list, so interested readers will have to look for it in the next book, to feature Athens, the Peloponnese, and the Aegean Islands. The many museums of New York City are a mere thirty minutes from my home, and I am a member of some of them and frequent many of them, often. Like Paris, New York is home to some of the most significant museums in the United States, among them the Metropolitan Museum of Art. The Met recently launched an extraordinary program that I think deserves an enormous amount of praise: the Timeline of Art History, which can be viewed by logging on to the Web site www.metmuseum.org/toah. As I write this, the timeline features art history through the year 1600 (after the birth of Christ), but it will continue to grow in scope and depth, eventually spanning art history through the present day. The timeline is a chronological, geographical, and thematic exploration of the history of art from around the world as illustrated especially by the Met's collection. Only museums the size of the Met and the Louvre could compile such a project, and now art history mavens and scholars around the world have access to an unparalleled compendium of art. (I should mention, for the benefit of readers who live far from New York and may be unfamiliar with the Met's extensive art collections, that the museum's French art departments are outstanding.) Of particular interest to a book on Southwestern France is the medieval art portion of the site, which includes a section on the Cloisters, located near the northern tip of Manhattan. The Cloisters museum includes the Pontaut Chapter House from Pontaut in Gascony (the museum purchased it in the early 1930s) and the cloister of St.-Guilhem-le-Desert, founded in 804 by Guilhem au Court-Nez, duke of Aquitaine and a member of Charlemagne's court. (A portion of the original cloister remains at St.-Guilhem, in a valley near Montpellier.) The timeline is nothing short of a major museum achievement, and it's an invaluable reference and research tool for students, educators, scholars, and anyone interested in the study of art history and related subjects. Once you start browsing, it's really difficult to stop. As I am still compiling my list of North American museums, I'd be grateful to hear from you if you'd like to share the specifics of a museum with a strong collection of French paintings, drawings, literature, letters, or decorative arts.

Négociants

This is the French word for "wine merchants," a key word to know with regard to Bordeaux wines in particular. According to *The Oxford Companion to Wine*, *négociants* "traditionally brought most of the wines they brought into their chais in or around Bordeaux (notably its Quai des Chartrons) to be matured and shipped out to export customers, notably in Britain or Scandinavia, either in barrels or after bottling. What the merchant supplied in addition to the mere buying and selling of wine was technical ability (his cellarmaster and team were likely to be considerably better technicians than the producers), and the financing of the grower. Since 1945, improvements in wine-making at all levels and since the 1980s, price increases and inflation levels which have made it impossible for even the biggest merchants to finance large quantities of wine, have transformed the role of the merchant from principal to broker. With the economic problems of the 1990s, and increased competition from other wine regions of the world, it seems likely that the merchants' other justification as advisor and selector, the intermediary who transmits changes in consumer tastes to producers, will once again become important."

O

Occitan

Occitan is derived from *langue d'occitan*—the language (or tongue) of the Occitan region of France, which long ago was defined as all of the south of France except the parts we know today as Roussillon and Gascony (the Provençal dialect should, in fact, be referred to as Occitan). The opposite of the *langue d'occitan*—or *langue d'Oc,* from which Languedoc takes its name—is the *langue d'oïl,* which refers to the dialects used in northern France. Both *oc* and *oïl* mean "yes" in their respective dialects, and both are from the Latin *hoc* and *hoc ille.* Michael Jacbos, in his excellent book *A Guide to Provence,* notes that "Provençal is a Romance language having much in common with Italian, Spanish, and French, but being particularly close to Catalan, the language spoken both in Catalonia and in the adjoining territory of Roussillon." René Weis, in *The Yellow Cross,* notes that Catalan "is the closest anyone can come now to the *langue d'oc*" that was spoken by the all the characters in his historic work on the Cathars. "The two are virtually identical." *Langue d'Oç* also refers to the land west of the Rhône to Toulouse, because during the time the popes were in residence in Avignon, the Rhône was the dividing line between land claimed by the popes—known as the Comtat-Venaissin—and that of the French kings. Lawrence Durrell, in *Caesar's Vast Ghost,* noted that Rhone boatmen actually referred to one bank of the river as "empire" and the other as "kingdom."

In discussing the *langue d'oc* versus the *langue d'oïl* in my *Provence* edition, I included an excerpt from Waverly Root's *The Food of France.* Root maintained that the dominance of the *langue d'oïl* over the *langue d'oc* was owing to the fact that the former became a written language, the literary language of its region, and the latter did not. "But a more important reason for the failure of the *langue d'oc* to become a language of literature is probably the paradoxical one that the south of France had become imbued with the Mediterranean civilization earlier than the north . . . Southern France had made Latin its literary language early. It was firmly rooted and hard to dislodge when the spoken tongues resulting from the collision between Latin and the tongues of Gaul began to crystallize sufficiently to be ready to become new languages. Latin was less firmly rooted as a written language in the north. It gave way more readily to the popular speech. And as this became a written language, and exchanges between the north and the south carried it southward before the *langue d'oc* had been committed to paper, the latter remained a dialect and the former became French." Additionally, both *langue* phrases divide north from south gastronomically, designating the north as a cuisine based on dairy products and the south as one based on olive oil.

An interesting festival I read about in Joy Law's *Dordogne* is the *Félibrée,* or "*Lou Bournat*" (le *Félibrige* was a movement founded by Frédéric Mistral which aimed to preserve the history, culture, and language of Provence). The fair takes place in a different commune every year, and the women of the designated commune make thousands of flowers from crepe paper that are then strung together across the streets (they apparently spend the winter months doing this, as it is quite time consuming and would otherwise never be completed in time as it takes place in late summer). Félibrée is an offshoot of the Félibrige, and *bournat* is a beehive, which symbolizes a group of busy like-minded people. Law notes that the festival "is a rather elaborate and expensive way of preserving the songs and dancing and re-creating the genuine gastronomic delights of the past," and she notes that other attempts to keep occitan alive are made by the Comité du Périgord de la Langue Occitane, "who fear that the patois spoken by Périgordins over seventy is dying out."

P

Packing

Some pointers that work for me include selecting clothing that isn't prone to wrinkling, like cotton and wool knits. When I *am* concerned about limiting wrinkles, I lay out a large plastic dry cleaning bag, place the garment on top of it, place *another* bag on top of that, and fold the item up between the two bags. The key here is that the plastic must be layered in with the clothing, otherwise it doesn't really work. ~If you're carrying a bag with separate compartments, use one for shoes; otherwise put shoes at the bottom (or back) of the bag opposite the handle so they'll remain there while you're carrying the bag. ~Transfer shampoo and lotions to plastic travel-size bottles, which can be purchased at pharmacies—and then put them inside a Ziploc bag to protect against leaks. ~Don't skimp on underwear—it's lightweight and takes up next to no room in your bag. It's never a mistake to have more than you think you need. ~Belts can be either rolled up and stuffed into shoes or fastened together along the inside edge of your suitcase. ~Ties should be rolled, not folded, and also stuffed into shoes or pockets.

Some handy things to bring along that are often overlooked: a pocket flashlight, for looking into ill-lit corners of old buildings, reading in bed at night (the lights are often not bright enough), or if you're staying at a hotel where the bathroom is down the hall, for navigating dark hallways at night (the light is usually on a timer and always runs out before you've made it to either end of the hallway); binoculars, for looking up at architectural details; a penknife/corkscrew; if you're camping, plastic shoes—referred to in the United States as jellies—which the Italians and the French have been wearing on some of their rocky beaches for years—for campground showers; an empty lightweight duffel bag, which you can fold up and pack and then use as a carry-on bag for gifts and breakable items on the way home; a plastic bag big enough for a wet swimsuit, in case your flight doesn't depart Perpignan or Toulouse until the afternoon, leaving you the morning to spend on the beach at Collioure.

Paris

As most visitors to the Southwest from North America will fly first to Paris, I thought I would take the admittedly bold (selfish?) opportunity to suggest that readers also take along a copy of my *Paris* edition. Like the other books in my little series, *Paris* is both an eye-opening companion for first-time visitors to the city and a seasoned one for those who know France's capital well. Even if you only have a day or two to spend in Paris, at either the beginning or end of a Southwest journey, I believe my *Paris* book will assist you in deciding how you most want to spend your time there. It will also bring to your attention some excellent guidebooks as well as related nonfiction titles and companion reading. I have found that no matter how large my home library is, I am always discovering books, both old and new, that deserve to be read. If you are as fanatical as I am about Paris, you probably approach a must-read book about Paris with the same anticipation that I do, regardless of whether that book is newly published or out of print. And books that are "old" to you and me are of course "new" to readers about to discover the moveable feast that is Paris. An excellent Web site I only recently discovered (three years after my *Paris* edition was published, unfortunately) that I believe may be worth your while to browse is www.bonjourparis.com. The site features "This Week in Paris" and "News from France" as well as a number of regular columns on a variety of topics; book recommendations; a marketplace; and sections on day trips, expatriates, language, history, museums and sights, rentals, wine, traveling impaired, and personalities.

A wonderful way to begin or end your immersion into the Southwest is to enjoy a meal at a restaurant that specializes in Southwestern cuisine. After all, Paris is home to restaurants featuring the cuisine from every region of France, and the Southwest is well represented. A few to choose from include Carré des Feuillants (14 rue de Castiglione, 1st arrondissement), Au Bascou (38 rue Réamur, 3rd arrondissement), La Table d'Aude (8 rue de Vaugirard, 6th arrondissement), Le Bar au Sel (49 quai d'Orsay, 7th arrondissement), La Fontaine de Mars (129 rue St.-Dominique, 7th arrondissement; I ate here on my last visit), A Sousceyrac (35 rue Faidherbe, 11th arrondissement), and Au Trou Gascon (40 rue Taine, 12th arrondissement), all of which are recommended by Patricia Wells in her indispensable book *The Food Lover's Guide to Paris* (Workman Publishing Company, revised and updated fourth edition published 1999; view www.patriciawells.com for updates on the Parisian food scene). And if you forgot to pick up some Southwestern culinary specialties (or if you tried but the shop was closed when you came by), two stores in Paris can accommodate: L'Ambassade du Sud-Ouest (46 avenue de la Bourdonnais, 7th arrondissement) and Le Comptoir Correzien (8 rue Volontaires, 15th arrondissement), both of which are also recommended in Wells's bible.

Parler

The French verb for "to speak, talk, or converse" and a useful word to know, even if it's only to inquire *Parlez-vous anglais?* (Do you speak English?). More to the point, remember not to speak loudly—in English *or* in French. It's simply not the custom. Parisians especially love to debate (sometimes at the expense of customers who are standing in a long line in a shop), but they rarely shout. If you're walking around or eating in a restaurant and you hear loud voices, they will invariably be American. Bruce Northam, in his book *Globetrotter Dogma,* which I cannot stop enthusing about, created a list of six American impulses to avoid if you do not wish to be viewed as the type of tourist known as unsavory. These are: "high-fiving everyone; wearing high-top sneakers and a baseball cap backward; talking incessantly, volume set on loud. Observation: There are *two* North American languages: English and louder; defending American football players against charges that they're overpadded, compared to helmetless, and possibly toothless, rugby players; giving an enthusiastic thumbs-up, accompanied by a lightheaded grin; prefixing your sentences with 'yo' and 'like.' Responding with 'totally' and 'definitely!' Then high-fiving again." In the States we may operate on the theory that the squeaky wheel gets the grease, but that doesn't fly in France. The French converse softly, and so should you.

Paseo

The *paseo* is the evening stroll, a very old and popular Mediterranean custom. In Southwestern France you will mostly encounter it in Languedoc-Roussillon and along the coastal areas of Aquitaine, as it is a custom well suited to a hot climate (though the evening stroll is quite popular in Toulouse also). I use the Spanish word here, *paseo,* though I'm not quite sure why; it simply seems to be commonly employed, though the French word for "a stroll" is *une promenade. Paseo* is also used in Spain and Morocco, and in Italy it is known as the *passegiata.* The evening stroll has historically served as a venue for young men and women to meet each other. *Everyone* turns out for this pre-dinner walk—grandparents, babies, teenagers, and toddlers. The *paseo* flows a bit better on straight stretches of cobblestones, macadam, marble, or whatever, but even in large cities like Toulouse, Bordeaux, and Montpellier, residents find a section of town for their walk. Sometimes elderly residents are not actually walking, but they gather on park benches and catch up on the day's news. It's a ritual not to be missed, and an essay in the wonderful book *The Walker Within* notes about this healthy habit that "were Americans to take up this custom, the rate of criminal violence would surely drop, for it's easier to gun down strangers than people with whom you've passed the time."

Pétanque

The game of *pétanque* is a ubiquitous symbol throughout the entire swath of southern France. *Pétanque* is referred to in the north as *boules,* a term with which readers are probably more familiar. I've been told the rules are slightly different between the two versions, but I've never been able to discern what those differences are. Some interesting facts I've read about *pétanque* are that it was the Romans who brought the game to Gaul, but the game's origins are in Egypt and Greece; the original balls were made of wood, and gradually, after players began hammering nails or studs into them, the balls were made entirely of metal; only a dozen balls are allowed to be thrown in one game, regardless of the number of players; the smaller ball in the game is made of wood and is called the *cochonnet* (little pig)—players attempt to throw their balls as close to the *cochonnet* as possible; in 1792, soldiers in Marseilles decided to play with cannon balls, but they set off a gunpowder store and literally blew themselves up—eight people died; though it seems uniquely French, *boules* is actually played all over Europe (in Italy it's known as *bocce*), Australia, North Africa, and parts of North America, and in 1996, a proposal was submitted to the International Olympic Committee to declare *boules* an Olympic sport. The best part about the game to me is that, like croquet and horseshoes, you can hold a drink in one hand while playing (though you'll rarely see the French do this—they retire to the nearby café after the game is over). The mail order catalog French Inspirations, by the way, offers a great *pétanque* set for about $35. The set comes with instructions and is packed in a carrying case. Call 800-440-1777 for more information.

Politesse

The French are generally well trained in the forms of *politesse* (politeness), and I find it refreshing, frankly, after much-too-casual American ways. Betty Lou Phillips, in *French by Design*, notes that "unlike Americans, the French have no difficulty drawing the line of familiarity, since the ways they address one another reflect how well they know each other. Whereas most Americans use familiar first names too soon after meeting and readily shorten the names of others without being invited to do so, the French mark distances and underline social differences with the formal *vous* (you). The more familiar *tu* (you) is reserved for family and closest friends." Phillips goes on to say that French children rarely misbehave in public, and the French generally are extremely conscious of liberties that might be disturbing to others. There are, thankfully, unwritten rules for cell-phone etiquette, and she reminds us that it is considered bad manners to call anyone after 9:30 P.M. or to phone a business associate at home on Saturday unless the person is also a close friend. (Tactful friends and family members reserve Sunday for their telephone calling.)

Hand in hand with *politesse* are good value, wealth, and discretion, all of supreme importance to the French. Again to quote Phillips, "Equating elegance with restraint, the French deliberately avoid material indulgences that are outward measures of success. Although they have a propensity for quality goods, most frown on anything that appears extreme. For them, comfort and tastefulness are paramount, not high-priced luxuries or extravagant ways . . . the French are more apt to judge each other by their good taste (*bon gout*) or lack of it. Instead, net worth is a private affair, and the French consider themselves keepers of a tradition to be guarded as fiercely as the family jewels, making discretion treasured." Odd to the French is the American habit of dividing a restaurant bill, Phillips notes. In France, restaurant tabs are controversy-free, as someone will always step forward and pay it (though they may quietly split the tab privately).

Prehistoric Remains

In addition to the world-famous cave of Lascaux, France is home to several prehistoric sites and museums, including the Chauvet cave in the Ardèche (which contains paintings 31,000 years old), the Cosquer cave in the Calanques between Marseilles and Cassis (featuring preserved images of animals, penguins, and horses for more than 20,000 years), the Archéodrome de Bourgogne near the Beaune-Tailly rest area on the A6 autoroute (featuring a reconstruction of 100,000 years of human activity in the region, with life-sized habitats), and the Baume Bonne cave in the Gorges du Verdon, where excavations have succeeded in revealing the Lower Palaeolithic age, 400,000 years ago. The most important Palaeolithic collection in France is in the Dordogne, the Musée National de la Préhistoire des Les Eyzies-de-Tayac. Les Eyzies-de-Tayac itself is known as the "World Capital of Prehistory," and the *musée* presents archaeological collections that are unique in the world, most of which come from the most prestigious prehistoric sites of the Vézère Valley. All of these treasures are displayed in the ruined château of Les Eyzies, dating from the sixteenth century.

I must confess that this museum satisfied all my curiosity about the *grottes* (caves) in the vicinity. I much prefer learning about prehistoric remains with the help of museums and books to actually visiting caves, which I don't like unless they have Roquefort in them. But caves definitely do appeal to many visitors, which is why Lascaux I, as it's called (the original cave discovered in September 1940), is no longer open to the general public. (It closed in April 1963 due to white disease, carbonic acid caused by human breath that was eating away at the paintings; admission is now limited to five prehistorians twice a week.) It's also why the Dordogne authorities constructed Lascaux II, located 650 feet below the original cave. Guided tours lasting about forty minutes are offered to the public, some in English. As I mentioned, I did not visit Lascaux II, and not even the wonderful Cadogan Guides authors could convince me to go, though they do enthuse about the visit, noting that "humble awe is a common response to this magical place, or even a sneaking suspicion that LSD guru Terence McKenna might be right (in his book *Food of the Gods*) that Upper Palaeolithic culture was built around magic psilocybin mushrooms, a healthy psychedelic experience lost with the climatic changes at the end of the Ice Age. Whatever the truth, more than 300,000 visitors a year get a glimpse into the world of their Magdalenian ancestors." If the crowds are too much for you, or if you are in the area during January and early February, when Lascaux II is closed, don't forget that it isn't the only prehistoric game in town. Remember that if you do visit an actual *grotte,* filled with Roquefort or with artifacts of a decidedly more valuable nature, bring along a heavy sweater or a coat—winter or summer, it's cold down there.

Readers especially interested in Lascaux may want to search for an article I was unable to include in this book entitled "The Lascaux Puzzle" (Roy McMullen, *Horizon,* Spring 1969). The accompanying color photos are reason alone to track this down, but the author raises two interesting points that are surprisingly given little attention elsewhere. McMullen states that to refer to Lascaux as the birthplace of art is to "trade a high mystery for a cheap piece of romanticism. Art is forever being born, and its birthplace is the nature of Homo sapiens." He continues that while it is no doubt true that the painters wanted their pictures to have a certain utility—perhaps to make hunting more plentiful or to explain the universe—to conclude that this utility was the *only* reason for painting is to dismiss what we know about the history of art and about human nature. "It is like assuming, for instance, that Fra Angelico painted almost entirely because he was a Christian and scarcely at all because he had a vocation—because he felt the typically hominoid itch to arrange forms and colors on a flat surface." McMullen also asks, for whom were the cave paintings painted? As he notes, evidence to support an answer is not lacking. If the present entrance to the cave is approximately the original one, the paintings were executed in dark passages and could have been seen only with the help of grease lamps and firelight. Also, in many places—too many for them to be called exceptional—the artists painted one animal on top of another, with no concern for the paintings' legibility. Finally, there is no indication that the cave was visited by a great number of people before its discovery in 1940. "Indeed, the signs of prehistoric frequentation seem to me quite compatible with the idea that the only human beings who went down there were the artists and their helpers or attendants." The fact that the paintings began to deteriorate only after they were exposed to modern crowds lends credence to this idea. McMullen concludes that "execution was all; looking was nothing," and that there was practically no public at Lascaux, nor at other decorated caves, as the evidence is about the same everywhere.

Q

Queue

Queue is the word for "line," and as Ross Steele notes in *When in France: Do as the French Do,* "French lines are disorderly affairs, and everyone seems to have a logical personal reason to break into the line (*resquiller*)." Though some public agencies have attempted to make people form a single line, known as *une file d'at-*

tente unique, it has largely failed. Steele explains that "lines publicly demonstrate the lack of discipline, the single-minded devotion to individualism, and the reluctance of the French to acquiesce to any group organization." Maintaining your place in line is something like survival of the fittest, and if you adopt the mindset of the French, you will, after several tries, fit right in.

R

La Résistance

The story of the French Resistance, as Freda White notes in her excellent book *Three Rivers of France,* "has still to be told. But the south-western region bears such visible scars of it that something must be said here. The region was south of the zone occupied by the Germans after the Armistice of 1940, though of course it was subject to the Vichy Government, whose policy wavered between passive acceptance and active collaboration." Even since the publication of my *Paris* edition, the French have come a long way in confronting their complicated wartime past, and a number of very good books have appeared over the last ten years or so addressing the issue. It would be difficult to prove that collaboration and vengeance were worse in one part of France than another, but surely some of the worst events occurred in Aquitaine and the Lot Valley. As White expands upon in her book, "the taste of blood grew sweet in the mouth of the Germans, and they took to seizing every man they met, whether a Resister or not, taking him to the nearest crossroads and shooting him. Scores of crossroads have little boards, where, in fading letters, are the names of four or six men, followed by the words 'Morts glorieusement pour la patrie, Juin 1944'—'Died gloriously for the country, June 1944.' If no men were available, for soon all the men fled on their approach to the woods and caves, they took women and children and killed them. At Paluel, near Sarlat, they took twenty-eight women of a hamlet, poured petrol over them and burnt them. Their orgy ended by the massacre of the people of Oradour in the Limousin, where they wiped out the whole population, burning them in the church." (Readers interested in learning more about Oradour should turn to an excellent source, *Martyred Village: Commemorating the 1944 Massacre at Oradour-sur-Glane,* Sarah Farmer, University of California Press, 1999, hardcover; 2000 paperback). As White concludes, "Both sides, when talking of the Resistance, say at some point 'One could not choose, in such times. There were good and bad in the Resistance.' There were indeed; it is certain that the Germans managed to plant plenty of spies in the Resistance bands, and that they were often betrayed by their own members. On the whole, however, the story is one of astonishing courage and loyalty throughout the whole population." I especially like that White's dedication reads "To the French Resistance of the River-Country / To those who died and are remembered / And to those who live and remember / I dedicate this book."

Rivers

As part of defining a visual image of a destination in my head, I like to memorize the major rivers of the area I will visit. For the Southwest, these include the Dordogne, Garonne, Lot (pronounced LOT-uh, with a long O as in *note*), Rhone, Tarn, and Vézère rivers. There are lots of companies—too many to list here—that organize river trips in the Southwest, both active and leisurely, in canoes, rafts, and large cruise boats. I have not yet been on a canoe or raft trip in the Southwest, though I would like to—the rivers are, for the most part, quite tranquil, perfect for someone like me (I once went rafting in northern California on the American River, considered to be moderate in rafting terms, and I was so petrified I molded my legs to the side of the raft thinking that would ensure I wouldn't fall out). So far my only Southwest river experience has been on the Garonne in Toulouse (Peniche Baladine, "la Dame de l'Eau"; 33.61/80.22.26; www.bateaux-toulousains.com), and I loved it! It was in the evening, the sun was going down, and it was beautiful. For those seeking more adventurous river thrills, there are dozens and dozens of companies to choose from—you'll find a great number of brochures displayed at local tourist offices and you'll learn of others in some guidebooks.

La Route de Saint Jacques

The pilgrimage route of St. Jacques or Santiago (St. James in French and Spanish) is among the most historically significant relics of the Middle Ages in Europe, especially in France where cathedrals were built (and towns grew) along the route. There are four major routes that cross much of France (the starting points were Paris, Vézelay, Le Puy, and Arles) and one smaller coastal route that began in Soulac (a little northwest of Bordeaux). The routes from Paris, Vézelay, Le Puy, and Soulac joined the more famous Spanish section, the Camino de Santiago, at Roncevaux (Roncesvalles), while the route from Arles crossed the Pyrenees at Col du Somport (Puerto de Somport) and continued on to Puente-La-Reina, just past Roncesvalles in Spain. The 733-kilometer (458-mile) route from Roncesvalles to Santiago de Compostela was declared a World Heritage Site in 1993. Currently, there are sixty-nine monuments on the route listed individually, and of that total fifty are in France, thirty-three within the Southwest. In 1189, Santiago was declared a Holy City, along with Rome and Jerusalem, by Pope Alexander III.

I devoted a considerable number of pages to the Camino de Santiago in Spain in my *Northern Spain* book, so readers may refer to that edition for more details and articles. A Web site I recently learned about that focuses more on sites and routes in Southwestern France is www.amis-st-jacques.org, the site of Les Amis de St.-Jacques. Some recommended books to read include *The Pilgrimage to Santiago* (Edwin Mullins, Interlink, 2001), *The Pilgrimage Road to Santiago: The Complete Cultural Handbook* (David Gitlitz and Linda Kay Davidson, Griffin/St. Martin's Press, 2000), *The Pilgrim's Guide to Santiago de Compostela* (William Melczer,

Italica Press, New York, 1993), *The Road to Santiago* (Michael Jacobs, Pallas Athene, London, 2002), and *The Way of St. James—Le Puy to Santiago: A Walker's Guide* (Alison Raju, Cicerone Press, 2001).

S

La Sabranenque

Founded by Henri and Simone Gignouxin in the 1960s, La Sabranenque is a non-profit foundation located in St.-Victor-la-Coste in Languedoc—on the other side of the Rhone from Avignon, a little north of the Pont du Gard—that is dedicated to restoring castles, rebuilding town walls, and reclaiming abandoned houses. I first read of La Sabranenque in an issue of *Travel Holiday* ("Will Work for French Food" by Christine Ryan), and I immediately wanted to sign up. La Sabranenque accepts volunteers every summer, for two-week stints at a cost of approximately $580. Ryan notes in her article that "even renting a villa, though, is not guarantee you'll get any closer to the heart of France than an offhand *bonjour* from the village baker. But that's exactly what La Sabranenque is all about. Based in St.-Victor and devoted to preserving the country's medieval ruins, this program puts you in touch, literally, with the stones and mortar of France's past . . . you become a part of St.-Victor-la-Coste—or as much as you ever could be, that is, without settling in for, oh, three or four decades." Ryan also notes that France has more medieval ruins than it knows what to do with, so many of them are simply collapsing, which is where La Sabranenque comes in. The basis of all projects is stone masonry; other techniques used can include any stage of historic restoration, from clearing of rubble to roof tiling. In between is stone cutting, flooring with tiles or wood, interior plastering, arch and vault construction, path paving, or dry stone walling. "Even shlepping rocks," Ryan says, "shows you just how hard it was to restore this village by hand—with no bulldozers or power tools—and how long it must have taken to build these structures in the first place. And those medieval contractors didn't leave just castles and villages like this behind, but immense cathedrals and monasteries and cities. You'll never look at Notre Dame—or even a simple Vermont stone wall—the same way again." Before I read this *Travel Holiday* piece, I had saved one of those "Letters on Travel" pages dated September 17, 1995, from the travel section of *The New York Times,* in which a reader wrote that three years prior she had the best vacation of her life . . . at La Sabranenque. This reader also added that she brought back more than good memories: as she learned the fine points of building a stone wall and where to pick the best fresh thyme, she fell in love with one of the supervisors, and they were married in 1994! (I just love stories like that.)

The directors of La Sabranenque are Henri Gignoux, founder and director of the International Center since 1967, and Marc Simon, an American who holds a B.A. cum laude from Princeton and a certificate in French language and civilization from the University of Avignon. There are two types of sessions offered, Volunteer and Visit (which features ongoing restorations of Mediterranean architecture from June to September) and Restoration Work (which is coupled with visits of the region during the months of March, April, May, and October). Both programs offer most afternoons free for one's own exploring and relaxation, as well as some regional visits to nearby towns and monuments. Volunteers must be in good health and eighteen years of age. Contact information: Jacqueline C. Simon, 124 Bondcroft Drive, Buffalo, N.Y. 14226; www.sabranenque.com.

Antoine de Saint-Exupéry

Saint-Ex, as he is more popularly known, was the author of *Le Petit Prince,* which continues to sell about three hundred thousand copies a year in France and over one hundred thousand copies in America—it's been translated into nearly eighty languages, making Saint-Ex the most translated author in the French language. He earned a pilot's license in 1922 and in 1926 joined the Compagnie Latécoère in Toulouse. Saint-Ex helped establish airmail routes over the French colonies in northwest Africa, the south Atlantic, and South America. In 1939, he became a military reconnaisance pilot, and in 1943, he joined the Free French forces in Algiers. On July 31, 1944, Saint-Ex set off alone on a flight across the Mediterranean but was never seen again, presumably shot down by the Germans. Though he was born in Lyons, Saint-Ex is somewhat of a son of the Southwest, and readers who want to learn more about his interesting and controversial life may want to consult *Saint-Exupery: A Biography* (Stacy Schiff, Knopf, 1994) as well as some of his books for adults, including *Airman's Odyssey, Flight to Arras, Night Flight,* and *Wind, Sand and Stars* (all available in paperback editions by Harvest).

Skiing

The Pyrenees, of course, offer not only good terrain for hiking but also for *faire du ski.* With altitude ranging from 4,250 to 8,500 feet, the mountain range is also one of the most varied in Europe. Readers anxious to include skiing in their itineraries will find more specific information in some guidebooks as well as from the Maison de la France offices in North America and on the Web sites of regional tourist offices in France. There are also ski resorts in and around the Massif Central and the Cévennes. I myself have not swished down any of these slopes, as I am rather a klutz on skis (the first time I ever went downhill skiing, I was afraid to hop off the chair lift, so I didn't, much to my husband's embarrassment). Rather, I excell at *après-ski,* and have spent many enjoyable hours watching *others* traverse the slopes.

Slow Food

Slow Food is very much an international movement, and though it is based in Italy (in the Piedmont region), France is very active in it. Slow Food is a wonderful response to American fast food. The movement was founded in 1989 and is active in forty countries with sixty thousand members and five hundred *convivia* (chapters). Slow Food U.S.A. has more than five thousand members and fifty *convivia.* Slow Food is for food and wine enthusiasts who care about and promote traditional foodstuffs from around the world and who "share the snail's wise slowitude." (The snail, appropriately, is the organization's symbol.) As Carlo Petrini, president of Slow Food, has stated, "Food history is as important as a baroque church. Governments should recognize cultural heritage and protect traditional foods. A cheese is as worthy of preserving as a sixteenth-century building." A highlight from the organization's manifesto is "In the name of productivity, Fast Life has changed our way of being and threatens our environment and our landscapes. So Slow Food is now the only truly progressive answer."

Several programs and divisions make up Slow Food: The Ark of Taste is a project aimed at documenting and promoting foods and beverages in danger of becoming extinct. The biennial Salone del Gusto in Turin is the largest food and wine event in the world, and its biennial Cheese in Bra (Italy) is the largest cheese show in the world. In addition, there are wine conventions and tasting sessions across the United States, and various food festivals around the world. As for publications, in addition to the excellent *Vini d'Italia* (published in conjunction with *Gambero Rosso*), Slow Food publishes *Italian Cheese,* the first guide to traditional Italian cheeses, with 205 artisanal specialties described and documented; *Slowine,* a seventy-page magazine reporting on wine culture around the world; and an outstanding and insightful journal entitled *Slow: The International Herald of Tastes,* which is published in English, German, Italian, and French. Slow Cities are a group of towns and cities in Italy committed to improving the quality of life of their citizens, especially with regard to food issues. You can view the entire list of Slow Food programs online.

Personally, I think Slow Food may save the planet, and it is one of the more worthwhile groups to support. Interested readers may join Slow Food U.S.A. by contacting the group by snail mail (434 Broadway, 7th floor, New York, N.Y. 10013), telephone (212-965-5640); e-mail (info@slowfoodusa.org), or by viewing its Web site (www.slowfood.com). A $60 membership entitles you to a personal membership in Slow Food International, four isues of *Slow,* four newsletters of *The Snail,* two issues of *Slowine,* invitations to all Slow Food events, and discounts on Slow Food publications and merchandise. (I have to admit I'm hooked on the snail pins and the aprons.)

Stendhal Syndrome

Named for the sick physical feeling that afflicted French novelist Stendhal after he visited Santa Croce in Florence, this syndrome is synonymous with being completely overwhelmed by your surroundings (my translation: seeing and doing way too much). Though it happened to Stendhal in Florence, it could just as easily have happened anywhere, and visitors who arrive with too long a list of must-sees are prime candidates. Even a relatively less traveled place—with not nearly as many attractions as Florence—may cause the overambitious to expire. My advice: organize your days, factor in how long it takes to get from place to place, and see what you want. There will be no quiz.

Studying in France

North Americans have quite a few learning opportunities in the Southwest, sponsored by colleges, universities, or other educational organizations. If you are a college-age student seeking a program, my advice is to select one that will allow you to stay a year or even longer. And if you have to change your major to go, do it—you won't regret it! A semester abroad is a great experience, but there is no replacement for staying a year. Alternatively, investigate attending a French college or university, and remember that studying in France isn't limited to studying the language (courses are also offered in the fine arts, photography, painting, business, literature, cuisine, wine, and so on) or to the young (plenty of programs welcome adults, and plenty of adults attend).

The place to begin your research is Learning Destinations, a company founded by Michael Giammarella (the company was formerly known as EMI International). Giammarella is a walking encyclopedia of programs in the Francophone world (including French-speaking Caribbean nations, and Italy and Spain, too), and is passionate about study abroad. He deeply believes that the experience of spending time overseas is essential for even the most basic levels of communication, cooperation, friendship, and appreciation of the world's peoples. Giammarella used to publish a thick directory of programs throughout France, but it became difficult to maintain. No matter: just tell Giammarella what region of France you're interested in, and he'll tell you what you need to know. Just a few of the programs he offers include a number of courses at the University of Pau under its Institut d'Études Françaises pour Etudiants Etrangers; a full program of short- and long-term language classes and a wine course at Bordeaux Language Studies (BLS), with ten years of experience and more than six thousand students from sixty-five countries; teenage (ages thirteen to seventeen) summer programs in Biarritz organized by BLS, including fifteen language lessons per week, a full-day excursion per week, and one surfing or sport activity per week; and language courses and au pair opportunities (for those eighteen to thirty) with families living in Bordeaux and surrounding towns in Aquitaine, sponsored by Aquitaine Service Linguistique. Contact information: P.O. Box 640713, Oakland Gardens, N.Y. 11364; 718-631-0096; fax: -0316; www.learningdestinations.com.

Worldwide Classroom is a great group I discovered when I was working on my *Venice* edition. I was browsing the excellent www.initaly.com Web site, and a link came up for Worldwide, which is among the largest international consortiums of schools, providing information about 10,000 schools in 109 countries. Contact information: P.O. Box 1166, Milwaukee, Wis. 53201; fax: 414-224-3466.

Remember that the French tourist offices here in North America have numerous brochures on language and cultural programs in France.

Surfing

Surfing is not a common entry in my books, but the Atlantic coastline along most of Aquitaine, including la Côte Basque, is actually prime surfing territory. Some of the beaches are actually considered to be of championship quality. Surfing first arrived here during the 1950s, and the first World Surfing Championships to be held in Europe took place in 1968 at Anglet on the Basque coast. Interested readers may also want to track down a good article, "Biarritz High and Low" (Anthony Weller, *Condé Nast Traveler,* June 2000). Weller spoke with Robert Rabagny, proprietor of Le Surfing, a restaurant-bar and surfing museum, who said that "Biarritz is now the California of France." Every July, Rabagny organizes the weeklong Biarritz Surf Festival, which sounds like something I'd like to attend if I was into surfing. Weller also revealed in his piece that "everyone used the word *discrète* about Biarritz—to distinguish it as forcefully as possible from the jet set Riviera."

Le Système D and la Débrouillardise

Le Système D is an expression that is rather like our phrase "beating the system." Author Ross Steele describes it as a "national pastime to find a way around a governmental regulation or administrative decision." The D stands for *débrouillard,* meaning "resourceful," from the verb *débrouiller,* "to untangle." Daily life in France, as those who have lived there know, requires familiarity with the art of *la débrouillardise,* and Steele reminds us that the French compliment *Il/elle sait se débrouiller* (He or she knows how to get things done) "expresses admiration for a person's resourcefulness."

T

Telephones

Remember that France is six hours ahead of Eastern Standard Time, seven ahead of Central Time, eight ahead of Mountain Time, and nine hours ahead of Pacific Standard Time. To call France from the U.S., dial 011 + 33 + the eight-digit local number (011 = the overseas line, 33 = country code for France, and the local number includes the appropriate city code). Note that when calling any city or town in France from the U.S. you must omit the initial 0. All phone numbers in this book include the 0, however, because readers may be making some phone calls while they are in France. Because I think it is obvious, numbers in this book also appear without the overseas access code (011); after you make a few phone calls or send a few faxes, you will have this memorized in no time. Perhaps less obvious for first-time visitors to France is the use of dots between digits instead of the hyphens we employ in the States. (Note also that the French often use a comma to separate digits in a price, such as 50,10, which is fifty paper euros and ten euro coins. Also, commas are used to indicate percentages, such as 60,15 *pour cent*.)

Terrorism

It is easy to refer to the days before September 11 as "normal," especially regarding international travel. But I don't believe we should pine for those days, which really were "abnormal," as events have shown us. American travelers—and Canadians, too—must accept the fact that we are no longer immune to terrorist acts, on our own soil or on that of other nations, and that this situation is permanent. The world changed irrevocably on September 11, and though I fervently hope it will become a better place, in time, for everyone, the world will not suddenly be a safe and welcoming terrain, especially for Americans. We must also accept that we will probably have to pay more to travel and to help pay for the new (and expensive) security systems and programs that have been installed in our airports and other public transportation centers. Additionally, I think we can count on travel taking longer than it once did (at every time during the year, not just during holidays), and we will need to practice the arts of courtesy and patience.

Western Europe is home to about fifteen million Muslim immigrants and while the majority are opposed to terrorism, their large presence does provide a convenient cover for terrorist cells as well as a recruiting ground. New groups that are moving into Europe have apparently been well trained in hopping from country to country in the border-free European Union, and are mostly self-financed through common criminal activities like credit card fraud, making it difficult if not impossible to follow a money trail. In an article I read recently, a French antiterrorism expert said a new threat now comes from the Caucasus; another official was quoted as saying, "Chechnya is just three hours away. This is not just a Russian problem. It's going to be more global."

At one time planning a trip to France did not require making a call to the U.S. State Department, but I urge readers planning a trip to Southwestern France to first read the State Department's profile. When I recently browsed its Web site (http://travel.state.gov/travel_warnings.html), I found a surprising amount of information about where embassies are located, crime, previous episodes of violence in France, medical facilities and insurance, traffic safety and road conditions, and the like. France has been included on the State Department's list of public announcements to Americans traveling abroad. (Public announcements are "a means to disseminate information about terrorist threats and other relatively short-term and/or trans-national conditions posing significant risks to the security of

American travelers. They are made any time there is a perceived threat and usually have Americans as a particular target group. In the past, public announcements have been issued to deal with short-term coups, bomb threats to airlines, violence by terrorists and anniversary dates of specific terrorist events.") Note that a public announcement is not the same as a travel warning, which is issued when the State Department decides, "based on all relevant information, to recommend that Americans avoid travel to a certain country." I mention all this not to create reasons for you to be afraid of traveling to France; rather, I've read that the State Department is extremely liberal in issuing travel warnings and public announcements, which is to say that it interprets *every* incident as serious. The State Department really cannot leave any stone unturned in its efforts to inform the public, so I think you should embrace a policy of "know before you go." Read up on everything, but do not allow yourself to be unnecessarily alarmed by insignificant incidents. I have found the State Department's consular information sheets particularly helpful—they're very detailed and less alarming. You may also call 202-647-6575 for information on travel warnings and public announcements.

Though some of the following tips may seem obvious, I think they are worth reflecting upon as you prepare for your trip. ~Register with the nearest embassy if it will make you feel better upon arrival. ~Pack clothes that don't make you immediately stand out from the locals. Don't bring that really comfortable sweatshirt with the American flag emblazoned on the front, or your favorite college T-shirt. ~Select either very expensive hotels or budget hotels. (The logic here is that moderately priced hotels tend to attract package tourists, a more obvious target.) I personally will not stay in an expensive hotel just to feel more secure. If I choose to stay at a high-end place, it will be because I want to, not because I'm afraid to stay at a more modest place. Thinking, aware travelers are always on their toes, regardless of the threat of a terrorist attack.

In the aftermath of horrific and senseless terrorist attacks—not only in New York and Washington, D.C., but in other cities and areas of the world—it strikes me profoundly that I refuse to be made to feel like a prisoner in my own city and my nation, and that places in the world like Southwestern France become ever more precious and exceptional, more important than ever to experience at least once. I will exercise caution and plan carefully, but I will continue to fly overseas. I believe that, contrary to one's initial reaction, staying home does not make us safe. The first goal of all terrorists is to intimidate and inspire fear in people. Staying home is equal to a victory, a major one, for terrorists. Again to quote Bruce Northam, "The world is a much safer place than it appears in the media. Like a Disney movie, there is always one evil character messing with the plot, but that's *not* reality. While exploring the planet it becomes obvious that, for the most part, we live in a self-policing world. People take care of each other. Good neutralizes the bad. It's embedded in human nature. . . . Get out of line. There is no time for a deadly outbreak of reserve." Francine Prose, in the last-page essay that is one of my favorite features of *The New York Times* travel section, has written what I think are the most sane reflections on terrorism. She reminds us that "travel alters and expands our perspective. By showing us that life really is different in other places, it provides a reality check against which we can measure the misperceptions and even prejudices we may have developed at home," and she concludes that "the events of September 11 have—or should have—turned us not just into patriotic Americans, but into citizens of the world. And we owe it to ourselves, and to our fellow citizens, to go out and see for ourselves this fragile, damaged and brave new world that, like it or not, we've come to inhabit." (Prose's essay appeared in the *Times* on September 8, 2002.) If terrorist attacks are always within the realm of possibility, then so are accidents in the mundane activities of our daily existence, such as walking out the front door and picking up the morning newspaper, standing on a ladder and cleaning the leaves out of the gutter, or carrying clothes a few blocks away to the dry cleaner—each of which carries the risk of falling down and hitting our head on the sidewalk or the stone steps or the fire hydrant—not to mention drunk driving accidents, street crimes, hate crimes, heart attacks, rape, or murder.

I compile books like this one because I have a deep respect for the people, the culture, and the religion of the particular place I'm immersing myself in, and I assume that my readers share this respect. I believe we are all, in a small way, promoting international understanding by reading about another place and traveling there. On days when I read the newspaper and the world seems particularly nasty, I remember that my friend Lindsay M. sent me the following lines from Shakespeare's *The Tempest* at eight o'clock in the morning on September 11, 2002: "How beauteous mankind is! / O brave new world / That has such people in't!"

Theft

Whether of the pickpocket variety or something more serious, theft can happen anywhere, in the finest neighborhood, on the bus, in a park, on a street corner. Southwestern France, unlike Provence and the Côte d'Azur, does not have a reputation for crime of any sort, not even pickpockets (excepting Toulouse, which requires travelers to be alert). It bears repeating not to wear a waist pack, which is simply a neon magnet for thieves.

Rental cars. Rental cars are easily identified by their license plates and other markings that may not be obvious to you and me but that signify pay dirt to thieves. Do not leave anything, anything at all, in a rental car, not even strapped under the seat, not even if you're parking it in a secure garage. My husband and I strictly follow one rule when we rent a car, which is that we never even put items in the trunk unless we're immediately getting into the car and driving away, as anyone watching us will then know there's something of value there. Hatchback-type cars are good to rent because you can back into spots against walls or trees, making it impossible to open the trunk.

Hotel rooms. Do not leave your passport, money, credit cards, important documents, or expensive camera equipment in your room. The hotel safe? If the letters I read are any indication, leaving your belongings in a hotel safe—whether in your room or in the main office—is only slightly more reliable than leaving them out in plain view. Sometimes I hear that valuable jewelry was taken from a hotel safe, which I find baffling as there really is only one safe place for valuable jewelry: your home. No occasion, meeting, or celebration, no matter how important or festive, requires bringing valuable jewelry. I happen to also find it offensive to display such wealth.

Pickpockets. Pickpockets employ a number of tactics to prey on unaware travelers. Even if you travel often, live in a big city, and think you're savvy, professional thieves can usually pick you out immediately. (They'll also identify you as American if you're wearing the trademark sneakers and fanny pack.) Beware the breastfeeding mother who begs you for money (while her other children surround you looking for a way into your pockets), the arguing couple who make a scene (while their accomplices work the crowd of onlookers), the tap on your shoulder at the baggage security checkpoint (when you turn around, someone's made off with your bags after they've passed through the X-ray machine)—anything at all that looks or feels like a set-up. I read about a twenty-four-page booklet entitled *Foiling Pickpockets & Bag Snatchers and Other Travel Related Crimes/Scams,* by Jens Jurgen, on the Web site www.travelaloneandloveit.com, maintained by author Sharon Wingler. Wingler notes that Jurgen details all the tricks known to thieves and con artists the world over, and she refers to his book as "a very inexpensive insurance policy." Though I haven't yet seen a copy, I intend to read it, and other interested readers may contact the Travel Companion Exchange, Inc., P.O. Box 833, Amityville, N.Y. 11701 to request the "Travel Safety/Pickpocket Booklet," currently $4.95 (if paying by check) or $5 (if sending cash).

If you've been robbed: If, despite your best efforts, your valuables are stolen, go to the local police. You'll have to fill out an official police report, but it will help later when you need to prove you were really robbed. Also, reporting a theft to the police alerts them that there is a persistent problem. You need to call your credit card companies (which is why you have written down these numbers and kept them in a separate place), make a trip to the American Express office if you've purchased traveler's checks, and go to the U.S. embassy to replace your passport.

Tipping

Tipping in France is not the mystery some people perceive it to be. At most restaurants and cafés the tip is included in the total, and you'll see this amount (noted as *service compris,* usually about 15 percent) as a line item at the bottom of your receipt. It is common to round up the bill, even if it is only a few euro coins; however, you are not obligated to do so. If you stand at the counter in a café, a tip is not typically included in the bill, so you should leave some change. If you're at a bar and end up in a deep conversation about vintages or fine spirits with the bartender, you might want to leave a little more. (At fancy hotel bars, however, it's expected to leave yet more.) If you're in a three-star restaurant and the *sommelier* has chosen a special wine for you, it's considered appropriate to give him or her ten percent of the price of the bottle. If the *maître d'hôtel* has been especially attentive, give him or her the equivalent of about five dollars. If you receive exceptional service at any establishment, or you want to return and be remembered, you should of course feel free to leave a larger tip.

As readers of my other books know, I have previously included tipping guidelines for a wide range of services and scenarios. I arrived at those suggested tips by reading all the information I had in my files as well as in some books, and then followed them up with personal experience. I have decided, however, that a few of my own tipping guidelines are quite personal (I *always* tip porters the equivalent of $1 per bag, for example, because I have a bad back and I so greatly appreciate the effort; but I recognize that not everyone feels comfortable with this), so I encourage travelers to do some reading on their own as well as seek the advice of *concierges* and front desk receptionists at inns and hotels or anyone you meet who you feel will share an honest opinion—sometimes this can be a waiter or waitress, or a shop clerk. Restaurants, bistros, and cafés aside, visitors should tip for the same services in France as they do in North America, such as a taxi ride, haircut, spa treatment, WC attendants, cloakroom attendants, concierge service, valet parking, theater usher, housekeeping and/or cooking services at a rented villa, and maid service at a hotel (I happen to feel this last is often the most overlooked service, and I am as generous as I can be when leaving a tip, usually about five dollars a day—but maids appreciate *any* additional gesture). I will simply add a few thoughts on tipping in this edition: ~Be prepared to tip by putting some small change in your pocket *in advance,* before you arrive at the hotel, for example, or before you go to the theater. ~If you do use the services of a concierge, it is considered appropriate to give a small amount per day, about five to ten dollars, for overall helpfulness and small tasks requested. However, for one-time-only tasks like obtaining reservations or tickets, it's expected to show your gratitude in a larger way, about $50 or $100—and even more, depending on the task. If you only use a concierge's services once, it's customary to tip on the spot. To thank a concierge for several services during the course of a longer stay, tip on your last day. Should you want to enclose your tip in an envelope marked with the concierge's name, make sure you hand deliver it or it may get shared among *all* the hotel's concierges; a nice gift—such as fine candy—is also an appropriate thank-you. ~I am a firm believer in maintaining a proper balance with regard to tipping. Excellent service should be awarded sufficiently, poor service should not, but excessive tipping is gross, and should be avoided. Wild tipping upsets the balance and destroys the concept of service. I know people who swear by the power of a twenty-dollar (or hundred-dollar) bill, but I think this should only be reserved for dire situations.

Toilets and Toilet Paper

In France, I never set out each day without stuffing some toilet paper in my pockets or bag. Public toilets—even those in some of the nicest places—can be abominable and sometimes do not have toilet paper (*papier hygiénique*). I have always found good, soft, American-style toilet paper in the bathrooms at American Express offices, which in the Southwest are located in Bordeaux and Toulouse. It is fairly common in France to use the toilet facilities at bars and cafés without also ordering something to eat or drink; but I've always felt a little guilty doing this, especially since the toilets are usually located at the back of the establishment and often down the stairs, so one can't slip in unnoticed. Therefore I typically plan on sitting down for a few minutes when I have to make a stop.

You may notice the prevalence of pay toilets throughout the South (and all over France). These are indicated by a sign at the top, *toilettes,* and are silver metal cabins you step into. As you might guess from the entry on car rentals, I am not the best of friends with these pay toilets, though I am proud to say I have used them successfully. I'm not alone, however, in my cautious approach to public toilettes: Polly Platt, in her great book *Savoir Flaire!,* wrote that she once decided to be brave and check one out. "The side where you insert your two francs didn't open. I kept pushing what looked like a door, and then began banging it, until a member of the CRS (the riot police) in battle gear appeared from nowhere. He thoughtfully advised me that the door was around on the end. Still dubious, I asked about the sign saying that children under 10 were not permitted to use. He explained that sometimes, when you're inside, the door doesn't open. Hmm. Would the CRS agent hear me banging from the inside? I abandoned the project." Platt goes on to note that in one of his syndicated columns, Dave Barry reported that a seven-year-old girl died in one of France's public toilettes. "Something to do with the automatic flushing and her lack of weight." Proceed at your own risk, dear readers.

Though less common, in the western half of Southwestern France so-named Turkish toilets are still found in cities of the Midi-Pyrénées. Often there will be a bucket in the stall for you to use for the disposal of used toilet paper (although these squat toilets will rarely have paper). Sometimes a Turkish toilet will flush, but this doesn't always mean you can flush toilet paper—if you see a bucket, you can assume that it's reserved for paper. Note that when some toilets flush they produce quite a wave, with the water coming up over the basin (and onto your feet). Guard against this possibility by not flushing until you're ready to step away, then flush as you simultaneously open the door of the stall.

Tour Operators

A list of full-service tour companies offering trips to France would fill a separate book, and it is not my intent to promote only one company or one type of trip. As the Southwest is not as heavily traveled as neighboring Provence or Paris, employing a tour operator may be a good idea for some readers, as its treasures and pleasures are less well known. I will be upfront and state that I am suspicious of those all-inclusive package tours. It's not only about price—for me, it's more about the accommodations and meals: those wonderful, boutique places I like to stay at are *never* part of any packages that I hear about, and I very much doubt that meals are any better than cafeteria food, making the whole package a poor value indeed. And regarding price, it's also true that packages are *not* always cheaper than if you made the arrangements yourself. I'm bothered by the fact that too many tour operators today (including biking and hiking tour operators) focus on luxury meals and accommodations. A great number of well-read and curious people are seeking personalized service and knowledgeable guides and do not need or desire five-star elegance every step of the way. I often wonder if the luxury-oriented companies aren't missing the boat in reaching even more clients; but that is, after all, how they maintain their business—there is much more wiggle room in negotiating rates with luxury hotels and inns, for example, and any sum above the negotiated rate is profit for the tour operator. All of this said, the combination of experience, insider's knowledge, and savvy guides that better tour operators offer is most definitely not found by searching the Web, for example; organizing trips like these requires a substantial amount of research and attention to detail, which some travelers do not always have the time or inclination to do (and for which they are willing to pay a great deal). Organized tours these days now offer travelers more free time than in years past, as well as more choice in meals and excursions.

Transhumance

Transhumance refers to the age-old seasonal migration of livestock—and the people who tend them—between low-lying lands and adjacent mountains. Transhumance was and still is "one of the most distinctive characteristics of the Mediterranean world," according to Fernand Braudel in his masterpiece, *The Mediterranean*. Braudel notes that in the Mediterranean region in the sixteenth century, "transhumance was confined above all to the Iberian peninsula, the south of France, and Italy. In the other peninsulas, the Balkans, Anatolia, North Africa, it was submerged by the predominance of nomadism or semi-nomadism." Nomadism, to clarify, involved moving an entire community—people, animals, and even dwellings—usually for long distances, and it has never been a way of dealing with enormous flocks of sheep. Braudel informs us that geographers distinguish between at least two different kinds of transhumance. Normal transhumance involved sheep farmers and shepherds who live in the lowlands. They leave the lowlands in the summer, which is an unfavorable season for livestock on the plains. Inverse transhumance is of the kind found in Navarra, in Spain, in the sixteenth century. Flocks and shepherds would come down from the highlands, the *euskari*. The lowlands served only for marketing purposes, when there was a market being held. This type of transhumance was "a frantic rush down from the mountains in winter . . . all doors were padlocked against these unwelcome visitors, and every year saw a renewal of the eternal war between shepherd and peasant." In 1938, a study was completed of all known cases of transhumance in the Mediterranean (unfortunately, I do not know if a more recent study has been attempted). All the known transhumance routes at that time were superimposed on a map of the Mediterranean region, and they measured about fifteen meters wide. The routes also bore different names in different regions, such as *cañadas* in Castile, *camis ramaders tratturi* in Italy, and *trazzere* in Sicily. In summation, Braudel writes that "transhumance implies all sorts of conditions, physical, human, and historical. In the Mediterranean, in its simplest form, it is a vertical movement from the winter pastures of the plain to the summer pastures in the hills."

Author René Weis notes that "the arch of transhumance, as the seasonal moving of livestock to regions of a different climate is known, stretched from Montaillou into Catalonia. Indeed, at the approach of winter the shepherds of the Pyrenees took their flocks all the way to the coast near Valencia. They did so across the Puymorens or Capcir mountains such as the Riucaut, and then headed south through the Cerdagne and across the Cadí range. Around Easter they would do the same trek in reverse and head back towards the summer pastures in the mountains."

Troubadours

As I noted in the introduction, it sometimes happens that I am unable to include particularly worthwhile articles in my books. At the eleventh hour of manuscript transmittal, Mark, the amazingly thorough production editor who has worked on all of my volumes, discovered that the piece I had selected to include on French troubadours featured poems originally written during the Middle Ages but more recently translated into English. Mark wisely noted that I did not have permission from each of the translators—who included Ezra Pound and Ford Madox Ford— and that now there was not enough time to secure those permissions. With regret, I had to delete the article, but readers interested in learning more about the troubadours should make a very big effort to search the archives at your local library for this excellent piece ("The Troubadours," by Frederic V. Grunfeld, *Horizon,* Summer 1970).

As Grunfeld noted, the troubadours "became the first poets in history to create a literature in a modern European language." He also reminds us that if the word *troubadour* has a faintly off-putting sound to our modern ears, this is because it was so heavily abused in previous centuries. "Somehow we find it hard to rid ourselves of the tedious image of the fat tenor *trovatore* in tights and tassels, inditing love songs to a lute while a chaste lady listens at a tower window. Nothing could be further from the true troubadours, who were more like the Rolling Stones than grand opera in their methods of operation and their way of looking at the world. Singing of love, sex, and politics, they were the underground press of their day—and the overground press, too, since there was virtually no other way of disseminating news."

A book highlighting Southwestern France without a major piece on the troubadours is an unfortunate omission. Again to quote Grunfeld, "It was the troubadours of Mediterranean France—a land of lentisk and asphodel, of olive, arbutus, myrtle, and euphorbia, and of nightingales singing in the medlars in June—who first introduced an air of elegance, like an attar of roses, into the rather brutish mating habits of the Middle Ages. They made love a condition of civilization, and vice versa." I hope readers will forgive this glaring omission, and allow me to explain further that the vast majority of writings on the troubadours are entirely too academic for all but the most dedicated scholars. I was fortunate to have received some expert advice and recommendations from Dr. N. M. Schulman, a medieval historian with a special interest in medieval France, and the author of *Where Troubadours Were Bishops: The Occitania of Folc of Marseille, 1150–1231* (Routledge, 2002), itself a major work, "half footnotes, half text," as she describes it. Schulman recommends the following titles for anyone interested in exploring the troubadours in further detail: *The World of the Troubadours: Medieval Occitan Society, 1100–1300* (Linda Patterson, Cambridge University Press, 1995; Schulman describes this volume as "probably the best English-language introduction to the region, scholarly but accessible"); *A Handbook of the Troubadours* (F.R.P. Akehurst and Judith Davis, University of California Press, 1999; this work—more than 500 pages in length—has been referred to as *the* book to read, in addition to an anthology of troubadour works, if you only have time or shelf space for one book on the subject); and *The Poems of the Troubadour Bertran de Born* (University of California Press, 1986, which is Schulman's favorite English-language edition of one troubadour's work). Additionally, Frederic Grunfeld refers in his article to an "indispensable collection" entitled *A Troubadour Anthology* by Anthony Bonner. After some sleuthing, I found a work by Bonner called *Songs of the Troubadours* (Schocken, 1972). This very well could be the same book— Grunfeld refers to the book as "forthcoming," and book titles often change before publication.

V

Vieilles Pierres
Literally, "old stones," a lovely French expression for the beauty of traditional things. The Southwest, from the Atlantic to the Mediterranean, is not just filled but

stuffed with *vieilles pierres*. It is an expression I take to heart, searching even in America for old stones and objects—even though "old" in the States takes on a different meaning than in France. Plastics, acrylics, metals, and other materials of our modern age have their place, and I sometimes marvel at their flexibility; but they cannot compare with *vieilles pierres*.

Vinexpo

Vinexpo is the world's premier wine and spirits exhibition, and it's been held in Bordeaux, every other year, since 1981. Though the convention is primarily open only to trade professionals, regular wine enthusiasts may sometimes be admitted as a guest of someone in the trade, so if you're really keen to attend and are a regular customer at a large wine or liquor store, ask the owner or manager if he or she would consider bringing you along. In October 2002, the very first Vinexpo Americas exhibition was held in New York, and I was fortunate to be invited. All I can say is, wow . . . what a feast! It's very overwhelming, but very exciting. I decided to concentrate only on the wines and spirits of the southwest, which were well represented not only by Bordeaux but Armagnac, Lillet, and a fairly large section devoted to the wines of Languedoc-Roussillon. Though Vinexpo Americas was represented by six hundred exhibitors from twenty-eight countries, it was still primarily dominated by the French, claiming 40 percent of the participants, followed by Spain, the United States, and Italy. The Vinexpo staff conducted some research studies, and revealed some interesting statistics: wine consumption in the United States has increased from 2 to 5 percent every year since 1995; in 2000, there were 19.2 million regular wine drinkers in the United States, 85 percent of whom drank wine at least twice a week; but, only 10 percent of that total drank 86 percent of all the wine consumed in the country (I maintain, as you'll read more about in the *Flavors and Tables of the Southwest* section, that this is because our vintners insist upon making pricey, boutique wines—forgetting completely about inexpensive, everyday wine—and therefore they are not raising new generations of wine drinkers). Regarding Bordeaux wine statistics, the Bordeaux Wine Bureau in New York reports that 85 percent of Bordeaux wines are red and 15 percent are white; the word *château* signifies a wine-producing estate with its own buildings. It is synonymous with the French words *domaine* and *clos,* but has no connection with any architectural use of the word; there are just 50 calories in a 2.4 ounce glass of Bordeaux—the same as in an apple; and the English word *claret* refers to dry red Bordeaux wine. If you are considering timing a trip to Bordeaux with Vinexpo, keep in mind that hotel rooms are booked nearly two years in advance, and restaurant tables about six months prior. For more information about Vinexpo, log on to www.vinexpo.com for details, and for Bordeaux wines, contact the Bordeaux Wine Burea, c/o Sopexa, 80 Maiden Lane, Suite 310, New York, N.Y. 10038; www.bordeaux.com

(a very good Web site that includes some articles about Bordeaux markets, wine schools, and vineyard visits).

W

Weather

Fall may be the most beautiful time of year in Southwestern France (many places in the world are wonderful at that time of year), but each season offers its own delights. Picking the "perfect" time of year is subjective; when it's rainy and cold—and it does get quite chilly in the winter months—you don't have the pleasure of picnicking and hiking outdoors or swimming at the beach, but prices drop and you'll have little trouble securing reservations at hotels and restaurants. Go when you have the opportunity, and that will be your experience, your France. It's true that peak season means higher prices and more people, but if you've determined you want to be in Carcassonne in July, then the cost and the crowds don't matter.

La Vie en Périgord

By Joyce Goldstein

༄

One of the best-known cooking school programs in France is La Combe en Périgord, the subject of this piece. Cooking schools continue to soar in popularity with travelers, and as classes are appropriately small, they tend to fill up fast. If you think you are remotely interested, act quickly! What is especially appealing to me about La Combe is that founders Wendely Harvey and Robert Cave-Rogers offer three distinctive programs: Guest Chefs' Program (which features leading American cookbook writers and cooking professionals), La Vie en Périgord (week-long programs created around seasonal specialties and events), and the Un-Programmed Program (for visitors who prefer to relax and do exactly what they want in this spectacularly beautiful corner of the Southwest). I credit the founders for the last one most of all because not *everyone* wants to participate in a cooking program, but La Combe is so achingly lovely that one shouldn't be discouraged from staying in this eighteenth-century country house. For more information, visit La Combe's Web site, www.lacombe-perigord.com, or browse the archives for the March 2003 issue of *Bon Appétit*, which featured an eight-page profile (with to-die-for photographs) of La Combe.

JOYCE GOLDSTEIN formerly owned the Mediterranean-inspired restaurant Square One in San Francisco and is the author of a great many cookbooks, including *The Mediterranean Kitchen* (William Morrow, 1989), *Mediterranean: The Beautiful Cookbook* (Collins, produced by Welden Owen, 1994), *Enoteca: Simple, Delicious Recipes in the Italian Wine Bar Tradition* (Chronicle Books, 2001), *Saffron Shores: Jewish Cooking of the Southern Mediterranean* (Chronicle Books, 2002), and *Sephardic Flavors: Jewish Cooking of the Mediterranean* (Chronicle Books, 2000).

Garlic confit, poached cod, scallops with roe, spiced carrots, and green beans with organic tomatoes sat on the table, and seven students in the spacious kitchen were deeply immersed in their studies: slicing fennel for a salad, mixing a mustardy vinaigrette, and sweetening a goat cheese mixture for a walnut cake. It was Saturday night, time to enjoy the spoils of a French vacation, and I was back in school. But as one student basted lavender honey on the ducks roasting in the ovens and I swatted away wasps on the patio beside a farmhouse in the Périgord Noir in Southwestern France, I knew I wouldn't want to spend Saturday night anywhere else.

The Périgord region, which is divided by the Dordogne River, is the home of ducks, foie gras, and walnuts and is located very near Bordeaux, so I knew that I was in good food and wine territory. Wendely Harvey and her husband, Robert Cave-Rogers, owners of La Combe en Périgord cooking school, custom-plan a week jam-packed with trips all over the region, exploring Dordogne history and culture, for each group that visits La Combe. We visited the caves near Lascaux, toured castles such as Château de Losse in Thonac, and strolled through beautiful medieval hill towns like Beaumont. Between antique shopping and wine tasting in Les Eyzies de Tayac, we sampled Périgourdine fare at small, nearby restaurants such as Aux Vieux Moulins in Les Eyzies, L'Auberge de Castel Merle in Sergeac, La Maynardie in Salignac, L'Auberge de l'Abbaye in Cadouin, and Chez Alain in Issigeac.

Our mornings were filled with culinary adventures. Months ago, when I had planned the recipes at home in San Francisco, I decided to make shopping for seasonal produce at the well-regarded Sarlat and St. Cyprien markets an essential part of the program. Although California is seasonally a bit ahead of the Dordogne, I hoped that there would be berries, artichokes, and asparagus in profusion, and I selected recipes that showed off those ingredients. Still, I wanted to leave things loose, so that if my students saw something at the market they wanted to try, we'd get it. After all, isn't that what cooking is about?

Our first dinner at La Combe was an informal one, with lots of small plates to share with many different tastes, but nothing tricky to prepare. We were close to the Spanish border, so a tapas-style menu with lots of wine was appropriate to break the ice.

White asparagus from the Dordogne is renowned all over France. And there we were, in a local supermarket surrounded by tables overflowing with gorgeous, fat white asparagus, as well as a few piles of green stalks. After the students in our group discussed the recipes and created a menu, we served the asparagus two ways: with a mint and almond vinaigrette and with a Spanish romesco mayonnaise. The white bean stew was big enough for two dinners, so we took the remaining mussels out of their shells and folded them into the bean mixture to use the next night. After cooking together and sharing plates, we definitely felt like a team, lounging around the patio and chatting about our lives back in the States, as Robert plied us with glasses of the local Bergerac wines.

My students were an interesting mix from San Francisco, Los Angeles, New York, and Modesto, California—some "foodies" who spent most of their waking hours cooking, or at least thinking about cooking, and others who cooked at home and were anxious for new inspiration. On a casual Friday with no class scheduled, we talked about the school and the region of Périgord.

La Combe, which means "little valley," opened in August 1999. After searching endlessly for the right location, Wendely and Robert found their property on a stretch of country road, in front of hills that contain some of the region's celebrated prehistoric caves. Built around a courtyard was a main house, a stone barn, and a *pigeonnier*.

I had befriended Wendely in San Francisco, where we worked together on many cookbooks, so I received monthly reports on La Combe's two-year renovation and the mysterious ways of French plumbers and electricians. Still, I was bowled over when I first stepped inside the house and saw the homey yet elegant kitchen. The four-hundred-square-foot room includes two stoves, three ovens, and a large island with plenty of work space. An antique walnut armoire and built-in cupboards with open-grill doors house dishes and equipment. I couldn't wait to start cooking.

But there was still a lot of Périgord to explore. At Le Moulin de la Tour in Ste.-Nathalène, we saw walnuts pressed into oil and tasted all of the nut-based products. Later that afternoon we visited a duck farm at St.-Crépin et Carlucet and witnessed the *gavage,* or force-feeding, of the birds in a huge barn hung with flexible hoses that funneled grain into the fowls. Despite the controversy surrounding the practice, we all seemed to accept it in the context of French culture and bought plenty of foie gras for dinner. Pan-seared, the foie gras was garnished with apple slices sautéed in Armagnac. Then, demonstrating with panache how to turn leftovers into a treat, we had a fabulous little gratin of white beans with mussels and artichokes, topped with toasted bread crumbs and grated cheese, as our first course. Wendely cooked a lovely osso buco, garnished with *gremolata* and served with pasta. Bread, cheese, a big salad, and a walnut cake dressed with raspberry *coulis* completed our meal.

Saturday's dinner was more formal, and we had a game plan. Since this was duck country, our main course would focus on roast duck with lavender honey and thyme, with a complement of produce gathered at the Sarlat market. Among the stalls that meandered through the gorgeous medieval town's streets, we found *cabillaud,* or cod; brilliant orange carrots; newly picked endive; fresh mushrooms; and feathery shoots of fennel. Although we had planned to cook fish with a confit of garlic, herbs, and cream, we discovered an unexpected treat at the market: giant, tender scallops with roe. Most of the group had never eaten them with the roe before, so despite the cost, we succumbed to temptation and added them to the *cabillaud.* It was a truly elegant first course. We smoked up the kitchen a bit, getting the perfectly crunchy skin on the ducks.

The dessert—a walnut cake layered with slightly sweetened goat cheese and fig jam—was so good that we saved the leftover cheese mixture and jam for breakfast.

You'd think by now that we couldn't eat another bite. But we were a hardy bunch and toured St. Cyprien market on Sunday with eagle eyes, selecting the best of the show for our last dinner. The students were learning about their personal palates and their areas of interest in the kitchen: my goal was to make them feel so confident and at ease that they could go into the kitchen and attack food preparation with enthusiasm and good technique.

Our centerpiece was a garlic-and-rosemary-spiked leg of lamb rubbed with a fantastic walnut mustard we found at the Sarlat market the day before. We were so enthusiastic about the mustard that Wendely tracked down Monsieur Quenel, the mustard man, in Siorac, so we could bring some home with us.

To accompany the lamb, we chose a medley of some beautiful artichokes, violet-hued spring onions, and little new potatoes— oven-roasted with herbs from the *potager,* or vegetable garden, and rubbed liberally with the garlic oil that we had from Saturday's confit. After an afternoon goat-cheese tasting, we decided to go easy on dessert: a simple almond sponge cake with berries and honey ice cream. Today, as I field emails from students who have whipped up romesco sauce or baked walnut cakes in their kitchens back home, I believe that the class was a success. I look back on our experience at La Combe as something I anticipate doing again.

The Kiosk—
Points of View

"It never occurred to me that [Hitler] might destroy France, because it would have been as hard for me to prefigure a world without France as survival with one lobe of my brain gone. France represented for me the historical continuity of intelligence and reasonable living. When this continuity is broken, nothing anywhere can have meaning until it is reestablished."

—A. J. Liebling, *The Road Back to Paris,* 1944

Voting with Your Fork

BY NANCY HARMON JENKINS

～

Freda White, in her wonderful book *Ways of Aquitaine,* noted in the final chapter, *"Envoi"*—such a lovely word, *envoi,* meaning "sending," "dispatch," "shipping," "parcel," "package," and "envoy"—that "if I were asked to put the elements of French civilization into a list, I should begin (1) conversation, (2) food, (3) love. For men, that is. For women, love comes at the top; and for all, religion is the joker and may turn up anywhere." White also opined, as others have, that "France puts eating in its proper place, and that is at the top of civilized occupations." She then shared an episode from her own travels in Poitiers: "I had tried a hotel recommended by a guidebook and found the rooms poor and the food uneatable. They served meat hard from the refrigerator; and moreover played a base though common trick by offering as *table d'hôte* a meal so nasty that their guests were forced to order much dearer items off the à la carte menu. I found a charming bed-and-breakfast hotel, but wanted impartial advice on restaurants. As I was changing money at the Crédit Lyonnais bank, I asked the woman cashier if she could recommend me a restaurant where I could eat modestly and decently. She blushed and said that she lived at home and did not know restaurants, but she would ask a colleague. He collected another, and in three minutes the entire exchange department of the Crédit Lyonnais was gathered in a passionate discussion. Then the senior, a most impressive person, came forward and said: 'Mademoiselle, we think you should try the Plat d'Étain. It is small and quiet and clean, and one eats well there.' They were as clever as bankers ought to be; for the Plat d'Étain suited my tastes exactly. I used it on my many visits to Poitiers. But dearly as I like them, I simply cannot imagine myself asking the staff of the Bank of Scotland in Edinburgh to tell me where to go for good food."

References to how the French feel about cuisine are not in short supply, and even if you've never been to France, you have undoubtedly heard anecdotes about the French and food. Yet I cannot refrain from sharing a few more from Mort Rosenblum, author of *A Goose in Toulouse and Other Culinary Adventures in France:* "Back when heads were piling up in baskets in a Paris square, and revolution in France shook the world as nothing had before, a pudgy, balding savant reminded citizens to keep their priorities straight. Great human events are fine, Anthelme Brillat-Savarin observed, but let's not forget lunch. . . . French society revolves around greengrocers who know each of their tomatoes personally and cheese sellers who can spend half an hour discussing the pros and cons of a particular slab of brie. On New Year's Eve, whatever the rest of the world does to celebrate, the French sit at large tables and eat themselves senseless. While others wondered where to be on December 31, 1999, Frenchmen were deciding which bottles of wine they would open. . . . Over centuries, the dinner table has remained an anchor for families and friendships, the heart of what is finest about France. Each course requires separate effort, part of a whole. Children learn their values and their manners at mealtime. Nothing important gets signed, sealed, or delivered without the clinking of glasses and the rattling of cutlery. And nothing is so sacred as Sunday lunch. In French, you only have to say 'dimanche midi.' The eating part goes without saying."

Call it a quality, a characteristic, or a quirk: I have gone to such lengths to emphasize this fixation with food to explain why I have included two pieces devoted to the subject in this section. This first piece, which was written in 1992, remains near and dear to my heart, never more so than now. In the fall of 2002 Island Press published a monumental work entitled *Fatal Harvest: The Tragedy of Industrial Agriculture*. Featuring essays by a number of environmentally concerned authors, the book is a wake-up call to Americans. In a review of the book for *Saveur,* writer Thomas McNamee notes that most of us simply do not realize the gravity of the situation, and that the biggest lie we've been fed is that industrial agriculture is the only means by which to feed the world, keep prices reasonable, and offer us the range of choices we demand. "Good land stewardship can feed the world far more generously than the present system of artificial fertilizers and disease-inducing pesticides. Organic crops grown on small family farms can be just as affordable as the mass-market produce equivalent, if we eradicate the favoritism that industry has bought from our legislatures. As for range of food choices, industrial agriculture is at this moment causing the extinction of thousands of varieties of crops, animals, and seafood." The good news is that there is good news—many individuals and organizations (such as American Farmland Trust, Earth Island Institute, Native Seeds, Organic Farming Research Foundation, and the Sierra Club) are tirelessly and creatively working toward realistic solutions. It's inescapable, however, that the vast changes that must take place in agricultural production and distribution require the muscle of Congress.

Edward Behr, editor of the wonderful quarterly newsletter *The Art of Eating,* has also written well and convincingly about the issue of food distribution. In issue number 63, 2003, Behr introduces readers to Eliot Coleman, apparently a well-known American market gardener (I admit that

Coleman's name was not familiar to me, but I'm happy I know of him now). According to Behr, Coleman absolutely believes that well-raised organic food is superior to conventional, but he also believes that the word *organic* is now "dead as a meaningful synonym for the highest quality food." Part of what Coleman feels is missing is a concern for freshness and ripeness. Coleman's vision of the ideal grower is someone who is motivated both by producing high quality and doing good *as well as* by the desire for profit. As Behr points out, however, these growers have been criticized "for being expensive boutique growers, for sounding morally superior, and for being unrealistic about how much money, time, and energy most people can afford to devote to shopping for food. (Of course, what it really costs to produce reasonably good food isn't necessarily what we are used to paying, and it involves a host of messy issues such as agricultural subsidies, erosion of top-soil, farm wages, the environmental cost of using so much petroleum-based fertilizer, and the effects of huge concentrations of manure created in large-scale farming.) Most American farmers now compete to produce as cheaply as possible in order simply to stay in business. How good can food be if the main goal is to reduce the cost of production?" Behr refers readers to an article that appeared in *Mother Earth News* a few years ago, in which Coleman proposed a new term, based on a Greek word, to promote better food: *authentes,* meaning "one who does things for him or herself," or authentic. For a food to be labeled "authentic," it would have to be sold directly by the person or family who grew it—there would be no middleman.

Allowing for those individuals or families who don't have the time or the inclination to do their own selling, I am personally very much in favor of this idea, and I'm proud to admit that when I lived in the San Francisco Bay Area for most of the 1980s, I had the same idea that Coleman continued to elaborate upon in that same issue of *Mother Earth News:* "Fresh fruits and vegetables, milk, eggs, and meat [would be] produced within a 50-mile radius of their place of final sale." I arrived at this thought because I was frustrated by the fact that whenever I went to a California supermarket, the very same mealy, picked-too-early tomatoes one finds everywhere else in the States were for sale in the produce aisle. *How is this possible?* I thought, in the state where nearly everything is grown, not only for North America but for the world? The little secret that food writers who enthuse about California's cuisine never tell you is that supermarkets in the Golden State are as bad as they are everywhere else, and frankly, it's inexcusable. If growers in California can't sell their produce directly to supermarkets, something's rotten, and I smell a huge, fat, and happy rat. (I am not referring here to the outstanding independent markets in the Bay Area, such as Monterey Market, Berkeley Bowl, and Rainbow Grocery, where shoppers are given specifics about how the tomatoes were grown as well as the name of the farmer who grew them!—Now *that's* establishing a connection between the grower and the buyer.) Eliot Coleman has more ideas worth exploring: "The seed and storage crops (grains, beans, nuts, potatoes, etc.) [would be] produced within a 300-mile radius," and only "traditional processed foods"— cheese, bread, wine—could claim to be "made with authentic ingredients." Coleman's vision would not mean that growers would cease to be organic, but instead of focusing on ways to combat pests and diseases, they would concentrate more on creating healthy plants and animals, which would be raised on pasture as much as possible. A definition of "authentic" as "local, seller-grown, and fresh" seems to me the only way to go forward.

But here's the thing of it, dear readers: the best way to effect change is to borrow two very valuable lessons from our French friends (and others around the Mediterranean). *Eat food in its season,* and *demand that our food be real,* that is, not pumped with hormones or filled with preservatives. Products that are certified organic are wonderful, though I do not believe they are always essential to eating well and healthy—there are plenty of artisanal food producers in North America who create their products with quality ingredients, without pesticides, and who are careful stewards of the land; though their products may not be designated organic, they deserve to be supported. G. Y. Dryansky, writing for *Condé Nast Traveler* some years ago, observed that "regarding food, the French have known for a long time what we Americans are coming to understand: that not just wine and water but all things have the taste—the character—of where they come from." If you spend any time visiting an outdoor *marché* in France, you will notice that vendors will ask you when you plan on eating the *fraises des bois* (wild strawberries), melon, peaches, or tomatoes you're about to buy. This is because the vendor will separate the produce according to when you should eat it: within a few hours, tonight after dinner, or tomorrow afternoon, for example. This is, of course, the way produce should be purchased. You will not find, therefore, strawberries picked before they are ripe, and no one would dream of selling—or buying—strawberries unless they were going to be eaten a day or two later, at the most. After you've tasted memorable produce you bought at a *marché,* accept nothing less when you return home! Fresh fruits and vegetables are meant to be eaten as soon after harvesting as possible. We have lost sight of the seasons because refrigerated trucks, trains, and planes can supply supermarkets with a vast array of foods all year; but just because supermarkets have a food in stock doesn't mean that that food is in season. (Remember that the raison d'être of supermarkets is to buy quantity at a reasonable price—quality and a short shelf life are not positive attributes to produce buyers.) You don't need to be a food scientist to know that refrigeration does not enhance flavor, and raspberries flown in from Chile are not fresh, just expensive and flavorless. It is not a virtue that lettuce can last a week in a refrigerator—if it does, that's lettuce I don't want to eat. I have great respect and admiration for working families, and though adapting the French tradition of buying less food more times a week requires a bit more thought and organization, I believe it is worth the effort. (I am a working mother, and I also compile the books in this series, so I do know what the word *busy* means.) The owners and managers of supermarkets will change the way they buy and distribute food only if customers are vocal about their demands and refuse to purchase the mediocre produce they offer. Rethinking the value we place on the food we eat is an exercise that can only reap benefits to *everyone* involved in the food chain.

NANCY HARMON JENKINS, a director of Oldways Preservation and Exchange Trust in Boston, is the author of *Flavors of Tuscany* (1998) and *Flavors of Puglia* (1997), both published by Broadway Books, and *The Mediterraean Diet Cookbook* (Bantam, 1994). Jenkins is also a contributing editor of *Food & Wine* and has written frequently for *The New York Times*.

Food matters—and not just because we all have to eat two or three meals a day. It matters because it is a profound and important way of connecting ourselves with the earth, with our history, with our communities, and with each other, of guaranteeing our health as individuals and as social animals, as well as the health of the world we live in.

In the second half of this century we have learned entirely new ways to grow and harvest and package and distribute and cook our food. These ways, on the whole, are not good for us or for the world we live in. They did not come on us all of a sudden, but evolved slowly from the conviction that the earth is ours to exploit without thought or fear of the consequences. We are wasting our heritage, denying our cultural connections to the earth and each other, and in the process missing out on one of the warmest and most enjoyable of human activities: the act of eating, the pleasure of the table.

If you eat, says Frances Moore Lappé, who spends a lot of time thinking about these things, you're involved in agriculture. Most of us don't know that; or if we know it as some vague generality, we don't act on it. As the poet and farmer Wendell Berry has pointed out, eating is the last act in "the annual drama of the food economy that begins with planting and birth." Haven't we all known at least one child who thought peas arrived from Mother Nature fresh-frozen in cardboard boxes? But how many grown-ups stop to think of pea pods rising from the seed, flowering and swelling on the vine, when we pick up a box of frozen peas to take home and throw in the microwave? How many of us can connect the way those peas taste with the soil in which they were grown, the pesticides and fertilizers that pushed them along, the processor's salt and sugar and imitation flavor additives that give them any taste at all?

The United States must feed the world, we are told, and we can't do it without chemical additives to our agriculture: fertilizers, pesticides and herbicides, growth regulators, and genetically engineered plants and animals that make possible bumper harvests of corn and miracle wheat and beef to feed the millions. The abundance of U.S. supermarkets, we are told, is the direct result of this, and the long-term result is the ability of American farms and farmers to provide cheap food for starving Africans, Asians, and even war-ravaged and politically debilitated Europeans. We have to keep dumping chemical fertilizers on the land because there is so little nourishment left in our soil that otherwise nothing will grow. We have to keep using poisons on our fields because we have so restricted genetic varieties in our food plants through monoculture (raising the same crop year after year on the same field) and other avaricious practices that otherwise nothing will flourish. Even if we had the will to do so, we are told, we cannot afford to cultivate organically, to practice, in the current politically correct phrase, "sustainable agriculture."

In truth, if we care about our future, we cannot afford to do anything else. The chemical runoff from the 845 million pounds of pesticides used annually on our fields has poisoned our well waters and aquifers and endangered the health of our farming communities. An enormous quantity of irreplaceable topsoil has been lost, washed or blown away each year because of our foolish methods of cultivation, monocropping, indiscriminately irrigating the wasted land, using chemical instead of organic fertilizers that build up the tilth of the soil. The strength of a species is in its diversity, and the loss of diversity in our food crops means that we rely on a decreasing pool of genes to withstand threats from insects or blights. When you have only two or three varieties of corn or wheat or cabbages or potatoes, a single rust or blight, a single insect infestation, can wipe out the crop, with disastrous consequences.

Almost every thoughtful person who cares about food knows that the American diet is a mess. Our chronic disease rates are high because as a people we eat far too much fat, too much salt and sugar, too much meat, and too little of the fresh fruits and vegetables, rice, pasta, beans, and whole grains that even our conservative, industry-minded government now says are good for us. We eat too much processed food, food over which we have no control. Most of the time we don't even know what we're eating because our labeling laws are limited in scope and full of loopholes that allow, for instance, high-fat products from hot dogs to mayonnaise to be marketed as "light" and "low-fat" simply because they have less fat than their even higher-fat counterparts.

Average consumption of red meat per person has declined substantially in recent years, but Americans in 1990 still consumed more meat, at 112 kilos per capita (that's nearly 250 pounds, or well over *half a pound per person per day*) than any other nation—way above the per capita figures for those traditional meat-eaters the Germans (89 kilos) and the British (71 kilos).

If your friends are like mine, they most likely say, "Oh, gosh, I almost never eat meat anymore." But the fact is someone is eating all that meat. Our appetite has created a voracious market that only the most questionable practices of intensive animal husbandry can satisfy. Feedlot beef, fattened on grain that could and should be put to more efficient uses, hogs and poultry raised on antibiotics and other drugs to make them grow fatter faster, veal calves that because of their deliberately weakened condition must be constantly medicated to keep them alive for slaughter, are all indications of tremendous waste, as well as of the threat to human health from the residues of such additives in our meat.

As international trade agreements proliferate, our food comes from ever-greater distances, creating not only an energy waste in the cost of transport but a further loss of control over how our food is raised and what goes into it before it reaches our markets. Meat for fast-food hamburgers is raised on former forest lands in Central America, plums and grapes are flown from Chile, raspberries come from New Zealand and radishes from Mexico. *Radishes* from Mexico? It's not as though radishes are terribly high on anyone's out-of-season must-have list, is it? Couldn't we all make a little vow to do without radishes this winter? They'll only taste that much better come spring.

The truth is that we *do* have choices and we *can* exercise control. Like sheep grazing in toxic pastures, we have become a herd of passive and uncritical eaters (the phrase, again, is Wendell Berry's), but it need not be so.

When we focus, we can choose, and what we choose, whether meat or fish, locally grown lettuce or imported radishes, Gala apples from industrial producers in New Zealand or New England apples raised by sustainable methods in orchards that also add pleasure to our landscape, makes a difference in the world around us.

Changing our diets is the answer to most of what's wrong with the way we eat. And dietary change, "kitchen-counter reforms," as Worldwatch Institute, a Washington think tank, calls it, is not difficult to effect. "Vote with your fork" is the axiom of Oldways Preservation & Exchange Trust, a group I work with that is trying to help us focus our attention and choose good foods that will create healthier bodies, healthier communities, and a healthier planet.

It's not difficult because it's a question of taste, or as people who are serious about their food like to say, the tomato question. Tomatoes—but it could be apples or oranges—have been bred for the market, bred to be harvested green, held for months in a cooler, gassed into ripeness but not into flavor, and hurtled to market still tough enough to withstand the rigors of the journey. But taste? Forget it. For taste you need a summertime tomato, raised in a field not too far distant and rushed to market, juices oozing but flavor intact. That's the tomato to choose.

Changing our diet is not difficult. We have made similar changes in the past, with cigarette smoking and with spitting—does anyone remember when bars and hotel lobbies routinely had spitoons for the convenience of gentlemen spitters? No more, and now they don't have ashtrays either. Unlike smoking and spitting, however, changing diets doesn't mean giving up anything but bad food. It does mean releasing a little time in your day to think about good food, to seek out producers and purveyors of pure and wholesome food, to spend some mental energy on its preparation. That's not deprivation. That's a blessing and a bounty.

Buy fresh, buy organic, buy local, buy seasonally. You don't have to be categorical about it: if your heart really does long for radishes and you're willing to put up with long-distance ones that have been raised with carefully modulated additions of lord-knows-what, then buy the Mexican radishes, for heaven's sake. But make the four rules part of your general mindset when it comes to food: fresh, organic, local, seasonal. And when you've done all that, take some time to think about preparing well what you've put time and money into acquiring.

Is this elitist? Selecting food wisely, eating with consciousness, eating with gratitude for the products on the table and for the skills of the farmer and the cook, is not elitist. (And in any case, what's wrong with elitism if we're *all* elitists?) Among life's greatest pleasures, after all, are those moments when we share with each other the sensuous delights of the table. These are the moments when strangers become friends and friends become lovers; when families become, in the fullest and richest sense, families; and when memories, strong, intense, and persistent, are given birth.

Food matters. Hungry people know that, but we don't always recognize it in America because most Americans, fortunately, are not hungry. On the other hand, most Americans don't eat well, and I know *that* because I'm an American and I do.

I eat well because I think about it. I think about shopping wisely, seeking farmers and purveyors who produce good wholesome food, and I think about cooking it well, so that the goodness of the food shines through and lends it an appeal that goes way beyond fancy sauces and elaborate presentations of expensive ingredients. No, I don't spend a lot of money on food, and yes, my children, both of whom are grown and living far away from my kitchen, also eat well, at least in part because they grew up in the certain knowledge that food matters.

I think of what Alice Waters, chef and owner of the restaurant Chez Panisse in Berkeley, California, said in the spring of 1992 when she received an accolade from a New York gourmet society. With characteristic modesty, she stated her credo: "I still believe from the bottom of my heart that good food is a right, *not* a privilege. What you eat can change your life: it nourishes our spirits as well as our bodies. Good food—pure and wholesome food, honestly grown, and simply cooked—may be the best hope to transform our society and our consciousness. It matters profoundly."

Let Them Eat Big Macs

BY DAVID DOWNIE

~

If the name José Bové isn't exactly household-known in North America, it certainly is in France. What readers may recollect better than Bové's name is the protest he staged, with a contingent of three hundred other farmers, on August 12, 1999, at the construction site of a new McDonald's in Millau, about 60 miles northwest of Montpellier. McDonald's is not only a symbol of American globalization but is most at odds with the values held by French farmers. A new McDonald's opening in a North American city or town is usually greeted with welcoming arms, but in Southwestern France it is tantamount to *une catastrophe*. On that day in August sheep farmer Bové drove his tractor into the side of the half-built McDonald's while his fellow farmers wielded their crowbars. Bové then drove to the police station, explained his action, and turned himself in, along with nine other members of the farmers' union, the Confédération Paysanne. It was at this point that the official war against *malbouffe* (junk food, which as Mort Rosenblum, in *A Goose in Toulouse*, defines as "any industrial, hormone-laced, genetically altered, or just basically cruddy nourishment") began. Bové served six weeks in jail for the McDonald's attack, and in November 2002 he was sentenced to serve fourteen months in prison for attacking a field of genetically modified rice at a research station near Montpellier. If perhaps you viewed these events as not having much relevance to you personally, you should know that just before Bové's protest, France banned hormone-laced beef imports from the United States, and the powers-that-be in Washington decided to retaliate by imposing a 100 percent tax hike on French luxury foods, including Roquefort cheese. If you love Roquefort as much as I do, you sadly lamented the rising price tags, which are now approximately twenty dollars a pound. Something about this picture seems grossly wrong to me: for rightly not wanting hormone-laden beef, the French are punished with a puncture to their prized Roquefort cheese, made in the same unadulterated way for hundreds and hundreds of years. As this piece attests, it *is* about the food.

DAVID DOWNIE has lived in Paris since 1986 and writes regularly for the travel section of the *San Fransisco Examiner, Paris Notes,* and *Salon.com*, the online magazine for which he serves as Paris correspondent. He has also contributed to many travel guidebook series, including Gault Millau, Fodor's, and Eyewitness Guides; he is the author of *Cooking the Roman Way: Authentic Recipes from the Home Cooks and Trattorias of Rome* (HarperCollins, 2002) and *Enchanted Liguria: A Celebration of the Culture, Lifestyle, and Food of the Italian Riviera* (Rizzoli, 1997). Downie's work has been featured in the *Paris* and *Central Italy* editions of *The Collected Traveler*.

The year is 1960. The place: a posh restaurant just waddling distance from the colonnaded Assemblée Nationale on the Left Bank. Over classic *poulet en demi-deuil*—chicken in "half-mourning" shrouded with garlic, black truffles, and an artery-plugging butter-and-cognac sauce—plump Gaullist parliamentarians discuss the Algerian War.

But something's wrong. The statesmen—there isn't a woman to be seen—shake their jowls and summon *le chef.*

"The truffles are sublime, monsieur," snorts a senior senator. "Regrettably your *poulet* tastes of fish."

"Fish?" gasps the chef, doffing his toque.

"How can we bring Général De Gaulle to dine here tomorrow?"

The chef crumbles into a velvet-upholstered armchair. "It's true, messieurs, I can no longer find chicken that tastes of chicken. The caged *poulets* eat fishmeal with hormones and taste of the sea. I may have to fall on my sword before the Général like Vatel!"

The senators drop their cigars; Algeria fades from their minds. François Vatel, chef to Prince Condé of Chantilly, chose suicide rather than serve Louis XIV substandard fare. "This is a national emergency," cries one parliamentarian, "a red emergency!"

Several months later Poulet Label Rouge—the Red Label—is created to certify top-flight French chicken. No fishmeal or hormones, no cages, nothing but the old-fashioned best. And soon—when the grain-fed free-range roasters have grown to edible age—the senators, *le chef, le général* himself (not to mention a grateful French nation), are smiling once again.

The preceding, of course, is fiction, though a similar scenario probably occurred circa 1960. Fiction or not, the Label Rouge system celebrates its fortieth anniversary this year, a testament to France's continuing commitment to agricultural excellence. The Label Rouge system is also a reminder, however, that the complicated battle against lousy food—what the French call *la mal-bouffe*—continues.

Bad food in France has been front-page news for the past year. Dioxin-tainted chicken, salmonella, listeria, and illegal hormones, not to mention genetically modified organisms (GMOs), have all made for daily reading. There is even a movie out, *La Vache et le President,* about a farm boy, mad cows, and the French president.

How could this have happened in the land of King Henri IV ("a chicken in every pot") or the magistrate-gastronome Brillat-Savarin ("Tell me what you eat and I'll tell you who you are"), namesake of the country's richest, 75 percent-fat cheese? A country that overthrew the ancien régime for lack of bread ("Let them eat cake"), then named a steak after Napoleon's plenipotentiary minister (Chateaubriand) and one hundred years later invented the Michelin Red Guides with their multimillionaire starred chefs? France, a lay republic where food—the last cultural ID card of vanished duchies and kingdoms—is sacred? Where *crise de foi* (crisis of faith) and *crise de foie* (liver crisis) are homonyms?

According to some French food experts, including feisty members of the Confédération Paysanne (an association of small-scale "peasant" farmers) who challenged the WTO in Seattle and attacked a McDonald's in Millau), the trouble really began in the late 1940s. This was when "industrial" or "American-style" farming first took root. With modern agribusiness came chemical pesticides and fertilizers, boundless fields *sans* hedgerows, battery breeding, and long-distance transport of products and live animals.

In truth, France's alimentary troubles began with the abandonment of countryside and village—classic French food is essentially rural (except urban haute cuisine)—during the industrial revolution. As many as 120,000 provincials per year poured into Paris in the late 1800s, turning the capital into a culinary crucible while bleeding the countryside; the slaughter of World War I simply sped up the process. French agricultural workers once numbered in the tens of millions. By 1960 there were 5 million; by 1980 only 1.8 million. In 1998, the latest year for which statistics are available, a mere 910,000 were left.

This tiny group now produces a fifth of the European Union's agricultural products, making France the world's second biggest food exporter (after the United States). Food products remain the country's largest single industrial sector, worth 816 billion francs (about $116 billion) in 1999. Over 67 million tourists a year visit France (25 million go to Paris alone), many of them still expecting to taste the most refined cuisine in the universe. And taste they will—foie gras, escargots, conserves, wine, and hundreds of tangy cheeses made from the raw milk so dreaded by the FDA. Visitors may also have to swallow *la malbouffe*.

For French cuisine, the late twentieth century was a roller coaster—the perceived lows sometimes coinciding (in critical American eyes) with trade wars, economic cycles, and unfavorable dollar-to-franc exchange rates. It's safe to say that French cooking bottomed out in the late 1960s or early 1970s, before the Label Rouge and other high-quality niche initiatives finally bore fruit.

Witness the cookbooks of the period. My modest collection includes a 1969 paperback titled *Cuisine pour toute l'année* by Monique Maine. Her introduction includes the following ominous observation: "There has been enormous progress in the food industry, packaged foods are now all of excellent quality, but, above all, frozen food has entered our lives." In other words, no more seasonal local specialties, just pop down to the "hypermarket" and stock up on canned or freeze-dried goodies.

As French hypermarkets began to spring up, so died village mom-and-pop shops. This accelerated demographic flight, or what the French dubbed the "desertification" of the countryside. The catchphrase *la malbouffe* was coined in the 1970s by prescient French nutritionist Joël de Rosnay.

Contrast these facts with the words of English food writer Elizabeth David. In her 1960 *French Provincial Cooking*—still considered one of the great French cookbooks—she is strangely, perhaps willfully, out of touch. "Changes brought about by modern methods of transport and food preservation have not destroyed [the] traditions of French provincial cookery," she writes. Destroyed? Perhaps not. Changed, yes indeed.

Seventeen years later, in her preface to the 1977 edition, David conceded, "Over the years, a certain amount of what I wrote about the provinces of France has inevitably passed into history. Nobody would pretend that the deep freeze isn't everywhere, or that restaurants don't sometimes serve disgraceful prefabricated sauces and inadmissible travesties of famous dishes . . . my inclination now is to try harder than ever for quality."

In her 1983 preface to the same cookbook, David recalled that by 1960, when the work was first published, the so-called *cuisine classique*—elaborately rich flour-based sauces with overcooked vegetables—had been outmoded since at least 1939. David looked with a mixture of alarm and wry amusement upon nouvelle cuisine. Was French food as a whole condemned to ridicule, she wondered, because of nouvelle cuisine's "airy little nothings accompanied by their trois sauces served in dolls' house swimming pools round one side of the plate"? No, decided David, "it is not so much the cooking that is wrong, except in the most blatantly arrogant establishments, as a certain coldness and ungenerosity of spirit." By the early 1980s the excesses of nouvelle cuisine were already clichés.

Just about anywhere in France today you find—often at the same time—the *haute cuisine* of the Michelin-starred chefs; the "classic" *cuisine bourgeoise* of the gastronomically attentive middle classes; remnants of *cuisine régionale* scattered around the provinces; improvised eclectic (a Franco-ethnic mix of store-bought, semiworked, and precooked ingredients); and something like *cuisine nostalgique-rétro*—what Grandma might have cooked (but never did), served primarily in the faux bistros of big French cities.

Add in the countless ethnic cuisines in France (some of the best Moroccan, Vietnamese, and Thai food found anywhere), and fast-food outlets (over 2,500 of them, including about 800 McDonald's), and you get the picture: it's like looking down into a churning food processor.

Meanwhile, Label Rouge now boasts 27,110 members raising or growing 429 types of high-quality produce (from chickens to snails, shallots to beef), and you can get certified organic or GMO-free foods in every supermarket in the land. Open markets thrive in big cities where nary a street is without its butcher, baker, and chocolate maker (not to mention greengrocer, deli, wine merchant, and so forth). A recent Louis Harris poll shows that 99 percent of the French describe taste (*le goût*) as a "strong cultural value," and 79 percent consider it the primary determinant in making their food purchases.

All this sounds like great news—a happy culinary cycle of novelty, reaction, and revival, with a welcome opening to the outside world. Bové, the militant co-founder of the Confédération Paysanne and coauthor of the current bestseller *Le Monde n'est pas une marchandise* (The World Isn't for Sale), insists that this cycle has been broken.

Bové believes the future of French food—and, by extension, of French society—is in mortal danger from wholly new factors. Among them are the European Union's peasant-crushing Common Agricultural Policy (CAP); the United Nations' sinister *Codex Alimentarius international food treaty;* unfettered global trade; environment-unfriendly agribusiness practices; hormones; mad cows; and GMOs. Another insidious threat allegedly comes from big-money fast-food chains, specifically McDonald's, which the French call "MacDo." "If we don't act now it's finished, it's over," the gravel-voiced Bové told me recently, tracing a doomsday picture with his ever-present pipe.

Bové's critics call his rhetoric scaremongering. But if everything's hunky-dory in French fields, kitchens, and dining rooms, then why is this fifty-year-old dairy farmer from Roquefort a national hero? Bové's book has been on the bestseller list for months. Wherever he goes, TV, radio, and newspapers follow. French people of all ages cajole him to autograph their T-shirts, their pants, their books—whatever's handy when he appears.

Bové and his fellow Confédération Paysanne activists have not merely touched a chord in food-worshiping France. They're playing a cacophonous symphony with choral complement. Furious farmers, rabid ranchers, disgruntled politicians from across the spectrum, and most of all, millions of wary shoppers have lined up behind him, making him a Gallic David against the global Goliath.

Bové's deification began in August 1999 in Millau, a bucolic dairy village outside Roquefort, when the stocky curd-wrangler with a horseshoe mustache led a wildly enthusiastic group of three hundred local farmers, environmental militants, and Confédération Paysanne activists in the "destruction," according to prosecutors, of an unfinished McDonald's franchise as police watched. Though several arrests were made at the time of the attack, a manhunt by French secret servicemen followed a few days later. Bové, along with a handful of fellow Confédération Paysanne militants, were tossed in jail for about three weeks. Thus began what Bové now sees as "$30 million worth of free publicity" for the Confédération Paysanne's peasant revolt against *la malbouffe* and its perpetrators.

In July 2000 an estimated forty thousand supporters showed up for Bové and his codefendants' hearing in Millau on charges of "ransacking" the McDonald's. But Bové's anti-MacDo crusade began in spring 1999, when the United States, faced with refusals by France to import American beef (as a result of feared growth hormone residues), applied punitive duties on dozens of French products. One of the hardest hit was Roquefort cheese. Roquefort makers sell 440 tons of their pocked blue curd to America every year at a wholesale value of 30 million francs ($4.3 million). Needless to say, local milk suppliers like Bové weren't happy. As if to add insult to injury, a new McDonald's franchise—nearly eight hundred Golden Arches already grace some 420 French towns—was under construction in nearby Millau, Roquefort's backyard.

The punitive tariff on so symbolic a food was viewed by Bové as pure provocation. Roquefort isn't just any *fromage*. In 76 B.C. the ancient Roman chronicler Pliny the Elder traveled to Gaul, reporting back about the peculiar mold-flecked cheese. Enlightenment philosopher Denis Diderot called Roquefort "the king of French cheeses." In 1925 Roquefort became the first French product to receive the coveted AOC (*appellation d'origine contrôlée*), devised to thwart counterfeiters.

"It was truly stupid for the American administration to take Roquefort cheese hostage in the hormone-beef trade war," Bové tells me in Paris, puffing away. "They represent two utterly irreconcilable types of farming. Doubling the import duties on a high-quality AOC to force us to buy hormone beef? It's folly."

Despite the confrontational tone, Bové and his Confédération Paysanne's gastro-crusaders did not target McDonald's simply because it's American. Nor is Bové your average French dairyman. He spent part of his childhood in California with his scientist parents. (They were doing agricultural research at the University of California at Berkeley.) He speaks fluent English and scoffs at attempts to discredit him by labeling him anti-American or cravenly nationalistic. "When I was in America last year I talked to farmers and consumers and our message got through," he says. "Texan cattle ranchers, non-GMO soy growers, Alaskan salmon fishermen—they've taken inspiration from European movements. I think there's an awakening of consciousness in America, too; things are beginning to move."

Bové and his federation targeted McDonald's, he says, because the chain serves what he calls "food from nowhere"—what he and many other Frenchmen perceive as corporate, cultureless, and rootless food. Menu items such as hamburgers or chicken nuggets, notes Bové, are "recomposed" from myriad sources; they're standardized, bland, sterilized. This, to his mind, is the antithesis of traditional French food and all that goes with it—the art of growing, eating, and cooking with reverence for the soil and the seasons. "In France the link to your roots is very much through food and cooking traditions," explains Bové, whose ranchland near Roquefort is encircled by eight-hundred-year-old stone walls. "In America there's no sense of an ancient civilization with a rural identity, etched over time into the landscape."

The notion that food is both sacred and site-specific is the root of the emotionally charged French concept of *terroir*. First applied to describe the association of grape variety and soil in winemaking, it has come to evoke the wholesome, earthy qualities of regional foods and cooking. The more France goes global and the more fast foods and hypermarkets there are, the more tenaciously the French adhere to concepts such as *terroir*, talismans against an uncertain future.

And for good reason. France's gastronomic future looks increasingly overweight. Researchers such as Dr. Philippe Froguel of France's prestigious CNRS and Institut Pasteur in Lille, believe that Europeans will reach American obesity levels in the next twenty years. "Half of Americans are overweight," Froguel told me. "A quarter are obese. Right now 30 percent of Europeans are overweight. However, European children are getting fatter all the time. Child obesity has doubled in France in the past five years, and obesity among young French adults has shot up 45 percent." Froguel, also a diabetes expert, adds that "atypical diabetes" (that is, juvenile diabetes)—an affliction associated in part with a genetic predisposition and in part with unhealthy eating habits—was unknown in France until 1999.

Why is this happening? According to Froguel, the French appear to believe they are increasingly under the sway of "MacDomination" and "Coca-colonization." The power of *terroir* would seem to be weakening. "Just because we've got these great French chefs it doesn't mean the mass of French restaurants is good," says a pragmatic Bové. "Responsibility for McDonald's popularity falls on French restaurants and bistros that are frozen in time, like in a [Robert] Doisneau photograph [from the 1950s] . . . Institutional restaurants are disgusting, school restaurants are revolting. In them we have tasteless, insipid, homogenous food, so kids prefer to eat at MacDo instead of the school cafeteria."

McDonald's France counters by claiming that its food is wholesome, its beef French (and hence hormone-free). Where the Confédération Paysanne sees economic and cultural domination, McDonald's sees sponsorship: it builds RonaldLand playgrounds for kiddies, donates money to charity, and offers seminars to teach French parents how to behave—according to McDonald's—like parents. It has annual sales of over $1.5 billion, and its restaurants employ about thirty thousand locals and "help animate" downtown areas that would otherwise be deserted (presumably because, as in America, suburban hypermarkets and malls have killed off traditional shopping areas in many French towns and cities).

All of which makes France's enduring Label Rouge glamorous and more important than ever. Now a $1 billion business, its labels distinguish the exceptional quality characteristics of everything from fruit to fish. As a consequence a Label Rouge chicken could cost 50 percent more than a nonlabel competitor. Slow-growing, slow-fattening species are favored. Farmyard guinea fowl from the Landes, for example, take ninety-four days to grow to slaughterhouse age, compared to the usual forty-five. Poultry must be slaughtered locally (within two hours or 60 miles of the farm). Herbivores are fed only top-quality grain; animals must be either "raised in the open air" or "totally free-range." A Label Rouge "farmyard porker raised in the open air," for instance, is better off than your average Parisian: it gets a minimum 50 square meters (about 530 square feet) to trot in—the size of an average one-bedroom apartment. "It is not an elitist social class thing," Dominique Chaillouet, a Label Rouge spokesperson, told me, "but rather a question of festive food. Even the poor buy Label Rouge for special occasions; it's a question of frequency."

The Agriculture Biologique or AB label, on the other hand, is an 8,100-member government-certified labeling scheme (recognized by the European Union) that imposes strict regulations on about three thousand organic products, concerning itself only with the healthfulness of its foods—no chemical pesticides, fertilizers, dyes, food coloring, or flavoring; only organic feeds and fodder; free-range conditions; limited use of antibiotics (no more than twice a year); respect for natural cycles; encouragement of biodiversity.

Bigger by far are France's prestigious AOC government-certified products, a 100 billion franc ($14.5 billion) market with 133,000 members. Many consumers mistakenly think AOCs apply only to wines. In fact there are dozens of other AOC food products, each with a specific charter to protect it. They include Vallée des Baux de Provence and Nyons olives and oil; Chasselas de Moissac grapes; Ile de Ré potatoes; Coco de Paimpol beans; green lentils from Puy; Grenoble walnuts; Vosges fir-tree honey; Bresse chicken and turkey; Camargue bulls; Haute Provence essential lavender oil; hay from Crau—and of course, Roquefort cheese. (Bové is the president of the Roquefort AOC.)

But the palette of "labelized" French products is wider still. It also includes IGPs (*indication géographique protégée*), which specifies the qualities or characteristics of a specific region or regional farming tradition. Then there are the AOPs—*appellation d'origine protégée,* which means the product comes from a particular region that is protected for a variety of cultural and environmental reasons. Just to confuse things further, some Label Rouge products can also bear IGP, AOP, or AB labels and vice versa. Add in supermarket "labeled" brands (Agriculture Raisonnée, reasonable farming, and Agriculture Durable), plus dozens of other products made to resemble authentic government-sanctioned quality labels, and consumers wind up in a daze.

There is one new label that has grabbed everyone's attention of late: GMO-free. In part because of the Confédération Paysanne's ongoing campaign against GMOs—militant actions have included ransacking grain silos and destroying crops—but also because of agitation from Greens across the continent, GMOs are a nonstarter in Europe. Most supermarket chains won't stock them, and "GMO-free" has become a favorite marketing gimmick. According to GMOs' supporters, science has been swept away by fear and emotion.

The glut of labels is symptomatic of French consumers' desire to be able to trace a product back to its origin. Once upon a time, before the advent of the hyper- or supermarket, you knew that your butcher and greengrocer got their goods from their cousins, the local pig farmer, snail and frog breeder, or oyster cultivator. Until there is a mass exodus from cities back to the countryside and a return of small specialty stores to deserted French towns and villages, labels and product traceability will remain important means of informing and protecting consumers. "This is a historic moment in civilization in terms of its relationship with agriculture and food," Bové told me, citing the EU agriculture commission's stated goal of eliminating millions of supposedly "inefficient" small-scale European farms.

Historic, indeed. Last weekend at Millau at least forty thousand pro-peasant, antiglobalization militants and sympathizers provided a large-scale indication that the EU will continue to face considerable challenges in carrying out any policies judged unfriendly to small farming. Bové's trial also provided a convenient opportunity for a miniature rerun of the anti-WTO demonstrations of last year in the United States. Millau, sited in the Tarn River region, was dubbed "Seattle on the Tarn."

Like the earlier "action" against McDonald's, this one was non-violent. The charge against Bové was redefined from "ransacking" to "dismantling" on the basis of photographic evidence and eye-witness testimony that indicated little damage had been done. Another charge, that Bové allegedly threatened to bomb the McDonald's, was dropped. Bové risked up to five years in jail and a 500,000-franc ($72,566) fine. But the magistrate hearing the case recommended a symbolic ten-month sentence with nine months suspended. Since Bové already spent almost one month in jail in 1999 following his arrest, he probably will not be incarcerated again. [Note that at press time, the end of Bové's story had yet to be decided.]

Meanwhile, the feisty dairy farmer continues to crisscross France, signing books and speaking to packed houses. He is less concerned about his destiny than that of his cause. "The real challenge is to face down the prospect of industrial agriculture's triumph, with a little niche market for tourists, so your American readers can still find a good Bordeaux, or a great cheese made by somebody somewhere," he told me in Paris, provocative as always. "But that will be a minimal niche market, for folklore, for tourism. Right now we still have a heritage that we can save in France, but we've got to radically change agricultural policy."

Others are more optimistic, pointing to the groundswell of support for the Confédération Paysanne and France's all-out fight within the EU to preserve "traditional French chocolate" made with only sugar and pure cocoa butter. France was also a key player last year in the EU's victorious battle with the WTO over raw-milk cheeses. (Had a U.S.-sponsored initiative won, the French would have been forced to stop making Brie, Camembert, Reblochon, and many other raw-milk cheeses with centuries-old pedigrees, and even nascent artisan U.S. cheese-makers could have been affected.) Says François Dufour, cofounder of the Confédération Paysanne, "I think we're stemming the tide, we're reversing things. It's not just the peasants, it's local people in various parts of France who're aware of the problems and willing to stand up and fight."

Battles over growth hormones, raw milk, GMOs, vegetable fats in chocolate, and countless other food-related issues are bound to continue. The feistiness of French farmers and consumers—the country's national symbol is a cocky rooster, after all—is the best guarantee that French food and cooking will continue to be excellent in the decades to come. In the meantime, I'm heading to my favorite local bistro for a bang-up 1950s-style meal Robert Doisneau would've loved.

Working to Put Blacks on France's Agenda

BY JOHN TAGLIABUE

∽

Immigration, as I noted in *Practical Information,* is a key issue in France. Here is a piece about an immigrant businessman pressing for changes in politics, with some success. One of the reasons I especially admire this piece, and Dogad Dogoui, is for the inclusion of the final line. I believe it is not debatable that some of the grievances raised by Islamic fundamentalists—including Osama bin Laden—are valid, especially those that address the gross inequities between the daily lives of Muslim immigrants and natives of Western societies. One doesn't have to be a rocket scientist to grasp that it's not enough to rid the world of violent terrorists: both they and the young and disenfranchised place little or no value on human life and are desperate for basic necessities and opportunities the rest of us take for granted. September 11 irrevocably changed our world forever, but until we give immigrants of every nationality and religion a confident vision for the future, we are merely raising generations of malcontents and potential terrorists.

JOHN TAGLIABUE is a staff writer for *The New York Times,* where this piece originally appeared.

T hey say, France is one and indivisible," said Dogad Dogoui, with characteristic deadpan humor, as he poked at a lunch of fish recently. "I say, yes, and with lots of people who are invisible."

After seventeen years in France, Mr. Dogoui is still uncomfortable with the French treatment of blacks. He is one of hundreds of thousands of nonwhite immigrants, mainly blacks and Arabs, whom France has absorbed over the years from its former colonies in Africa and the Caribbean. But French sensitivity to the Arabs in their midst, largely because of the potential for a spillover of violence from the Middle East, far outstrips that toward blacks here, he said. So last year, Mr. Dogoui, a stocky, cheerful man who earns a living advising foreign companies how to do business in France, founded a club for black business leaders. Now he is spearheading a drive to involve more blacks in politics.

French attitudes toward blacks, he conceded, are ambiguous. The cradle of human rights, Paris raised a statue early in the last century to Toussaint-Louverture, the black Haitian liberator. For years the French have regularly denounced American racism, and the road from Harlem to Paris was wide, inviting talented American blacks like the singer Josephine Baker, musicians like Sidney Bechet, and writers like Richard Wright, Langston Hughes, and James Baldwin.

Yet today blacks are not much on the French agenda, said Mr. Dogoui, thirty-eight, who migrated here from Abidjan, Ivory Coast. He thinks they should be. "For thirty years France has been changing," he said. "But they don't open their eyes and see it."

Officially, blacks number about 1.5 million of a total population of 59 million. But the unofficial number is higher, Mr. Dogoui maintains, and more come daily.

In national elections this year Christiane Taubira, a feisty economist from French Guiana, became the first black candidate for president, drawing 660,000 votes, or 2.3 percent of the total. But in French politics, Mr. Dogoui said, "blacks arrange the chairs at conferences and clean up afterward." No black person sits in the National Assembly or in regional parliaments. In all of France, he said, there are only about one hundred black city council members. "That's ridiculous," he said. "What does that mean, among thirty-six thousand towns and cities?"

The oldest of twelve children, Mr. Dogoui grew up in comfortable circumstances—his father was deputy director of the port of Abidjan. At one time he had wanted to emigrate to Quebec, but his father objected, saying the move would carry him too far from their close-knit family. He is now married to a French woman from Normandy; they have three children. In 1994, he became a French citizen.

After trying unsuccessfully to enroll in medical school, Mr. Dogoui studied psychology, but became drawn to public relations. He obtained his degree from the leading French school for public relations, making useful contacts while working as an intern in several government ministries. Earlier he had attended a Catholic boarding school in Normandy, where he cut his teeth on politics, founding an African students association and organizing an African film festival.

As a student, Mr. Dogoui supplemented an allowance from his father by working with other black and Arab immigrants in a packaging plant in a Paris suburb. While there, he saw how long hours on the factory floor prevented the blacks from overseeing their children's education. But what particularly troubled him, he said, was how the workers clung to an immigrant mentality, happy to have escaped African poverty and content with the simplest of jobs. "They forget that their kids are not immigrants," he said. They nevertheless showed enough concern to complain that the schools offered their children none of the extra help they needed or a place to study after hours. "It's not a financial question but a question of interest," Mr. Dogoui said.

While white pupils are encouraged to continue studying, black children are steered toward vocational training. He heard, he said, of black students telling their teachers they wanted to study medicine, only to be laughed at. "Black kids say, 'Why should I study journalism?'" he said. "There are no blacks on TV." Mr. Dogoui likes to tell a story about his ten-year-old son, who returned recently from a trip to London, where he visited stores with nonwhite owners. "They're bosses there," the boy told his father with an unmistakable note of wonder.

During a layover recently at the Amsterdam airport, Mr. Dogoui sat in a lounge with other business people. One-third of them were black, he said, yet he was the only French person. The others were from North America, Britain, and the Netherlands. France's largest corporations have no black directors or senior executives, he said, claiming competent blacks are unavailable. Yet as a corporate consultant advising North American and Scandinavian companies how to do business with French companies, Mr. Dogoui has observed how savvy businesses use blacks to increase their effectiveness in dealing with nonwhite countries or customers. Finding competent black executives should be "a challenge for French companies," he said. But it isn't one that they seem particularly eager to confront. "Sometimes it's racism," he said, referring to French companies. "But sometimes they just don't get it."

When asked whether the French people are racist, however, he reflected a moment before saying no. Some blacks see the French as racists, he said, because they distrust all French society. "I chose to adapt," he said, attributing his success to his mastery of the French language, which he spoke at home in Abidjan, and to an ease accepting people of other cultures that he inherited from his father. At boarding school and in college, he said, he met French students who were curious about Africa and its art, literature, and film. But the average French person, he said, shows little interest. France, he said, is "a strange country—closed, traditional, even on the left."

One goal of the business club is to create an investment fund to finance black start-up companies. France has room for ethnic African and Caribbean restaurants, Mr. Dogoui said, as well as hairdressers and cosmetics. French advertising lacks blacks, he notes, both in the advertisements and in the agencies, and has neither a major black newspaper nor magazine.

The goal of Mr. Dogoui's political movement is to discover talented blacks to run for office at all levels of government. He has no illusions about the difficulties they will face. For example, when the new prime minister, Jean-Pierre Raffarin, assembled his cabinet last spring, black leaders including Mr. Dogoui asked him to name a black minister for African affairs. They were refused. Blacks, he said, "are disappointed with the left," believing that the former Socialist prime minister, Lionel Jospin, did little for them. "And they mistrust the right." He favors no particular faction. "My dream," he said, "is to have blacks someday on the left, on the right, and in the center."

An optimist by nature, he fears nonetheless that, barring change, racial unrest could explode in France as it did in America in the 1960s. High-rise slums surrounding French cities are cauldrons of racial anger dominated by urban gangs. "And they are armed," he said. "You have to give young people hope."

A Place to Spend a Lifetime

BY LESLIE BRENNER

〜

It's hard not to be jealous of this writer—as she's married to a native of the *sud-ouest,* she probably doesn't have to wait too long between visits! And she's right in observing that even after years of exploring, there is still so very much to see, absorb, and comprehend.

LESLIE BRENNER lives in Los Angeles and is the author of *The Art of the Cocktail Party* (Plume, 1994), *Fear of Wine: An Introductory Guide to the Grape* (Bantam, 1995), *Essential Flavors: The Simple Art of Cooking with Infused Oils, Flavored Vinegars, Essences, and Elixirs* (Viking, 1999), *Greetings from the Golden State* (Picador, 2002), and *The Fourth Star: Dispatches from Inside Daniel Boulud's Celebrated New York Restaurant* (Clarkson Potter, 2002).

When I married into a French family of the Southwest ten years ago, foie gras was the first thought that went through my head—after, *bien sûr,* the notion that my husband was the love of my life, would make a wonderful father, and so on. Magnificent Bordeaux wines came closely in its tasty wake, followed by black truffles, toothsome *cèpes,* briny oysters, *confit de canard*, and comforting cassoulet. My first visit to my husband's homeland didn't disappoint. Yet I had no idea of the treasures I would find over the next decade as I came to know this magnificent region—and man, of course.

Traditional, solid, and soulful, the Southwest comprises a wide range of landscapes: beaches that stretch luxuriantly from the mouth of the Gironde estuary down to the Spanish border, the endless pine forests of Les Landes, vineyards of the Médoc, fairy-tale–like châteaus that dot the hilly banks of the Dordogne and Lot

Rivers from Beynac-et-Cazenac to La Treyne, the awe-inspiring gorges of Rocamadour and snowy peaks of the Pyrenees Mountains. Not to mention Sarlat, St.-Cirq-Lapopie, and Domme—a dense concentration of some of the most charming and beautiful villages in France. Somehow it's all pulled together by a spirit—no, not a spirit exactly; it's something less ethereal, more basic. Call it a soul. The earthy soul of the Southwest.

The people of the Southwest share as deep an association with their region as they do with the whole of France. Solid, dependable, and loyal, they can also be inscrutable. Though their language is peppered with patois, they're not often given over to flights of fancy. Southwesterners love head-to-head confrontation, whether it's rugby, a good argument at the dinner table, or bullfighting. Yet aggressive they're not, as evidenced in the bullring: in *la course landaise,* the animal is artfully sidestepped, dodged, and leaped over but never killed. Scratch the surface of the Gascon, and you'll find an inexhaustible warmth.

The pace of the Southwest is relaxed, and the main meal is still enjoyed at midday—especially on Sunday, when it can last until dinnertime! And the bounty for many of these tables comes from colorful, fresh food markets in the center of town. In the Southwest one discovers the unhurried pleasures of life. For instance, it is said that you have to be at least forty before you can truly appreciate Armagnac, the oldest brandy in France—six hundred years and still going strong—made in the heart of the Southwest. Begin your education by lingering over a glass and discussing the merits of a fine Armagnac with a winemaker in his cellar.

The prevalence of Romanesque buildings, with their unpretentious elegance, reflects the inherent solidity of the Southwest people. Between the twelfth and sixteenth centuries, as many as two million pilgrims crossed the region each year en route to the shrine of St.-Jacques-de-Compostelle (Santiago de Compostela) in northwestern Spain, stopping at a number of churches, including St.-Jean-Pied-de-Port (where several routes converge), St.-Sernin in Toulouse, Ste.-Foy in Conques, and Rocamadour. Scallop-shell motifs carved into stone or wood and pictured on signposts throughout the Southwest mark the routes.

And what could be earthier than the varied *terroir* of the Pyrenees—from the sheep farming of its hilly regions of Béarn and Bigorre to the jagged peaks that make for the most challenging cycling in the world (a famously difficult portion of the Tour de France passes through here every year) and some of the best skiing in Europe (there are forty winter resorts in the region).

Water is just as much a part of the soul of the place as is terra firma. How lovely to see the châteaus of the Tarn or the Dordogne via a leisurely trip in a canoe! The Southwest is a land of unspoiled rivers and lakes that beg for a swim, of oyster beds in Arcachon and man-made waterways. The Canal des Deux Mers and the Canal du Midi join up with the Garonne River and the Gironde estuary, connecting the Mediterranean to the Atlantic. Ah yes, the ocean. Along the Côte d'Argent, pine forests give way to windblown sand dunes (including the largest in Europe, the 330-foot-high Dune du Pyla), which slope down to some of the most graceful beaches of the Atlantic.

Even after my ten-year introduction to the Southwest, I feel I could spend a lifetime here exploring and getting acquainted.

Bibliography

The Mediterranean: History, Natural History, and Personal Narratives

Not all of Southwestern France borders the Mediterranean Sea, of course, but the sea has had an enormous influence on the region at large, so I include books on it here just as in my other editions.

The Ancient Mediterranean, Michael Grant, Charles Scribner's Sons, 1969. In this scholarly work Grant reminds us that a huge proportion of our civilized heritage, "almost in its entirety, came to us from the ancient Mediterranean—from Greece and from Rome and from Israel. This fact is given too little prominence today because so many other ancient cultures, some of them from much further afield, have now been discovered. Yet it still remains true that the Mediterranean was the region from which civilisation came our way."

The First Eden: The Mediterranean World and Man, Sir David Attenborough, William Collins Sons & Co., London, 1987. The four parts of this book deal with natural history, archaeology, history, and ecology, and there is very good coverage of Mediterranean plants and animals.

The Inner Sea: The Mediterranean and Its People, Robert Fox, Alfred A. Knopf, 1993.

Mediterranean, photography by Mimmo Jodice, essays by George Hersey and Predrag Matvejevic, Aperture, 1995.

Mediterranean: A Cultural Landscape, Predrag Matvejevic, translated by Michael Henry Heim, University of California Press, Berkeley, 1999. A beautiful, unusual book combining personal observations with history, maps, maritime details, people, and language.

The Mediterranean, Fernand Braudel, first published in France, 1949; English translation of second revised edition, HarperCollins, 1972; Abridged edition, HarperCollins, 1992. Still the definitive classic. *De rigueur.*

Mediterranean: From Homer to Picasso, Xavier Girard, translated by Simon Pleasance and Fronza Woods, Assouline, 2001. This recent book, perhaps in a category by itself, is divided into five chapters—representations, narratives, figures, places, and arts. I've been waiting for a volume just like this one, filled with color and black-and-white illustrations and photos. As stated in the prologue, "The Mediterranean," wrote Bernard Pingaud in the pages of *L'Arc* in 1959, "is nothing other than the image we make of it for ourselves. The unusual thing is that we all make an image of it for ourselves, and that it is still a magnet for all those who are lucky enough to discover it one day. Herein lies a secret. It is perhaps not the secret conjured up by the 'land where the orange tree blooms.' It is the secret of this image itself, the secret of a dream which paradoxically contrasts abundance and drought, merriness and poverty, moderation and excess, joy and tragedy. Who can say why we need the Midi? If the Mediterranean didn't exist, we would have to invent it."

The Mediterranean: Lands of the Olive Tree, Culture and Civilizations, text and photographs by Alain Cheneviere, Konecky & Konecky, New York, 1997. This is that rare coffee-table book that has both perceptive text and gorgeous photos.

Memory and the Mediterranean, Fernand Braudel, Alfred A. Knopf, 2001.

On the Shores of the Mediterranean, Eric Newby, first published by The Harvill Press, London, 1984; Picador, 1985, paperback. You have to travel with Eric and Wanda Newby to other places around the Mediterranean besides France— the former Yugoslavia, Greece, Turkey, Spain, Israel, North Africa, and Venice—but it's a pleasure every step of the way.

The Phoenicians, edited by Sabatino Moscati, Rizzoli, 1999. The Phoenician civilization remains mysterious, but this beautifully printed and fascinating paperback reveals a treasure trove of information in the form of essays contributed by a number of scholars. I don't know about you, but the last time I spent much time delving into the Phoenicians was in junior high school, so this volume has been a welcome addition to Mediterranean literature.

The Pillars of Hercules: A Grand Tour of the Mediterranean, Paul Theroux, G. P. Putnam's Sons, 1995.

Playing Away: Roman Holidays and Other Mediterranean Encounters, Michael Mewshaw, Atheneum, 1988.

The Spirit of Mediterranean Places, Michel Butor, Marlboro Press, 1986.

The Sun at Midday: Tales of a Mediterranean Family, Gini Alhadeff, Pantheon, 1997. Though Alhadeff's life was and remains partly Italian, this is a full Mediterranean memoir, beautifully written and one of my most favorite books.

Mediterranean Architecture and Style

Mediterranean Color: Italy, France, Spain, Portugal, Morocco, Greece, photographs and text by Jeffrey Becom, foreword by Paul Goldberger, Abbeville Press, 1990.

Mediterranean Lifestyle, photography by Pere Planells, text by Paco Assensio, Loft Publications; distributed in the U.S. by Watson-Guptill Publications, 2000.

Mediterranean Living, Lisa Lovatt-Smith, Whitney Library of Design, Watson-Guptill, 1998.

Mediterranean Style, Catherine Haig, Abbeville Press, 1998; first published in

Great Britain in 1997 by Conran Octopus Ltd., London.

Mediterranean Vernacular: A Vanishing Architectural Tradition, V. I. Atroshenko, Milton Grundy, Rizzoli International, 1991.

Villages in the Sun: Mediterranean Community Architecture, Myron Goldfinger, Rizzoli, 1993.

Europe

Age of Faith, Anne Fremantle and the editors of Time-Life Books, 1965. This is one volume in the "Great Ages of Man: A History of the World's Cultures" series. Like Time-Life's "Foods of the World" series, published at approximately the same time, these are wonderfully written and produced hardcover editions. Robert Lopez, who at the time of publication was chairman of medieval studies at Yale, wrote that "the thousand medieval years were not solely an 'age of faith,' nor is faith a uniquely medieval phenomenon. But the cathedrals were the most impressive monuments of that era; its greatest poem was a description of Hell, Purgatory and Paradise; Crusades were the only collective enterprises which temporarily rallied all nations; there were heretics and infidels but agnosticism was nonexistent or cowed into silence; the clergy was more numerous and influential in politics, economics, philosophy and other intellectual pursuits than it has ever been since. There is nothing wrong with the traditional formula of an 'age of faith,' provided we remember that the Middle Ages were many other things as well." This is not meant to be a definitive history of the Middle Ages; it's really a study of Christian life, with chapters on "The Light of the Church," "Conquest by Crusade," "Adventures of the Intellect," "Art Inspired by Faith," and "Winds of Change." However, it remains quite a good source for readers who are looking for a work of some depth—no doubt others will prefer more comprehensive and academic books, of which there is no shortage. The map of Stone Testaments to an Age of Faith includes the cathedrals of Conques and Albi, and there is a great, double-page photo of Carcassonne, which could almost have been taken today, it has changed so little. (The caption to this photo reminds readers that many medieval towns grew up beside a burg, or fortified place, situated on a river or seacoast. Outside the burg, mercantile settlers built a market and homes and constructed their own walls around them, and the people who lived here "soon acquired a definitive name. To distinguish them from the knights, clerics and serfs who resided in old burgs or unwalled villages, the people of the new towns were called bürgers in German, burgesses in English, and bourgeois in French. At first these terms embraced all economic levels. That they came to denote middle-class affluence was testimony to the new burgs' spectacular success." With a plethora of color and black-and-white photographs and a four-page chronology of events significant in the Age of Faith under the categories of church and papacy, society and economics, politics, philosophy, art, and literature.

The Crusaders: Warriors of God, Georges Tate, Harry N. Abrams, 1996. The quotation on the inside front cover of this little paperback (small enough to pack easily in a handbag) is worth repeating: "In the long sequence of interaction and fusion between Orient and Occident out of which our civilization has grown, the crusades were a tragic and destructive episode . . . There was so much courage and so little honor, so much devotion and so little understanding" (Steven Runciman, *A History of the Crusades,* 1954). I am aware that there are a great number of titles published on the Crusades (including the one just named), the finest of which, in my opinion, is Karen Armstrong's *Holy War* (noted below); but as fond as I am of her book, and as fine as all the other tomes may be, I think this one—in the wonderful Discoveries series—may be the best for the traveler who wants a good, concise history that can be read rather quickly. The author was director of the Institut Français d' Archéologie du Proche-Orient from 1980 to 1990, and he is currently director of the Archaeological Mission of Northern Syria. He is also a specialist in the East from the third century to the twelfth century. The book opens with a chapter on the Mediterranean world on the eve of the Crusades and concludes with Saladin's victory. Like other Discoveries books, this one is amply illustrated with color reproductions of artworks, maps, and black-and-white illustrations. For its size (192 pages) and price (about $12.95), this is a very good value.

The Decisive Battles of the Western World and Their Influence Upon History, J.F.C. Fuller, Eyre & Spottiswoode, London, vol 1: *From the Earliest Times to the Battle of Lepanto* (1954), vol. 2: *From the Defeat of the Spanish Armada to the Battle of Waterloo* (1955), vol. 3: *From the American Civil War to the End of the Second World War* (1956). Though I know it is incorrect to place this trilogy under the heading of "Europe," most of these decisive battles did, after all, take place in Europe, and truthfully I just haven't figured out yet how to categorize it. (Most likely I will create a separate heading for it, which it certainly deserves.) I came across this trilogy while I was reading a biography of Philip II by Sir Charles Petrie, in which Petrie referred to Fuller's account of the Battle of Lepanto as the single best one in print. By searching www. abebooks.com, I found the three-volume set available from a book dealer in the U.K., not surprisingly, and I'm happy to report that this is a stunning publishing achievement. Major-General Fuller was apparently the "pioneer of mechanization in the British Army" and is "known all over the world as the most fearless and penetrating of military critics." Fuller notes in the preface that "whether war is a necessary factor in the evolution of mankind may be disputed, but a fact which cannot be questioned is that, from the earliest records of man to the present age, war has been his dominant preoccupation. There has never been a period in human history altogether free from war, and seldom one of more than a generation which has not witnessed a major conflict: great wars flow and ebb almost as regularly as the tides." Not exactly uplifting, but he goes on to say, "yet one thing is certain, and it is that the more we study the history of war, the more we shall be able to understand war itself, and, seeing that it is now the dominant factor, until we do understand it, how can we hope to regulate human affairs?" How, indeed. France figures in all three volumes, although significantly less in the third. No matter: this set is worth your most determined efforts to obtain it. *De rigueur.*

Fifty Years of Europe: An Album, Jan Morris, Villard, 1997. At last count I discovered I'd read all of Jan Morris's books except three. Hers are among the very first books I distinctly remember as being responsible for my developing wanderlust. When I saw this volume, I thought, who better to be a reader's companion on a tour of Europe on the brink of the twenty-first century? She's traveled to all of Europe's corners more than, I believe, any other contemporary writer, and one of the most appealing aspects of this book is that she often includes multiple perspectives, relating her observations to the first time she visited a place as well as more recently. The final chapter, "Spasms of Unity: Six Attempts to Make a Whole of Europe, from the Holy Roman Empire to the European Union," is perhaps the best.

The Guns of August, Barbara Tuchman, Dell, 1962. I'm embarrassed to admit that I have neglected to include this classic work in previous editions of *The Collected Traveler.* It wasn't intentional; it's just that I have *so many* books in my house, and they are almost all shelved two deep on each shelf, so that it is impossible to see any titles at the back of the shelf without removing the books in front. Somehow, I simply forgot about *The Guns of August* when I was compiling my previous bibliographies because I couldn't see it on the shelf. It is an excellent, must-read account of the first days of World War I, and surely is, as William Shirer described it, "one of the finest books of our time." I was reminded of its relevance recently when I took it off the shelf and turned randomly to a page preceding the first chapter. The two quotations on the page were these: "The human heart is the starting point of all matters pertaining to war" (Maréchal de Saxe, *Reveries on the Art of War,* 1732) and "The terrible ifs accumulate" (Winston Churchill, *The World Crisis,* volume I, chapter XI), and it was impossible not to think of the conflicts of our own time, almost one hundred years later. *De rigueur.*

History of the Present: Essays, Sketches, and Dispatches from Europe in the 1990s, Timothy Garton Ash, Random House, 1999. The bulk of this insightful book is made up of "analytical reportages" that were originally published in *The New York Review of Books.* Ash admits that the phrase "history of the present" is not his but rather was coined by American diplomat and historian George Kennan in a review of Ash's *The Uses of Adversity* in the 1980s. The phrase is the best description for what Ash has been trying to write for twenty years, combining the crafts of historian and journalist. I really like the way Ash has written this book, with a chronology for each piece and diarylike sketches inserted throughout that are drawn from Ash's own notebooks and recollections.

Holy War: The Crusades and Their Impact on Today's World, Karen Armstrong, with a new preface, Anchor Books, 2002; originally published in hardcover in Great Britain by Macmillan, 1988, and subsequently published in revised editions in the United States by Doubleday, 1991 (hardcover), and Anchor Books, 1992 (paperback). It is of course impossible to fully comprehend the history of France without simultaneously understanding its role in the Crusades, and this newly reissued book is an excellent source. Armstrong notes that "it is important for Western people to consider these contemporary holy wars in connection with the Crusades, because they remind us of our own input, involvement and responsibilities." At the end of her preface, she adds that the Crusades showed religion at its very worst: "I was so saddened by the conflict between the three Abraham traditions that I decided to embark on the research for my book *A History of God.* [See my *Morocco* edition for details of this excellent work.] I wanted to demonstrate the strong and positive ideals and visions that Jews, Christians, and Muslims share in common. It is now over a millennium since Pope Urban II called the First Crusade in 1095, but the hatred and suspicion that this expedition unleashed still reverberates, never more so than on September 11, 2001, and during the terrible days that followed. It is tragic that our holy wars continue, but for that very reason we must strive for mutual understanding and for what in these pages I have called 'triple vision.'" *De rigueur.*

Paris 1919: Six Months That Changed the World, Margaret MacMillan, Random House, 2001. "For six months in 1919, Paris was the capital of the world. The Peace Conference was the world's most important business, the peacemakers its most powerful people. They met day after day. They argued, debated, quarreled and made it up again. They created new countries and new organizations. They dined together and went to the theater together, and between January and June, Paris was at once the world's government, its court of appeal and its parliament, the focus of its fears and hopes. Officially, the Peace Conference lasted into 1920, but those first six months are the ones that count, when the key decisions were taken and the crucial chains of events set in motion. The world has never seen anything quite like it and never will again." That, the opening paragraph of this monumental book, is enough, I think, to hook anyone at all interested in French and European history. MacMillan, the great-granddaughter of David Lloyd George, holds a Ph.D. from Oxford University and has written two previous works of nonfiction, *Women of the Raj* and *Canada and NATO*. Her book is not merely an updated work on the subject; rather, it is a landmark work of narrative history presenting an incredibly dramatic account of the days when much of the modern world as we know it was mapped out. The Paris Peace Conference is usually remembered for producing the German treaty, signed at Versailles in June 1919; but, as MacMillan notes, "it was always about much more than that. The other enemies—Bulgaria, Austria, and Hungary, now separate countries, and the Ottoman empire—had to have their treaties. New borders had to be drawn in the center of Europe and across the Middle East." Countries were created in 1919, such as Iraq and Yugoslavia, each with its own struggles that we still grapple with today. MacMillan argues here that the major players in Paris of 1919—including Woodrow Wilson, David Lloyd George, Winston Churchill, Lawrence of Arabia, and Georges Clemenceau—have been unfairly made the scapegoats for the mistakes of others who came later. She also debunks the widely accepted notion that reparations imposed on the Germans were in large part responsible for World War II. MacMillan reminds us that we know something of what it is to live at the end of a great war, because the voices of 1919 were very like the voices of the present.

The Penguin Atlas of Ancient History (1967), *Medieval History* (1968), *Modern History—to 1815* (1973), and *Recent History—Europe Since 1815* (1982), Colin McEvedy, Penguin Books. This is a brilliant idea: a chronological sequence of maps that illustrate political and military developments, which in turn illustrate history via geography. Each individual volume is remarkably fascinating, and the four volumes as a whole present an enlightening read. Maps appear on the right-hand pages while one page of explanatory text accompanies them on the left-hand pages. ~Also in the same series but compiled by different authors is *The Penguin Atlas of Diasporas* (Gerard Chaliand and Jean-Pierre Rageau, 1995). This book is equally as fascinating—perhaps more so, as I've not seen another volume like this—and it highlights Jewish, Armenian, Gypsy, Black, Chinese, Indian, Irish, Greek, Lebanese, Palestinian, Vietnamese, and Korean migrations. All of these are *de rigueur* for history novices and mavens alike.

The Road to Verdun: World War I's Most Momentous Battle and the Folly of Nationalism, Ian Ousby, Doubleday, 2002. The attack on Verdun on February 21, 1916, was, according to Ousby, the most enormous push "yet gathered in a war that had already proved a deadlock of concentrated force." This is a serious tome, not for the casual reader—and not without some criticisms, according to reviews—but most worthy nonetheless.

A Soldier's Story, Omar N. Bradley, Modern Library War Series, 1999. About five years ago the Modern Library introduced this war series with Caleb Carr as the series editor. In his overall introduction to the series, Carr makes several valid points about military history. He reminds us of the general attitude in this country during the 1960s and early 1970s, when admitting to an interest in human conflict was most unpopular. But he counterargues that military-history enthusiasts are often among the most well-read people we'll ever meet and that they are also usually quite knowledgeable in discussions of political and social history. "The reason for this," he writes, "is simple: the history of war represents fully half the tale of mankind's social interactions, and one cannot understand war without understanding its political and social underpinnings. (Conversely, one cannot understand political history or cultural development without understanding war) . . . military history is neither an obscure nor a peculiar subject, but one critical to any understanding of the development of human civilization. That warfare itself is violent is true and unfortunate; that it has been a central method through which every nation in the world has established and maintained its independence, however, makes it a critical field of study." Bradley's classic is not devoted exclusively to the Second World War in France (Sicily, Tunisia, England, and Germany are also covered) but the D-day assault and the liberation of Paris are dealt with at length.

France and the French

The Algeria Hotel: France, Memory, and the Second World War, Adam Nossiter, Houghton Mifflin, 2001. Though obviously an important book in terms of the history of all of France, Nossiter's impressive reportage is also significant to the Southwest as the first of the three chapters in the book is entitled "Bordeaux, Papon, and the Exigencies of Memory." Bordeaux, of course, as Adam Gopnick noted in one of his many wonderful missives for *The New Yorker,* is the city "where France goes to give up. It was where the French government retreated from Paris under fire from the Prussians in 1870, and again from the kaiser's armies in 1914, and where, in June 1940, the French government fled in the face of the German advance and soon afterward met not just the fact of defeat but the utter depth of France's demoralization." And, as Nossiter notes in this first chapter, "Bordeaux, the city without its own Resistance, went on to name more of its streets after Resistance heroes than any town of its size in France." Nossiter also relates that he walked into one of my most favorite chocolate shops in the world, Cadiot-Badie, which had been located in the allées de Tourny since the 1840s, to inquire about the building next door, at number 28, which had been owned by a M. Naquet, reputedly the wealthiest Jew in Bordeaux before the Second World War. Nossiter showed the proprietor of Cadiot-Badie a sheet of paper imprinted with Etat Français, Service des Questions Juives. I was dismayed to read that, "his face displayed mild consternation. He glanced around to see if anybody else was in his store. Then he saw that the paper had nothing to do with him. 'This Papon thing it's all coming too late, much too late,' he said. 'There are more important things to worry about.' There was a thin smile. 'I mean, not more important, but more . . .' He seemed relieved when I turned to go." The allées bears the name of the eighteenth-century governor who transformed Bordeaux into the attractive city it is today, and Stendhal apparently wrote of the pretty thoroughfare, "I don't know of a more beautiful place in France." It was no accident, Nossiter writes, that M. Naquet, who owned twelve buildings in Bordeaux, put some of his considerable fortune into a private house on the allées. "He was there because of everything the street symbolized in the life of his city. The story of M. Naquet was henceforth intimately entwined with that of the allées—more so than, say, an ordinary property owner's story would have been." I found this book impossible to put down, and was honestly disgusted by some of the people Nossiter spoke with, especially two elderly residents who were both of wine families: "We will never accept that a president drags us through the mud, saying that we were guilty of something. I won't accept that the French are accused of being coadministrators of the Final Solution! It's monstrous." "We have the feeling of not being heard. This is destroying the unity of our country. It's horrible. It makes me want to vomit." Nossiter notes, "Something was awry in perceptions of the war. They were not the Occupation's guilty ones, but its victims. How could this have been forgotten? It came back to them in a memory even more haunting than hunger and fear, banal concerns that affected all Frenchmen." It gets worse—these two continued ranting to Nossiter, and he writes, "She moved on to lament over the execution of Louis XVI. Confounded, I struggled to be sympathetic. This wasn't a joke. I mumbled something about the continuities of French history . . . 'I'll never understand how a people can cut off the head of its sovereign.'" To digress once again to Adam Gopnick's piece in *The New Yorker* ("Papon's Paper Trail"), which I so wanted to include in my *Paris* edition but Gopnick had already included it in his own, highly recommded book, *Paris to the Moon* (Random House, 2000, hardcover; Vintage, 2001, paperback), he notes that the jury at Papon's trial in the Palais de Justice had "used their imaginations to make some necessary retrospective law, and they had done it well. By saying that Papon didn't know where the trains were going, and also saying that he was guilty of crimes against humanity, they were making the right and courageous point. To deliver a child to the secret police is as large a crime against humanity as you ever need to find, no matter where you think he is going or what kind of car he is going to travel in. The men with stamps and filing cabinets now couldn't plead procedure any more than soldiers could plead orders; the *appareil* of the state would have to understand that their fiches represented people, whether they were Jews or Algerian demonstrators or refugees yet to come. The parallel paper universe now had a window." Read Nossiter's book. It's *de rigueur*.

Citizens: A Chronicle of the French Revolution, Simon Schama, Vintage Books, 1990. I don't believe there is a better account of one of the major turning points in European history than *Citizens*. It's not what I would call light reading, although it is absorbing, and it's not lightweight—at 948 pages it positively should not be packed in your bag—but if you are seriously interested in a complete, single-volume edition on the Revolution, this is it. Black-and-white illustrations, drawings, and photos throughout.

The Collapse of the Third Republic: An Inquiry into the Fall of France in 1940, William Shirer, Simon and Schuster, 1969. I wasn't surprised to find that Shirer (*The Rise and Fall of the Third Reich*) had written this book, only that I didn't know he had until about five years ago. It is, as you might expect, as thoroughly researched and revealing as *Rise and Fall,* and he carefully illustrates, point by point, how the fall of France was an absolute debacle. Until reading this I hadn't realized the extent of the utter chaos—the complete lack of communication among high government officials and between them and the public—that followed the news that the Germans were en route to Paris. As French historian Marc Bloch observes, "It was the most terrible collapse in all the long story of our national life." No photos but good maps.

Creating French Culture: Treasures from the Bibliothèque Nationale de France, introduction by Emmanuel Le Roy Ladurie, edited by Marie-Hélène Tesnière and Prosser Gifford, Yale University Press, in association with the Library of Congress, Washington, and the Bibliothèque Nationale de France, Paris, 1995. This beautiful volume, which accompanied an exhibit of the same name, is nothing less than a history of France as told through its documents, manuscripts, books, orchestra scores, photographs, prints, drawings, maps, medals, and coins. The creators of the exhibit developed a theme for this project, which is to explore the relationship between culture and power in France, and the project's scope covers twelve centuries, from the time of Charlemagne to the present. This makes for a gigantic tome (the book runs to 478 pages), but it is extraordinary. Some highlights include the "Letter of Suleyman the Magnificent to Francis I, King of France"; a drawing of Catherine de Medici as a widow; a first edition of *The New Justine, or The Misfortunes of Virtue,* by the marquis de Sade; the constitution of the Thirteen United States of America (French-language edition, printed at the behest of Benjamin Franklin); an illustration of devices used to lift the two large stones of the pediment over the main entrance of the Louvre; a map of the battle of Austerlitz; the handwritten "*J'accuse*" letter written by Emile Zola in defense of Captain Alfred Dreyfus, which was printed on the front page of *L'Aurore* on January 13, 1898; and five issues of *Resistance: Official Bulletin of the National Committee for Public Safety,* published between December 1940 and March 25, 1941. I love this book—it's a masterpiece, and one could get lost in it for hours. Also included are a chronology of the history of France and good color maps.

Culture Shock! France: A Guide to the Customs and Etiquette, Sally Adamson Taylor, Graphic Arts, Portland, Oregon, 1990. Each Culture Shock! edition is authored by a different writer, and each is eminently enlightening. This edition covers such topics as speaking and thinking in French, political parties, French film, the French attitude toward pets, the "no" syndrome, why things close for lunch, do's and dont's in a restaurant, visas and work permits, queuing, being a guest in a French home, money and banking, and office and business relationships. The Culture Quiz at the end of the book is particularly helpful. Although some of the information is directed at people who plan to be in France for an extended stay, this is a really useful, basic guide that I consider *de rigueur* reading even for a short visit.

Fragile Glory: A Portrait of France and the French, Richard Bernstein, Alfred A. Knopf, 1990. To my mind, *Fragile Glory* is the best overall book about France since Braudel's *The Identity of France* (below). *Fragile Glory,* too, is inexplicably out of print, and I do not know if it was ever published in paperback, but I do see the hardcover frequently in used-book stores. Bernstein was the Paris correspondent for *The New York Times* from 1984 to 1987, and his book explores Paris and the concept of *le tout Paris,* naming French children, his unique "R5 complex," the myth of the anti-American, immigrants, French aristocrats, politics and parties, Jean-Marie Le Pen, *les affaires,* and the French struggle with their past. By the final chapter Bernstein has laid the foundation for two major but sometimes contradictory conclusions: that France is still a nation greater than the sum of its parts, but that the French people are becoming more like everyone else, losing many qualities that made them *different.* Another candidate for the *de rigueur* list.

France on the Brink: A Great Civilization Faces the New Century, Jonathan Fenby, Arcade, 1999. As excellent as the other titles recommended here are, an updated book on France was in order, and we now have Fenby's volume to provide us with thoughtful fodder for the early twenty-first century. Journalist Fenby—who has written for *The Economist, The Christian Science Monitor,* and *The Times* of London and has been editor of the *South China Morning Post*—is married to a Frenchwoman and was named a *chevalier* of the French Order of Merit in 1990. He's been reporting on France for over thirty years, and in this work he presents a full array of the country's ills and contradictions, some of which are familiar (the Resistance was smaller than we like to think;

high unemployment; immigration; government corruption) but nonetheless remain for us to reconcile. Readers who haven't kept up with the France of today may be alarmed to discover that some classic French icons—berets, baguettes, accordions, cafés, foie gras—are fading. In his review of the book for *The New York Times*, European cultural correspondent Alan Riding wrote that "the entire book serves as a valuable introduction to contemporary France." I would add that it is also *de rigueur* reading.

French or Foe?: Getting the Most Out of Visiting, Living and Working in France, Polly Platt, Culture Crossings Ltd./Distribooks, Inc., Skokie, Ill., 1996; first published in 1994 by Culture Crossings, Ltd., London. Platt's on-the-mark book is without doubt the best of its kind, and I consider it *de rigueur* for anyone planning to live, work, or study in France and anyone who really, really wants to understand the ways of the French. Platt's own company—Culture Crossings—which she incorporated in 1986, provides training seminars and workshops for corporate managers and executives and their spouses transferred to foreign countries. There is no other book as comprehensive as hers, covering such topics as perfecting the *mine d'enterrement* (funereal expression) and de-smiling; French time; the customer is automatically wrong; what *non* really means; what to expect at a dinner party; the French family; *se débrouiller* and le Système D; the logic of French management; and so on. In addition to explanations, Platt offers her own personal tips, such as the Ten Magic Words (*Excusez-moi de vous déranger, Monsieur, mai j'ai un probleme*) and Persistent Personal Operating. Platt presents real people and situations in a clear and witty way. Irresistibly indispensable.

French Toast: An American in Paris Celebrates the Maddening Mysteries of the French, Harriet Welty Rochefort, St. Martin's Press, 1999. A little bit different than but equally as revealing as Polly Platt's books, this is an essential read. Though Rochefort has lived in Paris since 1971, and there a few quirks that are unique to that capital city, the topics she addresses here apply to nearly every corner of France. Rochefort is so endearing because she has a great sense of humor and humility, and she admits that she has made so many of the faux pas outlined here. Her mother-in-law hails from the Périgord, and throughout the book there are boxed interviews with Philippe, her husband (presumably also from the Southwest), who provides some candid insights. One that even casual visitors to France might benefit from is that there is not a tradition of customer service in France, especially in the area of computers. A friend of Rochefort's, who is a French professor at Amherst and a bona fide Francophile, recounted after his last trip to France: "The French have still not developed a culture of help for the consumer. We may complain in this country that service is going down the tubes, but they haven't even invented it yet, except in cheese shops and restaurants. The French pay a fortune for electronics, but when they break, the seller gives one of those Gallic shrugs that's a cross between 'It's not my problem' and 'A competent person wouldn't have done this.'" Another is that the French have a set of codes for polite behavior that is extremely complicated. "I know now, for example, that I have made many gaffes by being too candid. In France, for instance, there is no intrinsic merit in being frank and to the point." *De rigueur* for bona fide, and wannabe, Francophiles.

The Identity of France, Fernand Braudel, translated by Sian Reynolds; vol. 1: *History and Environment,* William Collins and Sons, London, 1988; vol. 2: *People and Production,* HarperCollins, 1988. This monumental work is phenomenal in its scope and originality. Braudel, who passed away in 1985, has been referred to as the "greatest of Europe's historians" and believed strongly in the necessity of world history. His genius was in his ability to link people and events across all time periods—in a single sentence. "Economic geography" was one phrase he came up with just before his death to describe his approach to history. And yet even he acknowledged that this was not quite right. In seeking to define the identity of France, he departs completely from any sort of chronological pattern. This unprecedented work is inexplicably out of print but is worth all efforts to track it down.

Mission to Civilize: The French Way, Mort Rosenblum, Doubleday, 1988. When Rosenblum wrote this book, he was senior foreign correspondent for the Associated Press in Paris. (I believe he is now a special correspondent for the AP and has also written three other wonderful books, *The Secret Life of the Seine, Olives,* and *A Goose in Toulouse.*) His career as a journalist took him to North and West Africa, the South Pacific, Asia, the southeastern United States, the Caribbean, the Middle East, Canada—all the former and present DOM-TOMs (*départements d'outre-mer* and *territoires d'outre-mer*). Yes, this book is about the French and France, but more specifically it is about the importance of *la mission civilisatrice* (read: colonization) to the French. Rosenblum explains the seemingly contradictory French foreign policy; the difference between a *mauvaise foi* and *mauvais caractère;* the *Rainbow Warrior bavure* (*bavure* being a hitch or foul-up, notably by officials or police, which is so common that a smooth operation is referred to as *sans bavure*); *beurs* and *beaufs;* the struggles in Algeria and Vietnam and the atrocities committed in both; and the presence of *"faites mon jour"* (make my day), *hypermarché,* (supermarket), and *le fast food* in the language. This book is by turns engaging, funny, and revealing, and though it's out of print, there are still copies out there. *De rigueur.*

Portraits of France, Robert Daley, Little, Brown & Co., 1991. As a naïve *étudiante* in 1979, I did not realize why the Rue Lauriston, where Hollins Abroad Paris had its school for thirty-plus years, was referred to as *sinistre* until I read

Daley's chapter "The Gestapo of the Rue Lauriston," and learned that 93 rue Lauriston was the site of an infamous den of torture and inquisition during World War II—not by the Nazis but by a gang of French convicts organized by Pierre Bonny and Henri Lafont. (Happily, though I have nothing but fond memories of my classes at 16, Hollins has since moved its school out of the sixteenth arrondissement altogether.) Daley has put together a miniature tour of French history and culture in this collection of twenty essays. The entry on drinking the 1806 Château Lafite in Les-Baux-de-Provence is one of the best passages about a wine experience I've ever read. While his portraits take readers to all corners of *l'hexagone*, even dedicated students of France may find some surprises here, as Daley has preferred to find his stories in places where most readers haven't looked before. There are, therefore, no sketches of the most typical French icons.

Realms of Memory: The Construction of the French Past, Pierre Nora, English-language edition edited by Lawrence D. Kritzman, translated by Arthur Goldhammer, Columbia University Press; vol. 1: *Conflicts and Divisions* (1996); vol. 2: *Traditions* (1997); vol. 3: *Symbols* (1998). Originally published in France in seven volumes as *Les lieux de mémoire* (Memory Places), this stunning collection is easily at the top of my *de rigueur* reading list. I would go so far as to say that if you read only these three volumes, you will have little need to read much else, and if you fancy yourself a knowledgeable Francophile and *haven't* read these, you'd best make a trip to the library or bookstore. This series is nothing short of a singular publishing event, hailed by *The Times Literary Supplement* in London as "a magisterial attempt to define what it is to be French." Not for the casual observer, but for anyone seeking a deep understanding and appreciation of France and the French, this is a valuable trio of books.

The Road from the Past: Traveling History in France, Ina Caro, Nan A. Talese (an imprint of Doubleday), 1994. What a grand and sensible plan Ina Caro presents in her marvelous book: to travel through France in a "time machine" (a car), from Provence to Paris, chronologically, and experience numerous centuries of French history in one trip. I envy her and her husband, Robert Caro (the award-winning biographer of Robert Moses and Lyndon Johnson), for making such an unforgettable journey. I always attempt to plan my visits chronologically no matter *where* I'm going, so I am especially partial to Caro's method. Her route in this book takes travelers through Provence, Languedoc, the Dordogne, and the Loire Valley and ends in the Île-de-France. Not only do we progress chronologically, but the sites she has selected best represent a particular age and are also the most beautiful examples within each historical period. Her chapter on Carcassone is among the best I've ever read. After seeing each historical period separately, viewing all the periods together in Paris is "an incomparable experience," as she concludes in her introduction. Caro's approach presents a unique way of looking at France, at history, and at travel.

Savoir Flair!, Polly Platt, Culture Crossings Ltd., London, 2000; distributed in the U.S. by Distribooks, Skokie, Illinois. If you're as big a fan of *French or Foe?* as I am, you will run out *immediatement* to find Platt's second installment of French-American relations. It's more like a natural continuation of her first book, but it's different: 211 *savoir-flair* tips are presented and expanded upon, and every one is worth reading and memorizing. Among the most interesting observations in the book is a chart of Franco-American cultural differences—it appears on page ten, and don't miss it. Platt wisely says of it that you don't have to be an anthropologist to see that the people in these cultures are different, which is why foreigners who don't know much about the French, and have a cultural need to simplify, fall back on tired stereotypes, such as: "The French are quarrelsome eggheads who are obsessed with sex and don't tell the truth." Platt says, "Quarrelsome? Instead of avoiding their differences, French people confront them, discussing, arguing, honing their critical skills. Eggheads? Intellectuals are admired; being a philosopher is a profession. Sex-obsessed?

They call it love, and male-female encounters are the ambrosia of their daily life." Another is "Wimps at war in 1940." Platt says, "They weren't. Far from it. This is the English version of World War II. Read a thin book which is the best existing WWII account from the French front, *The Strange Defeat* by the eminent French medievalist and executed (Jewish) Resistance leader, Marc Bloch. Read about the bravery of the French military in Bosnia and Vietnam, not to mention Napoleon's armies." I, for one, am going to track down *The Strange Defeat* as soon as I finish this manuscript. There are so many significant tips; I especially like tip No. 38: "You can bluff with certain words" (some expressions that sound awfully French and give the impression of possessing a full vocabulary: *Ça veux dire quoi, ça?* (That means what?), *Ça rime avec quoi?* (That rhymes with what?), and *C'est à dire . . .* (That is to say . . .). Further, if you want to agree in a very French way, then you say, "*C'est exact*" or "*Tout à fait*" (absolutely) or "*C'est clair*" (that's clear), "which doesn't mean necessarily that you agree, but that you heard and understood." These all are similar to three expressions that a French friend of Platt's claims a French person can cross the United States with and be congratulated on his or her perfect English: "If you look at it that way," "You've got a point there," and "Is that so?" I can run on endlessly about this book, as well as Platt's earlier bible. Extremely *de rigueur*.

Vichy France: Old Guard and New Order, 1940–1944, Robert O. Paxton, Alfred A. Knopf, 1972. It doesn't take long to discover that, among the number of books about Vichy, the definitive volume is Paxton's. If you're only going to read one, read this. An internationally recognized authority on this subject, Paxton was an expert witness at the trial of Maurice Papon in 1997 (see his editorial "Vichy on Trial," *The New York Times,* October 16, 1997). Understanding France during World War II is complicated at best but is essential for understanding France at all today. Paxton documents the inner workings of the Vichy government, the politics between Philippe Pétain, Pierre Laval, and François Darlan, and the surprisingly slow growth of the Resistance. The book's thesis that the Vichy government enjoyed mass support, at least initially, apparently came as somewhat of a shock upon its publication in 1972. As Paxton writes, "It is tempting to identify with Resistance and to say, 'That is what I would have done.' Alas, we are far more likely to act, in parallel situations, like the Vichy majority . . . The deeds of occupier and occupied alike suggest that there come cruel times when to save a nation's deepest values, one must disobey the state. France after 1940 was one of those times." Paxton also noted that "no one who lived through the French debacle of May–June 1940 ever quite got over the shock. For Frenchmen, confident of a special role in the world, the six weeks' defeat by German armies was a shattering trauma."

Office de Tourisme de Bordeaux
B O R D E A U X   T O U R I S M E

GRAND THEATRE
Samedi 25 Mai 2002 à 11h00
R.V.place de la comédie
Gratuit 0,00E (0,00F)

Placement libre

Réf 20390

036087

Bordeaux and Aquitaine

"Aquitaine is the Land of Waters . . . the traveller may look at a town or village, large or small, dominated by a cathedral of the Middle Ages or by a modern factory. Almost always it occupies the ground and bears the name it has owned for as long as written history runs. Looking again, the traveller will observe that its reason for being is a river or a spring."

—Freda White, Ways of Aquitaine

"Bordeaux, it is certain, is the most notable city of the eighteenth century, next to Leningrad. The tourist, escaping from the traffic, may take one of the side streets off the centre, and suddenly find himself in silence, between plain dignified houses, in which he can imagine families of unostentatious, immensely proud people who have traded in wine for a thousand years."

—Freda White, Ways of Aquitaine

Putting the *eaux* Back in Bordeaux

BY PIERRE VEILLETET

∾

Today Bordeaux is the fifth largest city in France, and yet as *Gourmet* writer Doone Beal noted in a 1988 profile, the city "must be among the least known in France: not only to foreigners but also to the French themselves." While I do think this is less true today, I don't often hear North Americans talking about Bordeaux. Many are just back from Paris, or Provence, or possibly Normandy or Burgundy, but rarely Bordeaux, which may be perceived as a plus but is also one of the reasons I wanted to compile this book: I think Bordeaux is a wonderful, beautiful, gently paced but ambitious city, as this contemporary piece attests. As Doone Beal noted in her 1988 profile, "With its uniformly elegant eighteenth- and nineteenth-century buildings, its broad tree-lined streets, and its handsome vistas (look which way you will, there is bound to be some plinth or edifice of flamboyant distinction topped by a statue), Bordeaux is a tonic of visual pleasure." For many years Bordeaux's historic waterfront, which is truly a stunning architectural achievement, was marred by abandoned warehouses that blocked the view of the Garonne River. By the time you read this, much of the largest urban renewal project in decades will have been completed, effectively giving the Garonne back to the city.

PIERRE VEILLETET, a native of Bordeaux, is an author and newspaper editor who writes frequently for the highly regarded *FRANCE Magazine*, where this piece originally appeared.

Anywhere you go in Bordeaux these days, you're likely to come across an excavation site. From the foundations of the old city, workers are exhuming amphora shards, coins dating back to the musketeers, even a dainty slipper—a petite size five—dropped perhaps by a young lady returning home from some glamorous ball. The other day an entire skeleton was found, well preserved and looking not a day over eight hundred. Of course, that's not much when you recall that Bordeaux itself is more than two thousand years old.

The sky of the Gironde is now bristling with cranes and strange billboards offering multiple-choice-style "tests" asking passersby to identify the proper location of a monument. (Carthage? New York? St. Petersburg? Las Vegas? Athens?) The correct answer, as you may well have guessed, is always Bordeaux. Could this apparent immodesty in fact betray an identity crisis? When a city scrutinizes its depths like the entrails of a sacrificed beast, when it compulsively compares itself to other places, doesn't that mean that it no longer has a very clear grasp of what it is or what it wants to become?

That's the case for Bordeaux, at least, which is entering the twenty-first century clad in a hardhat. Construction work is slated to last a decade and will alter the face of a city that has barely changed in a hundred years, if not more. Indeed, the past here is so present, so vivid, that the task of envisioning the future has always been put off until later.

The *bordelais* are keenly aware that Burdigala was already a well-established town when Paris was still a cesspool. It was first populated by a Celtic tribe, the Bituriges Vivisci; they, followed by the Ligurians and the Iberians, settled on a broad bend on the Garonne River three centuries before the birth of Jesus Christ. When the town fell to the Romans in the first century B.C., their descendants willingly collaborated with the occupiers, rapidly bringing prosperity to Burdigala and its vineyards. That idyll ended in A.D. 276, when barbarian tribes from the Rhine pillaged the "magnificent" Roman city. The Pyrenees have never been a very effective roadblock, and the early *bordelais* found themselves on an invasion route—after the Visigoths from the North, they were conquered by the Saracens and then the Normans.

In the mid-twelfth century the marriage of Eleanor of Aquitaine and Henry Plantagenet brought the province under England's dominion, assuring its fortune for three hundred years. Gascon and English were the languages of Bordeaux during this second golden age, when wine exports peaked. The *bordelais* reluctantly returned to the bosom of France in 1453, but they preferred their occupiers—which explains their longstanding, sometimes affected predilection for everything English. Bordeaux reached its third apogee during the eighteenth century, when trade with the West Indies made it the kingdom's leading port. Under the great intendants—powerful provincial administrators appointed by the king—the city was rebuilt to befit its new status.

Thus it could be said that Bordeaux is a more-than-two-thousand-year-old town built in sixty years—from 1730 to the French Revolution. Or less paradoxically, that following a great period of transformation, it showed the world the face with which it would henceforth identify. So strongly do people identify with this image that they consider it an unsurpassable achievement. They reproduce it—even pastiche it—ad nauseam. This compulsion, known as the *cas architectural bordelais,* refers to the creation of a style that would prevail over and even squelch any further development. By the mid-nineteenth century Bordeaux reached a fork in the road: to industrialize or not to industrialize. A city of merchants, it was either unable or unwilling to go the industrial route. Little by little it began to assume an air of faded splendor peculiar to cities such as Venice that gradually sink into genteel decadence, lounging around eating bonbons. Nevertheless, it had three more opportunities to call itself a capital, or in common parlance, the "capital of disaster." In 1871, 1914, and 1940—that is, at the beginning of three great wars—the government fled Paris in disarray to take refuge in Bordeaux. It was from there, on June 17, 1940, that General de Gaulle flew to London to launch his famous appeal to the free French.

Even a brief summary such as this would not be complete without noting three historical constants that have forged the local mentality—what is popularly referred to as *l'esprit de Bordeaux*. The first is that this bend in the Garonne has served as a port for thousands of years. It flourished because so many European migration routes intersected at this point: Celts, Vandals, and Visigoths; Marrano Jews from Spain and Portugal; immigrants from Ireland, Scotland, and Germany; all formed successive dynasties of wine traders known locally as *chartrons* or the "aristocracy of the cork." Rather than reject foreigners, Bordeaux has always been enriched by their contributions. By the same token, it hardly ever attempts to demolish its past; it simply builds on top of it, creating new layers.

The second and equally crucial constant is that all the city has ever really asked for over the years is to be left alone so that it could attend to business. Indeed, "the soul of Bordeaux is commerce," declared former mayor Lodi-Martin Duffour-Dubergier. The *bordelais* have always realized they were better off with a good contract than a bad dispute. They never had any qualms about collaborating with whoever seized control of the area, as long as they could be sure of a good business climate. The city's cosmopolitanism and religious tolerance are based on the same principle: individual liberties are the best guarantees of free trade.

Their mentality, in other words, is the antithesis of dogmatism. During the French Revolution the moderate Bordeaux-based Girondins insisted that no ideology could justify oppression or terror—and they paid for it with their heads. Many had been attorneys. Even today Bordeaux claims the second-largest number of lawyers in France—and still offers the same resistance to Parisian certainties.

Doubt is also a common characteristic of the people here. Not that the locals are especially skeptical—they simply like to form their own opinions, weighing the pros and cons and steering clear of extremes. Because of the traditional Gascon indifference to religion, for example, Calvinism *à la bordelaise* never exhibited the fanaticism for which it is known elsewhere. Indeed, from their Roman ancestors the *bordelais* inherited ideas about the law and freedom. From the English came a sense of practicality and a taste for independence. In 1274 Bordeaux invoked "human rights" in extraordinarily prescient terms: "We submit," declared its citizens, "that all men and all lands are inherently free and that any kind of servitude runs counter to common law."

Montaigne, the half-Jewish mayor of Bordeaux; Montesquieu, the aristocratic head of the parliament; and Mauriac, the Nobel laureate for literature—our illustrious "three M's"—are leading exemplars of this attitude. It's surely no coincidence that all three were well-to-do landholders and remarkably skilled businessmen. Montesquieu's wine and his *Esprit des lois* were both aimed at the same British market.

Last (and probably most obvious), from day one, Bordeaux has been nurtured by the grapevine. There's every reason to assume that will be the case until the end of the world—the only time we won't be able to sell the previous year's vintage. The wine and the town share the same name and are intrinsically intertwined. The former is the lifeblood of the latter. Occasionally we suffer from a bout of low blood pressure, but a couple of sunny summers and everything's back to normal.

"Bordeaux and wine" is a topic so vast that it can hardly be summed up in a hundred pages, let alone in a few words. Let's just say that the legacy that has been handed down from one century to the next—from Roman villas to Médoc châteaus, from monks to *chartrons,* from the Gallo-Roman poet Ausonius to Robert Parker—owes everything to providence, alchemy, tradition, snobbism, speculation, and yes, the nature of the soil as well as oenological advances. In other words, to people. Today there are twelve thousand vintners in the Gironde, and wine production is a culture in every sense of the term. Some sociologists disapprovingly refer to it as a monoculture. But in fact that's a misconception: today's economy has diversified, with more people employed by the aeronautics industry than by the wine sector.

Historically, though, wine has always been the salvation of the Bordeaux economy. Without it, the town would have had to roll up its sleeves instead of waiting for the grapes to ripen. Who knows if it might have become as industrious as Lille or as conscientious as Lyons? Growers were recently a bit shocked to discover that—surprise!—Bordeaux is no longer the only wine in the world. But why worry? Everyone knows it's still the best, right?

Bordeaux's tendency to weigh all the pros and cons of every issue may be to the city's credit, but it has a downside: procrastination. Infinite waffling. Endless stalling by committees. A passion for quibbling. Circles and networks that cancel each other out. Stendhal once observed that Bordeaux has more clubs than Geneva. France's first Masonic lodge, "Anglaise 204," was founded here.

Indeed, the city produces more orators, intellectuals, and artists than captains of industry. As for its much celebrated architectural splendors, Victor Hugo once famously declared: "Take Antwerp, add Versailles and you get Bordeaux." And Stendhal observed: "Bordeaux is inarguably the most beautiful city in France." So why tamper with a good thing? Hasn't wine taught us about patience? It took an order from Napoleon I before the city built its first bridge. Until then people crossed the river by *gabarre,* the gondola of the period. Before World War II members of the city government visited Antwerp to study the possibility of building a tunnel under the river. They're still discussing it.

Jacques Chaban-Delmas, a French Resistance general, friend

of Eisenhower, and prime minister under Georges Pompidou, was elected mayor of Bordeaux after the Liberation of France. "When the last tram stopped running in 1958," he once confided to me, "I felt like I'd brought an end to the nineteenth century!" Chaban was forced to practice emergency medicine. Practically the entire infrastructure of the city had to be updated: sewage, lighting, roads . . . There was so much to do that by the time he finished up his last term, some major projects had barely gotten started, including the refurbishment of the waterfront. Richelieu's "great port where one saw more than a thousand sails" hadn't existed for ages. Instead, it had become a derelict strip of land cluttered by warehouses.

Chaban's successor was Alain Juppé, another former prime minister. Juppé's big challenge since assuming office has been to bring a city that was three-quarters eighteenth century and one-quarter twentieth century into the twenty-first. Which takes us back to the steam shovels and to the hardhats whose faint light illuminates a little identity crisis: what's the best way to join one's century? Should there be a new look, and if so, what? The new mayor had a lucky accident of history working in his favor: Bordeaux was unscathed by industrial development. Its architectural heritage—the city boasts one of Europe's most extensive concentrations of registered buildings—remained intact and represented a relatively untapped source of tourism. Yet in some ways it actually proved to be a handicap: it's easier to tear up a horrible town like Bilbao and build a new Guggenheim and other spectacular architectural showpieces with no particular connection between them when the people themselves are yearning for a change in decor.

But what do you do when order and beauty have reigned for centuries? How do you change? What can you touch? With one or two exceptions (which, to tell the truth, were unnecessarily costly or overblown), Juppé left the city's cultural institutions alone. The

Orchestre National Bordeaux-Aquitaine conducted by Hans Graf, the Austrian maestro often sought out by film director John Huston, retained its prominence, as did the Théâtre National du Port-de-la-Lune. The pioneering Centre d'Arts Plastiques Contemporains, the first French institution to exhibit such modern artists as Frank Stella, Richard Serra, and Keith Haring, is no doubt less flamboyant than it was during the Chaban era, but it still draws more visitors than any other site in Bordeaux. On the other hand, the mayor's office revived the Fête Populaire du Vin, bringing the vineyard back into the city. Aware of its vulnerability in a global market, the wine industry certainly didn't mind.

But most notably, Juppé directly attacked Bordeaux's most recurrent problem: infrastructure and public transportation. Rather than draw the work out over a long period of time, the mayor opted for radical surgery: an incision ten miles long that turned the city upside-down. Traffic has become a nightmare. But while the local paper regularly reports protests and isolated bankruptcies, most people seem to be taking the inconvenience in stride. Sure they complain, but they admit that the construction is for a good reason— the city had fallen so far behind.

The mayor's efforts to renovate and develop the city's waterfront have been especially welcome. Indeed, what was not so long ago a forbidding no-man's-land separating the town from the river has been reclaimed and is being transformed into a user-friendly space featuring new tram lines, parks, a bike path, and a pedestrian walkway. Run-down warehouses littering the waterfront have been removed or converted into sleek convention centers, exhibition halls—even a popular disco. The neighborhood itself is unique in Europe. Picture graceful Louis XV stone facades adorned with lacy wrought iron extending for more than two and a half miles along the 1,600-foot-wide Garonne, the Old Man River of Southwestern France. Sublime, to be sure, but a little empty, a little cold . . .

Parisian landscape architect Michel Corajoud initially ran up against proponents of the status quo ("don't touch a thing") when he suggested planting trees to provide shade, rehumanize the place, and soften the light. His vision—not without poetry—has now won over most of the population.

People are less cautious when it comes to the swath of underdeveloped land on the other side of the river. Apart from the creation of an excellent contemporary botanical garden, everything has been more or less given over to the private sector. And what has been built so far is hardly brilliant.

But the most important aspect of these projects has yet to be resolved. After laborious negotiations, an agreement was finally hammered out to erect a drawbridge downstream from the town that would allow cruise ships to get by, but everyone knows that what Bordeaux really needs is another bridge. People get all worked up about this, though, because it would spell certain death for the centuries-old port and thereby alter the city's identity. Remember, it took Napoleon to impose the first span. One of these days Juppé will have to reopen the debate. It's safe to say that when that happens, city council meetings will be standing room only.

Grape Expectations

BY GENE BOURG

As enjoyable as Bordeaux is, visiting the surrounding wine country is essential to fully comprehending this corner of Aquitaine. After all, Bordeaux is known as the world capital of wine, and according to statistics from the Bordeaux Tourist Office, there are fifty-seven appellations in the region and 284,320 acres of vines; one out of every six jobs in the Gironde is devoted to the industry (12,000 growers, 400 dealers, and 130 brokers). There are six families of appellations in Bordeaux: Bordeaux and Bordeaux Supérieur; Côtes de Bordeaux; Saint Emilion, Pomerol, and Fronsac; Médoc and Graves; Golden Sweet Whites; and Elegant Dry Whites. The United States is the third largest importer, after Germany and the United Kingdom, of Bordeaux wines. Even if you don't desire to partake of the fruit of the vine, driving by the vineyards and through the small towns and villages is beautiful, at any time of year, and there are some renowned places to eat and sleep within each appellation.

It was in this article that I learned of Dewey Markham Jr., an American living in Bordeaux who arranges private tours of the châteaus (see entry under his name in *Practical Information*). As the article was written in 1998, I contacted Dewey and inquired if he still arranges tours for visitors and happily found that he does. My two cents on visiting wine estates anywhere in wine-growing world: unless you are a fanatic, it's really not necessary to spend time at more than three or four. The basics of winemaking, aside from all of today's advanced technology and fancy machinery, are essentially the same as they've always been. True, one château may prefer stainless-steel vats, while another employs barrels; one may have a fabulous art collection (a perfectly good reason to select one château over another!), while another displays vintage winemaking equipment rather like a museum. A few are interesting, but after a succession of estates, the distinctive features of the various châteaus begin to blur. My advice is to select two or three, possibly four, that you'd really like to visit and skip the others. Unfortunately, some of the best-known Bordeaux estates are not open to the general public, so unless you have the right contacts or have arranged for a private tour, there may be some châteaus you will not have the opportunity to see.

I have been asked on occasion to single out a winery or wine village that I particularly recommend. This is nearly impossible, of course, as serious wine collectors and mavens already know exactly where they want to go. Rather than select a winery, I will make special mention of St.-Émilion, a leisurely forty-five-minute drive from Bordeaux. To quote a favorite wine and food writer of mine, Jacqueline Friedrich (author of *A Wine and Food Guide to the Loire,* Henry Holt, 1996), "Wine villages as charming as St.-Émilion may exist but I don't know of any more charming." Note that visitors to wineries are typically offered one or two wines to taste, not an array as are offered at some California wineries, notably Robert Mondavi, for example. Also, it's a good idea to contact the wineries about a week or so in advance of your visit.

GENE BOURG, a freelance writer living in New Orleans, writes frequently for *Saveur, GQ, Food & Wine, Travel + Leisure, Food Arts,* and *Diversion,* where this piece first appeared. His interest in French culture stems largely from his Louisiana-French ancestry and from two years he spent in France during the 1960s, one in Paris, the other in Gascony. Bourg has also served as restaurant reviewer of the *Times-Picayune* in New Orleans for nine years, and he was editor of the 2002 edition of Gault Millau's *Best of New Orleans.* Additionally, he received the National Magazine Award for "Acadiana: Where Cajun Gets Real," a piece on Louisiana's Acadian food and culture that appeared in the January–February 1995 issue of *Saveur.*

The mood inside Le Lion d'Or, a restaurant in the heart of Bordeaux's Médoc wine district, was heady indeed. In a jammed dining room slightly larger than a one-car garage, wine-makers, château owners, and grape growers bounced from table to table, backslapping and swapping glasses of one another's wares. Emblazoned on the bottles were such legendary appellations as Margaux, Pauillac, St.-Estèphe, and St.-Julien.

The plates on the tables held the typically hearty local fare: roasted Pauillac lamb, *escargots à la bordelaise,* and paper-thin slices of rolled pig's stomach known as *grenier médocain,* a dish that perhaps only a native could love. But this was one of those nights when eating took a backseat to drinking.

Such impromptu parties erupt frequently at Le Lion d'Or, a favorite hangout of the Médoc wine trade. On this unusually warm October night the revelry was no doubt heightened by the fact that throughout the Bordeaux region wineries were winding up an annual *vendange,* or grape harvest, of historic proportions. Months of extraordinarily hot, dry weather in Southwestern France had produced grapes in a combination of quantity and quality that hadn't been seen for generations.

Bordeaux itself is the capital of a wine country encompassing 13,000 estates cultivating 284,000 acres (443 square miles) of vineyards. From cabernet sauvignon, cabernet franc, and merlot grapes come the legendary reds. The whites, made mostly from sauvignon blanc, sémillon, and muscadelle grapes, range in character from the crisp and fruity dry wines of the Graves district to the sweet, celebratory vintages of Sauternes. The 1997 grape harvest produced some 855 million bottles. This assures the prosperity enjoyed in recent decades by the towns and villages that line the region's two rivers, the Garonne and the Dordogne, which join the Gironde estuary before it meets the Atlantic Ocean.

If wine drives the Bordeaux economy, it also defines the city's character, so any time spent in the city of Bordeaux should include at least a day or two of travel through its surrounding wine districts. For me, the city certainly gained context after two days of side trips to some of the noble estates of the Médoc, the more unassuming properties along the Côtes de Blaye and the Côtes de Bourg, the fascinating medieval town of St.-Emilion, and a modest, family-operated winery in the Graves district.

Wine helps shape Bordeaux's gastronomy, too. In the better restaurants the wine in your glass is likely to be on your plate as well. Confectioners offer chocolate truffles spiked not with brandies or liqueurs but with Sauternes or St.-Emilion or any number of other wines from the region. In the glitzy new Place des Grands Hommes mall near the city's center, shoppers can finger the fabrics of Givenchy and Armani and try on the latest running shoe from the United States. But squeezed between the mall's purveyors of haute couture and trendy imports is a vendor of *canelés,* Bordeaux's traditional little cake resembling a miniature baba, soaked in red wine rather than rum.

The affluence generated in recent decades by the wine trade has transformed Bordeaux into one of the most beautiful cities in France. It may lack Paris's worldly sophistication and Marseilles's lusty energy, but Bordeaux can claim a self-assured panache all its own.

My first acquaintance with the city came in the early 1960s. In that era the impression it conveyed to a wide-eyed twenty-four-year-old was that of an interesting yet colorless and insular river town, with a population whose smugness underlined the limitless gradations of dark gray in the cityscape. This was where I first learned that a Frenchman's home could be not only his castle but his fortress as well. Among the few true French friends I was able to make in Bordeaux, I heard myself repeatedly referred to as "the American."

What I found when I returned last October was a Bordeaux that could actually sparkle, with not only a new cordiality among its people but also a fresh, vibrant look. In the outdoor cafés along the crowded pedestrian malls in the heart of the old town, smiles and banter were exchanged from one table to another. Forming the backdrop for the sipping and conversing were stately, ornate buildings from which several centuries' worth of grime had been gently scrubbed.

The ongoing cleanup all over Bordeaux is exposing the true, creamy beauty of the mostly eighteenth-century facades, crafted with stone from nearby quarries that now serve as aging cellars for wine. The Place de la Bourse, along the banks of the Garonne, basks in a newfound splendor that's revealed especially at night, when floodlights bathe its rediscovered sculptures, carved decoration, and gilded ironwork, sealing the quadrangle's reputation as one of the greatest examples of the Louis XV architectural style anywhere.

Closer to the city's heart is the broad expanse of the Allées de Tourny, bordered by offices, shops, and restaurants, and leading to the wide and lofty colonnade fronting the Grand Théâtre. *Grand* is certainly the word for this example of classic proportioning and ornamentation. Built between 1773 and 1780, the thousand-seat theater underwent a top-to-bottom scouring and restoration in 1992. Its sweeping central staircase, which inspired the one at Paris's Opéra, now provides an even more dazzling setting for the entries and exits of members of the city's wine aristocracy.

Farther downriver is the vast expanse of the Esplanade des Quinconces. Today its 145,000 square yards seems reduced to a more human scale, its walkways and lawns populated as they are by gaggles of locals and tourists. A fine vantage point from which to take it all in, I discovered, was a sidewalk table at the welcoming Bistro des Quinconces, with a cool glass of sauvignon blanc bottled within a half-hour drive.

These days jets and bullet trains put Paris only two or three hours away, virtually obliterating the distance between Bordeaux and the capital. What has not been obliterated, it seems, is the independent streak in the *bordelais* psyche. While Parisian trendies toss around the latest Americanisms, a bilingual *bordelais*'s English pronunciation usually finds its roots on Bond Street rather than Broadway, thanks to the city's historical social and commercial connections to Britain. At the Intendant wineshop on the Allées de Tourny, which boasts a treasury of classic reds and whites cradled around its beautiful spiral staircase, a salesman pronounced even the word *Bordeaux* as a Londoner would.

Collectors won't find many bargains in the racks of Bordeaux's wineshops, but at the Vinothèque de Bordeaux, at 8 Cours du XXX Juillet, and the Bordeaux Magnum, nearby at 3 rue Gobineau, they will find a good selection of inexpensive *crus bourgeois* and lesser known wines. The wines of Bordeaux are made to drink with food. And for its provender Bordeaux draws first on the riches of the Atlantic (37 miles west), the Gironde estuary, and the wide Garonne River that flows past the city. These waters offer up sole, shad, sturgeon, and baby eels to be cooked with parsley and garlic.

Cèpes and Foie Gras

Fans of prosciutto ham will find its rival in the silky, delicious *jambon de Bayonne,* brought up from the coastal town of Bayonne. From the Bassin d'Arcachon come luscious oysters, and from the fields and farms farther inland come the tasty beef of Bazas, the robustly flavored lamb of Pauillac, and the large and meaty *cèpe* mushrooms of the area's forests. The ducks and geese of the Landes region are preserved in their own fat to become succulent confits; their livers produce the world's finest foie gras.

Despite all of this bounty, Bordeaux seems to be only now developing a significant restaurant culture. For decades the town's gastronomic temple was the old Dubern, which can still be found on the Allées de Tourny. The ancient Le Chapon Fin on the rue Montesquieu, where Toulouse-Lautrec once broke bread, survives along with its old-fashioned ways.

But for someone with a serious hunger, the place to go is the decidedly rustic dining room of La Tupina, lined with exposed brick, chiseled wood, and quaint iron kitchenware. A prosperous-looking dinner crowd gathered around a glowing fireplace where chickens roasted and country soups bubbled. As I pulled up a chair, the lamb chops on another table looked too good to pass up. And they were, with their perfect char, crackly crust, and superb flavor.

Close to the city center, on the narrow, buzzing rue Buffon, I lunched at the Café Gourmand. Its name may be uninspired, but its breezily casual dining room displayed the latest in colorful downscale chic—antique prints and handbills on the walls, a bank of doors opening onto the sidewalk, and a young clientele filling the banquettes as fan blades whirred overhead.

The Café Gourmand's owner-chef is Bruno Oliver, grandson of France's legendary gastronomic scholar Raymond Oliver. Bruno brings his own youthful vigor to longtime staples of the Bordeaux diet. In the warmth of an early afternoon the chef sent out a bracing *salade croquante* of vegetables tossed with soft, spicy mussels; slabs of foie gras trading juices with sweet, late-harvest sauvignon blanc grapes; a *brandade de morue* that updated this traditional puree of cod and potatoes with a big dollop of tart *tapenade;* and for dessert a chilled soup of raspberries and strawberries made even cooler with fresh mint.

Afterward a few minutes' stroll led me to Old Bordeaux (St.-Pierre) and its thousands of lovely stone buildings. Its busiest thoroughfares, the rue Ste.-Catherine and the rue Porte-Dijeaux, are now among the quarter's pedestrian malls, cobblestoned and still divided down the middle by shallow gutters. Occasionally a street will lead to a square bustling with cafés and shops like the one I happened upon. Under the cloudless sky of a hot autumn day, the market umbrella shading my table was almost as welcome as the triple portion of ice in my lemonade. Perhaps the most pleasing space I came across in Old Bordeaux was the little Place du Chapelet, whose beauty would be remarkable even if it didn't contain the Eglise Notre-Dame, an exquisite example of the French Baroque style.

Any search for the soul of Bordeaux should extend to the outlying wine districts. In many ways this wine country is as different from California's—in both landscape and spirit—as one could imagine. Instinct and ritual have been embedded in the winemaking culture almost from the time the ancient Romans planted the first vines here, in and around the settlement they named Burdigala. For centuries most of the great wine estates were accessible only to the trade. But a few years ago many of them began opening their doors to the public. Tastings and tours are now available almost everywhere.

Rising from the iron-flat terrain of the Médoc district's coastline is a succession of châteaus that are as magnificent as those in the Loire Valley. In sharp contrast to this grandeur are the smaller estates southeast of Bordeaux, clustered around the Garonne Valley. Their scale not only makes them more approachable but allows for a more casual and interesting look at winemaking techniques.

A twenty-minute drive southeastward from the city along the

Garonne brought me to the Graves district and the village of Portets, with its makeshift billboards advertising tastings at several small wineries. Just off the highway stood the little Vieux Château Gaubert. The charming one-story main house, connected to its two little wings by open arcades, was built in 1796 as the country estate of a prosperous Bordeaux shipping merchant.

After a half-century of neglect, the château was bought in 1988 by a young vintner, Dominique Haverlan, and his wife, Hélène. They are still restoring the outbuildings, but the house itself is now a cozy abode for the couple and their two children. Dominique's personal tour of the vineyards, presses, and storehouses was delivered in halting but understandable English. It ended with a tasting of a half-dozen reds and whites from the Château Gaubert and three other properties he owns in Portets, which together produce some 220,000 bottles a year, a comparatively small output.

Similarly modest winemaking operations are found to the north, in the town of Blaye and along the slopes of the Côtes de Bourg district, across the Gironde estuary from the Médoc. Blaye's draw for travelers, aside from its winemaking, is its immense Citadel, surmounting a high bank of the estuary. The Citadel's ancient walls enclose not only a well-preserved medieval fortress but also a thriving village with a picturesque square that appears to have changed little over the centuries.

An hour's drive from Bourg brought me to St.-Emilion, its ramparts, roofs, and walls golden in the early-afternoon sun. Of all the attractions in St.-Emilion, the most awe-inspiring is its underground monolithic church, carved between the ninth and twelfth centuries from a single block of limestone. Beyond the tunneled path that serves as the church's entry is the cavernous nave, its walls nearly black with the patina that took a thousand years to create.

As sunset approached, I lazed with an aperitif at a café on St.-

Emilion's old Place du Marché. Then I took a short walk to Francis Goullée, a restaurant with an atmosphere as familial as its name, thanks to Madame Goullée's homey appointments and easy hospitality. From her husband's kitchen came a savory onion flan in a light tomato sauce, more foie gras and lamb, and a soul-warming dessert fashioned from little more than cool fresh cream and the famous local macaroons.

Leaving the restaurant near midnight, as the streets were emptying, gave me a chance to take in St.-Emilion's medieval beauty without the usual daytime distractions and crowds. On the Place du Marché the last customers languished at the café tables as I walked toward the ramparts at the town's edge. When I reached a suitable vantage point along the ramparts, the dark sky allowed only hints of what lay below. But I knew that westward was Bordeaux, where I'd started and where I'd find myself in the morning, eager for one final taste of the same kind of unhurried, and very approachable, pleasures I'd found all over the region.

Bordeaux in a Box

Hotels

The following hotels accept major credit cards and have English-speaking staff, telephones, TVs, and private baths or showers. All prices are for double rooms.

Bordeaux

Hôtel Burdigala. Not centrally located, but perhaps the city's most prestigious hotel address, with tastefully appointed rooms and dependable service. Pricey by local standards but worth it. 83 rooms. *115 rue Georges Bonnac; 33.5/56.90.16.16; fax 56.93.15.06. $150.*

Le St.-James. On the right bank of the Gironde, Le St. James offers luxurious accommodations and views of Bordeaux in the distance. But its severe contemporary design (concrete floors, lots of rusted ironwork) may not suit every taste, especially in these decidedly rural surroundings. 18 rooms. *3 place Camille Hostein, Bouliac (5½ miles southeast of Bordeaux on Highway D610); 33.5/57.97.06.00; fax 56.20.92.58. $160.*

Tulip Inn Bayonne Etche Ona. This eighteenth-century classic has spacious 1930s-style rooms. A few minutes' walk from the central Allées de Tourny and Cours de l'Intendance. 64 rooms. *4 rue de Martignac; 33.5/56.48.00.88; fax 56.52.03.79. $85.*

Médoc

Château Cordeillan-Bages. A deluxe hostelry inside the seventeenth-century wing of a major wine château, on five manicured acres with supremely elegant rooms, a luxury restaurant, and a wine school. 25 rooms. *61 rue Vignerons, Pauillac; 33.5/56.59.24.24; fax 56.59.01.89. $150.*

Relais de Margaux This modern, attractively decorated hotel with spacious rooms and manicured grounds is well located for touring the Médoc, but service is touch and go, and there is no restaurant. 64 rooms. *Chemin de l'Ile Vincent, Margaux; 33.5/57.88.38.30; fax 57.88.31.73. $170.*

St.-Emilion

Hostellerie de Plaisance. As beautiful and comfortable a hotel as you're likely to find in a village of St.-Emilion's size, with good service and spectacular views. Many consider the restaurant the best in town. 16 rooms. *Place du Clocher, 33.5/57.55.07.55; fax 57.74.41.11. $134.*

Restaurants

The following prices are per person and include service, tax, and a glass or bottle of modest wine. *Expensive* means $75 to $100; *moderate*, $35 to $75; and *inexpensive*, $20 to $35.

Bordeaux

Café Gourmand, *3 rue Buffon, 33.5/56.79.23.85 or 56.52.10.98. Moderate.*

La Tupina, *6 rue de la Porte de la Monnaie, 33.5/56.91.56.37. Expensive.*

Le Bistro des Quinconces, *4 place des Quinconces, 33.5/56.52.84.56. Inexpensive.*

Médoc

Château Guittot-Fellonneau. It's not mentioned in this article, but don't miss this authentic *ferme auberge* with lots of rustic charm and delicious local specialties that you can wash down with a robust *cru artisan* Haut-Médoc at about $10 a bottle. *Macau; 33.5/57.88.47.81. Inexpensive.*

St.-Emilion

Francis Goullée, *27 rue Guadet; 33.5/57.24.70.49. Moderate.*

Tours and Tastings

L'Ecole du Bordeaux in Pauillac offers lectures (in English) and visits to four wine châteaus: Cantenac-Brown in Margaux, Suduiraut in Sauternes, and Lynch-Bages and Pichon-Longueville in Pauillac. Price: about $10 per person. 33.5/56.59.24.24 or fax 56.59.01.89.

L'Ecole du Vin in Bordeaux offers tastings and instruction geared to all levels. For a catalog contact the Maison du Vin at 33.5/56.00.22.66 or fax 56.00.22.77.

Dewey Markham Jr., an American who lives in Bordeaux and has excellent access to the châteaux of the region, conducts private tours. He can be reached at 33.5/57.22.07.51 or by e-mail at *dmarkham@insat.com*.

France's Secret South Sea

BY ALEXANDER LOBRANO

∾

Though it's true, as the author notes here, that the Bassin d'Arcachon is a haven for the well heeled, it is also one of the few remaining stretches of coastal France that aren't swarming with foreign tourists—and definitely not Americans. Don't let the presence of the jet set intimidate you: the best features of this *coin de la France* are free—the gorgeous sand, the beautiful vistas, the tranquillity, the fresh air and bright sunshine—commodities in short supply that we *all* seek, no matter the size of our pocketbooks. I am not ashamed to admit that I love the Côte d'Azur as well as the *côtes* of Provence and Languedoc-Roussillon; but when I crave an unspoiled seascape and complete rest and relaxation, this sublime stretch of Aquitaine *côte* delivers. Feasting upon delicious seafood, especially shellfish, is a particular pleasure of the Bassin, and though you will have to open your wallet to do so, there are a number of no-frills places to choose from where you won't have to open it very wide. It's also true, as the author wisely notes, that it's almost impossible to find a place to stay in high season if you haven't reserved well in advance. But even if you can drive out only for the day from Bordeaux, it is more than worth the detour.

ALEXANDER LOBRANO lives in Paris and is European correspondent for *Gourmet*. He has also contributed to a number of other publications, including *Departures, Travel + Leisure,* and *FRANCE Magazine,* where this piece first appeared. Lobrano writes a weekly food column for *Time Out Paris* and edits the Paris *Zagat Survey.* His work has previously appeared in the *Provence, Cote d'Azur and Monaco* and *Morocco* editions of *The Collected Traveler.*

The huge hydrangeas bowing down to the powdery white sand are the same kaleidoscopic tones of pink, blue, and lavender as the sun fading on the wave-dappled inlet just steps from the terrace at Chez Hortense. Across the way, a mile distant, the Dune du Pilat, the largest sand dune in Europe, has a spectacular lunar glow too on this lush midsummer evening. But few of the impeccably groomed diners in this painstakingly casual and clearly affluent crowd—Ralph Lauren's polo player is galloping across half the chests in the room—are paying much attention to the magnificent natural setting.

It's the opening night of the season at the chicest restaurant in Cap Ferret, one of the chicest resorts in France. Just an hour from Bordeaux, the town lies at the tip of the long, thin peninsula of dunes and forest that forms the western arm of the Bassin d'Arcachon, France's beautiful and rather secret "South Sea." And though no one would admit it, there are people in the crowd who called days earlier from halfway around the world to make sure that they'd get a table on this most strategic of terraces. The inevitable denials of the natives notwithstanding, this is *the* night to see and be seen in a place where appearances count for a great deal.

To grasp "Ferret," as the locals affectionately call it, imagine a Gallic version of East Hampton, then add the perfect social graces and restrained elegance of the Bordeaux bourgeoisie and a sprinkling of aristocrats. Along with, *bien sûr,* the occasional scrupulously ignored celebrity—Bordeaux mayor Alain Juppé, Johnny Hallyday, Léon Zitrone, Jean-Paul Belmondo—adding a bit of glamour to the crowd.

What you won't find here, in large numbers anyway, are foreigners, and that is one of the things that makes this corner of France, the world's most visited country, so alluring. It's not that Cap Ferret is xenophobic, it isn't, but rather like several of the world's other exclusive summer communities—the German North Sea island of Sylt, or the gated pine glade of Point O'Woods on New York's Fire Island, a favorite with *New York Times* staffers—there's a very limited number of hotel rooms available, most of which are booked far in advance, so you either own your own digs or are forced into the dreaded category of day-tripper. And although Dutch and German campers may like to be near the ocean beaches, almost everyone else in this *franchouillard,* or super-French, *station balnéaire* is happier dallying on the Bassin d'Arcachon itself. Never mind that the residents of Pyla, the area's other furiously chic resort town at the entrance to the bay, make a firm point of their preference for the "pristine" (you get the implications insofar as the Bassin is concerned) Atlantic waters.

Pyla, with its large "Basco-Landaise" villas (half-timbered whitewashed houses with long, low rooflines built by three generations of the Gaume family), likes to imply that it's more "discreet" than Cap Ferret. And it's true that the great families of France—the Rothschilds, Debrés, Mauboussins, Taittingers, and Bettencourts—come here to escape the public eye. The only place you might catch a glimpse of the local *gratin* is over dinner at La Côte du Sud during the summer; out of season at La Cabane, where they grill meat on an open fire; or at Les Deux Chênes, known for its *cèpes.* Aside from these restaurants, though, there's little way for an outsider to experience the posh local life.

Pyla and Cap Ferret may be the Bassin's twin compass points of exclusivity, sharing a sort of anti–Côte d'Azur philosophy, but they tell only a small part of this lovely bay's story. This vast tidal basin—more than three-quarters (about 62,000 acres) of which is exposed at low tide—has been attracting vacationers since at least the fourth century, which is as far back as archaeologists have been able to date the Gallo-Roman ruins in Andernos-les-Bains, a large and well-established resort and oyster-producing town on the eastern flank of the lagoon. Here the powerfully simple Romanesque church of St.-Eloi sits on the shallow banks of the Bassin, and excavations have proven that the Romans had established a sort of rough-and-ready spa here using the salt- and mineral-rich mud to treat rheumatism and other maladies.

Odds are that the Roman *curistes* scarfed down an oyster or twelve as well, considering that the Bassin's most ancient vocation is oyster fishing. Originally the bivalves grew more or less wild here, but then in 1852 Vincent Coste, a local fisherman, designed the first oyster-seed collectors. Jean Michelet, another waterman, later developed the liming technique, painting concave tiles with lime and stacking them in the sea, making it easier to later detach the oysters that would cling to them.

Local lore claims that a whole new chapter in oystering began by accident in 1868, when a Portuguese ship sank in the mouth of the bay. The spawn of *les portugaises,* the deep, craggy oysters (as opposed to the traditional flat *belons*) that were clinging to its hull, were reputedly washed into the nutrient-rich waters and rapidly acclimated, eventually becoming the dominant oyster species. The truth, for once, is just as fascinating: the ship was carrying a cargo of oysters destined for Arcachon (the intention was to introduce them into the local beds) but had to take shelter near Bordeaux during a storm. Fearing that the oysters had died due to the delay, the crew tossed the lot overboard into the Garonne, and the shellfish eventually found their way to the Bassin on their own.

With the rapid expansion of the French railway network during the reign of Napoleon III, oysters were one of the many farm products that became popular with city dwellers, and at the emperor's orders, the Bassin d'Arcachon was carefully surveyed into allotments awarded to local fishermen and their families. The move provoked a huge boom that completely transformed the Bassin, basically changing it from a wild sea into a carefully managed one.

The whole bay became ringed with oyster-producing ports, the most famous being Gujan-Mestras, where a visit to the Maison de l'Huître offers a fascinating history of oyster farming. A critical date was 1970, when either an epidemic or mysterious natural causes wiped out the local *portugaises,* since replaced by a Japanese variety (*Crassotrea gigas*). Today the Bassin provides a livelihood for some four hundred *ostréiculteurs,* who annually produce up to fifteen thousand tons of oysters, about 10 percent of the total French production. Even more valuable than the adult oysters is the Bassin's spat, or oyster-seed, crop. Accounting for 70 percent of French production, it is exported to other regions of France as well as to European countries and Morocco.

The institution of organized property rights in the Bassin also led to the invention of a uniquely local construction, the *tchanquées*—wooden houses built on pilings as surveillance points so that the locals could make sure no one was making off with their shellfish. Only two of these picturesque bungalows survive, both on the Ile aux Oiseaux, the low-lying island in the middle of the lagoon. Just before sunset on a gentle June night, they're perfectly viewed during a tour in Joël Dupuch's aluminum *pinasse,* a type of wide, flat-bottomed boat with a very shallow draw that is indigenous to the Bassin.

Dupuch, a burly jovial man, is a sixth-generation oysterman who also has restaurants in Bordeaux and Dijon and was formerly vice-president of the Bordeaux Chamber of Commerce. Today he and his wife divide their time between Bordeaux and the wooden cottage overlooking the bay that he inherited from his family. "Our way of life here is very, very family-oriented," he says. "In Le Piquey, the village where we live, the same families have been sitting in the same place on the beach for generations. Everyone knows each other, so everyone knows it's 'their' spot." He goes on to explain that laws stipulate that the oyster beds can only be passed on to a family member or sold to another oysterman, ensuring great stability in the region. The same is true of fishermen's cottages. "It's almost impossible for an outsider to buy a cottage in L'Herbe, Le Canon, or any of the little towns on the western edge of the bay," notes Dupuch. Designer Philippe Starck did manage to buy waterview property in Le Piquey, just alongside the protected zone where Dupuch lives, but such lots are few and far between and are tremendously expensive—if you don't hear about them by word of mouth, there is little chance of your even making a bid.

"Tourists have to adapt to this place," declares Dupuch, who suddenly throttles the motor of his boat in response to something sensed below the opalescent surface of the sea at dusk. "We oystermen know this bay so well that the moment something changes, we notice it, just as we would notice if something were moved in our own bedroom." As the boat glides over a newly created sandbank, he continues, "Anyway, visitors are welcome, but they must adapt to us rather than the other way around. We don't want the Bassin to become gentrified. This isn't the Côte d'Azur, where tourism has created a rift between year-round residents and visitors. Here we have a unique social harmony. That is because our two primary industries—oysters and tourism—grew up together. Both of these populations realize that they have the same interests at stake."

Now the shoreline of Arcachon, the *grande dame* of the Bassin, comes into view. The town has become built up, with a year-round population of twelve thousand, but a few fanciful villas survive among the massive apartment buildings that went up during the 1970s. Nevertheless, a certain aura of gentility prevails here that harkens back to the days when ladies promenaded under silk parasols and the Moorish-style casino, now gone, attracted the crowned heads of Europe. Originally a tiny fishing village, Arcachon boomed when the Pereire brothers, clever *bordelais* bankers, bought and extended the Bordeaux–La Teste railway, which arrived in 1857. To create traffic on the new line, the brothers built a Grand Hôtel and a "Chinese" buffet restaurant, while another developer put up the casino. They then invited Napoleon III to come for a visit—a shrewd marketing coup that rapidly established the town's fashionable reputation.

Although the *ville d'été* along the seafront has been rather brutally modernized, the *ville d'hiver,* built inland to escape the winds, maintains an air of cosseted bourgeois leisure. Many of the villas here echo the Victorian architecture in Britain and North America with their fanciful neohistorical references and general frilliness— the same lacy wooden eaves, porticos, railings, and glass awnings found in Manchester or the Hudson River Valley abound in this leafy, private neighborhood. Puttering around these back streets is nice weekday entertainment, but don't even think about driving here on a weekend in high season, when an infernal system of one-way streets, nonexistent parking, and heavy traffic can combine to create chart-busting stress.

Otherwise Arcachon's most appealing attraction is its vivid and lively market, where you'll find all of the luscious bounty of Southwestern France's lavish cuisines—Basque, *landais, bordelais,* and *béarnais.* This very popular market is at its best on Saturday mornings, when the locals shop for weekend entertaining and tourists put together superb picnics, including takeaway platters of freshly shucked oysters, foie gras, Bayonne ham, Ossau d'Iraty sheep's milk cheese, fresh plums from Agen, and a variety of other delicacies. Even if you're not planning a picnic, you can stop in at one of the counters serving fresh oysters with a side of grilled sausage, a delicious local combo, along with everything from paella to *confit de canard*.

If you're staying in Cap Ferret, you can take the ferry over to Arcachon for a day, a far better idea than the long drive around the Bassin. If you do, you'll also experience another reason why this area is so wonderfully well preserved—to wit, the shifting sands at the mouth of the bay make it impossible to build a bridge between Pyla and Cap Ferret, preventing the closing of a circle that would surely lead to further development pressures.

As you return to Cap Ferret from Arcachon, the azure and topaz waters of the Bassin will be streaming—east or west, depending on the tide—into the ocean, and on a sunny day, with white sand beaches in the distance, it's almost hard to believe you're in France, for the whole scene seems Caribbean or Pacific in its lushness and beauty.

"It's true that there are mornings when I go down to the beach for a swim and find myself thinking that we have no reason to envy the Polynesians," says Benoît Bartherotte, whose *bordelais* family has been vacationing along the Bassin for three generations.

"Cap Ferret used to be so wild that we were practically considered Indians for coming here," he chuckles. "Fishermen would ferry us across from Arcachon, where my grandparents had a villa, to hunt and fish." Bartherotte later married the girl next door, Elisabeth (Zaza) Saige, who was also enamored of this strip of wilderness. "When we built our first cabin out here, we had no electricity or running water; we lived by candlelight," he says, sounding rather nostalgic for those days of bygone rusticity. "Unlike Le Touquet, Deauville, or Arcachon, which all became grand resorts during the reign of Napoleon III, Cap Ferret has always had a renegade personality."

An exuberant man with a delightfully Whitmanesque approach to life—in short, seize the day, live and let live, learn and enjoy yourself as much as you can while respecting other people—Bartherotte was a successful fashion designer in Paris, where he ran the Esterel house before selling and deciding to live full time in the family camp while pursuing other projects. He appears to take a certain pleasure in perpetuating the nonconformist myth of Cap Ferret—today he lives at the extreme tip of the peninsula with his large family in Walden Pond–like splendor in a complex of beautiful wooden cabins and houses set in a pine forest on the edge of the dunes. On any given day he can be seen roaring across the bay in his boat, picking up or dropping off friends or family on the giant sandbars at the mouth of the bay.

In fact, however, Bartherotte has invested much of his life and money in his personal passion for the cape by spending millions of dollars combating the major menace to its survival—erosion. A huge stone jetty, which Bartherotte has financed single-handedly, has prevented the sea from flooding the point of Cap Ferret. Indeed, a conference held this past August by the French National Hydraulic Center (SOGREAH) concluded that were it not for Bartherotte's sea wall, a major channel would have shifted 270 meters to the west, effectively wiping out the point. "The areas not protected by my wall are still being swept away," Batherotte says gravely. Then he grins. "So enjoy it while you can! Have you been to L'Herbe? Or Le Canon? They're the prettiest villages on the bay."

Bartherotte is right, of course. L'Herbe and Le Canon are intimate warrens of old weathered wooden cottages decorated with geraniums and hollyhocks often growing higher than their roof lines, and they have an unselfconscious charm that defies a calendar, to say nothing of a Palm Pilot. Wandering their narrow lanes, you get a gentle glimpse of an eternal summer of siestas, bathing suits drying on clotheslines, teakettles whistling, radios playing, half-read paperbacks abandoned face down on front porch railings, teenagers flirting, and seagulls crying.

Shy of romancing or marrying a native, the only way to go local is to stay at L'Herbe's winsome Hôtel de la Plage, a seaside boarding house that's so film-set perfect you half expect someone to call out "Lights, camera, action!" They won't, of course, so you'll be left in peace over your delicious supper of local oysters and *mulet en sauce verte* (mullet in green sauce, a local specialty). On a warm night, sitting outside, you'll see the lights of Arcachon twinkling across the bay, and odds are you'll feel very much like a privileged insider, which is exactly the way the natives want it. "You're very welcome here," says the sassy hostess, "just don't tell anyone else about us."

Carnet d'Adresses

Lodging

Cap Ferret became trendy only about ten years ago, so there are few hotels—and even fewer with charm. Most people either have second homes here or rent a villa. For lists of reputable rental agencies, contact the Arcachon Tourist Office (see Resources).

L'Hôtel des Pins. Simple and clean with a retro beach-house feel, L'Hôtel des Pins charms with its unassuming attitude, awning-covered terrace, and banks of fluffy hydrangeas. *23 rue des Fauvettes; tel. 33.5/56.60.60.11; fax 56.60.67.41. 14 rooms from €52.*

La Maison du Bassin. The most sought-after address on the peninsula, this seven-room hotel has made the pages of glossy shelter magazines and is booked months ahead during the busy season. Antiques, flea-market finds, and natural pine give it the feel of a seaside home, and each room is unique. The bar—

complete with pool table—is a popular place for before-dinner drinks, and the restaurant, with its flower-bedecked terrace, offers well-prepared local seafood. *5 rue des Pionniers; tel. 33.5/56.60.60.63; fax 56.03.71.47. Rooms from €84; tasting menu at €35 and à la carte.*

Carpe Diem. Those looking for a unique vacation experience may want to contact Benoît and Zaza Bartherotte, who live at the farthest point of the cape on a sublime stretch of beachfront property appropriately christened Carpe Diem. Benoît designed and built an adjoining seven-bedroom villa that they rent to friends—mostly movie stars and artist types—to help fund their ongoing battle to keep the encroaching sea at bay. *Carpe Diem, La Pointe, 33970 Cap Ferret; tel. 33.6/09.53.67.12. Weekly or monthly rentals.*

Dining

Vacationers in Ferret typically eschew urban sophistication in favor of a simpler lifestyle, so restaurants here tend to be unpretentious affairs. And frankly, what could be better than stopping in at an oysterman's shack where, for a mere €8 or €10, you can treat yourself to a dozen oysters, bread, butter, and a glass of white wine?

Chez Hortense. A Cap Ferret institution—people come from around the Bassin to savor the mussels (a house specialty) and the simply prepared yet wonderful fish. Proprietor Bernadette extends a warm welcome to all, but locals greet her with a kiss. *Avenue du Sémaphore; tel. 33.5/56.60.62.56; fax 56.60.42.84. A la carte about €45 to €50.*

Pinasse Café. Located near the ferry landing in downtown Cap Ferret, this waterside café features seafood and fish along with great views of the Bassin looking across to the Dune du Pilat. *2 bis avenue de l'Océan; tel. 33.5/56.03.77.87; fax 56.60.63.47. Fixed-price menu at € 23, à la carte about € 30.*

Sail Fish. This former boat shed has been turned into a trendy spot with good food and an ambiance to match. The rendezvous spot for hip *bordelais* and, more recently, Parisians; weekends are especially lively. *Rue des Bernaches; tel. 33.5/56.60.44.84. A la carte about €40.*

Hôtel de la Plage. Run by two feisty cousins, this place doesn't seem to have changed in decades. The only restaurant in the achingly picturesque fishing village of L'Herbe, it delights with no-nonsense cuisine, water views, and lots of local color. *Tel. 33.5/56.60.50.15. Fixed-price menus at €16 and €25, à la carte about €20.*

La Cabane d'Edouard. Run by a local oysterman, this casual wharfside eatery features the bounty of the Arcachon bay— oysters, mussels, seafood platters—along with expansive views of the Bassin. *Port de Claoey, Cabanes 1 and 3; tel. 33.5/57.70.30.44. A la carte.*

Resources

For complete listings of hotels, restaurants, special events, and activities around the entire Bassin d'Arcachon, contact the Office du Tourisme d'Arcachon, Esplanade Georges Pompidou, BP 137, 33311 Arcachon Cedex. Tel. 33.5/57.92.57.57; fax 357.52.97.77; www.arcachon.com; tourisme@arcachon.com.

Caroline Mattéoli's paintings are available at her studio (11 rue Magellan, 75008 Paris; tel. 33.6/60.76.18.79) or through Galerie Le Minotaure (2 rue des Beaux-Arts, 75006 Paris; tel. 33.1/43.25.35.37).

Bibliography

A House in the Sunflowers: Summer in Aquitaine (1991) and *A Harvest of Sunflowers: Living the Dream in the South of France* (1996), both by Ruth Silvestre, both illustrated by Michael Grater, both published by Allison and Busby, London. The first volume in this pair of books was published only one year after the wildly popular *A Year in Provence* by Peter Mayle, yet I never heard a word about it, perhaps because it was never published in the United States. Both books, detailing the author and her family's purchase of Bel-Air de Grèzelongue in the Lot-et-Garonne, are wonderful, and readers especially interested in this corner of the Southwest should make an effort to find at least one of these volumes. (I found mine at a Borders branch, so I don't believe they are obscure.) When one considers the great number of I-bought-a-house-in-Provence titles published, it is a bit remarkable that there are so few published on this *douce* corner of France. Silvestre may not be quite the wit that Peter Mayle is, but her experiences are as rich and poignant. What I like best about reading books like this is that I always learn of local French words and phrases that I would otherwise never encounter. Silvestre shares plenty of them, such as: *en fète* (what a nice way to say "in bloom"), *petit à petit, l'oiseau fait son nid* (little by little, the bird makes its nest), *fai calou* (Occitan for "it's hot"), *canicule* (heatwave), and my most favorite, *quand il y a du soleil, il y a de la joie!* (when there is sunshine, there is joy!). The family from whom Silvestre bought Bel-Air de Grèzelongue is kind and enormously helpful, and Silvestre learned much about the ways of the countryside from the *grand-mère*. Grandma says quite often, *C'est le système,* but careful observers of the French know that Grandma isn't the only one who has a *système* for almost everything.

Ways of Aquitaine, Freda White, W.W. Norton, 1968. Though White's definition of Aquitaine is different from anyone else's I've encountered (picture a square with Bordeaux in the bottom left corner, Nantes in the upper left, Bourges in the upper right, and Aurillac in the bottom right), there is much here that is relevant nonetheless. You'll find the excellent works by White—*Three Rivers of France* and *West of the Rhone* are mentioned elsewhere in this book—recommended in every good bibliography of the Southwest. White explains that as she had previously written *Three Rivers of France,* which focuses on the Dordogne, Lot, and Tarn Rivers, she purposely omitted the southern reaches of Aquitaine in this book. She also notes that Aquitaine, named by the

Romans, once "covered the great regions of central and western France, stretching north and south from the Loire to the Garonne, and east and west from the Rhone ridges of the Massif Central to the Atlantic. Later, the Roman rulers divided Aquitaine into two provinces, Aquitania Prima with Bourges as its capital, and Aquitania Secunda governed from Bordeaux." With black-and-white photographs and a detailed fold-out map glued onto the back cover. *De rigueur.*

Bordeaux the City and Bordeaux the Wine

In a departure from my other editions, I have decided to recommend books about Bordeaux wines here in this bibliography rather than the one in *Flavors and Tables of the Southwest*. Bordeaux is, after all, the central hub of Europe's wine trade, and it is the only city to lend its name to an entire wine-growing region. I don't think there is a book published about Bordeaux (the city) that isn't also about Bordeaux (the wine and the vineyards). And whether you drink wine or not, I think these words by Peter Mayle are worth keeping in mind during a visit to Aquitaine (and Languedoc-Roussillon as well): "The amount of work, much of it manual, involved in maintaining a great vineyard defies description. The initial investment is colossal. The risks of weather are beyond man's control; too much rain, no rain at all, hailstorms, freak winds, late frosts, early frosts. Everything can be done perfectly for eleven months of the year and destroyed overnight. I can never open a bottle of wine without thinking of the effort and skill and patience that have gone into it, and what a bargain it is."

The Bordeaux Atlas and Encyclopedia of Châteaux, Hubrecht Duijker and Michael Broadbent, St. Martin's Press, 1998.

Bordeaux: A Comprehensive Guide to Wines Produced from 1961 to 1997, Robert M. Parker Jr., Simon and Schuster, 1998. This Bordeaux encyclopedia is probably Parker's most famous book. (A few of his most notable others include *Burgundy: A Complete Guide to the Producers, Appellations, and Wines* and *Wines of the Rhone Valley,* both also published by Simon and Schuster.) Perhaps surprisingly, for those who are not yet familiar with Parker, his tone in this Bordeaux bible is quite inviting and personal, making even readers who are a bit intimidated feel right at home and ready to learn. In typical Parker style, he details vintages of each year and provides each with a numerical rating based on the hundred-point system he prefers; a score of 90–100 is equal to an A, 80–90 corresponds to a B, and so on. The bulk of the book is devoted to these ratings, though Parker does include a short history for each estate, including profiles of the owners, which to me are always interesting to read. There is also a section featuring hotel listings and contact information for each estate, which is helpful for those planning a trip to the vineyards. Though I admit that a Parker rating alone does not influence whether I buy a particular bottle of wine, and I tire immediately when someone recites endless Parker scores, I very much enjoy reading Parker's books and his newsletter, *The Wine Advocate,* and I have great respect for him. Parker has become, according to Jay McInerney, "the most respected, admired, and feared wine critic in the world, educating a generation of American consumers—myself included—and influencing the way that wine is made and sold around the world. A single point on his rating scale can be worth hundreds of thousands of dollars to a winemaker." When McInerney asked him to describe the "Parker Effect" on the wine world, Parker replied, "Lower yields, ripe fruit, an artisanal approach. Less is better. Let the *terroir* express itself. This is my legacy." McInerney added, "If this sounds a little technical, let me put it this way: the next time you open a bottle of wine, raise the first glass to Robert Parker, because, no matter what it is, it will probably taste better than it would have if the big man had stuck with corporate law."

Bordeaux: People, Power and Politics, Stephen Brook, photographs by Gary Latham, Mitchell Beazley, 2001. This is the most complete book I've ever seen on Bordeaux, as it is not only about the wine but also about the city, the old families with influence, the nouveaux riches, the corporations, and the future of the region. My favorite chapters are *"En Primeur,* the Ferrari Without Wheels: How Producers Market Their Wines and How This Influences Wine Styles and Prices" and "Think Bordeaux: The Culture of Hype—The Rituals and Ceremonies of the Professional Bodies and What They Represent." Brook is a leading authority on the Bordeaux region, and here he thoroughly reveals an honest, behind-the-scenes business side of the wine trade. If wine "business" seems dull to you, it isn't: how Bordeaux's wines are produced, marketed, and sold is incredibly fascinating, and Brook also provides plenty of vintner profiles, family trees, and interesting sketches on the power of the press, merchants, *négociants,* and consumers. (There are great photos, too.) *De rigueur* for serious collectors of Bordeaux and readers who want a solid understanding of the wines and the region.

Grands Vins: The Finest Châteaux of Bordeaux and Their Wines, Clive Coates, University of California Press, 1995. Master of Wine Coates here presents a compendium (816 pages) of selected Bordeaux wines, including summaries of each vintage, histories of each estate, maps, regional winemaking idiosyncrasies, and optimal drinking times for each wine. The fact that the book appeared in 1995 takes nothing away from this publishing achievement: it remains a significant read, though I do not recommend it for Bordeaux beginners.

Wine and War: The French, the Nazis, and the Battle for France's Greatest

Treasure, Don and Petie Kladstrup, Broadway Books, 2001. Though this wonderfully written and important book does not focus exclusively on Bordeaux, naturally the vineyards and the city figure large in a history of the World War II years in France. In fact, the Demarcation Line (maps of France illustrating the location of the Demarcation and Maginot Lines are the endpapers of the book) was drawn to include most of France's best vineyards. To finance the war effort, the Germans forbade wine shipments to anyone but the Third Reich, and set the prices they would pay, which were naturally low. They then sold the best wines to customers around the world, earning a hefty profit. This is the kind of book one cannot easily put down, and once I began reading it, I couldn't stop and was finished in three days. Tragically, it reads like a thriller, and like other tales of Nazi cruelty and atrocity, one can't help but shudder at what might have been. (It was bad enough.) Based on three years of research and interviews with the survivors, of varying ages, this project is really lots of stories woven together about remarkable people who made remarkable efforts to protect their wine, their economy, and their fellow citizens. The authors discovered that a wine-and-war connection actually dates back to the sixth century B.C., when "Cyrus the Great of Persia ordered his troops to drink wine as an antidote to infection and illness. Julius Caesar and Napoleon Bonaparte were believers too. Napoleon even hauled wagonloads of champagne on his campaigns, most of the time anyway. The reason he lost the battle of Waterloo, some say, was that he did not have time to pick up any champagne and had to fight on Belgian beer alone. Perhaps with that in mind, French soldiers in World War I were issued cases of champagne to keep close beside them in the trenches to keep their morale up. When World War II broke out, the French government sent utensils and recipes for making hot wine to the front." The authors also relate that the peasants who worked the vineyards have long believed there is a special relationship between war and grapes: "They had always said that the Good Lord sends a poor wine crop when war starts and a fine, festive one to mark its end. And they were right. 1939, the year World War II began, was a horrendous vintage, whereas 1945, *l'année de la victoire* (the year of the victory), was one of the best ever recorded." Fascinated as I was by these discoveries, it was really the individual stories that kept me glued to this book. One in particular is among the most poignant I've ever read: Gaston Huet, a noted Vouvray vintner from the Loire Valley, had the idea to organize a wine fête within the German POW camp where he and a million and a half other Frenchmen were being held. Despite numerous hurdles and setbacks, Huet and a group of his fellow soldiers managed to smuggle seven hundred bottles of wine into the camp, enough for every prisoner to have one glass at the banquet. Years later Huet recalled that the fête "saved our sanity. I don't know what we would have done without that party. It gave us something to hold on to. It gave us a reason to get up in the morning, to get through each day. Talking about wine and sharing it made all of us feel closer to home, and more alive." I simply had no idea that the Nazis paid so much attention to France's vineyards—they even appointed German agents for importing wine from France (the French called them *weinführers*)—who were responsible for selecting the wines and overseeing the shipments. Here, though, is where the Nazis made a mistake: the *weinführers* were definitely wine experts, but they were much more than that. "They also were friends of many French wine producers and merchants. Their connection through generations of doing business together had long since transcended commercial matters; they had trained in each other's firms and spoke each other's language fluently. They were even godfathers to each other's children." The *weinführers* also were keenly aware of something Maurice Drouhin stressed to his son at the beginning of the war: "One day, whether in five months or in five years, this war will be over, and France will still be next to Germany. We will still have to live together." The authors also provide some passages that reveal what Bordeaux, the Nazis' primary destination, was like after May 1940: "The Germans swept in like angels of death," said one resident, recalling how the sunlight glinted off their motorcycle goggles. Within hours they were setting up checkpoints, requisitioning homes and office buildings and taking control of the port. On hand to greet them was the French government which had fled Paris two and a half weeks earlier and turned the city into its temporary capital . . . Almost overnight, nearly everything about this ancient port city had changed. It bristled with gun emplacements; flags with Nazi insignias were draped everywhere. The port itself, a vital shipping point for Bordeaux wine producers for more than two hundred years, was now teeming with armed soldiers and being converted into a German naval base. The most dramatic change, however, was the population. Earlier that month, it had been 250,000. Now, crammed with refugees who had fled the German invasion, it was nearly a million." This long overdue chapter in French history made me cry, smile occasionally, and marvel often at the determination of the authors and the truly heroic French citizens, extraordinary in their ordinariness. *De rigueur.*

Wines of Bordeaux, David Peppercorn, Octopus Publishing Group, 2002. This revised and updated edition is a better book for readers who are just beginning to learn about Bordeaux than for Bordeaux experts. The sizable introduction is devoted to the basics of wine: aspects of production each month, grape varieties, understanding a label, the different châteaus, and the families behind the business. One of my interns described this volume as being similar to a Zagat's guide for Bordeaux wines—not a plus, to my mind. I do see her point, yet this is a good, compact overview for those Bordeaux enthusiasts not ready to take the plunge into Parker or another more substantial tome.

~The Aquitaine Tourist Office publishes one of the most outstanding tourist brochures I've ever seen, *Aquitaine: The Other South of France*. This forty-three-page booklet, in English, is divided into five sections: water (sea, coastline, rivers), land (forest, mountains, nature), stone (heritage, historical sites, towns, and villages), *terroir* (wine, gastronomy, celebrations, shows, and people), and practical information (reception and accommodation). A good map—and the Tourist Office defines Aquitaine broadly, as the map includes the Pays Basque—is provided on the inside front cover. You will find information on resorts, sports, houseboats and excursion boats, spas, nature reserves, hiking trails, tourist trains, prehistoric caves, towns of art, beautiful villages, wine châteaus, wine and cuisine classes, and festivals and events. The practical information section includes contact information for all the local tourist offices, mileage and average temperature charts, and resources for hotels, campsites, and *gîtes*. This booklet is almost as thorough as an actual guidebook, and I urge you to request one from the Maison de la France offices in North America. If the office nearest you no longer stocks it, contact the Aquitaine Tourist Office directly: Comité Régional de Tourisme d'Aquitaine, Cité Mondiale, 23 Parvis des Chartrons, 33074 Bordeaux Cedex, France. Additionally, the Aquitaine Tourist Office publishes theme brochures on such topics as campsites, golf, waterway tourism, thalassotherapy, cyclotourism, and more, and you may request these as well.

~The annual forty-page-plus *Bordeaux* booklet published by the Bordeaux Tourist Office is, like the Aquitaine brochure, a must-have. This excellent resource, also almost as good as a guidebook, is loaded with practical information on special events, itineraries in various *quartiers,* sites and monuments, museums, vineyards, hotels, restaurants, and nightlife and also includes a good map. This booklet is available from the Bordeaux Tourist Office (12 cours du XXX-Juillet; www.bordeaux-tourisme.com) and may also be stocked in limited quantites at the North American tourist offices.

~*Bordeaux: Découverte du Vignoble* is is an excellent fold-out brochure with a map of the area vineyards on one side and resources about Bordeaux wine on the reverse. This very useful publication is published by the Conseil Interprofessionnel du Vin de Bordeaux (CIVB).

~*Aquitaine en scène* is a fold-out calendar brochure published quarterly and features music, dance, theater, cinema, expositions, and *histoires* (narrated stories). It's printed in French, Occitan, and Basque, reflecting the region's inhabitants, but even if you can't read any of those you can probably figure out the date and time of an event you'd like to see. Readers who would like to know what's going on *before* they arrive should log on to www.aquitaine-en-scene.org for regularly updated listings.

Basque Country

"No word less describes Basques than the term separatist, a term they refuse to use. If they are an island, it is an island where bridges are constantly being built to the mainland. Considering how small a group the Basques are, they have made remarkable contributions to world history. In the Age of Exploration, they were the explorers who connected Europe to North America, Africa, and Asia. At the dawn of capitalism they were among the first capitalists, experimenting with tariff-free international trade and the use of competitive pricing to break monopolies. Early in the industrial revolution they became leading industrialists: shipbuilders, steelmakers, and manufacturers. Today, in the global age, even while clinging to their ancient tribal identity, they are ready for a borderless world."

—Mark Kurlansky, *The Basque History of the World*

The World According to the Basques

BY MARK KURLANSKY

❧

Here are two good pieces detailing some corners and cuisine of the French Basque lands. I included a few good articles on the Basque region of Spain, known as the Pais Vasco, in my *Northern Spain* edition, and I refer readers to that volume for a more thorough overview of the Basque lands. It's not that the Spanish portion of Basque country is more significant than the French, but it garners more headlines, for better or worse, so I devoted more attention to it in that volume.

Here are three key points to keep in mind when considering the Basques. First, the ETA (Euskadi Ta Askatasuna, Basque Homeland and Liberty) really isn't interested in you, the tourist. It's true that a car bomb in a Madrid parking garage in 2001 did harm some innocent passersby, but in general, it's government officials who are targeted—successfully, unfortunately. Second, when Basques speak of their homeland, they are referring to land that is on *both* sides of the Pyrenees, in France and in Spain—it's easy to forget that there are Basques in France, as most if not all terrorist attacks occur on Spanish soil. The three provinces that make up the Pays Basque in France are Labourd, Basse-Navarre, and Soule. In Spain the Pais Vasco has three official Basque autonomous communities: Guipúzcoa, Vizcaya, and Álava. But the province of Navarre is also mostly Basque—Mark Kurlansky, in his excellent book *The Basque History of the World,* notes that "an old form of Basque graffiti is 4 + 3 = 1." Finally, the Basque language ties the Basques of both Spain and France together more than any other element. A young employee at the San Sebastián tourist office told me that more Basque young people speak the language today than any generation within the last one hundred years. This is significant, since as recently as 1991, only about a quarter of the Basque population spoke Euskera. The young woman—who was in her twenties—at the tourist office explained to me that students in grades ahead of her were offered the choice of having classes taught in Basque or Spanish; but she and her peers were not given a choice, and all their classes were in Basque. English is now not only the secondary language of instruction but is mandatory for all students. As a result, she told me, there are actually a fair number of students who do not read or speak Spanish fluently, some not very well at all. These students are of course introduced to Spanish by television, film, literature, and periodicals, but more often they may view television programming and read newspapers, magazines, and books in Basque. And for students who live in the more rural areas of the Basque region, Basque may be the only language spoken at home.

After the September 11 tragedy and the Irish Republican Army's decision to disarm in the fall of 2001, ETA was the "sole significant guerrilla group in Western Europe," according to a report filed by *The New York Times*. The new Europe, with a single currency, has ironically given the Basques something they've failed to achieve on their own: a borderless zone uniting Basque provinces in Spain and France. This idea of borders, or rather the lack of them, is a new one for both Europeans and foreigners. Though H. V. Morton opined that one of the remarkable things about Spain is "the change from one region to another," there is almost no difference at all between the French and Spanish Basque border. Visitors to Fuentarribía (or Hondarribia) and St.-Jean-de-Luz, for example, do not necessarily feel they have crossed a border. Differences do, obviously, exist as one travels farther into Basqueland on either side, but there are more similarities than differences.

In October 2001 the ETA requested a referendum that would allow French and Spanish Basques (including those of Navarre) to cast votes for or against full autonomy. At that time Prime Minister José María Aznar argued that there is no distinction between terrorists who organize attacks on the World Trade Center and those who set off car bombs. His position has been that there must be no negotiation until ETA surrenders, and as I write this, no referendum has been held. Still, the "4 + 1 = 3" equation is definitely one to watch in the years ahead.

MARK KURLANSKY is the author of *The Basque History of the World* (1999), as well as *Cod: A Biography of the Fish That Changed the World* (1997), *Salt: A World History* (2002), all published by Walker & Co., and *Choice Cuts: A Savory Selection of Food Writing from Around the World and Throughout History* (Ballantine, 2002).

Noon is lunchtime in the little Basque village of Arnéguy: maybe fresh trout from the Nive River; *confit de canard*, a duck stewed in its own fat; sharp sheep's milk cheese, from the farm on the last mountaintop in France, served with black cherry jam from nearby Itxassou; and a bottle of red Irouléguy wine. When you're finished, it's almost two in the afternoon, and lunch is just beginning a few miles away in the little Basque village of Valcarlos. Here they serve trout from the same river, perhaps followed by a pigeon stewed in red wine—*salmi de paloma*—and a bottle of light red Navarra wine. The sharp mountain sheep's milk cheese comes without jam in Valcarlos. Then you could go back down the slope and it would nearly be the dinner hour in France, after which you could climb up again in time for a late supper in Spain.

To the Basques who live high in the Pyrenees near the frontier that separates Spain from France, there's only one difference between the two countries—mealtime. It is perhaps their one concession to European borders. The Basques are a people apart. No one knows where they come from. They have their own language, unrelated to any other known to human history and thought to be the oldest still spoken in Europe. They have their own traditions; their own breeds of cows, sheep, and pigs; their own sports, such as jai alai; their own food; even their own hat, the Basque beret. To visit Basqueland is, in a way, to see Europe as it might have been five hundred years ago, when the continent was divided not by the borders of countries but by the territories of tribal-like cultures.

Still, the adjective most often applied to the Basques—*mysterious*—is an unjust moniker for a fairly straightforward, pragmatic people. Thought to be one of the first peoples to discover North America, they were leaders in developing trade there, as well as in South America. They were southern Europe's first modern bankers, and the first industrialists, too; they made the iron fields of Vizcaya one of Europe's greatest steel centers.

The one thing the Basques have never had is their own nation. Seven provinces comprise Basqueland—and all but one have their own Basque dialect. They've never been united in a single country; currently three of the provinces are in France, and four are in Spain, although nearly all of the 2.9 million Basques live in Spain. The majority of Basques may want more autonomy, and a small minority has advocated the use of violence. For many years these armed separatists have exchanged attacks with the Spanish paramilitary and national police. The fighting almost never affects outsiders, however, and the Basques have unilaterally renounced the use of violence, producing an unofficial truce. Still, for many Basques, France and Spain are foreign countries. To them, the pass that connects Arnéguy and Valcarlos simply goes from the Basque province of Basse Navarre to the Basque province of Navarra.

Fear? What's Fear?

This most beautiful spot on the European continent, where reddish ferns grow on the slopes of the hills and rough outcroppings form jagged teeth on the crests, first achieved fame as many people and places do—with a well-written lie.

The *Chanson de Roland* (Song of Roland) is revered for the extraordinary beauty of its Old French verse. This epic poem is the heroic story of Charlemagne's nephew, who gave his life in the Roncesvalles pass, valiantly defending the tail of the Frankish column but outnumbered by two large Muslim armies. Roland died on the heights of the pass, so goes the poem, saving Europe from the Moors. To this day he is enshrined as an icon of French nationalism.

The real story is less noble: after crossing into Spain and taking several unguarded Muslim cities, Charlemagne ended his campaign at the first hint of resistance. While retreating to France in A.D. 778, he attacked and looted the undefended Basque city of Pamplona. The Basques, who in truth were the ones greatly outnumbered, waited to take their revenge at the Spanish entrance to the pass, in a pine grove known as Roncesvalles. (Roncesvalles is both the name of the pass and the Spanish name for the pine grove. Basques call the grove Orreaga; in French it's Roncevaux.) Hidden in the same woods where today Basque hunters shoot pigeon for *salmi de paloma,* they waited as Charlemagne's army climbed the heights and dropped single file into the pass. Swooping up from the forest with rocks and spears, they forced Roland's rear guard, sluggish with its heavy arms, down from the cloud-draped high ground. They probably killed every trapped Frank, including Roland. Then the Basques simply dispersed and went home to their mountain villages, leaving no army for Charlemagne to pursue.

The pass and the area around it have rested firmly in Basque hands ever since, even as it remained the preferred route to attack Spain or France, depending on the attacker. But the quest hasn't always been military. In A.D. 800 a religious hermit in the northwestern Galicia region of Iberia followed a shaft of brilliant light to a forgotten Roman cemetery and found a small mausoleum concealed by overgrown vines, weeds, and shrubs. Since beams of celestial light don't lead to just anyone's grave, he concluded that the tomb must be the burial place of Saint James—Santiago—brother of Saint John the Divine, author of the Fourth Gospel.

Since then thousands of pilgrims, mostly French, have crossed Roland's pass on their way to Santiago de Compostela in Galicia. Because this area of the Galician coast is known for scallops, a scallop shell—*coquille St.-Jacques,* as it has been called in French ever since—became the symbol of the pilgrimage. Even today a few backpackers mill about in St.-Jean-Pied-de-Port, scallop shells on their packs, as they prepare for the journey through the pass. In Roncesvalles, on the site of the battle, the modern-day pilgrims rest at the hospices and sanctuaries built for their medieval forebears. The High Gothic stone church, built in 1220, is small enough to be inviting and is awash in light filtered through long, leaded-glass windows—a perfect place for pilgrims to rest among the pines, pray, and contemplate the history of the pass, however they might imagine it.

The New Old Ways

During the first week of October, only dogs reside in the town of Irouléguy, near St.-Jean-Pied-de-Port, a village of lanes that seem to follow the meandering trails of sheep. It's harvest time, and the people of the village are in their vineyards, plucking grapes to make wine. Not that their fathers were winemakers. But their grandfathers were, and the tradition dates back to the Roncesvalles monks in the fourteenth century. The people of the area, like most peasants in southern France, made a little rough wine each year for themselves.

"Let us be what we are," a Basque named Esteban de Garibay implored the Castilian crown in the sixteenth century, and that has always been the Basque demand. Until the nineteenth century the Basques were ruled by their own laws in Spain, but when they lost autonomy, some of their traditions withered. The language started to decline. By the end of World War II, the winemaking had stopped.

Everything changed in the 1960s, when the Basques renewed their national aspirations, as well as their interest in recuperating and preserving their lost heritage. Today more Basque youths speak the ancient tongue than in any generation in one hundred years, and the past two decades have seen the greatest outpouring of Basque-language literature in history. In Irouléguy people turned their attention to wine, and by 1970 the area around the town was officially recognized as a French wine region. Today whole families work in their vineyards, most producing wine for a cooperative in nearby St.-Etienne-de-Baïgorry.

Thérèse and Michel Riouspeyrous were among the few who did not join the cooperative. Their label, Arretxea, comes from the Basque phrase *harri etxea,* "stone house," a reference to the family's home, built in 1658. To the Basques, a house (*etxea*) is more than just a house, it's a concept. It is built facing the east—and the sunrise—and symbols of the sun are often carved in the lintel over the door, along with the name of the founder and the date of construction. In Basqueland the house itself has a name, a name that is just as important as the family's name; even today people introduce themselves as being from a certain house, although the actual dwelling may have vanished several centuries ago. It remains the house of ancestry, of the clan—and the name is remembered.

The Riouspeyrouses' family house was nearly ruined when Thérèse and Michel bought it and restored its huge oak beams and spacious, high-ceilinged rooms. They began cultivating fifteen acres of grapes a decade ago. With classic Basque stubbornness, they spurn higher yields by shunning chemical fertilizers, using instead compost and sheep droppings acquired from local shepherds, just as their grandparents had. They feel wine loses flavor when the sediment is removed, so they do not filter their wine. In America this wine might be called organic, but to the Riouspeyrouses, it is simply the wine "of their house."

Invisible Borders

The village of St.-Jean-Pied-de-Port, with its medieval stone walls and little stone bridges over the gurgling Nive, is surrounded by imposing peaks draped every morning in gauzelike clouds. The town takes its name from its place as the last town before the Roncesvalles *port,* or doorway, as the local French call passes. The path leading from St.-Jean-Pied-de-Port toward the foot of the Pyrenees begins amid steep green pastures that look as soft as chenille. The narrow mountain trail leads up to the top of the last peak in France, and though it seems a thrilling climb to the sky, the altitude here is less than five thousand feet, not even as high as the tallest of New York's Adirondack Mountains.

Soon the traveler is in Arnéguy, tucked in a crook of the Nive. Like all Basque hamlets, Arnéguy is centered around a church and a jai alai court. When the border with Spain was tightly controlled, Basques from the Spanish side would line up along the little stone bridge over the Nive, which marked the border, and watch the Sunday matches. In those days a French flag flew over the little stone bridge, and gendarmes inspected papers and packages. There was also a customs house and a shop that sold products from all over France.

Once in Spain, the traveler begins a climb along the edge of a mountain to Valcarlos, where there is also a church and a jai alai court. Valcarlos is on the high slopes, and its people plant small gardens that drop down the hill. Wild apples grow in the woods.

As in Arnéguy, the houses, half a millennium old, are white and red—the white originally a protective wash of chalk, the red ("Basque red" to the French) once made from cow's blood. But in Valcarlos soldiers of Franco's Guardia Civil, wearing patent-leather three-cornered hats, inspected papers. There was a Spanish flag, and a store sold goods from all over Spain.

The customs house in Arnéguy is closed now, the gendarmes and Guardia Civil have left their stations, and even the flags are gone— all casualties of the expanding European Union. The stores are still there but without tariffs. In the next few years, the same EU currency will circulate in both towns. A traveler who does not remember will not be able to tell where France has become Spain.

The irony is that the newly united Europe has made possible what the Basques could not in the last 150 years: the rejoining of Basque provinces in Spain and France. The Basques, of course, are happy with this change—they have seen enough invaders, and most do not think the differences between France and Spain are worth fighting over. But they are traditional people, rooted in the past, and one pillar of their tradition has collapsed. So there are some who can't help but be nostalgic about the old mountain border. "You used to have to hide a little bottle of Pernod in your clothes and nervously smile at the customs official," says Jeanine Pereuil, a baker from St.-Pée whose shop makes only the Basque cake that her great-grandfather made. "Now it's not any fun at all to go across."

Essentials

You can fly to Basqueland via Madrid or Paris. From Madrid, Iberia and its affiliates fly to Pamplona and San Sebastián. From Paris, Air France serves Pau and Biarritz. But maybe the best way to get to the Roncesvalles pass is to arrive at one of the coastal cities near the border, rent a car, and take the stunningly beautiful roads (D918, D932) through the Nivelle and Nive Valleys. Almost every town on the way is worth visiting, and you'll pass roadside stands selling the wonderful local cheeses, jams, peppers, and hams.

The most comfortable hotel in St.-Jean-Pied-de-Port is **Les Pyrénées** (19 place du Général-de-Gaulle; 33.5/59.37.01.01; doubles from about $90). The rooms are nice, but what's really special is the hotel's elegant **Restaurant des Pyrénées,** which has earned two Michelin stars. (Fixed menus for two start at about $80.)

For a traditional and less expensive Basque experience, stay at the nineteenth-century **Hôtel Central.** Rooms in the back look out over the Nive River (1 place Charles de Gaulle; 33.5/59.37.00.22; doubles, about $53). The restaurant here serves mostly local food: try the trout or the *confit de canard* ($100 for two, à la carte).

Valcarlos has several places to stay, but the best bet is the moderately priced **Hostal Maitena** (34.9/48.79.02.10; doubles, about $38). Its restaurant has a spectacular view of the pass and serves local favorites, including dove and trout.

The wine growers' cooperative in **St.-Étienne-de-Baïgorry** is one of the rare French wineries that actually welcomes visitors and offers tours (33.5/59.37.41.33; through April, open 9 A.M. to noon and 2 P.M. to 6:30 P.M., Monday through Saturday; May through September, open every day).

The best way to engage Basques is to try to speak Basque, even if you can only muster a few simple phrases. English-speakers may be hard to find, but most Basques speak Spanish and French, regardless of where they live. Be sensitive to Basque sensibilities; if you refer to "being in Spain" when in fact you're in Basqueland, you'll annoy your hosts. Be aware, too, that many towns have names in both Basque and Spanish (or Basque and French); try to use the Basque name.

For information about Basque Country in France, call the Tourism Agency of the Basqueland in Bayonne, France (33.5/ 59.46.46.64); for Spain, call the Tourist Office of Donastia, the Basque name for San Sebastián (34.9/43.48.11.66).

This piece originally appeared in the March 1999 issue of *Travel Holiday*. Copyright © 1999 by Mark Kurlansky. Reprinted with permission of the author.

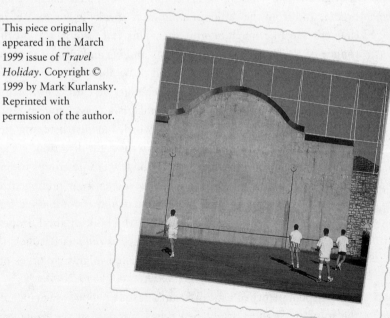

The Far Side of France

BY BRUCE SCHOENFELD

೬

BRUCE SCHOENFELD is an Emmy Award–winning television writer who contributes frequently to *Wine Spectator, Saveur, The New York Times Magazine, Outside,* and *Gourmet,* where this piece first appeared. He is also the author of *The Last Serious Thing: A Season at the Bullfights* (Simon and Schuster, 1992) and is currently working on a book featuring former tennis player Althea Gibson (to be published by HarperCollins). Schoenfeld travels often to Basque Country on both sides of the Pyrenees.

I'm driving over hills colored, like an artichoke, in varying shades of green. The windows of my rental car are open to the afternoon breeze, and from the radio an announcer speaks in staccato bursts that crackle like machine-gun fire. This is Euskera, the mother tongue of the Basques: laden with *x*'s and *k*'s and unrelated to any other language in the world. It's said to be almost unlearnable for adults, but to my ear that announcer must be calling a match of pelota, the Basque national game, which is a cross between tennis and handball. I can't understand a word, but just listening to it makes me giddy; I know I'm heading in the right direction.

The Basques, after all, are one of the few ethnic groups to have retained a strong regional identity in an increasingly homogenized Western world. And though the Basque region encompasses areas of France and Spain where Iberia joins the bulk of the European continent, many Basques identify themselves *only* as Basques, the lone European ethnic group to have resisted migratory urges and stayed put.

I've spent plenty of time in Spain's Basque region, which includes the stunning seaside city of San Sebastián, part of the Rioja wine appellation, and Bilbao, home to the Frank Gehry–designed Guggenheim Museum. There I've found that the unfortunate image of bomb-toting terrorists has little to do with the food-obsessed bankers and businessmen you are likely to encounter in the region.

I've also passed through the Pays Basque of Southwestern France, but only along the coast, usually stopping at Biarritz for a meal and a stroll along the beach on my way to Spain. Biarritz is a splendid old-world resort town, but with its wrought-iron railings, its American surfing schools, and its ascot-wearing men walking poodles, it is the international facade the Pays Basque shows to the world. The dinner menu at the restaurant inside the imposing Hôtel du Palais, which was built at the behest of the decidedly un-Basque Napoleon III, features veal *scaloppine* with spaghetti, Caesar salad, smoked salmon with sour cream and *blini,* steak tartare. I remember that food from Walt Disney World.

You have to travel over those verdant hills to find the real thing. The Basques have their own architecture; sports like pelota, goat races, and the flinging of heavy iron bars; even their own typography: the rounded letters, small *i*'s, and capital *A*'s that constitute a sort of national font. And they have their own food, from exquisite dishes at Michelin-starred restaurants to village specialties.

One of those specialties is cider, and I'm on my way to the town of Sare to meet an apple grower named Xavier Laussucq, who has promised to teach me about it. As I pull into the town square and park beside a tent with a striped awning, I see a woman there selling *gâteaux basques,* pastries filled either with cream or with a type of cherry grown only in the nearby town of Itxassou. I haven't eaten since breakfast, so I buy a slice of the cherry. When the woman hands it to me, I nearly drop it because of its surprising heft. The Basques are not a subtle people. Yet the crust is somehow flaky to the point of translucence, and the center is filled with the richest, darkest, most intensely flavored cherries I've tasted. If the packaged fruit pies of my youth were the gustatory equivalent of tinny AM radio, this is a fruit pie in glorious Dolby stereo.

Next, I head over to the Herriko Etxejo Edantegia, which for all its alarming consonants is nothing more than the bar next door. I've just been served a bottle of cider when Xavier Laussucq walks in. Taking one sip of my cider—a tart, rustic brew that tastes as if it has run head-on into grappa—he immediately invites me to his house for a bottle of his. "Mine is less green," he says. "More smooth."

Soon I'm standing in his driveway of mismatched stones, gazing at a typically ageless and immaculately kept Basque house, with whitewashed walls bisected by the timber beams that are always painted either green or red, the colors of Basque nationalism. "Built by a pirate," his wife volunteers.

Laussucq's cider seems no smoother than the bottle I had at the bar, but I'm distracted from all thoughts of apples by something dangling from the frame of the garage—strings of drying peppers, the renowned *piments d'Espelette*. The peppers of Espelette are a Basque phenomenon, like the cherries of Itxassou, the *jambon de Bayonne,* and the apples of Sare: they help define this singular nation-state without a nation.

I suddenly want to taste those peppers, to learn Euskera against all odds, to wear a red beret as the Basques do. I've been on the ground two hours.

The peppers of Espelette came from the Americas, carried back by explorers in the fifteenth century. The Basques didn't have the money to actually buy the spices, which in some cases were worth their weight in gold, so they planted the peppers instead. They grow unusually well in Espelette—a town of maroon-colored shutters with maroon-colored peppers dangling from the window frames—because it is hot and humid in the summer. "The mountains stop the clouds, so it rains quite a lot here," pepper grower Maritxu

Garacotche tells me. In August, he adds, the fields turn bright red, "the color of a matador's cape."

"Most hot peppers are nothing but fire," Garacotche says. But the Espelette peppers are not hot, not compared with the peppers of Mexico or Asia. Instead, they have an undercurrent of sweetness, a point of pride in this town. "This pepper has its own special flavor," he says. "We use it with meat and with fish, in traditional dishes like *axoa* [a stew of minced veal], and in our blood sausage. We use it in charcuterie, and we use it with eggs."

Sheep farmers, the Garacotches harvest peppers both as a hobby and as a sideline. They pick them in August and dry them for a month by putting forty to fifty on a strand and hanging them everywhere. Over the course of my stay, I will eat those peppers in almost every form imaginable. That night, in the dining room of the charming Hôtel Euzkadi, I have them roasted with sweet Spanish peppers in one course, ground into *axoa* for another, and in a sauce with a bit of tomato accompanying a *boudin noir* as a third. For each dish, they provide a different element: sweetness here, a hint of a bite there, some flavor, some complexity.

With the meal I drink Irouléguy, the wine of the Pays Basque, which is made from the sturdy but rather inelegant Tannat grape. (Later, I will have a transcendent bottle of this wine, made by Michel Riouspeyrous under the Domaine Arretxea label, but most Irouléguys I try are as interesting as a punch in the head.) For dessert I have a typical Basque dish—Itxassou cherries in a compote poured over the strong goat cheese called Iraty. So intense is the flavor of the cherries that I decide to set out the following morning on a pilgrimage to Itxassou.

It isn't much of a pilgrimage, distances being quite manageable in the Pays Basque. In twenty minutes I'm standing beside a cherry grower with the mellifluous name of Xan Estebecomena, looking out at his denuded trees. All three of the varieties unique to the area were harvested at the beginning of June, two weeks before my visit. And some have an incredibly short life span. The small, bright-colored Xapata is delicious for eating but spoils easily. "They're only good for two days, and they only ripen during that window in June," says Estebecomena, one of fifteen growers belonging to a cherry-producing cooperative. "People from Bordeaux to Toulouse come just to taste them." The other two varieties, Peloa and Beltxa, are dark and black and live on through the year as cherry compote. Estebecomena gives me a jar, then sends me off to the restaurant at the Hôtel du Pont d'Enfer, in Bidarry, for lunch.

To get to the hotel, I cross a medieval bridge spanning a small river. The restaurant itself isn't much to look at, with a cigarette machine stuck in the corner and advertising in Lucite stands on the tables. The cuisine is billed as rustic, and nobody is wearing a sport coat, much less a suit. Yet as it turns out, Estebecomena knows food as well as he does cherries. My lunch borders on magnificence.

I have local white asparagus, a spongy mushroom pâté of star-tling intensity, and *salmis de palombe,* a fricassee of wild pigeon. The pigeon meat is the color of clay, and the rich brown sauce, made with Madiran wine, makes me call for another basket of bread to soak up all I can. I struggle with the knife and fork, then give up and grasp the pigeon in my hands, tearing off hunks of meat with my teeth. My server, the chef's daughter, nods with approval. "Like a Basque," she says.

Any visitor to the Pays Basque will eventually pass through St.-Jean-Pied-de-Port, or Doninane Garazi to the Basques, who have spelled out their version of the name in flowers on a hillside in the city center. Propitiously located near the end of a mountain pass from Spain and at the intersection of three main highways and a river, it serves as the unofficial capital of the region. And Les Pyrénées is the best place to bunk within an hour's drive. There are postcard racks and souvenir shops along the town's main street, but also genuine bustle in the air, as if its citizens are going about important business.

The restaurant at Les Pyrénées lost one of its two Michelin stars this year, but by all accounts the food is as it has been for decades. Firmin Arrambide started cooking in his father's kitchen at the hotel when he was fifteen, which was thirty-nine years ago. His meals don't qualify as Basque cooking exactly, but as cooking born of one Basque's love of gastronomy. "Things don't have to be absolutely Basque to make Basque food," he says. "I take ingredients I like and I make dishes; I put Basque touches in what you'd call European dishes."

So my salad of pan-fried crayfish is served with a rich sauce of those ubiquitous Espelette peppers. A piece of sea bass, as meaty, moist, and noble as any steak, comes with beautifully undercooked local vegetables (artichokes, lima beans, and peas) that aren't a mere accompaniment but an integral part of the whole. For dessert, cheese and cherries are paired with grape and walnut bread that seems almost Scandinavian. Drinking a glass of local pear eau-de-vie, I nibble at exquisite petits-fours (and a miniature crème brûlée in a pan fit for a dollhouse), then watch dusk settle over the terrace. It isn't difficult to understand why the Basques want to preserve their heritage—and their way of life.

That thought recurs at a festival in the town of Hasparren when I watch a game of pelota. Five players on each of two teams, one outfitted in red and one in white, scatter across a blacktop as long as a football field with a high wall at each end and fling a hard ball back and forth (with wicker baskets or paddles or just their hands) until someone drops it and a point is recorded. Later, outside the Relais des Tilleuls, in the town center, I drink a beer as children in berets dance a *saut basque,* which is like the elegant Catalonian *sardana* set on fast-forward. I can be nowhere else in the world.

With the beer, I try a slice of the sweetly salty *jambon de*

Bayonne, which tastes like most any other good-quality ham. What I really want, I'm told, is Ibaïona ham, which is much rarer—there are only three producers who make it. Luckily, one of them, Louis Ospital, has his factory in Hasparren, so off I go.

Ospital is short and balding, dressed in jeans and a madras shirt. He explains that whereas *jambon de Bayonne* is made from a six-month-old pig that has eaten, as pigs are wont to do, whatever has come its way, Ibaïona comes from year-old pigs fed only cereal. Their meat is coated with a mixture of sea salt, garlic, and—sure enough—Espelette peppers, then hung for months in cold storage. After four to six more months at room temperature, Ospital rubs the Ibaïona hams with a flavorless red pepper from Spain. "Everything here has to be red, white, or green, the colors of the Basque flag, or it won't sell," he says.

Ibaïona tastes nothing like *jambon de Bayonne* or Italy's prosciutto or Spain's *patanegra.* It's more like a country ham, a Christmas ham, but stronger, saltier. I don't much care for it on the first bite, but by the third I adore it. "Very few restaurants serve it," Ospital says when I ask where I might eat it again.

Fortunately, the Auberge de la Galupe is one of them. In the town of Urt on the region's northern border, it's set in a seventeenth-century whitewashed house with a stone floor. The chef, Christian Parra, worked at New York City's Rainbow Room in the 1960s. He's half Basque, half *béarnais,* a huge man who roams the floor restlessly checking on his patrons. I eat a six-course meal in which each dish is perfectly prepared (though not by Parra, who never leaves my sight).

I have pan-fried mullet and then domesticated pigeon, which bears approximately the same relation to the wild pigeon I ate at the Pont d'Enfer that Arthur Miller does to Dennis Miller. I have ravioli with duck and local foie gras—and, as part of an artichoke ragout, morsels of Ibaïona ham, more delicate this time, but unmistakable. I stagger out into the sunshine at four o'clock, ready to play some pelota myself, if I only knew how.

On my last night in the Pays Basque, Spain and France are contesting an elimination match of the European soccer championship. I find myself in Chez Pablo, a one-room restaurant in the overgrown fishing village of St.-Jean-de-Luz. The televised match is on in the kitchen, and servers rush into the dining room with updates. Five miles from the Spanish border, Chez Pablo serves what purports to be Spanish food. The owner's grandmother had fled Bilbao when Franco assumed power in the 1930s and gone into business cooking the food of her homeland. I order a salad and a Spanish omelet, but the omelet is like nothing I've tasted, in Spain or anywhere else. It has onions and, yes, Espelette peppers—though not in the classic *piperade* that usually accompanies a Basque omelet, but laid across the top like Spanish sweet peppers. The tomato sauce underneath tastes like (and perhaps is) ketchup. I eat it with sangría, relishing every odd, multicultural bite.

The chef, who is also the owner, is uncertain of her soccer allegiance. "I have mixed blood and mixed emotions," she says, which strikes me as a succinct description of modern Basqueness. There are Basques on both teams, but there is, of course, no Basque team. As I finish my sangria, I hear a whoop of joy from the kitchen. One team or the other has scored a goal, I know—but which one, it is impossible to say.

Traveling the High-Low Country

The Basques are food-obsessed people—it's said that they spend a greater proportion of their paycheck on restaurant meals than any other ethnic group in the world, and almost every dining establishment in Basque territory is worth a visit.

For simple atmosphere and carefully prepared versions of local favorites such as veal stew and wild pigeon, try **Restaurant du Pont d'Enfer** (Bidarry; 33.5/59.37.70.88). In Aïnhoa you'll find great food at the **Hôtel Ithurria** (33.5/59.29.92.11), and in Sare at the **Hôtel Arraya** (33.5/59.54.20.46).

The region also has its share of Michelin-starred restaurants— nine at last count. The lone two-star is Christian Parra's **Auberge de la Galupe,** just off the quay in Urt (33.5/59.56.21.84), with fine renditions of Basque, *beárnais,* and French dishes. The one-star **Table des Frères Ibarboure** (chemin de Ttaliénia; 33.5/59.54.81.64), home to some of the most evolved plates of seafood around, is tucked into a residential area in Bidart, between Biarritz and St.-Jean-de-Luz. Try the rich codfish ravioli in vegetable broth, and a tuna *carpaccio* with phyllo in Asian spices. And chef Firmin Arrambide's Basque-influenced takes on classic French food make **Les Pyrénées,** in St.-Jean-Pied-de-Port (19 place du Général-de-Gaulle; 33.5/59.37.01.01), the standard for Pays Basque dining. (The rooms at this Relais & Châteaux property in an eighteenth-century inn border on the garish, but they're still better than anything else around.)

For accommodations in the village of St.-Jean-de-Luz, **Hôtel-Golf de Chantaco** (route d'Ascain, 33.5/59.26.14.76), an old and somewhat forbidding mansion set beside a formidable golf course, is the most lavish. A better choice might be one of the small hostelries by the port, such as **La Marisa** (16 rue Sopite; 33.5/59.26.95.46). The rooms are small, but the management are friendly and speak English.

Town festivals play a large role in the social life of the area. Call the Aquitaine Tourist Office in Bordeaux (33.5/56.01.70.00) to learn where and when you can don a beret and dance a *saut basque.*

Low-cost carrier **RyanAir** (London Gatwick; 33.5/44.541.56. 95.69; www.ryanair.com) serves some of the second-tier cities of Europe and has made travel to the Basque Country easier than ever, with nonstops from London Gatwick and similar outposts. Don't bother with the five-dollar sandwich from the vending carts in the middle of the aisle: the food, any food, will be better once you arrive.

The Basque Cake

BY MARK KURLANSKY

~

Though I prefer not to include excerpts from books in this series, on occasion I have made an exception. The following piece is the opening chapter of *The Basque History of the World* by Mark Kurlansky. When Kurlansky asked if I might consider including it in this edition, I pulled the book off my shelf and reread the chapter. I had forgotten how much I enjoyed reading the stories of St. Pée (and other towns) during World War II, as well as how fond I am of gâteau Basque (you'll find a recipe in *The Basque Kitchen* by Gerald Hirigoyen—see *Flavors and Tables of the Southwest*—but somehow it is simply *not* as yummy as the gâteau made on Basque soil).

MARK KURLANSKY, introduced earlier in this section, began his career as a foreign correspondent writing about the last years of Francoism in Spain, especially in the Basque provinces, and has returned there annually for the past twenty-five years. His book *Cod: A Biography of the Fish That Changed the World* won a James Beard Award for Excellence in Food Writing, and he is also the author of *A Continent of Islands: Searching for the Caribbean Destiny* (Perseus Publishing, 1993) and *A Chosen Few: The Resurrection of European Jewry* (Ballantine, 2002).

The truth is that the Basque distrusts a stranger much too much to invite someone into his home who doesn't speak his language.

—Les Guides Bleus Pays Basque
Français et Espagnol, 1954

The game the rest of the world knows as jai alai was invented in the French Basque town of St.-Pée-sur-Nivelle. St. Pée, like most of the towns in the area, holds little more than one curving street against a steep-pastured slope. The houses are whitewashed, with either red or green shutters and trim. Originally the whitewash was made of chalk. The traditional dark red color, known in French as *rouge Basque,* Basque red, was originally made from cattle blood. Espelette, Ascain, and other towns in the valley look almost identical. A fronton court—a single wall with bleachers to the left—is always in the center of town.

While the French were developing tennis, the Basques, as they often did, went in a completely different direction. The French ball was called a *pelote,* a French word derived from a verb for winding string. These pelotes were made of wool or cotton string wrapped into a ball and covered with leather. The Basques were the first Europeans to use a rubber ball, a discovery from the Americas, and the added bounce of wrapping rubber rather than string—the *pelote Basque,* as it was originally called—led them to play the ball off walls, a game which became known also as *pelote* or, in Spanish and English, *pelota.* A number of configurations of walls as well as a range of racquets, paddles, and barehanded variations began to develop. *Jai alai,* an Euskera phrase meaning "happy game," originally referred to a pelota game with an additional long left-hand wall. Then in 1857, a young farm worker in St. Pée named Gantxiki Harotcha, scooping up potatoes into a basket, got the idea of propelling the ball even faster with a long, scoop-shaped basket strapped to one hand. The idea quickly spread throughout the Nivelle Valley and in the twentieth century, throughout the Americas, back to where the rubber ball had begun.

St. Pée seems to be a quiet town. But it hasn't always been so. During World War II the Basques, working with the French underground, moved British and American fliers and fleeing Jews on the route up the valley from St.-Jean-de-Luz to Sare and across the mountain pass to Spain.

The Gestapo was based in the big house next to the *fronton,* the pelota court. Jeanine Pereuil, working in her family's pastry shop across the street, remembers refugees whisked past the gaze of the Germans. The Basques are said to be a secretive people. It is largely a myth—one of many. But in 1943, the Basques of the Nivelle Valley kept secrets very well. Jeanine Pereuil has many stories about the Germans and the refugees. She married a refugee from Paris.

The only change Jeanine made in the shop in her generation was to add a few figurines on a shelf. Before the Basques embraced Christianity with a legendary passion, they had other beliefs, and many of these have survived. Jeanine goes to her shelf and lovingly picks out the small figurine of a joaldun, a man clad in sheepskin with bells on his back. "Can you imagine," she says, "at my age buying such things. This is my favorite," she says, picking out a figure from the ezpata dantza, the sword dance performed on the Spanish side especially for the Catholic holiday of Corpus Christi. The dancer is wearing white with a red sash, one leg kicked out straight and high and the arms stretched out palms open.

Born in 1926, Jeanine is the fourth generation to make gâteau Basque and sell it in this shop. Her daughter is the fifth generation. The Pereuils all speak Basque as their first language and make the exact same cake. She is not sure when her great grandfather, Jacques Pereuil, started the shop, but she knows her grandfather, Jacques's son, was born in the shop in 1871.

Gâteau Basque, like the Basques themselves, has an uncertain origin. It appears to date from the eighteenth century and may have originally been called *bistochak.* While today's gâteau Basque is a cake filled with either cherry jam or pastry cream, the original bistochak was not a gâteau but a bread. The cherry filling predates the cream one. The cake appears to have originated in the valley of the winding Nivelle River, which includes the town of Itxassou, famous for its black cherries, a Basque variety called *xapata*.

Basques invented their own language and their own shoes, espadrilles. They also created numerous sports including not only pelota but wagon-lifting contests called *orgo joko,* and sheep fighting known as *aharitalka.* They developed their own farm tools such as the two-pronged hoe called a *laia,* their own breed of cow known as the blond cow, their own sheep called the white-head sheep, and their own breed of pig, which was only recently rescued from extinction.

And so they also have their own black cherry, the xapata from Itxassou, which only bears fruit for a few weeks in June but is so productive during those weeks that a large surplus is saved in the form of preserves. The cherry preserve–filled cakes were sold in the market in Bayonne, a city celebrated for its chocolate makers, who eventually started buying Itxassou black cherries to dip in chocolate.

Today in most of France and Spain a gâteau Basque is cream filled, but the closer to the valley of the Nivelle, the more likely it is to be cherry filled.

Jeanine, whose shop makes nothing besides one kind of bread, the two varieties of gâteau Basque, and a cookie based on the gâteau Basque dough, finds it hard to believe that her specialty originated as cherry bread. Just as the shop's furniture has never been changed, the recipe has never changed. The Pereuils have always made it as cake, not bread, and, she insists, have always made both the cream and cherry fillings. Cream is overwhelmingly the favorite. The mailman, given a little two-inch cake every morning when he brings the mail, always chooses cream.

Maison Pereuil may not be old enough for the earlier bistochak cherry bread recipe, but the Pereuil cake is not like the modern buttery gâteau Basque either. Jeanine's tawny, elastic confection is a softer, more floury version of the sugar-and-egg-white macaroon offered to Louis XIV and his young bride, the Spanish princess María Theresa, on their wedding day, May 8, 1660, in St.-Jean-de-Luz. Ever since, the macaroon has been a specialty of that Basque port at the mouth of the Nivelle.

When asked for the antique recipe for her family's gâteau Basque, Jeanine Pereuil smiled bashfully and said, "You know, people keep offering me a lot of money for this recipe."

How much do they offer?

"I don't know. I'm not going to bargain. I will never give out the recipe. If I sold the recipe, the house would vanish. And this is the house of my father and his father. I am keeping their house. And I hope my daughter will do the same for me."

This chapter originally appeared in *The Basque History of the World* (Walker & Company, 1999). Copyright © 1999 by Mark Kurlansky. Reprinted with permission of the author.

Biarritz

BY NAOMI BARRY

ے

Biarritz—I just love saying the name, and I love the place even more. Royal as its history may be, Biarritz is also one of the most down-to-earth beach communities I've ever visited.

NAOMI BARRY lives in Paris and has been a frequent contributor over many years to the *International Herald Tribune* and *Gourmet,* where this piece first appeared in 1970. She is also the author of *Paris Personal* (E. P. Dutton, 1963) and *Food alla Florentine* (Doubleday, 1972). Her work has appeared in the *Paris, Morocco,* and *Venice* editions of *The Collected Traveler.*

The Queen of Beaches and the Beach of Kings," proclaims the publicity. "Biarritz is so *snob,* it doesn't have to be beautiful," cracks a more acid observer. The royal background of Biarritz is enough to reel a republican head: Empress Eugénie dancing the fandango for her friends; Edward VII walking down the beach followed by his dog, Caesar; Alfonso XIII teaching French society ladies to curtsy for a costume ball. Other tableaux: Dowager Empress Maria Fedorovna arriving in a special train painted white, with one coach filled with flowers, and a booted, bearded Russian imperial porter at every door; and in the suite of the grand dukes, little Vladimir Nabokov coming all the way from St. Petersburg to build sand castles on the Basque coast. Did he spy his first Lolita playing on the golden crescent beach?

Even though most of today's kings are of cattle or cotton, I was a bit reticent about Biarritz. According to my theory of diminishing resorts, once a place is world renowned, I am at least twenty years too late.

But Biarritz is like a vintage Bugatti. The latest fashions come and go, but both the resort's and the car's high style endures. The houses and villas are a tribute to nineteenth-century "ugly," but the passage of time has given them a period charm. The tone of the town is discretion. A great deal goes on, but it is never screamed in your face. Society is closed: most of the parties take place in private villas, but one invitation is enough to make you a member of the clan.

The natural attractions of Biarritz are a sweeping bay and cliffs shaded by feathery tamarisk trees. Along the beach the neat lineup of striped tents resembles a picturesque row of Sahara kepis. On the rocky promontories at either end of the beach are the two bastions of elegance—the gleaming white Casino Bellevue and the brick-red Hôtel du Palais. The monumental Palais (but housing only two hundred bedrooms) is one of the celebrated hostelries of the world. It was built on the smoking ruins of the Villa Eugénie, which is supposed to have been much less grand than the present structure.

The Palais now belongs to the municipality and is open from the first of May until the end of September. Each September it is the setting for a sumptuous costume ball that is one of the annual society events of France. Themes for costumes and decors have been the Second Empire (a living tableau was a reproduction of the Winterhalter portrait of the Empress Eugénie surrounded by the crinolined ladies of her court), Goya, Edward VII, the toreador, and the grand dukes of Russia.

Even if you don't sleep at the Palais, spend a day at the kidney-shaped pool overlooking the Atlantic. A cabana around the pool rents by the season and is as desirably hard to get as a box at the opera.

A must is to have lunch one day at the pool restaurant where you help yourself to a selection of the forty-six delicious hors d'oeuvre. This luncheon stop is equivalent to checking in at headquarters. The doorman, a majordomo dressed in pristine white, is known affectionately as the Admiral. Try the new Beach Bar cocktail there, *Rayon Vert*. It is a lethal concoction of, among other things, Izarra (the golden liqueur of the Basques), blue curaçao, and *eau-de-vie de framboise*. When caught together in a glass, the combination evokes the famous green ray that streaks across the summer horizon of Biarritz at sundown.

The Spaniards discovered Biarritz around the 1830s, and they are still coming strong. They prefer the gaiety of the French Basque town to San Sebastián, their own summer capital a few miles down the coast. The irresistible pole is the Casino Bellevue, where Spaniards make up 70 percent of the clientele. Spain has no authorized gambling. Although Biarritz has a year-round municipal casino, the Bellevue, which is open from the first of August until the fifteenth of October, determines the season.

Several years ago a Spanish customs man bicycled to the casino at Hendaye, the first French town over the border. He won a felicitous two hundred dollars. The casino management offered him a taxi to Biarritz for the next evening where the gambling possibilities were greater. The little *douanier* won ten thousand dollars there. The Bellevue directors, eager to get it back, invited him with exquisite hospitality to return for dinner the following evening. Naturally, a taxi was put at his disposal. On his third night at the roulette wheel the customs man won twenty-one thousand dollars.

The journalists, who spend their summers at Biarritz for just such stories as this one, gleefully telephoned the news to their Paris newspapers. The Spanish government immediately clamped an embargo on such goings-on where their border functionaries were concerned. The *douanier* was forced to retire gracefully with his fortune to the Spanish side of the frontier. "He is probably a big promoter in Marbella today," chortled the correspondent of *Le Figaro*. "Without the help of his government, he would surely have lost it all."

At the Hôtel du Palais you don't have to lose your money at the gaming tables to spend it. A suite costs $120 a day. There is an additional charge of five dollars a day for your dog. The canines eat à la carte, just like everybody else. One Indian prince thought his cocker spaniel looked sad and asked the management to prepare a party in his rooms. At five o'clock in the evening fifteen thoroughbreds-in-lodging showed up for a spread of raw meats, cooked meats, little cakes, and rice.

A wealthy Spaniard who comes every year takes a sitting room and two bedrooms. One bedroom is for the man and his wife. The other bedroom, with twin beds, is for housing the maid and the family's boxer, who turns in every night like Little Red Riding Hood's Grandma Wolf.

Edward VII used the Palais as his summer palace for years. In

1911, while at the hotel, he named Herbert Henry Asquith the prime minister. A plaque in the lobby commemorates the event. To another plaque honoring Edward VII was recently added the name of Edward VIII. The duke of Windsor believed he had continued the family tradition in patronizing the hotel.

Sir Gladwyn Jebb's daughter was engaged at the Palais during the period that her father was British ambassador to France. Englishmen who can afford it are loyal to the Palais. So are rich South Americans who probably would never have succeeded if they hadn't emigrated from Spain.

The seven o'clock rendezvous is across the street from the Palais at Sonny's Bar, a glorified version of an English pub with oak paneling, coaching prints, and shining horse brasses. The pulchritudinous young crowd that gathers here belong to a special race of the bronzed and the beautiful.

In Biarritz everybody swims like a dolphin, and the more intrepid go in for surfing. The sport was introduced several years ago by Peter Viertel. The long rolling waves around Biarritz make it the best resort in Europe for riding the boards.

For a glimpse of Second Empire, pause for a coffee and pastry at the Miramar, which has a stunning view over the sea. The Miramar, established in the 1850s, has maintained a charming decor of the period. It makes its own chocolates, bonbons, *touron* (a sticky sweet almond confection), cakes, and cookies. The Spaniards, whose timetable is always a few hours behind everyone else's, rush in for their afternoon hot chocolate at about eight o'clock at night. They are served in a hurry, and the Miramar closes up.

Gastronomy in the grand manner reigns at the Café de Paris across the street from the Casino Bellevue. It is one of the great restaurants of France, and a meal here is worth a trip to Biarritz, even out of season. During World War I the casino served as a hospital for American officers. An enterprising fish merchant, whose market was situated where the Café de Paris is now, set up a bar to drink the health of the young Americans, as soon as they could totter out of bed. He then added a little restaurant.

In 1921 Robert Laporte, a youthful chef from the famous Chapon Fin in Bordeaux, took over the kitchens and stayed for twenty-six years. Laporte then bought the Biarritz airport restaurant, Relais de Parme, and made it the only airport restaurant in France to earn a star from the *Guide Michelin*. Private planes often radio the tower to order dinner at the Relais de Parme before taxiing in for a landing.

To Laporte's astonishment, the week he opened the restaurant "our crowd," led by the Windsors, followed him out to the airport in full evening dress. The duchess chided him for the globe lighting fixture in the ceiling, which made the place look like a bathroom. The lighting, of course, has since been changed to suit.

Papa Laporte's restaurant gets a great deal of business from motorists driving down to Spain on route N10. His specialties start with a *soupe de poissons,* which he describes as being more of a bisque, enriched as it is with egg yolk and fresh cream. It is a savory brew made from eight kinds of seafood including mussels and langoustines. He does a chicken in champagne, which is served with a crêpe wrapped around a banana that has been baked in butter in the oven. Another favorite dish is a *poularde à la crème,* deglazed with whiskey and accompanied by corn croquettes.

Five years ago Laporte returned to the heart of Biarritz by buying the Café de Paris. He placed his son, Pierre, whom he had trained himself, in charge. Pierre has been nominated one of the six most illustrious young chefs in France by those Bobbsey Twin guides of French gastronomy, Christian Millau and Henri Gault. Lithe, dark, and with a gleaming smile, the thirty-eight-year-old Laporte is probably the handsomest chef and restaurateur in the country. Off duty, dressed in a midnight-blue polo shirt and vermilion slacks with vermilion espadrilles to match, he is a striking advertisement for Biarritz. In addition, he speaks an enchanting Dublin English, which he learned as a student at Trinity College.

Pierre is an ardent surfer and fisherman. "If I am lucky enough to catch a *loubine* (a local variety of sea perch) at five in the afternoon and serve it to you at seven or eight in the evening. . . ." The result is so poetic that he is momentarily at a loss for words.

Sole, turbot, lobster, langouste, and langoustine are all freshly caught in the waters off Biarritz. One of the Lucullan delights of the Café de Paris is a brochette of langoustines. The tails are shelled, wrapped in bacon, and speared on individual skewers. They are so delicate and moist that they melt in the mouth. With them goes a sublime *mousseline* sauce flavored with chopped fresh tarragon.

The Café de Paris is a procession of subtle refinements. If you are courteous enough to telephone for a reservation, the management rewards you with an exquisite tablecloth. The "reserved" tablecloths are all different but of the finest fabrics and the most appealing patterns.

Dishes are presented with admirable little bouquets of fresh flowers arranged by Mrs. Laporte. To while away the time until your first course is ready, you are served a superb bowl of vegetables (artichoke hearts, giant mushrooms, and onions) marinated *à la grecque*. This offering is the restaurant's gesture of hospitality.

For Pierre, the first thing that counts in any meal is the bread. Dissatisfied with commercial bread, he sought out an old-fashioned baker in the nearby village of Bidart who still grinds his flour between two millstones. The flour, which contains both the germ and the skin, must be used within six days. The Café de Paris bakes its irresistible rolls twice a day, just before lunch and dinner. Another favorite dish is chicken and langouste, cooked together in a *sauce américaine*.

Pierre has a horror of conserves. If he must have a preserve of asparagus and *cèpes,* he puts it up himself. He also prepares the fresh foie gras from the neighboring province of Les Landes.

Pierre's passion, however, is sugar work. He spins it, he blows it, and he weaves it. His desserts are *beaux-arts* productions. For his daughter's communion he labored twenty-five hours to produce a basket of white flowers all made from sugar. White is the most painstaking color of all, because each petal must be sugar-soldered without the seams showing.

A remarkable tour de force is a flambéed extravaganza of oranges and ice cream. The entire show goes on at tableside before your eyes. One waiter brings in a bowl of sliced oranges that have been soaked in Grand Marnier. Another carries a free-form sculptured ice pedestal illuminated by a small electric bulb set into the base. Resting on the ice are silvered goblets containing hollowed oranges filled with balls of either vanilla ice cream or orange sherbet. Over the whole is a voluminous bridal veil of spun sugar. Into a long oval copper chafing pan go the oranges, the ice cream or sherbet, and the lacy threads of sugar. A dramatic flaming, and it is served forth—an unbelievable taste experience of hot and cold. As an example of his virtuosity, once when I was there Pierre quickly baked an open-faced apple tart in the shape of a fish. Head and fins were a *chausson* of apples. The glazed apple slices duplicated the scales.

Be sure to taste the excellent cheese *maison.* Runny cheeses such as Brie and Camembert are scraped of their crusts, macerated in cognac and Armagnac, strengthened with a little Roquefort, and enriched with a bit of fresh heavy cream. The new mélange is packed in a crock and topped with shelled walnut halves.

Pay a visit to the wine cellars, whose stock is insured for $170,000. Imperials of Bordeaux, equivalent to eight ordinary bottles, are served for big parties of eight to ten people. "The bigger the bottle, the finer the wine," says Pierre. A supply of white wine and champagne is kept chilled in a five-degree chamber, ready to drink on a moment's notice. In the guest book one happy customer rechristened the Café de Paris the Café de Paradis.

Biarritz has a popular-priced department store called Biarritz Bonheur. It's as good a nickname as any for this smiling seaside town.

Bibliography

The Basque History of the World, Mark Kurlansky, Walker & Co., 1999. By the time you reach the end of this book, you will know I am an enormous fan of Mark Kurlansky. (Two of his books I particularly love are *Cod* and *Salt,* highlighted in the *Flavors and Tables of the Southwest* bibliography.) Just as he did so successfully in his previous books, here he wonderfully weaves other stories—culinary, political, literary, and economic—into the history of the Basques. Kurlansky reminds us that the Basques are a puzzling contradiction, as they are Europe's oldest nation without ever having been a country. One of his most pertinent observations in this book is that "the Basques are not isolationists. They never wanted to leave Europe. They only wanted to be Basque. Perhaps it is the French and the Spanish, relative newcomers, who will disappear in another thousand years. But the Basques will still be there, playing strange sports, speaking a language of *k*'s and *x*'s that no one else understands, naming their houses and facing them toward the eastern sunrise in a land of legends, on steep green mountains by a cobalt sea—still surviving, enduring by the grace of what Juan San Martin called *Euskaldun bizi nahia,* the will to live like a Basque." Written in unerring and exhaustive Kurlansky style, this book is positively *de rigueur.* If you only have time to read one, this is it.

Postcards from the Basque Country: A Journey of Enchantment and Imagination, Beth Nelson, Stewart, Tabori and Chang, 1999. This hard-to-categorize book is lovely, unique, quirky, offbeat, and very personal. It's not a work of fiction, however; the reader is introduced to the Pays Basque (mostly) through pages of the author's diary, which are filled with musings on travel, the Basques, and her life. Each page is an individual collage, filled with paper ephemera such as stamps, old postcards, maps, timetables, and photos cut out of magazines. "From Biarritz to Bilbao, the Bay of Biscay is the heart of a Basque," Nelson notes. And about travel, she writes "You don't really long for another country, you long for something in yourself that you don't have or haven't been able to find." I'm fond of this little book, and it's a nice souvenir as well (and a great gift, too).

The Basque Series

Readers truly interested in the Basques simply must get to know the Basque Series, published by the University of Nevada Press in Reno. If you are curious, as I initially was, why this series—with over forty titles—is based in Nevada, it is because great numbers of Basques emigrated to Nevada as well as New Mexico, California, Arizona, Utah, Idaho, Oregon, Washington, Wyoming, and Colorado. An entire ethnographic display at the Museo Vasco in Bilbao is devoted to this theme, and Robert Laxalt related in his book *The Land of My Fathers: A Son's Return to the Basque Country* that when he and his wife visited his cousins in St.-Jean-de-Port, they lived on the Street of the Americans. They were puzzled by this because they thought they were the only Americans in the village, but they soon learned that the villas on that street were built in the 1920s and 1930s by Basques who had lived in the United States and worked as sheepherders for as long as ten or twenty years in the mountains and deserts of the American West. "The Basques who had come back with money and built their villas consorted mainly with each other in the bistros and on village feast days, sharing mutual experiences in towns named Reno, Fresno, San Francisco, Los Angeles, among others."

So the University of Nevada Press is a perfect home for these wonderful books, and I encourage anyone interested in learning more to read at least a few of the titles in this series. An eighteen-page catalog showcases the series (you may request one by contacting the university at Mail Stop 166, Reno, Nev. 89557-0076; 877-682-6657; www.nvbooks.nevada.edu). There are too many titles to list here, but the selection is quite remarkable. A few titles to represent the range of the list include *Chorizos in an Iron Skillet: Memories and Recipes from an American Basque Daughter; Basque Dance; A Travel Guide to Basque America: Families, Feasts and Festivals* (this would be particularly great, I think, for immersing yourself in the Basque culture before and after a trip); *The Basque Poetic Tradition;* several dictionaries (Basque to English and the reverse); *The Guernica Generation: Basque Refugee Children of the Spanish Civil War;* several bilingual children's books; and the complete works of Robert Laxalt, who passed away in 2001. I think it is fair to say you won't find a better selection of Basque fiction and nonfiction—published in English—anywhere.

I have not read every title, but of those I have, I especially love *A Book of the*

Basques (Rodney Gallop) and *The Land of My Fathers: A Son's Return to the Basque Country* (with photographs by Joyce Laxalt) and *Sweet Promised Land*, both by Robert Laxalt. In *The Land of My Fathers* Laxalt alternates traditional Basque maxims and beliefs with recent stories and events that illustrate the old tales. Among them are:

My cousin Eliza claims that the Basques have a masochistic nature. When it is time to work, the Basques approach it as though it were a flagellation. It is as if they are punishing themselves. Eliza feels that the Basques want to sweat and toil in the old way. *By the sweat of your brow,* she claims the Bible says. If you are working for someone, you must give it your all, or it will not be money honestly earned. But I know they are not punishing themselves. For them, work is a cleansing. The Basques derive pleasure from it. They emerge from work as if stepping out of a bath. There are smiles on their faces when a laborious task is done. When it is time to play—be it at jai alai, handball, or the running of the bulls—they will play as hard as they worked. They will think of nothing else.

I learned then what I always suspected. The Basques are not vindictive, but neither are they a forgiving people.

The Basques don't have much use for those who don't do their duty or ful- fill their obligation to family. These ne'er-do-wells are relegated to inscrutable silence and oblivion.

Among the Basques, to ask for a written contract implies a lack of trust. A man's word is a thousand times stronger because it commits his honor. The written law is intended to bring order to society, but the Basques already pos- sess that with unwritten tradition.

The Dordogne and the Lot

"It was a stroke of genius on my part to make the tour of the Dordogne region before plunging into the bright and hoary world of Greece. Just to glimpse the black, mysterious river at Domme from the beautiful bluff at the edge of the town is something to be grateful for all one's life. To me this river, this country, belong to the poet, Rainer Maria Rilke. It is not French, not Austrian, not European even: it is the country of enchantment which the poets have staked out and which they alone may lay claim to. It is the nearest thing to paradise this side of Greece. Let us call it the Frenchman's paradise, by way of making a concession. Actually it must have been a paradise for many thousands of years. I believe it must have been so for the Cro-Magnon man, despite the fossilized evidences of the great caves which point to a condition of life rather bewildering and terrifying . . . I believe that this great peaceful region of France will always be a sacred spot for man and that when the cities have killed off the poets this will be the refuge and the cradle of the poets to come. I repeat, it was most important for me to have seen the Dordogne: it gives me hope for the future of the race, for the future of the earth itself. France may one day exist no more, but the Dordogne will live on just as dreams live on and nourish the souls of men."

—Henry Miller, *The Colossus of Maroussi*

A Leisurely Meander

BY WILLIAM GRIMES

⁓

I love pieces about rivers, or any body of water really, especially those that follow a river's course from end to end. (Readers familiar with my *Provence* edition may recall "Relish the Rhone" by Clive Irving, in which he followed the Rhone from Switzerland to Stes.-Marie-de-la Mer.)

WILLIAM GRIMES is restaurant critic of *The New York Times*, and is also the author of *Straight Up or On the Rocks* (North Point Press, 2001, hardcover; 2002, paperback) and *My Fine Feathered Friend* (North Point Press, 2002).

The Lot may be the world's least goal-oriented river. It begins unpromisingly as a small spurt in the rugged uplands of south-central France, achieves creek status as it spills through limestone gorges and faults, and then, a full-fledged river, wanders in a tight series of loops before slowing down and strolling amiably toward the Garonne, late for the appointment and not even bothering to look at its watch. Before reaching its destination near Aiguillon, a straight-line distance of perhaps 100 miles, the Lot somehow manages to wander 192 miles. Virtually useless for navigation, regarded with condescension by fishermen, it offers a narrative line made up entirely of digressions.

From the outset, I used it as an excuse. In the course of a week I would drive alongside the Lot from start to finish, always keeping the river in sight. Occasional deviations would be allowed, but in general the river would define the journey.

The Lot rises due east of Mende, in the wild country once stalked by Robert Louis Stevenson and the persnickety Modestine, heroine of *Travels with a Donkey in the Cévennes*. Duty demanded a search for the first tiny streamlet, somewhere out on the arid scrub of Mont Goulet, but with the Cévennes National Park and the grim heights of Mont Lozère nearby, the impulse to deviate won out. Gaining new respect for Modestine with every mile, I urged my car upward toward the 5,500-foot summit, my foot on the accelerator and my heart in my mouth, as every hairpin turn opened onto a steep valley and sheer dun-colored cliffs, with the merest stone lip defining the road edge like the rim of a tin can.

On a clear day you can see the Mediterranean from Mont Lozère, a harsh, denuded block of granite that stares out over a receding perspective of folds and wrinkles. But not this day. At 4,000 feet, pushed by a biting wind, a fog rolled in and quickly enshrouded the car. I pulled over, walked to the edge of an escarpment, and stared into the abyss. The temperature had plummeted, and straight ahead the mist raced by in patches and tatters, whipped on mercilessly by the wind. The scene was sublime, in the Romantic sense: inspiring terror, awe, and a feeling of desolation.

Mende itself is the modest little capital of Lozère, France's least populated department. Like so many of the towns and villages along the Lot, it goes about its business more or less undisturbed by tourism. By guidebook standards it has few attractions. There is the cathedral, built in the fourteenth to sixteenth centuries, which you visit because it is large and it is there and then wonder once again why a mediocre church is supposed to be bliss for the tourist. Beyond that, the town offers only its town-ness: narrow twisting streets, sixteenth-century stone houses with overlapping oval roof slates arranged like fish scales, and the thirteenth-century bridge spanning the little Lot.

The package could not be more attractive. Nor could the setting: Mende sits on a shelf looking out on what used to be known as the roof of France, a savage region lacerated by continual strife: first the Hundred Years' War, then the sixteenth-century wars of religion, when Protestants and Catholics sacked and pillaged in turn, and finally by the revolt of the Camisards, a purely local affair in which aggrieved Protestants rose up in 1702 and waged guerrilla warfare for five years before being crushed.

After Mont Lozère the landscape west of Mende seems civilized, picturesque. The road still winds, the valleys are deep incisions, stone houses cling improbably to the brown rock face like outcroppings. But the gradually widening Lot exerts a beneficial, calming influence, even as it passes through a series of celebrated gorges west of Estaing. Here and there sweet-looking farmland appears, inhabited by unusually handsome cattle upholstered in brown velour.

The towns are small. Estaing, Entraygues, and St.-Côme-d'Olt (the Languedoc spelling of *Lot*) count as major stops. All have fewer than two thousand people. The even smaller towns depend upon a weekly market and a roving charcuterie truck for their shopping. And some villages are so tiny that a strange car causes a stir and sends the local dog into ecstasy.

Yet tourists have passed this way for a thousand years, bound for the cathedral town of Conques, a ten-mile hop south of the Lot. Perched high on an escarpment overlooking the gorges of the Ouche, Conques has been a magnet for tourists ever since its abbey came into possession of the relics of Saint Foy, a young girl martyred in Agen, 90 miles west of Conques, in the fourth century. There the relics were closely guarded until the ninth century, when, legend has it, a monk at the abbey of Conques swore to lay his hands on them. Posing as a pilgrim, he entered the abbey at Agen. He remained there for ten years, and eventually was entrusted with the care of the relics, which he spirited away to the mountain fastness of Conques.

In the Middle Ages a good set of relics was as valuable as an NFL franchise today. Soon Conques became a staging post for pilgrims en route to the supershrine of Santiago de Compostela in Spain, believed to be the burial place of Saint James the Apostle. In this golden age the present church was built, a noble structure in its own right but remarkable for its tympanum, a bas-relief of the Last Judgment over the front doors.

The tympanum offers two readings of the afterlife: Classic Comics on the lefthand heaven side, R. Crumb on the sin-packed hell side. Heaven is a bit stiff, like a convention of Rotarians, but hell offers a riveting panorama of torment and anguish. Pride, a knight in chain mail, is thrown from his horse by a demon with a fork, while another devil eats the brain of a figure representing Anger. In one panel a wretch is flayed alive by a shrew-headed demon as a colleague devours the skin. Some of the original color remains: blue for heaven, red for hell.

Conques has one masterpiece in stone, another in gold: the Trésor, the finest collection of medieval and Renaissance goldsmithery in France. Access seems rather casual. On a quiet Sunday morning a wheezing monk took my ticket and pointed me toward a room off the cloister, as though I had come to read the meter. After shuffling over and watching for a few minutes to make sure the loot wasn't being piled in the middle of the floor, he vanished, leaving me alone in Christendom's version of Ali Baba's cave.

The centerpiece of the Trésor is the Majesty of Saint Foy, a seated wooden figure wrapped in silver gilt and encrusted with jewels, antique cameos, and filigree. The figure, which contains the relics, has an uncanny presence, with its oversize head and staring enamel eyes, its features almost Byzantine. For sheer strangeness, however, it is rivaled by a silver reliquary in the form of an upright forearm, two of its fingers pointed heavenward in a surreal gesture of faith.

West of the turnoff to Conques, a strange madness seizes the Lot. It begins to describe fantastic loops as it flows through the white limestone plateaus known as *causses,* demarcating little tongues of land as it goes. These promontories made ideal defensive sites, and at Capdenac-le-Haut the Gauls may have made their last stand against Julius Caesar after he defeated Vercingetorix.

One of the best of the strongholds is the Château de Cénevières, fortified since the seventh century and owned by the Gourdon family from the thirteenth century right up to the Revolution. The story of this old pile is told with gusto and flair by Guy de Braquilanges, a direct descendant of the man who bought the château from the Gourdons in 1795.

The elderly Monsieur de Braquilanges, whose son takes the tickets, lectures in French, but his expressive body language (he traces all dates and numbers in the air with a forefinger) allows even the poorest speaker of the language to follow him. Pointer in hand, Monsieur de Braquilanges takes his visitors on a highly personalized tour of the castle and its artifacts, discoursing on Renaissance cooking methods, alchemy, Louis XV furniture, and the proper way to use a petard.

Special attention is devoted to the siege of Cahors, the ancient capital of Quercy that stands on its own little spit of land some miles to the west. In 1580 Antoine de Gourdon, a convert to Protestantism, carried off the furnishings of the town's cathedral, bits of which, including a thirteenth-century altar, can be seen at Cénevières.

Cénevières is convenient to La Pescalerie, sandwiched between a vertical limestone cliff and the diminutive Célé River, a tributary of the Lot. At La Pescalerie an old manor house has been transformed into a bliss-inducing hotel. The grounds present an allegory of leisure: the mentally stressed traveler can stroll down to the river along an *allée* overgrown with grape-laden vines. A flock of snow-white pigeons, with shuttlecock tail feathers, coo and chuckle soothingly. Under massive ginkgo trees, guests can sit by wrought-iron tables with a drink and contemplate the hotel's sweeping lawns and gardens. For exercise, I recommend a walk of perhaps twenty feet to the hotel's restaurant and a close inspection of the wine list, which is strong on the wines of Cahors.

Those bent on stirring may wish to see St.-Cirq-Lapopie, often—too often—described as the most beautiful village in France. The tour buses have picked up the scent. They ascend without cease the narrow road to the town center, where they disgorge their contents.

The town *is* beautiful, so steep that the roof of one house is even with the front door of the house behind it. But the former wood-turning center has fallen prey to the culture of Ye Olde Craft Shoppe. A set piece rather than a town, St.-Cirq feels a little soulless, lacking in mystery, except for the fact that André Breton, the surrealist prophet of "convulsive beauty," chose to take up residence here in his declining years.

A stone's throw away from St.-Cirq-Lapopie, near the Célé, lies the Pech Merle cave. Twenty centuries ago, Stone Age humans inscribed and painted bisons, mammoths, and horses on the walls and in one section of the cave left a footprint: a man's size six by the look of it. The cave lay undiscovered until 1922, when two teenage boys, inspired by the spelunking of the Abbé Lemozi, a local prehistorian, followed a narrow crevice to a series of vast underground chambers.

Today a maximum of seven hundred visitors daily take a ninety-minute guided tour past stalactites and stalagmites, strange disk-shaped concretions, and strangest of all, the dangling root of an enormous oak tree, a reminder of the vegetable world far overhead. During my visit the acoustics in the largest chamber were too enticing for one woman, who, with hands folded in front of her, sang a nice little French air to general applause.

Toward Cahors the atmosphere becomes southern. The slate

roofing gives way to red tile. And the Lot enters a new phase, sleepily making its way through low-lying farmland, vineyards, and orchards. The town of Cahors itself, pleasant and poky (although at twenty thousand inhabitants the largest town along the Lot), need not detain the river lover for long, however.

True, the cathedral, with its Romanesque doorway, has its admirers, and the fortified medieval Pont Valentré is justly celebrated. The town's covered market, moreover, is a wonderland of *quercynoise* and *auvergnat* produce: goose and duck foie gras, pork confit, regional cheeses like St.-Nectaire, *cabécou*, and Cantal, the wines of Cahors and Bergerac.

But the urban feel of Cahors, however muted, seemed alien to the river's spirit. I pressed on through the region that Waverley Root, the food historian, called the domain of fat, past billboards of happy white geese advertising roadside foie gras stands, past the signs pointing to tasting cellars all along the way, past the Château la Coste, a fortified site near Grézels whose Museum of Folklore and Wine offers a tantalizing menu of lectures on such subjects as "The Nut and Its Place in the Cooking of Quercy." Onward I drove, through the wretched sprawl of Villeneuve-sur-Lot to the heart of prune country and the final downward slide to the end of the Lot.

The last stretch of my trip, the run to the Garonne, was tinged with melancholy. By now the Lot and I had a history together, a bond of sorts, and the idea that the river would simply disappear into the Garonne, like a small company bought out by a multinational, seemed vaguely disturbing. But having missed the beginning I was determined to see the end.

It turned out to be tougher than expected. Aiguillon advertises itself as "Le Pays de Confluence," but unfortunately official policy did not seem to reflect grassroots feeling. A quick poll of the local population showed only dim awareness of the whereabouts of the confluence.

Desperate, I pulled over and shouted my question to a sun-burned laborer leaning on a shovel, who listened with the pleased expression of someone waiting for a punch line, then shrugged his shoulders and said, "I'm Portuguese."

A nearby yeoman in blue overalls, balancing what looked like a week-old cigarette on his lower lip, came to the rescue. He gave manically explicit directions, repeated them three times, offered tips on road conditions, commented on the weather, and may even have recited long declamatory passages from Racine, but his nearly impenetrable accent made it difficult to tell.

The confluence was just over thataway, down a farmer's road rutted by tractor tires and made squishy by a recent downpour. I jerked the car forward through the muck, lurching and bouncing deep into field and forest. Where was the confluence? Could two rivers meet and keep it a secret? The stream on my right—was that the Lot or the Garonne?

With the mud halfway up my wheels, I gave up and turned the car around. Through a fringe of trees, the river shimmered freshly in the sunlight, Corot-esque now. Broad and placid, it had time on its hands. I recognized the basic character traits. It was the Lot. And this was goodbye.

The Way of the Prune

The hero of the Lot Valley is small, dark, and handsome. It is a prune, the renowned *pruneau d'Agen*, the central character in innumerable tarts and flans, the source of delicious fruit brandy, a traditional gift carried by local folk when they visit friends or relatives in Paris.

Its origins are obscure. According to legend, the prune was brought by thirteenth-century crusaders from Syria to France, where it found hospitable soil and climate in the Southwest. First referred to in Renaissance texts, it became a valuable export by the seventeenth century and today is a mainstay of the economy in the Lot-et-Garonne and adjacent departments.

For nearly two hundred years the Agen prune has stood out as the prune without peer: plump, firm, and moist, packed with fruit flavor and overlaid with a nutty, smoky taste. The name is a bit deceiving. The prunes were once shipped through Agen, a port on the Garonne, and the wooden crates were stamped with the name of the town. But two-thirds of the *pruneaux d'Agen* come from orchards along the Lot River west of Villeneuve-sur-Lot.

The curious may follow the Prune Route ("Lot Vert, Prune Mauve"), marked by purple road signs, that wends its way through the orchards devoted to the plum known as the *prune d'Ente*. For the real story, however, it is essential to visit the Musée de la Prune et du Pruneau, by the side of the D911 near Granges-sur-Lot. The museum, which opened in the summer of 1990, is open from 8 to noon and from 2 to 7 Mondays through Saturdays, and from 3 to 7 on Sundays and holidays.

After paying the dollar admission, the visitor is invited to take a prune from a platter and is offered a printed information sheet in French or English. The guide, Nadège Chatras, who also operates the cash register in the museum store, leads her visitors to an outbuilding with old drying ovens, an antique sorting machine, and displayed on the walls, a collection of historic photographs. Her lecture, in French, covers the fine points of prune production and consumption.

The French enjoy their prunes in four principal ways: plain, dusted with sugar, stuffed with marzipan paste, or soaked in Armagnac. The Prune Museum shop deals in all types, as well as locally produced prune and plum brandies, and a prune-nut candy of its own devising called Prunandises. Roadside stands throughout prune country have similar wares on offer.

The industry has two professional organizations battling on its behalf: the Comité Economique du Pruneau and the Bureau National Interprofessionel du Prune. The latter, known as BIP, has as its motto *Au Service du Bon Pruneau d'Agen* (Serving the Fine Agen Prune). Both organizations believe their product to be the finest in the world.

The ideal prune, said Christian Amblard, director of the Comité Economique, should be fleshy, with a good plum flavor, and "of a color appropriate to the prune identity"—that is, black or blueblack. The *bon pruneau* should be moist enough for an agreeable feeling in the mouth, but not too moist to preserve well. The skin should have no rips, tears, or spots.

Monsieur Amblard dismissed the California prune as toughskinned and fibrous. In his casual disregard for rival claims he echoed the sentiments of my prune-loving *hotelier* in Pujols. "Other countries produce them," he said, "but only France understands them."

At Ease Along the Lot

The Lot Valley and its environs contain comfortable hotels in all price ranges; most have restaurants offering regional fare and characteristic wines. What follows is a selection; prices are very approximate and date from 1992, merely providing a guide to expenses. Some establishments are open only seasonally; because dates can change, it is well to call or write in advance.

Mende

A pleasant midscale establishment is the **Hôtel de France** (33.5/66.65.00.04), 9 Boulevard L. Arnault, 48000 Mende (Lozère). There are 28 rooms; a double costs about $50 a night, while a half-pension (room, breakfast, and lunch or dinner) ranges from $40 to $45 a person. The hotel is open from February 1 to December 15; the restaurant is closed Sunday nights and Mondays, except during July and August.

Conques

The **Hôtel Ste.-Foy** (33.5/65.72.80.30), 12320 Conques (Aveyron), overlooks the church of the same name. There are 34 rooms, which range in price from $45 for a double to $110 for a little suite; a half-pension ranges from $50 to $80 a person. Open from mid-March to mid-November.

Cabrerets

La Pescalerie (33.5/65.31.22.55), 46330 Cabrerets (Lot), has 10 rooms, ranging from $90 to $130. The restaurant offers set menus with such specialties as rabbit confit with tarragon, grilled duck with honey, or artichoke ragout with wild mushrooms for $35 to $45. Open from April 1 to November 1; the restaurant is closed midday Tuesdays.

Mercuès

Château de Mercuès (33.5/65.20.00.01), 46090 Cahors (Lot), is set in wooded countryside near Cahors, overlooking the valley of the Lot, with a swimming pool and tennis courts. There are 25 rooms, which range in price from $100 to $235, and 7 suites that cost from $180 to $330; a half-pension is $110 to $235 a person. The restaurant offers such specialties as ravioli stuffed with foie gras and truffles, salmon with saffron, and a *feuilleté* of caramelized pears; set meals are $35 to $50. Open from mid-March to mid-November.

Touzac

La Source Bleue (33.5/65.36.52.01), 46700 Touzac (Lot-et-Garonne), has 15 rooms installed in a fourteenth-century mill on the banks of the Lot, about equidistant from Cahors and Villeneuve-sur-Lot. Double rooms range from $45 to $70; half-board is $50 to $65 a person. Open from late March or mid-April to mid-November; closed Tuesdays.

Pujols

Hôtel Chênes (33.5/53.49.04.55), 47300 Pujols (Lot-et-Garonne), in a restful setting just outside Villeneuve-sur-Lot, has 21 rooms ranging up to $65. There is a swimming pool, but no restaurant. Nearby, however, **La Toque Blanche** (33.5/53.49.00.30) offers such specialties as sole stuffed with crayfish, duck liver with shallots, vinegar, and sherry, and cabbage stuffed with crayfish and caviar butter; set meals range from $25 to $45, and the restaurant is closed from the end of June to early July; at the end of November; and on Sunday nights and Mondays except in July and August.

At Home in Dordogne

BY FREDERIC RAPHAEL

༄

Here is a piece that, when I first read it in 1987, made me want to pick up and move to the (still) bucolic Dordogne.

FREDERIC RAPHAEL lives in the Dordogne and has contributed a number of articles to *The New York Times,* where this piece first appeared, over the years. He is also the author of approximately twenty books, including *The Necessity of Anti-Semitism* (Palgrave Macmillan, London, 1998), *Coast to Coast* (Orion, London, 1998), *Like Men Betrayed* (Viking, 1970), and *After the War* (Viking, 1989). Raphael's most recent published title in England is *Personal Terms: Journals 1951–1969* (Carcanet Press, 2001), which was deemed "a minor masterpiece" by the *Times Literary Supplement.*

The unadventurous truth is, I have never been a compulsive traveler; I would sooner stay than go. If invited to hike unforgettably through the Himalayas, I find urgent reasons to escape the sublime. Why risk yourself, I wonder, on the roof of the world when there is perfectly good accommodation on the first floor? Travel hopefully, if you will; I prefer to arrive.

We may have lived in more places than most people, but it is always a relief to find a house or a cottage to call our own, however briefly. I have filled exercise books with field notes about colorful discomfort in Central America, and I have typed bravely in a high wind on a Greek island, watched for hours by a peasant who had never seen an Olivetti before, but I have yet to regret solid walls, a sound roof, and a large measure of privacy. I never love my fellow creatures better than when I am secure from their noise and the smell of their cookery. Keenly though I enjoy holiday activities, my pleasure is immeasurably greater if I have first done a morning's work. In short, there is no place like home, or a home from home, which is why, from the moment I took one look at Dieppe and fell in love with France, I have always wanted my own place here. Others may like to play the tourist, the milord, the explorer; I like to play the resident.

When we had the chance to buy a house in France, we avoided anywhere within easy ride of an international airport or a modern highway. The great advantage of our corner of the Périgord, where we now spend much of our time, is that it is not near anywhere you might have heard of and it is really difficult to explain how to get here. It is not even to be found among the official *départements* of France, though it existed before they did. The Périgord belongs to *la vieille France,* and no Parisian bureaucrat is ever going to efface it with his neat rationalizations. Its etymology is Gallic, but its first inhabitants were literally prehistoric. People have lived in these wooded valleys and in the caves that riddle them longer than anywhere else in Europe.

Much of the old district called the Périgord is officially part of Dordogne, the southwestern *département* that takes its name from our greatest river, which rolls and twists in its limestone bed with the languorous majesty of a royal lover enjoying some delicious favorite. Overstatement? Erotic literature is a specialty of the region; Henry Miller called it "the cradle of poets." The high-flown and the earthy are happy neighbors: who but a countryman like Bertrand de Born could praise his mistress for having "a rabbit's supple loins"?

Love and war are the ancient staples of the Périgord. The troubadours piped and sang in the châteaus of men who lived, and died, by the sword and the ax. The swift Dordogne—don't swim in it too blithely—is turreted with ocherous castles in which Englishmen and Frenchmen, Normans and Périgourdins, Protestants and Catholics played savage hide-and-seek down the centuries. The town of Sarlat, with a modest uniqueness I am here to recommend, was sited well away from the great and dangerous river. It was founded in the eighth century, possibly earlier, by Benedictine monks. They built their abbey far enough from the water to be secure from the Norman marauders who came upstream from Bordeaux with empty boats and returned with full ones. Sarlat is only about four miles from the river, not too far to enjoy its commerce, but far enough to keep looters from its gates.

Our town, I must confess, has no supreme monument, no manifest masterpiece to make it all worthwhile. I could cite the strange twelfth-century Lantern of the Dead tower, with its mysterious and almost impenetrable upper room and its conical roof, or the

Cathedral of St.-Sacerdos, but what little French town does not boast an oddity as perplexing as the one, or a buttressed cathedral as soaring as the other? As you drive in from Montignac, where a facsimile of the Lascaux caves is well worth a detour, you may wonder what is so special about a town announced by the usual modern sprawl of suburban villas, gas stations, and supermarkets. It is much the same if you come the other way, after a visit to the beetling château of Beynac, out-beetled by the craggy château of Castelnaud across the river.

Sarlat's salvation, when you reach the ancient heart of it, lies in its constricted site. Unobtrusive in the folds of its surrounding hills, it could not grow obese even if it wanted to. To savor its unpretentious grandeur, do not so much look around you as look up (always good advice if you want to avoid seeing the same ads and the same chain stores in modern cities). Sarlat boasts no skyscrapers, but when it grew rich, its sixteenth-century citizens had to build upward. Three and four stories may not seem much, but the idiosyncratic moldings and the bold staircases, often around handsome courtyards, give the tight city both a lofty feeling of style and a much-needed sense of spaciousness.

When your eyes reach the crest of the buildings, you are rewarded by a rare skyline: instead of the routine tiles of the Midi, Sarlat's roofs are steeply decked with *lauzes,* serried slabs of rough local stone, laid on wooden rafters, black shadows pinched between them, which give the town an irregular uniformity. The streets are a medieval maze; despite the renovations of recent years, and the signposts, it is easy to follow a narrow alley, past weathered doorways and under eroded gargoyles, into a cul-de-sac, vivid with geraniums or window-boxed petunias—from which you must retrace your steps, if you can, in order to find your way to the main square or up to the municipal gardens, laid out according to the instructions of Louis XIV's gardener, Le Nôtre (though a talented assistant did the spadework).

One of the virtues of modern France is the care and ingenuity lavished on its provincial gardens. If you are driving south toward the Périgord from Paris, you should on no account fail to go into the center of Angoulême and look at the gardens in front of the town hall; they are a credit to the town council and taxpayers, who rightly look on a measure of flamboyance as a social asset.

The gardens of Sarlat are not what Le Nôtre made them—we should not be able to play in the annual tennis tournament if they were—but they are trim and colorful, and from their summit you can get a good view of the oddly elusive layout of the town.

Beyond it pesticides have not quite won the war against wild-flowers. In April the fields are yellow with cowslips. The hedgerows grow more ambitious and colorful with the months. Violets and marguerites, orchids and scabiosa, dog roses and poppies soon make it seem as if Renoir were still working here, incognito. By May the stark outlines of winter's poplars—trees planted, traditionally, for peasant girls' dowries—are fuzzed by the blue promise of sum-mer's foliage. Spring and early summer are a time of dramatic skies that can explode in sudden storms only to grow seductively calm and golden again at evening. Nothing is certain in the Périgord, but everything—from caustic heat to hailstones that dent car roofs—is possible.

Sarlat's foundation was a declaration of Christian faith and an assertion of Christian authority. The Saracens had yet to be defeated at Poitiers, well to the north, by Charles Martel in 732, when the town was first mooted. Its prosperity had no commercial base; it came from the abbey's revenues (its property extended as far south as Toulouse, over 100 miles away) and from the passing trade of pilgrims, happy to find a haven from the rigors of the Périgord forests and the danger of the bandits who roamed them. These brig-ands were called *routiers,* the same name now given to law-abiding truck drivers and to the restaurants that serve them—and to you, if you dare the garlic and the racy language. Most of the pilgrims were on their hazardous way to Santiago de Compostela, on the north-westernmost corner of Spain. A millennium later, after the Spanish Civil War, the flow was the other way: many refugees from Franco's regime settled in the Périgord, and their names, and French-speaking children, abound.

One of the charms of our region is that it is at once particular and cosmopolitan. Sarlat, with its pious tradition, was a bastion of the Catholics during the wars of religion—its brave citizens successfully resisted the great vicomte de Turenne when he besieged them in 1587—just as it had been a stronghold of the French during the Hundred Years' War with England. For brief periods the English held the town "For God," but they were eventually evicted and pushed back toward Bordeaux. They did not finally quit France until the fifteenth century, and then with no promise not to return.

Indeed, did they ever really go? The whole long valley of the Dordogne, which takes you past Monbazillac and Bergerac toward the great vineyards of St.-Emilion and the Médoc, has been filling the cellars of London and Oxford and Cambridge ever since wine merchants replaced soldiers of fortune as the representatives of Anglo-Saxonry in Aquitaine. English-speaking people may be foreigners here today, but they are scarcely strangers. In fact, there exists today in Bordeaux a flourishing organization called the Society for the Reattachment of Aquitaine to the Commonwealth. The area was never, argue these tea-drinking enthusiasts, so prosperous as when the region was under the English crown.

The church created Sarlat, and its princes enhanced the town's fame and beauty. Saint Bernard preached there in 1147, and the Lantern of the Dead tower was built toward the end of the century in honor of the miracle said to have occurred during his visit. In his excellent guide to the region, James Bentley tells the story of the saint blessing the bread of the *sarladais* faithful. Even in the twelfth century Christianity needed to prove its quality; there were heretics and schismatics, like the Albigensians, who disparaged the Roman Church. Bernard promised that all who ate the sanctified bread would recover their health. The bishop of Chartres, Geoffroy de Lèves, was apprehensive enough to add, as a cover, "if they eat in perfect faith." Bernard had no time for such escape clauses. "I didn't say that," he said. It seems that his faith was honored; the sick were healed and Sarlat acquired its singular adornment.

A later ecclesiastic, Pope John XXII, a native of Cahors, about 60 miles farther south on the pilgrim route, made Sarlat into a bishopric in the fourteenth century, and Cardinal Niccolò Gaddi, bishop in 1533, brought to his diocese a Renaissance intelligence and taste shaped in the Florence of the Medici. He also brought the workmen who gave his palace an Italianate splendor and set the style for the town houses of the merchants, who made secular Sarlat no less magnificent than its religious buildings.

The cardinal arrived at almost the same time as Sarlat's most famous son: Etienne de La Boétie was born in 1530. At the age of eighteen he wrote a brave and eloquent essay, *Discours sur la servitude volontaire,* which denounced tyranny and those who served it. He argued against the cowardice of those who said they were doing their duty because they obeyed a tyrant. Their real motive was graft: they agreed to be kicked that they might kick others. It says much for La Boétie's charm, no less than his courage, that he could go on to a brilliant, if short, career as a member of the Bordeaux *parlement,* of which he became a member when he was twenty-two. Alas, he died in his early thirties, nursed by the anguished Montaigne, whose essay on friendship is La Boétie's enduring monument (though the statue in Sarlat's Place de la Grande Rigaudie does its stony best). The Hôtel de La Boétie, the family home, is opposite the Cathedral of St. Sacerdos, and is probably the finest mansion, and the best preserved, in the town.

The tourist, you may gather, will find plenty to interest him in the old streets. Local histories brim with characters like the quietist heretic François de Fénelon and the versatile Fournier-Sarlovèze, on whose career Conrad based his story "The Duel." But as I have already indicated, Sarlat's special appeal to us is that it can be taken for granted. Splendid buildings, splendidly restored, have only so much claim on one's affections. What I love about Sarlat is enriched by its myths and by its respect for literature (its poets are commemorated on the wall of the *mairie*), but what I treasure is the Balzacian reality of its daily life—the rivalries of its *notables,* the transformation of the pharmacist and the oculist into a doubles pair whom my son and I confront across the net on August afternoons, the beauty of Mireille Garrigou as she promptly brings the soup to your table at the Hotel St.-Albert, and the charm of Jean-Michel, her husband, as he slides in a plate of asparagus as a bonus to your hors d'oeuvres for the sheer joy of generosity.

On summer Saturdays we get up early and leave our hilltop to go into "the big city" for coffee and croissants at the St.-Albert. We then attack the market, with its ephemeral show of the necessary and the unnecessary. There you can observe all the modulations of courtesy, from the nod to the handshake, from the peck on the cheek to the double or even (between first cousins) the treble kiss. The simple pleasures of recognition become, over the years, the illusion—perhaps the reality—of friendship, as Montaigne celebrated it. Sometimes, hearing us, a tourist will assume that we, too, are *de passage* and solicit, or offer, advice. When they ask us where we are staying, we answer, with a mixture of modesty and smugness, "We live here."

Of course, we also live elsewhere, but the Périgord has a warmth and a familiarity that never pall. In summer it is tropical and crowded, and Sarlat grows fat and fattens its tourists. The drama festival is ambitious and often of a high standard. In the local gymnasium not long ago I saw a production of Genet's *Les Bonnes,* performed, as he had preferred, by two entirely naked youths. It might have shocked New York, but the *sarladais* looked and listened to the brazen text without a trace of embarrassment. This is a place where writers are honored, a place to put down your suitcase and, if you're lucky enough, your roots.

Back to the Land

By Leslie Brenner

⤳

If a Frenchman's heart lives in Paris, his stomach resides in the Dordogne Valley, or so it seems from this wonderfully written piece. Though cuisine is at the heart of this writer's ramble, the Dordogne's other, equally impressive charms are revealed as well.

Leslie Brenner, introduced earlier, is a contributing editor of *Travel + Leisure,* where this piece first appeared. Regarding the amount of foie gras she consumed in her search for the perfect Dordogne repast, she notes, "I was amazed I could eat so much and still walk away from the table." Brenner is also the author of five books about food and wine, including *The Fourth Star: Dispatches from Inside Daniel Boulud's Celebrated New York Restaurant* (Clarkson Potter, 2002).

A restaurant opening in France's Dordogne Valley has nothing in common with one in Paris or New York. Instead of a gaggle of reviewers and industry insiders, you're more likely to find a roomful of farmers, bakers, florists, and children. At the decidedly unglamorous debut of La Ferme de Berle, a farm-restaurant near Collonges-la-Rouge, one spring evening last year, my husband and I sat on plastic chairs sipping homemade *vin de noix*. Through the room's picture windows we could see cows grazing in the pasture. At a long table for eight, an organic-beef farmer chatted excitedly with a postal worker; a shoe merchant and the town *pharmacienne* shared a tureen of choucroute garnie. Outside, Salomé, the chef's six-year-old daughter, played with her dog and greeted familiar faces.

I was introduced to the Dordogne Valley of Southwestern France, which includes the culinary region of Périgord, a decade ago by Danièle Mazet-Delpeuch, formerly palace chef to François Mitterrand. I had met Danièle in New York, and she had invited me to visit her family's 700-year-old stone farmhouse. I was tantalized by her descriptions of the countryside, the ancient villages built into the steep cliffs along the Dordogne River, the imposing châteaus and simple Romanesque churches, the well-preserved bastides, or fortified towns. But what intrigued me most was the food: truffles, cèpes (porcini), walnut oil and *vin de noix* (walnut aperitif), the renowned goat cheese *cabécou*, and, of course, ducks and geese and their foie gras.

The moment I arrived, I fell in love. Everything I tasted seemed like the best thing I'd ever eaten. And Danièle was the perfect host— more than just a devoted *gourmande,* she's an expert on every aspect of the region's food, and she was generous with her knowledge. Once, as we drove back to her farm in late afternoon on a one-lane mountain road, Danièle slammed on the brakes, walked around to the front of her tiny, beat-up Renault, and returned holding her prize by the ears: roadkill. The rabbit, she announced, was still warm and would make a marvelous pâté.

Ten years later I was back on that same road, this time accompanied by my husband, Thierry. I had returned to the Dordogne to seek out the region's best food, and aimed to enlist the help of my old friend.

In her lilac-scented garden, Danièle served us tea and *pain de miel* (honey cake) and talked of her plans to open a cooking school. Intense and fiery, she is also a solid, earthy woman of the *terroir* who calls herself "just a grandmother filled with recipes." Teaching cooking would be nothing new to Danièle—she was one of the originators of the "foie gras weekends" popular in the 1970s, when Parisians would come to spend a couple of days down on the farm.

Where could we get a great meal? "You're in luck," she said. "A friend of mine—*une vraie cuisinière*—is opening her farm-restaurant just outside Collonges tonight." For Danièle to call someone *une vraie cuisinière,* a real cook, was a great compliment.

Driving through the countryside, I was overwhelmed by the region's natural beauty. I remembered feeling the same way on my first visit. The landscapes leaned more toward the sublime than the subtle, with dramatic limestone gorges; curious loops in the river, called *cingles,* that bend in almost complete circles; and endless old-growth forests. It is a place that feels older than ancient, where the medieval *châteaux forts* seem but recent history next to the plentiful prehistoric sites.

Collonges-la-Rouge, a village built almost entirely from red sandstone, may just be the most beautiful spot in France. The setting sun cast a rosy glow on the village's red stones as we took a walk to admire the towered and turreted manor houses, the narrow footpaths, and the handful of artisanal shops. Collonges is one of the 144 "Plus Beaux Villages de France" scattered across the countryside. Founded in the eighth century around a church and priory, what you see today dates mostly from the eleventh to sixteenth century. During that period, as many as 2 million pilgrims passed through here on their way to the shrine of St.-Jacques-de-Compostelle (Santiago de Compostela) in Galicia; scallop motifs carved into several buildings mark Collonges as a stop on the pilgrimage route. We were surprised to have the town almost entirely to ourselves—a benefit of visiting off-season. After checking into the only hotel in Collonges, we headed for Danièle's friends' farm.

Unlike other "farm-restaurants" we'd been to, La Ferme de Berle really is a working farm—raising cattle and producing walnut products. The chef, Laurence Salvant, whose magenta-streaked hair marked her as a city girl (she's Parisian), greeted us warmly at the door. Her husband emerged from the kitchen in a denim apron covered with flour, having spent the day making bread. Jean-Jacques is a dark-skinned fellow with apple cheeks; his family has owned the farm since "*seize cents et quelques*" ("sixteen hundred–something").

We took our seats—next to the postal worker and the farmer—and accepted glasses of the house-made *vin de noix*. Along with these came a plate of hors d'oeuvres that Laurence called "*tartes berloises*": *grattons* (crisp duck skin), crème fraîche, walnuts, and bacon baked onto bread. Their salty richness was complemented by the velvety, sweet wine.

Choucroute à la Laurence came next, a mountain of tender sauerkraut made from cabbage grown on the farm, garnished with succulent sausages, steamed potatoes that tasted as though they'd just been pulled from the earth, and, for an iconoclastic Perigordian touch, a flavorful *confit de canard*. We sopped it all up hungrily with more thick slabs of bread.

Later, Laurence joined us for a glass of wine. Until now, she'd never cooked professionally, but she had long dreamed of opening a small-scale restaurant at home. "A friend said she had a cousin who was living alone on a farm," Laurence told us, "and he wanted to do meals there." They met, and when Jean-Jacques taught Laurence his grandfather's method of making bread in the wood-burning oven, she knew this must be love; they married soon after.

Much to our surprise, the extraordinary meal, including a decent bottle of wine, was only about $50. Delighted with the bargain, we put down a credit card. It took a few minutes before we realized that, of course, they didn't accept plastic. We promised to return the next morning with cash. Good thing they didn't make us wash dishes for our supper: the next day, Laurence told us she and Jean-Jacques had stayed awake washing up past 2 A.M.

As wonderful as our farm supper had been, we still craved a superlative four-course meal; though we'd arrived more than a week before, we had yet to find one. Some good meals, yes—foie gras served three ways at Le Relais des Cinq Châteaux, a modest restaurant in a hotel that stood amid corn and tobacco fields. Fat white and green asparagus in a balsamic vinaigrette dotted with *lentilles de Puy* at La Meynardie, a charming spot where we sat on the shady terrace of what was no longer a working farm. And, most notably, a picnic in La Roque-Gageac, made from ingredients purchased at the famous market in nearby Sarlat.

Our dinner at Le Centenaire, however, the region's only Michelin two-starred restaurant, in the Hôtel du Centenaire in Les-Eyzies-de-Tayac, had been disappointing. Though perfectly cooked and nicely sauced, my husband's thick-cut pork chop sat forlornly on the plate, barely garnished. My rabbit lacquered with cèpe powder was better, but not inspired. Both the cuisine and the décor seemed stuck in a time warp, circa 1964. The restaurant, like several others in the region, seemed to be coasting on its reputation.

Danièle offered to make us dinner, but I demurred (though I'm still kicking myself); I was bent on finding an extraordinary restaurant. We found one at Château de la Treyne, a graceful Relais & Châteaux property dating from the seventeenth century, set on a storybook-perfect site over the river near the village of Lacave.

The château's sixteen rooms are elegantly furnished, with jewel-toned brocades. Ours, named Henri IV, had an antique four-poster and looked out over the formal gardens. When we sat down to dinner, the room was bathed in the light of the sunset reflected off the river; the owner walked through, lighting candles. I started with a terrine of duck foie gras, accompanied by a purée of figs and an intense *gelée* flavored with Monbazillac, a sweet white wine. Since the region is famous for lamb, I couldn't pass up the fillet roasted with mustard and thyme and served with the kidneys. Thierry chose a *chartreuse de pigeonneau du Sud-Ouest* with truffle juice. The chef played up the natural gaminess of the bird, serving it rare with the foie gras; buttery Savoy cabbage was the perfect garnish.

The wine list was a gold mine for lovers of Bordeaux. We selected a 1995 Château Beychevelle—redolent of fruit and beguilingly complex. With wine remaining in our glasses, the cheese trolley was irresistible. After that, the *corne d'abondance*—a puff pastry with a *confit* of the ripest berries, *fromage blanc* ice cream, and a coulis of Muscat de Rivesaltes—was altogether light, bright, and ethereal.

Our dinner at Château de la Treyne was as formal as La Ferme's was rustic. The only sign of chef Stéphane Andrieux came the next morning as we pulled out of the gravel-lined parking lot. The door to the pretty blue-and-white-tiled kitchen was open, revealing Andrieux and his small team starting work on that evening's dinner.

I found the earthy Périgord cooking of my dreams in "bastide country," about a half-hour drive west of Lacave, in Monpazier. Founded in 1285 by Edward I of England, Monpazier is one of the region's most striking fortified towns: I was immediately won over by its geometric beauty. In contrast with other members of "Les

Plus Beaux Villages," this was a functioning town, with appliance stores, shoe-repair shops, and a weekly outdoor market.

The day we arrived, the market filled the square; farmers, cheesemongers, and *charcutiers* had come from every corner of the valley. At one stall, two young men in jeans sold *saucissons secs*—dried sausages made from pork, boar, or rabbit. "*Goûtez, goûtez!*" they shouted, holding out samples on the ends of their pocketknives. I recognized one cheesemonger from the market at Sarlat; he was hawking his wares from behind a wheeled dairy case that held flats of ash-covered logs and aged, hockey-puck-sized disks of *cabécou* (a fresh, mild goat cheese with a soft rind and creamy center). On the far side of the market were the fishmonger and butcher, and farm stands filled with neatly stacked white asparagus, bunches of tomatoes on the vine, and baskets of perfumed strawberries. Nearby, a group of old men in berets gossiped and argued.

Now that our appetites were piqued, I asked the concierge at our low-key hotel if she could recommend a restaurant for dinner. She sent us to La Bastide.

That evening, crossing the now-empty square, we entered a narrow side street paved with cobblestones and lined with shops more utilitarian than touristy. We walked into La Bastide to find a table in the bar filled with locals, all of whom seemed to be friends of the house. Huge vases of roses and Queen Anne's lace cheered up the slightly dowdy, pink-tablecloth dining room; copper pots and bowls hung on the walls. When I asked for the four-course "*saveur du terroir*" menu, the waitress's mouth turned up in a half-smile; she was pleased that I was ready for the full experience.

My first course, the *foie gras frais au torchon*—an expertly seasoned duck liver—was rich and velvety, perfectly smooth. Then came an admirable *omelette aux cèpes*. The mushrooms, cooked slowly in goose fat, were silky, soft, and plump. *Confit de canard* was next, deeply flavorful, with golden-brown skin, and garnished with diced potatoes sautéed in garlic and more goose fat. After *salade à l'huile de noix* and just-ripe *cabécou,* who could even consider dessert?

The back of the menu listed chef Gérard Prigent's artisanal producers: chickens from Durou farm in Rampieux, ducks from La Quercynoise in Gramat, *verjus* from Domaine de Siorac in St.-Aubin-de-Cabelech. I hadn't seen this kind of producer credit on any other menu in the region. Intrigued, we returned the next morning to have a chat with the chef. As it turned out, Prigent is one of only two chefs in the Dordogne to have received official certification from the Ministry of Tourism as Les Cuisineries Gourmandes des Provinces Françaises, which requires members to use traditionally produced ingredients of the region in 70 percent of their dishes. Over espressos, Prigent told us how he happened upon Monpazier some thirty years ago. He had stopped for a drink in a café and, after soaking up the atmosphere, said to the waiter, "It's beautiful here—do a lot of people come through?" The waiter replied, "Yes, but the problem is we don't have a single restaurant." The young chef was inspired to open La Bastide. Today Monpazier has a population of 531—and seven restaurants. Prigent is now ready to retire, but will do so only if he can find someone who shares his dedication to classic cooking. That might be difficult. "In our profession, we make less and less money," he said, "and we have fewer and fewer qualified people."

After hearing Prigent's concerns about the future of the region, I was anxious to visit Château des Reynats, just outside Périgueux, where a promising young chef was cooking. My father-in-law, who lives in Bordeaux, had sent me an article about Philippe Etchebest a few months earlier, when the chef received his first Michelin star.

We checked into the run-down nineteenth-century château, wondering what a great chef could possibly be doing in a place like this. Our top-floor room was shabbily furnished in faded red brocades, without a snippet of style. Looking for escape, I went down to the "bar"—a couple of worn armchairs and two tables—for an apéritif. Though I was sitting just a few feet from the receptionist, she was chatting with the bellman, and no one offered me a drink. Finally I had to ask. As I sipped my Ricard, several couples stopped by the front desk. "Oh, we really love our room!" one woman said. "Love the décor," a second couple said. They all seemed to be in a great mood. I looked around for a hidden video eye: Was I on a Gallic version of *Candid Camera*?

In the château's restaurant, L'Oison—with its crystal chandeliers and heavy red curtains—I ordered the multi-course chef's tasting menu. Etchebest's cooking was no less than stunning. He used regional ingredients in a very modern way, and his flavors were clean and surprising. The result was much lighter and more refined than traditional Perigordian cuisine. A delicate ravioli of langoustine in a frothy cream sauce sat atop julienned cucumbers tinged with cumin. Lasagne of seared foie gras and wild mushrooms were heightened by an extravagant black truffle emulsion. And could those crunchy little garlicky matchsticks actually be cèpes? The sleek tableware from Spain—a white Bidasoa porcelain plate with an oversized rim and a teacup-sized depression in the center—contrasted with the décor of the room as much as Etchebest's cooking did. A trio of Grand Cru chocolate desserts attested to his skills as a pastry chef as well.

The next morning I asked to see some other rooms in the château, determined to solve the conundrum of the gushing guests. The tour was led by Etchebest, who, as I learned, is general manager as well as chef; he and his wife, Dominique, have undertaken to turn around the long-neglected hotel. Besides putting in his new menu, he told me, they were two-thirds of the way through renovating the rooms. The entire second floor was finished, and he showed me the new rooms. Whimsical (Louis XV chairs upholstered in tangerine-hued crushed velvet), and playing on local themes (the Dordogne room has furniture made from sticks and rocks), they were more stylish and appealing than anything else we'd seen in the Dordogne. These were the rooms occupied by the giddy guests; bad luck had put us on the floor that had yet to be redone.

Much of Château des Reynats' renovation will be completed by the summer of 2003. And five euros says Etchebest will be the region's next big star.

The Facts

The Dordogne Valley straddles three official regions in Southwestern France (Aquitaine, Limousin, and Midi-Pyrénées) and three distinct *départements* (Dordogne, Corrèze, and Lot). Spring and early fall are the best times to visit this area. In May, the Dordogne Valley is resplendent with lilacs and wisteria; white asparagus and strawberries make restaurant menus irresistible. In fall, cèpes are plentiful (though many establishments close for winter in early November). Summer is lovely too, if you don't mind sharing the place with lots of French vacationers. Get good maps (we suggest Michelin)—the smallest roads are the most beautiful, but navigating them can be a challenge.

Where to Stay

Château de la Treyne. A château on 300 acres of parkland and forest, with sixteen quietly elegant guest rooms. DOUBLES FROM $168; Lacave; 33.5/65.27.60.60; www.relaischateaux.com.

Château des Reynats. The new owners of this formerly run-down castle are making it the most stylish hotel in the region. DOUBLES FROM $125; avenue des Reynats, Chancelade-Périgueux; 33.5/53.03.53.59; www.chateau-hotel-perigord.com.

Hôtel Edward 1er. A nineteenth-century manor house with small but charmingly furnished rooms. DOUBLES FROM $58; **5 rue St.-Pierre, Monpazier; 33.5/53.22.44.00.**

Where to Eat

Ferme de Berle. Dinner on the farm, with Laurence and Jean-Jacques Salvant's family recipes. DINNER FOR TWO $41; **Berle, Collonges-la-Rouge; 33.5/55.25.48.06.**

Le Relais des Cinq Châteaux. Unpretentious, traditional Périgord cooking. DINNER FOR TWO $53; **Vézac-en-Périgord; 33.5/53.30.30.72.**

Restaurant La Meynardie. Three- to five-course menus served on the pretty terrace of a farmhouse. DINNER FOR TWO $62 **Paulin, Salignac-Eyvigues; 33.5/53.28.85.98.**

Château de la Treyne. Chef Stéphane Andrieux's refined dishes shine in this romantic setting. DINNER FOR TWO $147; **Lacave; 33.5/65.27.60.60.**

Restaurant La Bastide. Traditional Dordogne specialties. Don't miss the *foie gras au torchon.* DINNER FOR TWO $72; **52 rue St.-Jacques, Monpazier; 33.5/53.22.60.59.**

L'Oison. Philippe Etchebest's innovative preparations are the valley's most pleasant culinary surprise. DINNER FOR TWO $62; **Château des Reynats, avenue des Reynats, Chancelade-Périgueux; 33.5/53.03.53.59.**

Where to Shop

In Sarlat, stores on the place de la Liberté offer delectable foods such as foie gras and truffles. On Wednesdays and Saturdays, the outdoor market—one of the best in the Dordogne—fills the square.

Elie-Arnaud Denoix. *Vin de noix* (labeled *apéritif de noix*) and plum eau-de-vie, in lovely gift bottles. **Collonges-la-Rouge; 33.5/55.25.44.72.**

Entre Cour et Jardin. Bright jacquard table linens; local pottery in earthy colors. **36 rue St.-Jacques, Monpazier; 33.5/53.22.61.30; www.couretjardin.com.**

Moulin de la Tour. A sixteenth-century water mill with virgin walnut, hazelnut, and almond oils for sale. Tours available. **Ste.-Nathalène, Sarlat; 33.5/53.59.22.08.**

What to Do

Musée National de Préhistoire. An impressive collection of cave paintings, Neanderthal skeletons, and tools in a thirteenth-century fortress. **Les Eyzies-de-Tayac; 33.5/53.06.45.45.**

Grotte du Grand Roc. Guided walking tours of prehistoric caves that tunnel deep into a hillside. **Les-Eyzies-de-Tayac; 33.5/53.06.92.70; www.grandroc.com.**

Lascaux II. The 17,000-year-old Cro-Magnon cave paintings at Grotte de Lascaux have been closed to the public since 1963. See replicas here instead. **Montignac; 33.5/53.35.50.10.**

La Maison. Learning to cook Périgord classics with Danièle Mazet-Delpeuch. CLASSES FOR TWO (INCLUDING ALL MEALS AND ONE-NIGHT STAY) $190; **Chavagnac; 33.5/53.51.00.24.**

Five Stops You Shouldn't Miss

In 1982, Charles Ceyrac, then mayor of Collonges-la-Rouge, formed Les Plus Beaux Villages de France, an organization dedicated to preserving France's most beautiful villages. Acceptance into the group isn't easy: besides good looks, a town must have architectural and historical interest—and fewer than 2,000 inhabitants. Of the 144 member towns, an impressive concentration lies in and around the Dordogne Valley. Driving the small country roads that connect them is an ideal way to see the best of the valley. Collonges-la-Rouge is perhaps the most spectacular of these; Monpazier, with the concentric rectangular layout that typifies the bastide, runs a close second. Here are five of my other favorites:

Domme. On a bluff high above the Dordogne River, this thirteenth-century bastide is notable for its views of the luminous green farmlands and surrounding villages, as well as for its unusual lamb chop–shaped town plan. Because of its central location, Domme fills up with tourists in summer, but in spring, when the simple houses are covered with purple wisteria, quiet prevails.

La Roque-Gageac. Seen from the banks of the Dordogne, tiny La Roque appears to emerge whole out of a rocky cliff. Ancient houses with *lauze* (stone slab) roofs climb straight up the bluff. Take the narrow path to the right of the postage stamp–sized post office to the top of the town. There you'll find troglodyte caves— if you brave the rickety wooden staircases leading up to them.

Loubressac. Also designated an official Village Fleurie (flowering village), Loubressac is a hill town with walled gardens, exuberant pink hydrangeas, pretty ironwork lanterns, and fruit trees that bloom in springtime. In every direction, the village has breathtaking views of the green valley below.

Autoire. Ringed by rocky, verdant cliffs, Autoire is a cluster of striking medieval half-timbered houses with steeply pitched shingled roofs, several of which were built by nobility from nearby St.-Céré in the fifteenth and sixteenth centuries. A dramatic square clock tower dominates the sleepy, quintessentially Quercynois town.

Carennac. Larger and livelier than many of the others, Carennac borders the Dordogne and has its own little babbling creek flowing through town. The larger manors have pointed towers and turrets, and gardens filled with pale apricot roses. A trail leads down to the river, where it follows the tranquil banks. (Since Loubressac, Autoire, and Carennac are closely grouped in the eastern end of the valley, the three towns make a good circuit for a day trip.)

Bibliography

At Home in France: Tales of an American and Her House Abroad, Ann Barry, Ballantine, 1996. Yes, here is yet another I-bought-a-house-in-France-and-I'm-going-to-tell-you-all-about-it book, but like the others I recommend, it's also very much worth reading. The author's house is near Carennac in the Lot departement, which "is usually overlooked by guidebooks (pray that it continue, I secretly hope), which tend to focus on its westerly neighbor, the Dordogne." I was hooked on the author's story about "that postcard-size patch of the world and the people who inhabited it" partway through the introduction, in which she explained *le grand mur de Chine*. It seems when she first visited the Lot, in 1971, it was as a houseguest of friends who were restoring a farmhouse. When the friends had to return to Brooklyn, she stayed on a bit, and her one obligation in their absence was to oversee the construction of a stone wall by a local mason. The purpose of the wall was to discourage the neighbor's cows from roaming across their property. Other neighbors were not shy about mocking the wall, but it was nonetheless completed. "One evening not long after the completion of the wall, I was standing by the kitchen window, washing greens and slicing tomatoes for my dinner salad, and gazing approvingly at *le grand mur de Chine*. Suddenly the large, doleful eyes of a cow met mine. The great beast froze for a moment, the enormity of its face captured in the frame of the open window. I could feel the warm current of its breath. The cow passed, and was followed by another, and another. Eventually, the whole herd plodded before the window, some taking a sidelong, disinterested glance. They had chosen the inside track of *le grand mur* at the far end—their well-worn route—to wind their way back to the familiar barn. *Le grand mur de Chine*—I could hear the gleeful echoes." I also loved the time Barry bought entirely too much delicious bread from a *boulangerie* in the Dordogne village of Meyrals. She stopped off at the house of her friends, the Hirondes, and asked if they had a freezer so she could store a portion of the bread there until the end of the week, when she was returning to the States. "They stared at me, barely masking their incredulity. The notion of freezing bread—in a country where you went daily for your noon and evening *baguette*—was apparently a novel one. They didn't have a freezer, but the Servais did." Madame Servais did agree, cheeerily, to freeze the bread, but not without Monsieur asking, "YOO 'AVE NO BREAD IN YUR COUNTREE?" Throughout the book Barry is loyal to her adopted region and rarely ventures outside of it, which I appreciate; she does, however, relate one wonderful visit to Provence, in which she raves about a place that is special to me, too: Les Hospitaliers in the tiny village of Le Poët-Laval. But upon crossing the border into the Lot, "I marveled again at the singular character of the region: the old stone houses with red-tiled roofs, the gentle landscape, the colors. The very air, it seemed, was unlike any other. I took a deep breath and drank it in. In all of France, I was reassured yet again, this was exactly where I wanted to be."

The Cave of Lascaux: The Final Photographs, Mario Ruspoli, Abrams, 1987. Ruspoli had the great fortune to meet one of the four boys who discovered Lascaux on September 12, 1940. The remarkable thing is that he and two cameramen were given only ten minutes in the shaft of the cave to take what really are the final photographs. Their scientific mission, spread over three years, was to film *Corpus Lascaux,* a cinematographic monochrome of the famous cave, made at the request of the French Ministry of Culture. The book relies on the latest scientific information available (as of 1987) to tell the story of what is known about the sanctuary of Lascaux. "The Experience of Filming," on page 182, is especially fascinating. Ruspoli remembers a remark by prehistorian André Leroi-Gourhan, that "modern people confronted with the prehistoric world were 'like martians visiting the cathedrals of a vanished civilization.'"

Dordogne, Joy Law, Pallas Athene, London, 2000. Occasionally, I receive queries from friends and colleagues and letters from readers who tell me they are only willing or able to read a limited amount about a destination, and they want to know one, possibly two, books I would recommend. Usually, I have a difficult time arriving at only one or two books, but in the case of the Dordogne, I have no difficulty at all: this wonderful, wonderful book by Joy Law is most definitely the single volume I recommend. Hand in hand with a guidebook—to inform you of specifics regarding opening hours, hotels, restaurants, prices, etc.—visitors will have everything they need. Chapters include "The River," "The Land," "Caves, Celts and Périgueux," "Churches, Castles and Bastides," "Chateaux and Bourgs," "From Classical to Modern Times," "Life in Périgord," and "Sans Beurre et Sans Reproche." Additionally, Law has provided a gazetteer of the Dordogne, a chronology, a list of rulers and governments of France, and a twenty-nine-page practical information section (on yellow paper at the back of the book), which includes a two-page alphabetical listing of market days (note that even if this book had been published fifty years ago, the market days schedule has not and does not change, so readers may count on its accuracy). With black-and-white photographs and illustrations, floor plans, maps, and a twenty-four-page insert of color photos. Readers who love this book as much as I do may be happy to discover that Pallas Athene publishes other travel and history books equally as essential as this one (visit www.pallasathene.net to learn about its other publications, which are distributed in the United States by Trafalgar Square in Pomfret, Vermont). *De rigueur.*

From Here, You Can't See Paris: Seasons of a French Village and Its Restaurant, Michael Sanders, HarperCollins, 2002. This is a wonderful book, and I really hope you'll read it. Sanders set out to spend a year in and around a small, chef-owned restaurant in a rural setting somewhere in Southwestern France. He "wanted to capture the life of a restaurant through the wax and wane of the seasons, taking divergent paths to explore in some depth what made the region unusual along the way." Interesting enough, I suppose, but it's been done almost ad nauseam. Thank God for us that what Sanders found "was a far broader, more nuanced picture of a restaurant that had not only played a large part in saving a village but in so doing had come to be in many ways its focal point, the restaurant at the center of this very small world. The more I began to explore the story of La Récréation, the more I realized how intertwined it was with that of the village and its people, and how both in turn reflected far deeper and quite powerful changes going on throughout rural France and Europe as a whole. In Les Arques and the département of the Lot surrounding it, I found a lonely piece of France caught squarely in the headlights of the global economy, the real effects of forces not abstract at all, but writ large on the faces of its inhabitants." If you haven't yet pored over a map of the Dordogne and the Lot, you'll have to if you want to identify the village of Les Arques, a village that has "fewer than fifty houses, and whose entire listing in the regional phone book takes up less than a single full column on a five-column page." Sanders informs us that the year-round population of Les Arques is about thirty people, almost entirely elderly and retired; of the commune as a whole, 169. Without revealing all the details of this rather remarkable story, I will simply convey that two factors are responsible for the renaissance of Les Arques: *le patrimoine* (cultural heritage) and *la bonne chère* (good eating). Les Arques has a museum (devoted to the Russian émigré painter Ossip Zadkine, a contemporary of Picasso and Braque, among others) and a renowned restaurant, La Récréation (run by Jacques and Noelle Ratier; Jacques previously worked for Andre Daguin in Auch and Roger Vergé at Le Moulin à Mougins on the Côte d'Azur). Sanders was drawn to Les Arques initially because of La Récréation; I, too, had read of it, but I'm sorry to say at the last minute I changed my route during my last visit to the Southwest, and I only discovered this book upon my return. If I had read it before I departed, I would have made this "forgotten corner of Southwestern France" my base. Sanders reminds us that "the Lot is still part of that France in which it is hard to find a bad meal and even harder to find a bad meal at an exorbitant price," a statement with which I have to agree. La Récré has earned one fork in Michelin; but Jacques is neither competing at the high or low end of Michelin criteria—he's not competing at all actually, just doing what he likes. But he is at a place I imagine many restaurateurs holding a Michelin fork or two are also at—the crossroads of either continuing or changing. Besides being an absolutely wonderful read, this book also includes an appendix of good addresses—most valuable, of course, for the Périgord-Quercy area. Sanders wisely notes that good guidebooks steer visitors to notable museums and architectural wonders, so instead he's tried to inform visitors to "those places to eat and stay, and things to do that you could only learn from someone who's been there." Within this appendix, he recommends visiting farms, a piece of advice I, too, would highly recommend you do. Look for the signs saying *visite à la ferme*. "In and around Les Arques, you can visit foie gras raisers and goat cheese makers and, a little farther afield, many vineyards and even a snail farm. Though they would never say this, I will. Buy something! These busy farmers are taking time to give you a unique look at what they do even though it is not always convenient. Respect their effort by supporting it, even in the most modest way." I see from the length of this recommendation that I have perhaps gone on a bit long. Upon reflection, no, I haven't: Sanders's book is a most worthy read. *De rigueur.*

Three Rivers of France: Dordogne, Lot, Tarn, Freda White, photographs and commentary by Michael Busselle, Pavilion, 1996; first published in Great Britain in 1952 by Faber and Faber Limited. I couldn't decide where to include this wonderful book but ultimately decided that even though it is a book of the entire Southwest, the Dordogne is the first river mentioned, and so it seemed like the right place. This work is simply the very best book on the entire region (though the Tarn only flows through the upper corner of Languedoc). As Michael Busselle notes in his introduction to the 1996 edition, "Like almost everyone who has traveled in the south-west of France, I have been aware for many years that *Three Rivers of France* is the definitive book on the subject."

The Pavilion edition is paperback and includes stunning color photographs as well as a "Guide for the Modern Traveller" and a section of practical advice. White herself noted that "after dawdling for a short time in a country such as this of the south-western rivers, the wise traveler will know far more about France than if he had never left the capital." The same could be said for reading her book, which features individual chapters on the lower, middle, and upper Dordogne, the Lot and upper Lot, the Tarn, before history, the people, the land, the weather and wind, the builders, the Resistance, and food and drink. In closing, White states, "The Dordogne is a romantic river. The Lot is a magical river. The Tarn is a breath-taking river. Oh, happy Traveller, you have the choice of three." Indeed. *De rigueur.*

A Village in the Vineyards, Thomas Matthews, photographs by Sara Matthews, Farrar, Straus & Giroux, 1993. When this book first appeared, I thought to myself, "*Another* I-went-to-France-and-bought-a-house-and-it-happened-to-be-near-a-vineyard book?" But I had to give this one a try as it was published by a most esteemed publishing house, and I felt that if some wise editor at FSG thought this was a worthy story, then surely so would I (it also helped that the three endorsements on the jacket are contributed by three of my most favorite French food/wine authorities, Kermit Lynch, Patricia Wells, and Jancis Robinson). It is, of course, a very worthy story, and the author—though I didn't immediately recognize it at the time—is a senior editor and New York Bureau Chief of *The Wine Spectator*. So yes, the book is definitely about wine, but abstractly, providing more of a backdrop to a much richer story of people and the lives they lead in a tiny village called Ruch, in the heart of the Entre-Deux-Mers wine-growing region. Near the very end of the book, Matthews expresses that he and his wife had come to France to find "the past alive in the present," and on the holiday of Toussaint, they visited the village graveyard along with everyone else. "Some of the graves held remains of families with no living members left in town. Were they tokens of ruptures with tradition, evidence that the town had lost touch with its roots in the past? No, I thought, not when nearly every grave was heaped with flowers, many with multiple bouquets, and the ground looked like a tapestry of love and respect. The fabric might be worn in spots, but the weavers were still at their looms. A wonderful book, with nice black-and-white photos.

Booklets and Brochures

Périgord Noir: Dordogne–Sarlat–Vézère is a high-quality, sixty-four-page color brochure published by the Club Hôtelier du Pays de Sarlat, an organization of thirty-six member hotelkeepers founded in 1995. The member inns are all independently owned and operated, and adhere to the ten principles in its Quality

Charter. This is actually a good resource for some wonderful places to stay in the area, and I wish I'd known about it before my last trip. The booklet itself is printed in both French and English, and I have only seen a few of the hotels mentioned in other books. "To market and promote the image of the Périgord Noir" is one of the hotels' ten principles, and therefore this brochure also includes a six-page color-photo collage, *Couleurs Perigord Noir,* as well as sixteen pages of practical information for visitors to the region. I'm not sure if Maision de la France offices in North American stock copies of this worthwhile publication, but readers may browse the Web site www.hotels-sarlat-perigord.com to see if it may be ordered by mail.

Sarlat et le Perigord Noir: Guide Touristique is a thirty-four-page color pamphlet I found very helpful. It's in French, and I'm not sure it's available outside of the Office du Tourisme in Sarlat, but it's published annually and can be fairly easily deciphered. Specific information regarding sites and gardens to visit, outdoor activities, theme parks, *stages artistiques, goûters à la ferme,* and *visites gourmands* is provided, and in addition, eight *circuits*—with maps—are proposed, including Vallée de la Vézère: au pays de Cro-Magnon, Circuit des Jardins, Circuit des Bastides, and Circuit en Périgord Quercy.

Corners of the Midi-Pyrenees

"Cradle of French viniculture, the region called the Midi stretches from the mouth of the Rhône just west of Marseille down to the Spanish border south of Perpignan, varying in width from 20 to 100 kilometers. Although no two Frenchmen will agree on the exact boundaries, there is no disagreement on the connotations of the word: the Midi is the south of deep blue skies contrasted against the ocher-red rock and the subtle shades of silvery grays and greens of the scrubby pine-like vegetation along the Mediterranean the locals call the garrigue."
—Alexis Lichine,
The Wines and Vineyards of France

Medieval Conques Continues Its Long Homage to Saint Foy

BY ROBERT WERNICK

～

Mort Rosenblum, in *A Goose in Toulouse,* writes that he had long perceived Conques to be among the few rural French towns where the residents seemed to have a clear sense of what is important in life. Though in more recent years he reached the conclusion that the people of Conques perhaps strayed a bit from that path of good sense ("a single man in a small place, elected by a handful of voters to a six-year term, can put an indelible blemish on six-hundred-year-old splendor"), Conques is still very much worth visiting. Like Rocamadour, a sister pilgrimage village, it receives great numbers of tourists, especially during the summer months. (If you, too, find yourself there in the summer, my advice is to arrive early—you will be rewarded with at least *some* quiet time to explore before all the tour buses arrive.) Rosenblum also relates that in 1991 a headline in an article about Conques that appeared in the *International Herald Tribune* read, "Does a Medieval Town Need the Twentieth Century?" Rosenblum wisely observed that "as the twenty-first century approached, it seemed a pertinent question that might be applied to a great deal of France and things French."

ROBERT WERNICK divides his time between Paris and Georgia and has been a frequent contributor to *Smithsonian* (where this piece first appeared) for many years. Wernick has written about a wide variety of subjects as well as many Mediterranean destinations. His work has previously appeared in the *Central Italy* and *Provence* editions of *The Collected Traveler.*

F ides, or Faith, was the name of a twelve-year-old girl who lived in the Roman province of Aquitania, in what is now the little French city of Agen. She was raised as a Christian, and when the soldiers of Rome one day in the year 286 demanded that she worship an image of the emperor Maximian, she refused to betray her God. They tied her to a griddle and stretched the griddle over a bonfire. An attendant angel, moved by the little girl's plight, sent down a thick cloud to cover her nakedness, and the cloud dampened the fire. Inflexible in his wickedness, the Roman officer in charge of the proceedings ordered her dragged to an executioner, who chopped off her head. Pious hands collected body and head, and eventually her bones were placed in a handsome sepulcher in Agen, and pilgrims came from great distances to behold it, often being vouchsafed miraculous cures as a result.

Such was the tale which was known through all Western Christendom in the early Middle Ages. Nowhere was it listened to more avidly than at the monastery of Conques, in south-central France, a hundred miles or so northeast of Agen and perched on a cliffside in a forested wilderness. This monastery had owed its foundation to a Frankish nobleman named Dadon, a brutal ruffian even by the standards of his time. But eventually a wave of shame and remorse came over his obdurate heart. He became a hermit, living on roots and berries, lacerating himself in a frenzy of penitence. His harsh repentance reached the ears of the king of Aquitania, Louis the Pious, son of the great Charlemagne; the king came to pray with the hermit and left him money to build a monastery on the site of his rude dwelling. The king was pleased by the site, a shell-shaped ledge scooped out of the mountainside, and he named it Conques, from the Latin *concha*, meaning "shell."

The monks who came to live there received many marks of favor from powerful patrons, but their monastery did not enjoy the fame they thought it deserved. Few pilgrims were willing to make the dangerous voyage there through the ravines of what was then the province of Rouergue and is now the department of the Aveyron. Since the time of the Gauls, this has always been considered one of the most depressed regions of all France, the poorest in natural resources. Until the popularization of Roquefort cheese in the last century introduced a bit of prosperity, its history was one of periodic famine and, as a consequence, of emigration to more favorable economic climates.

What was needed, the monks reasoned, was something both physical and sacred, a material manifestation of holiness. An idea took root. They sent a young smooth-talking brother named Ariviscus to join the monastery of Agen. He stayed there ten years and so gained the confidence of his superiors with his piety and zeal that they appointed him guardian of the tomb of Saint Fides, her name now Gallicized to Foy (*foi*). That night, when all the others were asleep or at prayer, so the story goes, he broke open the tomb, scooped up the bones of the saint, and fled over the hills to Conques.

The monks of Conques were proud of his exploit and wrote accounts, both in verse and in prose, of what they called the Furtive Translation of the holy relics. It may sound shockingly larcenous to modern ears. But the monks, in their hardheaded medieval way, regarded it as an act of piety. If Saint Foy, they reasoned, had not wanted her bones removed, she would have stopped Ariviscus dead in his tracks.

Miracles from a Playful Saint

Miracles began to happen. Saint Foy restored sight to the blind. She listened to the prayers of poor Christians who had been held as slaves in Spain. When they acquired their freedom, they came to lay their chains at her feet—immense heaps of iron that the monks later melted down and fashioned into the ornamental grilles that close off the chapels of the church to this day. She played girlish tricks as well, as when she woke up the old night watchman to tell him the lamp had gone out by her shrine. After he had dragged his arthritic old bones over the stone floor he found that she had relit the lamp herself.

Stories like this brought pilgrims to Conques, thousands of pilgrims, many of them bearing rich gifts for the saint. The monks decided that her bones needed to be properly housed, and they would make a reliquary statue to contain them. The thirty-three-inch statue, called the Majesty of Saint Foy, which the monks produced in their workshops, was an extraordinary object: wood encased in gold, sparkling with a dazzling profusion of jewels, stiff, oddly shaped, and oddly proportioned, with great staring eyes of blue-black enamel, totally hypnotic to pilgrims come to contemplate it.

Centuries later scholars argued over the nature of this work. For some it was a pagan idol redecorated to serve as a Christian saint. For others it was a purely Christian work. In 1954 a team of experts under the direction of Jean Taralon, now the head of Monuments Historiques de France, took the Majesty apart and studied it in detail over the better part of two years. They concluded that the Majesty was a combination of the long-dead Roman and the burgeoning medieval art.

The torso of the statue, they found, was made of two blocks of yew wood, very roughly chiseled—journeyman carpenter work. Over this a skilled goldsmith had placed a gold repoussé case worked into highly sophisticated designs. Then a fourth- or fifth-century Roman head, perhaps a mask or the portrait bust of an emperor, was joined to the saint's torso. To the medieval artist, incorporating a pagan work of art into a Christian sacred object was not unusual. No matter that the head was too big for the body, or that the neck reared back at an unnatural angle. They were not interested in representing the little girl who had been martyrized. They wanted a statue of the saint, triumphant in heaven, ready to grant favors to her supplicants. The fierce eyes and the jutting jaw were to them marks of power and glory, just as they had been to the fourth- or fifth-century sculptor who first fashioned them.

The original Roman head had worn a wreath of laurel. The monks removed this and replaced it with a gold crown. They seated this composite figure on a gold throne, and over the centuries it was repeatedly repaired, reconstructed, redecorated. The quadrifoliate window in the stomach, which allowed the faithful to see the skull of the saint, was carved in the fourteenth century. The outstretched arms with hands holding little tubes for flowers or palm leaves were added in the fifteenth century: the shoes not until the nineteenth century.

And all the while, century after century, pilgrims added their private treasures to the glory of the saint: earrings, necklaces, bracelets, pieces of rock crystal, cameos of Roman emperors, gems of all kinds—sapphires, rubies, emeralds, carnelian, jasper.

An extraordinary treasure grew up around the statue of the saint. A magnificently crafted Saracen saddle was fitted whole into the decoration of a large silver cross. There were reliquaries for other bones, or for splinters of the True Cross or other treasures of doubtful authenticity: the skull of the prophet Habakkuk, three hairs of the Virgin Mary, the umbilical cord and foreskin of the child Jesus. Legends were embroidered to fit all of them. A triangular reliquary was said to have formed part of a letter A (opposite); this in turn was said to be the first in a series in the shape of all the letters of the alphabet from Alpha to Omega that Charlemagne ordered for the most worthy monasteries of his kingdom, Conques getting the pride of first place. The Charlemagne story is probably an invention, but it was true that only kings or princes could have afforded these magnificent gifts to the saint. The skull of Saint Foy was wrapped in Byzantine silk colored with the rare and expensive purple dye reserved for the use of imperial families.

The great days of Saint Foy and of Conques came in the eleventh and twelfth centuries, when interminable files of pilgrims used to tramp across France on their way to the tomb of the apostle James at the church of Santiago de Compostela in Spain. The hardest and stoniest, and therefore the most popular, of the pilgrim routes led through Conques. There the footsore pilgrims would halt to drink from the spring that gushed under the church—a twelfth-century guidebook says that no one could praise this water highly enough—

and there the image of the saint would be borne triumphantly through the crowd amid the ringing of bells, the blaring of trumpets, and the frenzies of mass devotion.

To accommodate the increasing crowds, the monks tore down their old low-ceilinged church early in the eleventh century and built another, in the awesome new Romanesque style. (Construction proceeded slowly and was not completed until about 1130.) Working on a narrow ledge, they were cramped for space, but what they sacrificed on the ground they made up for in height: the vaults of the nave soar to more than seventy-two feet. Conques was one of the five most important pilgrimage churches, built to receive great crowds and processions.

Sculpture on medieval churches was meant to be a permanent sermon in stone, spelling out for frequently illiterate pilgrims the teachings of the church. The sculpture at Conques has been amazingly well preserved. The combination of a fairly mild climate and the sheer isolation of the spot has protected it. The church itself is surprisingly complete and relatively intact. The ensemble of 124 figures on the tympanum over the west door—some of them still bearing blue and ochre traces of the polychrome decoration that once covered them—remains almost unchanged.

The capitals of the columns inside the church trace the history of sculpture in France during the late eleventh and early twelfth centuries and, testifying to the vast creative imagination of the medieval artist, include abstract geometric and foliate designs as well as animated renditions of monstrous animals and the human figure in action.

Medieval sculpture tended toward the ideal and the generalized. It usually preferred images of sin or sanctity to portraits of any particular sinner or saint. The sculptors at Conques were passionately earthy and realistic. They loved the details of life around them, and whether creating angels or fabulous monsters or scenes from the daily round of existence, they were capable of amazingly lifelike effects. When two warriors smote each other with their huge swords as they frequently did, according to the customs of the time, you can almost hear the clash of steel.

When the itinerant sculptors came to creating the figures that would populate heaven and hell on the tympanum, they drew inspiration from a variety of influences from the past—Carolingian, Roman, Byzantine, and even Greek. Many of the faces, however, have a startlingly familiar look to anyone who has wandered around Paris. There is a simple explanation. The population of the Aveyron has been remarkably homogeneous since prehistoric times, because few were ever tempted to move into this inhospitable region. Hundreds of *aveyronnais* peasants, fleeing the wretched life of rural poverty, came to Paris in the nineteenth century and opened shops selling coal, wood, and alcoholic beverages. The coal and wood trade has languished, but the drinks still flow. Enter a traditional-looking bistro in almost any quarter of Paris; chances are you will see leaning over the counter a shrewd, work-lined, immensely practical *aveyronnais* face that might have come right off the stones of the church at Conques.

Episodes that could have inspired scenes on the tympanum have been recorded in old chronicles. When the sculptors wanted to show Pride riding to a fall, their thoughts might have turned to the familiar figure of Rainon, a local baron and great villain who was riding full tilt to knock down an inoffensive monk when his horse stumbled. Rainon broke his neck. Is it Rainon who appears for the rest of time on the right side of the tympanum, among the damned, falling like an enormous worm in chain mail from his horse into the fires of hell? Above him there is a devil gathering up a group of tonsured figures in a net. Everyone at Conques thought they could recognize in these figures portraits of Bishop Bégon of Clermont and his nephews, who in the tenth century had shamelessly plundered the treasures of the church.

Paradise is generally less interesting than hell in works of art.

But even here, in the faces of the elect, the sculptors have added a certain spice out of their own irrepressible verve. One is most likely Charlemagne the emperor, being led uneasily into heaven by some supremely confident monks. The woman beside him has been identified as his sister, with whom he was supposed to have committed incest. It was a way of reminding the powerful of the Earth that one manner of acquiring salvation was generosity to monks like those of Conques.

Treasures Preserved by Guile

There are fashions in pilgrimages as in everything else, and the vogue of Santiago de Compostela gradually faded. Conques complaisantly went back to being a little village on the verge of nowhere, a fading monument in the wilderness.

The treasures of Saint Foy remained. But gold and silver and jewels and such treasures have always been irresistibly alluring to kings and conquerors and thieves in the night. It took guile and foresight and an abiding faith to keep those treasures intact down to our own day.

They somehow survived the Hundred Years' War, when the land was periodically ravaged by pitiless bands of Englishmen and brigands. They survived the wars of religion of the sixteenth century, when the Huguenots were destroying churches out of a zeal for religious purity. They set fire to the church at Conques and would have hammered its treasures to bits in their fanatic rage if the monks had not taken the precaution of hiding them under stones in the church floor. (Some were so well hidden that they were not found again until workmen making repairs stumbled upon them three hundred years later, in 1875.)

They were again in mortal danger during the French Revolution. The revolutionaries regarded statues, caskets, and such as relics of ancient superstition; they loved to chop off the heads of stone kings, and besides they had an appetite for gold and silver to pay for their wars. One day in 1792 the people of Conques heard a report that the authorities in Rodez were coming up to make an inventory. Knowing what that meant, they disguised themselves as bandits, broke into the church at midnight, and carried off everything of value. When the soldiers arrived from Rodez, they were sent off on a wild-goose chase after the robbers. Meanwhile the treasure was divided up among trustworthy families. Some objects were walled up in chimneys, and some were buried in vegetable gardens where they suffered badly from the damp. The Majesty of Saint Foy was tucked away in a cellar.

All remained hidden for forty years, the secret of the hiding places being handed from father to son, and no word of it ever reached the outside world. By the time of the next revolution, in 1830, there were no monks left in Conques, not even a priest, and the church itself had lost most of its roof and was piled with debris. The French government proposed to tear it down as a measure of public safety. By rare good fortune the inspector they sent to the spot was the young novelist Prosper Mérimée (author of *Carmen*). He made a slow and exceedingly painful journey over the roadless mountains and was overwhelmed when he found "such riches in such a desert." On his recommendation the government decided to restore the church instead of destroying it. It was overrestored to some extent—the two towers on the west front are the work of a nineteenth-century architect and add a needless heaviness to the whole—but at least it was saved. Once they saw that the government no longer intended to loot the church, the townsfolk brought back the hidden relics into the open air.

Nothing much has happened in Conques since then. A lovely little village suspended in time, a genuine relic of ancient days, it is inhabited today, like most remote villages in France, by a handful of elderly and retired people. The monastic community that once numbered more than a thousand souls has shrunk to three brothers of the Order of the Prémontrés, who guide the busloads of tourists through the dark underground room where the Majesty of Saint Foy and all the other treasures are now kept in glass cases with electronic burglar alarms. Aside from such visitations, a deep sleep has fallen on the ancient shrine.

It has become something of a tourist attraction in recent years, and in summer its narrow cobblestoned streets are full to bursting. But the tourists have to leave in the evening because there is only one hotel in town and a wise government policy permits no new building nor any change in the local architecture. The streets empty out then, and as the dying sun lights the dark tile roofs of the village clustered around the tawny limestone and pink sandstone of the church, it takes little effort of the imagination to move backward a millennium in time—and, while the great bell in its tower booms out the call to evening prayers, to envision the scene with a mass of weary pilgrims shuffling over the mountains to venerate the little saint with her triumphant imperial eyes.

Figeac's Flair for the Egyptian

NANCY BETH JACKSON

ༀ

The medieval town of Figeac is not given sufficient coverage, in my opinion, in most guidebooks, let alone in periodicals, so I was happy to see this piece in print a few years ago. I admit it isn't quite as beautiful as Sarlat or St.-Cirq-Lapopie, or as dramatic as Rocamadour or Cordes-sur-Ciel; but Figeac hosts a wonderful outdoor market, its architecture is well preserved and unique (some of the pale stone buildings in the old town feature beautiful, open-lofted roof areas known as *soleilhos*), and its Musée Champollion is home to a "small but exquisite collection of Egyptian antiquities," as the author rightly notes in this piece. (Also, standing in the Rosetta Stone courtyard is, well, for lack of a better word, really cool.) The Figeac Tourist Office (located in the Hôtel de la Monnaie in the place Vival), offers an impressive schedule of guided tours from April through September. In addition to *visite générale de la ville* tours, there are tours with particular themes, such as the art of stained glass, the grand merchants of Figeac, art and architecture of the Middle Ages, and following in the footsteps of Champollion. At other times of the year the tourist office is happy to arrange tours for groups small and large.

NANCY BETH JACKSON formerly lived in Aynac in Southwestern France and is working on a biography of Champollion.

I owe apologies to all the houseguests I hustled through Figeac, which has been a trading center for Southwestern France since at least the eleventh century. My excuse is that I was so busy renovating a water mill in a nearby town that I missed what was right next door. The town for me was pork chops, pâté, and nut cake from the busy Saturday market under a pavilion that looks like the old Les Halles. I never thought to play tourist. When guests came, I chose Cahors, Souillac, and Rocamadour for their outings unless we were shopping for dinner or needed a bank.

Not that tourists don't stop in Figeac. The interminable traffic lights at a bridge over the Célé make sure motorists at least brake, but now I know that travelers who pause longer can find themselves on a slightly discombobulating detour into Egypt.

Here men in berets play *boules* next to an obelisk; an optician's billboard shows Nefertiti in aviator glasses; chocolate boxes and baguette wrappers display the portrait of a nineteenth-century Egyptologist; and hieroglyphics pave a Romanesque courtyard. Bookshops, too many it seems for a population of ten thousand, fill their windows with translations of the Book of the Dead and pharaonic art on papyrus. The compact local museum displays mummy cases worthy of a Cairo exhibit.

Even in the early 1800s, only a hiccup ago by both Egyptian and local standards, Warburthon's work on Egyptian hieroglyphics was available at a village bookstore, established in 1773 by an itinerant *dauphinois* bookseller who set up shop after marrying a local girl from nearby Faycelles. The peddler was Jacques Champollion, a shadowy figure who may have been just wandering through with his cart when he slowed for a pretty face. What is known is that his youngest child, whose fame was predicted before his birth by a local seer, was Jean-François Champollion. Fascinated by Egypt since childhood, Champollion broke the Rosetta stone's hieroglyphic code and opened up millenniums of history to scholars and tourists.

What Champollion has done most recently for Figeac under a socialist mayor is help revitalize a burg that suffered declining population and a decaying town center—until national politics and local pride worked together to revitalize the economy and refurbish a local hero. For over a dozen years, starting in 1984, as I renovated the mill about thirty minutes north of the town, I watched Figeac spruce up and develop what amounts to a Champollion cult. But only after I moved to Egypt myself in the early 1990s did I begin to appreciate Figeac's favorite son and the town.

Freed from chipping away old stucco and irrigating vegetable patches, I have since returned to Figeac on vacations to learn about Champollion, his birthplace, and nearby archaeological sites where he and his much older brother, Jacques-Joseph, labored. Like them I became enchanted with the prehistoric burial chambers that resembled pyramid construction and a fortress town where the brothers dug in search of Uxellodunum, the legendary site where Caesar finally defeated the Gauls.

Charles Boyer, the actor born here in 1899, has only a modest plaque on the stone building where he was born. Champollion has his own square, a museum in the renovated family home, and a gargantuan Rosetta stone created by the American artist Joseph Kosuth that covers the floor of a medieval courtyard near the museum. It is hard to walk through town without seeing Champollion's dreamy-eyed three-quarter profile staring out of shop windows. Local merchants even issue a credit card in hieroglyphics.

But Champollion, who left Figeac for studies in Grenoble when he was only eleven, was not always so honored here. Three years after his death in Paris in 1832, an obelisk in his memory was erected in Figeac's Place de la Raison, a graveled space occupied by an abbey's cloister before the revolution. Nothing came of plans approved by Napoleon III in 1867 to add a statue.

Until 1934, when masons renovating a store uncovered a stone painted with the word *Librairie* and the Champollion name, local people weren't even sure of the location of the bookshop, which was run by the sisters of the family while the brothers reached intellectual heights in Grenoble and Paris. Now the storefront at the site is a bar called the Sphinx.

The family's home was only a few degrees away from ruin when a group of Figeac citizens decided to rescue it in the early 1970s. After François Mitterrand was elected president in 1981, the socialists adopted Champollion as one of their heroes, perhaps because he had once been sent back to Figeac in internal exile for supporting Napoleon, the people's emperor.

Champollion, however, is an unlikely political icon. He spent his exile setting up free classes for children, excavating Roman ruins at Capdenac-le-Haut, and puzzling over a rubbing of the Rosetta stone, which had been discovered by Napoleon's soldiers.

Champollion never saw the stone itself, a hunk of black basalt carved in Greek, hieroglyphics, and an ancient Egyptian script. A French Army officer had uncovered it at an old fort at Rosetta near Alexandria in August 1799 during Napoleon's invasion of troops and scholars. The British claimed it as booty when they ousted the French in 1801. For nearly twenty years, while the stone sat in the British Museum (where it remains today), scholars across Europe followed one false lead after another as they tried to match the two Egyptian inscriptions to the Greek.

Before I lived in Figeac, I had heard only vaguely of Champollion, whose claim to deciphering the Rosetta stone I later learned had been challenged by an English physician and scholar named Thomas Young. The two men were remarkably alike: child prodigies who grew up with family members other than their parents. But while ancient Egypt consumed Champollion from boyhood, Young explored it as one of many intellectual diversions, publishing his preliminary findings anonymously. Aware of Young's research, Champollion discarded some of his own theories, suffered a fit of inspiration that left him in a coma, and revived to announce that he had broken the hieroglyphic code after years of investigation.

Young never visited Egypt, but seven years after announcing his key to the hieroglyphics, Champollion launched a major expedition up the Nile paid for by the king of France and the grand duke of Naples with a spirited crew of French and Italian scholars, including the artist Nestor L'Hôte. I read Champollion's journal in a nineteenth-century edition at the American University in Cairo. A librarian in the rare books library laid the book like a jewel on a green felt tabletop and left me alone with Champollion, who whispered in my ear from the antique pages. More than 150 years separated our stays in Egypt, but the only thing dusty about his words was the cover.

His journal shares his joy in seeing all that still remained of ancient Egypt. He and his cohort sang arias and danced across the sands at midnight on their way to the Temple of Dendera, scaring the wits out of a poor Egyptian peasant who thought he had met up with devils. Champollion's delight is obvious as he describes setting up camp in a Valley of the Kings burial chamber and arranging for an obelisk to be moved from Luxor, ultimately to the Place de la Concorde in Paris. His journal is full of exhilaration, but the trip left him exhausted and ill. He returned to Paris in March 1830 and died two years later in his forty-second year. His grave in Pere-Lachaise cemetery in Paris is easy to find under an obelisk, but it is in Figeac that he is met at every turn.

To avoid the annoying traffic lights, I usually park above the town in the Place de Foirail, the old animal market near Notre-Dame du Puy, an impressive church reconstructed in 1658. I amble down and huff back up cobblestoned streets with gutters down the middle. I pause at hidden gardens behind heavy wooden doors with the traditional iron knocker of a woman's hand. Until I came as a tourist, however, I rarely considered the towers, arcade facades, and half-beamed architecture all around me. Now I always stop at the Champollion Museum, pause in the Rosetta stone courtyard landscaped with papyrus plants, and appreciate the museum's small but exquisite collection of Egyptian antiquities.

If I shopped until lunchtime, I used to have few choices. Today a welcome addition to the town's wide selection of fast-food places and restaurants is La Cuisine du Marché, run by Joel Centeno, the son of Basque immigrants, who worked his way up in Toronto and Palm Beach before returning home to the Lot with his Canadian wife, Nathalie. In a region of rustic inns, La Cuisine du Marché has sunlight streaming through plate glass filling medieval arches, chefs chopping in full view behind yet more glass, and *plats du jour* worthy of a photo. But the noontime crowd is totally local.

The restaurant is midway between the market pavilion and the seventeenth-century gilt wood sculptures in the chapter house attached to St.-Sauveur, a treasure so ignored it is usually in the dark unless someone pushes the light-timer. How had I missed the chapter house all those years? Now I never go to town without dropping by to see the infant Jesus sleeping on the cross or contemplating the strangely contemporary faces of seventeenth-century workers the sculptor used as models in the thirteen-panel series on the passion of Christ.

I knew more about Conques, the dramatic Benedictine abbey isolated high in the hills almost due east, than I did about Figeac. Figeac was probably a Roman site, but just when the town's own Benedictine monastery was established is suitably clouded in legend. Supposedly a flock of doves flying in cross formation led Pepin the Short to the site in 753, but more likely it was a great-grandson who ordered the monastery built nearly a century later as a supply base for Conques.

A rivalry soon developed between the sister abbeys—Conques, possessor of the relics of Saint Foy d'Agen, and Figeac, a prosperous market and a more convenient stopover on the pilgrimage route to Santiago de Compostela in Spain. It took a Council of Nîmes edict in 1096 to separate them officially, Conques taking the high road of pilgrimage and Figeac going on to trade woolen cloth, wine, and honey with England, Cyprus, and the Middle East by the thirteenth century. One merchant, Guillaume de Bonnes Mains, set forth on his own personal crusade, sailing to Alexandria to buy Jerusalem. He failed, but the importance of Figeac's medieval merchants is remembered in the bourgeois architecture.

In the early fourteenth century the Church handed Figeac over to Philip the Fair, who established a royal mint; today a building called the Hôtel de la Monnaie houses the tourism office and a small museum of Roman artifacts. The town pasted itself up the cliff between St.-Sauveur near the river and Notre-Dame du Puy, whose aerial views were said to have been selected by the Virgin herself.

Today facades, bastardized over the centuries, are being returned to their original design as architects transform medieval houses into apartments for both rich and poor. The result is not Disney's Epcot but a small city with an often unlikely mix of young and old, panhandlers and bourgeois tourists, jazz and Gregorian chants,

Rollerblades and cobblestones. It remains a major market town, not just for the Saturday fair where vendors sell everything from live rabbits to rubber shoes and clowns parade on stilts, but also the big Leclerc discount store across the Célé near Capdenac-le-Haut.

In addition to getting to know the town, I used Figeac as a base for exploring the Roman wells at Capdenac and the strange Needles of Figeac, thirteenth-century obelisks that may have been erected to mark the boundaries of the Benedictine territory. One Sunday drive led me to a dolmen, a megalithic stone construction dating probably from about 2100 B.C. to 1700 B.C. Three of them can be seen near the village of Faycelles, where Champollion's mother was born.

Not long before he died, Champollion visited Figeac in search of the fresh air he thought would cure him and to visit with the sisters in the bookshop. Already the lane, not much more than an alley, where he had been born, had been renamed Rue des Frères Champollion.

"I am happy to be breathing air less impregnated with the miasmas of high civilization; my lungs are better and my work, too," he wrote in the autumn of 1831, the year after returning from Egypt. Anyone who has ever gathered chestnuts or searched the forest floor for *trompette des morts* mushrooms in the Lot fall knows the feeling. Before returning that November to Paris, where he had established the Louvre's Egyptian collection, he did what would be his last work—adding to his hieroglyphic dictionary and reclassifying the sequence of pharaohs after seeing a hieroglyphic chronology on site in Abydos. He died the following March.

"Thus, the little town, cradle of his mother and himself, had always been destined to be the place of his last discoveries," wrote a German biographer, Hermine Hartleben. "It was there that the pioneer of Egyptian studies traced his last lines of faith for the future development of the science he created." And nobody in Figeac is about to let the world forget it.

Planning a Visit to the Town

Getting There

Figeac is about 350 miles south of Paris by car, most of it by autoroute. There are trains from Paris (usually taking five to six hours) and Toulouse (about two hours). The city center is a short walk from the station. The Toulouse airport is a two-hour drive from Figeac.

Sightseeing

A well-marked self-guided walking tour starts at the Musée Champollion, 5 rue Colomb. Follow the keys.

The Tourist Office, Place Vival, open all year, offers guided tours in French with English audiotapes available. It also has tours to nearby villages, including Faycelles, where Champollion's maternal relatives lived.

The Musée Champollion, a few steps from the market square, varies its hours according to season, but is always closed for a lengthy French lunch and on Sundays and holidays. It also closes on Mondays except in July and August.

The big market of the week is Saturday. The city's well-designed Web site at www.quercy.net/figeac has information on sightseeing, as well as tour schedules and events. Click on the British flag for information in English.

Excursions

Figeac is a good base for exploring the Lot, Célé, and Dordogne Valleys as well as for visiting its splendid sister abbey-town, Conques. The region has endless vineyards, prehistoric sites, caves, Gallic-Roman and Romanesque art, and outdoor activities. Outstanding summer music festivals are held in St.-Céré and at the Château de la Rauze in Le Bourg, northwest of Figeac.

Lodging

Hôtel du Château du Viguier du Roy, 52 rue Émile Zola, 46100 Figeac (33.5/65.50.05.05; fax 65.50.06.06), is top of the line in the center of town, with 21 rooms and suites, pool, and cable TV— and a medieval tower. Be sure to ask about the gargoyles. Doubles about $107 to $208.

Liffernet Grange, Lunan, 46100 Figeac (33.5/65.34.69.76; fax 65.50.06.24). This six-room bed-and-breakfast with pool is on a hillside four miles south of town toward Capdenac-le-Haut. Anthony Nielson, who is English, and his French wife, Dominique de Lamothe, also run a wine-exporting business. A double costs about $58 with breakfast.

Places to Eat

La Cuisine du Marché, 15 rue Clermont (33.5/65.50.18.55), run by Joël Centeno, specializes in fish; fresh daily. Menus range from about $11.50 to $38.

La Puce à l'Oreille, 5 rue St.-Thomas (33.5/65.34.33.08), has tables by a walk-in fireplace in winter and in the medieval courtyard in summer. When I started going there in the late 1980s with small children and elderly aunts equally pleased by the menu and ambiance, I paid around $7 for a prix fixe lunch. Menus start at about $12.50 today. I still favor the pork chops.

For the best in traditional menus, drive north a few miles to **Chez Marcel,** rue du 11 Mai 1944 in Cardaillac (33.5/65.40.11.16), whose dukes left behind a château well worth a look. Menus are about $13 to $30 with five rooms to rent upstairs if you just can't go any farther after a copious lunch of foie gras, duck confit, Quercy lamb, garlicky green beans, and hot apple pie—and plenty of Cahors wine. Why the Marcel of Chez Marcel became a legend among local antiques dealers is obvious in the decor.

Roaming Through the Rugged Cévennes

BY SUSAN SPANO

~

The "Frugal Traveler" column is a regular feature of the *New York Times* travel section, and I usually read and clip those that pertain to Mediterranean locales. The primary goal of the column is to reveal the planning and taking of a trip on a modest budget—an appealing idea, but sometimes the focus is so much on the money spent or saved that other aspects of travel and experiencing a place are overlooked. Overall, however, the column provides useful suggestions and advice, and it is a welcome feature of the newspaper. This one in particular, highlighting a trip to the Cévennes (not widely covered apart from brief mentions in guidebooks), is a good resource for readers interested in visiting this national park. (Note that this report was published in 1994, and all prices are as they were originally quoted. I do not believe the prices will have changed drastically in the intervening years, and as this is a piece about planning around a budget, it's doubtful that the accommodations or eating places the writer mentions have been transformed from budget establishments to *grand luxe*.)

SUSAN SPANO has been writing the "Frugal Traveler" column of *The New York Times* travel section for a number of years.

In the fall of 1878 Robert Louis Stevenson and a donkey he called Modestine set out on a 135-mile trek across the Cévennes Mountains, a region of soaring peaks, wild upland plateaus, long ridges covered with Spanish chestnut trees, and deep green valleys at the southern end of the Massif Central in France. Along the way he "slept rough" in a bedroll under the stars, kept watch for the infamous "Beast of Gévaudan," a vicious, flesh-eating wolf-man first sighted in the area in 1764, ruminated on subjects like love, history, and religious tolerance, and took notes for a book published the following spring called *Travels with a Donkey in the Cévennes*.

Ever since I first read that splendid little volume, I have wanted to hike in the Cévennes. I knew that Stevenson's twelve-day adventure cost him eighty-five francs. How much more expensive might a trip there be a hundred years later? I wondered. After all, the Cévennes remains one of the poorest regions in France—Gaul's Appalachia, inhabited by people who squeeze a living from hardscrabble farms, raising sheep and cows, keeping bees, and harvesting chestnuts, as well as by a fair number of British expatriates lured there by low real-estate prices. The native *cévenols* are rugged, insular people, many of whose Protestant forebears fought the army of the Catholic French crown during the eighteenth century War of the Camisards. Today, as then, there are few towns of any size in the Cévennes; gas stations and grocery stores are rarities, movie theaters nonexistent—though first-run films are sometimes shown in village halls, a little like traveling circuses.

But in July and August the solace is broken by tourists, who come to the mountains to hike, drive, bicycle, and kayak in the Parc National des Cévennes. Established in 1970 (and declared a UNESCO World Biosphere Preserve a year later), it encompasses 226,000 acres of the Cévennes' most impressive scenery, including 5,500-foot Mount Lozère, 5,000-foot Mount Aigoual, and 3,000-foot Causse Méjean, a lonely limestone plateau bordered on the north by the great gorge of the Tarn River. Myriad trails wander through the park, and it is also traversed by 12 Grandes Randonnées, France's enviable 25,000-mile network of long-distance footpaths, which occasionally follow ancient sheep tracks and lumber roads as they cut through the Cévennes on their way toward the Pyrenees, Alps, or Atlantic coast.

In *Travels with a Donkey* Stevenson wrote, "I travel for travel's sake . . . the great affair is to move." So in early May, after spending a week sightseeing in Paris, I boarded a TGV in the Gare de Lyons, which took me to Nîmes in about four and a half hours for $144 round trip, second class. As the train sped south, the rolling spring-green hills of central France yielded to the rocky, vermilion-toned fields of Provence, dotted with poppies, as in Van Gogh. In Nîmes, where it was ninety degrees and brutally sunny, I rented a little Peugeot with four on the floor for $40 a day including unlimited mileage, tax, and insurance. (Without insurance the price would have been $27 a day.) Then I headed northwest via the N106, D982, and D6 into the craggy, arid mountains, trying to resist the temptation of driving too fast on the crazily curving roads.

At the town of St.-Jean-du-Gard, the D9 climbs atop the Corniche de Cévennes, a high, fifty-mile ridge with show-stopping views of the endlessly mounding peaks to the north—greener and more alpine than those to the south—and hamlets with names like Le Pompidou and Barre-des-Cévennes, built almost entirely of leather-colored flint and granite and perched on narrow terraces where it seemed only a goat would have the nerve to go.

Three hours after leaving Nîmes I descended into the town of Florac in the valley of the Tarn River, where the national park makes its headquarters in a seventeenth-century château. I felt dazed and breathless from the drive and almost went off the road when I caught sight of the Rocher de Rochefort, a huge, spindle-shaped rock that juts from the near-vertical sides of the Causse Méjean above town. Florac, population 2,100, is by far the busiest town in the region, with seven hotels, many cafés and restaurants, a tourist information office, and at least two sporting-goods stores.

I could well imagine it mobbed with visitors in the high season, but in early spring relative quiet prevailed. Its cobblestoned streets, walled kitchen gardens, and rustic bridges over a stream called Le Pêcher were appealing. Nonetheless I drove on, in search of a place to stay that was a little more out-of-the-way. When I saw a small sign for the Auberge le Boufadou about a mile north of town, I turned off the highway toward the hamlet of Bedoues.

At first Le Boufadou didn't thrill me, for it lay across the road from an unsightly campground (where an electrical hookup costs around five dollars) and had been recently built in pseudo–Alpine chalet style, with three guest rooms on one floor adjoining a restaurant. But the mistress of the inn seemed genuinely pleased to make my acquaintance, and the room she showed me, with a low double bed covered by a pink chenille spread, lace curtains, shower, sink, and toilet, was immaculate. And when she told me the price—$27—my jaw nearly dropped. Dinner in the restaurant, cooked by her and served by her bashful teenage daughter, cost another $17 and included a salad with beets and chestnuts, a small, bony, locally bred trout on a bed of sautéed carrots and potatoes, peach cake, a slice of deliciously gooey Roquefort cheese, red wine, and a *café noir*. Afterward I climbed up the hill to Bedoues, inspecting a lovely eighteenth-century church with a tall, slim steeple straining toward heaven, smelling the white and purple lilacs, and placing a call to my brother in Los Angeles from a phone booth by a barn, where the cattle kept lowing. Then I wandered into the campground and found the crystal-clear Tarn River flowing at its edge, leading me to envy the campers—tacky trailers, lawn chairs, and all.

The next four nights in other Cévennes hotels, *logis,* and *chambres d'hôtes* (the French version of B&Bs) stand out in my mind as one of my best experiences of rural France—not to mention my cheapest. I stayed in three more places in the course of a five-day sojourn in the Cévennes, never spending more than $36 a night, and ate to the detriment of my figure, sometimes paying more for an evening meal than for accommodations—the *cévenols* have their priorities right.

My favorite place to stay, where I spent two nights, was the auspiciously named Grand Hôtel du Parc, which lies along the main street in Florac and has a lovely garden and swimming pool. I avoided the more expensive new wing and chose a $25 room on the fourth floor of the old (where there was no elevator)—earning a tilted nose from the proprietor. But up there, where the hall was tiled with linoleum from the 1930s and the communal bath was pink and deep, I found a little piece of paradise.

My room had faded floral paper on the ceiling and walls, a lusciously soft double bed, wood floors, a big Art Deco armoire, and a casement window overlooking the rooftops of Florac and the Rocher de Rochefort—an enchanting prospect, fit for a fairy-tale princess. Modest plastic dividers set the sink and bidet apart from the rest of the room, and the toilet was about fifteen steps from the door. The food at Florac's Grand, served with a country-style pomposity that I found endearing rather than irritating, was slightly more expensive than that at Le Boufadou, and not as good—but what a place to come home to after a long day's hike.

I ate in many places, too—the mountain air made me do it. The best restaurant I tried was La Lozerette in the hamlet of Cocures, east of Bedoues, with a stylish dining room full of lilacs, guttering candles, and taped jazz, where on subsequent nights I tried $17 and $28 fixed-price menus, which featured such items as creamy cauliflower soup, more trout, veal wrapped in marrow, chocolate truffles, and an exquisite nougat chestnut glacé slathered in strawberry sauce. I stayed in a room above the restaurant there, as well—on the top floor, under the eaves. It was small, with two single beds pushed together, had been redecorated too recently for my old-fashioned taste, and cost $36.

My daily expenses averaged $72, and I could easily have made the trip even more cheaply. Had I brought along a sleeping bag, I could have plotted a long course through the mountains, walking all day and sleeping at one of the hundred or more *gîtes d'étapes* along the trails in the national park. A little like youth hostels, these are often run by *cévenol* farm families, with communal bunk rooms, where a bed for the night costs $5 to $10 and a home-cooked dinner around $10. If Stevenson were still around, this is the way he would have done it.

I fell into a routine of my own, rising early, breakfasting in my hotel (a big cup of café au lait and croissants with butter and jam cost $4 to $5), and then heading into Florac for another café au lait at the Brasserie du Globe, with umbrella tables on the esplanade. There I studied maps I bought at the park headquarters and bought provisions for lunch on the trail—usually delicious pastries filled with cheese or ham.

One sunny sixty-degree morning, when the fruit trees had suddenly burst into bloom, I set off on the GR 43-86, which cuts along the northeast edge of Florac, and walked north for five miles into the foothills of the Cévennes, seeking several prehistoric menhirs, or stone monuments, marked on my map. I never found them, but my picnic lunch in a field of bright yellow broom overlooking an ancient-looking farm complex called the Manoir Issenge was one I won't soon forget.

Another day I drove along D907 at the base of the Tarn Gorge, took a two-hour boat trip (with three other passengers and a guide) from the village of La Malène through the river's narrows for $16, and then hiked up the steep side of the Causse Méjean, a four-mile journey that took me to the Roc des Hourtous, where the most dramatic stretch of the Tarn Gorge spread out before me. The fair weather held, so on my third day in the mountains I walked along the GR 72 northeast of the village of Barre-des-Cévennes—a wild, desolate thirteen-mile circuit with smashing views of the Mount

Lozère range. On the fourth day I rested, touring the region around Mount Aigoual behind the wheel of my Peugeot.

Alas, things went downhill on my last night in the mountains, which I spent at a sixteenth-century guesthouse east of Barre des Cévennes owned by an English couple who were about as welcoming as a chunk of *cévenol* granite. My room was fine and with breakfast and dinner cost only $36; but the food was abysmal, and while I was sitting on the patio watching the sun set, a spider bit me and my forearm swelled to an alarming size. By morning I was right as rain, and feeling philosophical about my recent travails. After all, I'd roamed freely and blissfully through the Cévennes, and never once met up with the Beast of Gévaudan.

Bottom Line

Preparations

I bought a round-trip ticket to Paris in April at a cost of $469 through Council Charter, 205 East 42nd Street, New York, N.Y. 10017; 212-661-0311 or 800-800-8222.

My round-trip Paris-Nîmes TGV ticket cost $144, calculated at 5.6 francs to the dollar; I bought it at the Gare de Lyons in Paris several days before I left for the Cévennes and had a reserved seat for the four-and-a-half-hour trip.

I reserved a rental car before leaving for France by calling the Kemwel Group, 800-678-0678. The rate for an economy-class car for five days was $198.35, with unlimited mileage, tax, and insurance. In Nîmes I picked the car up at the Citer rental agency, 1010 avenue du Maréchal Juin (33.5/66.29.04.12)—a $5 taxi ride.

Information on the Parc National des Cévennes can be obtained from the park headquarters, B.P. 15, 48400 Florac; 33.5/66.49.53.00. The Florac Office of Tourism is at avenue Jean Monestier, 48400 Florac; 33.5/66.45.01.14.

L'Auberge le Boufadou, 48400 Bedoues, 33.5/66.45.08.40, no fax, is about five miles northeast of Florac on the D998. It has three guest rooms with private baths for $27 a night and a restaurant where a Continental breakfast is $5.

Grand Hôtel du Parc, 48400 Florac, 33.5/66.45.03.05, fax .66.45.11.81, has 58 rooms costing from $15 to $48, a swimming pool, garden, and restaurant. (Breakfast is $4.50.)

La Lozerette, Cocures, 48400 Florac, 33.5/66.45.06.04, fax .66.45.12.93, has 21 rooms from $36 to $55, a restaurant, and a pleasant garden.

The Rush of the Slow

BY SUSAN HACK

∾

Of all the nautical locales one may choose from in France for a house-boat holiday, the clear winner for me is the Canal du Midi, also known as the Canal of the Two Seas as it was originally intended as a commercial waterway connecting the Atlantic to the Mediterranean. (Not unintention-ally, the canal allowed French ships to avoid the hefty tariffs levied by Spain for use of the Straits of Gibraltar.) Floating on the canal is a wonderful stress-reducer for those of us with lives that are too harried; but what I like best about the Canal du Midi are the trees—apparently, forty-five thousand planes, pines, poplars, and fruit trees were planted along the edges of the canal. According to the January 2002 newsletter of My French Store (www.myfrenchstore.com), the trees not only provided shade but also lim-ited the "evaporation of water during the summer months, which are hot in this southern region of France. Also, the roots of the trees would help strengthen the riverbanks, and the leaves would form a layer in the bottom of the canal to reduce the risk of water infiltrating the soil." For more information about companies that arrange barge cruises, see the Canal du Midi entry on page 39 of *Practical Information*.

Susan Hack is a contributing editor at *Condé Nast Traveler*, where this piece first appeared. She lives in Paris and Cairo, and her work has been featured in the *Paris* edition of *The Collected Traveler*.

It's a warm May afternoon on a leafy canal in the South of France, and I've gotten off our barge to bicycle along the sun-dappled towpath. Casting off from the bank, the captain motors beside me at four miles per hour, slow enough for a clutch of downy ducklings to keep abreast of the curved bow, where my five-year-old daughter stands with my husband, laughing and tossing baguette crumbs into the water.

Four miles an hour may be a sensible pace for newborn ducks or a 104-year-old Dutch *tjalk* aptly named *La Tortue* (The Tortoise), but it feels way too slow for a hot-pink Peugeot mountain bike. A few brisk miles later I pass a cherry orchard and three generations of farmers merrily picking.

"*Venez, ramassez avec nous,*" calls out Jean, the six-foot grandfather, in Spanish-lilted French, inviting me to share this southern rite of spring. Soon my fingers are dripping with dark red juice, and I'm chatting with the women about jams and *clafoutis,* watching children fill baskets and shirttails with ripe fruit.

The Canal du Midi has that "slow down and smell the . . ." effect, its languid banks overgrown with red poppies, yellow irises, and (*quel cliché!*) wild white roses. Ironically this was once a seventeenth-century superhighway, a miraculous shortcut between the Atlantic and the Mediterranean, enabling sea captains to avoid the Spanish coast and conquer nature by sailing across dry land. Proclaimed in 1666 under Louis XIV, the water-obsessed Sun King, the Royal Canal of Languedoc took fourteen years to dig; 328 aqueducts, bridges, locks, and tunnels and a brand-new Mediterranean port made it Europe's biggest civil engineering project since the Roman era. Rechristened the Canal du Midi after the French Revolution, the 149-mile-long waterway carried thirty thousand passengers annually, until the construction of the Bordeaux railway in the 1850s drove the horse-drawn packet boats out of business. Traffic revived a bit in the 1920s with the advent of diesel-fueled longboats. But the biggest of this century's iron-hulled bulk carriers could never fit into oval locks designed for seventeenth-century *barques,* and commercial shipping ended in 1979. After two decades of uneven maintenance, the canal was added to the UNESCO World Heritage list in 1996, a guarantee, one hopes, for its future preservation.

Pleasure cruising, in any case, has given the canal a new lease on life, though you'd never guess that this is France's most popular pleasure boatway, so well do the winding miles absorb the hotel barges, motor yachts, and retro-looking *pénichettes.* Every now and then a houseboat passes us, part of the slow processional bearing honeymoon couples, families, and not a few lone men and their dogs. We call out *"Bonjour!"* and toast our good fortune to be traveling this shimmering green aisle between a double row of plane trees, transported not just through physical landscape but into a relaxed and convivial state of being.

Rising and falling through eighty-six locks, the Canal du Midi crosses the torrid plain bounded by the Pyrenees, the Massif Central, and the flamingo-rich Rhône delta. This is the old province of Languedoc (literally *langue d'oc*), whose name denotes the language in which *yes* is pronounced *oc* instead of *oui.* One of France's least industrialized regions, Languedoc is often bypassed for more fashionable Provence, which is a shame, since the *garrigue* is as wild and the sunflowers as pretty as in the land of Peter Mayle.

Our journey starts with a rendezvous in Carcassonne, the twelfth-century fortress whose fifty-two towers and two miles of curtain walls formed the backdrop of Kevin Costner's *Robin Hood: Prince of Thieves*. Into this souvenir-riddled disjunction between chivalrous past and Hollywood present stagger our jet-lagged friends from New York, Alison and Rory O'Connor—luggageless, thanks to a missed plane connection. The photographer Michael McDermit pulls up in a cloud of dust, only to find that since he doesn't have a hotel reservation in Carcassonne's medieval town, his car is not allowed within the city's gates. Our 170-mph TGV from Paris arrives on schedule, though the swaying carriages make my daughter, Sophie, lose her breakfast three times. Anchored close by, in the village of Trèbes, *La Tortue* seems a welcome haven from our compendium of modern travel disasters. "This would be great," sighs Rory, collapsing into a deck chair with a caviar canapé and a glass of champagne, "except that my mind's still somewhere over the Atlantic."

I'd originally wanted to drive a houseboat along the entire canal, from Toulouse all the way to the Mediterranean port of Sète, until Scott, my husband, brought up the subject of bilges. "Don't you need to pump them?" he asked back home in Paris. "That doesn't sound relaxing to me."

Instead, we've booked a one-week charter on *La Tortue,* a ninety-five-foot former cargo barge, whose British captain, Paul Pasco, has lived on the canal for seventeen years. He's proposed traveling from Trèbes to Béziers, through fifty-two miles of vine-covered plain. Fifty-two miles seems an awfully short program, especially for Alison and Rory, who've traveled more than three thousand miles just to get here, but then *La Tortue* is offering something more than transportation from point A to point B. "It's an antistress cruise that works best on hyped-up businesspeople," Captain Pasco says. "The first day they're up at six A.M., anxious to get off the barge and go somewhere. By the third day, all they want to do is sit on deck watching the scenery."

In this hyperactive age of supersonic Concorde jets, the very idea of a sub-walking-pace cruise leaves some people feeling antsy. To placate the restless, Captain Pasco offers a busy range of possible onshore activities, including wine-tasting, horseback riding, and white-water kayaking (though not hot air ballooning, inadvisable because of Languedoc's mistral and tramontane winds). In addition, he keeps bikes on board and a minivan on call, along with a cheery guide, Barry Gray, who's abandoned an archaeologist's career in Canada to marry the love of his life, a Frenchwoman named Véronique. Barry lives in the nearby village of Nissan-lez-Ensérune, where he's restoring an eighteenth-century windmill. His van appears magically along the towpath after breakfast or lunch, in case anyone feels compelled to tour a Cathar castle or two.

The next morning, we cruise gently across a seventeenth-century canal bridge (strange sensation, floating on a bridge with a river perpendicular beneath us) and pass through our first triple staircase lock beside the ruins of a mill. We spend the day traveling eastward, the vineyards of Corbières on our right, the start of Minervois wine country on the dark hills to our left. Sophie, who goes to French kindergarten, knows that a fig tree is a *figuier*, but the word for grapevine, in either French or English, escapes her. "Mom, look at all the *grapeiers*," she offers.

Rory, a TV producer back in New York, has already eased into bliss mode, happy to hang out on deck, threatening to eat bugs for Sophie, cracking the spine of a fat novel. Scott, a journalist, immediately sides with Rory in the R and R department, turning off his cell phone and unpacking a set of watercolors. The canal's water world also works its seductive power on Alison, a magazine editor, who debarges not to sightsee but to walk along the bank, gathering purple malva, yellow broom, and fragrant honeysuckle and lavender.

La Tortue moors for the evening under centuries-old sycamores, but a strange spire rising beyond the tree line moves Michael and me to go exploring. On close inspection, the curious structure turns out to be a nineteenth-century wine baron's folly, a decrepit "château" whose mansards, captain's lookout, and octagonal witch's-hat tower eerily recall the house in *Psycho.*

Instead of Tony Perkins we discover a friendly French farmer. "My parents bought it in 1925, and I lived there as a child," says Jean-Pierre Malis, the current owner, who has decamped with his own family to a more sedate 1880 stone cottage across the lawn. "In those days everyone wanted to put his own mark on the landscape, but for me it's a burden. You can't imagine what it would cost just to put up scaffolds to fix the roof. I wish a rich American would buy it and cart it away."

Despite his farmer's tough lack of sentiment, Malis is a gracious and loquacious host, rushing back to his kitchen to fetch us crystal glasses of bubbly Blanquette de Limoux. France's oldest sparkling wine, it was invented by Benedictine monks in the sixteenth century. The Blanquette's not a vintage to make Robert M. Parker cry, but it's a lovely getting-to-know-you drink and sets our new friend talking about Languedoc wine.

In the late nineteenth and early twentieth centuries, Malis tells us, farmers grew rich off the demand for cheap *vin ordinaire,* which soldiers and workers drank at a per capital rate of five liters a day. Languedoc and neighboring Roussillon, along the Spanish border, still produce more than half of France's red table wine and 10 percent of that consumed globally. But recognizing that Coca-Cola has become the world's bulk beverage and that wine gluts don't help the economy, the French government has encouraged farmers to upgrade their cooperatives and rip out undistinguished vines. In the last fifteen years Languedoc-Roussillon has earned thirty-two *appellation d'origine contrôlée* distinctions, including Minervois, Corbières, Faugerès, and St.-Chinian, primarily carignan, syrah, grenache, cinsaut, and mourvèdre mixtures.

Malis has planted cabernet sauvignon and chardonnay on his 320 acres, which he sells to transplanted Australian vintners who bottle pure *cépages* locally using Australian techniques. "They label it WINE MADE IN FRANCE, which of course is much more prestigious than WINE MADE IN AUSTRALIA," he winks. His real passion is rice, which he grows on paddies swamped with canal water. Sunset finds us discussing paella with this French new-world winemaker, watching egrets wade amid green shoots.

The first independent American traveler on the Canal du Midi was Thomas Jefferson, who voyaged from Sète to Toulouse in May 1787, taking voluminous notes on architecture, wine, and canal society. "Of all the methods of travel I have ever tried, this is the pleasantest," he wrote, having loaded his carriage onto a horse-drawn bark to avoid the jolts of the era's roads. "I walk the greater part of the way along the banks of the canal, level, and lined with a double row of trees which furnish shade. When fatigued, I take seat in my carriage where, as much at ease as if it were my study, I read, write and observe."

In the 1970s British canal enthusiasts began waxing lyrical about forgotten French waterways; their low-budget, drive-your-own-houseboat disciples earned the canal its nickname, Le Canal Anglais. Today the houseboat-rental business is growing 15 percent a year. Forty percent of the new clients are French families turning up their noses at beach vacations to follow the siren call of *tourisme vert*.

After years of catering to wealthy American retirees (*La Tortue* once hosted a party whose youngest member was eighty-seven), hotel barges are attracting more active passengers, many of whom like to combine onboard relaxation with invigorating bike tours. The chief difference between the two forms—self-drive houseboat and hotel barge—is something akin to the difference between driving an RV through a national park and booking a luxury safari.

Aboard *La Tortue* we never have to sweep the deck, wash the dishes, pump the bilge, or risk rope burn while tying up for the night. The three sleeping cabins, equipped with twin beds and private bathrooms, are a bit cramped. But the five-course meals are fabulous, and we get to eat them outdoors.

Captain Pasco is right. By day three we've fallen into our anti-stress routine: wake, eat breakfast, cruise, moor for lunch, cruise, moor for dinner, talk the hours away, and fall asleep to the sound of nightingales and crickets. Sophie is having so much fun without TV or even other kids to play with that Scott and I begin to wonder whether we should bottle canal water to use as an antiboredom elixir. She dangles a cane fishing pole over the side of the boat and keeps company with local wildlife, including ducks and swans, spiders with metallic green abdomens, coypus (cousins to the muskrat), and a toad that, paralyzed by the early morning cold, is unable to hop off the towpath.

There's a slight traffic jam at the next lock, the Ecluse de Puicheric, so we walk ahead to chat with the stout red-headed *éclusière*. The reinforced iron doors still turn on seventeenth-century heelposts, but the introduction of electricity in the 1980s means that fifty-one-year-old Marie-France Deschamps no longer has to hand-crank the gates. The daughter of a barge captain, she sweated away her youth in the vineyards and much prefers the laid-back life on the canal. "To work in fresh air, by my own little house, is something very agreeable," she says, footsteps away from her hibiscus-framed door.

While Sophie makes friends with Marie-France's apricot poodle, Scott and I watch houseboats negotiating the lock. At Dad's command, two teenage girls leap in unison off the deck of their *pénichette* and neatly tie up the bow lines. Then there are the parents who encourage their seven-year-old to drive a hundred thousand dollars' worth of rented yacht into the seventeenth-century stone-lined chamber. Maneuvering *La Tortue* into position, Captain Pasco stares coolly at the tyke, wincing at Marie-France's shouts and the unmistakable sound of scraping paint.

Our chief navigational hazards are low bridges, which cause our captain to let off ear-shattering blasts from his foghorn. A sun-weathered Willem Dafoe look-alike, he has kept us plied these past few days with champagne, local red, white, rosé, and sweet muscat wines, and an alarmingly high proportion of France's two-hundred-plus cheeses. Our party is now so relaxed and oversated that mere shouts of "Look out! Hey! Mind your head!" no longer suffice as warnings against decapitation. But the horn—originally designed to pierce northern pea soup—does the trick.

Languedoc is known for hearty country fare like cassoulet, but *La Tortue*'s chef, Peter Shaw, has been whipping up such complex dishes as a duet of silver sea bream and red mullet with a brandy and ginger *zabaglione,* and a fillet of beef with *galette* of puy lentils and a pepper sauce with a port reduction. His little secret is that he lives life at more than four miles an hour. Unbeknownst to us, a relay of vehicles shadows the barge. Before we wake up, Peter zips off to village markets and back, buying farm-fresh ingredients, which he supplements with herbs from a garden on *La Tortue*'s deck.

On day four we finally roust ourselves to go on an outing with Barry. At the weekly market in Olonzac, two miles from the canal, we buy fixings for a picnic lunch: paella, cheese, and quails stuffed with sausage and muscat grapes. The quail-roasting man insists that we eat the birds immediately, right there in the town square, because they must be eaten as hot as possible, but instead we get in Barry's van and head to the fortress town of Minerve, site of an infamous massacre of Cathar heretics in 1210. Over the aeons the Cesse River has punched a tunnel through the base of the limestone cliff beneath the town, but the riverbed is dry in the summer, and we eat on the floor of the gorge at the tunnel mouth, sitting on large white stones. Wandering the dark tunnel afterward, we come across small birds bathing in clear water. "Cesse pools!" Barry quips.

Up in the village Barry introduces us to a museum curator who speaks Occitan, the old troubadours' language, now undergoing a cultural revival after government attempts to suppress it back in the 1930s. To my untrained ear, Occitan sounds like a cross between Spanish, French, and Italian—"*Bonjorn, Madomaisela*"—but in actuality it's more akin to modern Catalan.

Occitan was the mother tongue of Pierre-Paul Riquet, the Canal du Midi's builder, remembered throughout Languedoc as "the last of the Romans" because he fulfilled Caesar's dream of linking the Atlantic and the Mediterranean. In an era when most men were dead by the age of forty, Riquet started construction at the advanced age of sixty-three, sinking his whole fortune into the fourteen-year project. He was a tax collector rather than a trained engineer or architect, and his disparate talents included negotiating water rights with recalcitrant farmers, organizing twelve-thousand-man battalions of workers, and accurately locating the separation points of complex watersheds. He died in 1680, two million livres in debt, the canal just shy of completion, the words "one league to go" on his lips.

Though it's tempting, just staying on board would feel like an amusement park ride on a liquid conveyor belt. Fortunately, the people who live along the canal are so open and friendly that it's easy to break down that passive tourist barrier. It's a moving experience, talking to people whose defining childhood memories are of World War II dogfights over the vineyards, of their parents' resistance against the Nazis, and of fearful encounters with German soldiers, who tossed grenades into the Canal du Midi as a perverse form of relaxation.

Sadly, many of the villages we pass through feel like empty stage sets, deserted by the young. The vacuum of shuttered wine-growers' houses is only partly filled by artists and summer residents. With their sun-bleached walls and communal washstands for the grape pickers, towns like Capestang and Colombières have a sleepy, elegiac feel, ancient loudspeakers atop the mayor's office scratchily calling out matters of civic importance, such as "The peach seller has arrived. The horse butcher, Monsieur Selponi, is here." Then I see Leonardo DiCaprio's face staring out from a magazine cover on a newsstand, and my illusion of timeless isolation collapses.

We spend our last day in the Grand Bief, a lockless section that winds like a true river around the land's natural contours. Flood breaks obscure the lovely switchback views for the little *pénichettes,* but from *La Tortue*'s high deck we're able to look out over a Mediterranean panorama of vineyards, peach orchards, and pantiled red roofs. There's an eighth-century B.C. Iberian settlement on a hill to our left, and past the remains of an old Roman road, the Via Domitia, I see a double line of plane trees marching toward Béziers, as well as the railway that will soon speed us back to Paris.

On the canal bank, just past the village of Poilhes, we meet Jean-Charles Tastavy, a forty-five-year-old winemaker who can trace his Languedoc roots back eight hundred years. He prunes and sprays according to the cycles of the moon and makes his best merlot by fermenting uncrushed grapes, each red globe becoming "a little bottle of wine." As we sip glasses of the earthy liquid, Tastavy shows us how he slips inside twenty-foot-tall nineteenth-century oak hogsheads to clean them. "When I was twelve, my father assured me that if the head can get in, the rest will follow," he grins, showing us a tiny hatch and demonstrating his rubber-man technique. "It's like childbirth in reverse."

It's too bad we can't turn back the clock ourselves, for now we must wistfully bid *La Tortue* adieu. After a week of slow-motion pleasure, we're rushing again, frantically searching the cabins for lost toys and sun hats, snapping last-minute group photos, all the while watching the time so we don't miss trains and planes. Even the unperturbable Captain Pasco seems a bit frazzled as he calculates the time and distance of a minivan ride to Béziers, where our Paris-bound TGV stands at the platform. Kisses, handshakes, promises to write. A final glimpse of the green-hulled barge, the baby ducks, and the wild roses. But as farewells go, this one's not so bad. By traveling so slowly, we savored the best moments of this trip. At four miles an hour, nothing passes in a flash.

Insider's Gascony

By Nancy Harmon Jenkins

~

It is perhaps a sad and happy fact that Gascony is little highlighted, appearing infrequently in periodicals and not allotted much space in guidebooks. I have been thwarted in my efforts to extoll its virtues in this book simply because there is not an abundance of material from which to choose. Charles Neal, in his excellent book *Armagnac* (which is both the name of the spirit and the region that is at the center of Gascony), writes that "Today, on a typical summer afternoon, fluffy white clouds sprawl across Armagnac's deep blue skies. Fields are scattered along its gently rolling countryside like colored squares on a velvet-covered checkerboard. Sunflowers turn toward the hot sun in one field. Several hundred yards away, corn stalks hang limply. Golden wheat fills another square and reflects the sun's golden brilliance. Further on, long rows of green vines stretch across its crumbly soil toward the jagged horizon. Armagnac is an agricultural region, isolated from busy highways and main railway lines. Its inhabitants are closely rooted to the earth and center their lives around the products that have sprung from its soil for centuries." The beauty and character of Gascony should not be measured against its small presence in this book, and I urge visitors to the Southwest to include Gascony in their itineraries—you won't regret it!

NANCY HARMON JENKINS, introduced previously, is a contributing editor of *Food & Wine,* where this piece first appeared. Her work has also appeared in the *Morocco* and *Central Italy* editions of *The Collected Traveler.*

When I travel through the Southwest of France—which is not nearly often enough—I try to stop for a night or two in the tiny hamlet of Camont on the banks of the Canal Latéral à la Garonne, the water road that runs past Toulouse to Bordeaux through the heart of Gascony. Camont, a pleasant but otherwise undistinguished cluster of farm buildings, is a worthy detour simply because it is home port for *The Julia Hoyt,* a restored Dutch barge, and her captain, Kate Hill, an American who has made the boat, the canal, and Camont her home for the last dozen or so years. And she shares it all with guests who take part in her culinary tours.

Picture this: a spare but comfortable farmhouse, its walls a patchwork of burnished river stone and mortared brick, built and rebuilt over several centuries, with a pigeon tower attached. A two-story kitchen lies at one end, with a fireplace that runs the breadth of the room and a refectory worktable almost as long. Outside the kitchen is a garden with a riotous mix of roses and nasturtiums, herbs and greens, that reaches down to the canal. Then there's the canal itself, sixty feet wide, its turbid waters moving languorously northwest to Bordeaux's Atlantic coast, seventy-five miles away. The century-old cargo boat, tied up at the end of the garden, is a splendid sight with Kate at the helm and DuPont, her black, long-legged Labrador mix, sitting at attention beside the wheel.

Just to lie in bed in the farmhouse at night listening to the frogs and the lapping water should be reason enough for a stop. But Kate also knows that to understand a region's culture and way of life, you have to know the cuisine in ways that go far beyond merely learning recipes.

"You can't separate daily life from daily food," Kate says over a glass of chilled Floc de Gascogne, a locally produced combination of Armagnac and grape juice. Sitting at a table on the sun-dappled flagstones of the kitchen terrace peeling garlic cloves for *tourain d'ail,* a rich pureed garlic soup, she muses about what brought her to this place and why she stays: "Both the life and the food here are simple and easy. But a recipe on its own doesn't communicate that, so I try to tell stories about food, to show how it's part of our accumulated history together. After twelve years here, I feel I've only scratched the surface—but at least I know now how much deeper I still need to go." She takes obvious pleasure in imparting her knowledge to clients who spend a few days or a week at the farm, tasting, cooking, and learning.

Questions are inevitable, of course, and each brings on a burst of laughter. "Where did I learn so much about food? On Route 66 in Kingman, Arizona, at the Skyline Truckstop Diner & Motel," Kate says. "My parents ran the diner after my father retired from the Navy. I was sent out to bring in the customers: 'Sir, my mom's cherry pie just came out of the oven. Wouldn't you like to try it, sir?'

"How did I become a barge captain? In Honolulu, where I was born, my father was the captain of the admiral's barge. There's not a direct connection, but still . . .

"How did I get here? A long, slow route: from Holland, where I purchased the barge in 1986, it took five months along canals and rivers to reach Toulouse, where the Canal à la Garonne meets the Canal du Midi—where, you might say, the Atlantic meets the Mediterranean. It was very labor-intensive," she adds wryly. "But you could also say I was looking for a cuisine with a real identity."

And she found it in Gascony, a French culinary heartland where foie gras and duck confit are still made by farm women and sold at the farmhouse door, where Armagnac is distilled by small producers and aged in casks made from local black oak until it is honey-colored and almost honey-flavored, too—"the liquid embodiment of all things Gascon," Kate says.

In Kate's culinary tours, a typical day might begin with a bicycle ride to a nearby farm for Madame Sabadini's omelets and home-cured sausages and hams. A lunch excursion for foie gras might include a visit to an antiques market in a nearby town and end with a stop at the dairy across the Garonne river where Madame Bordin makes wonderful fresh, as well as slightly aged, chèvres from the thirty-six milking goats her husband tends. Then it's back to Camont for a lesson in how to use chèvre in the kitchen, perhaps in a savory tart, the creamy cheese garnished with pine nuts.

A Saturday market trip could incorporate an impromptu tasting at the home of an artisanal Armagnac producer whose wife cooks lunch while guests sit at the kitchen table. Or the day might be given over to a trip to Lectoure, where friends of Kate's have revived the ancient production of woad, a plant once used to make blue dye. Not only are the woad-dyed linens and laces at Bleu de Lectoure exquisite, but the stop provides an opportunity to learn about the original source of the region's wealth.

A tour always includes lessons from Vétou Pompèle, Kate's chief culinary assistant. The last time I was at Camont, in May, Vétou sent her son and his girlfriend out after dinner to gather armfuls of fragrant acacia blossoms. Then she made dessert fritters, beating up a batter for dipping the delicate, cream-colored flowers, frying them in hot oil and sprinkling them with a pinch of sugar. It was the epitome of what Kate had been talking about, a recipe so simple you can hardly call it a recipe, so tied to this place and the time of year that you can't imagine it anywhere else, so delicious that your hand keeps reaching for just one more, just one more.

Reprinted with permission from *Food & Wine* magazine, April 2002.
American Express Publishing Corporation. All rights reserved.

Bibliography

Little Saint, Hannah Green, Random House, 2000. "She is the sacred center. Around her the wheel of the story with its thousand starry spokes spins." So begins the introduction to this beautifully written, unforgettable memoir about author Green, her husband, Jack, the time they spent in Conques over twenty-plus years, and the short life and horrible death of Sainte Foy. This unique book is quite difficult to describe, and I defer to the editor's copy on the jacket, in which it is summarized as "part history, biography, celebration, meditation, inspiration. It is an ode to joy, death, the earthy, and the spiritual." It's also a travel book that I recommend as *de rigueur* to anyone venturing into this corner of the Midi-Pyrenees. It was, in fact, as travelers that Green and Jack first came to Conques, in the springtime of 1975, "to have our hearts caught unaware—Jack a painter, a Californian by birth, I a writer, an Ohioan from an old Swedenborgian and Episcopalian background, a stranger to saints; and yet I was given through Sainte Foy, in this remote and ancient place of pilgrimage, the gift of seeing into that zone which has been held sacred since the beginning of human consciousness." Green notes that in advance of their first trip to Conques, she read what little she could find about Sainte Foy in the Michelin and Blue Guide volumes, "but had I learned more in advance, I still would not have been prepared." I myself found this to be entirely true, for nothing, really—not even all the gorgeous color photos I saw in other books—prepares one for the jewel-encrusted statue of Sainte Foy and the tragic story of her life. This is the only book in English, that I know of, devoted to Conques and Aveyron, and I would probably recommend it for that reason alone; but as it happens there is another reason to urge you to read it: it's a gem. (By the way, if you don't find the book in the travel section of your favorite bookstore or library, check in religion—it is sometimes shelved there, and though after reading it your sense of faith my be renewed, it is not in any way a book about finding God.)

Midi-Pyrénées, text by Samuel Sadaune, photographs by Richard Nourry, Editions Ouest-France, 2002. This attractive and well-written paperback is one volume in the *Itineraires de Découvertes* series. In French, the series is widely available in bookstores and museum shops throughout the Southwest. I haven't seen the books in English yet, but this of course doesn't mean they won't be translated. Other related titles include *Le Canal du Midi, Les Chemins de Compostelle en Terre de France, Le Languedoc-Roussillon,* and *Le Pays Cathare.* This Midi-Pyrénées edition was especially helpful to me in planing my last trip—I was fortunate that French friends sent it to me a few months before my departure. Each chapter features a theme, such as *Triomphes de l'art Roman* and *Bouquets de Bastides et de Villages* and includes a good map allowing for visitors to plan a route for taking in the related sites, villages, towns, or natural areas. If you read even just a little French, I think you will find the text not too challenging and the books very good—I wish I had the entire collection in my posession.

Midi-Pyrenees: Region of Passions, Éditions Milan, Toulouse, 2001. Were it not for Elfie Majoie, who works as a North American liaison for the Midi-Pyrenees tourist office and is co-founder, with her husband, of DMI Tours (one of the best and most personal tour operators specializing in the Southwest; www.dmitours.com), I might not have learned of this wonderful, 246-page hardcover. A number of journalists and scholars have contributed excellent essays on various topics unique to the Southwest, and these are paired with beautiful, full-color photographs. Not available in North America, this book is found in bookstores and museum stores throughout the Southwest.

Travels with a Donkey in the Cévennes, Robert Louis Stevenson, Marlboro Press, 1996. Modestine, Stevenson's donkey, has become one of the great characters in travel book literature, just as this 1879 book has become a travel classic. Stevenson penned this wonderful read when he was in his late twenties, supposedly to earn a quick buck. Whatever his reasons, it's a *de rigueur* read for visitors who'll be in and around the Cévennes. Stevenson was apparently very interested in discovering the land of the Camisards, Protestants who were severely repressed under Louis XIV. A reviewer from France wrote that this work is a "perfect example of what tourism can and must be: the discovery of the visited people's mentality, culture, way of life, and the connection of these with the surrounding nature . . . one has to live with the people, no matter how little, to eat the people's food and to be in contact with the people in order to discuss general and particular subjects and to understand their way of thinking and behaving. Thus tourism becomes an adventure even in the heart of the most civilized country and only a couple of miles away from a railroad."

A Walking Tour in Southern France: Ezra Pound Among the Troubadours, edited by Richard Sieburth, New Directions, 1992. In 1958 Ezra Pound discovered a cache of writings he had scribbled into a small notebook during the summer of 1912, when he set out on foot to observe the troubadour landscape of southern France. Editor Sieburth decided he wanted to try his hand at decipherment (it had been attempted twice before) but reached the conclusion that the "only path of interpretation lay through the roads of France." So, armed with the corresponding Michelin maps and the same guidebooks that Pound had consulted (Baedeker's, the 1877 *Guide Joanne to the Pyrénées,* and Justin Smith's 1898 *Troubadours at Home*), Sieburth retraced Pound's itinerary, "discovering in the process that in almost every case the actual details of observed geography clarified the most puzzling cruxes of the manuscript." This, then, is the final work, accomplished by the "pedestrian" method of scholarship, one that I personally find incredibly appealing. That said, you should know that this work is a bit academic, and though I love the old postcard images featured throughout, I would have preferred the inclusion also of contemporary color views of the same towns and landscapes. The walk was completed in two portions, one in Languedoc-Roussillon and the other in the central Midi-Pyrénées, including Rodez, Albi, Toulouse, Cahors, Domme, Sarlat, Brive, and so on. The real value of this book to me is in Pound's commentary on the troubadours. He writes that "if a man of our time be so crotchety as to wish emotional, as well as intellectual, acquaintance with an age so out of fashion as the twelfth century, he may try in several ways to attain it. He may read the songs themselves from the old books—from the illuminated vellum—and he will learn what the troubadours meant to the folk of the century just after their own. He will learn a little about their costume from the illuminated capitals. Or he may try listening to the words with the music, for, thanks to Jean Beck and others, it is now possible to hear the old tunes. They are perhaps a little Oriental in feeling, and it is likely that the spirit of Sufism is not wholly absent from their content. Or, again, a man may walk the hill roads and river roads from Limoges and Charente to Dordogne and Narbonne and learn a little, or more than a little, of what the country meant to the wandering singers, he may learn, or think he learns, why so many canzos open with speech of the weather; or why such a man made war on such and such castles. Or he may learn the outlines of these events from the 'razos,' or prose paragraphs of introduction, which are sometimes called 'lives of the troubadours.'" Appendix I of the book focuses on "Troubadours: Their Sorts and Conditions" (very revealing, for those especially interested) and Appendix II features three of Pound's translations.

Booklets and Brochures

The Comité Regional du Tourism for the Midi-Pyrénées, based in Toulouse, has published a set of excellent color brochures that are among the most complete and useful I've ever seen. The tourist office defines Midi-Pyrénées quite broadly: an area extending from Barbotan-les-Thermes to the west (in the Gers) northeast to Souillac (just south of Brive-la-Gaillarde and west of Rocamadour), across to Laguiole (in the Auvergne) south to include the Parc Naturel Regional du Haut-Languedoc, westward to Toulouse, and including the entire area south from the Ariège Pyrénées back over to Tarbes (just east of Pau). As a result these very thorough booklets are also useful for areas where there is some overlap. In "Discovering the Midi-Pyrénées: An Introductory Guide to Southwest France," the Comité president notes that "there isn't a period of history that has not left its mark on us. The dawn of mankind is recorded in the mammoths and bison of the Niaux and Pech-Merle caves. Ancient civilisations have left their mark at Montmaurin, while Albi's rose-red cathedral is witness to the bloody Cathar wars of the Middle Ages that ended in such tragedy. The historic figures of our land are still alive in people's memories. Among the best known is Ingres whose work is beautifully preserved at Montauban. And there is also Figeac's Champollion, the first to decode the secret language of Egyptian hieroglyphics. Our landscapes are hugely varied—from the lonely sparse *causses* to the lush valleys of the Gers and the lofty peaks of the Pyrenees . . . This and the other major brochures in the series are available at Maison de la France offices in North America and at the Toulouse tourist office.

~Albi's tourist office has published a great ten-page brochure outlining four *circuits* highlighting the heart of old Albi, different stages of Albi's development through twenty centuries of history, a stroll along the banks of the Tarn, over the pont-Vieux and Pont-Neuf, with superb views over Albi, and religious heritage. Each *circuit* is accompanied by a map, and one page is also devoted to arts and crafts.

~*Le Tarn en Poche,* published by the Comité Départemental du Tourisme du Tarn in Albi, is an eighty-page booklet with tons of information on outdoor sports; family activities; monuments, châteaus, and museums; special events and festivals; markets, restaurants, and *fermes-auberges;* occitan culture; *discothèques* and dancing; *naturisme* (otherwise known as nudist colonies); cinemas; and *idées week-end.*

DOMAINE
GRAND GUILHEM
Chambres d' Hôtes
avec piscine
4 Epis NN

Commune de Cucugnan

Le Château de Quéribus
&
"Le Sermon du Curé de Cucugnan"

Spectacle en continu toute la journée
au THÉÂTRE ACHILLE MIR - CUCUGNAN

Billet à conserver en cas de contrôle

N° 146787   Tarif **Adultes**

Sur les routes du Pays Cathare

Languedoc-Roussillon

"The Languedoc and Roussillon region is one of France's best-kept secrets. While Provence and the Côte d'Azur just across the Rhone have been living it up, attracting movie stars and the masses, its less pretentious neighbor has remained in comfortable obscurity. And so much the better for those in the know: a dramatically varied landscape, two distinct, proud cultures—Occitan and Catalan, a tradition of heresy and steadfast rebellion, and age-old customs all combine to make this a region deservedly unmatched in its romantic associations, at once epitomizing and contradicting everything that is France. Now shaking off centuries of sleepy neglect, Languedoc and Roussillon is emerging as one of the most enticing parts of the country, its remote villages and little-travelled byways affording a much-needed window onto a rural culture no longer found in northern France."

—Brian Catlos, *The Rough Guide*
to Languedoc and Roussillon

From Toulouse to the Mediterranean

BY DOONE BEAL

～

DOONE BEAL lives in London and has written about many Mediterranean destinations for *Gourmet,* where this piece originally appeared.

Bounded on the south by the Pyrenees and on the east by the Mediterranean, France's Languedoc-Roussillon is a land of vineyards and more vineyards, of rolling hills and of peaks crowned by medieval castles. Its orchards, forests, and rivers are punctuated by drowsy villages and rambling abbeys.

A natural gateway to the Languedoc-Roussillon (the region encompasses, and takes its name from, two adjacent but historically separate provinces) is the city of Toulouse. On the Garonne River and the Canal du Midi, roughly halfway between the Atlantic and the Mediterranean, this one-time capital of the old Languedoc was for centuries a rich trading post and port. The mainstay of the city's prosperity today is a huge aerospace industry.

Its skyline etched with towers, domes, and steeples, Toulouse is an architectural feast. Most of the handsome rose-red brick buildings in the old center—*hôtels particuliers,* churches, and the massive Capitole, or Hôtel de Ville—date from the sixteenth, seventeenth, eighteenth, and nineteenth centuries. Among the city's many churches, the most dramatic is Les Jacobins, distinguished by its fretted thirteenth-century tower and "palm tree" vaulting. Twenty-two ribs radiate from the main column, creating a space of soaring light and height, spare and unadorned save for stained-glass windows.

The Basilica of St.-Sernin, one of the largest Romanesque churches in France, was in medieval times an important stop for pilgrims en route to Santiago de Compostela. A particularly enchanting view of its exterior can be had from the gardens of the Musée St.-Raymond, a small treasury of Greek and Etruscan, as well as Roman, remains, from sarcophagi to jewelry. The sixteenth-century building was formerly one of several residences for students of the university, which was founded in 1229 and remains very much a part of the life of Toulouse.

The fountains flashing among the trees in the Place du Président-Wilson are a useful beacon from almost any vantage point; in the center of the fountain, surrounded by nymphlike muses, is a statue of the seventeenth-century Languedoc poet Godolin. (Toulouse was home to many of those musical and poetic troubadours of the Renaissance whose language, *langue d'oc,* still informs the local tongue.)

At lunchtime the cafés of the Place Wilson beckon: Le Capoul, maybe, which is part of the very pleasant hotel of the same name. There are also several inexpensive café-restaurants on either side of the Capoul. Another, more elegant, option, Vanel, on nearby Rue Maurice-Fonvieille, is highly rated. We began there with truffled foie gras, and I followed up with *filets de rougets, sauce civet à la moelle de boeuf:* an unlikely but seductive combination of red mullet and beef marrow. My partner chose venison with tiny, long-stemmed yellow mushrooms. A velvety red Gaillac was a perfect foil to both dishes, and we finished with cinnamon ice cream and puff pastry filled with caramelized apples.

The two central bridges over the Garonne River—the Pont Neuf and the Pont St.-Michel—offer some of the loveliest vistas of Toulouse, and between them lies a historic *quartier* that includes the Rue de la Dalbade and its diverse mansions, most notably the grandiose and gorgeous Hôtel de Pierre (now divided into private apartments). We spent one morning in the nearby Musée des Augustins, housed in a disused monastery and a chief repository of the statuary, paintings, and other adornments rescued from convents and churches demolished in the nineteenth century. Then it was time for lunch and a change of scene. We had made reservations at the Beaux-Arts: built in a semicircle, with classic mirrors, potted palms, and plush banquettes, this bustling old brasserie overlooks the Garonne and the Pont Neuf. A seafood stall—displaying oysters, clams, cockles, and crabs—on the corner of the building boded well. We ordered a dozen *palourdes* (clams akin to littlenecks), crab with mayonnaise, *magret de canard* with prunes, and finally a delectable honey-glazed nougatine. People were still streaming in as we left at half past three.

In a corner of the Place du Capitole, set back from the busy thoroughfares, stands the elegant Grand Hôtel de l'Opéra (originally a seventeenth-century convent), where we stayed. Under the same ownership as the hotel, the Grand Café de l'Opéra and the restaurant Les Jardins de l'Opéra compete for hotel guests' custom. The decor of Les Jardins is a tour de force—Art Nouveau with a glass roof and masses of greenery—but the evening we dined there the restaurant was all but empty. Although the individual Grand Marnier soufflés were a triumph, there were some disappointments in both food and service. Maybe the setting, the Michelin two-star rating, and, above all, the prices pitched our hopes too high. By contrast, the Grand Café across the courtyard is friendly, informal, and well-patronized at all times. It was clearly a favorite of the artistes who once performed at the Opéra and whose signed photographs line the walls. The extensive menu includes a delicate *carpaccio;* grilled sardines; cassoulet; and a memorable salad with warm goat cheese. In short, the café is twice the fun at half the price: the old adage that you get what you pay for does not always hold water.

One hears much, in this region of France, of the Cathari, a

medieval Christian sect. Its members were regarded as heretics by the established Catholic Church, and in 1209 Pope Innocent III mounted against them what was known as the Albigensian Crusade. Brutal and vicious, the war continued for over a century, and the ruined hilltop castles of the Languedoc-Roussillon testify to its horrors to this day.

Among the first Cathar cities to fall to the Crusaders was Carcassonne, which had become, under the suzerainty of the counts of Toulouse, not only a wealthy community in its own right but one of the largest fortresses in Europe. Thus it was a tempting prize (religious zeal was not unmixed with greed). Carcassonne proved to be a hard nut to crack, but the inhabitants finally surrendered in August 1209. The city was later refortified, but, with the 1659 Treaty of the Pyrenees—by which the whole of the nearby Roussillon was returned to France after five hundred years of Spanish rule—Carcassonne's strategic value ebbed. The ramparts would have fallen into ruin were it not for the intervention in 1835 of Prosper Mérimée. Inspector general of historic monuments for Louis-Philippe (as well as the author of *Carmen*), Mérimée initiated the restoration of Carcassonne, enlisting the aid of the architect Eugène Viollet-le-Duc.

Seen from the lower town, which itself dates back to the Middle Ages, the towers of the Cité (as the citadel is known) loom like an operatic stage set on the hill above. The Cité's audience of visitors—to extend the metaphor—runs into the thousands in high season; Carcassonne is a tourist magnet, on the same order as, say, St.-Paul-de-Vence but of much greater historic significance. The approach is over a drawbridge and through the Porte Narbonnaise, from which radiate winding cobbled streets, flights of steps, and some picturesque squares, all strewn with souvenir shops and cafés.

Facing the graceful basilica of St.-Nazaire is the Hôtel de la Cité, built on the site of an old episcopal palace in 1909, when its then-handful of rooms accommodated the foreign dignitaries and visitors from Paris who came to see Viollet-le-Duc's restoration. (Their maids and chauffeurs usually stayed in the more modest Hôtel Dame Carcas, now part of the same building and linked to it by warrens of passages and corridors.) The Hôtel de la Cité was renovated only a few years ago into a luxury establishment, faithfully redecorated with fleur-de-lis wallpaper, chandeliers, coats of arms, and mullioned windows. The hotel also boasts one of the finest restaurants in the area, La Barbacane. Chef Michel Del Burgo, who apprenticed with Michel Guérard, has a light touch; langoustines roasted with sea salt came with a green salad so delicate that it tasted like a bouquet of freshly gathered spring flowers. Two more delights were the fillets of red mullet (under a *concassé* of fresh tomatoes and basil and crispy slices of onion) and roast pigeon stuffed with risotto. Among the desserts was a dark, deliciously bitter chocolate soufflé.

Visitors can walk the *lices*—a rough path that threads between the double fortification—or take the guided tour of the ramparts, but it isn't necessary to join the crowds in order to savor the scene. The Hôtel de la Cité has terraced lawns and gardens from which one can see at close quarters the Tower of the Inquisition and enjoy a marvelous view of the countryside. There is also a pool, which at the height of a baking summer would be bliss indeed. Guests who stay, as we did, in the small but perfectly adequate Hôtel Dame Carcas may enjoy the facilities of its bigger and more opulent sister.

Immediately outside the Porte Narbonnaise, the Auberge du Pont-Levis is a genuine country restaurant: quiet, calm, and gracious, with a tree-shaded dining terrace. The hosts are the Pautard brothers—Olivier, the *chef de cuisine,* and Thierry, the *pâtissier.* We began with a guinea-fowl terrine and an excellent salad of grilled eel. The pièce de résistance was a roasted quail stuffed with quail livers, chopped pork, bread, and herbs. To finish our fruity red

Roussillon (Languedoc-Roussillon produces nearly one-third of France's wine, including the popular Pays d'Oc varietals just becoming available in the United States), we chose from a cheese board that included several varieties of *chèvre* as well as a creamily pungent local sheep's-milk cheese.

Although one can venture from Carcassonne into the wildly beautiful country that lies to the south and east, we found Perpignan to be the more practical base for touring. A relaxed city 45 miles southeast of Carcassonne and just 9 miles from the Mediterranean coast, Perpignan is divided by a grassy-banked canal spanned by small bridges as well as major ones. The staff of the Park Hôtel, where we settled, was always welcoming and always ready with advice as to where to dine. In fact, two of the best eating places in town are right on the spot: the Bistrot du Park and Le Chapon Fin. At the latter, chef Eric Lecerf's terrine of red mullet and his roast John Dory with truffles justify his one-Michelin-star status. He is also responsible for the dreamy lobster gazpacho that is a specialty of the Bistrot, which has a menu based chiefly on seafood. There one could make a complete meal of the splendid *plateau de fruits de mer.*

A major city of the Roussillon and once the province's capital, Perpignan rose to prominence as Carcassonne was declining. The city's most important landmark is the Palais des Rois de Majorque; the palace was built in Perpignan's golden age, between 1276 and 1344, when it was the continental capital of the kings of Majorca and a trading post between Languedoc, Spain, and the Balearic Islands. The immense fortified building contains elegant courtyards and is now used mainly for concerts.

Along Quai Sadi-Carnot, the dark red brick of Port de Notre Dame leads into the pleasing maze of the old city and to the cathedral. Globular lamps, brightly painted shutters, and wrought-iron balconies line the narrow streets, which are a hodgepodge of bookshops, chic little boutiques, and the occasional pharmacy: splendid grazing territory where losing your way is a joy rather than a hazard. With a shock of pleasure I came upon the Saturday market in the Place de la République—not only spring vegetables but flower stalls: a bouquet of scents and colors, with irises, tulips, daisies, carnations, roses, freesias, and lilies.

The old quarter of Perpignan is a diverting jumble of architecture: a single building might range from the thirteenth to the seventeenth century. The Loge de Mer, a former trade exchange, dates to the fourteenth century; looking at it, I wondered not for the first time whether I was in France or Spain or even Italy. In any event, it is the center of a lively street life, where a brass band might strike up on a Saturday afternoon or a procession might materialize.

We fared well at La Passerelle—named for the footbridge that spans a bubbling cascade in the canal—on Cours Palmarole. This calm restaurant specializes in fish; oysters and plates of *fruits de mer* as well as the *parillade,* a grilled selection from the catch of the day. Our own choice was delicious seafood in puff pastry with a cream and champagne sauce and a piquant dish of baby red mullet. We walked back to the Park Hôtel after lunch along the Promenade des Platanes, a cool and shady little forest of plane trees.

Perpignan and the surrounding countryside were territories long disputed by France and Spain, and there is a strong Catalan influence in both language and food. Here olive oil supplants the goose and duck fat of the rest of the Languedoc, anchovies from Port-Vendres spice the hors d'oeuvres, and the area is a veritable orchard of cherries, peaches, and apricots, apples and pears, not to mention the vineyards that extend in every direction over valleys, plains, and hillsides. It is here, too, that one comes closest to the eastern range of the Pyrenees and the majestic Pic du Canigou, snowcapped all year save for high summer. The Roussillon reminded me of Provence and Tuscany as they were some forty years ago.

Not that civilization is lacking in the country. One brief excursion was to Céret, a picturesque walled town of sun-dappled squares that bestrides the River Tech. From before World War I into the 1930s, Céret drew the same painters who frequented the coastal village of Collioure, 20 miles to the east: Miró, Matisse, Dufy, Cocteau, Chagall, Braque, and—the longest runner of them all—Picasso. The new Musée d'Art Moderne features works by all of them, including some rare Picasso ceramics.

Our visit preceded a splendid lunch at the restaurant Les Feuillants, where Didier Banyols cooks and his wife, Marie-Louise, is sommelier. Self-taught, Didier produces imaginative interpretations of such local food as medallions of lobster in a creamy clam sauce and turbot with *cèpe* cream sauce and asparagus. (Along with the recipe that he was kind enough to share with me, Didier gave me a useful tip: to almost any savory sauce he adds a last-minute squeeze of lemon juice and a pinch of curry powder.) With our main courses we drank a tangy Roussillon rosé, and with the dessert—poached raspberries and strawberries—a glass of chilled Muscat de Rivesaltes. There are three bedrooms for those lucky enough to find one available and, in the courtyard, a brasserie with a simple menu.

Another day we took the scenic main road west from Perpignan to Quillan and then looped north, through the town of Couiza, along secondary roads that ramble through the heart of this spectacular scenery. The terrain ranges from forests of pine, cedar, and fir to vistas of rolling hills and bare uplands backed by the distant peaks of the Pyrenees. Route D613 then meets D212—marked "of doubtful quality" on Michelin's map, but well paved—which winds steeply down, via Auriac, to the pretty town of Cucugnan. I had a marvelous wild boar *en casserole* at the Auberge de Cucugnan, but this is also tour bus territory—the big attraction being the nearby Château de Peyrepertuse. Another Cathar stronghold, Peyrepertuse is as well known for its truly mind-blowing view as for the ruined towers, stark against the skyline. Almost at the castle's base is the village of Duilhac and the willow-shaded terrace of the Auberge du Vieux Moulin, where, with hindsight, I would have had lunch. (No bus could get near it.)

Of all the cloisters we visited, the most romantic are those of the Prieuré de Serrabone, high above a valley along a detour from the main route to Prades. This golden stone priory, dating back to the eleventh century, is set amid gorse and wild lavender and shaded by olive, chestnut, and pines. The capitals of the Romanesque cloisters, carved from mottled white and rose marble, depict griffins, lions, and apes—even Bacchus—with a wry humor typical of the period, rather like that which produced the *misericords* beneath the choir stalls of medieval churches.

Although Prades, too, possesses some renowned architectural attractions—including an elaborate Catalan-style high altar in its Eglise St.-Pierre—the city is most often associated with cellist Pablo Casals and the music festival dedicated to his memory, which takes place in July and August. The concerts are held in an auditorium within the precincts of the Abbey of St.-Michel-de-Cuxa, a few miles south of town. (The abbey's cloisters are incomplete: the missing pieces form part of the Metropolitan Museum of Art's Cloisters complex overlooking the Hudson River in New York City.)

Just beyond Prades is the fortified town of Villefranche-de-Conflent, where the rivers from three different valleys—the Têt, the Cady, and the Rotja—meet and rush over the white rocks beneath the covered ramparts. Villefranche has recently become a tourist draw, as the shops that line its medieval streets bear all-too-telling witness. But the Eglise St.-Jacques, its Baroque interior adorned by fine paintings, is one of the most beautiful in Roussillon. Tucked in a peaceful square nearby, the Auberge St.-Paul, formerly a thirteenth-century chapel, is sheltered from the hubbub. On a sunny day we lunched outside, in the shade of a huge plane tree. The enthusiastic young owners, Charles and Patricia Gomez, reverse the traditional French roles: he is the host and sommelier; she is the chef, and a talented one. Our meal included boned roast pigeon with asparagus and morels and a fillet of turbot with sea urchin coral, but the star turn was a starter of quail eggs and puréed asparagus topped with a puff-pastry hat.

Half an hour's drive west of Perpignan, the corniche road of the Côte Vermeille, so named for the golden color of the soil, twists above the sea, linking Cerbère in the south, almost on the Spanish frontier, with the anchovy-fishing village of Port-Vendres and then dropping down into Collioure, the coast's main resort. It is not hard to see why this quintessentially Mediterranean town, with its embracing mountains—navy and emerald at times, dark violet at others—the old church on the waterfront, and the fortified château, seduced those painters who commuted between here and Céret. Today, the stout, slanted masts of the gaily painted fishing boats vie with tall, slender yacht masts; and pollarded plane trees share the main promenade of the Vieux Port with shops, cafés, and restaurants.

The Hôtel Les Templiers cannot have changed much since its inception in the early twenties, when the artists first discovered it and were befriended by the patron, René Pous. The bar echoes with the slither of cards and the click of dice as old men talk in their sharp Catalan, seemingly oblivious to the art around them. The inn's walls, stairways, and upper corridors are covered with a priceless collection of paintings—reputedly about a thousand canvases in all. This tribute to his father is zealously maintained by Pous *fils,* Jojo. Nothing, but nothing, is for sale, although next door, at La Casa Catalana (owned by Jojo's wife, Térésa), one can find good prints of some works, including a much-treasured Dufy.

The Hôtel Les Templiers has a canopied dining terrace, as does the neighboring Hostellerie La Frégate, though La Frégate has the more comfortable interior restaurant of the two. Both establishments offer simple guest accommodations. One cannot go very far wrong in Collioure with such local seafood as the Frégate's milky-fresh *flétan* (halibut), served on a bed of braised leeks with an impeccable *beurre blanc,* and *riz noir,* which proved to be a black paella colored by the cuttlefish ink with which it is cooked. Paella, incidentally, is traditional on this coast on festival days, when immense pans of it bubble away beneath a canopied market stall, as much for the benefit of the stall holders as for the passing visitor. This is part of the town's appeal: save for the high summer season, when the crowds do gather, Collioure—like so much of the seductively varied Languedoc-Roussillon—has managed to keep its own identity.

Hotels and Restaurants

Auberge de Cucugnan, 2 rue de l'Auberge, Cucugnan; 33.5/68.45.40.84

Auberge Pont-Levis, Chemin des Anglais, 11005 Carcassonne; 33.5/68.25.55.23; fax 68.47.32.29

Auberge St.-Paul, place de l'Eglise, Villefranche-de-Conflent; 33.5/68.96.30.95

La Barbacane (*see* Hôtel de la Cité)

Bistrot du Park, 18 boulevard Jean-Bourrat, Perpignan; 33.4/68.35.48.18

Brasserie des Beaux-Arts, 1 quai de la Daurade, Toulouse; 33.5/61.21.12.12

Le Capoul (*see* Le Grand Hôtel Capoul)

Le Chapon Fin, 18 boulevard Jean-Bourrat, Perpignan; 33.4/68.35.48.18

Les Feuillants, 1 boulevard La Fayette, 66400 Céret; 33.5/68.87.37.88; fax 68.87.44.68

Le Grand Café de l'Opéra (*see* Le Grand Hôtel de l'Opéra)

Le Grand Hôtel Capoul, 13 place Président-Wilson, 31000 Toulouse, 33.5/61.10.70.70; fax 61.21.96.70

Le Grand Hôtel de l'Opéra, 1 place du Capitole, 31000 Toulouse; 33.5/61.21.82.66; fax 61.23.41.04

Hostellerie La Frégate, 24 quai de l'Amirauté, 66190 Collioure; 33.5/68.82.06.05; fax 68.82.55.00

Hôtel Dame Carcas, 15 rue Saint-Louis, 11000 Carcassonne; 33.5/68.71.37.37; fax 68.71.50.15

Hôtel de la Cité, place de l'Eglise, 11000 Carcassonne; 33.5/68.25.03.34; fax 68.71.50.15

Hôtel Les Templiers, Collioure; 33.5/68.98.31.10; fax 68.98.01.24

Lingering in the Languedoc

BY LINDA WOLFE

∾

The Hérault is probably the least known (to North Americans) area of Languedoc; it is given little coverage in guidebooks, so I was especially happy when this piece appeared.

LINDA WOLFE is a journalist and author who visits France frequently.

I've been to France often, and happily, but never have I been as enthralled as I was on a trip last June to the valley of the Hérault River in Languedoc. In part it was the landscape. All around were dramatic vistas of distant, rugged mountains and deep ravines, punctuated by placid vineyards and sprawls of mysterious stone towns. In part, too, it was those towns, which up close proved to be twists of narrow streets that climbed to ancient châteaus and seemed untouched by modernity.

I was in the Hérault to visit cousins who had rented a house—sight unseen, from a newspaper ad—in the tiny town of Brissac-le-Haut, population forty. I had flown from Paris to the nearest big city, Montpellier, and there my cousins met me and drove me to their house 28 miles away, along a route that started out straight but soon became steep and filled with what the French call *lacets*, shoelace turns.

"Let's show Linda what to expect," said Ellen, who would prove to be our resident tour guide, and made Bob, who would turn out to be both principal driver and navigator, stop a couple of times so that I and yet another visiting cousin, Natalee, could get a feel for the area.

First we walked around the delightful town of Les Matelles, a vertical scramble of cobbled streets and shuttered houses. I'd seen many such vertical château towns in other areas of France, but generally they had been gussied up with boutiques, artisans' shops, and restaurants. Les Matelles had no such contemporary touches; nor, it would turn out, had Brissac-le-Haut or most of the towns we were to visit in the region. Indeed, Les Matelles appeared to be empty of all human commerce, although its stoops and doorways testified otherwise, the stoops sprouting pots of petunias, geraniums, and thigh-high fragrant rosemary bushes, the doors sporting the *cordibelle,* a huge dried sunflower that is a regional emblem.

Although it was late afternoon, the hottest time of day, Ellen goaded us upward for perhaps fifteen minutes until we reached the château. Worth the detour, worth the climb. From there we first saw the stern, towering mass of the local limestone giant, the Pic St.-Loup, 2,138 feet high.

Our next stop was St.-Martin-de-Londres, which has a renowned eleventh-century church and a lovely medieval square, its splashing fountain and leafy trees providing coolness and shade for shoppers and café sitters. There we bought bread for dinner and an amazing confection: a local baker had sculptured the Pic St.-Loup in meringue and dark chocolate. Then at last we headed for Brissac-le-Haut.

It was early evening as we entered the town, another upward thrust of narrow and cobbled streets. Bob and Ellen's place was a stone house built in the late sixteenth or early seventeenth century, with thirty-inch-thick walls and a vaulted ceiling. The house was simply furnished and its kitchen was primitive, but none of us minded, for as dusk descended, we sat on the stone terrace with its panoramic view and dined on pâtés, *saucisson,* the astounding local blue cheese, our Pic St.-Loups, and a terrific Languedocian red wine that Bob swore had cost only two dollars in a *supermarché* in nearby Ganges. Better yet, after dinner—in the eerie crepuscular light that lasts, in June, till ten—we climbed again. This time it was to Brissac-le-Haut's own château, a majestic hulk that was begun early in the eleventh century.

Like the Château de Brissac, many of the castles in the region were built in that distant century, a time when Languedoc was emerging as the center of a lively, sophisticated, and literate civilization. The troubadours wrote in the *langue d'oc,* which was different from the language spoken up north, the *langue d'oil.* By the beginning of the thirteenth century, great power and wealth were assembled in Languedoc, and the area had become home to a number of religious sects that denied some of the sacraments and beliefs of the Roman Catholic Church.

One such sect, Catharism, whose followers were later known as Albigensians, inspired the genocide and outrageous land grab known as the Albigensian Crusade. A marriage of convenience between the papacy in Rome and the nobility in northern France, it was a crusade that tortured and burned alive many residents of the area, most of them not Cathars at all, confiscated their goods and property, and left local communities in disarray. Indeed, some say, that disruption long ago is why Languedoc is still one of France's poorest and least developed areas. Wherever one goes in the Hérault, one hears tales of the butchery and of the Cathars—how good and pure they were, how they were early feminists (women as well as men were permitted to administer last rites), and how, although they were forced to deny their faith, their religion continued underground, reemerging centuries later in the beliefs of the Huguenots.

I didn't know anything about the region's tortured history that first night when we stood in the Château de Brissac's shadow. I would learn about it later, when we began touring, and meeting local residents—who, by the way, were extremely friendly and willing to put up with feeble French.

That first night, Ellen planned our week, and we fell asleep soundly, the extraordinary heat of the day having given way to an evening so cool that we had to get out extra blankets. We awoke the next morning to sheep bells—this is an area where one of the biggest events of the year is the spring transhumance, when the flocks are driven into the uplands; it's like a New England leaf-turning weekend, for the event is so popular there's even a toll-free phone number to call to get the date.

From then on, we were always on the go. Languedoc is home to some of the great historic sites in France, cities like Béziers, Carcassonne, and Nîmes, but we decided to concentrate on less-known places. We saw the geological wonder of the area, the Cirque de Navacelles, a circular valley carved out of the mountains by glaciers that looks for all the world like a landscape on the Moon yet harbors at its seemingly unreachable bottom a town of secretive-looking old stone houses. (No wonder the Cirque was, as I later learned, a stronghold of the French Resistance.)

We saw the winding forested trails of the Cévennes National Park, through which Robert Louis Stevenson traveled on a donkey and which today are favorites of energetic hikers and climbers. We saw La Couvertoirade, a walled village built in the twelfth century by the Knights Templar, which, with its small towers and modest ramparts, looks like a mini-Carcassonne; and the haunting St.-Guilhem-le-Désert, a town set amid scenery so spectacular, you think for a moment you are at Yosemite. St.-Guilhem has not just cliffs and canyons but also an eleventh-century church built to commemorate Guillaume, a friend of Charlemagne's who in the ninth century retreated to this remote and decidedly spiritual outpost to mourn his wife and repent a life of conquest. The church is exquisite, even though most of its cloister was sold to the Metropolitan Museum of Art in New York, which made it part of what we know as the Cloisters.

Additionally, we saw innumerable picturesque towns that do not, for the most part, seem to be listed in guidebooks: towns like

St.-André-de-Buéges, where there is a brooding twelfth-century church; Pégairolles-de-Buéges, high up on a lonesome cliff; and St.-Jean-de-Buéges, with a view from its ruined castle of such hidden lush valleys that we all thought at once of our favorite childhood book *Lost Horizons.*

Then one day we ventured to the eastern edge of Languedoc and saw—though *experienced* would be the better word—the Pont du Gard. The astounding ancient Roman aqueduct comes upon one suddenly. Ellen, Natalee, and I had been chattering in the car, reliving girlhood memories, when suddenly we heard Bob shouting in uncharacteristic awe, "Look! Stop talking and look!" And there, out of nowhere, it was.

Henry James, who loved the Pont du Gard, had had a similar experience. He wrote, "You are very near it before you see it; the ravine it spans suddenly opens and exhibits the picture." Yes. And yes again to his taut description of the three tiers of the monumental bridge: "They are unspeakably imposing." Although it is said to be one of the most visited sites in France, that late afternoon we could see it with no one at the bridge except ourselves and a few people parading the distant top tier.

The Hérault also offers abundant and very good wine, producing more than any other region in France. And there's excellent, not very expensive food. We especially enjoyed eating at the local farms (called *mas*), which serve their own produce. A favorite was the Ferme-Auberge du Domaine de Blancardy, where the meal was all duck—from the *plateau gourmand* that starts the meal with duck *rillettes,* smoked breast meat, and foie gras, to the main course choices of *confit de canard, aiguillettes,* or *magret grillé.*

Another favorite was La Ferme des Moreaux, where an architect and his wife, André and Anne Damiean-Moureaux, drop-outs from big-city life, raise their own lamb and free-range chickens, grilling the meat over an aromatic fire in a huge circular medieval-style grill.

They also bake their own dark bread and grow *plantes médicinales,* herbs with which to flavor the meats. There are also more formal restaurants, like the elegant Muscardine, which serves what the kitchen calls *nouvelle cuisine languedocienne,* the pretty Abeuradou, on the grounds of a château at Pont-d'Hérault, or the captivating Auberge de la Vallée, where the chef misses not a seasonal trick. The night I was there, he had whipped up a fine spicy, tomato-based *sauce armorigue* for the first crayfish of the season.

As much as I saw in the Hérault, I would love to go back. For I never did get to see the museum of Cévennes life in Le Vigan, or the prehistoric village at Cambous. I was a week too late to see the sheep ambling up the mountains. And although spring slipped into summer while I was there and the hills began to turn from green to pale purple and gray, I didn't get to swim in the now no longer icy waters of the crystalline Hérault River.

Finding Your Way Through the Valley

Getting There

Montpellier, the best starting point, is about a one hour and fifteen-minute flight from Paris. You will need a car to explore the region. There are several car-rental companies at the Montpellier airport.

When to Go

Late spring and autumn generally offer sunny, dry weather, as does the summer, although it can be very hot. The winter is cold and bleak.

Where to Stay

There are many small hotels in the region, and most are inexpensive. I did not stay in any of them, but I visited a few. The most attractive I saw were these:

L'Auberge les Norias, 254 avenue des Deux Ponts in Cazilhac, 33.5/67.73.55.90; fax 67.73.62.08. The hotel has 11 very comfortable rooms in a pretty inn that overlooks the Hérault River. A double room is $61; one room with terrace is $65.

The Château du Rey, at Pont-de-Hérault, 67.82.40.06, has 12 rooms and one suite in a castle built in the thirteenth century and first renovated as a hotel by the famous nineteenth-century architect Eugène Viollet-le-Duc. A double room is $98. The restaurant L'Abeuradou, 33.5/67.82.49.32, is in the hotel.

Where to Eat

The prices given are for three-course dinners for four, including wine. Reservations are necessary at these restaurants.

La Ferme-Auberge du Domaine de Blancardy, 33.5/67.73.94.94, is just outside Ganges on the road to Nîmes. Specialties are homemade pâtés, duck confit, grilled *magret* of duck, and the Domaine's own wines. Dinner was around $100.

L'Auberge de la Vallée, 33.5/67.73.11.90, is at St.-Jean-de-Buéges, 29 miles north of Montpellier. Specialties are fish, seafood, regional dishes, and game in season. The chef will also prepare bouillabaisse, paella, cassoulet, or couscous on order. Dinner was $123.

La Ferme des Moreaux, 33.5/67.73.12.11, is on the road to St.-Guilhem-le-Désert at Causse de la Celle. The restaurant specializes in "medieval cooking," with such dishes as leek tart, lamb grilled over an open hearth, pork cooked in honey, and tomatoes Monsieur Seguin, filled with goat cheese. Dinner was about $100.

Reading

The best guide to the area is still Freda White's *West of the Rhone: Languedoc, Roussillon, the Massif Central* (Norton, 1964).

A lively book that discusses the history of the region (among others) is *The Road from the Past: Traveling Through the History of France,* by Ina Caro (Doubleday, 1994).

This piece originally appeared in the July 16, 1995, travel section of The New York Times.

The Light of a Lost Star

BY GULLY WELLS

❧

It was in this excellent piece that I learned of the book *The Perfect Heresy* by Stephen O'Shea, which fed my interest in the Cathars. As Wells wisely notes, "It isn't really worth exploring the fascinating world of the Cathars unless you've done some reading before you arrive."

By the way, a truly worthwhile Web site to browse for an amazing amount of information on the Cathars is www.cathares.org. The site is in French, but some of the links, notably the tourist office of the Aude, have English translations. In addition to the ten villages, fortified sites, châteaus, seven abbeys, three grottoes, seven megaliths, and twelve *circulades* highlighted, there is information provided on accommodations and restaurants, photos of the castles, a dossier on topics such as the Inquisition, and a boutique offering music, posters, postcards, jewelry, and so on.

GULLY WELLS is a contributing editor at *Condé Nast Traveler*. She writes often about France, and her work has appeared in previous editions of *The Collected Traveler*.

It was the most terrifying building I had ever seen: enormous, monolithic, red brick. Its grim walls were punctuated by buttresses that evoked the cylinders of a (loaded) gun, its windows nothing more than sinister elongated slits. There were watchtowers on top of the bigger buttresses, and another tower, almost as high as the walls themselves, rose up like a skyscraper from the roof until it really did seem to graze the deep blue sky above.

Architecture as intimidation. This building was going to impose its will on you whether you liked it or not. It reminded me of the harsh, triumphalist style favored by the Soviets, or a medieval version of something Albert Speer might have created for his patron, Hitler. But the most astonishing thing about this deeply disturbing edifice was that it wasn't a fortress or a high-security prison. It was a church. The Catédrale de Ste.-Cécile in Albi, to be precise.

I took a few steps back and looked up, squinting into the harsh southern sunlight, barely able to see the top of the tower. If this really was a cathedral (which it was), where were the intricate jewel-colored rose windows, the gargoyles, the statues of the saints, the facade carved with such elegant precision that it seemed more like lace than stone? Accustomed to the stupefying beauty of Chartres, Notre-Dame, and Rheims, I was affronted by the sheer brutality before my eyes. Who had built this? And why was it unlike any other cathedral in France?

About twenty-five years ago I read a book called *Montaillou,* by the French historian Emmanuel Le Roy Ladurie, which told the story of the religious persecution of the inhabitants of a tiny village in the foothills of the Pyrenees at the beginning of the fourteenth century. The people of Montaillou were followers of the Cathar religion (of which more later), a Christian heresy so threatening to the Catholic Church that it had to be eradicated by whatever means. The Church tried reason (sic), it tried debate, it tried bullying, it tried burning them at the stake, but when none of this worked, the Church got serious. Pope Innocent III declared war on the heretics and organized, with the help of King Philip Augustus, a series of crusades. Crudely put, the pope was after souls and the crusaders wanted land, so it was a win-win plan. And since the Cathars were scattered all across a region of

Southwestern France called the Languedoc, whose principal town was Albi, these battles became known as the Albigensian Crusade.

War fueled by religious fanaticism takes on an even more brutal aspect (as we now understand all too well), and this was no exception. When the city of Béziers fell to the crusaders in 1209, Arnold Amaury, the monk who was one of the crusaders' leaders, was asked how their swords were to distinguish between Catholic and Cathar. In response, he uttered the infamous words "Kill them all. God will know his own."

In the end, which came in 1244 with the siege of Montségur, these battalions of heavily armed men won the war, and although there were a few remote places such as Montaillou where a handful of believers hung on, Catharism had largely been destroyed by the mid-thirteenth century.

Which brings us back to the cathedral in Albi. Construction began in 1282, nearly forty years after the defeat at Montségur, and ended only in 1392, more than a century after the heresy's eradication. And yet the bishop of Albi, Bernard de Castanet, still clearly felt that the cathedral had to assert and confirm the absolute victory of the Church over the heretics of the past, present, and future—such was the mysterious power of the Cathars. In the haunting words of Le Roy Ladurie, "Today Catharism is no more than a dead star, whose cold but fascinating light reaches us now after an eclipse of more than half a millennium."

Over the years, I read more books about the Albigensian Crusade, and the Languedoc became one of those places you stuff into the overflowing filing cabinet in your mind, under the heading "Must visit someday." I'd seen photographs of Cathar castles, which seemed to grow out of the grim, gray stone of the mountain peaks, their ruins still standing guard over the countryside in case the murderous crusaders returned. And I tried to understand the Cathar religion—the word comes from the Greek *katharos,* meaning "pure." Put at its very simplest: there are two gods, with the evil one (or devil) ruling the physical world, including mankind, so that everything with material form is by definition evil, and a greater, good god ruling the spiritual world and having no earthly form, existing only as an idea in the minds of men.

The very concept of two gods was heretical, but worse was to come. Since the Cathars rejected the material world, what use did they have for an organized church, prayers, mass, or any of the trappings of the Catholic Church? Women were regarded as the equal of men, and since they did not recognize Church marriages, why not sleep with whomever you wanted to? It was a deeply subversive faith because it rejected all hierarchy in this world as the work of the devil. What could be more threatening to society? Obviously, they had to be destroyed.

My father, an architect, told me about the walled city of Carcassonne, where he'd spent his honeymoon in 1949. And one night last year I had dinner with a French friend whose only and all-consuming passion is wine. Madame Folle de Vin was going to introduce me to a wine from a region she was quite sure I'd never heard of: the Languedoc.

Once known for producing huge quantities of the worst wine in France, she told me, it had recently started to change. A bottle of Château La Voulte-Gasparets 1997 was ordered and had disappeared by the end of the evening. I scribbled in my notebook the name and the wine region, the Corbières, so that it too could go into the filing cabinet.

And then, a few months after that dinner, I was flipping through the Michelin. The map of France is dense with the red rosettes of starred restaurants, but there are deserts, such as the Languedoc, with only the occasional red oasis. One, it turned out, was in the Corbières, in a tiny hamlet called Fontjoncouse, a long way from any town but near the château that had produced the unforgettable wine. Two beckoning stars.

After a quarter century, it had all come together: the Cathars, the castles, the medieval towns and monasteries, and now the kind of food and wine that makes this experience the perfect balance between nourishing body and soul.

Carcassonne was my gateway to the Languedoc-Roussillon (the name for the modern French region). It is still possible to approach this city and see it shimmering in the distance, surrounded by farm-land. With its turrets and towers and honey-colored walls, Carcassonne seems to float on a hilltop. (In fact, there are two Carcassonnes. The one on the hill is called La Cité. The other—the "new" one founded in the fourteenth century but greatly expanded since—lies hidden in the valley.) Approaching La Cité, you have this glorious moment when you imagine you've time-traveled back a thousand years. You will never see such a perfectly restored/pre-served medieval town again, but once you get inside those beautiful crenellated walls, the hell begins.

The parking lot is down beside the old moat, which makes sense. Who in his right mind would drive through the snaky alleyways that wind up through the town? The answer is, anyone staying at the Hôtel de la Cité, inside the walls (whose guests tend to drive Mercedes, Ferraris, and BMWs), and the guys who deliver fresh shipments of beer, ice cream, pottery cats dressed in lace dresses, plastic swords, and T-shirts printed with knights in armor. The rest of us are on foot. As I set off up the main street, I felt as though I were being wafted along by the crowds. My feet hardly seemed to touch the ground as a gang of German teenagers and a gaggle of elderly Japanese women surged up the hill right behind me.

The Eglise St.-Nazaire, consecrated in 1096, dominates La Cité and is a cool, peaceful refuge from the hordes. The nave is soft, rounded, and Romanesque, while the choir, which was built in the thirteenth century, is Gothic. As far as I could see, there haven't been too many renovations in the interior decorating department since. I stopped in front of a vast rose window composed of all the colors of the sea: aquamarine, cobalt blue, turquoise. It was like swimming in the Grenadines.

In horrific contrast, a stone bas-relief on one wall was a picture of pure mayhem: on one side, knights on horses with lances; on the other, hand-to-hand combat. I imagined it was crusaders attacking the Cathars during the siege of Carcassonne in 1209, fresh from the slaughter at Béziers. This is one of the strange sensations you get when visiting these Cathar strongholds, once the scene of bloody battles and massacres—but so long ago that history has softened the pain. The streets of Carcassonne used to run with blood, but today there's nothing worse than candy wrappers and spilled Coke.

My father had told me about Eugène Viollet-le-Duc, who had been responsible for the restoration of Carcassonne in the mid-nineteenth century. The truth is that he got a bit carried away and couldn't resist adding a few touches of his own, like some crenellations tacked onto the church belfry, as well as turret roofs whose shape is apparently inauthentic and whose tiles should have been brick, not slate. The slightly tedious argument about restoration versus preservation has been going on ever since.

After a day battling the crowds in Carcassonne, I was ready for the remote foothills of the Pyrenees and my pilgrimage to the village of Montaillou. The early morning sun was shining as I headed due west, but the closer I got to the mountains, the more dismal the weather became. Mist turned to fog, drizzle to rain.

If Montaillou seems like the back of beyond today (and it does), it is almost impossible to imagine what it must have felt like a hundred years ago. The only thing in the whole hamlet that was open was a little store. On the cluttered shelves, there was a mix of local produce, *confit de canard* in glass jars sealed with a layer of fat, honeycombs in wooden boxes, and *foie gras de canard* in a terrine, as well as books, postcards, and pamphlets all about . . . the Cathars. The heretics who were once burned at the stake have been transformed into a lucrative marketing tool for local tourism. A poster advertised a reenactment of some medieval garden party, with the ruined castle as the backdrop and the guests lounging around on the grass, dressed in "Cathar" costume.

The lady behind the counter told me that this festival was held every year, but, sadly, I had missed it by a couple of days. "*Quel dommage,*" I murmured as if I really meant it, and then asked my new friend if she spoke Occitan, the original language of the Languedoc. She laughed and said that she wasn't old enough or young enough to have been taught it. *Les vieux* grew up with it, and *les jeunes* were taking it up—people like her, in the middle, had missed out. Madame seemed genuinely pleased that it wasn't going to disappear completely. She told me that now you can study it at school and at university, and there are even a few hours of Occitan TV each day on France 3.

And what of the Cathars? She pointed proudly to a signed photo of professor Ladurie that hung next to the poster, and then to the stack of paperback editions of his book on the table. Just as I was turning to leave, a middle-aged man with steel gray hair walked in, and Madame leaped to her feet and introduced me to *le maire,* Monsieur Clergue. The name was strangely familiar, and then I remembered that the priest in Montaillou at the time of the inquisition was Pierre Clergue, who must have been this man's ancestor.

The fascination of *Montaillou*—the book, not the place—lies in its detailed description of just about every aspect of the lives of the villagers in the early fourteenth century, from their eating habits, religious beliefs, love affairs (and methods of contraception), and health and medicines, to their squabbles over a pig.

The village was one of the last holdouts of Catharism, and the bishop of Palmiers, determined to root out the heretics once and for all, ordered an inquisition. The villagers were questioned about not just their religion but every aspect of their lives, and the answers were taken down and carefully preserved. When the bishop became pope, these records were transferred to the Vatican, where they remain to this day. The documents were rediscovered in the early twentieth century, but it was Ladurie who made brilliant use of them in his book—and incidentally helped the people of Montaillou make a living from something other than sheep and ducks.

On the way back to Carcassonne, the fog cleared and I could see the deep-green valleys—not a house in sight, completely deserted but strangely beautiful and soothing. I was interested to learn that Occitan seemed to be making a comeback, even if only a modest one. The people of the Languedoc have always felt themselves separate from "France" to the north—the region was incorporated into the rest of the country only in the Middle Ages.

The north-south divide lasted well into the twentieth century (just as it did in Italy), with *le nord* regarding the Midi as somehow less civilized. Part of this division is about language. The name of the region comes from the Occitan word for "yes," which is *oc,* and led to *langue d'oc.* (In the rest of France, the word was *oïl,* which evolved into *oui.*)

If the French can get agitated about regional languages, then what about food? And wine? Not to mention cheese? Wasn't it de Gaulle who prided himself (just for a change) on being able to govern a country that produced 246 different cheeses? With these thoughts in mind, I knew that I must be hungry. I was on my way to meet Monsieur Two Star, Gilles Goujon, at his Auberge du Vieux Puits in Fontjoncouse.

As you drive south toward the Mediterranean and east toward

the Rhône, the scenery changes completely. The misty valleys give way to brick-red soil, vineyards, and rocky hilltops, their crests looking like rows of giant dragon's teeth. The Corbières is (I imagine) a bit like Provence before it became Provence, and the serious business here is quite clearly wine—not tourism. So what was a Michelin two-star restaurant doing in a village every bit as tiny and remote as Montaillou?

The answer lies in the French passion for food. They are happy to drive for hours and hours if they are sure that a sublime meal will be their reward. The restaurant was right by the side of the road, just outside the village of Fontjoncouse. Not big, not small, and if you didn't know what you were looking for, you'd probably drive right past it. Madame Goujon was behind the desk, and Monsieur was, of course, in the kitchen.

The dining room was warm and elegant, with a terra-cotta floor and pale shell-pink linen, so welcoming that you wouldn't think twice about bringing your dog and your two-year-old in her stroller. And by the end of the evening, I must have counted six kids ranging from newborn to about eleven, and at least four dogs ranging from Labrador to a puppy of indeterminate parentage. All perfectly behaved.

The menu and the wine list were entirely from *le terroir,* and what better *terroir* to plunder? I put myself entirely in the hands of Madame Goujon. The buttery galette with trout (from the market in Minerve) to begin, then *pintade* (from Monsieur Garros in the village of Bugarach) with couscous, which meant it must be time for some red wine. The sommelier suggested a Château La Voulte-Gasparets 1997. Wonderful, especially with the next course, which was cheese. There were at least thirty varieties, many of them goat, some sheep, and every single one either from producers who were practically neighbors or from the market in Lézignan, all of ten miles away.

Since the Auberge opened in 1992, local farmers have become friends; neighbors have become suppliers of wild mushrooms, fruit, honey, baby vegetables; and word has spread that there is a passionate chef in Fontjoncouse who will buy only the absolute best you have to offer. But if he likes you (and your *framboises*), he may just do a barter and exchange a few baskets for a dinner like no other you have ever tasted.

Not too far from Fontjoncouse, just inland from Narbonne, up a long dirt road and surrounded by thick woods and vineyards, lies the Abbaye de Fontfroide. A Cistercian abbey, it has been in this valley for more than a thousand years, and even though there aren't any monks left, these honey-colored stone buildings—the enormous refectory, the more intimate cloister, the chapter house—still exude a palpable feeling of calm, serenity, and religious devotion. I fell in with a handful of people being bustled around by the guide and, once we got to the rose garden, "lost" myself behind a hedge and let my thoughts wander back to Montaillou.

Jacques Fournier, bishop of Palmiers, who had conducted the inquisition, went on to be named the abbot of Fontfroide and then rose even higher, becoming Pope Benedict XII. The abbey where I was lolling so happily in the sun had been at the very center of the war against the Cathars. Seven hundred years ago this peaceful backwater had been the headquarters of a violent crusade. The whole might of the Catholic Church had been marshaled against the heretics: churches, abbeys, monasteries, and castles were built; soldiers fought battles; the Church burned people and, of course, eventually won the war. And yet by some ironic twist of history, the heretics were never truly destroyed, and the "cold but fascinating light" of the Cathars, who left behind no churches, monuments, or artifacts and scarcely a written word, still has the mysterious power to haunt both our memory and our imagination.

Cathar Country

If you crave glitz and glamour, then the Languedoc is not your kind of destination. But if you can appreciate a vast, empty expanse of southern France with a long and thrilling history, amazing architecture, wine that has gone from *ordinaire* to *extraordinaire* in the last decade, and great local food (the most famous dish being cassoulet), then this is the place for you.

Albi

On the banks of the Tarn, La **Réserve** is comfortable and, if you want to be in the city, convenient. 33.5/63.60.80.80; www.relaischateaux.com; doubles, about $112–$217. Only an hour south, the **Château d'Aiguefonde** is both interesting and beautiful, having been brilliantly restored by Paul de Vilder, who is also the chef and host. When he joins you after dinner to help you plan your next day's activities, you feel as though you are staying in a private home—which indeed you are (33.5/63.98.13.70; perso.wanadoo.fr/aiguefonde.chateau; doubles, about $104–$169).

No restaurants are outstanding, but two are recommended: the **Moulin de la Mothe,** which overlooks the river (33.5/63.60.38.15; entrées, about $19–$33) and **L'Esprit du Vin** (33.5/63.54.60.44; prix fixe, about $27–$43).

Béziers

You can lunch on mussels and local wine at one of the endless sidewalk cafés in the central market, or be extravagant and dine at **L'Ambassade,** where Patrick Olry cooks some of the most ambitious food around in an ultracool, ultramodern setting (33.4/67.76.06.24; entrées, about $20–$37). **Framboisier** is also good—try the warm oysters in a champagne sauce (33.4/67.49.90.00; entrées, about $34–$77). Just a few miles north, in the tiny village of

Maraussan, another talented young chef, Jean-Luc Santure, has given **Parfums de Garrigue** a country feel. The place is surrounded by vineyards, and, as at all of these restaurants, the wine list includes the best local bottles (33.4/67.90.33.76; entrées, about $20–$30).

Carcassonne

The huge, faux-Gothic **Hôtel de la Cité** delivers comfort and style on a grand scale. A private garden and pool overlook the ramparts (33.4/68.71.98.71; www.hoteldelacite.orient-express.com; doubles, about $209–$243). The more formal of its restaurants, **La Barbacane** is easily the best place to eat in town (entrées, about $21–$30). Try the simpler one, **Chez Saskja,** for a light lunch (entrées, about $9–$14).

On the way to nearby Cavanac, the **Domaine d'Auriac** is a nineteenth-century estate with a large house that has since been turned into a comfortable hotel. Golf, a pool, and a one-star Michelin restaurant are on-site (33.4/68.25.72.22; www.relaischateaux.com; doubles, about $100–$330). In Fontjoncouse, a good hour from Carcassonne, the superb eight-room **L'Auberge du Vieux Puits** is owned and run by the Goujons, who serve by far the best and most ambitious food in the entire region. Plan to spend the night: you don't want to have to maneuver those roads after a bottle of wine and a glass of Armagnac (33.4/68.44.07.37; fax .08.31; doubles, about $86; prix fixe, about $45–$64).

Mirepoix

This especially charming village west of Carcassonne has a main square surrounded by late-thirteenth- to fifteenth-century half-timber houses that jut out, forming covered arcades. Stay at the **Maison de Consuls,** which dates back to the fourteenth century (33.5/61.68.81.81; doubles, about $60–$75), and eat at any of the brasseries around the square. There's also a great open-air market on Saturdays.

READING

It isn't really worth exploring the fascinating world of the Cathars unless you've done some reading before you arrive. The most accessible book is *The Perfect Heresy* by Stephen O'Shea, a brilliant and gripping history of the Cathar movement that reads like a thriller (Walker Books, 2000). The classic *Montaillou,* by Emmanuel Le Roy Ladurie, is more academic and focuses on one hamlet. Still, it gives you an insight into the daily lives, loves, and religious beliefs of the people of Montaillou in the fourteenth century (Knopf, 1979).

As guidebooks go, the *Insight Guide* to the southwest of France is indispensable, as is the *Michelin Green Guide. Languedoc and Roussillon* from **Hachette Vacances** is also worth having.

Carcassonne, City of Stone

BY ALAN RIDING

Ina Caro, in her wonderful book *The Road from the Past: Traveling Through History in France,* notes that she put off for years visiting Carcassonne because she had heard (accurately) that it was too touristy, overly restored, and a "Disneyland caricature of the Middle Ages." You will undoubtedly read the same, but I think that like Caro (and me), you will find that you don't care. Don't allow the tourists and shops to deter you—like walking through the tourist village on Mont St. Michel in Normandy, you'll be rewarded if you just keep on walking onward and upward. The author of this piece refers to the tourist train that makes a little journey around the outside walls of Carcassonne, and so does Caro—the first thing she and her husband did at the gates of Carcassonne was to hop on that little train. "If you want to know how a fortified city defended itself against besiegers, believe me, by the time your little train has completed its circuit of the walls, you will know. The tour could have been called 'All You Ever Need to Know About Concentric Medieval Defensive Fortifications.' And even if you couldn't care less about medieval defensive fortifications, you should take the tour anyway, because the beauty of medieval construction, in direct contrast to classical architecture, which preceded it, and Renaissance architecture, which followed, is the unplanned evolution of its parts in reponse to changes in warfare—changes that took place over a period of a thousand years." Caro continues by stating that by circling Carcassonne on the train, "you are circling the history of France from the fall of the Roman Empire to the rise of the French monarchy; you are seeing the evolution of medieval construction, which had its roots in the colonization of the province by Rome in the first century B.C., when the Senate established Carcassonne (Carcaso) as an outpost to guard the trade route (the Via Aquitania) between Narbonne and Toulouse. Carcaso's site, located in a gap between the Montagne Noire to the north and the foothills of the Pyrenees to the south, was selected because of its impregnability. And it was made even more impregnable by massive walls built by the Romans over the next three hundred years." Though I typically shun a tourist train, I completely endorse Caro's enthusiasm for this one. Additionally, I also share her enthusiasm for the Hôtel de la Cité, which is within the walls of Carcassonne and is a member of the same hotel family (Orient Express group) as the Cipriani in Venice. The Hôtel de la Cité is one of few premier hotels in the Southwest, and even if you decide it is too much of a splurge, I encourage you to plan for a drink or a meal there—as well as a walk around its spectacular pool.

ALAN RIDING is the European culture correspondent of *The New York Times* based in Paris.

In a country so rich in châteaus, palaces, cathedrals, and monuments, it may be bordering on hyperbole to suggest that the fortified town of Carcassonne is the most breathtaking sight of all. Suffice it to say that, seen from afar, it offers the extraordinary spectacle of a medieval fortress that seems to have changed little over the centuries. Imposing, impregnable, and perfectly preserved, with massive stone ramparts, towers, and barbicans adding to its authority, the town dominates a large area from its hilltop position. No wonder the Black Prince took one look and abandoned his plan to attack it.

Today Carcassonne can be entered peacefully, although the illusion of being back in the Middle Ages quickly evaporates. La Cité, as the walled town is known here, is one of provincial France's most popular tourist spots, drawing over two million visitors a year. Most spend only a few hours here, which explains why the main street into the town is lined with shops selling postcards, plastic medieval armor, ice cream, and sandwiches. Most also come in the steaming-hot school vacation months of July and August. In May or September, without the heat or crowds, La Cité is a far gentler experience.

The one image that does not change is that of the great fortress on the hill. And that sight alone justifies any detour. Gustave Nadaud, a nineteenth-century French songwriter, wrote, "You should not die without seeing Carcassonne," and it was this panoramic view that he had in mind. Today we can add to that image the ramparts at night, bathed in light, floating magically on the horizon, beckoning like a dream castle in a fairy tale. Visitors who watch the spectacular Bastille Day fireworks display on July 14 each year may even be forgiven for thinking of Disney. But La Cité was here first, by about 1,700 years.

The first settlement on the hilltop in fact dates back to around the sixth century B.C., although it was not until much later that the Romans constructed defensive positions on the site, with the first circle of ramparts and barbicans built in the third century to deter the barbarians. By then, La Cité's location astride the broad valley that leads to the Mediterranean between the Massif Central and the Pyrenees had given it immense strategic importance. In the fifth century the fortress was captured by the Visigoths, who strengthened it further, holding it until it was overrun by the Franks in the eighth century. For four hundred years, it came under the suzerainty of the counts of Toulouse, 60 miles to the west. Then once again it changed hands and destiny.

In the twelfth century a dissident Christian religious movement known to its enemies as the Cathar heresy became influential in the region. Its attacks on the Catholic establishment for corruption and other forms of immorality enraged the Vatican, which eventually ordered a punitive crusade. The pontiff, Pope Innocent III, promised forgiveness of sins to all who joined the offensive, while the French king, Philippe II Auguste, hinted that captured land would be distributed to the crusaders. On July 22, 1209, the so-called Albigensian Crusade sacked nearby Béziers, killing thousands of its inhabitants. One week later, it laid siege to Carcassonne until the fortress's leader, Viscount Raymond-Roger Trencavel, surrendered on August 15, 1209.

A monastic account written in 1218 described what would prove to be a turning point in the history of La Cité: "The crusaders considered how best to take the town. If it were destroyed like Béziers, then all it contained would be lost. So they decided to allow all the inhabitants to go free provided they left the town naked. Thus all their booty could be preserved for the new viscount. So it was done. All the inhabitants left the town carrying nothing but their sins. The Count of Montfort then took over, to the glory of God, the honor of the Church and the ruin of the heresy."

In 1240 Trencavel's son tried to recapture La Cité, but by then a second, outer circle of ramparts had been built and the inner wall had been raised. It proved invincible, and the royal troops drove off the attackers. Soon after, two villages that had sprung up at the foot of the ramparts were razed and their population housed in a new town one mile away on the opposite bank of the Aude River. Known variously as Ville-Basse and Bastide-St.-Louis, it too was fortified, although it was often attacked and burned (by the English forces led by Edward, known as the Black Prince, among others). La Cité was never again conquered, its ruler safe inside his own castle, the Château Comtal, within the larger fortress. The town's military importance, however, gradually dwindled until, by the nineteenth century, its stones were being carried away to be used in other construction.

At this point La Cité could easily have suffered the fate of scores of Cathar castles that stand in ruins on hilltops around this area of Languedoc-Roussillon. Fortunately, the writer Prosper Mérimée, who was serving at the time as inspector general of historic monuments, came to the rescue, proposing its restoration. In 1844 the influential French architect Eugène Viollet-le-Duc arrived here to oversee the town's restoration. He did a remarkable job, although he did stir a controversy by adding touches of his own, such as conical-shaped roofs to barbicans that were previously open to the skies. In fact, even now some purists sniff that what we see today is a nineteenth-century creation. But they are too severe. La Cité may look more like a Loire Valley château than it did in medieval times, but Viollet-le-Duc deserves credit for the fact that it exists at all.

I recount all this history because, almost like the levels of an archaeological excavation, the different epochs of La Cité can still be seen today. For example, different-sized stones record work done on the ramparts in the third, thirteenth, and nineteenth centuries. Further, the thirteenth century has taken on new relevance here of late, with the region assuming the identity of *le pays Cathare,* as if that were the most important moment of its history. Certainly it is not difficult to find people here ready to argue that the Cathars were unjustly crushed, that they were innocent victims rather than devilish heretics.

This period in the town's long history and more form part of the guided tours of La Cité's towers and ramparts that leave regularly from the gates of the Château Comtal. The tours visit areas not otherwise open to the public and help bring alive the history of La Cité. A little "train" on rubber wheels and several horse-drawn carriages offer twenty-minute visits to the moats and ramparts.

The other monument not to be missed is the Church of St.-Nazaire. There was a church at the site as early as the sixth century, although the earliest remains—a splendid Romanesque nave—date from the twelfth century. With Carcassonne brought under the control of the French monarchy in the thirteenth century, the church was largely rebuilt to conform to prevailing Gothic fashions. The graceful narrow columns around the apse and transept make the church seem even taller than it is, while its magnificent north and south rose windows, dating from the thirteenth and fourteenth centuries respectively, cast beautiful light at dawn and sunset.

Wandering around the narrow streets of the overbuilt town offers a few surprises. A new Greek-style amphitheater behind St. Nazaire offers a busy program of classical and pop concerts in July each year, followed by a medieval show in August. Nearby, at 3 Rue du Plô, there is the Musée de l'École, a delightful little museum housed in an old primary school that shows how French classrooms looked seventy or eighty years ago, flip-up desktops and fountain pens included.

Vacationing children, on the other hand, are more likely to be drawn to the Cartoon Museum, on the Rue du Grand Puits, which shows how cartoons are made. The presence of familiar Disney characters seems doubly justified here: some say La Cité inspired the set of Walt Disney's 1959 movie *Sleeping Beauty*. Older children may prefer to cross the street to see the museum dedicated to the Cathar Castles and Instruments of Torture. It matters little that, except for the early thirteenth century, La Cité was untouched by the Inquisition or torture. Both are privately run museums aimed at the passing tourist.

Inevitably, outdoor cafés and restaurants take full advantage of the splendid setting, with the shaded Place Marcou a popular spot for a snack. Fortunately, there are also ample opportunities to taste the cuisine of this region, notably its famous cassoulet and foie gras. Les Coulisses du Théâtre and La Marquière are among the better restaurants, although serious gourmets should head to La Barbacane, the restaurant at the Hôtel de la Cité. The hotel, which occupies a former bishop's residence, is also the best within the fortress, its gardens offering a good view of the Ville-Basse and beyond.

Carcassonne's tourist office is eager to draw visitors to the "modern" city, but perhaps the only reason to go to Ville-Basse is to see the market that fills the Place Carnot on Tuesday, Thursday, and Saturday mornings. Fruits, vegetables, cheeses, meats, and a rich selection of pâtés and terrines serve to remind that, no matter how much they complain about their economic troubles, the French continue to master the *art de vivre*. Indeed, for a taste of farm life, there are a number of *fermes-auberges* in the area that offer lodging and excellent meals for reasonable prices.

Still, for me, the best reason for leaving La Cité is also the main reason for approaching it—to peer once again in amazement at its majestic profile, to wonder what medieval peasants and warriors alike thought when they saw it, and to know that, generations hence, it will still be there. In that sense, then, there is no hurry to see it. On the other hand, don't forget Gustave Nadaud's sound advice: "You should not die without seeing Carcassonne."

Getting There

Visitors can take a train from Paris or almost anywhere in France, connecting in Toulouse or Narbonne. Or you may take a plane from

Paris, either to Toulouse, where you can make connections with the train or rent a car, or direct from Paris to Carcassonne by TAT/Air Liberté.

Sightseeing

Château Comtal. One-hour tours in English leave at 11 A.M. and 1, 3, and 5 P.M., with tickets costing $5.35; $3.50 for those 12 to 26, free for those under 12. Tours of the ramparts by "train" or by carriage are about $5.

The **Church of St.-Nazaire** is open daily from 9 A.M. to 7 P.M. There are free organ concerts at 5 P.M. on Sunday through September 14.

Musée de L'École is open daily in summer from 10 A.M. to 6 P.M. Admission; free for children under 12.

Cartoon Museum and **Cathar Castles and Instruments of Torture,** rue du Grand Puits, are both open daily 10 A.M. to 8 P.M. through September; from 9 A.M. to 7 P.M. October through June. Admission.

For more information: Carcassonne has two **tourist offices,** one in Ville-Basse, at 15 Boulevard Camille-Pelletan, 33.4/68.10.24.30; fax 68.10.24.38; the other in La Cité, at Porte Narbonnaise, 33.4/68.10.24.36; fax 68.10.24.37.

Where to Stay

Hôtel de la Cité, 1 place St.-Nazaire, Cité de Carcassonne; 33.4/68.25.03.34; fax 68.71.50.15. Occupying a former bishop's palace, with splendid gardens leading up to the ramparts, this hotel likes to boast of the rich and famous who have stayed here over the decades. It offers respite from the crowds at the same time as being a few steps from the sights.

Domaine d'Auriac, route de St.-Hilaire, Carcassonne; 33.4/68.25.72.22; fax 68.47.35.54. This former wine *domaine* on the outskirts of Carcassonne has been converted into a first-rate hotel, with a swimming pool, tennis court, and ample shaded gardens. A perfect place to relax between sorties to La Cité, it looks onto an eighteen-hole golf course.

Hôtel Dame Carcas, 15 rue St.-Louis, Cité de Carcassonne; 33.4/68.71.37.37; fax 68.71.50.15.

Hotel le Donjon, 2 rue du Comte Roger, Cité de Carcassonne; 33.4/68.71.08.80; fax 33.4/68.25.06.60. Linked to Best Western and popular with Americans, this 37-room hotel is well situated for visiting La Cité. Many of its rooms have views over the ramparts or along moats.

Château de Cavanac, route de St.-Hilaire; Cavanac; 33.4/68.79.61.04; fax 33.4/68.79.79.67. This château about three miles from Carcassonne has just 15 rooms, all decorated differently and charmingly. For anyone visiting the region by car, this is an ideal jumping-off point for an outing to La Cité.

Hôtel des Ramparts, 3 place du Grand Puits, Cité de Carcassonne; 33.4/68.71.27.72; fax 33.4/68.72.73.26. A friendly little hotel in the heart of La Cité, it faces the ramparts of the Château Comtal.

Where to Eat

La Barbacane at the Hôtel de la Cité, 1 Place St.-Nazaire, Cité de Carcassone; 33.4/68.25.46.47. This somewhat formal restaurant with one Michelin star focuses extensively on duck and *foie gras de canard,* regional favorites. On weekdays, it offers a businessman's lunch for about $30; in the evenings, its three-course *menu de saison* costs about $47; its *menu dégustation,* about $70. A bottle of wine is $13 and up.

Domaine d'Auriac, route de St.-Hilaire; 33.4/68.25.72.22. Dinner on the hotel's terrace overlooking its gardens is a summer evening's delight. Its cuisine also has one Michelin star, with its *foie gras poilé* with mushrooms worth a return visit. Menus from about $32 to $65, with wine from $17.

La Marquière, 13 rue St.-Jean, Cité de Carcassonne; 33.4/68.71.52.00. This pleasant second-floor restaurant on a quiet street in La Cité offers fixed menus from about $16 to $47. It is also strong in local wines, among them those from the Corbières, Minervois, Fitou, and Cabardes areas; $11 to $25. To accompany foie gras, the sweet white wine from Muscat is a good substitute for Sauternes. Dinner for two without wine about $83.

Les Coulisses du Théâtre, 15 rue St.-Louis, Cité de Carcassonne; 33.4/68.47.63.39. This restaurant opposite the Hôtel de la Cité has the added attraction of a shaded garden for lunch or dinner. Like many restaurants in Carcassonne, along with the required cassoulet and foie gras, it offers a variety of lobster dishes. A meal for two with a bottle of local wine: about $50.

L'Écurie, 1 rue d'Alambert, Ville-Basse Carcassonne; 33.4/68.72.04.04. A friendly family restaurant in Ville-Basse, this is a good place to mix with local residents. It offers delicious regional dishes and good local wines. Menus from about $28 to $43; wine from $13.

Bar le Sénéchal, rue Viollet-le-Duc, Cité de Carcassonne; 33.4/68.72.33.42. This open-air café opposite the Château Comtal offers a variety of snacks; its *pâtés fraîches au foie gras de canard* should not be missed. Dinner for two with wine: about $20.

Bistro'Fruit, place Marcou, Cité de Carcassonne; 33.4/68.25.52.33. One of several outdoor cafés in the Place Marcou, with a *cassoulet bistrot*—for just $15—that was among the best I have tasted. A meal for two with wine: about $33.

Fields of Dreams

BY ALAN BROWN

～

It isn't often that a travel piece appears and I act immediately upon something the writer recommends; but when this article was published in *Travel + Leisure*, I was in the middle of planning a trip to the Corbières area of Languedoc-Roussillon and wasn't quite satisfied with the way it was shaping up. I read about and drooled over the inviting photographs of Domaine Grand Guilhem and fired off a fax *tout de suite*. It was a good thing I acted so quickly: only two rooms were still available, and if I had selected other dates later in May, the *gîte* was fully booked. I am unable to find any more words of praise in my thesaurus to describe how wonderful Grand Guilhem is and how utterly wonderful and restful is the Corbières. Gilles and Séverine Contrepois, the lovely *patrons* of Domaine Grand Guilhem, are remarkably kind and exceptionally knowledgeable about their corner of Languedoc-Roussillon—they will enthusiastically help visitors plan a thorough and memorable trip through the area, and they happily make lunch and dinner reservations. (For more details about Le Grand Guilhem, see *Good Things, Favorite Places*.) The other suggested inns, restaurants (one a Michelin two-star), and purveyors mentioned in this article are also highly recommended. If you have a solid background in Cathar history, you don't need much else but this piece to explore this uncrowded, always sunny, blissfully untouristy part of France.

ALAN BROWN writes frequently for *Travel + Leisure,* where this piece first appeared.

In the old days, when people went to the Corbières, they said they were going to the *garrigue*," my French friend Florent Morellet says, referring to the dusky green scrub that blankets the Corbières' rocky hills. "Because the *garrigue* is nothing, and the Corbières was nowhere." At this very moment we are heading "nowhere": west on the autoroute from Montpellier into a chunk of Southwestern France tucked between the Mediterranean and the Pyrenees. The gregarious Florent, who owns a popular New York restaurant of the same name, insists the Corbières is "the next Provence."

Back in the Middle Ages its rugged remoteness lured both heretical sects and monastic orders. In recent decades nonconformists and disenchanted urbanites have been drawn here by the region's almost narcotic beauty and its still-affordable land. And though the Corbières is an easy drive from airports in Montpellier, Toulouse, and Carcassonne (even Barcelona is only a few hours away), most guidebooks contain a scant page or two on the region.

Better known as a wine appellation than as a clearly defined region, the Corbières is a craggy square of southernmost Languedoc, bordered by the curve of the Aude River to the north and west. The small city of Narbonne at its northeast corner—technically outside the Corbières—serves as a gateway to the area; otherwise it is sparsely populated. In a week of crisscrossing the dramatic river valleys and jutting peaks, we hardly pass another car.

A quarter century ago Florent's brother Christophe and his wife-to-be, Dominique, bought a ramshackle old *bergerie*—sheepfold—here to live out their back-to-the-land fantasies. They had no electricity or plumbing, they bathed in a stream, and for income they raised goats and made cheese. "The first time I visited, they were so 'ecological' they wouldn't even let me use toothpaste," says Florent with a laugh. While we talk, we leave the autoroute at Narbonne and plunge into a pastoral landscape of vineyards and, yes, *garrigue*.

His ebullience barely dimmed by jet lag, Florent can't stop exclaiming over the fields of red poppies, the bright yellow *genêt,* or flowering broom, along the roadside, the cypress trees— "almost black in this light"—and everywhere vines green with spring promise. Grapes have always been grown here, but until the 1980s the Corbières produced only cheap bulk wines. Then the winemakers got serious. Today vines of grenache, syrah, carignan, and other varietals blanket the countryside, and the Corbières is gaining recognition for its robust reds ("better than Côtes du Rhône," Florent declares). It is now the Languedoc's largest appellation. Ambitious young vintners continue to arrive, raising the quality bar.

On the heels of the winemakers have come the restaurateurs and innkeepers, joined by Florent's brother and sister-in-law, who sold their goats and recently opened an inn just outside Lagrasse, the Corbières' prettiest town. Tourists have been trickling in to taste the region's wines and to explore its medieval abbeys and hilltop castles, but this is still largely uncharted territory. It seems something of a miracle to have a region of such charm nearly to ourselves.

It is dusk when we arrive at Christophe and Dominique's inn, La Fargo. In 1996 they bought a ruined centuries-old forge on a gentle slope in the Orbieu River Valley. Four years ago they opened a restaurant, and by 1999 the six guestrooms were ready. A sturdy sandstone structure, La Fargo sits surrounded by well-tended gardens. My high-ceilinged room adjoins a small orchard of fig, cherry, apple, and grapefruit trees; plump kumquats grow just outside the door. I throw open the windows, which frame a romantic view of the hills. The evening air is fragrant with rosemary and thyme, and the frogs are making a racket. Christophe and Dominique bought the inn's furnishings in Bali; my firm, comfortable teakwood bed is covered with a lovely *ikat* spread. The last thing I remember is Dominique calling from the hallway: "Breakfast at nine." Still in my travel clothes, I sink back and fall into a deep sleep.

When I wake, the sun is shining and a white apron flaps on a clothesline in the cool wind. I pluck a handful of cherries on my way to breakfast. Seagulls sail by, reminding me that we're close to the Mediterranean. Christophe, a tall man with a mop of graying hair and an open face, is mowing the border of a grove of young oak trees. A previous owner planted them a few years back with truffle spores on their roots. Turning off the mower, Christophe shows me how to spot the trees where the spores are growing: the ground near their trunks is almost free of vegetation. "But it will be years before we can harvest the truffles," he says.

Dominique, reserved and slender, with long dark hair, is setting a table on the terrace, putting out honey from their own hives. Bowls of her homemade jams—fig, lemon, apricot, strawberry— keep the napkins from blowing away. Christophe fetches toast and coffee, Florent appears with an armful of maps, and we all sit down to breakfast and to plan our day.

In New York, Florent described the Corbières to me as "a pioneer area." Most of the people we meet here have left more conventional lives and jobs behind and started anew. There is something of the romantic about them all, especially the winemaking couple down the road from La Fargo. "In the eight years we've been here, we've had one earthquake, one fire, two floods, and a bad frost," says Alain Quenehen with a laugh, his blue eyes sparkling in his tanned face. "When you're a winemaker, your wealth is outside, so anything can happen. You have to be Zen, be cool."

Alain is the essence of cool, as is his partner, Natacha Devillers.

The walls of the dining room in their château, which dates as far back as the ninth century, are covered with photographs of jazz legends and of themselves sitting in clubs, always cheek to cheek. Natacha herself designed the eccentric lampshades.

Twenty-two years ago in Paris Natacha dialed a wrong number and got Alain. They talked until four in the morning and then every day for a week. They've been together ever since. And for twenty-two years now, on the anniversary of that fateful misdial, Alain has proposed marriage. Natacha always turns him down. "If I marry him," she says, "he'll stop proposing."

In 1993 they gave up their city jobs and moved to the Corbières to open a winery. Two years later Château Prieuré Borde-Rouge produced 9,000 bottles. This year brought 90,000. The reds, which are luscious and lusty (no surprise, considering the makers), are made from carignan, grenache, and shiraz grapes.

"Come see our babies." Alain, who is disabled, zips out the door in his wheelchair. We follow. Close to the house, young shiraz vines are just peeking out of a field of dark soil. "Aren't they beautiful?" Natacha says proudly. "They're only three months old."

Alain and Natacha have two guestrooms, and I briefly toy with the idea of booking one in the fall and pitching in on the grape harvest. Who wouldn't want to be part of this household, even if only temporarily?

There may be a shortage of high culture and modern conveniences in the Corbières, but the people here more than make up for that lack. Whether in the markets or in their own shops, everyone seems to have time to talk, and our visits to vintners and cheesemakers all have the relaxed feel of dropping in on friendly neighbors.

When Florent and I drive over to visit Chantal Donnet, we find her elbow-deep in a stainless-steel vat of sheep's milk, stirring with bare hands. Pretty and trim, her blond hair tucked back into a net, she wipes off her hands to welcome us. (Beauty experts, take note: the skin is soft and smooth.)

Twenty-six years ago Chantal and her husband, Jean-Gabriel, left Montpellier to move down to this lush valley outside the village of Villetritouls. She studied cheese-making while he took a sheep-herding course. (Only in France!) Now they're the only makers of sheep's-milk cheese in the Corbières. "Contrary to what people think, sheep are temperamental, much more difficult than goats," Chantal says. Opening a door in the floor, she invites us into her cellar. "Our cheese is organic, but we don't call it that because my husband doesn't want to belong to the 'organic church,'" she says with a smile. The air is cool and moist, and the smell is heady. Rows of round cheeses sit aging on shelves. "See how the wooden shelves breathe," she says. "When it's humid, they absorb water from the air. When it's dry, they release it. It's magic."

Chantal is clearly a woman happy in her work. But clouds are gathering on the horizon. "The EU is making things difficult. They don't understand that unpasteurized cheese is actually safer. It's alive. It reacts, changing constantly," she says. "The day the EU tells me that I have to use plastic shelves instead of wood, I'll quit making cheese."

Before leaving, we enter her shop to sample her cheeses. "And you must try our yogurt; it's real, not like American yogurt," she says, dribbling a neighbor's honey on top. "Food for the gods." Florent and I taste it and sigh in unison.

Everywhere we go people offer us Corbières honey, extolling its virtues, calling it the best in France. It is even whispered that the honey one buys in Provence actually comes from the Corbières. And no one produces better honey, everyone agrees, than Geneviève and Henri Jean Poudou, elderly siblings who are, Florent tells me as we drive to their house outside Lagrasse, "like characters in a fairy tale, those people who live in a shoe."

Monsieur and Mademoiselle Miel, as they're called, do not in fact reside in a shoe. But for more than sixty years they have lived and made honey in the same cottage where they were born, which is hidden in a dark, overgrown hollow. A stream runs right under the house, turning the ancient water mill that provides them with electricity—all very Brothers Grimm.

"I started working with bees when I was six months old," says Geneviève, a stout, white-haired woman. Sitting us down, she feeds us samples of their ten kinds of honey. Each has a strong, seductive, sometimes smoky taste. The *garrigue* variety is like a viscous stew of herbal flavors. "Our honey is a living product, good for your health, not like America's pasteurized honey," she assures me, repeating a refrain that runs through all our encounters here. A dapper customer comes in and bows to Geneviève, addressing her as "Mademoiselle." She grins like a girl, showing off a mouthful of straight white teeth. "Dentures," Florent whispers, but I'm not so sure. Rumor has it that she and her brother live only on honey and milk. Rumor also has it that she was once engaged but jilted her fiancé because she couldn't bring herself to leave her hives.

"In France, you know, women were traditionally not allowed to work with bees," she tells us, as if she's read my mind and wants to set the record straight. "Bees were thought to be angels, and women were impure. Only in the Corbières, where women were considered descendants of the Virgin Mary, were we allowed." Her smile is beatific as she hands me a spoonful of rosemary honey. I smile back at Saint Geneviève. It's no wonder she didn't marry. What man could possibly compete with such a heavenly calling?

Wine, honey, and cheese are not the Corbières' only notable culinary offerings. The region offers simple but good fresh food. During our visit we have two extraordinary meals. The first is at La Fargo, whose elegant yet informal restaurant takes its cue from the surrounding landscape. In warm weather tables are put out under a vast arbor of kiwi vines, and Christophe cooks local lamb with rosemary on the wood grill. One evening he serves it with fava beans and sautéed onions and a dish of asparagus and prosciutto topped with shaved Parmesan. Dominique and Christophe's twenty-two-year-old son, Duncan, home for the summer from school in Montpellier, makes what must be the best (and richest) *gratiné* potatoes I've ever tasted. And for dessert Dominique bakes an orange cake that, on its own, would explain why the restaurant attracts customers from all over the Corbières and beyond.

While La Fargo exudes a comfortable rusticity in both its food and decor, L'Auberge du Vieux Puits, the ten-year-old restaurant in Fontjoncouse that was awarded a second Michelin star in 2001, goes in for more pomp and formality—but Corbières-style. The night we dine there the service is genuinely warm and friendly. Chef Gilles Goujon earned his toque in three-star restaurants in Cannes and Marseilles before coming to the Corbières. His cold fava bean soup and smoked trout—filled *galette* topped with sparkling salmon eggs and surrounded by a moat of frothy green grape juice are sublime. And both are included in the bargain prix fixe menu that the maître d' practically insists we choose over the pricey à la carte. The young wine steward not only picks superb local wines for us but brings me a wine map of the Corbières and marks it with his favorite vineyards. Later, when I ask which is the best, he opens a bottle and pours me a generous glass, on the house. Florent and I end up closing the place, and even then we leave reluctantly.

Most of the travelers who make it to the Corbières wander down here from the walled city of Carcassonne, just outside the Corbières' northwestern border. Once a stronghold of the Cathars, a heretical sect of the twelfth and thirteenth centuries, it has been restored into something of a medieval confection, but is jammed with souvenir shops and busloads of tourists.

Hunted down and persecuted by the Church, the Cathars took refuge in the Corbières' dramatic hilltop fortresses, known now as "Cathar castles" (erroneously, for they were built before the time of the Cathars). The region's roads are dotted with signs reading LE PAYS CATHARE, and there seem to be castle ruins around every bend. Those at Termes, Quéribus, and Peyrepertuse are three of the best known. Florent and I spend an afternoon hiking up to the last, which has spectacular views stretching from the Pyrenees to the Mediterranean. How anyone managed to build anything on these towering and perilous peaks is beyond me.

In fact, it may be the wedges of cold, forbidding rock that gave the Corbières its name—from *cor*, a pre-Celtic word for "stone," explains Jean-Pierre Mazard, a blue-eyed, genial vineyard owner with a wine-barrel chest, whom Florent and Christophe call Monsieur Corbières.

In the village of Talairan, where his family has lived for twelve generations, Jean-Pierre has done up Domaine Serres-Mazard's tasting room as an eccentric history museum. "He channels the Corbières," as Florent wryly puts it. When we enter, he actually picks up a waiting pointer and taps the snout of a mounted boar's head. "There are more wild boars in the Corbières than people," he begins.

The lecture is intriguing, as is his collection of memorabilia and photographs. But when he sits us down to watch his slide show on wild orchids, Florent invents a fib about a pressing appointment (hard to imagine in the Corbières) and suggests we move on to the wine tasting. "But behind the wines, there are people and nature," Monsieur Corbières protests. "It is important to know these things to really appreciate the wines." He moves on amicably and opens one of his reds. Holding a glass up to his nose, he inhales deeply. "Smell this one—it has the aroma of the *garrigue*."

Wine, not blood, apparently runs through his veins. Even on the subject of his beloved daughter, Marie-Pierre, he expresses himself with grapes. "A painter has his brushes; I painted a portrait of my daughter in wine," he says, handing us glasses of the honey-hued dessert wine he created in honor of her upcoming wedding. "Marie-Pierre often wears more than one perfume"—Florent winces here— "so I mixed six different grapes. Like her, the wine is warm and convivial and has character."

On the way back to La Fargo, the car trunk filled with bottles of wine, I cast an appraising eye on every roadside house. Though Americans have yet to discover the Corbières, the British and Dutch have started to snatch up old houses at bargain prices. Now I, too, am tempted. On our last day, when Dominique and Christophe invite us to their own house for a farewell lunch, I know the kind of house I'm looking for.

As Florent and I drive up the unpaved road, high jazz notes gurgle in the hot dry air. Duncan is playing the saxophone in his open-air bedroom. And I think that their house, the once-crumbling *bergerie* ("It had only one room with a roof, and we all slept there," Florent recalls), is like a jazz improvisation, with whimsical nooks and crannies spinning off a main theme. Though it's only a short drive from La Fargo, the rambling stone house and the isolated valley it overlooks seem a more primitive world, one of weird, Jurassic-sized succulents and gnarly trees, its air heavy with herbs. A windmill towering over the property (which, along with the solar panels on the roof, is the family's only power supply) creaks like a giant cicada.

Christophe and Dominique's twenty-six-year-old daughter, Rachel, an art restorer who lives in Tuscany, is setting a table in the garden. We sit down to a long, lazy lunch, with a huge salad, cheeses and meats, cherries from their trees, and endless glasses of chilled Corbières rosé. Languidly we discuss the different meanings of words in French and English. For dessert, Dominique has baked a chocolate cake, and Jérôme, a friend from Paris, has brought an *oreillette,* a Corbières specialty: an airy crêpe deep-fried in sunflower oil and sprinkled with sugar.

I move to a hammock under the trees. Florent, a dedicated sun worshiper, takes off his shirt and stretches out on a stone wall. Duncan asks his sister to give him a haircut, which, we all agree, he desperately needs. He drags a chair into the sun and ties a towel around his neck, and she starts snipping away.

I close my eyes and drift off. When I open them, I'm alone. I hear distant splashing and laughter. Following a narrow goat path down the hill, I come to a place where the stream tumbles over rocks into a wide swimming hole. Jérôme sits in the shade, smoking and reading. Rachel is building a miniature raft, lashing twigs together with grass. Constructing a sail of rosemary branches, she launches the craft over the waterfall, only to have it catch in some rocks. She hikes her summer dress up to her sun-browned thighs, wades in, and huffs and puffs at the rosemary sail until the raft breaks free and is carried away by the current. I lie back on a flat, sunwarmed rock and nap again. And I dream of the *garrigue.*

The Facts: The Corbières

The weather in the Corbières is Mediterranean, similar to that of Provence. Summers are hot and dry. The tourist season doesn't start until late May; most inns and restaurants are closed for the winter (typically November through April).

Flying into Toulouse (two hours away by car) or Montpellier

(one and a half hours) is the most convenient route to the Corbières; Barcelona (three hours) and Carcassonne (thirty minutes) are also options.

Hotels

La Fargo, *St.-Pierre-des-Champs; 33.4/68.43.12.78; fax .68.43.29.20; www.chez.com/lafargo; doubles from $48; dinner for two $40.* Christophe and Dominique Morellet's old Catalan forge, south of Lagrasse, has six rooms with Balinese furnishings, an orchard, and a popular, elegant restaurant with a terrace.

Domaine Grand Guilhem, *Chemin du Col de la Serre, Cascastel; 33.4/68.45.86.67; fax .68.45.29.58; www.thelin.net/gguilhem; doubles from $57.* Four charming rooms in a nineteenth-century château (plus a cottage). The musician-owners, both former Parisians, hold regular music and wine nights.

Lou Castelet, *33 place de la République, Fabrezan; 33.4/68.43.56.98; lou.castelet.free.fr; doubles from $61.* A beautiful château with gardens on the edge of a lovely village northeast of Lagrasse. Rooms are spacious and elegantly furnished.

Domaine du Haut Gléon, *Villesèque-des-Corbières; 33.4/68.48.85.95; fax .68.48.46.20; www.hautgleon.com; doubles from $59.* A sprawling winery near Fontjoncouse whose former shepherds' and grape harvesters' quarters have been turned into chic guest rooms and vacation houses.

Restaurants

L'Auberge du Vieux Puits, *Fontjoncouse; 33.4/68.44.07.37; dinner for two $90.* Chef Gilles Goujon's restaurant, possibly the finest in the Corbières, earned two Michelin stars last year, but he hasn't let it go to his head. The service is warm, the food sublime.

La Bergerie de Fontfroide, *Fontfroide; 33.4/68.41.86.06; lunch for two $26.* A lovely courtyard bistro with outdoor tables, on the grounds of the Abbaye de Fontfroide, near Narbonne. Fresh, local ingredients are highlighted. Lunch only.

Purveyors

Most wineries and other producers of regional specialties welcome visitors but do not have regular hours, so call ahead. Wine maps are available in English from the Syndicat de l'AOC Corbières (Maison des Terroirs en Corbières, Boutenac; 33.4/68.27.73.00; www.aoc-corbieres.com).

Château Prieuré Borde-Rouge, *Lagrasse; 33.4/68.43.12.55; www.borderouge.com.* Alain Quenehen and Natacha Devillers coax luscious reds and whites out of the Corbières *terroir.*

Fromage de Brebis, Fermiers des Corbières, *13 avenue de la Matte, Villetritouls; 33.4/68.24.04.95.* Chantal Donnet's *fromagerie* has a shop where you can buy her cheese and yogurt.

Moulin de Boysède, *Lagrasse; 33.4/68.43.10.10.* Geneviève and Henri Jean Poudou welcome visitors and shoppers to their honey-cultivating operation. Call ahead.

Domaine Serres-Mazard, *Talairan; 33.4/68.44.02.22; mazard. jean-pierre@wanadoo.fr.* Jean-Pierre Mazard pours oak-aged red, rosé, and white wines in his tasting room–*cum*–history museum near Lagrasse.

Château Les Palais, *St.-Laurent-de-la-Cabrerisse; 33.4/68.44.01.63; chateau.les.palais@wanadoo.fr.* Seven generations of the de Volontat family have been making wine in this twelfth-century former convent attached to the abbey at Lagrasse. (The tasting room has served as both a chapel and a stable.)

Bordering on Genius

By Clive Irving

∽

Almost a hundred summers ago, Henri Matisse found in the little fishing village of Collioure a brilliance of sunlight and color that changed his art. In this piece, the writer explores not only Collioure but the Pyrenees that lie just beyond, and he finds Matisse's inspiration and much more.

In the February 2002 issue of *Condé Nast Traveler,* writer Ron Hall contributed a piece entitled "In the Shoes of the Fisherman," in which he identified seven perfect Mediterranean fishing villages, each of which still retained "charm in abundance, a pretty waterfront, an active fishing fleet, a lively fish market and good seafood restaurants, and, of course, it should not be too messed up by tourism." One of the seven villages he profiled was Collioure, which also gets my vote for one of the most perfect villages I've ever had the pleasure to visit.

CLIVE IRVING is a contributing editor of *Condé Nast Traveler,* where this piece first appeared in the November 1997 issue. His work has also appeared in the *Provence* edition of *The Collected Traveler.*

How close can you get to understanding an act of artistic revelation by seeing the place that ignited it? Often, it seems a dubious exercise. Art transfigures so much that the original material is apt to seem banal against what imagination has done with it. Mont Ste-Victoire, for example, was and is an unexceptional chunk of Provençal limestone unless you see it through Cézanne's obsessed eye. Collioure, however, is a different story. You can't look down on this small medieval harbor without instantly connecting with the color storm it generated in Henri Matisse's mind in the summer of 1905.

The harbor, on the Mediterranean just short of the Spanish border, is a crucible of light. In June, the sun is caught in and focused by a bowl of terra-cotta, the roofs of the old town. In 1905, when Matisse came here and painted his way out of all earlier inhibitions and into the style of the Fauves, the "wild beasts," it was this hue of flammable terra-cotta that electrified his work. "No doubt," he told a friend, "you will be surprised to see a beach of this color, in fact the sand was yellow. I realized that I had painted it in red and the next day I tried with yellow. This was impossible by that stage and that is the reason why I returned to red" (*La plage rouge,* 1905). Well, that's okay then. Even the terraced hill above the harbor turned to red and bled into the roofs (*Les toits de Collioure,* 1905–6). Today that same terrace, planted with vines, is still stubbornly green, though fringed with mimosa in June.

As Matisse struggled at the margins of color and light over a series of summers, he worked his way southwest from St-Tropez, where he first sketched the idea for what became, painted in Paris, *Luxe, calme, et volupté,* to Collioure, which was—and is—a very different place, as great a concentration of the unFrench as you'll find in France. Collioure is Catalan, but that's only the beginning of it. This is also the ancient kingdom of Roussillon, as well as falling within the region of the eastern Pyrenees, which has a distinct mentality of its own. All of this makes the citizens of Collioure assertively independent of Paris. Just how much so was made clear to me in 1974, when I happened to be eating down by the harbor. In the middle of my lunch, the streets suddenly erupted in a joyous riot. What had happened? *"Le president est mort!"* they cried, and, indeed, President Georges Pompidou was hardly cold before the whole of Collioure was *en fête,* so much did they despise him and everything that rule from Paris stood for.

That was my second visit to Collioure. The first, in 1961, had been memorable for a different reason. The modest harborside hotel where I stayed had a staircase hung with original Picassos. Such insouciance. It's unimaginable now that even the most forti- fied hotel in the world could risk hanging an original of any worth anywhere. But this is now and that was then in Collioure, an artists' town where playing the muse had made it blasé about genius: Derain (co-Fauve of Matisse's), Braque, Picasso, Foujita, to name but a few who passed through.

It's not, however, the wildest of Matisse's Collioure paintings that stays in my mind. It's a simple study of an open window (*Porte fenêtre à Collioure,* 1914). Deceptively simple, in the way that the Great Pyramid is simple. This painting's vertical fields of jet and shades of green seem to foreshadow the way Rothko arranged his blocks of color. But the really arresting quality of the Matisse— something I apprehended only by being there—is the way it conveys temperature through light. In the intense shade of the shuttered window is a reclusive force, light shrinking from light.

"My aim is to convey my emotion," Matisse said—the words of a man whose innovations tended to drain him. Something about Collioure in that first summer had hot-wired him. With a few brushstrokes, he put an unbridgeable distance between himself and the "uncertain shimmer" of Impressionism. By 1914, with the half- shuttered window, he was more constrained but more intense, too.

Photographs of Collioure at the turn of the century show a beach stacked with fishing boats, Catalan barks with a triangular, Arab-style sail centrally hinged to a single mast, their hulls striped in vivid primary colors. The scale of the port has changed very lit- tle since then. The narrow four- and five-story buildings have the kind of inner geography that has mutated in a characteristic French way over the generations, from teeming tenement, to pension, to apartment (the Matisse family was photographed in 1911 in what looks to be a congenially crowded ménage, probably part of a whole floor), to *hôtel du commerce,* to rental apartments, and now, more and more, to fancy ateliers for which the ever-resilient shell has been gutted, replumbed, and made to smell sweeter. I hate to say it, but one of the things lost to my sentimental nose is that old taint of walls lacquered with the ineffable sediment of kitchen, cognac, and less wholesome emissions.

I had trouble locating the place where the Picassos once hung. The essential clue, decisive in the end, was that the staircase had risers that were tiled in the Portuguese style. In 1961 the restaurant and bar had been a bit *faux-bohème,* but then so was I. Guys hung out there who looked like they lived as I wanted to live, painting badly and eating well. There was a large, convivial table where you could drown in a terrine of *soupe de poisson* and carafes of local *rouge* were passed around.

At the time, my wife was *enceinte,* but she entered into the communal spirit with gusto, since she had two to feed. Alas, it did not end well. The feast proved to be emetic. She had suddenly to flee up the staircase toward the rather basic toilet, but didn't make it. The Picassos were witness to her agony, but *le patron* was unfazed, and we'd always looked on that night as a fragment of youthful abandon.

This experience had left my wife with an indelible memory of the tiled risers, and after several false starts we did find the staircase, central to a hotel called Les Templiers. The bar, if not the Picassos, was still there and was now hung with passable local works. It wasn't the place that had changed in any saddening way; it was just *les temps,* and, of course, us.

This beautiful littoral, squeezed from the west by the Pyrenees into a subtropical haven with marine air and light somehow infused with a backdraft of mountain fragrance, is called the Côte Vermeille (Matisse's pigment). Maps dictate that it begins in the north at Argelès-Plage and runs south for about fifteen miles to Cerbère, just short of the border of Spanish Catalonia. It is not, however, as cohesive as this might suggest. A long sweep of fairly flat coastal plain extends southwest in a crescent and includes Argelès-Plage. This part of the coast is heavily developed. Resorts favoring blanched and receding tiers of concrete grip the beaches, and behind them is camping country, now replete with RV parks. Then, abruptly, the foothills of the Pyrenees intervene. From way out on the coastal plain you can spot one of Collioure's watchtowers on a salient, but the town is well hidden almost until you reach it. The assiduous road builders of France have created a seamless new highway that diverts traffic around Collioure. The once-coagulated streets are as quiet again as they were in 1961.

It's all too easy to be so seduced by the languorous ways of the town that you forget about the mountains behind it. But there came a time when I felt I had to break free of this pleasant torpor and head up into the eastern Pyrenees, something I had never done with any dedication. As soon as you reach the foothills, you're immediately conscious of Le Canigou. To the Catalans this particular mountain seems to exercise a mantric pull. Le Canigou's saw-edged spine runs more or less laterally, west to east, forming a natural barrier between France and Spain. It is said that on a clear day, from the top of Le Canigou, you can see as far as Barcelona to the south and Marseilles to the north (which, if true, is as near to Marseilles as I, for one, would want to be). The Spanish Catalans call the mountain Canigó and, since they see its southern slopes, feel its better nature. On the French side, I found it lugubrious in aspect. That could have been because, as I followed the valley of the Têt River west, Le Canigou was snowcapped, and the snow conspired with a northwest wind to produce La Tramontane, a cold, dry gale that whipped through the valley, lashing at the vineyards on the eastern hills.

All the way from the Mediterranean to the Atlantic, there are thermal springs in the rupturing geology of the Pyrenees, where mountain meets valley. Old spa towns are dotted in the rumpled skirts of Le Canigou on both the north and south sides. The spas were state subsidized and used to have the air of a fading *petite bourgeoisie* whose addled livers were in need of regular purging. That is changing, now that the wellness fad has hit France. I stayed at Molitg-les-Bains, which is built around a narrow gorge above the town of Prades. Twelve sulphur springs gush water with temperatures between seventy-seven and one hundred degrees. According to my 1914 Baedeker, they were much celebrated "for the treatment of mucous and skin diseases and rheumatism."

Le Grand Hôtel Thermal occupies several terraces above the springs. Inside, it has the carbolic, no-nonsense approach of a correctional center for the out-of-shape. This was altogether too rigorous for me. Instead, I opted for the Château de Riell, a luxury retreat with a Michelin star for its restaurant, sitting high above the spa in its own park. A nutty architect built it originally for a doctor as a pastiche castle over what were once, it is alleged, medieval dungeons (now an annex of the restaurant for those who get a kick out of feasting in macabre surroundings).

La Tramontane made dining outside impossible, although the gardens were lush with roses, palms, Alpine edelweiss in the last stages of bloom, and, growing wild, cactus and the vivid, short-lived purple mullein. The appearance of palm and pine together shows how the gardeners try to get the Mediterranean to cohabit with a more astringent climate, but the park at the château was on the margins of the milder air. Barely a mile above the spa, the small village of Molitg, centered on a twelfth-century church with a campanile, was more austere than any on the coast. Beyond it, the tree line thinned to high moorland and bald gray limestone.

When I left Molitg-les-Bains to drive deeper into the French Pyrenees, this hardening of the land increased.

Louis XIV's geographers fixed the height of Le Canigou's summit, correctly, at 9,135 feet and assumed, incorrectly, that it was the highest of the Pyrenees. The first paved road to penetrate the eastern Pyrenees, the route I now followed, was decreed by Napoleon in 1808 and completed in 1866. It was a formidable achievement, involving several difficult ascents and one pass, at Souterrain, that to this day requires hairpins layered like the folds of the intestine. The engineers who then found themselves on a high plateau had been preceded by Sébastien Le Prestre de Vauban, engineer-general to Louis XIV, no respecter of subtle landscaping, who left his mark with the daunting and hideous hulk of the Mont-Louis fortress, which had been built to face the border and two peaks greater than Le Canigou: Puigmal d'Err (9,545 feet) and Puigmal de Sègre (9,325 feet).

Napoleon had military reasons for the road. The French had always favored drawing the border between France and Spain, as far as possible, along the summit line that begins with Le Canigou. The historical weight of this border is more profound than its physical shape—it was "the first boundary which the French national consciousness, at its awakening, clearly perceived," said the French geographer Roger Dion. Conversely, the Spanish kings were reliant on it to keep at bay the plague of the French Revolution.

But when the border had to bisect accessible plains and valleys, it was obviously a lot more porous. Napoleon's road was built to reach a strategically sensitive canton, the Cerdagne to the French and Cerdanya to the Spanish. It happened that once I crested the summit of Napoleon's road, now Route Nationale 116, the doleful influence of Le Canigou receded, the clouds lifted, and on the vast plateau of the Cerdagne, framed in broad alpine pastures and horizons of white peaks, it felt as zestful as Switzerland in summer.

One of Europe's wackiest pieces of map-making has always riled the politics of the Cerdagne. A tiny Spanish enclave, centered on the town of Llivia, had been marooned inside France after a treaty of 1660. The Spanish agreed to cede thirty-three villages to France, but the people of Llivia protested that they were a town, not a village. Their fate was to become this detached and defiant outpost, complicated by the unbordered allegiances of Catalonia, where regional culture frequently took precedence over nationality.

Looking for Llivia, I discovered that the French, to this day, will not help. The only road leading to it was perversely signposted only to a nearby French town. After I figured this out, the badly cambered and pitted French road suddenly became an impeccable two-lane blacktop at exactly the point where there was once a border post. This was an omen, swiftly enlarged by the appearance of Llivia itself. The town was encircled by new chalet-style apartment blocks. Spanish Cerdanya was more than a different way of spelling the name: alongside the French Cerdagne, it looked like a neighbor who had suddenly come into money.

I knew that, as in much of rural France, depopulation was emptying Roussillon. The old French peasant culture had virtually disappeared from the Cerdagne. In one village that had twenty-nine functioning estates in 1955, one remained in 1985. This plays through in ways that deplete the culture. For example, Saillagouse, the last French town I saw before Llivia, used to be renowned as the regional center for charcuterie. Typically, this supported small, specialized farming. I found only one decent charcuterie in Saillagouse, and one brasserie with an authentic regional menu. People were buying baguettes from the *supermarché*.

The true nature of the Spanish boom was evident as soon as I reached the heart of Cerdanya. In 1985 the Cadi massif, as impervious a barrier as Le Canigou, was breached by a new road tunnel. Barcelona is now an easy two-hour drive. In winter this has wrought a sea change: the slopes of the Spanish Pyrenees have become one of Europe's fastest-growing ski areas. All along the valleys the chalets rise with gray-slated roofs and orange pine shingle, emblem of Spanish Catalonia's affluent age.

On the southern flank of Le Canigou, the prosperity, so lacking on the French side, was seeping into what had once been a remote, Romanesque town—Camprodon. Real estate flyers were everywhere, with garish renderings of mountainside apartments aimed at the weekenders from Barcelona. But so far, the new money hasn't tainted the old center of Camprodon. It clusters at the confluence of two rivers, the Ter and the Ritort, at about three thousand feet. Camprodon has known a boom before. In the nineteenth century, with the coming of a railroad spur, it became a fashionable retreat from the heat of the Barcelona summer. Catalan versions of Newport or Southampton "cottages" were built on the edge of town, with large, landscaped gardens and paddocks around a grand central boulevard planted with plane trees.

Later this century, the railroad was closed as Spain became comatose under Franco. Now, with new and faster roads, the old estates are again alive with the play of fat cats. The old town, of medieval scale, is being spruced up, and its main shopping street, the Cal València, has chic leather boutiques alongside the *xarcutería* selling local hams, sausages, cheeses, and Catalan pastries encrusted with pine nuts—an abundance that is in stark contrast with the scene in Saillagouse, on the other side of the mountain.

Camprodon's gift for street life is expressed in four small, shaded squares, each with its own character: one dominated by a classic *modernista* hotel, one used for the weekly market, one for café life, and the fourth adjacent to two churches, one of which, the Església del Monestir de Sant Pere, is an exquisitely plain tenth-century Romanesque classic. You can get a fix on the town's relationship with the two rivers by climbing to the apex of a sixteenth-century humpback bridge with a lookout tower, the Pont Nou, spanning the Ter just short of where the Ritort joins it. The upper Ter Valley, curving sinuously west, leads to a ski resort, Vallter 2000. Last year there was skiing until the end of May.

So far, Camprodon has seemed able to absorb change without being vulgarized, trying to contain the needed renovation within its traditional fabric. It may be one of the oldest conceits of travel that remoteness is good, that the loss of remoteness, like the loss of innocence, is sad and—maybe—even sinful. However, like the people of Camprodon, most of those who live in remote places always seem to me to become a lot more sociable when the warm light of the outer world finally beams in.

Be that as it may, Spanish Catalonia demonstrates something else: the transcendence of regions over states. Like northern Italy, where the Lombard League has asserted a decisive influence on national politics, Spanish Catalonia has a political and economic dynamic of its own that it has used to win cultural independence. In Camprodon it was a mistake to use the Spanish *Buenos días*. Nobody was hostile, but they responded quite differently to the Catalan *Bon dia*. Catalan is now the official language.

Typical of this lightly worn but firm attitude of cultural identity was Gerard Gimenez, a young ranger at the Aigüestortes National Park, the deepest point I reached in the Pyrenees and by far the most spellbinding. I met Gerard in the park's eastern gateway, the small town of Espot. We went off in a deconstructing four-wheel-drive by way of a loping track of rock shards, trying to make the snow line. At seven thousand feet we ran out of road. A jeep, abandoned, blocked the way—at precisely the point where the first sorbet-textured snow encircled a shallow lake.

Gerard knew the jeep. It belonged to another ranger, who lived a further thousand feet up, in a park shelter with his wife and young family. Through a telescope, he indicated the shelter, in a way which suggested he envied that kind of arrangement.

I dipped a hand into the lake, and for a few seconds the icy water coated my palm like an ephemeral, lubricious spinning of silk. The lake was one of a series that filtered the last of the snow runoff, a natural drainage system descending in stages until, lower down, the water was checked by a dam. Between each of the lakes, the water ran through tight granite gullies, creaming white at the edges but fast and clear in the current. Way above us were the three distinctive, spiky peaks, compressed together like a sculpture group, whose profile has become the decal of the Aigüestortes park.

The park is a rare protected enclave in the Pyrenees, the only one in Spanish Catalonia. It was established in 1955, after the construction of hydroelectric plants badly scarred the forests of pine and fir. It provides a habitat for rare herds of Pyrenean chamois (through Gerard's telescope, I glimpsed a stag foraging on a high ridge), as well as scores of other species of animals, birds, and flora. The creation of the park under Franco seems remarkably green for a Fascist. I was ready to give him that one, until Gerard took me for a walk on a broad road that had been cut through forest to a dam. He explained that it was built with a great deal of sweat for a one-way drive by Franco, who was opening the dam. The *caudillo* then left by the public road, having made a point about power by insisting on arriving from the opposite direction.

Gerard spoke Catalan and workable English. He made the polite and pragmatic concession that Catalonia was "a nation but not a state." In March of 1996, when the Socialists lost power in Spain after thirteen years, the sixteen seats in the Madrid parliament held by Catalans became pivotal to the viability of the new Conservative government, and Jordi Pujol, the Catalan leader, has made the most of it, securing for his people increasing regional autonomy. Gerard echoes Pujol, whose rallying cry is "We are a distinct nation with our own language, culture, and traditions."

Gerard didn't seem happy with my theory about the end of remoteness. He's from Barcelona, the dynamo driving the boom. (Catalonia generates forty percent of Spain's industrial exports.) But he had come up here into the deepest Pyrenees to live in a small, remote village of fourteen people and had noticed the irony of the fact that when Barcelonan money colonized villages as weekend retreats, it was the newcomers who wanted to then close the gate on further development, not the villagers, who had suddenly catapulted from rural poverty to a modern way of life. Gerard is a biologist, and he has an ascetic bent, suited to these elemental satisfactions. He lives contentedly with a dog as companion, and he worries about the fragility of human ecosystems as well as natural ones. He told me about a Pyrenees enclave, Aranes, of no more than three hundred people, where they still speak their own unique Romanesque language. As new roads are blasted through tunnels under the Pyrenees, cultures such as this, preserved by remoteness, will wither.

Later that day, driving through a mountain pass with the mimosa extending for thousands of feet on either side and the afternoon air becoming torrid, the scent was as unctuous as a glass of Sauternes. I pulled off the road at an overlook. Thunderheads were brewing. The spectrum of temperature and color was astonishing to an eye unused to mountains—from pasturelands with rich new grass down in the river basins up to the dissolving snow line. The heat pushed to ten thousand feet and vaporized the snow, and the vapor mutated into the nimbus, shot through at its base with the tint of a falling sun.

This could never be mistaken for an alpine light. There was too much heat, edging into the brilliance of the Mediterranean. The mimosa, cascading through the valleys all the way down to the coast, made a single, connecting color between the highland domains and the sea. Before the sea, though, the coastal plain. It opened up beyond the cherry orchards of Céret, a town of tiled loggias with a bullring, and then I went across the plain on a long, narrow road that was shaded by gnarled plane trees all along its southern edge, through St-Génis-des-Fontaines and St-André, the air thickened with heat. In Collioure that evening, I sat on a terrace and saw the sun fade into a storm line over the mountains, leaving a long, broody Mediterranean twilight. Then, in the dusk, a lone, plangent saxophone played across the water from somewhere in the old town, "We'll meet again . . ." I really hope so.

High on the Pyrenees

Collioure's excellent information center, behind the Plage Boramar, has a map that locates key scenes of the nineteenth-century Fauve storm. It includes, to give just one lovely example, a church razed by Vauban, the remorseless fortress builder, which was replaced by the seventeenth-century church of Nôtre-Dame-des-Anges. The site incorporates a lighthouse as belltower and is at the end of the Plage Boramar. I found it closed for renovation, but when open, it must be seen for its five Baroque altarpieces by the Catalan master Joseph Sunyer.

Perhaps the best way to explore the eastern Pyrenees is to use any or all of the following five places, all within a few hours of the border, as your base.

Collioure

The best-sited hotel is the **Relais des Trois Mas/La Balette,** developed from three Catalan farmhouses on the southern slopes, with views of the harbor from every room. The restaurant can be chaotic. Our photographer, Brooks Walker, was photographing a plate of anchovies when it was snatched from under his lens by the waiter and served to another table, even though it was his dinner as well as a prop. The restaurant's location redeems it: its terrace leads directly to a small, gravelly topless beach, La Balette (33.4/68.82.05.07, fax .38.08; doubles, $80–$150).

Molitg-les-Bains

Of several hotels clustered around and above the thermal spa here, the nineteen-room **Château de Riell** is the most luxurious (the others have a rather medicinal flavor). All rooms have mountain views, and there is a finely landscaped park and a Michelin one-star restaurant. Open April through October (33.4/68.05.04.40, fax .37; doubles, $160–$220).

Bolvir

Well placed for skiing and alpine cool in summer, Bolvir is a harbinger of the Catalan leisure boom, and Spanish hospitality gets no more stylish (or expensive) than at the 11-room **Torre del Remei,** once an aristocratic country estate. A little like a Bavarian *schloss* on the outside, it is avant-garde Barcelona on the inside. Rear suites are best, especially No. 2. At about 3,600 feet, the estate is part of the high meadows of Cerdanya; cowbells are the only jangling you'll hear (34/72.14.01.82, fax .04.49; doubles, $160–$195).

La Seu d'Urgell

This is a good base for reaching the Aigüestortes park, two hours away from the 38-room **El Castell,** where the Tàpies family serves

Catalan cuisine at its finest. Lower rooms are best. The hotel stands above the town, which is congested but has a fine medieval heart (34/73.35.07.04, fax .15.74; doubles, $100–$160).

Camprodon

Now a winter sports center, it has several well-waxed but aging hotels. The better choice is the simple, comfortable **Edelweiss** on the edge of town, but the restaurant cannot match the town's bodegas for atmosphere and authentic *xarcutería* (34/72.74.06.14, fax -05; doubles, $65–$85).

The Ecstatic Anchovy and Other Sensations

There are anchovies, and then there are Collioure anchovies. Things are done with this fish in Collioure that elevate it from mere pizza topping to art. Specialized ateliers in Collioure fillet, cure, and marinate the fresh fish with a variety of secret recipes, often packing them in salt. You can sample them at the counters of two curers, Roque and Desclaux, adjacent to each other on the rue des Treilles, at the northern end of town—but not for long. Alas, the new carbolic regime of the EU has decreed the end of the cottage industry within Collioure, where women filleted and stacked the fish between leaves of brown paper. They will soon move to a plant out of town. Will the flavor survive?

The finest anchovies I tasted in Collioure were at a backstreet restaurant called **Nouvelle Vague**. The marinade was sharp, the fish succulent. But the best dish here, and the best of my trip, was a *rillettes de lapin* with fig confit (33.4/68.82.23.88; entrées, $10–$15). Collioure's other signature dish is the *crème catalane*, a *brûlée* dessert made of lemon, vanilla, and fennel-seed custard. Particularly excellent were those at **Nouvelle Vague** and **La Frégate**, in the harbor (33.4/68.82.06.05; entrées, $19–$32).

At the hotel **Torre del Remei**'s restaurant, what appeared to be a vegetable terrine was actually a reworking of a classic Catalan appetizer, *escalibada*—aubergines, peppers, and onions layered and served with a subtle mustard sauce. Also notable here was the Scandinavian salmon marinated for a day and a half in mountain herbs, sugar, and salt (34/72.14.01.82; entrées, $12–$20).

El Castell serves strong local flavors: cassoulet with Catalan sausage, pig's trotters in jelly. The flawless restaurant has an outstanding cellar, particularly strong in vintage reds from the Ribera del Duero—notably the prized Vega Sicilia at a fair price. Beyond mundane needs is an 1890 Rioja (34/73.35.07.04; entrées, $15–$30).

Languedoc: Is There Life After Provence?

BY CHRISTOPHER PETKANAS

༄

Here is a collection of five singular places to stay in northern Languedoc, just across the Rhône from its more high-profile neighbor. As this piece appeared not all that long ago, in 2000, I have kept the prices the author provided as they were. I do not believe they will have changed drastically, but you should not only confirm the rates but inquire as to the number of rooms, meals offered, and seasonal closings.

CHRISTOPHER PETKANAS is a contributing editor for *Travel + Leisure*, where this piece first appeared. He is the author of *At Home in France: Eating and Entertaining with the French* (see *Good Things, Favorite Places* for a thorough description) and is someone who stays in *a lot* of hotels, inns, and guesthouses.

After driving more than two hours, it did not seem likely that Garrigues—a village that looked as if it had been evacuated—was going to produce the *raffiné* inn that a friend of a friend had promised, using words like *oasis, haven,* and *you've never seen anything like it.*

Le Mas Parasol finally revealed itself on the other side of a scarred plank door, which was set in a towering stone arch and painted, a long time ago, an unbeatable olive green. Everywhere my glance settled—on box shrubs clipped into topiary globes, on patinated vintage park chairs—assured me Le Mas Parasol had not been oversold. It was built in 1793 as a farmhouse in a style typical of agricultural dwellings in and around the not-too-distant Cévennes Mountains. A two-story structure in luminous beige limestone, the inn has an exterior staircase leading to a loggia that wraps around three sides. Looking at the surrounding plain from here is like watching a fire: you can't take your eyes off it.

Six guestrooms, some with exposed stone walls and arched ceilings, face a central courtyard. Decorative elements run to stenciled friezes, tailored upholstered headboards, the odd antique Provençal rush-bottomed armchair, richly worn surfaces, salvaged doors, and quantities of Designers Guild's signature color-zapped textiles from London. Parked outside in the garden is Parasol's newest accommodation: a self-sufficient, smartly rehabilitated Gypsy caravan with its own salon.

Several nights a week owner Geoffroy Vieljeux dons an apron to tempt his charges with lamb shoulder confit, potatoes prepared in the manner of a *tarte Tatin,* and turnovers filled with salt cod. Vieljeux's deep knowledge of the Languedoc's finest restaurants ensures that, the rest of the time, no one goes hungry.

Rue Damon, Garrigues; 33.4/66.81.90.47; fax .66.81.93.30; doubles from $70.

Domaine des Clos

There were as many *Tintin* coloring books littering the communal breakfast table as copies of *Côte Sud*. Two-fisted coffee bowls were filled and emptied, filled and emptied. Children gave their complete attention to dissolving Poulain powdered chocolate in milk—the national breakfast of the precaffeinated. The assembled four young families gave off a confident, all's-right-with-the-world air of preppiness. And they all seemed to know one another. They did—but they'd met only seventy-two hours before. Each had come to Domaine des Clos, a sprawling eighteenth-century farmhouse on a wild windswept plain 82 miles southwest of Avignon, to say goodbye to summer. Having checked in as strangers, they checked out as friends, numbers exchanged, rendezvous promised.

It was just this affectionate atmosphere that Sandrine and David Ausset dared to hope might result from their warm-hearted renovation of the Domaine. Five sunny, color-washed guestrooms and four apartments are winsomely and intelligently appointed with brass and iron beds, muslin hangings, vintage marble-topped dressing tables, and terrazzo floors. The crunchy, snowy coverlets are sewn by the *maîtresse de maison* herself, and light fixtures are cleverly designed using old agricultural implements, including sconces fashioned from rusty hoe blades. Sparkling white bathrooms are edged in Tunisian tiles painted with a charming pinwheel motif.

Though the guestrooms share one well-equipped kitchen, don't worry about pileups—the laid-back people drawn to the Domaine are no more interested in traffic jams than you are. While breakfast is prepared by Sandrine, who makes her own luscious fruit-packed *confitures,* the kitchen is heaven for travelers who tire of eating in restaurants day after day—even when the restaurants are great.

Who hasn't dreamed of making *pistou* with basil they buy themselves at a southern French market?

One morning I skipped across the Rhône to Tarascon and the Musée Souleiado Charles Demery, the Provençal folk museum run by the Souleiado fabric family. Lunch in Arles at the Grand Hôtel Nord-Pinus was an excuse to revisit the hotel's rakish vest-pocket bar, where a mounted bull's head hangs above a vitrine displaying a sequined matador's jacket. In the afternoon I stopped for a beer in trendier-than-thou St.-Rémy-de-Provence and spied a Monaco princess. But thoughts of the following morning at the Domaine occupied me more than my brush with royalty: would I make a friend at breakfast?

Route de Bellegarde, Beaucaire; 33.4/66.01.14.61; fax .66.01.00.47; doubles from $46.

Château de Ribaute

Just as I lifted my finger to press the intercom, two high-pitched toy poodles struggled through the bars in the iron gate, beating me out to announce my arrival at Château de Ribaute. Striding vigorously across the gravel courtyard behind them was Countess Françoise Chamski-Mandojors, the most unlikely owner I have met in eighteen years of guesthouse-going in France. A brisk, commanding woman of a certain age, she wore slim cropped trousers; below them peeked out the racehorse ankles that many French aristocrats manage to take with them to the grave. Her discreet gold jewelry caught the sun, and even at fifteen meters I could tell she was wearing Guerlain.

Located 22 miles northwest of Nîmes, Ribaute was built in the thirteenth century on the foundations of a Benedictine priory and adapted in the eighteenth century for a life that had more to do with the pursuit of pleasure and beauty than protection. Many French guesthouses claim to deliver the subtle niceties of staying in a private house, but few succeed with the ease, grace, and abundance of Ribaute—the centerpiece of a pleasant agricultural village without a single shop. The walled garden in which the pool is set attains that rare ideal—looked-after but not *too* looked-after. Lounging under the century-old Judas trees, firs, maples, and horse chestnuts is as cooling as an iced vervain infusion. Snuggle down with a volume from Count Ladislas's tower library on nineteenth-century domestic life in the Languedoc, and you may never get up. Unless it's to idle in your room. While there is no shortage of fanciful Louis-Philippe armchairs or sleigh beds, striped glazed percales and Patrick Frey *toiles* cancel any threat of fustiness.

Meals are skillfully cooked by the Chamski-Mandojorses' daughter, Julie, a thirty-year-old hotel school graduate whose dedication to keeping the château afloat must be encoded in her DNA. Duck terrine studded with hazelnuts and vegetable *tagines* are served in an abidingly grand dining room hung with Compagnie des Indes porcelain and a portrait of a relation who lost his head, literally, in the Revolution. In summer the scene shifts to the courtyard, whose arcades seem to exhale cool air.

Place du Château, Ribaute-les-Tavernes; 33.4/66.83.01.66; fax .66.83.86.93; doubles from $76.

Le Vieux Castillon, Castillon-du-Gard

Fifteen miles northeast of Nîmes in the hill town of Castillon-du-Gard is a hotel whose discreet, unhotel-like facade could easily be mistaken for a village house. The three interconnected buildings in honey-colored stone (the oldest dating from the twelfth century) exhibit a kind of cubist chaos. Le Vieux Castillon's proud, embattled beauty is much like that of the Languedoc itself.

Nothing prepares guests for the charms within. Discovering how the hotel's various wings join up is an enchanting surprise. One link is a grassy courtyard planted with olive trees, cypresses, and oleander. Another is a hyphen of a footbridge that vaults over a cobblestoned pedestrian passageway, where locals can be observed on their way to buy *Le Figaro*. With such low-key amusements, it's easy to imagine spending a week at Le Vieux Castillon without so much as a shadow of ennui darkening the pages of your vacation paperback.

The languorous rhythm of my own stay at the hotel suggested itself almost immediately after I set down my bags. A third of my time was claimed by poolside naps overlooking the grapevine-carpeted Vallée de St.-Hilaire. Another third was reserved for deconstructing chef Gilles Dauteuil's Mediterranean cooking, which cleverly manages to be both earthy and sophisticated (if rather pricey). And one-third was spent wandering through Castillon-du-Gard, population 816.

Despite being cradled in the bosom of the Midi, Le Vieux Castillon isn't the kind of hotel that lets its hair down; the thirty-three guestrooms and two suites have a slightly impersonal quality, with interior shutters, candlestick lamps, and cheerful buffalo-check fabrics. While service is generally acceptable, the personnel at reception could learn from their colleagues in the restaurant. The young maître d's and waitstaff are the best that France has to offer.

Who goes to Le Vieux Castillon? Across from me at lunch one day sat a distinguished couple in their seventies, the man in a jacket, tie, and immaculately polished shoes, his wife sporting a superbly pinned chignon. A dangerously tanned woman of a certain age in a coquettish sundress teetered by in Perspex sandals with heels like needles; she smooched a skeletal chihuahua. At the pool a few well-behaved children amused themselves quietly.

And everyone but me was French.

Castillon-du-Gard; 33.4/66.37.61.61; fax 33.4/66.37.28.17; doubles from $150.

In a canyon on the leafy edge of the Tarn, the fifteenth-century Château de la Caze was built for romance, even if its three towers, moat, and crenellations suggest a more defensive purpose. In 1488 a local demoiselle with a generous dowry was inspired by her new husband's good looks and gallantry to build a castle that would serve as "a setting and refuge for their love." Four years later the couple took possession of their imposing nest and found it bewitching. I was alone at La Caze, but I can still attest to its sexy vibe.

La Caze is a magnet for travelers seeking to live out their Renaissance fantasies. Horses once clopped through what is now the main hall, moodily lit by lanterns suspended above a Gothic pew. The floor is a checkerboard of beige, black, and brown paving stones polished to a high gloss. Twelve guestrooms and seven suites are filled with handsome Louis XIII furniture: beds with rope-turned posts and fleur-de-lis-patterned headboards, settees covered in magnificently faded needlepoint. "Soubeyrane" has a tower bathroom and the finest view of the Tarn; "Melchior" and "Nuptial" have their own terraces. La Caze also offers six shipshape apartments in a modern annex—ideal for families—with striking views of the château and the cliffs beyond. The wrought-iron beds, tables, and armchairs were made by a craftsman in nearby Lunel. No corners were cut: doors are of solid oak, and there are towel dryers in the crisp, fresh bathrooms.

Meals at La Caze are served by a friendly and capable young staff. Breakfast brings the celebrated honey of the Méjean Causse, made by bees that feed on thyme, white clover, and borage. At dinner the signature dish is trout with smoked *lardons* and Puy lentils, an interesting idea that, like much on the menu, needs refining and sharpening. Other dishes reflect the region's wealth of wild mushrooms: *cèpes,* chanterelles, *mousserons,* morels.

Kayaking and canoeing are practically at La Caze's doorstep. A day trip from the château took me to Générargues and the Bambouseraie, a forty-two-acre park where 150 species of bamboo are cultivated. I returned to the inn with tacky back-scratchers but also a load of terrific baskets and trays. At night, the canyon air was so pure that I slept with the leaded windows open. Waking at dawn, I saw a wild boar nuzzling the banks of the Tarn.

Route des Gorges du Tarn, La Malène, Ste.-Enimie; 33.4/66.48.51.01; fax 33.4/66.48.55.75; doubles from $110.

Bibliography

Instructions for Visitors: Life and Love in a French Town, Helen Stevenson, Washington Square Press, 2000. I was drawn to this book because it is one of the few novels or memoirs set in Languedoc-Roussillon. Happily, that's not the only reason to recommend it: it's a wonderfully written book for travelers, as well as a heartfelt story of the author's love affair with Luc, famous for stating, *"Le village, c'est moi."* I was quickly caught up in Stevenson's story by page nine, where she writes about seeing the Pyrenees after the long train ride down from Paris. "Snow caps the summit from October to May, catching a few minutes of peachy light every morning. The sun sets behind it in the evening. An insurance company tried to buy the mountain once, because they'd heard that Virgil had said it was the most beautiful mountain in the world, but no one could work out who to buy it from. So the insurance company bought a mountain in the Alps instead. That's the difference between the Pyrenees and the Alps: you can buy the Alps. Don't miss the recorded voice saying, 'Perpignan, ici Perpignan.' It rolls and chimes; there are bells and the white flutter of an agitated sea in her diction. She is waking you with a caress and a catch in her throat. It is a voice that makes you feel hopeful for small things. Welcome to Perpignan. Welcome to Catalunia." I continued on, of course, and found myself laughing out loud at a few places and actually crying at another. More even than a personal story, this is an excellent snapshot of a small village in a fairly remote part of France.

Montaillou: The Promised Land of Error, Emmanuel Le Roy Ladurie, Vintage, 1979; originally published in France under the title *Montaillou, village occitan de 1294 a 1324,* by Editions Gallimard, 1975; published in the United States by George Braziller, 1978. *Montaillou* is, as you'll find, always included in recommended reading lists—justifiably, as it is not like any other book on the subject of Catharism. Ladurie presents an engrossing, incredibly detailed view of the hilltop village of Montaillou, in the Pyrenees very close to the Spanish border. Montaillou is rather legendary in the history of Catharism in France, as it was the last village to actively support the Cathar heresy. By 1229 nearly every trace of Catharism had been brutally wiped out across southern France (mostly in Languedoc, which until 1271 did not entirely belong to the kingdom of France). But the Albigensian heresy still showed signs of life as late as 1318. According to Ladurie, "The Inquisition of Fournier and his colleagues, based in Carcasonne (Languedoc) and chiefly in Pamiers (Ariège), finally succeeded in flushing out this last pocket of resistance, by means of a detailed inquiry followed by some burnings at the stake, many sentences of imprisonment and still more penalties in the form of yellow crosses. (Just as medieval Jews wore the yellow star, so condemned heretics were forced to wear on their backs big crosses made of yellow material sewn to their outer garments.) Catharism never recovered from this final blow in 1320. The prisoners of Montaillou were the last of the last Cathars. But it was not an absolute end. For the brave fight put up by the peasants of Ariège to preserve the remains of their heterodox beliefs after 1300 foreshadowed the great Protestant revolt two centuries later." By way of explanation, Ladurie notes in his introduction that "though there are extensive historical studies concerning peasant communities there is very little material available that can be considered the direct testimony of peasants themselves. It is for this reason that the Inquisition Register of Jacques Fournier, bishop of Pamiers in Ariège in the Comté de Foix (now southern France) from 1318 to 1325, is of such exceptional interest. As a zealous churchman—he was later to become Pope at Avignon under the name Benedict XII— he supervised a rigorous Inquisition in his diocese and, what is more important, saw to it that the depositions made to the Inquisition courts were meticulously recorded. In the process of revealing their position on official Catholicism, the peasants examined by Fournier's Inquisition, many from the village of Montaillou, have given an extraordinarily detailed and vivid picture of their everyday life." Thus we learn of the ecology and environment of Montaillou, the life of shepherds in the Pyrenees, the body language and sex of the inhabitants, the libido of the promiment Clergue family, marriage, childhood, death, cultural exchanges, concepts of time and space, morality, wealth and labour, and magic and the other world. Ladurie uses italics throughout the text to set apart the actual recorded transcripts of the villagers, and one begins—or I did, anyway—to know some of them quite well. He ends this impressive study by noting, "Today Catharism is no more than a dead star, whose cold but fascinating light reaches us now after an eclipse of more than half a millennium. But Montaillou itself is much more than a courageous but fleeting deviation. It is the factual history of ordinary people. It is Pierre and Beatrice and their love; it is Pierre Maury and his flock; it is the breath of life restored through a repressive Latin register that is a monument of Occitan literature." *The Perfect Heresy* (below) is a broader and more accessible history of Catharism in southern France, but I highly recommend *Montaillou*—and I highlight it as *de rigueur*—to those readers who crave more or are especially interested in medieval French history.

The Perfect Heresy: The Revolutionary Life and Death of the Medieval Cathars, Stephen O'Shea, Walker & Co., 2000. I was torn about where to feature this book, since I feel it is significant enough to appear under the heading of French history; but I decided to include it here so it would stand out a bit more than in the crowded *The Kiosk—Points of View* bibliography. I will go out on a limb and state that if—*quel horreur*—someone told me I could bring only one book with me, this would be the one I would pick, and not with that much difficulty (after, of course, I found a way to smuggle Freda White's *Three Rivers of France* into my suitcase). This is one of those books you stay up late at night reading with a flashlight, or I did anyway. (I *really* need to get one of those mini reading lamps.) Emmanuel Le Roy Ladurie commented on O'Shea's book that it is "the work of a connoisseur of Languedoc, is written for a wide readership, and draws on his personal experience of France's southern region." It is also incredibly unputdownable and may make you sweat, shiver, or cry because it is an utterly sad reminder of the religious intolerance that haunts us today as well as a reminder that no matter how difficult life is in the twenty-first century, things really were much worse in the Middle Ages. As O'Shea notes, "Popular culture, drawing on the Gothic imagination of the nineteenth century, has exploited that notion; in Quentin Tarantino's *Pulp Fiction,* to take a well-known example, an enraged mobster hisses at an enemy, 'I'm gonna get *medieval* on yo' ass!' Just the word makes us wince." I believe the history of the Albigensian Crusade is a blot on French history even greater than the Vichy France years during World War II. Without giving away too much, O'Shea relates the nightmarish destruction of Béziers, where scholarly consensus estimates there were fifteen to twenty thousand victims: "Everyone in the town, from graybeard Cathar Perfect to newborn Catholic baby, was put to death in the space of a morning. In the days before gunpowder, to kill that many people in so short a time required a savage single-mindedness that beggars the imagination. To the crusaders bitter about the lost booty of affluent Béziers, there was consolation to be had in knowing that they had done God's work so efficiently. Personal salvation had been ensured by this stunning victory. In his letter to Innocent, Arnold marveled at their success: 'Nearly twenty thousand of the citizens were put to the sword, regardless of age and sex,' he wrote. 'The workings of divine vengeance have been wondrous.' A threshold had been crossed in the ordering of men's minds." It is this battle at Béziers about which the most famous line in Cathar history is said to have been uttered. "Professional opinion is divided on whether Arnold Amaury actually said, in the vernacular, 'Caedite eos. Novit enim Dominus qui sunt eius' (Kill them all. God will know his own). That lapidary phrase was most likely the invention of a pro-crusade chronicler writing thirty years after the fact. What is certain is that there is no record of anyone, certainly not Arnold Amaury, head of the Cistercian order and the loftiest representative of the vicar of Christ, trying to halt or even hinder the butchery that was about to begin. Not even Count Raymond, who is thought not to have taken part in the sack of the city, is mentioned by the chroniclers as attempting to discourage the crusader bloodlust." I will be honest here: the story doesn't get better; there is no Hollywood ending. One begs for it somehow not to be true, yet it tragically is. *De rigueur.*

The Yellow Cross: The Story of the Last Cathars' Rebellion Against the Inquisition, 1290–1329, René Weis, Alfred A. Knopf, 2001, hardcover; Vintage, 2002, paperback. Again, as with the other books on the subject of the Cathars, I have featured this excellent title here as the lands of Occitan Catharism stretched from Genoa in Italy in a swath across Languedoc-Roussillon to Valencia in Spain. The word "Cathar," Weis tells us, probably derives from the Greek *katharós,* which means "pure" or "purified," and the Cathar theology may have been influenced by Eastern metaphysics. This is the most recent work to be published of those recommended here, and it's impressive. The hardcover edition includes an insert of color photographs, some that Weis took himself of various mountain passes, trails, and sites that fascinate because of their seeming simplicity and ordinariness. Weis has created a work as detailed as *Montaillou,* though it does not focus on a single village or fortress, rather on the Cathar "twilight," as he refers to it, between the years 1290 and 1329. Weis states that "the intention of this book is to discover what really happened on the ground during the d'Ablis and Fournier Inquisitions, and to that extent researching the story turned into a kind of detective work. It did not seem to be enough, for example, to state that the whole of the village of Montaillou was arrested on a given day in the late summer or early autumn of 1308. I wanted to find out why it had happened at that particular time, whether there was a significant connection between this and an earlier raid on the village in May that year, and how the Inquisitorial posse managed to take the village unawares. As always, wherever Montaillou is concerned, it was crucial to understand the role that the most powerful family in the village played in this series of events. They sat, spiderlike, at the centre of the resistance network against the Church during the years from 1290 to 1320, and they were fabulously wealthy. That they played a decisive part in the recrudescence of Catharism has long been known, but quite how their power operated through its links with the Inquisition has never been fully appreciated. Nor has it been adequately explained how they eventually fell from grace, when they had so successfully weathered the initial storms of the Inquisition which destroyed the Cathar ringleaders." The name of this family is, as noted previously, Clergue, and seven centuries later they remain pre-eminent in the present-day skeletal village of Montaillou. One of the Clergues is apparently actively promoting the village's Cathar heritage; but Weis notes that the battle to revive the standing of Montaillou "may already be lost. To date there is no café here to welcome visitors, and the indigenous population is shrinking at an alarming rate. Indeed, the entire Ariège is being depleted of its people, notwithstanding the regional power's efforts to staunch the haemorrhage from the villages. There are no teenagers in Montaillou, and the only children are those who spend time here during the summer in the *colonie de vacances* which occupies the corner where once the outer medieval track intersected with the track running from the square of thirteenth-century Montaillou." Precise as Weis endeavored to be in this book, he was flexible enough to recognize that "as Jack London and George Orwell had done when trying to join the lives of the poor and dispossessed in London, one can never truly be there as long as the chance of getting out remains entirely a matter of choice. Just as it was only ever possible to be tramp-in-disguise rather than the real thing during a few weeks of well-intentioned research, so it was impossible now to experience the harshness of life in the medieval Cathar Languedoc. And not only did the Cathars struggle with the elements in a way that I never did or could, but this entire drama was played out against the background of a savagely repressive regime that thought burning people was not necessarily wrong. Jacques Fournier reputedly wept grievously (*multum plangebat*) for having to burn the Valdensian Raymond de la Côte whom he knew to be a good man; but burn him he did." *De rigueur* for those who have read *The Perfect Heresy* and want to continue reading a related work in greater detail.

West of the Rhone: Languedoc, Roussillon, the Massif Central, Freda White, Faber and Faber, London, 1964. Another essential Freda White volume.

Flavors and Tables
of the Southwest

*"Clearly, there is no question of turning back the clock, but experience shows that elements of the less intensive, more environmentally friendly way of family farming practised in this part of France for centuries are worth saving. Without these smallholders, we will be left with an empty landscape—*un paysage sans paysans*—without grain-fed, free-range chickens, hand-made* cabécou *cheeses, sourdough bread, and vegetables that are worth eating, and without the rural culture that produces them. The Dordogne has largely escaped industrialization: it still has small farms, artisan food producers and genuine* produits du terroir.*"*

—Vicky Jones, *Dordogne Gastronomique*

"The cuisine of Languedoc has been described as having developed from two influences—the cooking of Rome, which would be natural for this old member of the Roman Empire—and the cooking of the Arabs, who for nearly eight hundred years held substantial portions of Spain, just beyond the Pyrenees, and left traces of their presence in all phases of Spanish culture."

—Waverly Root, *The Food of France*

Savoring Foie Gras at the Source

BY JASON GOODWIN

∾

A book about Southwestern France without mention of foie gras and cassoulet, the subject of the following two pieces, would be incomplete indeed. Some readers will say, if asked, that they don't care for foie gras; I have friends and colleagues who scrunch up their noses at it. I admit it has been only in the last ten years or so that I discovered that I not only like foie gras but *love* it; I, too, used to scrunch up my nose at this rich delicacy. The truth is, I had never tried it, which makes me suspect that at least half of my friends and colleagues haven't either. Mitchell Davis, author of *The Mensch Chef* (Clarkson Potter, 2002), introduced a recipe for "Whole-Roasted Foie Gras with Apple and Caramelized Onion" with the observation that "one of the most interesting things I learned while working on my last cookbook, *Foie Gras: A Passion,* is that much of the European—and especially French—tradition of raising geese, fattening them, and cooking with the fat and the fattened liver comes from Ashkenazi culture. Jewish women in medieval Europe would raise and fatten geese as sources of income. The rendered fat, *gense schmaltz* in Yiddish, would be used to cook just about everything, sweet and savory, almost as a substitute for lard. And the prized liver would be reserved for special occasions, such as the Passover seder. I take great pleasure in knowing that the historical antecedent of modern-day chopped liver was actually foie gras." So I say, if you've never tasted it, give foie gras a try (and definitely if you are a guest in someone's home and it is offered to you).

JASON GOODWIN writes frequently for *The New York Times,* where this piece first appeared, and is also the author of *A Time for Tea: Travels Through China and India in Search of Tea* (Alfred A. Knopf, 1991); *On Foot to the Golden Horn* (Henry Holt, 1995); and *Lords of the Horizon: A History of the Ottoman Empire* (Henry Holt, 1999).

Officially, foie gras has no particular home. The Jews may have brought the secret of its production from Egypt in biblical times; for a long time they produced foie gras in Alsace. Norman farmers make foie gras. From eastern Hungary, too, from the Puszta, a giant prairie mown by geese, foie gras is sent to France for blending with the local product. All you need, after all, is a goose. And a funnel. And the disingenuous belief, perhaps, that the goose won't mind being gorged so fast that the grain must be massaged down its throat.

Nonetheless, foie gras is regional. It is something that is made in parts of Europe; in one part of France it is what they make, period.

As you travel south through France, you cross an invisible border that isn't quite the Loire, because the Loire is too far north; and not the Dordogne; on the Dordogne you are already in foie gras country. Foie gras appears as the steep slate roofs and kiln-dried bricks of northern France disappear; as you meet clay tiles—steeply raked, at first, then gradually stretching out like bathers on a sunny day—you will have crossed into a land of stone walls, clay-tiled roofs, and windows that have dwindled to keep out summer heat and winter cold.

And the farther you drive into the Southwest, the less you see of that celebrated French symbol, *le coq,* and the more you see of another bird, *l'oie* (pronounced rather like the French word *roi*), the goose. You see geese lumbering live in fields and honking at barn doors; you see them hanging, plucked, by the neck in *boucherie* windows. Against the flashy, arrogantly strutting cockerel, the Southwest sets the goose, slow, ponderous, and generous.

The foie gras heartlands are roughly defined by the Dordogne city of Périgueux in the north and the Pyrenean foothills on the Spanish border; Toulouse to the east, Auch to the west. FOIE GRAS VENDU ICI—the message flashes by on a painted board nailed to a roadside tree. VENTE DIRECTE, says another, without further explanation beyond that familiar painted shape, or outline cut in tin. Sooner or later you ought to stop and follow the profile of the goose into the farmyard, or to one of the factory shops set up along the road, where you find cans of the precious fatted liver. Foie gras is a notorious luxury that goes with champagne and caviar, bears' paws and white truffles, and you may find it anywhere, at any time of year. Liver is eminently perishable; for years foie gras has been canned (see listing) and sent around the world.

Some people say that foie gras should be eaten six months after canning, a little aged; indeed, the producers used to keep cans back for a few months before they sold them. But advances in packaging have made it possible to have foie gras fresh almost anywhere in the world—and nothing is better than that.

There's a nutritional theory, an elaboration of "you are what you eat," which holds that if you eat too much foie gras—if you wolf down a whole can, however small, on your own—you may feel a little like the unhappy goose itself. Foie gras is sociable: it needs to be shared. The wealthy have taken to foie gras because, in a life in which they can have too much of everything, foie gras sets a limit. The amount one person can eat is so restricted that it could be called the jewel of foodstuffs, precious and small.

At the same time a whole foie gras, fresh, is immense, and perhaps that is one reason why the poor man likes it. A good fatted goose liver weighs a couple of pounds; an ordinary goose liver just a few ounces.

As winter sets in, fresh foie gras starts to appear in the markets; it is traditional winter eating for country people. Mirande, southwest of Auch, in Gascony, holds perhaps the most famous foie gras fair in late winter, but any market town in the region will boast foie gras stalls. The livers lie on the bench, yellowy-gray, firm as cold butter, taking the smallest imprint from your finger when you press (as French housewives do). A little fat seeps out, beading around your fingerprint. This is the best kind, and you can't fail to be impressed by its football size (or appalled by what you pay for a shaving in a smart restaurant). A decently fat kind of foie, a solid two-pounder, will cost around $35 at market. And ten of you will later stagger from the festive board, dreaming no doubt of brisk walks in the open air, of sleep, of French irregular verbs; of anything but food.

But first the liver must be cooked.

I know many French home cooks who feel anxious about the business, but the *vendeuse* at the market in Mirepoix assured me that nothing could be easier. She spoke the rubbery, plangent French of the south, sounding all the word endings that we learned not to pronounce in school. So I listened very carefully to her recipe; I even made her repeat it, because this was not the moment to feign polite comprehension.

First I must scrape away the gall, that small green stain that appears on the liver's surface, awkwardly half-hidden between the lobes. Rinse the liver in cold water, pat dry, and stand overnight in a pan (never aluminum) beneath a generous sprinkling of salt—not a coating, nor a pinch. Sea salt, of course. The following morning rinse off the salt and bring the liver to the boil in a pan of cold water. Gently simmer for half an hour. *Et voilà!*

I did it, trembling, just as she said. Only I got into a tangle over the time, and we had it hot for supper, after all.

It was like—well, it was a different animal, that goose liver. It had the same pinkish coloring as the canned foie gras, the same grainless self-possession of a fat cheese. It was hot, but the real difference was that I had cooked it. Foie gras had been stripped of its starched collar; no longer a morsel to tempt a jaded millionaire, an affair of linen and silver to be enjoyed anywhere in the world, it had become a wintry feast for greedy Southwesterners, a gutsy, fork-in-fist treat. Six very greedy people had it with fresh white bread grilled as toast, and salad. We started with the Sauternes, thick, sweet, and chilled; but we finished the bottle only for form's sake. That fashionable accompaniment for foie gras, so excellent in restaurants, now seemed dubious and off-key. We turned eagerly to the full-blown local red instead.

Foie Gras is perhaps the essence of Southwestern cooking. The region is the goose's fief. In northern France butter is the cooking medium—delicate, a trifle cool. In the South, in the real Midi, in Provence, where forage is reduced by dry earth and stone, they use oil from sunflowers or olives grown on tough, tinder-dry trees (and scrubby pungent herbs for flavor). But in the Southwest fat's the thing: lard, goose, and duck fat.

The corollary should be a coronary, but according to a World Health Organization study, fewer *toulousains* die from heart disease than the average Frenchman (let alone American). Chemically, goose fat is more like oil than butter. But the idea that foie gras may actually do you good—suggested in a paper presented in 1991 by a French researcher, Dr. Serge Renaud, to a convention of duck and goose producers—remains unproved. A gourmand friend in Paris reacted to my temerity in cooking a foie gras with amusement that barely cloaked his disapproval. He pointed out that there was foie gras that melted in the mouth and foie gras that regrettably melted in the cooking, dwindling to a shadow of its former self. It is almost impossible to tell between the two in the raw, and the risk ought to be left to a professional. I'd offended him: it irritated him to think of celestial foie gras being treated in a homely way by an amateur. Piqued myself, I bought another foie gras in the market, rinsed, salted, rinsed, and blanched it—and baked it in a hollow pumpkin with a handful of chopped shallots: sublime liver and onions. It was rather good.

Guide to a French Delicacy

Varieties

Foie gras is made either with goose liver or with duck liver. Goose liver is more expensive, because breeding and feeding take more care, and the taste is delicate and unctuous. Duck liver has a stronger flavor. Foie gras comes traditionally from the Southwest of France (Périgord, Landes, Lot, and Béarn) and the Alsace region; the Vendée is beginning to produce it. The most prized comes from Gers, Landes, and Béarn.

There are many different ways to prepare foie gras. *Foie gras cru* (raw) has to be cooked within a week or two. It can be found in most foie gras shops in Paris but is essentially for home cooks or chefs. It should not be confused with *foie gras frais* (fresh, meaning half-cooked, or *mi-cuit*).

Since it is lightly cooked but neither sterilized nor pasteurized, *foie gras frais* is thought to have the purest taste and is the current favorite in France. It is also the most expensive. It keeps for two to three weeks. U.S. Customs prohibits the importation of fresh foie gras; according to French sources, some American aficionados try to avoid confiscation by having it wrapped as a present.

The other types are *semi-conserve* and *en conserve*. *Foie gras semi-conserve,* or partly preserved, is cooked and pasteurized but not sterilized and can keep in the refrigerator for up to six months. *Foie gras en conserve,* canned, is the most long-lasting, cooked at temperatures high enough to sterilize it. Some consider glass jars better for the taste than metal for canned versions.

Official Names

Another source of confusion is the official appellations, as opposed to the methods of cooking. *Foie gras entier* means the product is 100 percent liver and an entire lobe, or part of it. The term *foie gras* alone signifies 100 percent liver, from large pieces of lobe pressed together. *Bloc de foie gras,* sold either in *semi-conserve* or *en conserve,* canned, is reconstituted from pieces and purée.

Serious producers of foie gras scorn *mousse de foie gras,* or *pâté de foie gras,* often mixed with chicken or ham. Marcel Montigny, head of the gourmet counter at Fauchon in Paris, says that canned foie gras is the best choice for travelers, even though he feels canning foie gras is "almost a crime against gastronomy."

The label should state where the product comes from, and that it contains 100 percent *foie gras d'oie* (goose liver).

Shops in Paris

There are many places in Paris to shop for foie gras; here are a few, giving prices for *foie gras d'oie* only.

Fauchon, 26 place de la Madeleine, 1st arrondissement. Hours: 9:40 A.M. to 7 P.M. Monday through Saturday (closed Sunday); 33.1/7.42.60.11; Métro, Madeleine. Prices: *foie gras d'oie frais entier* from Périgord, $230 for a kilo. (All prices have been converted on the basis of 5.3 francs to the dollar. A kilo is equal to 2.2 pounds.) *Foie gras d'oie entier truffé* (with 3 percent truffles) from Périgord, $121 for 410 grams or 14.35 ounces; *bloc de foie d'oie* from Alsace, $103.70 for 11.5 ounces. Fauchon charges about $18.80 to ship a kilo (2.2 pounds) to the United States by air mail or $83 to ship overnight.

Labeyrie, 6 rue Montmartre, 1st arrondissement; 33.1/45.08.95.26. Hours: 8 A.M. to 6 P.M. closed Sunday and Monday; Métro, Les Halles; *foie gras frais,* or *mi-cuit,* $94.30 for 2.2 pounds; *foie d'oie mi-cuit des Landes,* $132 for 2.2 pounds; *bloc de foie gras d'oie en conserve,* $51.30 for 1.1 pounds.

Foie Gras Luxe, 26 rue Montmartre, 1st arrondissement. Hours: 6 A.M. to 6 P.M. except Sunday and Monday; 33.1/42.33.28.15.; Metro, Les Halles; *foie gras d'oie entier des Landes,* $94.30 for 2.2 pounds.

Carrefour (supermarket), 1-3 avenue du Général Sarrail, 16th arrondissement; 33.1/46.51.46.11; Metro, Porte d'Auteuil; open daily. *Foie gras d'oie mi-cuit Larnaudie*, $124.50 for 2.2 pounds.

A Savory Bean Classic: Cassoulet from Languedoc

BY ANN PRINGLE HARRIS

As the author of this piece notes, there's a lot of history in a dish of cassoulet, and different versions all claim to be *vrai* (true). Paula Wolfert, in her book *The Cooking of South-West France,* says of cassoulet that it is "one of those dishes over which there is endless drama. Like bouillabaisse in Marseilles, paella in Spain, chili in Texas, it is a dish for which there are innumerable recipes and about which discussions quickly turn fierce." What only a handful of food writers have noted over the years is that cassoulet, like its cousins *adafina* in North Africa and *fabada* and *cocido* in Spain, is a revised *cholent,* the slow-cooking bean stew that observant Jews the world over prepare for the Sabbath. (*Cholent* can be made on Friday and eaten for Saturday lunch without having to turn on the oven, which is forbidden until sundown on Saturday evening, as an oven in use goes against the proscription of doing work.) To again refer to cookbook author Mitchell Davis, he relates that he once saw a sign at New York's Second Avenue Deli that read, "The French Have Cassoulet, We Have Cholent." Davis also has a rabbi friend who grew up in an Orthodox home and whose mother made a different *cholent* every week of the year. One of the best examples of how food is inextricably linked with history occurred during the terrifying years of the Spanish Inquisition. Sephardic Jews were often turned in to inspectors by their gentile neighbors, who reported that the stove wasn't lit in a particular house on Friday night, or a housekeeper might report that there was no pork in the *cocido* or *fabada*. Over the years a variety of meats, including pork, have been added to these hearty bean stews, and on whatever day of the week you partake of them, you can be assured of not being hungry for many hours.

ANN PRINGLE HARRIS writes frequently for the travel section of *The New York Times,* where this piece first appeared.

The French like to think of their classic dishes as having been born, not made. Thus cassoulet, the famous bean casserole of the Languedoc region in Southwestern France, is said to have been born in Castelnaudary, about midway between Carcassonne and Toulouse. The legend is that during the Hundred Years' War, when Castelnaudary was being besieged by the English, the starving inhabitants pooled their few provisions—white beans, lard, sausage, and *confit d'oie,* or preserved goose—and cooked them in an earthenware pot in a wood-fired oven. And so was born cassoulet.

The legend is still appropriate, first because the basic ingredients of cassoulet remain the same, and second because it is truly a feast for the famished; no light eaters need apply. Not only is it a meal in a dish, but the dish itself is by tradition a rather large, high-sided bowl that comes to the table amply filled. Also by tradition, diners may be invited to serve themselves, family style, cassoulet being a triumph of country cooking rather than haute cuisine.

There are three regional versions of cassoulet—so say people who have made French food a lifetime's study, people like Waverly Root (*The Food of France*) and Julia Child (*Julia Child and More Company*). In the original version, that of Castelnaudary, the beans and seasonings are said to be baked only with pork products (rind, shoulder, sausage, ham, lard). The Carcassonne version calls for pork plus cuts from a leg of mutton, while the Toulouse version uses pork and mutton plus Toulouse sausage (made of coarse-cut pork) and preserved goose or duck.

That's the historical view, which of course flatly contradicts the birth legend lovingly recounted on many a Castelnaudary postcard and bill of fare. No matter. History is regularly revised and reinvented, and today's chefs seem to follow their own instincts about cassoulet rather than hew to a rule book.

Cassoulet in Toulouse is frequently listed on the menu as *à la mode de Castelnaudary,* and in a tour of those cities and Carcassonne I found preserved goose or duck, sometimes both, in every cassoulet I tried, and mutton or lamb in none of them. Which is not to say that mutton or lamb might not be used if they were on hand, especially by a home cook who has a gift for improvisation and leftovers to deal with.

Improvisation has no doubt led to a large number of popular recipes that differ from the original classics. Tomato or tomato concentrate, for example, called for in many recipes, drew a negative shrug from several chefs I talked with, as did mention of some of the spices and herbs listed in various cookbooks. Garlic, onion, salt, pepper, bay leaf, and a bit of fennel are what chefs from cassoulet's home towns seem to prefer.

Which spices and which meats to use are, however, almost secondary issues. What counts for serious cooks is the beans. They should be moist but not mushy, firm but not dry, well separated from one another but flavorfully blended with all the other ingredients. If they fall short of these requirements, the cassoulet is not a success, no matter how good the goose, duck, or sausage that went into it. In the past the white beans used in cassoulet were grown in the Lauragais section of Languedoc, and the *lauragais* also furnished the goose and duck. Today, although the goose and duck may be local, the beans are much more likely to come from the Vendée, on the Atlantic coast of France, or from Argentina.

According to Patrick-Thomas Bernabé, director of the hotel and restaurant Le Donjon, in Carcassonne, two types of white beans are generally used in cassoulet: *coco* beans, so called because they are shaped like coconuts, and *lingots*—literally, ingots, also named because of their shape. The starch from the beans is important, too, said Mr. Bernabé, because as it leaches out and blends with the juices of the meats used, it helps to form a good top crust. A *chapelure,* or bread-crumb topping, is not favored by chefs in the cassoulet region, who rely on long, slow baking to assure a good blend of flavors and a crisp top crust. To prevent the beans from drying out as the dish bakes, however, many chefs poke holes in the crust from time to time and add a bit of stock or boiling water to the mixture.

The making of cassoulet might be compared to a tactical plan of battle in which one flank is moving into position while another is opening fire. While the beans, thoroughly picked over, are soaking or simmering, there are the meats to be raised and boned, and the sausage to be boiled. And then there are the various steps that must be taken to preserve a goose or duck: cutting it up, salting, seasoning, and refrigerating the pieces for a day or so, then cooking them in their own grease, which has previously been rendered from the skin and fattier cuts.

All of this advance action is building up to the moment when everything must be assembled for the final step, oven baking, which typically takes about an hour at 400 degrees, longer if the ingredients were refrigerator-cold before assembly. Small wonder that even in Castelnaudary food shops display in their windows tins of *confit d'oie* and jars of *haricots blancs.*

In the hotel Restaurant Le Centre et Le Lauragais in Castelnaudary, though, almost everything that goes into cassoulet is prepared from scratch. On a tour of the kitchen, the proprietor and chef, Jean-Jacques Campigotto, pointed out cold rooms where meats are kept, machines where sausage is ground, gas-fired ovens in which cassoulet bakes, and hot tables on which the pots are put to rest. "Cassoulet must rest," said Mr. Campigotto, who considers a forty-eight-hour rest optimal; "it cannot reach its full flavor without rest." The house cassoulet at Le Centre et Le Lauragais features confit of goose and confit of pork, both of which are preserved in the restaurant's kitchen.

The restaurant, a pleasant room with white-enameled wood moldings and a dark ceiling from which small spots of light sparkle like stars, manages to serve everything at the right degree of heat, even though dishes come up from a basement kitchen. The secret is an efficient use of the dumbwaiter and, opposite it, the hot table where dishes are placed for the few seconds that may intervene before they arrive at the table.

Another family establishment that specializes in cassoulet is the Auberge du Pont Levis, just outside the Narbonnaise Gate to the old city of Carcassonne. Soft lighting, pink tablecloths, fresh flowers, and, in summer, an outside terrace make this an attractive dining spot, and the cassoulet, made with preserved duck, is very good. A first course of puréed artichoke and puréed leek chilled in alternating ribbons, like a slice of marble cake, is just light and delicate enough to whet the appetite for heartier fare to come. Henri Pautard, who has operated the inn since 1973, is proud of the fact that his two sons, Olivier and Thierry, are now his partners and chefs.

Since cassoulet is considered peasant cooking, restaurants granted stars by the various rating systems seldom feature it; you have to do a little searching. In Toulouse the search led to Le Colombier, in an old section of the city. The main building material in Toulouse is brick, and Le Colombier's arched brick wall and decorative tile floor give it a true *toulousain* feel.

Cassoulet at Le Colombier, containing both Toulouse sausage and preserved duck, was nevertheless listed on the menu as being prepared in the style of Castelnaudary. It was slightly milder in flavor than cassoulet in Carcassonne, where seasoning tends to be assertive. The wine suggested as an accompaniment, a Château Bellevue La Florêt, was local and very good. In fact, wine enthusiasts might like to combine their cassoulet sampling with tastings of some of the wines of the region—Minervois and Corbières, and Blanquette de Limoux, sparkling or still. Not *grands crus,* as local people readily admit, but good provincial wines to go with a classic provincial dish.

If You Go

The following restaurants make a specialty of cassoulet. Prices for two people, calculated at 5.44 francs to the dollar, are for an appetizer, main course of cassoulet, dessert, and wine.

Le Donjon, 2 rue Comte Roger, Carcassonne; 33.5/68.71.08.80. Stone walls, beamed ceilings, and tapestry-covered chairs give the dining room a medieval feel that goes with its location in the old walled city. Closed Sunday. About $60.

Auberge du Pont-Levis, at the Narbonnaise Gate to the old city, Carcassonne; 33.5/68.25.55.23. Light airy dining room with an outside terrace that is opened in good weather. Closed Sunday night and Monday in February. About $80.

Restaurant Le Centre et Le Lauragais, 31 cours Republique, Castelnaudary; 33.5/68.23.25.95. An attractive spot that draws local residents as well as guests of the hotel. Closed Sunday night and Monday. Open every day from Easter to mid-November. About $50.

Les Palmes, 10 rue Maréchal Foch, Castelnaudary; 33.5/68.23.03.10. A mural of alpine and seaside scenes brightens an otherwise rather dark dining room. Closed Friday night and Saturday. Open every day from Easter to end of October. About $50.

Le Colombier, 14 rue Bayard, Toulouse; 33.5/01.62.40.55. Exposed brick walls and a decorated-tile floor evoke the atmosphere of old Toulouse, but service can be slow. Closed Saturday and Sunday. About $100.

Roquefort: King of Cheeses

BY FRED FERRETTI

⌇

As I mentioned in *The Kiosk—Points of View,* I am a devotée of Roquefort, and when I'm eating it, I usually declare it my most favorite *fromage* in the world. If you love Roquefort as much as I do, I urge you to visit the caves and take the Roquefort Société tour (which is only in French, but during the film you are given a headset with a running English translation). According to Mort Rosenblum in *A Goose in Toulouse,* the 1.7 million cheeses that pass through Roquefort Société's eleven-story vaulted Cave de la Rue "outnumber tourists by a mere ten to one. In France, food draws, and this is the Lourdes of cheese." (Société also turns out 70 percent of all the Roquefort produced in France.) If you don't prefer Roquefort, I think you would also really enjoy the tour as it is one of the most unique in France, and it's also a highlight of a visit to this region.

FRED FERRETTI, as a contributing editor, has filed a great many articles for *Gourmet* over the years on a wide variety of cuisines and destinations, many of them Mediterranean. Working on this piece provided his first encounter with the sublime combination of Roquefort and Château d'Yquem, and he concluded it would not be his last. Ferretti's work has appeared previously in the *Paris* edition of *The Collected Traveler.*

The vistas on the journey west from Montpellier to Roquefort across the South of France change as one moves inland from the Mediterranean: sloping vineyards and groves of olive trees give way to crags and cliffs of limestone, then evolve into the raw beauty of a virtually barren expanse of rock-strewn plateau known as the Causse du Larzac. "Roquefort begins here," Jean-Claude Ricard told me with a sweeping gesture of his hand as we motored along the strange flatness. "It is the rocks—*on* the rocks, *in* the rocks, *under* the rocks—that make the cheese."

There seems little disagreement among those for whom cheese is an obsession that Roquefort is the finest in the world (though the makers and fans of Parmigiano-Reggiano would surely tell a different story). "What is better than Roquefort?" asks Pierre Androuët, the master of Parisian cheesemongers, in his *Complete Encyclopedia of French Cheese*. Ivory-colored, with deep blue-green marbling veins and a texture like butter, Roquefort possesses a subtle flavor that develops in both strength and intensity once inside the mouth. Equally at home with a bold Hermitage or an aged Bordeaux, the cheese is perhaps at its luxurious best with a great, silken Sauternes—in particular with such as Château d'Yquem, as I was to discover.

Jean-Claude, like his father and grandfather before him, is proprietor of Vernières Frères, one of only eight makers of Roquefort in existence. He had volunteered to collect me at the Montpellier airport and to drive me the almost 150 miles to Roquefort-sur-Soulzon, the only place where that glorious cheese is produced. We were en route.

The stark, flat land atop the Causse du Larzac is interrupted at random by tall, angular limestone formations weathered smooth by years and winds and jutting upward from among scattered boulders and piles of loose stones. Except for occasional patches of sage, verbena, and clover, vegetation is sparse in this rugged country, where posted road signs continually warn of sheep crossings.

We descended from the plateau along a switchback road into the green valley of the River Soulzon, then climbed upward again. Halfway up a mountain called Cambalou, which sits between this plateau and the neighboring Causse de Lévezou, we came to a small one-road village. "Roquefort-sur-Soulzon," announced Jean-Claude. "We are here."

In this remote niche of Southwestern France where it is created and where it ripens, Roquefort is revered as "*le roi des fromages et le fromage des rois*" (the king of cheeses and the cheese of kings). Given its history as a delicacy beloved by the Roman conquerors of Gaul; exacted annually as a tribute by Charlemagne; and decreed as unique by a succession of French kings, it is an appellation that cannot be denied.

Much mystery and lore attend Roquefort, the enveloping taste of which is the legacy not only of the milk from the special breed of sheep, the Lacaune, from which it is fashioned, but also of the limestone caves in which it ripens. Though there are scores of blue-veined cheeses, Roquefort is the only one derived from ewe's milk. The cheese ages and develops its veins of mold in the caves of Cambalou, a series of damp and drafty caverns beneath the village that were formed naturally by fallen rock millions of years ago.

The Lacaune ewes that provide the thick milk are an odd-looking breed, with long drooping ears and wide chests. Bigger than average sheep, they can be as heavy as 150 pounds, and their wool is so sparse as not to matter. Yet each ewe has the capacity to produce almost three liters of milk in a single day.

Roquefort, a name secured by the French government, is produced in the Rouergue district in the *département* of Aveyron, where these sheep graze. Milk is gathered by twenty-six hundred or so farmers in an area that extends about sixty miles in every direction from Roquefort-sur-Soulzon and takes in both sides of the border separating the provinces of Midi-Pyrénées and Languedoc-Roussillon. French law allows that milk from Lacaune sheep to be used in making Roquefort may also come from a tiny corner of Aquitaine, along the Spanish border, and from the island of Corsica—but from nowhere else.

All of this I learned over a lunch in a warm, roughhewn restaurant of arches and stone, La Braconne, in the market town of Millau, about a half hour north of Roquefort-sur-Soulzon. Millau is the headquarters of the Confédération Générale des Producteurs de Lait de Brebis et des Industriels de Roquefort, the governing group of the Roquefort makers. A busy place, its streets are lined with shops and cafés and bordered by shade trees. On Wednesdays and Fridays a fine tented market sprouts around the fountain in the town's principal square, Place du Maréchal Foch, and there, among the fruits and vegetables and the special mushrooms of the *causses* called *oreillettes* (or "little ears"), you can find small patties of ewe's-milk cheese called *pérails,* as well as *flaunes,* sweet tarts of ewe's-milk curd flavored with orange-flower water.

In the middle of Millau, on its own *place,* is the International Hotel, which served as base for my explorations of Roquefort. It is a comfortable, friendly hotel with a good restaurant presided over by Pierre and Jean-François Pomarède, whose roasted *filet d'agneau de nos causses* is quite delicious indeed.

From Millau we drove west, up and onto another of the region's *causses,* that of les Ségalas, passing as we went several *lavognes*— man-made catch basins that hold rainfall, providing the sheep with drinking water. Just outside the village of Clapies we came to the farm of Jean-Marie Bousquet, who, with his wife, Bernadette, and their son, Frederic, tends seven hundred Lacaune and milks them on land that has been in his family for 120 years.

The sheep graze on the scarce vegetation of the *causses* from May through November, then on grain and bales of hay. The milking season begins at the end of December and peaks from February through July, when the milk in Jean-Marie's flock (one of the largest in Roquefort) yields as much as fourteen hundred liters daily.

The raw milk is collected and transported to dairies throughout the region. Farmer Bousquet's, along with that of eighty other farmers, is taken to the dairy of Vernières Frères, a short distance away in the town of Villefranche-de-Panat, where it is chilled at once. Supervising the dairy is Jean-Pierre Lauzet, who tests a sample from each farmer's delivery and microscopically examines it for antibodies and bacteria count. Milk deemed satisfactory is passed through steel tubing, warmed to 85 degrees Fahrenheit (30 degrees centigrade), and poured into huge vats. Rennet and the spores of *Penicillium roqueforti,* which will eventually cause the formation of the veins, are added at this point. The rennet thickens the milk into curd, which is then broken into pieces and packed into cylindrical molds that are punched with holes, stacked, and allowed to drain for two days. The cheeses are then removed from the containers and taken to the *saloir,* or salting room, where they are rubbed generously with salt and placed on racks to sit for five more days. At this point they still are not Roquefort, according to Lauzet.

After the salt is brushed off, the cheese is passed through a *piqueuse,* a device with long, pointed spikes for punching holes. This allows air to enter and assists in formation and expansion of the veins throughout the body. The cheese is tested once more and, when approved, taken in "loaves," as the drum-shaped cheeses are called—between 250 to 1,000 a day—to the caves beneath Roquefort-sur-Soulzon.

It is the limestone upon which all of the Roquefort region sits that is responsible for this unique cheese—a circumstance of nature perhaps best explained in the caves of the Société Anonyme des Caves et des Producteurs Réunis. Until the middle of the nineteenth century the production of Roquefort was largely a cottage industry of individual workers who watched over their cheese from *cabanes,* small huts set at the mouths of the caves. In 1842 these artisans came together to form the Société Civile des Caves Réunis de Roquefort, subsequently the Société Anonyme des Caves et des Producteurs Réunis, which for many years was the only maker of the cheese. This is no longer the case, as seven others are now authorized to fashion Roquefort. Société, though, is still the largest producer (responsible for 70 percent of all Roquefort made) and has the largest caves. It manufactures more than fifteen different brands— five million loaves annually—each of which is confined to individual caves and made with its own strain of *Penicillium roqueforti.*

The caves of Société are open to the public and offer tours and tastings. A representative of the company, with the aid of dioramas and exhibits (in English as well as French), takes visitors through the history of the cheese. As far back as 4000 B.C., I learned, a tradition of making cheese from sheep's milk has existed on the land that is now Roquefort-sur-Soulzon. Roquefort, the guide explains, came into existence as a result of romance—which, of course, is how the French would wish it. A tale, believed and sustained with the retelling, is that about two thousand years ago a shepherd left his lunch of bread and curd cheese in a cave so that it would remain cool while he tended his flock. Outside he noticed a beautiful young woman who so attracted him he could do naught but follow her. Alas, she disappeared over the horizon, never to be seen again. The shepherd, returning to the cave, found that his lunch had virtually fused: the bread was covered with a fine mold, the curd marbled to a soft green. He was so hungry, though, a feeling heightened by sadness over his unrequited love, that he decided to eat anyway. *Voilà!* Roquefort was born.

Also illustrated in the cellars of Société is the chronology of the cheese. Pliny the Elder, in his *Natural History* of A.D. 77, mentions how important the veined delicacy was to the Romans in Gaul and to Rome itself, where it was sent regularly. In the eighth century, it is said, Charlemagne demanded two mule loads of Roquefort as a Christmas tithe at his palace in Aix-la-Chapelle; and in the Middle Ages, word has it, rents in the area were reckoned either in silver or in Roquefort cheese.

In 1411 Charles VI granted Roquefort its first appellation, a grant confirmed by at least five successive monarchs. In 1925 a special law was enacted by the French Parliament affirming the *appellation d'origine* of Roquefort, and in 1961 a court in Millau set the limits of the zone for ripening cheeses to the Cambalou caves underneath the town of Roquefort-sur-Soulzon.

In Société's caves, bread is "baked" inside jars with strains of mold, then stored there. Within a few months the bread disintegrates and the blue-green spores of *Penicillium roqueforti* form. This is what is added to the milk with the rennet.

The eight makers of Roquefort—Société des Caves, Vernières Frères, Le Papillon, Gabriel Coulet, Constans-Crouzot, Fromageries Occitanes, Carles, and Yves Combes—all fashion their cheeses in the same basic manner, though variations in the way the mold spores are cultivated and added do exist, resulting in slight differences in depth of flavor and saltiness.

The caves also differ. Some have high ceilings; others are low, arched, and narrow; and still others, no more than corridors. Because virtually the entire mountain of Cambalou is a tower of loose stone, the caves contain hundreds of fissures, or *fleurines,* through which cool, damp air flows steadily. This combination of factors creates an atmosphere that remains at about 95 percent humidity and at a constant temperature of about 48 degrees Fahrenheit.

The cheeses come from the dairies to these caves, into which heavy shelves have been built, and there the ripening begins, the cheeses slowly transforming into Roquefort. After a few weeks the loaves are carefully wrapped in heavy, pliable foil of tin—only tin.

Within this wrapping the cheese continues to ripen, the veins coursing through the interior and the texture softening to a creamy consistency.

The master ripener of Société des Caves, Maurice Astruc, a gnome of a man with a sweeping mustache, says it is most important to remember that the cheeses, all of unpasteurized milk, "are always living." In his caves he has posted a sign of caution for the *cabanières* who tend the cheeses: MANIPULEZ LE FROMAGE AVEC SOIN, it reads—"Handle the cheese with care."

The loaves, now Roquefort, stay in the caves for about eight months. They are then unwrapped from their tin shells, the accumulated mold around the outside is removed, and they are rewrapped, this time in aluminum foil, for further packaging and shipping.

Some cheeses are aged longer than eight months, for the longer they age, the creamier and more intense they become. When they are aged *too* long, however, they can become dry and will crumble when cut. (Ideally the veins of a Roquefort should be larger at the center of the cheese and well spread throughout the interior and toward the edge.)

The secret to proper aging is to know precisely how long to ripen, which is why someone like Maurice, who ages by instinct, is so valuable. "The stones are the most important," he says, "and the *fleurines*. But also important is the wood of the shelves—it must be oak." (In the cellars of Le Papillon, however, just down the slope from Société, proprietor Gerard Alric and master ripener Jean-Pierre Biros have constructed a cave without wood. Only plastic containers and steel shelving rest up against the stones in their facility, for they believe this to be more hygienic.)

One evening during my stay I sampled some Société cheeses, cooked in several preparations in the kitchen of Roquefort's Grand Hotel, a fifteen-room establishment that is open six months a year, from April through September. From a menu studded with dishes utilizing Roquefort, the chef made a rich *gratinée d'huitres au Roquefort* (oysters with melted Roquefort) and a rough-textured terrine of chicken and partridge livers. I also tasted fresh ewe's-milk cheese from Corsica. The last was pleasant, to be sure, but without the strength and depth of cured, ripened Roquefort.

"Ripened with *wood,*" insists Maurice Astruc, who will not consider tampering with centuries of tradition. He has aged some of his loaves for as long as thirteen months, he says, and to prove how fine they can be when aged with loving care, he led me to his Cave Baragnaudes, at least a hundred years in use, with oak shelves as old as the cave. He set out slices of three of Société's offerings: a ten-month-old Roquefort des Maîtres Affineurs (the company's main export brand and the one we usually receive in the United States); Le Grand Affineur Maria Grimal (sold in specialty foods shops), also aged ten months; and a Baragnaudes, named for the cave in which it ripens, which he had aged for thirteen months.

"My icebox," said Maurice, reaching into a cool *fleurine* in the cave wall. He pulled out bottles of Château d'Yquem '84, uncorked them, and told me he was certain I was to "taste paradise."

This master of Roquefort did not overstate all that much. Paradise? Well, perhaps not, but the combination of the aged cheeses—particularly the Baragnaudes—with the Yquem, cooled perfectly by nature in his private *fleurine,* was brilliant, sensual, exquisite. It is this memory I carry, of Roquefort in that cave hundreds of feet below the village of Roquefort-sur-Soulzon. My palate refuses to forget.

Hotels and Restaurants

La Braconne, 7 place du Maréchal Foch, Millau; 33.5/65.60.30.93

Grand Hôtel and Restaurant, 12250 Roquefort-sur-Soulzon; 33.5/65.59.90.20

International Hôtel and Restaurant, 1 place de la Tine, Millau;
33.5/65.59.29.00

In a Glass, a Swashbuckler Called Armagnac

BY R. W. APPLE JR.

∽

My first sip of Armagnac was in 1990, the same year I also first tried eau-de-vie. I like them both, but do have a preference for Armagnac. (It's also a prettier color, eau-de-vie being clear.) Before that I knew absolutely nothing about it. I asked Charles Neal, whose definitive book on Armagnac is detailed in the bibliography to recommend a few Armagnac varieties for complete novices, which I suspect are most of us. He suggested two from Bas-Armagnac, Château de Briat Hors d'Age and Domaine Boingnères Réserve Spéciale, and one from Tenarèze, Château de Pellehaut Réserve. I also couldn't resist asking Neal about his most favorite Armagnacs, and he selected three from Bas-Armagnac: a vintage of Domaine Boingnères Folle Blanche, a vintage of Francis Darroze Domaine de St. Aubin, and a vintage from Château de Ravignan. By the way, if you have trouble finding Neal's essential book, visit www.armagnac.fr for a brief history of Armagnac, a list of some producers, and recipes for dishes made with Armagnac as well as for aperitifs and digestifs. I believe the site is maintained by the Bureau National Interprofessionnel de l'Armagnac, and it's completely in French. While not a replacement for Neal's book, it's one of the few Armagnac resources around, and appears to be authoritative. As the author of this piece implies, Armagnac remains little known and little tried. *C'est dommage*, as it is truly something special. You will not have much trouble finding Armagnac in Gascony and across the Southwest, and when you do, don't hesitate to try it.

R.W. APPLE JR. travels often to France and, happily for readers of *The New York Times*, shares the gastronomic details of his *voyages* with us.

To tell the truth, I don't remember when I had my first swig of Armagnac, but I know when I really fell for the stuff. It was a rainy day in the fall of 1971, or maybe 1972, at a restaurant in Villeneuve-de-Marsan, a little crossroads town about halfway between Bordeaux and the Spanish border. The food was excellent (two stars in the Michelin guide, as I recall) and the wine copious. But it was the encyclopedic Armagnac list that bowled me over.

I was a semiretired war correspondent at the time, a two-fisted eater yet to learn the more recherché points of food and drink. I knew I was in the Armagnac-producing region, but I had no idea I was at the very heart of it, at the nexus, at the epicenter. It turned out that this place, called Darroze, was to Armagnac exactly as the Second Avenue Deli is to corned beef.

I was too green to choose intelligently among the fifty-plus offerings, and too thirsty not to ask for help. So the kindly patron, Jean Darroze, picked an Armagnac for me that I found fascinating—bold, yet full of velvety finesse. When I said something subtle and worldly like "*Zut alors!*" he smiled, suggested I stay the night, and asked me to his cellar.

To Ali Baba's cave, you might well say. I eyed, sniffed, and tasted Armagnacs both young and very old, some dating back one hundred years. Mr. Darroze showed me how to shake the bottle and watch the foam that formed; if it lasted too long, that was a sure sign, he said, that the booze had been doctored. "Notice how the aroma lingers in the glass even after the liquid is gone," Mr. Darroze said after we had sampled one bottle. "*C'est un vrai!* It's a real one!"

Today the Darroze clan is the first family of Armagnac. One of Jean Darroze's sons, Francis, an international rugby star in his youth, spent three decades building up unrivaled stocks of the best his region has to offer. Armagnacs bearing a plain tan Darroze label slowly found their way onto the drinks trolleys of the best restaurants in Europe and a few in the United States.

Francis retired recently, and his son Marc, thirty-three, took over the family business. One of Francis's brothers, Claude, owns a classic restaurant in Langon, south of Bordeaux, offering a vast array of wines and Armagnacs, and his daughter, Hélène, owns a chic, innovative place on the Left Bank in Paris. Both have stars in the current Michelin guide.

Hooked by "le Roi Jean," as his friends called the patriarch, I have been happily tasting Armagnacs ever since. Almost without exception, I have found, the best ones come from the westernmost of the three Armagnac districts, known as Bas-Armagnac. (The other two are called Haut-Armagnac and Ténarèze.) The best of the best come mostly from a sandy area only 10 miles from east to west and 20 miles from north to south—from villages with evocative names like Labastide and Arthez, Hontanx and Le Houga, scattered along the border between the two most important Armagnac-producing *départements,* Gers and Landes.

Although Armagnac antedates cognac by more than two hundred years, having been introduced in the sixteenth century, it has had to play Avis to cognac's Hertz for generations. The cognac region, north of Bordeaux, is five times the size of the Armagnac region. Worldwide cognac sales are twenty-five times as large as those of Armagnac; in the United States the ratio is 120 to 1. But in France competition is keener, with cognac outselling its rival only three to one.

There are fundamental differences between the ways the two brandies are produced. For cognac, wine is distilled twice, but for Armagnac, it is distilled only once, and at relatively low temperatures, which helps foster robustness of flavor. Cognac is aged in white oak, Armagnac in black oak with more pronounced tannins.

As a result, Armagnac is racier, rounder, and fruitier than its cousin from the north, with an earthier, markedly more pungent aroma. Much of the best of it is sold unblended—the product of a single artisanal distiller in a single year, or vintage. Vintage cognac is rare; skillful blends are the norm, usually produced by large *nego-ciants,* or shippers. Armagnac, therefore, has more *goût de terroir,* as the French say. It is more rustic and thus more identifiable with a single piece of land.

If a sip of cognac transports the drinker to the lounge of a London club, a sip of Armagnac evokes the swashbuckling aura of D'Artagnan and his fellow Musketeers, who, like foie gras, rugby, and bullfights, hold a central place in the culture of this part of France, which is known as Gascony.

This is a profoundly rural area, isolated from the main highways and rail lines of France. Its people cling to the old ways, and its undulating landscape has been little touched by the modern world. As Montesquieu said of his beloved estate, not far north of this area, "Here nature is in its nightgown, just getting out of bed."

But as we drove west from Condom to Villeneuve-de-Marsan in the summer of 2002, my wife, Betsey, and I passed fewer fields planted with vines than on past visits. More plots were planted with golden sunflowers, destined for the oil mill, and tall green corn, destined to fatten ducks and geese.

According to some estimates, as little as fifteen thousand acres are now devoted to growing the grapes used in distilling Armagnac. Thousands of acres, we were told by knowledgeable people, have been ripped out by small farmers in need of more reliable cash crops.

"People make cognac for profit, but they make Armagnac for love," said Michel Guerard, the noted chef, as we sat in the garden of his Michelin three-star restaurant, Les Prés d'Eugénie at Eugénie-les-Bains, just outside the Armagnac zone. "Like champagne, cognac is a corporate drink, with tremendous marketing resources behind it. There have been several efforts to assemble big combines in Armagnac, but no luck. Gascons just aren't joiners. More and more, sadly, Armagnac has become an esoteric drink, a drink for connoisseurs who have the patience to smell out good producers."

In fact, crisis grips the region. Sales of Armagnac are falling steadily. "With the market in turmoil, Armagnac is becoming a depressing subject for many farmers to talk about," writes Charles Neal, a California importer of premium wines and spirits, in his excellent, privately printed 1999 study, *Armagnac: The Definitive Guide to France's Premier Brandy*. "The financial compensations for products of the vine are extremely unpredictable." (A copy of Mr. Neal's book may be obtained by sending a check or money order for $33 to Flame Grape Press at 710 Eighth Avenue, San Francisco, Calif. 94118.)

The independent producers and their unblended, carefully aged spirits have been hardest hit; Armagnacs less than five years old now account for 85 percent of worldwide sales. The consumer, Mr. Neal asserts, "wants something that doesn't exhibit tremendous personality," so much Armagnac is reduced to 80 proof with water, rather than letting time and natural evaporation do their work, and sugar and other substances are added to "round off" the flavor.

But adulteration has undermined authenticity while helping sales only slightly. Social and political trends have hurt as well. "For me, Armagnac is the *bijou* of brandies," said Michel Trama, who stocks a dozen Armagnacs, including a half-dozen of the very best, at his restaurant, L'Aubergade, in Puymirol, east of the Armagnac region. "Historically, it's our regional drink. But not many people order it here anymore. If they're driving, they're afraid of the cops. And if they're not, they may order a whiskey after dinner, because it's chic. I sell a cognac once a night, an Armagnac twice. It's depressing, but it's true."

A few independents have managed to swim against the tide, finding means to distribute high-quality Armagnac reasonably widely and to earn consistent if modest profits. Among these are the Domaine de Jouanda at Arthez, owned by the de Poyferré family, which once owned part of Château Léoville-Poyferré, a second growth in the commune of St.-Julien in the Medoc; the Domaine d'Ognoas, also at Arthez, owned by the Landes government, where distillation is done in a magnificent copper still, made in 1804; and the Château de Lacquy, in the hamlet of that name, which has been in the de Boisseson family since 1711. Annual output is small—at the Domaine d'Ognoas, only about thirty barrels of amber liquid, with aromas of vanilla, prune, cinnamon, and licorice.

One domaine is linked to another by roads no wider than the driveways in American suburbs, often shaded by plane trees, with their distinctive dappled, two-tone bark. Some villages have unusual pyramid-capped church towers; others have squares surrounded by medieval stone arcades.

We stopped in Labastide, a charming village built in 1291, for coffee with two of the more colorful figures in the Armagnac trade, Marguerite Lafitte and her daughter, Martine. In the jolliest way possible, they teased us with tales of inexplicable Anglo-Saxon behavior—for example, how Armagnac samples sent to the United States were held up on one occasion by customs but cleared the next time when the container was marked "Holy Water from Lourdes."

Naturally, Armagnac from the family's Domaine Boingnères was served with the coffee, though it was still early afternoon. One of the most intriguing was a rich, refined 1975 made wholly from colombard grapes, which Martine described as the grape of the future for Armagnac. It is more widely used for wines; ugni blanc, folle blanche, and bacco are the more usual Armagnac grapes.

Bacco is the subject of considerable controversy. It is a hybrid, a cross between folle blanche and an American vinifera grape called noah, developed by and named for a local schoolteacher in the 1930s. European Community officials, hostile to hybrid grapes, are trying to outlaw its use; some producers argue heatedly that bacco alone can give Armagnac the full-blown character they seek. Others have torn out all their vines, as the Lafittes did in 1991.

Although *negociants,* who buy and usually blend spirits produced by others, are less important here than in Cognac, there are several of consequence, including Samalens and Trépout. Some, like Janneau and Sempé, have undergone wrenching changes of ownership. But none can match Darroze, mostly because of the unusual way the firm does business.

Darroze does no distilling. It does no blending. Its trade consists of buying individual barrels from the finest artisan distillers when they become available, sometimes a barrel at a time, sometimes more—as in 1976, when Francis bought the entire stock, about three hundred barrels, of the Domaine de St.-Aubin at Le Houga. That was the coup that made him famous.

Once the casks were kept in Francis Darroze's garage. Now six hundred of them from thirty domaines, each chalked with the producer's name, lie on two levels in a modern chai, the older ones downstairs, where the atmosphere is humid, the younger ones upstairs, where it is drier. As the Armagnacs are coaxed toward their prime, which he defines as roughly twenty-five years after distillation, Marc Darroze bottles that for which he receives orders and no more. The producer's name goes on the label together with the vintage, as well as the firm's name. On a separate back label the date of bottling appears—a vital detail because spirits do not improve once they leave wood and enter glass.

"We get good stock," said Marc Darroze, who spent part of his apprenticeship in Sonoma County, California, "because we respect the little farmers who make it. We use their name, we never blend their stuff with someone else's, we use no water or additives. That's all very important to these guys."

Using up-to-date office systems, Mr. Darroze has brought the firm into the new century, strengthening sales in Britain, the United States and recently, Russia. Two days a month, he drives into the backwoods, looking, as he said, "for barns with dark roofs," caused by the mold that grows as Armagnac evaporates. Sometimes he finds a widow who sells him a few barrels.

We tasted some old bottles together, including a 1965 from Eauze, which hinted delightfully of cacao and tobacco. That Armagnac, he said, "was the work of my father, and now I work for my son"—Clément, then just twenty months old.

France's Southwest, Worth a Detour

BY FRANK J. PRIAL

∽

Sometimes I'm asked why I included this piece or that in my anthologies, or why I saved a particular article in the first place. Most of the time my reasons are obvious and clearcut, but the truth is that occasionally, the most I can say is that a piece was simply interesting or well written rather than significant historically. I was compelled to save this piece because I really like (and purchase whenever I find them) the wines of Roussillon, as well as the writer Patrick O'Brian, and that's all. Reason enough, though, to share news about an area of good-value wines and an area featuring "a trove of undiscovered treasures."

FRANK J. PRIAL is the wine columnist for *The New York Times* who travels to France frequently. He is the author, most recently, of *Decantations: Reflections on Wine* (St. Martin's Press, 2001).

A few years ago I had lunch with an eighty-three-year-old winemaker in Collioure, a onetime fishing village turned tourist haven on the French Mediterranean coast, not far from Spain. "This one is the wine of the year, and this one is five years old," said my host, who was no ordinary *vigneron*. He was Patrick O'Brian, the novelist of the Napoleonic wars at sea. I had gone to talk to him about his long career and was astonished to find that he tended a little vineyard behind his home and was almost as proud of his wine as of his books.

I should not have been surprised. Wine is an integral part of life in the Roussillon, as that part of France is called even by Anglo-Saxons like Mr. O'Brian, who died in 2000. But unlike his novels, its best wines are little known elsewhere. Perhaps that's about to change. In the last three or four years, there has been, if not a flood, then a respectable stream of exciting wines from the Roussillon. What's more, with a little effort, you can find some of them right here on our shores.

The Romans made wine in this corner of the Mediterranean, and the Phoenicians and the Greeks had vines here before them. The locals speak Catalan, which they insist was the language of the Roman armies, and they think of themselves as Catalans first and French second. The border here has always been porous. Ask people what their capital is, and they are as likely to say Barcelona, 90 miles to the south, as Perpignan, which is, in fact, the capital of the Roussillon region.

Like the Central Valley of California, the Mediterranean coast of France has long suffered from its association with cheap wine. The stuff was made from poor-quality high-yield grapes like aramon, then turned into alcohol and burned off by the government. Farm subsidies are hardly an American invention. Traditionally, the appellation for this wine was *vin de table,* and it was sold by alcoholic content. An 11-degree wine was cheaper than a 12-degree wine, which was, in turn, cheaper than a 12.5. In shops in working-class parts of Paris, customers still bring their own plastic jugs and ask for five liters of *onze* (11) or *douze* (12). Three decades ago, the French government began to encourage growers in the Languedoc-Roussillon to plant better grapes. The results have sometimes been astonishing.

High land prices in Bordeaux, Burgundy, and the Rhone Valley prompted talented young winemakers to look seriously at regions they once would have scorned, like the Mediterranean littoral. Vast cooperatives have in many cases been replaced by small well-tended estates, whose owners make their own highly individualistic wines. These people brought modern winemaking techniques to the region and better grapes, notably syrah, to supplement and often replace the native grenache and carignan.

But even in the bad old days, wines of some distinction could be found in the Roussillon. This is the home of Banyuls, Rivesaltes, Muscat de Rivesaltes, and Maury, the so-called *vins doux naturels,* or natural sweet wines. These are wines made by adding grape brandy to wines while they are still fermenting. The wines are made from local red and white grapes, dominated by grenache. They are popular all over France, but a lot are still sold at stands or from trucks along the back roads of the region. About 90 percent of all the inexpensive sweet wine made in France comes from Roussillon.

The region's three red wine appellations are Côtes-du-Roussillon, Côtes-du-Roussillon Villages, and Collioure. A pioneer in making fine wines in the Roussillon is the Daure family at Château de Jau in Cases-de-Pène, northwest of Perpignan. Many Americans know its Jaja de Jau, a light red picnic wine. Only a few know its excellent Talon, a big rich blend of about 90 percent syrah and 10 percent mourvèdre.

One of the most important producers in the region is the Domaine du Mas Blanc at Banyuls, known for rich full-bodied red wines, mostly based on syrah and mourvèdre with grenache, cunoise, and other grapes in some of the *cuvées.* Among them, all bearing the Collioure appellation, are Clos du Moulin, Cosprons Levants, and Les Junguets, all deep, dark, intensely fruity wines. The domaine also produces relatively expensive banyuls, including hard-to-find older vintages. Banyuls-sur-Mer is actually a commune within the Collioure appellation. The Daures are also part of the Collioure scene with their Clos de Paulilles. Here, too, Banyuls is the principal wine, but they produce a delicious rosé probably all from syrah, with the charm of a rosé and the elegance of a good red.

Since Roussillon wines are not easy to find in this country, at least not yet, the best way to sample them is where they are made. This distant corner of France is a trove of undiscovered treasures. The coastline is overrun with tourists in summer, but they disappear in the fall, and the rugged backcountry is relatively untouched all year round. Henri Matisse and André Derain started what came to be known as Fauvism in Collioure around 1905. Pablo Casals lived at Prades in exile from the Franco regime, and Picasso lived and worked at Ceret, an exquisite country town, about 10 miles inland from Collioure. Much of the work he did here, around 1911, can be found in Ceret's gemlike museum. Its collection also includes little-known works by Braque, Soutine, Chagall, and Miró.

Les Feuillants, a Michelin one-star restaurant in Céret, offers classic Catalan dishes and has a terrific collection of the best local wines. None by Patrick O'Brian, I'm afraid, but then, that's a memory I prefer to keep just for myself.

Eat Yourself Slim the French Way . . .

BY NAOMI BARRY

⌁

Peter Mayle, in his book *French Lessons,* notes that "I have no doubt there are good chefs working in spas throughout France, but the godfather of them all is Michel Guérard, one of the first modern celebrity cooks. He became a household name in France more than twenty years ago when he invented *cuisine minceur*. This was based on the thought—revolutionary in those days, and not all that common even now—that a regime could actually be pleasant. You should be able to eat real food, drink a little wine, refresh your system, and take some pleasure from the normally dreary process of inner cleansing and weight loss." Here is a piece that is about food, of course, but is also very much about Guérard and his wife, Christine, who, according to a photo caption in the piece, "grew up within the family property near Toulouse in an old-fashioned, old-world way. She learned about the trees, flowers, and herbs of the countryside. From the family cook, she learned to make preserves. She studied in Spain, Paris, and England, and worked a year in Mexico before her father turned over Eugénie-les-Bains to her to build up." The destination spa Michel and Christine created in the Southwest remains the talk of food lovers and health seekers nearly thirty years later. About Eugénie the town, Mayle also noted that it "calls itself France's premier *minceur* village. It has also been called 'Guérardville,' because the maestro's influence is everywhere . . . it is a small industry built on a paradox: eat, drink, and lose weight."

Readers should note that a special three-day menu—with recipes—accompanied this piece, which first appeared in *House & Garden*. I chose not to include the menu simply because I feel the recipes are less interesting than the Guérards themselves, and that most readers would skip over them; if you are curious about the recipes, you should visit your local library and see if it's available on microfiche or perhaps even in a bound copy format. One recipe, however, for the signature Tisane d'Eugénie, I did include, as well as a list of Guérard's principles of cooking.

NAOMI BARRY, introduced previously, lives in Paris and contributed many articles to *House & Garden*, where this piece first appeared in 1975. She is also the author of *Paris Personal* (E. P. Dutton, 1963) and *Food alla Florentine* (Doubleday, 1972). Her work has appeared in the *Paris, Morocco*, and *Venice* editions of *The Collected Traveler*.

This nature-defying miracle has been realized by Michel Guérard—the most deliciously inventive French chef of our generation—at Eugénie-les-Bains, a charming hideaway in Southwestern France where smart Parisians are slimming down in an atmosphere of festive gaiety.

The first step was a personal history. Guérard wanted to lose weight to win the girl. (He is now married to the willowy Christine.) While paring down the avoirdupois, however, he had to keep his balance. Working in a professional kitchen can be fury and violence, demanding stamina and cool control. The usual programs had reduced him to a state of nervous distemper followed by disastrous eating binges.

Guérard turned his back on the doctors and the specialists and decided to test-pilot his own way. He went at the problem like a chemical researcher in a kitchen laboratory, applying his usual logic, imagination, talent, and taste. He is enough of an artist to admit his trials occasionally result in error.

It is an established fact that on approximately a thousand calories a day, even "too too solid flesh" eventually will melt away. From his own case Guérard had observed that prolonged deprivation and boring repetitiveness had a depressing effect upon the spirit. He set about to develop delectable dishes—strong on flavor, short on fat— the sum of which would fit within the desired calorie count. An occasional excess could be countered the next day.

His goal was a *regime minceur* (slenderness regime) with sensory excitement. The new repertoire is rapture to the palate and delight to the eye. Non-weight-watchers effusively praising an *estouffade* of milk-fed lamb with tiny onions and purée of green beans or a *navarin* of lobster have no idea they belong to the category of Non-Fattening Spectaculars.

To rise from a beautifully set table, lightly but satisfied, is a savvy way for civilized people to eat. The three-course meals are designed for total pleasure, including the aftereffect. Never before have I followed a regime supposedly good for me without having my mind riveted to the image of a chocolate cake. Guérard has not renounced the principles of French haute cuisine. Rather he has employed every trick and technique to adapt French haute cuisine to the dynamics of contemporary life. Instead of bemoaning the absence of bread, potatoes, and foie gras, one is captivated by Guérard's unexpected combinations, subtle counterpoint of flavors, and stunning composition of elements on each plate.

In a typical day's menu at Eugénie-les-Bains, the meals have been designed to be as interchangeable as dominoes. Rigidity is not part of the Guérard personality.

No beverages are served with meals, as it is felt that liquids tend to prevent proper chewing. Midmorning and before dinner, you are given a tall glass of Tisane d'Eugénie. Should you have it at the bar, where other guests may be having a Scotch or a Campari, you will not feel out of place. The Tisane is presented with the glamour of a planter's punch in a tall frosted glass garnished with a slice of apple, a slice of orange, a grape, a chunk of pineapple, and a sprig of fresh mint. (Christine knows every herb and plant of the area and its medicinal properties, having been taught by an elderly botanist.)

For the past ten years Michel Guérard has played the Pied Piper of Gastronomy, leading gourmets into unheard-of territories. In 1965 he opened his first restaurant, the Pot-au-Feu, on a Simenon-sinister street in the dreary Parisian suburb of Asnières. (He couldn't afford the high rent in the chic quarters of town.) Within weeks, *le tout Paris* was seeking directions to the culinary genius who was boiling up a storm in that dismal location on the outer fringes. Within two years the real out-of-towners were telephoning from New York for advance reservations, but even a dramatic long-distance call couldn't assure one of the coveted forty places.

In 1974 Guérard was dispossessed. The building of the Pot-au-Feu was slated for demolition. To the dismay of his partisans who cried he would be forgotten, he announced he was leaving Paris for Eugénie-les-Bains, a deep-country hamlet of 150 persons, to help Christine with the hotel and spa that belonged to her father, who was rejuvenating a chain of five watering places in the region.

The Guérard-istes now are streaming to Southwestern France. Easiest access to Eugénie is Pau, 50 kilometers away. The Pau airport now hums with an international buzz and an exchange of hails and farewells from Guérard friends who are coming or going. When there is no room on the Pau line, the Eugénie-bound fly to Bordeaux or to Biarritz and drive from there.

The late Christian Dior used to say that the lines of a future collection could be discerned in his collection of the season before, provided you had the eyes to see. Guérard's lightening refinement of French cuisine has been en route for some time. In an article published by the *International Herald Tribune* in July 1973, I found that at the recommendation of Paul Bocuse, I had tried a "sea bass *au varech*," a Guérard creation that has won the accolade from the top professionals of France as the discovery of the year. The fish is steamed under a heavy tangle of a particular seaweed sent to Asnières daily from Brittany. This *varech* imparts its moisture to the bass and infuses it with incomparable flavor of the sea. There is no other seasoning. The dish is a sublime of simplicity.

"When the bass is scraped of its seaweed and its scales, Guérard serves a small bowl of *sauce vierge*. This is olive oil acidulated with a little lemon juice, to which has been added chopped tarragon, chervil, crushed coriander, and a few bits of peeled and seeded tomato for color. Because he feels that potatoes or rice are boring accompaniments to fish, Guérard has arranged each individual 'platter' with a fan of fresh asparagus tips." After that lunch Guérard told me he had been inspired by the delicacy of Japanese cuisine and the lithe energy of the Japanese.

At that same Pot-au-Feu luncheon, I had eaten a lobster salad, in which each element maintained its distinction. Reading the description now shows it was a forerunner to Eugénie-les-Bains. "The dominant note is lobster served in generous chunks. Carrots, sliced paper-thin and previously treated to a suggestion of simmer without destroying the freshness of taste, lend an important touch of orange to the color scheme. Green beans, crunchy and barely cooked, have their place here as well. From the Chinese, Guérard has adopted the rule that vegetables, even when cooked, should still be raw enough to resemble 'just picked.' "

Vegetables "just picked" figure largely in the menus at Eugénie-les-Bains. Often running them through the blender seems to bring out the very essence of artichokes, string beans, watercress, leeks, cauliflower, mushrooms. Only salt is used, to bring out the innate flavor. He obtains tonalities of flavor by introducing surprising additions . . . puréed pear to puréed spinach or puréed cauliflower to puréed leeks.

The blender has become a necessary extension to his good right arm. Sauces have always been one of the elegant accomplishments of French haute cuisine. Guérard's contribution is a collection of superlative sauces, more taste than substance. He does not deny the rich goodness of fresh butter and cream. For his *regime minceur* he thickens his sauces with puréed mushrooms, a combination of puréed vegetables, or a low-calorie white cheese the French call *taillefine*. So successfully has he adapted the sauce of one of his famous Pot-au-Feu dishes—*duckling au poivre vert*—that only an exceptional palate or someone forewarned would detect the difference. The similarity of visual appearance makes it possible for a weight-watcher to eat opposite a non-weight-watcher without feeling cheated of all the fun.

The blender has become his magic wand, transforming vegetables into unctuous purées. "It is useless to incorporate butter or cream," he says, "for they cause the natural flavor of the vegetable to disappear. Finally, parboil them or steam them and salt at the moment you put them in the blender. That is all. Infinite combinations are possible. I very much like a mélange of carrots, mushrooms, celery, and onions. The artichoke can be remarkable provided you cook it whole, then remove the leaves and pass only the bottom round in the blender."

Simple cooking is somewhat of a misnomer. It is not the same thing as easy cooking. Guérard's food at Eugénie-les-Bains is referred to as simple because it is purified of all the elements of grease and fat that might make it heavy. The efforts involved often surpass what is known as *grande cuisine*.

Yet as he points out, it is a return to *grande cuisine,* which demanded that every particle of fat be meticulously skimmed from a sauce. "Then a lot of people began to neglect this golden rule, alas," he said. "In a traditional pan-fried steak, how many people remember to throw away the cooking butter?"

In the hierarchy of his present kitchen tools, a sharp knife ranks after the blender. A great deal of time is spent on chopping, dicing, slicing, and mincing. For instance, minced mushrooms can be cooked in a few turns around a Teflon pan because the many exposed surfaces give forth the maximum of inherent moisture. Furthermore, the infinitesimal bits of green pepper or red pimiento or orange carrot are necessary for their esthetic value. In his presentations, Guérard is closely allied to the Japanese.

Individual portions are composed on plates the size of platters. "I like comfortable plates," he says. The use of oversize plates he borrowed from the Troisgros brothers (having first asked their permission). It started years ago when he found he could not style a serving of pot-au-feu in the dining room but needed the comparative calm of the kitchen to make an artful arrangement. A commodious plate gives him the opportunity for special effects with everything from salads to desserts.

Feasting the eye is an important element of nourishment, particularly in a *regime minceur.* Automatically you slow down to admire and contemplate. Eating slowly is a key to oral satisfaction and leads toward the desirable state of less is more. "To cook well you cannot be stingy. But I reproach useless excess, the constant temptation to add a little something more in the belief that it will be better, when on the contrary just the reverse is true." He seemed to be paraphrasing Gertrude Stein who once commented that some people think if perfection is good, more perfection must be better.

At Eugénie-les-Bains, Guérard uses only the finest chickens, ducks, eggs, lobster, crayfish, beef, veal, lamb, fruits, salads, vegetables. Some come from his property. Others he searches out in the colorful farmers' market in nearby Mont-de-Marsan. The herbs and flavorful grasses are at hand in the kitchen garden and in the meadows just beyond the kitchen door.

If you can go, it will be a glorious experience in gastronomic finesse. The success of Guérard's experiments can be judged in the laughter and convivialty of the dining rooms where everybody is having a wonderful time, slimming *à la française*.

A Few Principles of Michel Guérard

Low-calorie food must taste so good and look so good that psychologically you never feel deprived but mentally prefer it. In time, you well may.

You can have haute cuisine with a low calorie count—approximately one thousand calories a day.

A feast for the eye is an important element of nourishment. Every Guérard dish is a stunning composition. Automatically you slow down to contemplate and admire it. Eating slowly is a key to oral satisfaction.

The judicious use of a blender gives a creamy texture without resorting to cream.

You need sharp knives, a blender, and a Teflon pan.

Vegetables are sliced and diced so fine, they can be cooked in a few turns around a Teflon pan without the addition of any fats.

Sauces are one of the delights of French cuisine and are featured in Guérard's Eat Yourself Slim regime. As thickening agents, he uses puréed vegetables or low-calorie white cheese (in France *taillefine;* in America farmer cheese, diet cream cheese, ricotta, yogurt cheese).

In this lighter way of eating, there are no potatoes, rice, noodles, or bread.

Every lunch and dinner is a three-course meal, ending with a dessert made with an artificial sweetener.

The Tisane d'Eugénie—an infusion of five health-giving herbs and plants—is served several times a day: at breakfast, before lunch, before dinner. The tisane is a natural diuretic. It is presented with the charm of a planter's punch, in tall glasses garnished with a slice of apple, a slice of orange, a grape, a chunk of pineapple, a sprig of fresh mint.

Meats can be grilled without fat or oil by giving them a fast dip in water. The evaporating moisture will keep them from sticking to the pan.

To banish hunger pangs for familiar but fattening foods, Guérard offers a variety of pleasurable taste surprises and the excitement of totally new culinary inventions.

Seasoning is vital: salt, pepper, and generous doses of fresh herbs. Much of the sensory excitement comes from the seasoning.

Tisane D'Eugénie

A natural diuretic made with equal parts of heather flowers, corn-silk, cherry stems, horsetail, and uva-ursi (bearberry). Prepare as you would tea: pour boiling water over herbs, steep at least 5 minutes, pour off tisane and serve, or chill to serve cold. Garnish with any combination of the following: slice of apple, slice of orange, a strawberry, a grape, a chunk of pineapple, a sprig of fresh mint. Ingredients are available at herb-and-spice or health food stores.

One Region, Two Friends, Thirty-eight Favorites

BY ELIZABETH THRUSH

～

Here's a wonderfully informative piece to treasure: a personal *carnet d'adresses* for the culinary specialties of the Gironde, the Pays Basque, the Dordogne, and the Landes shared by Bordeaux restaurateurs Jean-Marie Amat and Jean-Pierre Xiradakis. You will read about a few of these suggestions in other sources, but most of these are insider tips that I, for one, am extremely grateful to receive. The foodie roadmap starts here: it doesn't get much better than this.

ELIZABETH THRUSH is a pen name for Karen Taylor, editor of *FRANCE Magazine*, where this piece appeared in a special issue devoted to Bordeaux and Aquitaine.

They have been close friends for more than thirty years, yet they couldn't be more different. Jean-Marie Amat is tall and thin, a rather cerebral fellow who chooses his words carefully, enriching a conversation with thoughtful comments and sensitive observations.

Jean-Pierre Xiradakis is short and, well, a bit round, a down-to-earth, exuberant character whose famous anecdotes keep friends in stitches for hours. Their professional styles are just as diametrically opposed. Until recently, Amat was the creative visionary presiding over the St.-James hotel and restaurant, a luxurious, cutting-edge "village" that offered exquisitely sophisticated and refined cuisine, the hippest bistro for miles around, and the design talents of architect extraordinaire Jean Nouvel.

Xiradakis, meanwhile, has transformed a good chunk of Bordeaux's Rue Porte de la Monnaie into a picture of rustic charm. First there was La Tupina, a sort of farmhouse imported into the city complete with stone hearth and hand-cranked spit. Known for its hearty and generous fare, La Tupina has now been joined by a retro-style grocery store and a wine bar whose decor delights with witty nostalgic touches. Coming soon: a bakery.

Yet as unlikely as it may seem, this improbable duo has a lot in common—not the least of which is a penchant for practical jokes. (In their youth, they once put up "for sale" signs in the windows of other Bordeaux restaurants and had quite a reputation for hilarious crank phone calls.) On a more serious note, these two restaurateurs share a deep love for their native region and the conviction that no cuisine can be a success unless it is prepared from carefully selected ingredients.

The groundwork for this belief was laid in the early 1970s, when the pair became curious about Armagnac. "Every restaurant carried it back then," recalls Amat. "But it wasn't great. We discovered it could be excellent." Indeed, Xira, as everyone calls him, would set out on Saturdays to visit producers and would bring back bottles that he and Amat would taste that evening. Eventually they were both featuring a number of Armagnacs on their wine lists. "It sounds so obvious, but no one had ever done that before," says Xira.

"That experience taught us that a very ordinary product can be quite extraordinary, if you find the person who makes it right," recalls Amat. Thus began what Xira calls their "detective days" of combing the region, seeking out regional products and the people who still knew how to make them properly. "Today, there are *appellation d'origine contrôlée* designations and other quality labels," he explains, "so finding good products is no big deal. But back then it was gumshoe work!"

In the 1970s Amat was the first to put *agneau de Pauillac* on his menu, and the two chefs proudly claim credit for reviving *boeuf de Bazas, haricots tarbais,* and other nearly forgotten products. "We even brought back Gironde caviar," says Amat, "although it didn't last long because sturgeon fishing was soon banned. But for a few years we had the real thing." His one regret is that they never managed to revive *les petits pois de Cerons,* a wonderful little pea still grown in a few places in Spain.

On the following pages Amat and Xira share some of the gastronomic treasures they have unearthed throughout Aquitaine. Organized geographically, each section features items you will find on local menus, shops that still offer authentic local specialties, and a few *petits restos* that share their philosophy of excellence.

Prices are per person, exclusive of wine. Be sure to call ahead for hours of operation and reservations, if necessary.

La Gironde

Local Specialties

Caviar. Amat and Xiradakis remember hearing about the days when the Gironde was chock full of sturgeon, but by the early 1980s it had been overfished, and stocks became so depleted that catching them was banned. In the 1990s a few entrepreneurs here started raising sturgeon in fisheries, sometimes with very good results. The best caviar, of course, comes from producers who give their fish the highest-quality feed and the best care and who have mastered the salting process. As for taste, good Aquitaine caviar compares favorably with the best Russian and Iranian brands, although it has a somewhat less pronounced taste.

Oysters. The Bassin d'Arcachon, with its twice-daily tidal flows, is ideal for raising oysters. The waters are generally calm and rich in nutrients, and low tides expose the beds, making them easy to tend. Oysters from this area are prized for their fresh, salty taste. One *ostréiculteur,* Eric Larrarthé in Canon, raises "bonsaied" oysters. Known as *noisettes,* these bivalves are adults that have been deliberately kept small. (They used to be called *boudeuses,* or "pouters.") About half the size of a regular oyster, they appeal to kids and others who are not great oyster enthusiasts and to those who don't like the "milky" texture that larger oysters sometimes get in the summer months.

Agneau de Pauillac. For generations shepherds from the Pyrenees have brought their sheep down from the mountains in the fall to graze in the Gironde's vineyards and fields. In the spring they head back to the Pyrenees—although these days they make the trip by truck. But now as then the milk-fed lambs that are too young to make the journey are sold to local butchers. Known as *agneau de Pauillac,* this tender meat is very white and fatty with a distinctive nutty taste.

Gourmet Destinations

St.-Emilion. Macaroons have been a specialty in St.-Emilion since the seventeenth century, when nuns in a local convent began making them from almonds imported from Italy. Today you can buy *macarons* at a number of shops, but Madame Blanchez's are the best. She toasts and grinds her own almonds and has that artisanal touch that makes all the difference. *9 rue Guadet; 33.5/57.24.72.33.*

Soulac-sur-Mer. Since 1927 Judici has been run by the same family, who still use the same traditional recipes to make their delicious ice cream and fresh-fruit sherbet. Good ole vanilla and chocolate are perennial favorites in the *glace* department, though sorbet flavors—peach, apricot, pear—change with the seasons. *15 rue de la Plage; 33.5/56.09.81.48.*

Lege-Cap-Ferret. Customers quickly become addicted to Frédélian—their *glace caramel aux craquelins* is simply to die for. And this pâtisserie is one of the few places that still know how to turn out an excellent *canelé*. A *bordelais* tradition, these tiny cakes are at once rustic and refined—slightly crispy on the outside, soft and tender on the inside. *33 boulevard de la Plage; 33.5/56.60.60.59.*

Restaurants

L'Envers du Decor. This contemporary bistro is run by François des Ligneris, proprietor of nearby Château Soutard. Guests will find good, unpretentious dishes that change daily according to what's available at the market, along with a convivial atmosphere and an extensive selection of reasonably priced wines. A favorite with St.-Emilion wine-growers, who can often be seen here with five or six bottles on the table, tasting and comparing notes. *11 rue du Clocher, 33330 St.-Emilion; 33.5/57.74.48.31; closed weekends. Fixed-price menus at €14.95 and €25 and à la carte.*

La Guinguette. As the name implies, this no-frills Médoc eatery is near the river's edge. A great place to stop in for a seafood snack—

try the local shrimp during the summer season—and a glass of chilled white wine. *Port de Macau, 33460 Macau; 33.5/57.88.08.12. Fixed-price menus at €13 and €17 and à la carte.*

Le Lion d'Or. If you're looking for a French chef with attitude and the kind of authentic bistro that has become an endangered species, this is the place to come. Located in the Médoc, it is patronized by nearby château-owners, who have their own private lockers to store their wine. (They usually leave a bottle for the patron, who has amassed an impressive collection.) The food— regional cooking with an accent on lamb and duck confit—is simply extraordinary. *Place de la République, 22460 Arcins; 33.5/56.58.96.79. A la carte about €35.*

Le Pays Basque

Local Specialties

Piments d'Espelette. Chili peppers, brought back from America by Spanish conquistadors, have been grown in Espelette for centuries. About thirty-five years ago André Darraidou, a restaurateur and mayor of the town, decided to revive the tradition by using these mild yet flavorful peppers to spice up his cuisine. His brother jumped on the bandwagon, launching what has become the popular Fête du Piment, still held the last Sunday of October. The media took note, tourists started to come, and now the entire town is draped in garlands of drying peppers. In 2000 *piments d'Espelette* earned the AOC label, and there is even an official— nudge, nudge—Confrèrerie de Piments d'Espelette. Xiradakis is a proud *chevalier:* "It's the only medal I've ever received!" he admits.

Sheep's Milk Cheese. In the Pyrenees shepherds in different valleys make their own renditions of *fromage de brebis,* which now bears the AOC Ossau-Iraty label. Taste varies according to the altitude at which the sheep graze (which determines their diet) and how long the cheese has aged. Some are kept as long as two years, becoming increasingly dry and pungent. Sliced paper thin, *fromage de brebis* is delicious paired with *confiture de cerise noire* (see below).

Black Cherry Jam. Found throughout the Basque Country, *confiture de cerise noire* is a celebrated culinary tradition in Itxassou, where it is made from Beltza, one of three local varieties of black cherries unique to the town. Not a palate-pleaser when raw, the fruit makes a luscious jam for spreading on morning baguettes or serves as a sweet counterpoint to sharp cheese.

Gourmet Destinations

Oloron-Ste.-Marie. People are known to drive 100 miles to the Artigarrède pastry shop just to pick up a cake known as Le Russe, a heavenly confection made with almond paste, meringue, and praline-butter cream. Other pastry shops make Le Russe, but everyone who has tasted Artigarrède's agrees that no one makes it better. *1 place de la Cathédrale; 33.5/59.39.01.38.*

Bayonne. Chocolat Cazenave, a family business since 1854, serves lots of goodies, but the hands-down favorite at this *salon de thé* is the frothy hot chocolate served with a little pot of freshly whipped cream on the side. *19 rue du Port Neuf; 33.5/59.59.03.16.*

St.-Jean-de-Luz. There is not a sweet tooth in this town that doesn't know the Pariés pâtisserie, famous for its award-winning *kanougas,* chocolate- and coffee-flavored caramels sometimes made with bits of grilled cacao or coffee beans. Another house specialty is *mouchous.* Basque for "kiss," they are made of two macaroon-type cookies stuck together. *9 rue Gambetta; 33.5/59.26.01.46.*

Hôtel du Chêne. Simple, impeccably clean, and surrounded by beautiful Basque countryside, this curious little hotel-restaurant seems stuck in the 1950s. Basque to the bone, it is a meeting place for locals who gather here for *l'apéro* after church. Breakfast (with fabulous homemade black cherry jam), lunch, and dinner can be enjoyed under a canopy of wisteria. *Place de l'Eglise, 64250 Itxassou; 33.5/59.29.75.01; fax 3.59.29.27.30. Fixed-price menus from €15 to €25 and à la carte.*

Euzkadi. Like his parents and grandparents, André Darraidou runs this little *auberge* that originally catered to those visiting the nearby livestock market. Darraidou has kept the spirit of the place intact but has updated the regional cuisine his parents served. The result is generous portions of honest, authentic food and an ambiance that is a favorite with locals, who sometimes gather at the bar and belt out a few Basque songs. *285 route de Karrika a Nagusia, 64250 Espelette; 33.5/59.93.91.88; fax 59.93.90.19. Menus from €16 to €26 and à la carte.*

Chez Pantxua. Overlooking the ocean with views of St.-Jean-de-Luz, this traditional seafood restaurant is a family affair going back two generations. The owners' patronage of the arts can be seen in the excellent collection of Basque paintings on display; some date back to the early 1900s and were traded for meals. The menu features family-style Basque and Spanish dishes that are simple yet well prepared—try the *zarzuela,* a mix of fish and shellfish in a lobster bisque. *37 avenue Commdt. Passicot, 64500 Ciboure; 33.5/59.47.13.73. A la carte only, about €33 to €35.*

La Ferme Ostalapia. A restored seventeenth-century Basque farm, this restaurant offers hearty country fare served on a terrace facing La Rhune, the highest peak in the western Pyrenees. Featuring Basque and Spanish cuisine, the place has a special aura, thanks to its congenial owner, Christian du Plessis. Considered *the* local address by the vacationing who's who. *2621 Chemin Ostalapia, 64210 Ahetze; 33.5/59.54.73.79; www.ostalapia.com. A la carte about €25 to €30.*

La Dordogne

Local Specialties

Walnut Oil. Originally the traditional oil used in Bordeaux, *l'huile de noix* was eventually replaced by peanut oil shipped in from French colonies in Africa, then by olive oil. It is fragrant and delicious but must be used quickly because it rapidly turns rancid. Xira gets his supply from Jean-Pierre Bordier, a third-generation producer who cold-presses his walnuts—as well as hazelnuts and almonds—at his sixteenth-century mill. *Moulin de la Tour, 24200 Ste.-Nathalène; 33.5/53.59.22.08; fax 53.31.08.33.*

Chestnuts. Once a veritable treasure for local peasants, *châtaignes* provided food for both men and animals and could keep for a very long time. These versatile nuts can be puréed or roasted, made into soups, or candied for desserts. There is even a chestnut flour used to make cakes and pastries.

Truffles. Dordogne, and more specifically Périgord, is famous for its black diamonds, which are still painstakingly hunted and gathered by hand. From December to mid-March people bring their haul of precious fungi—sometimes only one or two cradled in a checkered handkerchief—to sell at the weekly market in Lalbenque, about 18 miles south of Cahors. The event kicks off every Tuesday afternoon at two-thirty; beforehand many repair to the Hôtel du Lion d'Or, famous for its omelettes and other truffle-laced dishes. *104 rue Marché aux Truffes, 46230 Lalbenque; 33.5/65.31.60.19; reserve at least a month ahead.*

Sarlat. In the past families in the Périgord made their own *vin de noix,* which became known as "Périgord Port." Today the Distillerie de la Salamandre is one of a handful of companies producing the aperitif, which is made from crushed green walnuts mixed with wine, sugar, alcohol, and various flavorings such as vanilla, orange peel, or cinnamon. Sold under the name "Le Gatineaux," it is at once sweet and bitter. Salamandre's other products range from eaux-de-vie made from local fruit (pears, plums, cherries, raspberries) and fruit marinated in liqueur. *Tours of the distillery can be arranged. Les Tissanderies; 33.5/53.59.10.00.*

Sorges. For the past twenty-five years Isabelle and Guy Meynard have run La Ferme Andrevias, where they raise some twelve hundred geese and tend a twenty-two-acre walnut grove. Visitors can see the entire process involved in making foie gras, from the arrival of day-old goslings to the force-feeding that begins at four months. Those who'd rather skip the details can head straight for the boutique and pick up a fabulous *pâté de Périgord* (truffled foie gras) or other homemade products (*confit d'oie, sauce périgeux*) sold only on the farm. *33.5/53.05.02.42.*

Bézenac. *Pâtissier* Raoul Lucco has concocted an extraordinary *gâteau aux noix;* unlike most versions, which tend to be rather dry, this moist walnut cake will keep as long as two weeks. Another original creation available at Les Gourmandises de Lucco is the Louvre, a caramel mousse with bits of pear and a walnut dacquoise. *La Couture; 33.5/53.29.25.33.*

Restaurants

La Maison des Peyrat. A thirtysomething lawyer—and a granddaughter, daughter, and sister of lawyers—Nathalène Arnaux broke with family tradition when she decided to refurbish a fourteenth-century hospice, turning it into a charming *auberge.* The restaurant, open only to hotel guests, serves a contemporary take on regional cuisine. *Le Lac de la Plane, 24200 Sarlat; 33.5/53.59.00.32; fax 53.28.56.56; www.maisondespeyrat.com. Rooms run from €60 to €80; breakfast is €8, dinner €17.*

Au Fil de L'Eau. This delightful riverside bistro in Brantôme, "the Venice of Dordogne," belongs to Régis Bulot, who also runs the nearby Relais & Châteaux, Moulin de l'Abbaye. Duck and fish are the stars of the show here, including the seasonal *friture d'ablettes,* small local fish fried whole. *21 quai Bertin, 24310 Brantôme; 33.5/53.05.73.65. Fixed-price menus at €21 and €26.*

Les Ecuries de la Passée. After years of running a restaurant lauded in guidebooks, Jean-Pierre Malaurie decided to concentrate on making foie gras, which he sold to luxury gourmet purveyor Petrossian. Then in 1996 he opened Les Ecuries de la Passée, housed in renovated stables. (Wine is kept in old stalls; customers dine in the former attic.) The decor mixes massive old beams with contemporary art, and the cuisine is equally distinctive—Malaurie works with the only remaining professional fisherman (actually, a fisherwoman) on the Dordogne, offering local pike, carp, perch, and the ever popular *friture de goujon.* A self-declared chauvinist, he features mostly Bergerac wines and, yes, still makes his own foie gras. *La Passée,*

24220 St.-Cyprien; 33.5/53.29.46.73. Fixed-price menus from €20 to €35 and à la carte.

Les Landes

Local Specialties

Ducks 'n' Chickens. The Landes is ideally suited to raising poultry: corn is produced here, there are wide-open spaces, and the climate is consistently mild, a big plus when it comes to fattening ducks. Perhaps for all these reasons the Landes can lay claim to a wide variety of poultry breeds. The chickens that end up on Xiradakis's famous roasting spit hail from here—they are yellow in color, rich in taste, and a bit tougher than your average chicken. Understandably so, he says—they've spent their lives running marathons through the pine forests!

Foie Gras. The Landes is a big producer of this delicacy. Quality and price vary; according to Amat, great foie gras comes from geese and ducks that have been fed well, treated well, and are, well, happy. Raw foie gras (*foie gras frais*) must be cooked within two or three days; *demi-cuit* and *cuit* foie gras, however, can be put up in jars or canned. The best are deftly seasoned and properly cooked—meaning not too much. Always look for the IGP label, which certifies the origin and quality of foie gras from Southwestern France.

Cèpes. People in the Southwest love these mushrooms, which are found growing wild in oak forests in the Landes as well as Dordogne. (Scientists have been looking for a way to cultivate them but haven't had much luck yet.) Every fall when the season begins, people can be seen treading gingerly through the woods, basket in hand, seeking out their little treasures. Back home, their booty can be prepared a thousand ways—raw, sautéed, stuffed, grilled, added to soups and salads . . .

Gourmet Destinations

Onesse-et-Laharie. Berdoulet Frères offers an award-winning *pastis landais*—not to be confused with the Provençal beverage celebrated in Pagnol films. Some *pâtissiers* do, in fact, make this briochelike pastry with *pastis,* although others prefer rum, vanilla, or other flavorings. What do Berdoulet Frères use? All they will say is that it's not *pastis. 312 rue des Ecoles; 33.5/58.07.30.21.*

Dax. Since 1906 Philippe Cazelle's family has been making madeleines the old-fashioned way, without preservatives. Sold locally and by mail order (only in France), these delicious little cakes must be consumed within five or six days—that is, if you can manage to hold on to them that long! *6 rue Fontaine Chaude; 33.5/58.74.26.25.*

Peyrehorade. Monsieur Barthouil still makes *saumon fumé* the way his father did when he founded the family business in 1929, using alder wood and brick smokehouses and ensuring that each fillet is smoked just long enough. Some of the salmon still comes from the nearby Adour, although fishing restrictions have made it so rare that the price is high and availability is limited. Barthouil's other products—foie gras, confits, *rillettes, tarama*—are similarly made using traditional artisanal methods. *378 route Hastingues; 33.5/58.73.00.78.*

St.-Sever. To produce his celebrated foie gras, Michel Dubernet works with local farmers who agree to raise their ducks and geese according to strict criteria that ensure the best quality. Local suppliers also provide the raw ingredients for his other homemade gourmet products, which include *confit de canard,* pâtes, and ham. *31 rue Lafayette; 33.5/58.76.19.48.*

Restaurants

La Plancha. A simple retro-style seaside restaurant where the food is as wonderful as the views. Grilled fish is the main attraction here, served with a special house sauce made from wine vinegar, garlic, and *piments d'Espelette. 115 promenade Océan, 40440 Ondres; 33.5/59.45.24.06. About* €25.

Chez Simone. A former truck stop, Chez Simone was reinvented twenty years ago by Bernard Paysan, who trained with the Landes's most famous chef, Alain Dutournier of Paris's Carré des Feuillants. The menu features Landes specialties—*garbure, confit de canard, magret de canard,* and of course foie gras every which way. A favorite with locals, who come to celebrate special occasions. *Bourg 40180 Bénesse-lès-Dax; 33.5/58.98.70.22. Fixed-price menus from* €10 *to* €26 *and à la carte.*

La Ferme aux Grives. Michel and Christine Guérard opened this idyllic country retreat in 1993, restoring a traditional *maison landaise* and turning it into a restaurant with authentic regional decor and cuisine to match. Located near Guérard's three-star restaurant, La Ferme is known for its duck and steaks grilled in the open hearth, as well as its spit-roasted suckling pig. With their characteristic perfectionism and attention to detail, the Guérards have taken a nostalgic dream of a bygone era and made it a reality. *111 rue Thermes, 40320 Eugénie-les-Bains; 33.5/58.51.19.08. Fixed-price menu at* €39.

Bibliography

Cookbooks

Like so many other cuisines, French cooking cannot be separated from French history. Really good cookbooks—ones that offer tried and true, authentic recipes, as well as detailed commentary on the food traditions of the country or region and the history behind the recipes and the ingredients unique to the cuisine—are just as essential to travel as really good guidebooks. In the Winter 1985 issue of *The Journal of Gastronomy*, Josef Konvitz noted in a piece entitled "Does Clio Have Taste?" that "food has always offered people of diverse backgrounds an opportunity to share company. May an interest in the history of food and drink nurture respect and understanding among all who are concerned about gastronomy!" I read these cookbooks the way other people read novels; therefore the author has to be more than just a good cook, and the book has to be more than just a collection of recipes. All of the authors and books listed below fit the bill, and because they are *all* my favorites, I feature them alphabetically rather than in order of preference. I use each of them at different times throughout the year, and I couldn't envision my kitchen without a single one. The Mediterranean cookbooks are in some ways the most interesting, because, as Claudia Roden notes in her book *Mediterranean Cookery*, "Looking for the imprint of the past in the Mediterranean can be fascinating and helps to explain why a dish on one side of the sea is like another on the other side. But it is even more exciting to discover the extraordinary regional diversity of the area. For here unity does not mean uniformity. Obviously a Berber village clinging to a rock has a different way of interpreting a stew from a city like Granada. The Mediterranean has many faces: eastern and western, Christian and Muslim, one intimate with the sea, one with the desert, one which knows the mountains and one which looks beyond the olive trees at northern Europe, one which is rooted to the land, another which glitters with ancient grandeur. And regional cooking reflects them all." I do not provide lengthy descriptions of these titles as I think it is sufficient to state that they are nearly all definitive and stand quite apart from the multitude of Mediterranean and French cookbooks crowding bookstore shelves. I have also included a few books and articles that aren't strictly cookbooks but are equally interesting and relevant nonetheless.

Mediterranean Cookbooks and Food

A Book of Mediterranean Food, Elizabeth David, Penguin, 1988. In her introduction, David shares an observation by Marcel Boulestin that it is not really an exaggeration "to say that peace and happiness begin, geographically, where garlic is used in cooking." She herself notes that "from Gibraltar to the

Bosphorus, down the Rhone Valley, through the great seaports of Marseilles, Barcelona, and Genoa, across to Tunis and Alexandria, embracing all the Mediterranean islands, Corsica, Sicily, Sardinia, Crete, the Cyclades, Cyprus (where the Byzantine influence begins to be felt), to the mainland of Greece and the much disputed territories of Syria, Lebanon, Constantinople, and Smyrna, stretches the influence of Mediterranean cooking, conditioned naturally by variations in climate and soil and the relative industry or indolence of the inhabitants."

Cod: A Biography of the Fish That Changed the World, Mark Kurlansky, Walker & Co., 1997. The first single-subject book I read about a culinary ingredient was *Peppers: A Story of Hot Pursuits* by Amal Naj (Alfred A. Knopf, 1992), and I discovered I was crazy for this type of book. So years later, when I discovered *Cod*, I knew I would love it, and indeed I did. I couldn't stop talking about it, in fact, just as I couldn't stop talking about all the wonderful things I learned about peppers. The fascinating story of cod crisscrosses the globe from Newfoundland, New England, the Basque coast of Spain, Brazil, West Africa, and Scandinavia, but the Mediterranean is never very far from the thread. Kurlansky notes that "from the Middle Ages to the present, the most demanding cod market has always been the Mediterranean." Fresh or dried salt cod is a ubiquitous Mediterranean staple (except in the Muslim countries), making an appearance in such dishes as *bacalao a la vizcaina* (Basque Country), *sonhos de bacalhau* (Portugal), salted cod croquettes (Italy), *brandade de morue* (France), and *taramosalata* (Greece), among others. (Kurlansky provides recipes for each.) *De rigueur.*

The Feast of the Olive, Maggie Blyth Klein, Aris Books (Addison-Wesley), 1983.

From Tapas to Meze, Joanna Weir, Crown, 1994.

Invitation to Mediterranean Cooking: 150 Vegetarian and Seafood Recipes, Claudia Roden, Rizzoli, 1997.

Mediterranean: The Beautiful Cookbook, Joyce Goldstein, Collins (produced by Welden Owen), 1994.

Mediterranean Cookery, Claudia Roden, Alfred A. Knopf, 1987.

Mediterranean Cooking, Paula Wolfert, HarperCollins, 1994.

The Mediterranean Diet Cookbook, Nancy Harmon Jenkins, Bantam Books, 1994.

A Mediterranean Feast: The Story of the Birth of the Celebrated Cuisines of the Mediterranean, From the Merchants of Venice to the Barbary Corsairs, Clifford A. Wright, William Morrow, 1999. An outstanding and exhaustively researched book. If you only want to read one book on Mediterranean cuisine, this is the one. Wright reveals that "I wrote this book in an attempt to extend one man's—Fernand Braudel's—vision, love, and scholarship, and I augmented it with my own research and love of Mediterranean food, in the hope of providing a guide to the Mediterranean that has not been attempted before. The weaving of history and gastronomy in *A Mediterranean Feast* was meant to reveal the culinary structure of the Mediterranean—its rugged contours, oppressive reality and blue delight—through the eyes of geographers, travelers, historians, and cooks, what Braudel means by 'total history.' Braudel's writings were an attempt to seek out the 'constant' of Mediterranean history, the structures and recurrent patterns of everyday life that provide the reference grid. For myself, and this book, the constant is the food of the Mediterranean, its cuisine and recipes."

Mediterranean: Food of the Sun: A Culinary Tour of Sun-Drenched Shores with Evocative Dishes from Southern Europe, Jacqueline Clark and Joanna Farrow, Lorenz Books, 2001. Though there are a few common recipes in this volume, a great number of them do not appear in other Mediterranean cookbooks, and the ones I've tried have been really delicious.

Mediterranean Light, Martha Rose Shulman, Bantam, 1989.

The Mediterranean Kitchen, Joyce Goldstein, William Morrow, 1989. A unique feature of this wonderful book is that Goldstein indicates how, by changing only an ingredient or two, recipes can go from being Italian, say, to French, Portuguese, or Moroccan, an approach that illustrates the core ingredients that all countries in the region share and that also allows for more mileage out of nearly every recipe.

The Mediterranean Pantry: Creating and Using Condiments and Seasonings, Aglaia Kremezi, Artisan, 1994. Among the Greek recipes (the author is an internationally known expert on Greek cuisine) are a number of staples good especially for recipes of the Midi, such as flavored olive oils, pasta with olive oil, anchovies, fennel, and roasted garlic and pepper paste.

Mediterranean Street Food: Stories, Soups, Snacks, Sandwiches, Barbecues, Sweets, and More, from Europe, North Africa, and the Middle East, Anissa Helou, HarperCollins, 2002. I was so happy when this book was published because, though some street foods are included in a number of Mediterranean cookbooks, they have not really been given the pride of place I think they deserve. Street foods are so much a part of the Mediterranean lifestyle, and Helou presents a great variety of recipes for soups; snacks, salads, and dips; pizzas, breads, and savory pastries; sandwiches; barbecues; one-pot meals; sweets and desserts; and drinks. Halou grew up in Beirut, then moved to London, and later to Paris, where, "even if the city is not by the sea, it is the capital of a Mediterranean country with a culture and a way of life, at least in the south, that are closer to mine . . . As for eating in the street, I was back in business. Whether it was time for breakfast, lunch, or dinner, there was always an ambulant vendor, a hole in the wall, or a café opening onto the street providing fun and tasty specialties to eat." Helou does not include a delicious street snack I had once in Béziers, a seafood pie called a *tielle*. If you run across what you think might be *tielles* (I suspect they are not unique to Béziers), try them right away, unless you're allergic to seafood, keep kosher, or something. *Tielles* are most yummy and very filling, perfect at around ten-thirty or eleven o'clock in the morning.

Mostly Mediterranean, Paula Wolfert, Penguin, 1988.

Olives, Anchovies, and Capers: The Secret Ingredients of the Mediterranean Table, Georgeanne Brennan, Chronicle Books, 2001. As Brennan notes, some of the Mediterranean's humblest snacks and dishes deliver a sense of gustatory well-being completely out of proportion to their simplicity because "the traditional uses of three preserved ingredients, olives, anchovies, and capers, give the food an endless variation of character and depth." In addition to recipes (a few I particularly liked include Anchovies and Lemon on Black Olive Bread, Anchovy Stuffed Eggs, and Pan-Seared Salmon with Capers and Green Peppercorns), Brennan provides information on the cultivation and preservation of olives and capers (and a good brine recipe for salt-curing olives) and the fishing for and preservation of anchovies.

Olives: The Life and Love of a Noble Fruit, Mort Rosenblum, North Point Press, 1996. "An olive, to many, is no more than a humble lump at the bottom of a martini. Yet a closer look reveals a portrait in miniature of the richest parts of our world. Olives have oiled the wheels of civilization since Jericho built walls and ancient Greece was the morning news. From the first Egyptians, they have symbolized everything happy and holy in the Mediterranean. But it is simpler than all that. Next time the sun is bright and the tomatoes are ripe, take a hunk of bread, sprinkle it with fresh thyme, and think about where to dunk it. I rest my case." Provençal olive oil is addressed in this wonderful book—none from Languedoc-Roussillon—but it is still a *de rigueur* read.

Salt: A World History, Mark Kurlansky, Walker & Co., 2002. Here's another fascinating volume from Kurlansky, this time the single subject being one humans and animals cannot survive without. Kurlansky reminds us early on in this book that "salt is so common, so easy to obtain, and so inexpensive that we have forgotten that from the beginning of civilization until about a hundred years ago, salt was one of the most sought-after commodities in human history." (Note that the low cost of salt does not apply to today's designer salts, such as *fleur de sel,* which is handmade, somewhat labor intensive, and "traditional in a world increasingly hungry for a sense of artisans.") One thing I love about books like this is the wealth of trivia one discovers: under Kurlansky's microscope, no stone is left unturned. I usually walk around for weeks asking "Did you know . . . ?" questions to anyone who will listen, and then I reel off all the amazing things there are to know about cod or salt. For example, did you know that salt makes ice cream freeze, removes rust, seals cracks, cleans bamboo furniture, kills poison ivy, and treats dyspepsia, sprains, sore throats, and earaches? (As an aside, readers interested in more myriad uses for salt should get a copy of the nifty *Solve It with Salt: 110 Surprising and Ingenious Household Uses for Table Salt,* Patty Moosbrugger, Three Rivers Press, 1998.) Besides practical uses, salt is believed by Muslims and Jews to ward off the evil eye, and bringing bread and salt to a new home is a Jewish tradition dating back to the Middle Ages. "In Christianity, salt is associated not only with longevity and permanence but, by extension, with truth and wisdom. The Catholic Church dispenses not only holy water but holy salt, *Sal Sapientia,* the Salt of Wisdom." As the title indicates, this is a worldwide story, but it's very much a Mediterranean story, too. Kurlansky writes that "the entire coast of the Mediterranean was studded with saltworks, some small local operations, others big commercial enterprises such as the ones in Constantinople and the Crimea. The ancient Mediterranean saltworks that had been started by the Phoenicians, like power itself, passed from Romans to Byzantines to Muslims. The saltworks that the Romans had praised remained the most valued. Egyptian salt from Alexandria was highly appreciated, especially their *fleur de sel,* the light crystals skimmed off the surface of the water. Salt from Egypt, Trapani, Cyprus, and Crete all had great standing because they had been mentioned by Pliny in Roman times." Finally, as in *Cod,* Kurlansky warns of what can happen with a seemingly endless resource due to greed and short-sightedness. The lovely French coastal village of Collioure, where artists such as Matisse spent many happy days, once had eight hundred anchovy fishermen; now it has none. I was humbled when I learned that the La Baleine sea salt I've been buying for years is owned by Morton's; and I was surprised to learn that most of the salt mined today is destined for de-icing roads in cold-weather places around the world. *De rigueur.*

Zingerman's Guide to Good Vinegar and *Zingerman's Guide to Good Olive Oil,* both by Ari Weinzweig, Zingerman's/Dancing Sandwich Enterprises, 1996. Here is a duo of little paperback books in the *Zingerman's Guides to Good Eating* series that are seriously addictive and positively must-haves in your kitchen. Truly, there have been a multitude of books and articles written about olive oil and vinegar; I've read nearly all of them, and rarely do they address the questions consumers have about these two Mediterranean comestibles. Look no further if you love olive oil and vinegar as much as I (and Ari Weinzweig) do. The olive oil guide offers answers to such questions as, What is extra-virgin anyways? Why does one olive oil sell for $10 and another for $30? How long can you store olive oil? And—my favorite—how come my Italian grandmother didn't use extra-virgin olive oil? Ari's answer is, "Though it will come as a surprise to many (and certainly no offense is intended), most of the Italians who immigrated to this country didn't use very good olive oil after they arrived. Most of them were poor, and even in Italy at the turn of the century the best extra-virgin olive oils were costly. In poorer households, which didn't have their own olive trees, it was common to use refined oils that were not particularly good. They were affordable, though, and these were the oils most immigrants could afford to bring with them to North America. Even those Italians who used the best extra-virgin oils in Italy couldn't find them in this country. Olive trees don't grow on the Lower East Side or in Brooklyn. The only place in this country in which olive trees grow is California, and most growers there planted olive trees to produce table olives, not oil." In addition to some wonderful recipes, Weinzweig includes two pages of cool olive oil trivia (did you know that 95 percent of the world's olive trees are grown in the countries of the Mediterranean? And that it takes about eleven pounds of olives to produce a liter of olive oil?). The vinegar guide addresses questions like, Can you really taste the difference? What's wrong with the stuff in the supermarket? And, what can you learn from the label? Included in the "additional array of excellent vinegars" is Banyuls, the incredible vinegar from Southwestern France. Weinzweig writes, "I let the sample of this wine vinegar sit on my desk unopened for nearly two months. I kept meaning to taste it. But the label wasn't particularly interesting and I'd never heard of it, so I never quite got around to it. Finally one day I brought it home, opened it up, poured a little of the light amber liquid in a bowl, dipped a bit of bread in, tasted it, and . . . it blew me away. Banyuls is one of the best vinegars I've ever had." Also provided is a list of ten things to do with vinegar (besides washing windows).

Culinary Classics

Cooking with Daniel Boulud, Random House, 1993. If this were merely a good cookbook with good recipes, I would not single it out for special mention; but the fact is that it is an extremely outstanding cookbook with incredible recipes. A feature that any French (or Mediterranean) cook would appreciate and admire is the Seasonal Markets Lists found at the end of the book. If there was ever a more inspiring way to emphasize the importance of cooking foods in their proper season, I haven't found it. Our supermarkets make it easy to forget that foods do still have seasons in which they grow and thrive and are harvested. (Just because supermarkets sell asparagus and plastic tomatoes in January doesn't mean they're in season—they're only inferior, tasteless, and flown in from somewhere else.) There are also *great* recipes interspersed between these lists, my favorite part of this incomparable volume. Daniel Boulud is one of the greatest chefs of all time, but he is very down to earth, not at all highfalutin'. This cookbook is among the best ever published.

The Physiology of Taste or Meditations on Transcendental Gastronomy, Jean

Anthelme Brillat-Savarin, translated by M.F.K. Fisher and with illustrations by Wayne Thiebaud, Counterpoint (by arrangement with The Arion Press), 1994, distributed by Publishers Group West; original translation copyright 1949, The George Macy Companies, Inc.

French Cuisine and French Food Traditions

Blue Trout and Black Truffles: The Peregrinations of an Epicure, Joseph Wechsberg, Alfred A. Knopf, 1953. At some point, those who are interested in reading about cuisine or France or both eventually discover the writings of Joseph Wechsberg. *Blue Trout and Black Truffles* is a classic, in the same culinary category as A. J. Liebling's *Between Meals.* Though Wechsberg writes about Vienna and Budapest in this wonderful volume, the greater part of the book is decidedly devoted to the eating places and vineyards of France. Some of the chapters appeared first in *The New Yorker, Holiday,* and *Gourmet,* and they are all sheer delight to read.

Chez Panisse Fruit, Chez Panisse Vegetables (both HarperCollins), and any of the Chez Panisse family of cookbooks (these include the *Chez Panisse Cookbook, the Chez Panisse Menu Cookbook,* and *Chez Panisse Desserts*) by Alice Waters. I have neglected the cookbooks of Alice Waters in my previous books, and it was only recently that I realized why: I don't find them to be very user-friendly. It is not my intention to be an overzealous critic when I state this, but I am a fairly accomplished home cook, and I have a passion for good cookbooks. I have found over the many years of Chez Panisse publishing that I always begin with a great desire to love and cherish each book, only to end by admiring the text—and finding it inspiring—but not many of the recipes. However, upon reflection, Alice Waters is too much of a champion of fresh, seasonal cuisine in America to omit from these pages, and plus I think she is a swell human being. Writing about *Chez Panisse Fruit* in *The Art of Eating,* contributor James MacGuire notes that "Waters's writing may be low-key, but her ardor is undiminished. The introduction describes the way she begins writing a book. 'I throw open the window,' she says, 'I start to flail my arms, and scream: Pay attention to what you're eating! And then I calm down a little and try to explain why this matters so much to me.' Readers are warned of 'extremely noxious agricultural chemicals' sprayed on commercial strawberries and reassured that she buys strawberries harvested by 'well-paid unionized workers' (shades of Cesar Chavez and the 1960s). Waters, as much as anyone, has made American chefs pay attention to high-quality, small-scale organic growers. Those growers remain a tiny minority, and this book is part of her effort, slowly increasing in success, to persuade everyday cooks to do the same." (As an aside, I have read elsewhere about those noxious chemicals sprayed on strawberries, and in a list I cut out of a magazine highlighting organic foods that are worth the money, strawberries topped the list as one item in particular that should never be purchased unless they are certified organic.) The *Fruit* and *Vegetables* books are beautifully produced with artwork that is suitable for framing. The other Chez Panisse titles are not quite as attractive (most do not have any photographs), though they are all of high quality.

The Cook and the Gardener: A Year of Recipes and Writings from the French Countryside, Amanda Hesser, W.W. Norton & Co., 1999. Hesser is a reporter for the "Dining In/Dining Out" section of *The New York Times,* and this is an account of her year in Burgundy, when she cooked for Anne Willan, cookbook author and founder of Ecole de Cuisine La Varenne. It's also the story of the gardener and his wife on the château property, and it brings readers and cooks a reminder that the stuff of a garden—our own, from a farmers' market, or the supermarket—should never be very far away from a kitchen.

The Cooking of Provincial France, M.F.K. Fisher (with Julia Child as consultant), Time-Life Books, 1968. The collaborative effort to produce this book (one of the volumes in the Foods of the World series) was extraordinary, the likes of which we'll probably never see again. (A separate, spiral-bound recipe booklet accompanied each hardbound volume.) This is long out-of-print and hard to find, but it does turn up at tag sales and in used bookstores.

The Food of France, Waverly Root, introduction by Samuel Chamberlain, illustrations by Warren Chappell, Vintage, 1992; originally published in hardcover by Alfred A. Knopf, 1958. Root says in the first chapter that "eating habits are part of our social habits, part of our culture, part of the environment, mental and physical, in which we live." He proves exactly that as he makes way around France, revealing the ways in which French food has shaped the French character. The Southwest is well represented: the section entitled "The Domain of Fat" contains chapters on the Central Plateau (Périgord, Auvergne, Marche, Limousin, Guienne) and Languedoc; "The Domain of Butter" discusses the Bordeaux country; and "The Pyrenees: Butter, Fat, Oil" covers Gascony, the Basque Country, and the Roussillon.

French Country Cooking, Elizabeth David, A Jill Norman Book (Dorling Kindersley), London, 1987; originally published by John Lehmann, 1951. Although I don't cook much from this book, I've learned a lot from it, and with the beautiful color reproductions of food artworks by Bonnard, Gauguin, Chardin, Signac, Monet, Renoir, and others, it is one of my most treasured volumes.

French Lessons: Adventures with Knife, Fork, and Corkscrew, Peter Mayle, Alfred A. Knopf, 2001. As Mayle notes in his introduction, he "can't pretend to have done more than scratch the surface of French gastronomy," but the surface he did scratch is enlightening and entertaining. For this culinary journey Mayle traveled to all corners of France to attend the sort of wonderful gastronomic *fêtes* and *foires* that make visiting France so rewarding. In the Southwest he attended the annual Marathon du Médoc, which takes place in the Bordeaux vineyards, and he spent a week at Michel Guérard's Les Prés d'Eugénie in Eugénie-les-Bains. Especially interesting is the final chapter, "The Guided Stomach," which is about Michelin's Red Guide. I presume readers are aware that the awarding (or loss) of Michelin stars is taken quite seriously in France. As Mayle notes, "What has always struck me about these annual dramas, which are widely reported in France, is that, in the most important sense, the decisions made by the guide are accepted. People may disagree—in fact, as it is France and as it concerns the stomach, they invariably *do* disagree—about a star being given or taken away. But I have never known anyone to accuse the guide of unfairness or bias. It is trusted. I find this remarkable in a world where corruption is constantly being uncovered and is now more or less taken for granted in every activity from politics to bicycle racing." Best of all for travelers, the final chapter, "Last Course," is a list of all the fairs, festivals, restaurants, and places detailed previously, with contact information for each.

Glorious French Food: A Fresh Approach to French Classics, James Peterson, John Wiley & Sons, 2002. I have been a big fan of Peterson's *Essentials of Cooking* (Artisan, 2000), so when I learned of this book I had a feeling it would be a winner, and it is. Peterson writes that "friends and colleagues seem perplexed when I tell them I've written a book about French cooking. They're gentle and discreet, and instead of just coming out with, 'Why yet another book about French food?' they ask how my book differs from other books about French cooking and why I would put so much energy into such a thing. The more chauvinistic among them imply that I'm wasting my time, since cooking in America is now better and more inventive than cooking in France and French cuisine is too rich, complicated, expensive, and pretentious. These are the same people who tell me that California wines are the best in the world and who react to any contrary statement with annoyance. I write about French food not because I think it's intrinsically better than food anywhere else in the world, but for reasons that have to do with more than just how food tastes. We all have the French to thank for encouraging a culture that takes a more than hedonistic interest in eating and drinking." I would not classify this as a book for beginners, but one of Peterson's best qualities is that he instructs and explains so thoroughly that even enthusiastic novices will have success with his recipes.

A Goose in Toulouse and Other Culinary Adventures in France, Mort Rosenblum, Hyperion, 2000. Like Rosenblum's *Olives,* this wonderful book is also a *de rigueur* read. I thumbed through *Roget's Thesaurus* for some time trying to select at least one adjective to describe this work accurately but gave up when I reread an endorsement on the back cover by Paul Theroux, who refers to it as a "banquet." A number of chapters focus on aspects of the Southwest: "Roquefort on the Run," "Another Roadside Attraction," "Battle of Bordeaux," and "A Goose in Toulouse." It is *de rigueur* because it is also about larger issues than food. To share only one quotable passage from the first chapter: "Globalization has a distinct American accent, but to the French, the U.S. model is no answer. They are troubled by America's income disparities and lack of a social safety net. They worry when French kids kill people, or themselves, in the name of imported American cults. *Le drive-by,* for a gang shooting, is not only a new French word but also an occasional reality. French society works. City streets are safe at night. Villagers take pride in their old stones and fresh flowers, preserving traditions for themselves rather than the tourist trade. It is not for nothing, Frenchmen of a certain age assure themselves, that an old German metaphor denoting profound well-being manages to remain fresh: 'Happy as a god in France.'"

Great Pies and Tarts, Carole Walter, Clarkson Potter, 1998. This thick volume is a very good overall baking book with many flawless recipes for open fruit tarts, French fruit tarts with pastry cream, and the like.

Larousse Gastronomique: The World's Greatest Culinary Encyclopedia, Clarkson Potter, 2001. The ne plus ultra of encyclopedias but also a cookbook, with four thousand recipes. With the exception of fiddleheads and ramps, absolutely everything I've consulted this gigantic book for I've found. The endorsements on the back cover are enough to convince any culinary enthusiast to drop $75 on this 1350-page tome; but for me it was the discovery that my husband's cousin, Amy K., who attended cooking school and was later employed at a restaurant in Paris, owned only two or three cookbooks in addition to a well-thumbed copy of *Larousse Gastronomique.* She told me that it's nice and even useful to peruse and consult cookbooks, but that a kitchen without *Larousse* is incomplete.

Martha Stewart's Pies and Tarts, Clarkson Potter, 1985. Nearly all the recipes in this very good book are in the French style. I've made every recipe but two; this volume is really the one that helped me become an accomplished baker.

Mastering the Art of French Cooking, vol. 1, Julia Child, Louisette Bertholle, and Simone Beck, Knopf, 1961; vol. 2, Julia Child and Simone Beck, 1970.

M.F.K. Fisher, Julia Child, and Alice Waters: Celebrating the Pleasures of the Table, Joan Reardon, Harmony Books, 1994. Although this book is a tribute to three women who changed the way Americans think about food and cooking, it is also about the common thread that inspired and united them: France and *la cuisine française.* I found it absolutely fascinating, and I was surprised to learn the degree to which they were pioneers in the food world. It's no exag-

geration to state that the Food Network exists and thrives today because of
Julia Child's PBS television series; that cookbooks and food publications are
more popular than ever because of M. F. K. Fisher's passionate writing on gastronomy; and we have more farmers' markets across the country (twenty-eight
in New York City alone!) due to Alice Waters's insistence upon fresh, seasonal
food. *De rigueur* for anyone interested in food, France, and America.

The Pie and Pastry Bible, Rose Levy Beranbaum, Scribner, 1998. Though this
  book is a definitive volume on pies and pastries of *all* types, it contains many
  recipes for French and French-style creations. (Beranbaum is also the author of
  A Passion for Chocolate, featuring fabulous—and rather challenging—recipes
  from the famous Bernachon *chocolatier* in Lyon.)

The Soups of France, Lois Anne Rothert, photographs by Don Smith, Chronicle
  Books, 2002. Of the many refined and delicious creations of French kitchens,
  both in the home and at restaurants, soup holds a special place I think, revered
  by peasants and aristocrats alike. Certainly for me, when I think of French cuisine, the first course I think of is always soup. This might have something to
  do with the fact that when I first arrived in Paris as a student, my adopted
  French family picked me up and took me to their home in the rue de Grenelle
  and served me dinner: a big bowl of the most yummy and satisfying spinach
  soup, accompanied by a baguette, salad, and a glass of wine. So it seems a
  cookbook devoted to French soups is overdue, and very welcome. From the
  Southwest, there are twenty recipes from Bordeaux, the Dordogne, le Pays
  Basque, and Languedoc. Rothert also provides an interesting note about *garbure,* one of the best-known French regional soups outside of France. "Cooks
  on the farms of Béarn and Gascony insist on a few 'musts': the indispensable
  ham bone with some small amount of ham still attached (*trébuc*), a morsel (at
  least) of preserved duck or goose (confit), hunks of country bread, and an
  abundance of seasonal vegetables." She adds that "many French writers refer
  to the large Southwestern corner of France, which includes the old provinces
  of Gascony, Béarn, Auvergne, Languedoc, Rouergue, Roussillon, and the
  Basque Country as the Occitane. *Garbure* is typical of that entire region, where
  many people lived year in and year out at a poverty level, often too poor to own
  simple soup porringers, even though soup was the foundation of their cuisine.
  Consequently, many families built tabletops of thick walnut slabs (walnut trees
  were plentiful!) into which they carved a shallow bow, *un creux dan le bois*
  (hollow in the wood), for each member of the family. Often their soup spoons
  were made of wood as well. Many regional museums exhibit these poignant
  glimpses of another time." This is a very soul-satisfying cookbook; however, I
  remain puzzled why the publisher felt a book about soups could sustain a $50
  price tag. Perhaps I am off the mark; the book is large, printed on fine quality
  paper and is filled with color photographs. But after all, the author notes that

"two additional pleasures of preparing a batch of soup are its inherent frugality and the healthful nature of its components. Both your body and your checking account will feel restored."

The Taste of France, Robert Freson, Stewart, Tabori & Chang, 1983. This is my most favorite overall French cookbook. Fabulous photographs by Freson (who also took the photos for *Patricia Wells at Home in Provence*) are paired with text by leading food writers including Anne Willan, Alan Davidson, Jill Norman, and Richard Olney.

La Varenne Pratique, Anne Willan, Dorling Kindersley, London, 1989; first published in the U.S. by Crown Publishers, 1990. Sometimes a cook just needs photographs, and this excellent volume has more than twenty-five hundred of them.

Basque Cuisine

The Basque Kitchen: Tempting Food from the Pyrenees, Gerald Hirigoyen with Cameron Hirigoyen, photographs by Chris Shorten, HarperCollins, 1999. Few Basque cookbooks are available in North America in English, so if you're eager to start cooking from one, this is it. The Basques, as you'll discover, have an enormous respect for food, equal to the French—"To know how to eat is enough" is an old Basque phrase. In addition to the full range of recipes, from appetizers and salads to sweets (and the ones I've tried are outstanding), the Hirigoyens also provide a "Notes on Ingredients" section, a culinary guide to the Basque Country, and mail-order sources for Basque foods and related items (most helpful).

The Basque Table: Passionate Home Cooking from One of Europe's Great Regional Cuisines, Teresa Barrenechea with Mary Goodbody, Harvard Common Press, 1998. Barrenechea is chef and owner of the widely acclaimed Marichu restaurants in New York City and the New York suburb of Bronxville, in Westchester County. Though I've never met Barrenechea personally, it seems to me that the adjective that best describes her is *passionate*— as in "passionate about Basque cooking and culture." In the introduction to this excellent cookbook, Barrenechea states that Basques believe their food is the best in the world. "After traveling all over Spain and abroad and falling in love with other cuisines, I have come to the conclusion that Basque cooking justly deserves its reputation as being among the best." Certainly anyone who has spent even a short time in the Basque Country, on either side of the Pyrenees, knows this to be true, and those who have not yet visited the region will quickly arrive at the same conclusion. "For Basques," Barrenechea continues, "food is a major topic of conversation—with the taxi driver, with fellow bus passengers, with friends lying on the beach. Listen to a conversation between Basques, and most likely you will hear what they had for dinner the previous night, what they will have for lunch that same day, or where you can get this or the other unusual ingredient. We Basques happily live for our next meal!" In addition to all the recipes for appetizers, first and main courses, and desserts, there is a section called "Basque basics"—my favorite—which offers fifteen basic sauces and flavorings that every good Basque cook worth his or her salt relies on "to turn a good meal into a spectacular one, a simple dish into a memorable one." A most inspiring cookbook.

Life and Food in the Basque Country, María José Sevilla, New Amsterdam Books, Lanham, Md., 1989. Though this book contains recipes, it is more a valuable history and testament to food traditions held sacred by the Basques. Chapters include "Market Day at Ordicia," "The Life of a Fisherman," and "The Gastronomic Societies." Of French-Basque cooking specifically, Sevilla says its main characteristic "is that it is an inland cuisine, relying on the fruits of the soil, with a bias towards dishes using meat, together with maize, the cereal which came to revolutionize the life of the Nation when it arrived from the Americas; these are the twin pillars on which depends its success. This is an obvious contrast to Spanish-Basque cuisine which, although it also incorporates inland dishes, is at its most characteristic when it creates delicious dishes using the fruits of the sea."

Southwestern French Cooking

Dordogne Gastronomique, Vicky Jones, foreword by Anne Willan, Conran Octopus, London, 1994. This excellent cookbook is one in the *Gastronomique* series developed by Conran Octopus and distributed by Abbeville Publishers in North America. Unfortunately, I recently learned it is out of print, as well as the others in the series; but as it's so good and one of the few books dedicated exclusively to the Dordogne (and to Bordeaux), I encourage readers to search for it in used-book shops and through used-book dealers. Each book in the series is hardcover and features loads of color photographs, recipes unique to each region, excellent accompanying text focusing on cuisine, history, and cultural traditions, and a most valuable visitor's guide at the back of each book, which includes restaurants, places of interest, specialty purveyors of the region, market schedules, and vineyard visits. This book is divided into sections featuring Périogord Noir, Périgord Blanc, Quercy, Bergerac and the River, and the Bordelais. Though I admit I use this book more for information than for cooking, I have made a few of the recipes, which turned out well.

The Cooking of Southwest France: A Collection of Traditional and New Recipes from France's Magnificent Rustic Cuisine and New Techniques to Lighten Hearty Dishes, Paula Wolfert, The Dial Press, Doubleday & Company, 1983.

To address the lengthy subtitle of this must-have book, Wolfert acknowledges one of the most important *trucs* she received from a French cooking teacher, André Guillot, who taught her that "there need be no incompatibility between great food and good health—that I have a responsibility toward my readers to think of their health as well as their delight—and that one *can* lower the quantity of fat in a dish without sacrificing any of its flavor." She continues in the introduction by stating, "The great cliché about the dishes of the South-West is that they are good but heavy and therefore not healthful. I disagree emphatically, and I have made a special effort in this book to include recipes that have been lightened. Please read what I have to say about 'fighting fat with fat' and about 'double degreasing' principles." Wolfert, one of my favorite food writers and cookbook authors, is nothing if not definitive, and this volume, like her brilliant book on the cooking of Morocco, is the definitive work on the cooking of the Southwest. She has divided this book up into chapters featuring specific types of food (such as soups, *pot-au-feu,* and *garbures;* light supper dishes; ducks, geese, and game; and so on) as well as one on basic preparations (stocks, sauce bases, bread) and—my favorite—"The Taste of the South-West" (including foie gras, truffles, Armagnac, *jambon de Bayonne,* walnuts from the Périgord, cheeses, and so on). About confits (from the French *confire,* to preserve), Wolfert relates that "'a Gascon will fall to his knees for a good confit' goes the saying." She explains that confits are simply preserved meats (duck, goose, pork, hen, wild birds, turkey, rabbit, or whatever) that have been salted, then cooked in and stored in fat. "But to preserve a meat is to make it into something quite different, to create an entirely new taste and texture. Confit is a phenomenon that really has no close counterpart in the rest of French cuisine. The nearest parallel I know is the Moroccan *khelea,* spiced dried beef or lamb that is cooked in and subsequently sealed in oil and rendered fat. I believe that the central culinary role of *confit* in far-flung areas of the French South-West is only one particularly telling clue to the importance of the North African influence throughout this part of France over many centuries." It's true that Wolfert offers many methods for lightening up some of these traditionally heavy recipes, though she notes an exception to *cassoulet,* "whose very essence is its richness and which, if lightened, would simply not be the same." I have actually made *cassoulet* without any pork or beef products—I used chicken sausage and goose fat—and I thought it was delicious and rich.

A Culinary Journey in Gascony: Recipes and Stories from My French Canal Boat, Kate Ratliffe, Ten Speed Press, 1995. Ratliffe writes in her introduction that for years, her answer to the question "Where are you and the boat?" was "Somewhere in Southwestern France. No one had ever heard of Castelnaudary, Agen, or Moissac. They thought that Toulouse was some artist's last name and Bordeaux was just a good red wine." In my experience, this is still true today, though less so. When I returned to the Southwest last year to revisit places and discover new ones, very few of my friends and colleagues were familiar with cities and towns other than Bordeaux, Toulouse, and Biarritz. They had most likely heard of the Dordogne region—though they couldn't name a single town within its boundaries—and some wine enthusiasts knew of Corbières (though they didn't recognize Languedoc-Roussillon), but Gascony? All the more reason this book, one of the few published in English devoted to the cuisine of Gascony, is somewhat *de rigueur* for anyone seeking to discover the region's specialties. I say "somewhat" because the book is the author's personal culinary journey: this is not a definitive tome of Gascony cuisine the way that Paula Wolfert's book (above) *is* the bible on Southwestern cooking. (I sometimes wish that Charles Neal's *Armagnac* (below) could somehow be bound with this volume, as the two titles together present a much fuller historical and gastronomic guide to this celebrated culinary region.) The canal boat referred to in the title is the *Julia Hoyt*, and readers may recall that this *péniche* is the very same boat referenced in "Insider's Gascony" by Nancy Harmon Jenkins in *Corners of the Midi-Pyrenees* (though Kate Ratliffe is now Kate Hill). The *Julia Hoyt*—which the author refers to as her "one-table restaurant and two-room hotel"—typically traverses eighty-eight kilometers, twenty-one locks, nineteen villages, and six courses along the Garonne. Ratliffe writes that she began learning about the cuisine of Southwest France in 1988, when she sailed into the Garonne River valley. "Since living here I've learned to cook and eat only by the seasons. Coming from California, a place where strawberries are available year-round and asparagus is cultivated for winter consumption, I had a lot to learn. Here, the farm to market system in place for over 700 years has taught me not to buy artichokes in September or look for lamb in August. Instead, we eat our weight in sweet round melons in July, juicy strawberries in May, and wait for wild mushrooms when they arrive with the game in autumn." I prefer her observations like this one more than I do the recipes, even though a number of local farmwives and chefs welcome her into their kitchens to teach her recipes and *trucs* (I have, however, thoroughly enjoyed her *barques de catalan, tarte de tomates matelot,* and *fromage en douce* over the years.) In 1991, Kate founded European Culinary Adventures, a land-based cook's tour of regional cuisine and culture, and she has also since opened the French Kitchen Cooking School at Camont, the two-hundred-year-old restored Gascon pigeonnier perched on the towpath near Agen. Readers interested in their own journeys on the *Julia Hoyt* or to participate in one of Kate's culinary schools may contact her at Long Village, 300 SW Second Avenue, Corvallis, Ore. 97333; 800-852-2625; phone and fax: 978-535-5738; www.juliahoyt.com. Reading this book, with its color photographs, maps, and reminiscences, is both an introduction and a souvenir of Gascony.

La Cuisine Secrète du Languedoc-Rousillon, André Soulier, Les Presses du Languedoc, 1997. While this cookbook is completely in French, it is wonderful to even find a cookbook specifically for the Languedoc-Rousillon region. It contains quite a bit of information in addition to the recipes and even includes wine choices to accompany the dishes.

Of Related Interest

The Cheese Plate, Max McCalman and David Gibbons, Clarkson Potter, 2002. I love *Cheese Primer* (see below) and couldn't really imagine a more perfect book about cheese; but when *The Cheese Plate* was published, I realized that *Cheese Primer* could, in fact, be complemented with a book that featured color photographs and even more information on creating cheese courses. McCalman is America's first *maître fromager* (cheese sommelier) and helped to create the successful cheese programs at the celebrated restaurants Picholine and Artisanal in New York. Though he is a nut for so many of the world's finest cheeses, McCalman has said of French cheeses that "without prejudice toward any other country, it must be stated that when it comes to cheese, France is King." A beautiful, practical book.

Cheese Primer, Steven Jenkins, Workman, 1996. Though not exclusively about French cheeses, cheeses from France figure large in this excellent cheese bible. Jenkins—the first American to be awarded France's Chevalier du Taste-Fromage—created and/or revitalized the cheese counters at such New York food emporiums as Dean & DeLuca and Fairway. In addition to presenting the cheeses of France and twelve other regions of the world, he explains how cheese is made, the basics of butterfat, and the seasons that are best for making and eating cheese. (Yes, most cheeses have a season, which is determined by pasturage—vegetation that cows, goats, and sheep have been eating at the time of milking.) For travelers, Jenkins provides the names of cheeses—many never exported—to try. This is the most comprehensive book on cheese I've ever seen. *De rigueur.*

The Joy of Coffee: The Essential Guide to Buying, Brewing, and Enjoying, Corby Kummer, Chapters Publishing (Houghton Mifflin), 1995. A comment I hear often from people who visit France, Spain, and Italy is that the coffee is so much better there. In my opinion it's not the coffee that's better but the quality of the dairy products used. Coffee, after all, doesn't grow in the Mediterranean, and roasters and vendors can buy excellent beans as easily as anybody else around the world. Anyway, if you're a coffee drinker, you can judge for yourself, and I've included this book here for those who want to know more about the elixir they love. Kummer, who is a well-known food journalist, covers coffee plantations, cupping, roasting, grinding, storage (the best place, if you drink it every day, is not in the freezer, as many people mistakenly believe), and brewing, plus separate chapters on espresso, caffeine versus decaf, and a country-by-country guide. There are also recipes for baked goods that pair particularly well with coffee. (I've made almost all of them and can vouch that they are especially yummy.)

French Restaurant and Food Guides

A word about guides that rate eating establishments: understand that they are all subjective, and that one should not be a slave to them. Ed Behr, in an article about Italy in his fall 1999 newsletter *The Art of Eating,* noted that the two most influential food guidebooks in Italy are *Espresso* and *Gambero Rosso Ristoranti d'Italia,* while the Michelin Guide effectively fills tables at establishments awarded the most stars. The Slow Food guides are used by those looking for more traditional places, but Behr found that the Italian guides are widely seen as corrupt, whereas Michelin is seen as having too obvious a French bias. Wine and food industry friends of Behr told him they rarely if ever follow the guidebooks because they don't agree with them; rather, they follow leads from people whose palates they trust. "There's no perfect way," Behr concluded. I couldn't agree more, which is why I emphasize the importance of trusting the authors not only of food guides but of hotel guides, too. I very much respect the guides I recommend here, but I typically follow the opinions of rather picky critics with exacting standards—I am not a fan of the popular single-city Zagat survey guides, for example, because they are compiled not by critics but by the general restaurant-going population, the majority of whom do not cook, read cookbooks, or travel and wouldn't know an authentic Southwestern dish if it hit them on the head. Behr has written that Zagat "has all the defects of democracy," and William Grimes, restaurant critic of *The New York Times,* has written about "the self-levitating phenomenon that I think of as the Zagat Effect, in which a restaurant, once it has achieved a top rating, continues to do so year after year, regardless of the quality of the food. Diners flock to it, Zagat guide in hand (either literally or metaphorically) and, convinced that they are eating at a top-flight establishment, cannot bring themselves to believe otherwise." Once I have determined that I trust a food or wine writer, I will happily follow his or her leads, knowing that I will eat and drink well if not always fabulously. It's true that places that appear repeatedly in numerous guides can sometimes slip in quality; but if you set out with an optimistic, not-too-beholden attitude, I think you'll agree with these critics' opinions and have some very excellent meals indeed (and hopefully discover some good places on your own that you'll share with me!).

The Food Lover's Guide to France, Patricia Wells, Workman, 1987. Although this book is over a dozen years old, I still highly recommend it. Many of the restaurants, *fromageries, charcuteries, boulangeries,* and shops selling *spécialités régionales* of the Southwest are not only still in business but thriving.

About Wine in General

Bacchus and Me: Adventures in the Wine Cellar, Jay McInerney, Lyons Press, 2000. You might, as I did, initially scoff at this work by McInerney, of *Bright Lights, Big City* fame. But whoever said fiction writers can't also write about wine, and knowledgeably? This book is actually a collection of columns that originally appeared in *House & Garden* (one appeared in *The New Yorker*), and though McInerney covers the wider world of wines, including sparkling and sweet, he notes that "Bordeaux was my first love as a wine drinker" and "I have more Bordeaux in my cellar than any other kind of wine." The collection includes five individual pieces on Bordeaux wines (including one titled "Bordeaux on a Budget," which is devoted to second labels of first-growth châteaus) and another on Sauternes, which features his oft-quoted line, "Not since Baudelaire smoked opium has corruption resulted in such beauty." There are also essays on what to drink with turkey and cheese, half bottles, food and wine combinations, and "Grape Nuts," a section of profiles on people who have influenced the oenology world. My favorite of these is "The Host," about Bruno Borie of Château Ducru Beaucaillou. McInerney asks Borie about the rosebushes that mark the end of each row of vines, a common sight in Bordeaux vineyards. (I personally took quite a few pictures of these vine-and-rosebush rows because I thought they were so pretty.) "There are three theories about that," Borie tells McInerney. "One is that the roses were like the canaries in the coal mines—early-warning systems for disease. Another theory is that they were planted so that the horses would know when to turn, at the end of each row." "And the third theory?" He smiles and takes a long drag. "Perhaps they're just there because they're beautiful," he says. "We have forgotten about gratuitous acts of beauty." Apparently, some of us haven't forgotten.

Great Wines Made Simple: Straight Talk from a Master Sommelier, Andrea Immer, Broadway Books, 2000. In 1997 Immer, one of only nine women in the world to qualify as a master sommelier, was named Best Sommelier in America. This book features wines from Bordeaux frequently, those from the greater Southwest much less so, but it is an essential volume nonetheless. A great companion volume is Immer's *Great Tastes Made Simple* (Broadway Books, 2002), where she concentrates on matching food and wine and provides recipes and explanations for why certain wines pair so well with certain types of food. Chapters cover peak-fresh food, earthy flavors, smoky and meaty, acidic accents, sweet, spicy, and hot, cheese, desserts, and classic matches. She also provides some mail-order sources if you have trouble finding some of the specialty food items she recommends. If you would like to receive her monthly *Great Tastes* newsletter, join her *Buying Guide* tasting panel, or share your food and wine experiences, log on to Immer's Web site, www. greatwinemadesimple.com. Most important, Immer asks, "Can wine make food even better? It stands to reason, because we know that the Europeans, justly famous for their eating and drinking lifestyle, have been enjoying wine with their meals—daily, not just on special occasions—for millennia. And we're talking lunch *and* dinner. I think every food lover and wine drinker yearns for a shot at those frequent flavor and pleasure possibilities. I also think that most of us feel stymied by one or more of these obvious hurdles: wine confusion, cost concerns, and, most frustrating of all, the rules." Immer rightly points out that drinking wine with meals represents a conscious choice on the part of the diner to spend more than he or she would on an alternative beverage, such as beer, milk, soda, iced tea, water, whatever. And though many diners (myself included) have decided that the extra expense is worth it, "still, the cost consideration is a real incentive for anyone to want to increase his or her odds of pairing success, and I've found that is true regardless of budget. Working in luxury hotels and restaurants, I've waited on my share of moneyed moguls, tycoons, and trust-fund types. They want good deals, too, *especially* if they're trying something new to them, as is so often the case with wine. It's universal: everyone wants to feel he or she is getting his or her money's worth." Which is where Immer's *Wine Buying Guide for Everyone* (Broadway, 2002) comes in. For this refreshingly honest little guide (it's approximately the same shape as the Zagat guides), Immer surveyed wine professionals and ordinary consumers to identify the most popular and available wines on the market. The result is a compilation of more than four hundred top wines that are available around the United States in stores and restaurants. No vintage bottles are listed; these are current, ready-to-drink wines. (An Immer insight: "Ninety-five percent of the quality wines on the market are meant to be consumed within one to three years of the harvest [the vintage date on the label], while they are young, fresh, and in good condition. Most wines do not get better with age, so why wait?") I am an especially big fan of Immer's observation that the American wine publications lack "someone with a little authoritative perspective validating the average person's taste and budget." It seems to me that American vintners have collectively decided to ignore the concept of everyday wine and concentrate instead on wines that begin to be priced at $15–$20 a bottle. They clearly don't understand (or don't care to) that in order to create a nation of wine drinkers, the industry must continually raise new generations of wine drinkers. I mean no disrespect to American vintners; but this is an important concept and is essential to understanding much of the culture in France and elsewhere. Creating pricey boutique wines is an exciting, creative challenge for vintners, but in wine-drinking countries consumers drink wine every day, at least with one meal and more often with two. Wines, therefore, must be priced accordingly. Readers who have visited France previously (or Italy, Spain, or Portugal) may have noticed that the vast majority of wines available for sale—whether at a *supermarché* or in a small specialty shop—are priced under ten dollars, many under five. At bars, a glass of wine is priced between one and four dollars, and even at many restaurants a good bottle of wine costs about ten dollars. People who live amid vineyards simply take a plastic jug to a vintner and have it filled with the local red or white. When my brother and sister-in-law visited Provence, they enjoyed a red wine one evening at an inn where they were staying; when they asked about it, the *patron* told them it was from the vineyard down the road, so the next day they set out to buy a few bottles. The price? Three bucks a bottle. To this day they maintain it was among the best table wines they've ever had. While it's possible to find a few American wines under ten dollars a bottle, I personally have found them undrinkable. (You know the kind—they give you a headache before you've finished one glass.) Dear readers, if you have found a favorite everyday American wine under ten dollars, please write and let me know about it; and if, like me, you haven't, be vocal and let the vintners of our nation know that we will support their efforts in making quality inexpensive wines that we can drink every day. Finally, read Immer's book for some great, affordable wine recommendations!

Michael Broadbent's Vintage Wine: Fifty Years of Tasting Three Centuries of Wine, Michael Broadbent, Harcourt, 2002. Broadbent, it may fairly be said, has had one of the most extraordinary careers in the world of wine. He "quite possibly knows more about fine, old wines than anyone else alive, and he writes about them with unparalleled expertise." Broadbent's two editions of *The Great Vintage Wine Book* are the definitive reference books on fine, rare, and old wines, and are considered the bible for collectors and wine traders. He has the distinctive honor of being one of only a handful of wine connoisseurs to be named a Chevalier de l'Ordre National du Merité by the French government. In this unique volume, which is decidedly not for wine novices, Broadbent provides his catalog of tasting notes for wines from almost everywhere in the wine-growing world. The section on red and white Bordeaux wines occupies a full 205 pages. Positively *de rigueur* for serious oenophiles.

Jancis Robinson's Wine Course, BBC Books, London, 1995.

Pairing Wine and Food: A Handbook for All Cuisines, Linda Johnson-Bell, Burford Books, 1999.

The Pleasures of Wine, Gerald Asher, Chronicle Books, 2002. Asher, who has been wine editor at *Gourmet* for over thirty years, writes warmly and wonderfully about wine and leaves readers with the notion that wine is much more than a beverage. As he notes in the introduction to this splendid collection, "wine, the thread that binds these essays together, is actually a prism. Through it we see the world—and ourselves—in a different light. If we pay attention, it gives us the measure of Spain's economy and tells us where the money that allowed Chile's first families to establish their prestigious nineteenth-century wine estates around Santiago came from. Just by tasting the wines we can grasp the difference between classical, rank-conscious Bordeaux and voluptuous, democratic Burgundy. We can read California history in the evolution of its wines, and take the pulse of the organic farming movement by noticing how grape growing is changing." I love this book, as well as Asher's *Vineyard Tales* (see below), simply for itself—I enjoy reading about wine, even if the wine being featured is one I've never even sipped. But I especially love this one for the nuggets of wisdom Asher sprinkles throughout, wisdom that emphasizes his enthusiasm for life and the people and things in it. He reminds us that novelist Iris Murdoch once said that the purpose of wine is to stimulate the flow of talk. "She urged against fine wine in favor of an indefinite supply of something cheaper. I take her point—the spirit of hospitality is better served by a pint of Beaujolais than an ounce of some rarity. But she may have missed an equally important truth: Within reason, the better the wine—and the food—the better the conversation." Southwestern wines featured in this anthology include Cahors, Château Margaux, Côtes de Castillon, and Armagnac.

Tasting Pleasure: Confessions of a Wine Lover, Jancis Robinson, Viking, 1997. The wines of Bordeaux are mentioned frequently throughout the book, and though wines of Languedoc-Roussillon aren't referred to as frequently, Robinson does reveal in one of the chapters that she and her family have, or at one time had, a house in Languedoc.

Vineyard Tales: Reflections on Wine, Gerald Asher, Chronicle Books, 1996. "Sauternes: The Sweet Life" and "Haut-Brion: A Most Particular Taste" are two chapters relating to the Southwest.

Wine People, Stephen Brook, The Vendome Press, 2001. I saw this lovely book one day while I was browsing at one of my most favorite bookstores, Rizzoli on 57th Street in Manhattan. I was surprised that I had not previously heard of it, and I was immediately smitten by its premise, a collection of forty portraits of individuals involved in all aspects of wine production and consumption. The profiles are not limited to proprietors and producers, but also include wine merchants and traders, wine writers, a collector, an auctioneer, and a sommelier. Brook is a contributing editor for *Decanter,* and is the author of a number of books, including *Sauternes and Other Sweet Wines of Bordeaux,* a book I'm sorry to say I have not yet read. He reminds us that "wine is more than a business; it is a culture that binds together the aristocrat and the peasant, the producer wedded to his soil and the sharp-eyed city merchant, the cautious grower and the extravagant consumer. It is a major source of conviviality. A raised glass can bring down, if only temporarily, national boundaries. Wine unites continuity and flux. It remains essentially the same product enjoyed on the slopes of the Caucasus Mountains and around the Mediterranean shores four thousand years ago and yet it is constantly evolving, steadily improving in overall quality and gradually shifting in style to meet the supposed tastes and expectations of consumers. That is what makes wine so fascinating a subject." Brook has aimed for diversity in this collection, though he admits that it proved impossible to include individuals from every single wine-growing region of the world. From the Southwest, Brook has chosen Alexandre de Lur-Saluces of Chateau d'Yquem; Corinne Mentzelopoulos and Paul Pontallier of Chateau Margaux; Jean-Michel Cazes of Lynch-Bages; and Claire Villars of the Taillan group of *négociants*. "The Critics" featured include Robert Parker and Jancis Robinson, and in the category of "Wine for Pleasure" is a profile of Noel Bajor, head sommelier at the Louis XV in Monaco, "which is about as good a job as any sommelier can hope to secure." It occurs to me that while this is a worthy read for wine enthusiasts, it would make a superb gift—with bottles of wine from the producers mentioned—for a special birthday, wedding, or any major cause for celebration.

The World Atlas of Wine, Hugh Johnson and Jancis Robinson, Mitchell Beazley, London, 2001. When this book was published, I bought it as a birthday gift for my brother-in-law, Gordon. It wasn't long after, however, that I wished I had bought a copy for myself as it is truly an absolute must-have volume. The previous four editions were authored only by Johnson, and were amazingly authoritative and excellent. But with the addition of Robinson, readers have the great fortune of a dream team of brilliant wine writers, and the book is now nothing less than astonishing. Twenty-eight pages are devoted to Bordeaux; four to the area bordered by the Dordogne and stretching to Toulouse; two to eastern Languedoc; two to western Languedoc; and two to Roussillon. I believe that even readers who are not interested in wine but love maps and geography will find this to be an engrossing volume. I waited a few months, but could hold out no longer and finally bought a copy of this stunning book for myself. I have since pored over it, getting lost in it again and again, and I think you will, too.

French and Southwestern Wines and Spirits

Alexis Lichine's Guide to the Wines and Vineyards of France, Alexis Lichine, Knopf, 1989, 4th edition. Lichine—former wine exporter, grower, and winemaker (Chateau Prieuré-Lichine), author, and all-around wine authority—

really knew how to bring wine to life. He notes early on in the book that "from time immemorial, the world's greatest wines have come from France. Though not large in size, for the diversity and quantity of wine it produces France could be a continent. . . . There is hardly a corner of the country that does not offer its own distinctive wines and cuisine, history and scenery, in almost equal measure." Even though this book is out of print (Lichine passed away in 1989, and Prieuré-Lichine was sold in 1999), it can still be found at some wine shops and bookstores. This is a book for both travelers and wine buyers, and the chapter on Bordeaux is excellent.

Armagnac: The Definitive Guide to France's Premier Brandy, Charles Neal, Flame Grape Press, San Francisco, 1998. My good friends Dan and Leslie introduced me to Charles Neal and his French wife, Nathalie, some years ago. At the time, Neal was already a published author (*Tape Delay: Confessions from the Eighties Underground* and *Sumac*), and he was working on the manuscript for *Armagnac*. Nathalie's parents, André and Simone Daubin (to whom the book is dedicated), were the founders of the highly regarded Chez Simone in Montréal du Gers (Chez Simone is most definitely worth a detour—though the elder duo retired in the mid-1990s, the restaurant is now in the capable hands of Nathalie's brother, Bernard, and his wife, Véronique. Nowadays, Chez Simone is known not only for the best rustic cuisine in the area but also offers some refined *plats* with Basque touches. It's mentioned often in guidebooks, both in France and abroad, and I believe it is arguably the best restaurant in the Gers, if not in all of Gascony. Telephone: (33.5/62.29.44.40). With the assistance of the Daubins, Neal was fortunate to be introduced to many Armagnac producers, as well as a host of other food and wine purveyors. Neal is also a wine and spirits importer who specializes in estate-bottled wines from appellations in Southwestern France. Readers may want to browse his Web site, www.charlesnealselections.com, to view what I feel is one of the most diverse and unique assortments of Southwestern libations available in North America (note, however, that Neal's definition of the Southwest does not include Languedoc-Roussillon, and he also offers cognac and calvados from Normandy; by law, Neal may only import and distribute wines and spirits to wholesalers, retailers, and restaurants, but he is able to direct you to shops in your locale that carry his wines). Returning to the specific spirit at hand, Armagnac, for those who do not know, "was France's first brandy. Because of its concentrated, complex aromas and tremendous length, it also remains first in the hearts of true connoisseurs. Armagnac's closest relative is cognac which, although often compared, is distinctly different, not only with regard to its soil type, climate, and grapes, but also its distillation procedures, aging methods and, of course, resultant taste . . . Armagnac and cognac, while both brandies, have about as much in common as Bordeaux has with Burgundy or Barolo has with Brunello." Though Neal devotes approximately 176 very detailed pages to Armagnac producers, for me the most informative and fascinating part of the book are the sections that appear first, addressing the customs and character of the Armagnacais, Gascons throughout history, grapes, barrels, distillation, caramel, and notes on Armagnac today. The producers section is, however, a great resource for travelers as many producers do not export their releases, and they're available only at the domaines. Neal reminds us that "France is often called the garden of Europe because every square mile is cultivated for a particular purpose. The reasons for these divisions stem back centuries when surveys proved that some areas were more suited to particular products than others. Henceforth, regions around France tend to have specific flavors due to the individual products grown within each one. This is of particular interest to the traveler who can, over the course of a week, enter numerous distinct areas and be spoiled by their highly original foods, wines, and spirits." Neal also notes that many people, some French included (although probably not anyone from Burgundy), consider Gascony to be the most important gastronomic region of France. "Certainly two of France's most important chefs— André Daguin, former owner of the restaurant at the Hotel de France in Auch and the first to serve *magret de canard* (duck breast) like a steak, and Landes native Alain Dutournier, chef and owner of Carré des Feuillants in Paris, have their roots in the Armagnac region. Michel Guérard, although not a native, owns the culinary mecca Les Prés d'Eugénie in Les Landes and has made Gascony his adopted home." Whether you've tried Armagnac before or not, whether you're interested in learning about it or not, this book is one-of-a-kind and about much more than an elixir—it's one of the few books devoted to the entire region of Gascony, and is a *de rigueur* read.

Hachette Atlas of French Wines & Vineyards, edited by Pascal Ribéreau-Gayon, with the collaboration of the Institut National des Appellations d'Origine, foreword by Robert Parker, Hachette, 2000; distributed in the United States by Sterling Publishing Co. Perhaps nothing further need be said about the merits of this book than the following endorsement by Robert Parker: "France has long been the world's standard-bearer for wine quality. Not a single producer of wine from anywhere else in the world would offer his or her product without first measuring it against the yardstick established by French viticulture. This comprehensive book splendidly chronicles and describes the wines of France. It is to be applauded loudly by anyone with a fondness for that country's diverse and dynamic viticulture." Though I believe *Larousse's Wines and Vineyards of France* (below) is a more definitive book, this volume has been published more recently, and features more contemporary issues and methods (the contribution by the INAO, that appears in the front of the book, is also outstanding). Like the *World Atlas of Wine,* this is a book to get lost in, happily.

Languedoc Roussillon: The Wines & Winemakers, Paul Strang, photographs by Jason Shenai, Mitchell Beazley, London, 2002. Strang is recognized as one of the leading experts on the wines of the South of France, where he has lived for many years. Strang's first, and excellent, book (*Wines of Southwest France*) is detailed below; his second, *Take 5000 Eggs,* a book on the markets of Southern France, I have not yet seen (I believe it, too, was published in Great Britain), but I would wager that if you see a copy you should make off with it. This volume is noteworthy not only because of its esteemed author but because it is the only illustrated book devoted entirely to the Languedoc-Roussillon region. As Strang notes, "Languedoc-Roussillon is the largest vineyard in the world, its production exceeding that of Australia or Bordeaux." Even the late Alexis Lichine wrote that "the Languedoc-Roussillon vineyards are to wine what the Middle East is to oil." Strang presents individual chapters on each of the most important wine-producing areas in the region, including Minervois, Corbières and Fitou, Banyuls and Collioure, and Costière de Nîmes.

Larousse Wines and Vineyards of France, Arcade Publishing, Little, Brown and Company, 1991. Both a dictionary and an encyclopedia, this tome (640 pages) is, in my opinion, the best single volume on French wine-growing areas. It's sadly out of print, but this comprehensive work covers every topic relevant to French wine and was written by sixty-eight authors, each one a specialist in his or her chosen area of expertise. You will still find it a trusty authority whenever you refer to it.

Wines of Southwest France, Paul Strang, Kyle Cathie, London, 1996. Only a handful of authors have attempted to write books about Southwestern French wines that do *not* include Bordeaux. Strang offers a full discourse on the process of winemaking and the history of the industry in the lesser-known wine-growing areas of the Southwest. His commentary is very informed, yet the narrative reads almost like a travelog, and the reader quickly detects that Strand is passionate about his subject.

FONDATION BEMBERG

LA RONDE JOYEUSE
MANEGE ENFANTIN
Dir.: R. SANCERNI
BON POUR 1 TOUR
Ticket non remboursable

Auberge Occitane

Good Things,
Favorite Places

"French people spend a lifetime leisurely combing their country, documenting yesterdays, carving out a private world where warmth and comfort are integrated in their own way. Without fail, a passion for France and a love of family and one another guide them."
> —Betty Lou Phillips, *French by Design*

Restorative Powers: The French Heritage Society Turns Twenty

BY TRACY KENDRICK

∽

I introduced the French Heritage Society in the *Practical Information* section, and here's a piece—published in 2002, on the occasion of FHS's twentieth anniversary—that explains the very good works that these good *amis de France* accomplish.

TRACY KENDRICK is an editor of *FRANCE Magazine,* where this piece first appeared.

Visiting the châteaus of the Loire Valley, it is easy to conjure up images of aristocratic life in pre-Revolutionary France. But how often does one actually have a chance to sample that lifestyle? Such an opportunity recently presented itself to members of the French Heritage Society (FHS), which celebrates its twentieth anniversary this year. To mark the occasion, the group organized a series of Loire Valley tours for its members. FHS prides itself on being able to open doors ordinarily closed to the public; accordingly, participants enjoyed access to private homes, gardens, wine cellars, and art collections. The highlight of the celebration was a day-long marathon of activities: artisan demonstrations, an elaborate *déjeuner sur l'herbe* in the celebrated gardens of the Château de Villandry, and a formal dinner and ball at the Château de Chenonceau, complete with horsedrawn carriages, heralds, and midnight fireworks.

There was serious business behind all this pleasure: raising funds for FHS's preservation projects in France and the United States. FHS started out as an offshoot of Vieilles Maisons

Françaises (VMF), one of the first French organizations devoted to protecting privately owned historic buildings. An American women's group in Paris took an interest in VMF, eventually leading to the creation of the New York–based Friends of Vieilles Maisons Françaises (FVMF). Unfortunately, the name proved to be somewhat of a handicap; not only difficult for Americans to pronounce, it had no resonance for them. "When I made a presentation," remarks Executive Director Jane Bernbach, "I'd spend vital minutes explaining where our name came from instead of telling people about our projects."

Furthermore, in the mid-1990s, FVMF began turning its attention stateside. "America's French heritage is very widespread, thanks to groups as diverse as Huguenots and trappers," Bernbach remarks. "It stretches not only down from Canada, but up from Louisiana, and there's a whole lot of it in the middle as well. Nevertheless it has received little attention, except in small pockets. We want to change that."

In an effort to improve its chances of success, FVMF officially became the French Heritage Society at the beginning of this year. Besides being user-friendly for Americans, the new name makes it easier for the organization to broaden its sphere of activities; this past January, for example, it signed an agreement to be the sole U.S. fundraiser not only for VMF but also for two other major preservation groups in France: the Demeure Historique and the Comité des Parcs et Jardins.

FHS, which currently has some two thousand members in sixteen chapters—fifteen throughout the United States and one in Paris—is clearly poised for expansion. Thus far it has raised more than $8 million (including matching funds) for projects on both sides of the Atlantic. For its twentieth anniversary, it has set an ambitious goal of raising $1 million to finance twenty new projects—fourteen in France and six in this country.

In order to receive a grant, a project must meet certain criteria. As well as representing French culture in some way, it must be both landmarked and open to the public. Furthermore, matching funds—from a government entity or some other source—must be available. A committee of French and American preservation experts reviews each proposal; some forty were submitted for the six U.S. slots available this year.

Among those to make the cut were the eighteenth-century French bread ovens at Fort Ticonderoga in New York, the only extant structure of its kind in this country, and several structures in Sainte Genevieve, Missouri, a town founded by French settlers in 1735. One of the most high-profile projects in France will be the restoration of a thirteenth-century stained-glass window at Chartres cathedral. Located a vertiginous three hundred feet above the choir, the window depicts scenes from Mary's life. The panes need to be removed, cleaned, and glued back together in places where they had broken while being dismantled for safekeeping during the two world wars. The price tag: about $180,000.

While preservation is FHS's raison d'être, the group is also involved in a variety of complementary activities with a more human emphasis. Its chapters host events ranging from wine tastings to private viewings of works of art recently acquired by local museums. For those looking to go farther afield, FHS organizes annual tours in France. This year's were especially elaborate, but all trips offer access to privately owned, architecturally and historically significant homes.

One of the group's goals for the future is to put its contacts and experience to use in the corporate world. "We can help businesses establish connections—both social and cultural—at a high level," explains Bernbach. "I'm not talking about incentive trips—that's not what we do. And we're not going to set up a convention center in someone's private château. But when an American company is establishing itself in France, it's good if they can become part of the local community, and they often need help doing that. We're also trying to encourage them to give grants in a specific region where they have, say, a factory so that they become associated with preservation."

Most important, however, is passing on the preservation torch through education. An FHS exchange program enables French and American students—usually undergraduates—to spend three weeks learning about restoration, landscape architecture, or the decorative arts in a landmarked building. While staying in a château with a French family, an American student might help replant a garden or catalog a library.

For the more initiated, FHS offers annual week-long seminars in France on subjects such as Romanesque architecture in Provence, eighteenth-century townhouses in Bordeaux, or Art Nouveau in Nancy. Next year's topic will be Louis XV architecture in the Ile-de-France. Though similar to member tours in that they include visits to private collections and gardens, the seminars are open only to individuals—curators, private collectors, professors—with some expertise in the relevant field.

Finally, there is the Richard Morris Hunt Fellowship, cosponsored by the American Institute of Architects. Named after the first American architect to study at the Ecole des Beaux-Arts in Paris, the six-month work/study program is open to French and American architects pursuing a career in historic preservation. The 2001 fellow, American Raymond Plumey, was whisked around to no fewer than 135 preservation sites throughout France. "I worked for about half a dozen architects and the Ministry of Culture," he explains. "I'd be assigned to a certain office for a period of two weeks, and the chief architect would take me to see different projects. I'd attend meetings and talk to contractors and then document everything I saw." He hopes to use what he learned to further a mission close to his own heart: safeguarding the history of East Harlem.

Perhaps the best example of FHS's dual goal of preservation and education is Laura, a Creole plantation in Vacherie, Louisiana. Built by a French family in 1805, it was reopened in 1994 after lying abandoned for nearly a decade. FHS helped re-create the plantation's garden according to its original design and assisted the current owners in tracking down artifacts and memorabilia in France. The group also sends a student to Laura every summer to work as a tour guide or research the plantation's history.

Last year that student helped translate the memoirs of Laura Locoul Gore, for whom the plantation was named. The document became the basis for the book *Memories of the Old Plantation Home,* which spans two hundred years in the life of the property, from its founding to the treatment of slaves to attacks by Yankee gunboats during the Civil War. A model of successful restoration, Laura has become one of the most popular tourist attractions in the area.

Good Things, Favorite Places

Granted, it's quite personal, but this is my list—in no particular order and subject to change on any day of the week—of some favorite things to see, do, and buy in Southwestern France. Singling out "bests" and "favorites" inevitably means that something I very much like will be forgotten—which is why I emphasize that this is by no means a definitive list; rather, these are some wonderful things that I am happy to share with you here in the hope that you might also enjoy them, and that you will reciprocate by sharing your discoveries with me.

A word about shopping: I am not much into acquiring things, so as a general rule shopping is not one of my favorite pastimes; but I do enjoy buying gifts for other people, especially when I'm traveling. To borrow a quote from a great little book called *The Fearless Shopper: How to Get the Best Deals on the Planet* (Kathy Borrus, Travelers Tales, 2000), shopping is "about exploring culture and preserving memory—the sights, sounds, smells, tastes, tempo, and touch of a place." Most of what I purchase, therefore—even for myself—falls into the culinary category, because for me, food and drink are inextricably linked to a place. Food and drink can be extended, of course, to tabletop items such as pottery, for which I have a particular weakness. Though inferior ingredients and carelessly prepared food can never be masked by a beautifully set table, to me a delicious meal is even better when it is served in vessels, on dishes, and with utensils unique to its origins. Every time I open the little glass jar of *confiture des figues,* the tins of anchovies and foie gras, or the container of *piments d'Espelette* in my pantry, I am instantly transported back to the shops where I bought them, and I remember as if it were yesterday all the delicious meals I had across Southwestern France. Though almost anything one can buy today is available almost anywhere in the world, I believe you can't buy memories—each time I serve olives in the small ceramic bowl with a separate compartment for the pits, I think of the lovely seaside town of Collioure, where I found it; and when I set my table with the beautiful ceramic plates I bought in Anduze and St.-Quentin-la-Poterie, there is no doubt that, for an evening, my family and friends and I are in the Southwest. To quote again from Kathy Borrus, "I am surrounded—not by things but history and culture and memory." Even the *supermarchés* of France sell beautifully packaged items of yummy stuff that in the United States are either hard to find or expensive or both.

A word about stores: business hours being what they are in France, you might want to adopt my motto, "When in doubt, buy it now." I learned years ago that the likelihood of being able to retrace my steps to a particular merchant *when it was open* was slim. If you spy a yummy treat or savory in the window of a pâtisserie or charcuterie, or some local pottery, a painting, a bottle of hard-to-find-at-home Bordeaux or Corbières wine, or *anything* that has your name all over it, *allez* (go) and get it, for Pierre's sake. One has regrets only for the roads not taken, or in this case the object not purchased! It bears repeating that some shops do not open until the afternoon on Monday, and nearly all retail businesses are closed entirely on Sunday. Saturday is the tricky day of the week: some stores are open only until lunchtime, not to reopen again until Monday. During the summer months many establishments will close for a longer period during the afternoon and stay open later in the evening.

Aquitaine and Bordeaux

~Arcachon, the Bassin d'Arcachon, and Cap Ferret, along the Atlantic coast just southwest of Bordeaux. Arcachon itself, a popular seaside resort notable (justly) for its oysters, is extremely pleasant, especially the boulevard de la Mer; but don't miss the excursions out to Cap Ferret (stopping in at the chapel of the Algerian villa) and the Dune du Pilat. (The Atlantic Coast edition of the Michelin Green Guide—featuring Poitou, Aquitaine, and the Basque Country—plots out a nice, reliable route to both.)

~Canelés, especially those from Baillardran in Bordeaux. Canelés, are little gâteaux (cakes) that are caramelized and a little tough, almost rubbery, on the outside and almost meltingly soft and airy inside. These delicious, unique treats, a specialty of Bordeaux, are named after the corrugated ridges—canelé means "corrugated"—of the copper molds in which they're baked. Canelés are rather difficult to describe accurately, but they represent one more model of something simple, sophisticated, and subtle that the French do so well. Canelés are not overly sweet, and they're very dense, with a delicate flavor (ensuring they will never be popular in the States). I would simply say to you that you really must try one, or some, and though you'll find canelés on breakfast tables and in pâtisseries across the Southwest, they are at their best in Bordeaux. Baillardran is widely regarded as making the best canelés, and happily there are a number of other locations in the city (I think as many as eleven) and conveniently at Bordeaux's Mérignac airport (halls A and B) and at the Gare St.-Jean (departures hall), so you don't even have to make a special trip to try them. Most visitors will probably discover Baillardran at its premier location, in the Galerie des Grands Hommes (in the Grands Hommes quartier, 33.5/56.79.89; to learn of Baillardran's other Bordeaux boutiques, visit its Web site, www.baillardran.com). Baillardran bakes three types of canelé: tendre, croustillant, and croquant, the differences among them being that each is baked longer—croquant is the most bien cuit and nearly crunchy on the outside. The very best thing of all is that you can buy the copper molds (I bought a set of ten), and Bailladran provides a copy of the recipe, in English (the recipe makes enough batter for ten individual *canelés*.) Note, however, that the baking temperature given refers to the British equivalent.

~Musée d'Aquitaine, Bordeaux. I am a big fan of good ethnographic and history museums, and the Musée d'Aquitaine is among the best. Tracing the life of Aquitaine Man from prehistoric times to the present day, the permanent collection is displayed on three levels and includes sections devoted to prehistory, Egypt and the Mediterranean, Gallo-Roman treasures, the Middle Ages, the South Pacific, and Africa. As interesting and well presented as these are, however, the real reason to visit the museum is the exhibits relating to Aquitaine in general (including Béarn, the Landes of Gascony, the Gironde and its vineyards, and Arcachon and its oyster farming) and the city of Bordeaux in particular. The museum is located at 20 cours Pasteur, 33.5/56.01.51.00; fax .56.44.24.36; www.mairie-bordeaux.fr.

~La Vinothèque de Bordeaux. There are many, many shops devoted to wine in Bordeaux, and I have been welcomed at those I've visited and have enjoyed my time browsing in all of them. But while many shops are clearly intended for international buyers quite knowledgeable about Bordeaux wines, La Vinothèque, a family business since 1922, is my favorite for learning about Bordeaux. Perhaps, on the two occasions I visited, the staff was in a particularly helpful and happy mood; my questions were patiently and enthusiastically answered. The staff members I met all spoke English quite well, and it helped that the large store stocks such a thorough selection of Bordeaux. They seemed genuinely interested to learn of the wine châteaus I planned to visit, shared their opinions of them, and offered suggestions of places to eat and visit nearby. La Vinothèque also offers a good selection of beautiful corkscrews, and wines are shipped worldwide. The attractive shop is located on the same block as the tourist office at 8 cours du 30 Juillet, 33.5/56.52.32.05; fax .56.51.23.46.

~Le Bar du Port de la Lune, Bordeaux. Port de la Lune (Moon Port) is so named because it flanks a crescent formed by the river. (This crescent shape also inspired the Bordeaux coat of arms.) This is where many of the cruise boats and wine excursion steamers dock, and it's become a hip nighttime spot for a mostly thirty- or fortysomething crowd. Le Bar in particular is a jazz spot, but there are also a theater and a few other watering holes/restaurants in this neighborhood across from the old abattoirs (slaughterhouses). The music's great and the prices are decent, and though it's known among tourists, it doesn't have that tourist feel at all. Le Bar is open seven days a week until two in the morning and is located at 59 quai de Paludate, 33.5/56.49.15.55.

~Musée des Arts Decoratifs, Bordeaux, is a memorably beautiful museum built by Bordeaux architect Etienne Laclotte for the marquis de Lalande. The museum is in an eighteenth-century town mansion and features outstanding collections of furniture, ceramics, glass, wrought iron work, and silver and goldsmith art. The history of the eighteenth century is presented in the collection of royalist souvenirs from the Jeanvrot collection. Even if the decorative arts are not your thing, I still recommend a visit, if only for the opportunity to walk around the former mansion. Few of us have friends, family, or connections that would grant us permission to visit the splendid private mansions of Bordeaux; the Musée des Arts Decoratifs, located at 39 rue Bouffard, provides that opportunity.

~Cadiot-Badie, Bordeaux, is on a very short list of the most beautiful shops I've ever stepped inside in my life. It's an old-fashioned *chocolatier* and confectionery, founded in 1826, with beautifully painted and molded pastel walls and ceilings, and even if you are not a fan of sweets at all, at least take a peek inside its artfully arranged windows. Being an unabashed fan of fine chocolate, however, I did more than look in the windows—and parted with some money in the process. Though *all* of the chocolates I tasted were exceptional, the store's specialties include *bouchons bordelais* (individually wrapped chocolates in the shape of corks, sold individually or as gifts packed in a wooden basket) and *truffes de Bordeaux* (my favorite: devastatingly delicious little deep chocolate truffles blended with wine and rolled in sugar that is almost purple in color). There are many, many items that are beautifully and creatively packaged for gift giving, including some assortments in deluxe wooden boxes. And of course one may select as many *délices* as one wants in a small bag for nibbling throughout the day. Cadiot-Badie is located at 26 allées de Tourny, 33.5/56.44.24.22; www.cadiotbadie.com.

~Le Grand Théâtre, Bordeaux. The Michelin guide notes that this theater is "among the most beautiful in France," and it truly is. This might not necessarily be obvious when viewing the outside of the building, which has a neoclassical facade and twelve Corinthian-style columns. (Those twelve statues represent the nine muses and three goddesses, Juno, Venus, and Minerva.) It's impressive, but not nearly as much as the interior. Unfortunately, due to a full schedule of year-round performances, visitors are not permitted to wander around at whim—you must purchase a ticket at the tourist office for a guided tour. The tours are offered throughout the day and are in French only, but don't let this stop you: even if you can't understand a word, you'll feel fortunate to have seen this beautiful work of art. The theater was built between 1773 and 1780, and the *salle de spectacle* was restored in 1991 to its original blue and gold colors. The Grand Foyer is the work of Jean Burguet, with a lovely, cherub-filled ceiling painted by Adolphe-William Bouguereau. The staircase, which is a single flight of stairs that then divides into two flights on either side, is a design that was later copied by Charles Garnier when he designed the Paris Opéra. The tour is scheduled to last for about an hour (mine was about fifteen minutes longer because our group asked a lot of questions and the guide was happy to answer them), and visitors are led upstairs, down the back stairs, nearly everywhere in the building—it's one of the most worthwhile tours I've ever experienced, and there are several photo opportunities that would otherwise not be available. Le Grand Théâtre is located a short walk from the tourist office, on the place de la Comédie (where the allées de Tourny, the cours de l'Intendance, and the rue Sainte Catherine all meet).

~Bordeaux Découverte, an ongoing promotion offered by the office de tourisme de Bordeaux, is one of the best values I've encountered anywhere. It's a tourist package (for individuals, not groups) that includes two nights in a double room at a two-, three-, or four-star hotel; a two-hour guided tour of Bordeaux; a guided tour and tasting at a wine château; a pass that provides free access to main sites, monuments, and museums; a pass that provides three days of free city bus transportation; and a complimentary bottle of wine and a souvenir gift. The price of the package is dependent upon the hotel selection, and 2002 prices were 74 euros per person for a two-star hotel, 109 euros for a three-star, and 152 euros for a four-star. The thing is that, unlike the majority of other packages, the participating hotels are among the best in Bordeaux, including the Burdigala, Normandie, Majestic (my favorite), and Mercure Meriadeck. The tourist office staff request that travelers reserve the package of their choice ten days in advance, and readers may request a booking form and more details directly from the office's Bureau des Visites Guidées, 12 cours du XXX-Juillet, F-33080 Bordeaux cedex; www.bordeaux-tourisme.com.

~A glass of Lillet, anywhere in Bordeaux . . . and beyond. Lillet, for readers who may not know, is "the aperitif of Bordeaux since 1872." I find that there are still a fair number of people who've never tried Lillet, which is a shame as it's a delicious and refreshing drink. I credit my parents for my familiarity with it as they had Lillet in their liquor cabinet for years. Lillet was born in the small village of

Podensac, in the Graves vineyard area, not far from Sauternes and just a few miles from Bordeaux. A fellow named Jean de Lillet moved to Podensac from Saint-Morillon in 1680, and his descendants, Paul and Raymond Lillet, founded a fine wine, liqueur, and spirits shipping company—Lillet Frères—in 1872. Lillet the drink—which is available in both *blanc* and *rouge*—was created in 1887. Making Lillet takes about twelve months, and there is no standard recipe: grapes from the Bordeaux region's best vineyards (about 85 percent) are blended with fruit liqueur (about 15 percent) to create each cuvée. The fruit liqueur (made from fruit and fruit peels) is concocted by Lillet from sweet oranges from Spain, bitter oranges from Haiti, green oranges from Morocco and Tunisia, and cinchona bark from Peru. After all this is blended, Lillet is aged in oak barrels for an average of eight months. Lillet is very popular in Aquitaine, and appears on all the café menus of Bordeaux. I believe that if more people tried it, they would like it as much as I do. I prefer *blanc* best in warm weather, and the rouge during the cooler months, at both times of year served straight up with a slice of orange, lime, or lemon. Fortunately, Lillet is widely available in North America (it's imported by William Grant and Sons, 800-752-8970, www.GrantUSA.com), and is moderately priced. Lillet has created a brochure, in English, featuring a number of recipes for cocktails as well as some for fruit desserts, veal, and cooked foie gras (the peaches with Lillet *blanc* is really *délicieux!*). Browse the Lillet Web site (www.lillet.com) for more information, but better yet, buy a bottle, invite some guests over, and indulge in a Southwestern feast.

~Driving along a local *route du vin*, whichever one you choose. My only vineyard trip has been on the D2 to Pauillac in Haut-Médoc. I loved driving on the gently curving two-lane road, passing through the villages of honey-colored stone, and viewing the beautiful wine châteaux. Not every route looks the same, of course, but it's hard to imagine that any would disappoint.

~Hotel Majestic, Bordeaux. What a lovely hotel the Majestic is! I am anxious to visit Bordeaux again, and when I plan my trip, the first call I make will be to the Majestic. This three-star, forty-nine-room inn is steps away from the tourist office and the Grand Théâtre, and a few more steps away from the Esplanade des Quinconces and the Allées de Tourny, but is on a quiet street. The building itself is a formerly private eighteenth-century mansion and has many charming features, notably a beautiful and unusually shaped staircase. In 1843, Victor Hugo lived in the mansion, and either at the end of the nineteenth century or the beginning of the twentieth (the staff isn't quite sure), the mansion was transformed into a hotel under the name Grand Hôtel Metropole Excelsior. Later, just before the Second World War, it acquired the name of Majestic. Charles de Gaulle lived at the hotel in June 1940. The reception staff at the Majestic was remarkably warm and welcoming to me, my daughter, and my friend Amy, and they were all enthusiastic about their city and the nearby vineyards. One staff member in particular, a young fellow whose name I neglected to note (at the time I visited, he was the only male on the front desk staff, and I hope he's still there), was particularly knowledgeable about Bordeaux's history, especially during the years of the Second World War. The Majestic has a nice little lobby and breakfast room, as well as its own private parking garage. (There are two other garages close by, as well as an airport shuttle.) In addition to the guestrooms, which are individually decorated, there is one suite available at the Majestic. There are grander and more historic hotels in Bordeaux, but I can't imagine staying anywhere else, and I think you'll find the hotel to be an unbeatable value. Contact information: 2 rue de Condé, 33000 Bordeaux, 33.5/56.52.60.44; fax .56.79.26.70; www.hotel-majestic.com.

~La Belle Epoque, Bordeaux. Sometimes, even when you have read about a great number of restaurants and made a few reservations, you just want a recommendation from someone local, some-one you have a feeling you can trust. So it was with my discovery of La Belle Epoque brasserie, recommended by that young fount-of-knowledge fellow at the Majestic (mentioned just above). Not only did he immediately and enthusiastically recommend La Belle Epoque, it was literally a five-minute walk from the hotel. We arrived at that all-too-early hour of seven-thirty, but my four-year-old daughter couldn't wait any longer. We were clearly the first diners of the night—the restaurant staff was still eating their com-munal meal at a table near the door—but we were kindly ushered in and made to feel comfortable despite the hour. By nine o'clock there wasn't an empty table in the entire place, and we were the *only* tourists. Many of the customers knew the hostess and even other diners, and we enjoyed one of the most delicious and memorable meals of our lives. The kitchen specializes in *cuisine traditionelle bordelaise.* With our aperitifs (Kir Royale and Lillet), we shared lit-tle toasts spread with foie gras and duck pâté as well as bacon wrapped around prunes, then made room for *huitres,* quiche, a local fish roasted in a round terra-cotta dish with basil, leeks, and carrots, and a steak that we proclaimed "outstanding." La Belle Epoque is not at all trendy, and its cuisine is not adventurous, but each dish is made with care. The staff is very attentive without being annoying (the hostess is also exceptionally friendly to children), and the restaurant itself is charming and warm. (The main dining room is painted and decorated by someone named Viellard; I don't know anything about Viellard, but the room is lovely.) This is the kind of place I'd feel proud to introduce to out-of-town guests, yet it also has the feel of a neighborhood café. I am at a loss to explain why this wonderful find isn't mentioned in any of the guidebooks I used; but perhaps that explains why we were the only tourists. Note that the restaurant is also open on Sunday for both lunch and dinner. Contact information: quai Louis XVIII, 33.5/56.79.14.58.

~La Tupina (Basque for "cauldron") is referred to in many surveys of Bordeaux-area restaurants. Raves for the place, which Patricia Wells in the *International Herald Tribune* in 1994 referred to as "the second-best informal restaurant in the world," abound, and they're all true: secure a reservation in advance (if you don't want to make it yourself, ask someone on the staff of your hotel or inn to make one for you well before your arrival), or you will likely miss out on an unforgettable *bordelais* experience. (The room with the long table and pots and pans hanging from the ceiling and the big stone hearth behind it all is the kitchen of my dreams, and I'm willing to bet it will not fail to satisfy some of yours, too). For more descriptive information about La Tupina and chef Jean-Pierre Xiradakis, readers may want to track down a few good articles: "Bordeaux Superior" (*Saveur*, David Case, December 1999) and "The Flavors of Bordeaux Speak for Themselves" (*The New York Times*, R. W. Apple, August 28, 2002. In the *Saveur* piece, Case emphasizes that in the 1970s, when nouvelle cuisine was all the rage in France, Xiradakis began to worry that no one would care anymore about real cuisine. At that time he started seeking out culinary products that had nearly vanished from the Southwest. "You see," he noted in Case's article, "the threat is not simply about taste. It imperils greater social values. Throughout history, food—hunting, gathering, and preparing—has been humanity's prime occupation. There was a lot of work, but it brought people together, and even inspired celebration." Xiradakis has been a vocal advocate for embracing both traditional and contemporary methods in the pursuit of true, authentic flavors and the very best culinary raw materials, and he opines that "restaurateurs have an obligation to defend the traditions of their region." Contact information: 6 rue Porte-de-la-Monnaie, Bordeaux 33000; 33.5/56.91.56.37; fax 56.31.92.11; www.latupina.com. By the way, after seeing both Tupiña and Tupina on its Web site, I learned from the press relations office that originally, the restaurant did employ the Spanish tilde in its name, but that now it is officially omitted and is referred to as La Tupina.

Dordogne

~Walnuts rolled in cocoa powder, available throughout the Dordogne. Walnuts are a specialty of the region—be sure to try several varieties of walnut cake when you come across it at pâtisseries, outdoor fêtes, and restaurants—so it's not surprising to discover their pairing with chocolate. But it *is* perhaps surprising to discover that cocoa-covered walnuts are remarkably delicious, even sublime. Once I tried them, I made a point of buying a small bag whenever I spied some. Two shops stand out as a cut above the rest: R. Mertz (33.5/53.59.00.85), specialty chocolate shop in the rue de la Republique in Sarlat; and Le Gourmet Quercynois, a regional specialty shop in St.-Cirq-Lapopie. (None of the packages I have bear the store's phone number or precise address, but St.-Cirq is so small it would be impossible for one to miss this wonderful little emporium.) At the shop in Sarlat, not only were the cocoa-rolled walnuts excellent, but the other chocolate creations were superb as well. R. Mertz offers a large selection, including equally yummy chocolate disks with whole walnut pieces on top and a variety of attractively packaged chocolates wrapped especially for gift giving. The chocolate-nut creations at Le Gourmet Quercynois are packed in little gift bags and are called *chocolanoix*. In addition to these addictive bonbons (it is impossible to stop eating them once you begin), Le Gourmet Quercynois is also a good place to pick up tins of foie gras, nut oils, and lots of other *délices,* such as chocolate-covered and Sauternes-dipped raisins (described by my friend Amy as simply "Oh. My. God.").

~Godard shops, throughout the region. Godard (*specialiste du foie gras*) is the leading retail outlet for foie gras, pâté, and related specialties—such as dried truffles, mustards, and other condiments—of the Dordogne. You'll soon begin to recognize the Godard logo of a fat goose waddling along, as there are Godard shops in nearly every town. Another well-known purveyor of foie gras and related items is Rougié, whose products are found in fine *épiceries* as well as at its main store, Boutique Rougié, 5 rue des Consuls, Sarlat; 33.5/53.59.24.68. While I have encountered very few locals in Godard, I do think the stores are pleasant places to shop, and the quality of the products is quite good. I have purchased a number of gifts at Godard—including a particularly nice pack-aged set of three different patés and a Laguoile spreading knife—and have not been able to resist buying a few things for myself, and everything was excellent.

~Walnut oil, "all of the Périgord in a bottle," according to Paula Wolfert. You'll see it in shops and at village fêtes all over the Dordogne, but to me the best place to buy it is *à la ferme*—at fam-ily farms where you may sometimes be shown how the oil is pressed. Don't worry if you don't speak any French—there's only one rea-son why you'd turn down a farm's little lane, and it doesn't take much translating to purchase a bottle or two of oil. When you get it home, remember to store the oil in the refrigerator and to use it up within about three or four months—unfortunately, nut oils of any kind just don't have a long shelf life, but you'll enjoy every drop of it while you have it.

~The *bastide* of Domme, and especially the view out across the countryside from the terrace. When I visited, the village was cele-brating its annual Honneur à Notre Elu fête (read more about under "Festivals" in *Practical Information*), a festive weekend-long event with contests, music, carousel rides, and food, of course. The Esplanade, an inn bordering on the little *place* with the terrace, must have one of the most advantageous plots of land in the world. Though I have not stayed there, my good friends Luc and Lorraine have, and they had the same view from their room's window as visitors have from the terrace—reason alone to book in advance. Contact information for the Esplanade is 33.5/53.28.31.41/fax .53.28.49.92.

~Restaurant La Poivrière, Domme. Not as lovely as the Esplanade, La Poivrière remains a good restaurant to know about in Domme, serving well-prepared local specialties. The fairly extensive menu features enough fish, duck, meat, and salads to satisfy just about everyone, and there are a number of local wine selections. It's wise to reserve ahead, as tables on both floors can fill up fast, especially in summer. Contact information: place de la Halle; 33.5/53.28.32.52 (telephone and fax).

Languedoc-Roussillon

~Hugo Vermenlen studio, La Cité, Carcassonne. Among all the tourist shops in Carcassonne, this little studio of painter and graphic artist Vermenlen stands out for, well, not standing out. Vermenlen, originally from Holland, has made his home in Southwestern France for many years. Etching is his favorite medium, and hanging in the studio you'll see wonderfully detailed and fine views of Carcassonne. I bought one that was already framed, and it was a very good value at about forty dollars. Vermenlen is especially interested in townscapes, rural landscapes, animal pictures, allegories, and representations of mythological scenes. He has also been a tarotist for more than twenty-five years, and fans of these beautiful cards will find lovely sets in his studio, which is located a 8 rue St. Sernin.

~Domaine Grand Guilhem, Cascastel, Corbières. I learned of the wonderful, wonderful Grand Guilhem in an article that appeared in *Travel + Leisure*, and I can't stop talking about it. I am not bragging when I say that I have stayed at a great number of lodgings, and as readers of my other books know, I have enthused about most of them. But I not only enthuse about Grand Guilhem, I dream about it, for in this *gîte* I think I have finally found that perfect combination of style, comfort, and remoteness, qualities that are rarely found together. Admittedly, I have also stayed at a few places in Provence that nearly match Grand Guilhem, except that very few corners of Provence are still remote, and in fact most are downright chic. Cascastel is not chic. It's not even about-to-happen, which is the point. Gilles and Séverine Contrepois left Paris in December 1997 headed for a new adventure, a new life. They found Domaine Grand Guilhem and transformed it into a place so lovely and comfortable that it's hard to break away from the breakfast table each day (or the pool or the sitting area in the room named "Muscat"). But *les sites cathares* beckon, as do the dozens of Corbières vineyards and tasting rooms, the Pyrenees, la Côte Vermeille, Carcassonne, the abbey at Fontfroide . . . and Gilles and Séverine know everything about everything in the region and will happily assist you in planning your daily itineraries. Each of the six rooms at Grand Guilhem has a unique name and each is decorated differently in the warm colors of the South with classic but hip touches. The sitting room on the second floor is done up in a lovely Moroccan fashion and is a delightful spot to sit and read quietly. Unlike at other inns or hotels, no one room in particular is a cut above the others—each room is unique unto itself and has its special amenities. (The room I shared with my daughter, for example, was small and almost plain, but its adjoining bathroom-*cum*-sitting room was enormous and colorful; my friend Amy's room was quite large—big enough for four to six people—while the bathroom was nicely appointed but of an ordinary size.) As I noted, the village of Cascastel is refreshingly nondescript. The vines that the Contrepoix family inherited with the property have produced a few good, everyday drinking wines. Bottled under the label *Les Maîtres Vignerons de Cascastel,* one of the reds won a local award for excellence. Gilles told us he believed his wine would improve over the next few years, as will nearly all the wines from Corbières. Prices at Grand Guilhem are modest and an exceptionally good value. I am absolutely counting the days until I'm able to return. Contact information: Domaine Grand Guilhem, Séverine et Gilles Contrepois, 11360 Cascastel; 33.4/68.45.86.67; fax .68.45.29.58; www.thelin. net/gguilhem.

~Miellerie des Clauses (11200 Montséret; 33.4/68.43.30.17; fax .68.43.35.15), Corbières. I learned of this honey farm from Gilles and Séverine at Domaine Grand Guilhem. The honey served at the Grand Guilhem breakfast table is without doubt among the best I've ever tasted, and I think it is nearly in the same league as Greek honey, often reputed to be the best in the world. The flavored honeys are what stand out at Miellerie des Clauses: the *citron* variety makes me swoon and is unbelievably delicious stirred into plain yogurt; the *noisette* tastes almost like chocolate, it's so rich; and there are about a dozen others. I couldn't believe my good fortune to learn that I could actually visit the farm, buy the honey (and other related products, such as *pain d'épice* and the most wonderful soaps) direct, and see an actual honeycomb. (There's a large, glassed-in sample inside the barn/shop, with bees moving all about.) The drive to the *miellerie* is also an off-the-beaten-path treat. The farm is located off the D613, and the directions are simply to follow the signs for the *miellerie*. Unlikely as this may seem, you can't really get lost, as the signs do indeed lead you to the farm, even if it occasionally seems as if you're in the middle of nowhere (you are) and that you don't have any idea how to return to a main road. (It may be helpful to know that the *miellerie* is close to the Abbaye de Fontfroide.) The farm is open *tous les jours de l'année* (every day of the year), from eight A.M. to noon and again from two to six P.M. and is very much worth a detour.

~Auberge du Château Bonnafous, Villesèque les Corbières. Gilles and Séverine recommended this country inn for dinner one night, and it truly was wonderful. Madame and Monsieur Christophe Michel are the proprietors of this simple hotel-restaurant that is typical of so many unsung places in France. In other words, it may never get a mention in Michelin, but each day's menu is fresh, local, and seasonal—and delicious. Peter Mayle, in *French Lessons,* wrote of places just like Bonnafous when he opined that "they are not always the most fashionable of restaurants, nor are they the most eulogized by the guidebooks. But they have something about them that I—not to mention a few hundred thousand French customers—find irresistible. A very distinct character, the comforting feeling that you and your appetite couldn't possibly be in better hands." Bonnafous may not receive anywhere near a few hundred thousand French customers, but the locals know Bonnafous and love it, and believe it or not, it's a good idea to make a reservation (it's one of the few restaurants in this part of the Corbières), or there is a good chance you won't get a table. Bonnafous is open every day during the summer and is closed on Sunday night and Monday at other times of the year. Contact information: route de Durban, 11360 Villesèque Les Corbières; 33.4/68.45.88.20; fax .68.45.51.78.

~*Lucques olives vertes à l'ancienne.* Pronounced as if you're saying the French name *Luc,* these delicious olives grow nowhere else in the world but in the *départments* of the Aude and Hérault. My friend Catherine T., a native of Rodez, boldly proclaims Lucques as the best olives in the world. They certainly are outstanding and are very recognizable by their nearly perfect crescent shape. Many food shops and specialty stores sell Lucques throughout Languedoc-Roussillon; the brand I bought was L'Oulibo, which was awarded the *médaille d'or* in 2001.

~Nomade, Collioure. All the guidebooks mention espadrilles, the colorful Catalan roped sandals, as a specialty of Collioure, and you'll see dozens of them in the shops there. While I have not visited the Musée de l'Espadrille in St. Laurent-de-Cerdans (very near the Spanish border), I do like traditional espadrilles; as for their traditional color scheme, notes the Hachette Vacances guide: "These are a hymn of praise to the south, whether they are the 'blood and gold' combination in homage to spices or inspired by the deep blue of the Mediterranean." Nomade, a fairly large shop in the rue Vauban, had a wider selection of espadrilles than others in town, and many that were not Catalan in color at all. I spontaneously tried on three pairs of espadrilles, all made under a label called *Simplement l'Été,* a phrase that had me before I even tried on the shoes. But the sandals fit beautifully, and I bought all three pairs, an act I never commit at home. The *patronne* of the shop also sold well-made handbags, and she clearly had the most stylish shop in the village. Nomade is located at 14 rue Vauban; 33.4/68.98.02.32.

~Le Chemin du Fauvisme, Collioure. The tourist office in Collioure publishes a map indicating a Fauvist painter's walking route around the old part of town. As you walk along, you come across framed prints of famous and less-so canvases by Derain, Matisse, Vlaminck, Dufy, and others, which are placed at the precise spots where the painters set up their easels.

~Atelier des Remp'arts and Majolique, Collioure. These two sister shops specialize in *ceramique artisanale* (handmade ceramics), and their wares seem to stand out among the shops in lovely Collioure. The pieces are bright and contemporary and, naturally, largely feature a seashore theme. The owner and his staff are extremely friendly and helpful, and they carefully wrap each fragile selection. (They will arrange shipping, too.) Though there are some items available in both shops, the selection does vary in each store, so if you like pottery you should browse in both. I was especially fond of the small olive and hors d'oeuvres bowls, as well as a number of serving platters and decorative items. If you're in the shop on the rue Mailly and are paying with a credit card, you have to bring your receipt to the shop on the rue St.-Vincent, where it is properly approved, then walk back to the other store to pick up your purchase. One boutique is located at 12 and 14 rue Mailly, the other at 7 rue St.-Vincent. The telephone number for both is 33.4/68.82.48.64; www.majolique.com.

Midi-Pyrenees

~*Le jugement dernier* (the Last Judgment) mural inside the cathedral of Ste.-Cécile, Albi. It is positively the most blatant form of religious propaganda you'll ever see, and one you'll never forget. Ina Caro, in *Road from the Past,* adds that the cathedral is "unlike any cathedral in France; and because of the circumstances that led to its construction, I would conjecture that it is unlike any other cathedral in the world."

~Musée Toulouse-Lautrec, Albi. Fans of Lautrec will feel they've died and gone to *le septième ciel* (seventh heaven) when viewing this comprehensive collection, the mother lode of Lautrec's oeuvre. Allot a fair amount of time for the museum—it's quite large, and to this day I regret that when I visited I had to rush through because my daughter had reached her expiration date for the afternoon. There is much here to contemplate, and even if you do not prefer Lautrec's work, he is a native of these parts and there-fore deserves to be appreciated. The museum is housed in the beau-tiful Palais de la Berbie, itself and its *jardins* worth a visit. The *palais* is located right next door to Ste.-Cecile, and the telephone number is 33.5/63.49.48.70.

~The village of Belcastel, approximately twenty to thirty min-utes from Rodez, and its hotel-restaurant du Vieux Pont. Belcastel is one of those stunning villages one dreams about, yet it is not nearly as well known as others in the Midi-Pyrenees. The reason Belcastel is on the map, so to speak, is because of its one-star Michelin restau-rant. Le Restaurant du Vieux Pont is actually the childhood home of

Nicole and Michèle Fagegaltier. The dinner I had there was memorable, the staff was particularly helpful and welcoming (even with a three-year-old child in tow), and I look forward to dining there again. But it's in Belcastel itself that I would make a detour. When we left the restaurant that night, the castle atop the hill was lit up, the river was loudly gurgling along, the air smelled sweet and fresh, the little hotel (only seven rooms) on the opposite side of the stone bridge looked so appealing, and all was beautiful and tranquil . . . I just couldn't believe a place like this existed. My friend Amy announced with what seemed like her most definitive tone that she was, from this minute forward, planning an upcoming mile-marker birthday in Belcastel, and we were officially all invited. Whether or not we do gather there for her birthday, I am returning to Belcastel for my own celebration, in honor of its tiny corner of paradise on earth. Contact information: Hotel-Restaurant Vieux Pont, 12390 Aveyron, 33.5/65.64.52.29; fax .65.64.44.32.

~A walk up the very steep main *rue* of Cordes-sur-Ciel, and the fabulous view all around from the top.

~Rowena Maybourn Block Printing, Cordes-sur-Ciel. We walked past this lovely shop while catching our breath up the hill and were compelled to visit because the window display was so appealing. Maybourn, who originally hails from London, has studied and now beautifully re-creates the ancient Indian art of block printing. The wall hangings and monotypes in the gallery are stunning and are all inspired by the Middle Ages. There is also a nice selection of beautiful cards featuring Maybourn's prints on the front with wonderful quotes on the inside. One card I selected featured, appropriately, a *chanson de troubadour* from the thirteenth century: "When I see the flower, the green grass and the leaf and I hear the birds singing in the grove, out of the joy of another creature that I receive in my heart, my own song is renewed, reborn, it grows and increases. I do believe that no man can have any worth if now he does not want to have love and joy for everything rejoices and is born again." Maybourn is a pleasure to talk with about her work, and she's also very enthusiastic about her adopted corner of France. The gallery is located at 4 Grand'Rue de la Barbacane 81170; 33.5/63.56.03.76.

~Les Délices du Terroir, Cordes-sur-Ciel. Les Délices is a great shop to browse if you're searching for some local culinary specialties, for gifts, or for something for yourself. It's not the only shop in the village, but I think it has the best selection. You can't miss it at 24 grand rue Raimon VII, 33.5/63.56.15.49.

~Hôtel-Restaurant Le Combalou, Roquefort. Combalou is the name of the mountain that is framed perfectly by the windows of this good little restaurant, about five minutes from Roquefort. The view is grand, and visitors may choose from a number of simple but well-prepared *plats,* most with Roquefort cheese as the star ingredient. Contact information: Lauras, 12250 Roquefort; 33.5/65.59.91.70; fax .65.59.98.18.

~L'Abbaye de Moissac, about halfway between Agen and Toulouse. Michelin only awards Moissac two stars, but I believe that is because the town itself—which suffered greatly during the Hundred Years' War, the wars of religion, and the Revolution—also was destroyed by a fire in 1930, which killed over one hundred people and wiped out over six hundred buildings. Indeed, the town can be downright dismal, especially on a rainy day, but when you reach the abbey, you will understand why *it* is a three-star destination. All the guidebooks cover the abbey and its history amply, so I won't repeat its significance here. I do want to mention, however, that the Fodor's guide refers visitors to a staircase just off one of the corners of the cloister—don't miss it! It's not that hard to find, but you may have to walk around much of the cloister before you find the right corner. You will be rewarded with a climb to a quiet and architecturally beautiful alcove almost with a view into the center of the church, complete with the best view of the Marc Chagall stained-glass window. I almost gave up on the staircase, but my friend Amy insisted that we find it, and I am eternally grateful to her that we did. By the way, if you wonder why there are postcards of grapes in the bookstore, it's because Moissac is now famous for its pale golden *chasselas,* "France's finest dessert grapes."

~The village of Monestiés, about 15 kilometers from Cordes-sur-Ciel. Friends from Rodez took me to this lovely, little-known village, "*l'un des plus beaux villages de France,*" to see the Chapelle St.-Jacques (also called de l'Hôpital), dating from the fifteenth century, and its unique treasure inside, *la mise au tombeau et la Pietà.* If an itinerary isn't carefully planned, a visitor may well conclude (about churches in particular), "Seen one, seen 'em all." The simple yet beautiful interior of this little church, however, is exceptional, and there is not another like it anywhere, according to my hosts. On either side of the tomb are five individually carved, full-size figures. The whole ensemble is made of stone, of a type known as *calcaire,* which was then painted in lustrous colors, as if to replicate Italian majolica. The other thing to note about Monestiés is that it's one of those perfectly kept villages, not thronged with tourists, yet with its own *office de tourisme,* reminding me once again that the French, possibly more than anyone else in the world, are extremely proud of their *patrimoine.* There are dozens, if not hundreds, of villages just like Monestiés throughout France—you will, I hope, write and tell me about one or more that you have visited, perhaps by accident. Such places all share certain timeless qualities, giving me hope that France may continue to be a guiding light to civilization in the years ahead. The telephone number at the chapel is 33.5/63.76.19.17, but if there is no answer, inquire at the tourist office.

~La Place du Capitole, Toulouse. There are, of course, many grand *places* and *plazas* in the world, and to a list of my favorites I would have to add the Place du Capitole. It is really the only grand *place,* in the true sense of the word, in all of Southwestern France, and it is a most enjoyable hangout. A number of simple cafés line the arcaded side opposite the Le Capitole building, all of which are better for drinks and ice cream than for serious meals; but I relish a seat at one of the *place*'s tables at any hour of day or night.

~La Salle des Illustres et ses Fresques and the Salle Henri Martin, Le Capitole, Toulouse. Though the interior of the most prominent building in Toulouse—Le Capitole—is touched upon briefly in guidebooks, I doubt many visitors take the time to step inside. I deduce this because when I visited, I encountered only eight other tourists, some of whom were French, and we had this magnificent building all to ourselves. Admission is *gratuit,* surprisingly, and as you climb the wide stone staircase to the upper floor, you sense you are in for a treat, as the frescoes above are so colorful and bright. The Salle Henri Martin is a room full of this symbolist painter's work celebrating the Languedoc countryside and the four seasons of the year. Of these, my favorites are *L'Eté ou les Faucheurs* and *Les Bords de la Garonne,* depicting a promenade along the banks of the Garonne and featuring painter Jean-Paul Laurens and France's famous socialist politician, Jean Jaurès. I wasn't able to linger here as long as I wished because preparations were in progress for a party to be held there later that evening (what fortunate guests!), but I cannot wait to return, and I would highly recommend you include a visit as part of your Toulouse itinerary.

~Le Capoul, Toulouse. Inexplicably, to my mind, this excellent *brasserie–salon du thé* is not mentioned in any of the guidebooks I consulted for Toulouse. On the two occasions I visited, I was struck by how good the service was, how good the food was, how pleasant the restaurant was, and how many locals gathered there. Sure, there were a handful of tourists—the restaurant's location on the lovely Place Wilson ensures that it will receive a fair number of tourists; but especially on Sundays, when many restaurants are closed in

Toulouse (including those at the Grand Hôtel de l'Opéra, below), Le Capoul is a popular spot among *toulousains*. On my first visit Amy, my daughter, and I sat indoors as it was pouring rain outside, and we enjoyed some local and traditional brasserie specialties—such as cassoulet and *steak frites*—amid the warm and gay atmosphere prevailing around us. On our second visit the weather was glorious, and we sat outside under the covered terrace, enjoying one of the restaurant's specialties: its oyster and shellfish bar. A variety of oysters are available, types I'd never before tried, and some of the assortments are served with delicious chopped red onions in a vinegar marinade, butter, and slices of dark bread. One of the highlights at this meal was the starter course of gazpacho with a big dollop of crab *blancmange* in the center. All in all Le Capoul seems to be an utterly reliable place, and it will be the site of my next meal in Toulouse. Contact information: 13 place Wilson; 33.5/61.21.08.27; fax .61.21.96.70.

~La Fondation Bemberg, Hôtel d'Assezat, Toulouse. The Bemberg is on my short list of favorite small museums in the world, and I enthusiastically recommend it as a must-see in Toulouse. I am still amazed that it took so many years for me to learn of its existence, let alone of its outstanding permanent collection. Collector Georges Bemberg, whose family was originally from Germany, developed a love for beautiful objects at a very young age. His collection, which he decided to preserve in its entirety as a foundation in the late 1980s, includes one hundred Old Master paintings (including Van Dyck, Cranach, Titian, Veronese, Canaletto, Guardi, Longhi, and Tiepolo), one hundred bronzes, two hundred pieces of furniture and *objets d'art* dating from the sixteenth, seventeenth, and eighteenth centuries (including a superb collection of Italian majolica), and more than 150 modern paintings and drawings. The modern collection knocked my socks off and includes nearly all the great names of the modern French school: Boudin,

Pissarro, Degas, Fantin-Latour, Sisley, Cézanne, Monet, Morisot, Caillebotte, Gauguin, Signac, Toulouse-Lautrec, Vuillard, Rouault, Matisse, Dufy, Marquet, Derain, Braque, and Bonnard (an entire *room* full of Bonnards, in fact; Bemberg managed to buy more than thirty Bonnard canvases). Modigliani, Utrillo, and Picasso round out the modern collection. According to the museum catalog, "What sets Georges Bemberg's collection apart is in fact all its charm and personality; it is nothing but a truthful reflection of the collector's tastes and temperament. Mr. Bemberg chose each painting, each object, solely on the basis of its beauty and the emotional effect it aroused in him." The emotional effect this museum had on me was great; I could not pull myself away, especially from those Bonnard canvases, notably *Marine, Still Life with Lemons,* and *Midi Landscape.* As if the collection needed any gilding, the Hôtel d'Assezat is an architecturally significant gem in its own right. The beautiful residence was originally built in the second half of the sixteenth century for Pierre Assezat, a merchant who made his fortune in Toulouse's then-flourishing woad (*pastel*) trade. The mansion, which has belonged to the city of Toulouse for more than two hundred years, represents the Renaissance in its general composition as well as the doric, ionic, and corinthian orders. A visit to the Bemberg is most satisfying and memorable—though it isn't overwhelming, be sure to allow enough time to wander leisurely. Note that the reception area doubles as a small gift shop, with good books (many in English), cards, and posters. Address: 18 rue de Metz; www.fondation-bemberg.fr.

~La Fleurée de Pastel, Toulouse. Just a minute's walk from the Bemberg is this wonderful, lovely shop celebrating a glorious period in Toulouse's history, the time when it was known as the Blue City. In the middle of the fourteenth century Toulouse became the European center of indigo dyeing. The leaves of the woad (*pastel*) plant, a member of the mustard family, produce an exceptional color of blue—also known as majestic blue—after they are harvested, wetted, and fermented. Woad has actually been known to man since the stone age and was very highly prized in Renaissance Europe. By the fourteenth century Toulouse and Thuringia (in Germany) were the *pastel* capitals of Europe, and by the fifteenth century thirty to forty thousand tons of woad were being shipped from Toulouse to many cities of Europe (especially England and northern Italy, which couldn't produce enough to meet the demands of their cloth industries) as well as to Byzantium and the Islamic world. But it wasn't always so: according to Michel Pastoureau, historian and author of *Blue: The History of a Color* (Princeton University Press, 2001, a fascinating and beautiful book; if you are even remotely interested, the color blue has a unique story, and the book features nearly a hundred related reproductions of artworks from Pompeii and Picasso to Degas and Manet), "Dyeing was done in red and yellow long before blue was used. Although blue is present in natural elements that go back almost to the earth's formation, it has taken humanity many long years to learn how to reproduce and use it. Perhaps this explains why blue remained a second-rate color in the West for so long, with hardly any role in social life, religious practice, or artistic creation. Compared to red, white, and black—the three basic colors of all ancient cultures—blue had little symbolic meaning and thus was poorly adapted to transmitting ideas, evoking emotional or aesthetic responses, or organizing social codes. Nor could it be used for even the basic tasks of classifying and establishing hierarchies, which are functions of color in all societies. And it couldn't be used for religious purposes—unable to evoke a response on earth, it certainly couldn't communicate with the beyond." At the height of Toulouse's woad production, Pastoureau relates, "numerous documents attest to violent conflicts between merchants of madder (used to make red dye) and woad, reflecting the economic stakes of changing fashions in color. In Thuringia madder merchants went so far as to ask glass-makers to depict blue devils in stained-glass windows as a way of discrediting the new fashion for blue. Farther north, in Magdeburg, capital of the madder market for Germany and the Slavic countries, hell itself was painted blue in frescoes in order to associate the rival color with death and pain. But all this demonizing of blue went for naught. Woad triumphed in the West, and as of the mid-thirteenth century red tones began giving way to blue in fabric and clothing, to the chagrin and great detriment of the madder merchants." The original method for preparing woad involved hand-pulling the leaves and crushing them into a mustard-smelling pulp in a circular stone woad mill. This pulp was formed into balls (*coques*), which were then laid on trays under cover to dry. After the balls were dry, they were crushed into a powder and wetted. They were then formed into balls again (at this stage they were referred to as *cocagnes*) and rotated frequently to encourage fermentation. (According to the Rough Guide, the prosperity that the woad plant brought to Toulouse and many of its surrounding towns and villages caused the region to be referred to the *pays de Cocagnes*, which apparently is a bit of a play on words, as the word *cockaigne* also means "land of plenty.") The rotating stage of woad production required great skill and a watchful eye, as too much heat would destroy the dye. The final blue compost was barreled and sent to the dyer for fabric dyeing. This entire process took from nine to twelve months. Under Napoleon the process was drastically reduced to six months and then to six days. (He needed the dye for uniforms and enforced a blockade that prohibited the flow of supplies; he was singlehandedly responsible for the increased production of woad in Toulouse.) But after the Portuguese discovered indigo in India, Toulouse's corner on this market began to shrink and was eventually wiped out entirely. Today woad has started to grow once again, and its leaves still produce a most unique and beautiful shade of blue. To return again to historian Pastoureau, blue is today the West's favorite color: "This is true despite gender, social origins, profession, or cultural baggage: blue dominates all the others. The principal manifestation of this popularity is in dress. In all the countries of Western Europe, and indeed in the entire Western world, blue in all its shades has been the most popular dress color for several decades (ahead of white, black, and beige)." Can you imagine packs of Gauloises in any other color? A great number of merchants in Toulouse made their fortunes from the woad trade, and thankfully, a few of their *hôtels particuliers* are still standing and open to the public. La Fleurée de Pastel, in fact, now occupies the Hôtel Pierre Delfau, the original private mansion of woad merchant Pierre Delfau. (His merchant logo, a heart with a double cross on top, appears above the entrance to the shop.) The store that oozes quality and history and is filled with one-of-a-kind items. Among the selections are silk scarves of all sizes, dyed, of course, in that spectacular blue; a great assortment of drawing crayons, pencils, and inks; fine notepads and sketchbooks; woven and knit items for men, women, and children; books, postcards, posters, and journals; tabletop linens; and a selection of soap and beautiful combs, all handmade in the Pyrenees. For about thirty cents you can also buy a packet of woad seeds; my mother promptly scattered the ones I bought in her backyard, and soon she had a veritable instant meadow. La Fleurée de Pastel deserves to be better known. The doors at the back of the shop open out onto a pretty courtyard, and the two elderly women who manage the shop carefully wrap your purchases with ribbons and logo stickers. Address: 20 rue de la Bourse (just off the rue de Metz), 33.5/61.12.05.94 (telephone and fax).

~Readers especially interested in the color blue and woad production may also want to know about the Route Historique du Circuit du Pastel au Pays de Cocagne, a route that is detailed in a brochure one can find on the front counter at La Fleurée de Pastel. I did not take this journey myself but would very much like to. The brochure states that the route, found in Michelin map 82, includes Albi, Gaillac, Graulhet, Lavaur, Le Château de Magrin, Magrin, Le Château de Loubens, Puylaurens, Ste.-Julia de Gras Capou, Revel, Toulouse, Villefranche-de-Lauragais, Le Château de Montgeard, Mazères, Mirepoix, Le Château de Caudeval, and Lectoure.

~Grand Hôtel de l'Opéra, Toulouse. Guidebook authors and travel writers will all inform you that the Grand Hôtel is the nicest lodging in town, and they're all right. But if "nice" were its only attribute, I wouldn't single it out for mention here. The facts are that the Grand Hôtel is in arguably the best location in Toulouse; the staff is extremely welcoming, kind, and attentive, ready to help solve any problem guests may have; and though the hotel is a three-star establishment, its prices represent a good value—value I rarely come across. The Grand Hôtel is simply among the nicest hotels I've ever had the privilege of staying at in the world, and judging from its guest registry, I'm not the only one who shares this opinion: Catherine Deneuve, Luciano Pavarotti, Yves Montand, Yehudi Menuhin, Elie Wiesel, and John McEnroe are among the Grand Hôtel's celebrated guests. The guest bedrooms are tasteful and unique, with no two alike (though I don't think I would want one of the rooms overlooking the *place,* as these are bound to be quite noisy at night), but the hotel's other amenities really make it special: the grand and beautiful lobby; the bountiful breakfast served every morning; its two restaurants, the Grand Café de l'Opéra and the renowned and pricier Les Jardins de l'Opéra (*both* are closed on Sunday); the outdoor courtyard and gardens; the only driveway entrance off the busy *place* (a *very* important bonus if you're arriving in a rental car); the bar; and its fitness and meeting rooms. I am personally indebted to the wonderful staff for being so attentive to my daughter when we stayed there on two occasions. Alyssa was forever losing her sweater and one of her stuffed animals (and someone always found them for us), and when we had finally checked out and were about to step into a cab to the airport, one of the kind porters handed Alyssa a little box of chocolates wrapped in a pretty ribbon from one of Toulouse's fine *chocolatiers*. When you first arrive at the Grand Hôtel and walk through the interior courtyard, you sense that you are in a quiet oasis in the middle of the city, and you truly are. Contact information: 1 place du Capitole, 33.5/61.21.82.66; fax .61.23.41.04; www.grand-hotel-opera.com. The Grand Hôtel is also a member of the Concorde Hotels group (www.concorde-hotels.com); North American residents may also make reservations by dialing 800-888-4747 or 212-752-3900 in New York.

~Hôtel du Taur, Toulouse. A change in my itinerary found me having to make same-day reservations at a hotel in Toulouse, and even though I had already spent a night at the Grand Hôtel, I wasn't due back there for another week, and the staff reported it was fully booked. I selected the Hôtel du Taur from the Lonely Planet guide and was told I would be given the last two rooms. (This was a Friday.) The Taur is a perfectly fine two-star hotel about twenty steps off the Place du Capitole. I found the staff to be very helpful and considerate and the location, of course, superb. The two rooms I reserved only hours before were not shabby or faded the way they are at some other two-star establishments, and the clientele was a mix of older and younger travelers from around the world. Upon entering the hotel, you have to walk up a fairly long flight of stairs to reach the *rez-de-chaussée,* and there is no bellhop to help with your bags, so keep this in mind whether you plan in advance or simply show up unannounced. (There is no elevator.) Contact information: 2 rue du Taur; 33.5/61.21.17.54; fax .61.13.78.41; www.hotel-du-taur.com.

~The city of Rodez, historic capital of the Rouergue River Valley. Rodez, approximately two hours northeast of Toulouse, is technically on the edge of the Midi in Aveyron. It's not often mentioned in articles about the Southwest, even though it is close to classic villages and sites of the region (Conques, St.-Cirq-Lapopie, and Roquefort). It makes a great base from which to tour the eastern half of the Southwest, and it's a gentle introduction to the Aveyron, which I plan to explore further in another edition. The defining aspect of Rodez is its imposing Notre Dame cathedral that sits atop a hill in the historic center of town. The enormous Gothic structure can be seen from quite a distance, and everything in Rodez emanates from it. The tourist office, located atop the hill near the cathedral, offers some good complimentary brochures of walking tours around the cobblestoned old town, including a seventeenth-century episcopal palace, a twelfth-century chapel, and a number of wonderful private houses dating from the fourteenth, fifteenth, and sixteenth centuries. Gastronomes will be happy to know that one of the few Michelin three-star restaurants in all of the Southwest is not far from Rodez (though it is firmly in the Auvergne): Michel Bras.

~Hôtel Libertel (46 rue Saint Cyrice, 12000; 33.5/65.76.10.30; fax .65.76.10.33; www.libertel-hotels.com), Rodez. Libertel hotels are a member of the Mercure hotel network, and both are members of the Accor group (www.accorhotels.com). Libertel hotels do not, generally speaking, represent the qualities I look for in accommodations—the properties and the rooms are not charming, historic, or beautiful—but I'm happy that this well-run chain exists. Sometimes when planning an itinerary, you just have to stay overnight in lodgings that aren't particularly appealing, and other times the place(s) you most want to stay are fully booked. You can always count on Libertel hotels to be very clean, conveniently located, and reasonably priced. This Libertel Rodez is the only Libertel/Mercure/Accor property I've stayed at in the Southwest, and it is consistent with its sister properties where I've stayed elsewhere, perhaps even a bit nicer. A nice perk for travelers with rental cars is that the hotel staff has made arrangements with one of the city parking garages—about a two-minute walk away—for hotel guests to park at a discounted rate. (This privilege comes with one restriction: multiple comings and goings aren't permitted at the special rate, so drivers may depart and return to the garage only once in the course of a day.) Many Accor group hotels are located outside of towns and cities, but the Libertel Rodez is located in the heart of the St. Cyrice district and is therefore within walking distance (uphill, though) of the cathedral.

Le Pays Basque

~H et C, Biarritz. H and C are the initals of Huguette Tozzi and Catherine Moutet, proprietors of this chic shop filled with gorgeous linens and a few other tabletop items. This store stands out not only for the flair its owners have in abundance but for the high-quality linens in Basque patterns and colors, which are very appealing. You can be sure that a purchase from H et C is unique—to my knowledge, these fabrics are not exported to North America. The shop is located at 1 avenue Foch, 33.5/59.24.50.69.

~The Grand Hôtel in Saint-Jean-de-Luz (Basque name Donibane Lohizune). After a recent four-year renovation, this beautiful light pink and white Belle Époque palace is positively the most enticing monument in town. Even if its room rates are more than your wallet can bear (double rooms are about $150–$285), don't miss a walk through the public rooms, or a visit to the bar or restaurant. The Grand is right on the beach, too, and it's a *batiment* with a history: *le tout l'Europe* flocked here after Louis XIV selected the pretty coastal village as the spot for his marriage to Maria Teresa of Spain—in 1660. If you somehow tire of the charms of Saint-Jean-de-Luz, you can explore nearby Biarritz or even San Sebastián, another beautiful city also with royal claims to its fame. Contact information: 43 boulevard Thiers, 64500 Saint-Jean-de-Luz; 33.5/59.26.35.36; fax: .59.51.99.84; e-mail: direction@luzgrandhotel.fr; the www.saint-jean-de-luz.com Web site has a hotels section, and the first hotel that appears is the Grand Hotel. Vintage and contemporary photos are featured and visitors may click on the English version of the text.

~Bayonne, which, other than its name, has absolutely nothing in common with Bayonne, New Jersey, is not written about much, or at least not as much as its glitzier neighbors, Biarritz and St.-Jean-de-Luz. Bayonne is also more than a little-visited, pretty place: it was founded in the fourth century and was established at the junction of two rivers, the Nive and the Adour, which divide the city into three sections. Five of Bayonne's original twenty medieval towers still remain, and until 1907, it was prohibited to build outside the city walls. Residents had no choice but to build up as opposed to outward, and the old half-timbered houses (many painted oxblood red to protect the wood from bad weather) are beautiful. The well-regarded Musée Bonnat, in Petit Bayonne, features works by Rubens, El Greco, Murillo, Goya, Ingres, and Degas. Bayonne is also on the culinary map, as it's famous for its ham (you can tour a ham "workshop") and chocolate—Bayonne was the first town in France to manufacture *chocolat*. Jewish refugees fleeing the Spanish Inquisition brought their skills to Bayonne in 1496, along with cocoa beans and recipes that had been brought back from South America to the Spanish court. The Basque liquor, *Izarra*, is also native to Bayonne. All in all, the city is a lovely detour, and you won't find many Americans strolling the streets.

Bibliography

Fiction

The Anchor Anthology of French Poetry: From Nerval to Valéry in English Translation, edited by Angel Flores; introduction by Patti Smith, Anchor, 1958, 2000.

Baudolino, Umberto Eco, translated by William Weaver, Harcourt, 2002. Eco's epic tale has as its backdrop the Middle Ages of (mostly) France, Italy, and Constantinople; woven into the story are the Crusades, troubadours, and power struggles between the pope and the emperor.

Birdsong: A Novel of Love and War (Random House, 1993, hardcover; Vintage, 1996, paperback), *The Girl at the Lion d'Or* (Vintage, 1999), and *Charlotte Gray* (Random House, 1999, hardcover; Vintage, 2000, paperback), all by Sebastian Faulks. These wonderfully engaging novels span the generations and the years between the First World War and the present day and are the kind that sweep you off your feet, filled with life and death issues, love, war, survival, surrealism, and romanticism, similar to works such as *The English Patient, Corelli's Mandolin,* and *A Farewell to Arms.* Though the Southwest is not the trilogy's focus, any one of these volumes makes a great immersion read about an immensely significant period in France.

Cyrano de Bergerac, several editions available.

In Our Strange Gardens, Michel Quint, translated from the French by Barbara Bray, Riverhead Books, 2001; first published in France by Éditions Joëlle Losfeld as *Effroyable jardins,* 2000. The title of this lovely little paperback is from a battlefield poem of the First World War: *"Et que la grenade est touchante/Dans nos effroyables jardins"* (How touching this fruit/In our strange and terrible gardens) by Guillaume Apollinaire. In French *grenade* means both "pomegranate" and "grenade," the fruit and the missile being of roughly the same shape. Printed in both English and French, Quint tells the tale (based on his father's life story) of two cousins in the Resistance toward the end of World War II. The book opens at the trial of Maurice Papon, in Bordeaux, and is simply one of the more ordinary—and therefore more affecting—memoirs of this period. The book ends in Bordeaux, too, before the Papon trial has officially ended. "So we shall see if the dignity of a court that has allowed a torturer like him to enjoy a few more crumbs of freedom, as if he had an exclusive right to the time, the eternity stolen from those he deported—we shall see if this crimson and ermine dignity has a sense of humor, a sense of the macabre. The name of the accused? I vaguely recall a brief reverberation, like that of a contemptuous slap, and—even that I hope to have forgotten by tomorrow, so as to remember only the names of the people he deported from life."

The Lost Upland: Stories of Southwest France, W. S. Merwin, Henry Holt, 1992. For many years Merwin, a distinguished poet, writer of prose, and winner of the Pulitzer Prize, lived in a stone house in a village of the Southwest. For this book he has divided the stories up into three narratives of small-town life, "Foie Gras," "Shepherds," and "Blackbird's Summer." In each one what is remarkable are the characters themselves and their development. One has to assume that many of them are based at least a little on Merwin's neighbors and the acquaintances he's come to know over the years. Their various types remain in my head and are not easily forgettable, so that when I am stopping in the small villages and towns of the region, everyone I meet seems to embody one of them. Besides the characters, the book is simply in and of the land in a way I've rarely encountered in literature. Yes, one has to classify it as fiction, but it is true in the ways of nonfiction, and I would choose this one first, together with his *The Mays of Vantadorn,* if I were faced with a severe space restriction.

The Mays of Ventadorn, W. S. Merwin, National Geographic Directions, National Geographic Society, Washington, D.C., 2002. This slender hardcover is one edition in the Literary Travel Series, launched a few years ago. The series features works by some of the world's most prominent and highly regarded literary figures, and each edition captures the spirit of travel and of places for which *National Geographic* is renowned. For this edition Merwin focuses on an area in south-central France, bordered more or less by the Limousin, Aquitaine, the Midi-Pyrénées, and the Massif Central, and the tale he relates is part memoir, part history, and part a portrait of the rugged landscape of Languedoc. Merwin weaves his own personal observations with a chronicle of Bernart de Ventadorn and the troubadours of twelfth-century Languedoc, bards who once ruled a world where kings were poets and vice versa. Richard the Lion-Hearted and Eleanor of Aquitaine are also part of this chronicle, which includes a number of poems and brings us to the World War II years. Merwin tells of troubadours known as the "four from Ussel" and learned that the family had not died out; a junior line had continued into the twentieth century.

Seven Men of Gascony, R. F. Delderfield, McBooks Press, 2001; originally published in the United Kingdom by Werner Laurie, 1949; first published in the United States by Bobbs-Merrill Co., 1949. I learned of this book—and lots of others published by McBooks Press—from a catalog my husband received in the mail. I had never heard of McBooks; my husband received the mailing because he's a big fan of the Aubrey-Maturin series by Patrick O'Brian. McBooks publishes many volumes of historical, maritime, and military fiction by writers who are not as well known as O'Brian. (Mediterranean ports of call figure largely in many of O'Brian's Aubrey-Maturin novels, published by W. W. Norton; though I am not as knowledgeable about the series as my husband is, he says the books would make splendid companion reading for any of the destinations featured in *The Collected Traveler.*) *Seven Men of Gascony* is somewhat unusual in that most of the incidents recorded in the story are true, episodes that were written down at the time or years later by officers and men of the Grand Army of Napoleon. The book focuses on Napoleon's last six years, and the central characters are, as Delderfield notes, spun from fact. Two subsidiary characters, Marshal Lannes and Marshal Ney, are now enshrined in French history, and their names are carved on the Arc de Triomphe. Delderfield encourages readers to learn more about these two "remarkable men": "they are worth contemplating, for men of their caliber are lamentably rare in the Europe of today." Delderfield concludes that "this book is only a fragment of the First Empire legend, and in writing it I intended to commemorate the gallantry and the hardihood of a million unknown men who marched, fought and died during the years when France challenged a continent." McBooks contact information: McBooks Press, Inc., 10 Booth Building, 520 North Meadow Street, Ithaca, N.Y. 14850; 888-266-5711; www.mcbooks.com.

The Three Musketeers, Alexandre Dumas, several editions.

General Art Reference

As noted in the excellent guide *The Traveler's Key to Medieval France,* there are very few important museums in Southwestern France—even those in Bordeaux are something of a disappointment for visitors who've previously been to the museums of Paris. Yet this part of France does have much to offer. "The dramatic landscape of the Pyrenees (which has been much less spoilt than that of the Alps) may attract your attention more than the architecture or artistic treasures, but you should not overlook the fact that the region also has two of France's finest painting collections—at Bayonne and at the beautifully situated and once thriving mountain resort of Pau." There are also, of course, the justly famous Bemberg Foundation and Augustinian museum in Toulouse, the fine Musée Fabre in Montpellier, the modern art museum in Céret, and the single-artist museums devoted to Toulouse-Lautrec (Albi), Ingres (Montauban), and Goya (Castres). Following are some very good art reference books that are described more fully in my previous editions.

The Art Pack, Christopher Frayling, Helen Frayling, and Ron Van Der Meer, Alfred A. Knopf, 1992.

From Abacus to Zeus: A Handbook of Art History, James Smith Pierce, Prentice-Hall, 1977.

History of Art, H. W. Janson, Anthony F. Janson, sixth revised edition, Harry N. Abrams, 2001.

The Illustrated Age of Fable: The Classic Retelling of Greek and Roman Myths Accompanied by the World's Greatest Paintings, Thomas Bulfinch, Stewart, Tabori and Chang, 1998.

The Oxford Companion to Christian Art and Architecture: The Key to Western Art's Most Potent Symbolism, Peter and Linda Murray, Oxford University Press, 1998.

The Panorama of the Renaissance, Margaret Aston, Harry Abrams, 1996.

The Architecture of Silence: Cistercian Abbeys of France, photographs by David Heald, text by Terryl N. Kinder, Harry N. Abrams, 2000. This absolutely stunning book is a gem, and features the twenty-two Cistercian abbeys of France. Of these, five are in the Southwest: Flaran, Fontfroide, Silvanès, Loc-Dieu, and Boschaud. Abbeys with which readers may be most familiar are Sénanque, Silvacane, and Le Thoronet in Provence, but all of them are beautiful and interesting in their own way. As noted in the introduction, "To visit a Cistercian abbey is to make a voyage of discovery, but not necessarily a physical voyage. It may be an inward voyage, where one discovers a part of one's own being, an inner experience from which one seldom returns unaltered. Depending on the investment made by the traveller, it may be a brief and pleasant diversion, or it may invite a change in the direction of one's life." What drew me to this book was the title, first of all, and the fact that I had previously visited that trio of abbeys in Provence, and I could barely drag myself away from them, especially Sénanque and its billowing, intoxicating fields of lavender. The gorgeous black-and-white photographs in this book "awaken a longing for a quieter, simpler existence," and for that reason alone it is worth picking up this volume. In some cases, all that is left of the original abbeys are ruins, though even these are beautiful. Happily, all five in the Southwest are intact and waiting for your visit.

The Barbizon School and the Origins of Impressionism, Steve Adams, Phaidon Press, London, 1994. Though the impressionists were not thick on the ground in the Southwest as in other parts of France, there are works scattered about in a few museums. This important book highlights some of the still relatively unknown painters who greatly influenced the impressionists: Charles-Emile Jacque, Theodore Rousseau, Narcisse Diaz de la Peña, and Georges Michel. These landscape painters, followed by Corot, Courbet, Daubigny, and Millet, had been coming to Barbizon (a small village on the edge of the Forest of Fontainebleau, about 40 miles southwest of Paris) nearly fifty years before the word *impressioniste* was first uttered in Paris.

Castle (1977) and *Cathedral* (1981) both by David Macaulay, both published by Houghton Mifflin. Though Macaulay is known as a children's book author/illustrator, his brilliant books are most definitely satisfying for adults. Among his numerous titles I've singled these two out because they are so appropriate to medieval architecture. Macaulay is a former teacher and architect, and his pen-and-ink illustrations are among the best in the world. Readers of any age will learn (or learn more) about how castles and cathedrals were built, stone by stone, as well as day-to-day life inside and outside of these structures.

Fauve Painting: The Making of Cultural Politics, James D. Herbert, Yale University Press, 1992. This book goes beyond the usual comparisons of fauve canvases to analyze them within the political and cultural trends of their time.

The Fauves: The Reign of Color, Jean-Louis Ferrier, Éditions Pierre Terrail, 1992. This book features the works of Matisse, Derain, Van Dongen, Braque, and Dufy.

French Art: Prehistory to the Middle Ages; The Renaissance, 1430–1620; and *The Ancien Régime: 1620–1775,* all by André Chastel, translated by Deke Dusinberre, Flammarion, 1995. Chastel was adviser to André Malraux, founder of the French Inventory of Historical Monuments, editor of the prestigious *Revue de l'Art et de l'Archéologie,* and a professor at the Sorbonne and the Collège de France. With more than four hundred exquisite color illustrations, these books are simply the most detailed, most beautiful, and therefore the best available on French art, unmatched in their thoroughness.

The History of Impressionism (1946) and *Post-Impressionism: From van Gogh to Gauguin* (1956), both by John Rewald, both published by the Museum of Modern Art. This one is still, in my opinion, the best overall volume on the impressionist movement. Rewald is a noteworthy name in modern French art history circles.

Romanesque and Gothic France: Art and Architecture, Vivianne Minne-Sève and Hervé Kergall, Abrams, 2001. This gorgeous and scholarly volume is a *tour de France* during the Middle Ages. It's beautifully produced (as Abrams books always are) and the authors set each landmark within the culture, politics, and society of the times. The Southwest is significantly featured.

Romanesque Art in Europe, edited by Gustav Künstler, New York Graphic Society, Greenwich, Conn., 1968. "Romanesque art was the first pan-European style since the fall of the Roman Empire, and it began as a deliberate revival of Roman, imperial art. When Charlemagne was crowned Emperor of the West in 800, he set out to be a second Constantine, and fostered a new development of painting, scholarship and architecture based on Roman or Early Christian models." So begins the first chapter in this excellent book. The author then notes that "South-western France is one of the richest areas for Romanesque sculpture in all of Europe." Included among the beautiful black-and-white photographs are architectural gems of Toulouse, the Pyrénées-Orientales, Moissac, Basses-Pyrénées, Beaulieu-sur-Dordogne, Souillac, and Conques.

The Traveler's Key to Medieval France, John James, Knopf, 1987. It is a real pity this book is out of print because it is the most outstanding, traveler-friendly volume ever published on the subject. My advice is to go to every length to either borrow this from the library or find a used copy somewhere. "The Middle Ages is wondrously silent, and it is our pleasure to make it talk" is the opening phrase of this paperback, sized just right for a handbag or other *sac.*

The author presents a thorough yet succinct historical background, and a directory featuring an alphabetical description of churches. There is simply no other book I've found that is so well written, informative without being overly academic, and handy for travelers to carry around. Perhaps the best endorsement for this excellent book is the final paragraph of the introduction: "This is a guide not to all medieval architecture but to the essential issues which inspired it. It is the story of the community of believers who expressed their faith in some of the most magical buildings on earth and for a short time lived with a mystic sense of God's presence. The ultimate decay of these ideals and the annihilation of the society that produced them in pestilence, war, and religious chaos was a sad, if almost inevitable conclusion. Perhaps the message is that, like Icarus, we may approach the highest only for a brief moment and should not be surprised if the sequel appears as another expulsion."

Art Books of Related Interest

The Artist in His Studio, Alexander Liberman, Random House, 1988. This hard-to-categorize book is a splendid record of Liberman's visits to a number of artists—thirty-one of them, nearly all of whom were French or worked in France—in the 1940s after the war. Liberman felt compelled to personally meet these artists and take photos in their studios because he feared that if he didn't, there would be no trace of the remarkable flowering of painting and sculpture the first half of the twentieth century had witnessed. No doubt he was also moved to do so by World War II's annihilation and destruction. A unique book, filled with color and black-and-white photographs and the text of Liberman's conversations with each artist.

The Voices of Silence, André Malraux, translated by Stuart Gilbert, Doubleday, 1953. This wonderful book has long been among my favorite art volumes. Malraux's text, accompanied by a plethora of black-and-white photos, covers a diverse range of artworks. Out of print but worth tracking down; I frequently see copies in used bookstores.

Single-Artist Books and Museum Catalogs

The following definitive volumes (some are comprehensive catalogs that accompanied museum exhibitions) are worth a special effort to track down. Some of these titles are *catalogues raisonnés,* or they represent an artist's work in the Southwest.

Jean-Auguste-Dominique Ingres

Portraits by Ingres, edited by Gary Tinterow and Philip Conisbee, The Metropolitan Museum of Art, 1999.

Albert Marquet

From Fauvism to Impressionism: Albert Marquet, Universe Publishing, a division of Rizzoli, 2001; published to accompany an exhibition of the same name at the Centre Pompidou, Paris, 2001, and at the Columbia Museum of Art (South Carolina), Museum of Art (Fort Lauderdale), Georgia Museum of Art (Athens), Dixon Gallery and Gardens (Memphis), and the McNay Art Museum (San Antonio) from late 2001 through early January 2003.

Henri Matisse

Henri Matisse: A Retrospective, John Elderfield, Museum of Modern Art, 1992.

Matisse and Picasso, Yve-Alain Bois. Foreword by Joachim Pissarro, Flammarion, 1998; published to accompany the exhibition "Matisse and Picasso: A Gentle Rivalry" at the Kimbell Art Museum, Fort Worth, Tex., January 31–May 2, 1999.

Matisse and Picasso: A Friendship in Art, Francoise Gilot, Doubleday, 1990.

Matisse, Picasso, Miró: As I Knew Them, Rosamond Bernier, Knopf, 1991.

Pablo Picasso

Though Picasso is known mostly for his Spanish heritage and the years he lived and worked on the Côte d'Azur, his relevance to a book on the Southwest is that he was a regular attendee of the bullfights at Nîmes, and spent some time in the village of Céret (the modern art museum there features some of his work) as well as in the coastal town of Collioure (on one wall of the bar at the hotel Les Templiers there are a few photographs of him taken when he visited Collioure—if memory serves me, I think there might also be a painting or two). The books I recommend below represent a small selection of biographies and memoirs. I selected these in particular because references to Céret, Collioure, or both are included, or because they are simply engrossing reads about a fascinating artist. I have not included any art books or museum catalogs as connoisseurs of Picasso's art will already have several or a great number in their possession, and art history students will have no trouble finding these as art books on Picasso are plentiful (you may also refer to my *Paris* and *Provence* editions for a more complete list of other recommended books). There is not, to my knowledge, a single edition devoted to the artworks Picasso created while he was in Languedoc-Roussillon—these works appear in museum retrospective catalogs and other books encompassing his vast output during his long life.

A Life of Picasso: Volume I, 1881–1906 (1991) and *Volume II: 1907–1917* (1996), John Richardson, Random House. Positively the most definitive volumes on Picasso—and two more are to follow in the planned four-volume set. Not for casual fans, but for those with a serious interest in the life and works of Picasso.

Life with Picasso, Françoise Gilot and Carlton Lake, McGraw-Hill, 1964 (hardcover); Anchor/Doubleday, 1989 (paperback). In his introduction to this engaging book (once I began reading it I was incapable of putting it down), Carlton Lake says of Gilot, "I realized that she had an infinitely deeper and truer appreciation of Picasso's thought and work than anyone I had encountered."

Picasso: A Biography, Patrick O'Brian, W. W. Norton, 1994. If you only know O'Brian for his wonderful Aubrey/Maturin novels, you're in for a treat as he is a longtime admirer of Picasso and an accomplished nonfiction writer as well (O'Brian also lived for many years in Languedoc-Roussillon). Of particular interest in this volume is the significance O'Brian attributes to Céret, "a little town in French Catalonia, not far from Matisse's Collioure; it lies in the Pyrenean foothills, a remarkably green, well-watered spot, famous for its cherries." Picasso initially visited Céret to see his old friend Manolo, who by 1908 was an established sculptor represented by David Kahnweiler, also Picasso's art dealer. O'Brian informs us that "although Ceret had been politically French since the time of Cardinal Richelieu, and although politically it had been Spanish before that time, it remained stubbornly Catalan, and both Picasso and Manolo were entirely at home there. They had the familiar language all around them; the bullring was a natural feature of the town; and on holidays the people danced the *sardana,* the only dance that Picasso approved of, to the sound of the harsh archaic oboes and the little drum." O'Brian singles out two particular works, *La Clarinette* and *L'Accordéoniste,* that Picasso painted in the summer of 1911, and he adds that at Céret, "Picasso returned to his Spanish ways, working all day and going to the café at night. The Grand Café where he met his friends is still there under the shade of its enormous planes, in whose upper branches the untiring scops owl utters its single note throughout the warm and tranquil night: the marble tables alas have long since been washed clean of Picasso's innumerable drawings, but a few of the paper napkins that he tore into wonderful shapes and patterns (a lifelong habit) have survived. Yet though he loved conviviality the Grand Café did not see him every night: sometimes his town-bred friends sat there without him; they were happiest with their feet on a pavement and for them a hillside was something to be viewed from a distance. But Picasso loved the country, and he was a tremendous walker: one evening he and Manolo, lost in talk, went on and on until they found themselves at Le Perthus, at the frontier itself. They could go no farther, for Manolo was liable to be taken up the moment he set foot in Spain, imprisoned and made to do his military service; but it was quite far enough, since even if they had gone through the vineyards it was at least twelve miles there and twelve miles back." If Richardson's works above are more than you desire, this is the volume to pick up, and my only criticism of it is that O'Brian refers to Françoise Gilot's book as "a bore," a comment I find both untrue and unfair.

Toulouse-Lautrec

Toulouse-Lautrec: A Life, Julia Frey, Phoenix (a division of Orion Books), London, 1995; first published in Great Britain in 1994 by Weidenfeld and Nicolson.

Gardens

The Garden Lover's Guide to France, Patrick Taylor, Princeton Architectural Press, 1998. Of the more than one hundred private and public gardens featured in this paperback volume, nineteen are in the Southwest. While I personally would prefer more historical and background information about each garden highlighted, visitor information and servicable maps are included, as well as color photographs of each garden. There is also a glossary of French garden terms at the back of the book.

Design and Decorating

At Home in France: Eating and Entertaining with the French, Christopher Petkanas, foreword by Marie-Helene de Rothschild, photographs by Jean-Bernard Naudin, Phoenix Illustrated, London; first published in 1990 by George Weidenfeld and Nicolson, London, distributed in the U.S. by Sterling Publishing Company. All about *l'art de recevoir,* the art of receiving or enter-taining as practiced by the French. Though recipes are included, this is a cook-book/lifestyle book unlike any other. Petkanas, who writes for *Travel + Leisure,* presents eighteen individuals or families who are famous for their *recevoir* hospitality, three of whom entertain in the Southwest.

Country Houses of France, Barbara and Rene Stoeltie, Taschen, 1999.

French Provincial Furniture, Robin Ruddy, Schiffer Publishing, London, 1998.

Really Rural: Authentic French Country Interiors, Marie-France Boyer, Thames and Hudson, 1997.

Shopping/Les Souvenirs

When I'm looking for singular gifts, including culinary items, I've enjoyed con-sulting *The Riches of France: A Shopping and Touring Guide to the French Provinces,* Maribeth Clemente, St. Martin's Press, 1997. This is the most thorough book I've seen on the subject, and there are separate chapters on Languedoc-Roussillon (which includes the Cévennes, the Hérault, and what the author refers to as Catalonia, which includes Collioure and other French towns near the Spanish border), and the Southwest (which includes the Pays Basque, Bordeaux, the Dordogne, Agen, Albi, Toulouse, Roquefort, Cordes-sur-Ciel, Laguiole, and Millau). I have referred to this book for at least half a dozen regions of France, and Clemente's recommendations have proven exceptionally helpful in searching for unique gifts for business colleagues, friends, and family.

Travel Anthologies, Journals, and Other Good Things

~Before-the-euro coin bracelet. I will be eternally grateful to my good friend Lorraine for the gift of a one-of-a-kind bracelet featuring an assortment of coins from all the countries that adopted the euro in 2002. Lorraine knows that I have been a nut for coins (and subway tokens) for many years, so when she saw this unique bracelet, she knew it had my name all over it. It's designed by Peggy Huyn Kinh, who, as I write this, is *directrice artistique* of ready-to-wear and accessories for Balmain. According to an article in *Madame Figaro,* Kinh's talents have also been recognized at Celine and Patou, and she now has her own boutique in Paris at 11 Rue Coëtlogon, 75006 (33.1/42.84.83.83; fax .42.84.83.84; info@phk.fr). The coin bracelet (which features the original coins, not facsimiles, so they are of differing size and weight) was designed in sterling silver. I do not wear silver as well as I wear gold and brass, so I took mine to a jeweler in New York City's Diamond District and asked her to transfer some of the coins, together with some favorites I'd collected, to a gold link bracelet. Whether the bracelet is silver or gold, it's a creative memento of francs, lire, pesetas, and so on, and each time I wear mine, I am bombarded with compliments. I have been stopped on the street several times by passersby inquiring where I bought it.

~Editions Clouet/Avenue A Cards, Inc. My intern, Wing Mai Sang, discovered this wonderful shop at New York's annual Bastille Day street festival. On our visit to the store, we found a selection of French travel posters, postcards, notecards, tin boxes and plaques, and calendars, many of which feature Southwestern destinations. These are not vintage or antique editions, but many are worthy of being framed. The owners, who are French, are happy to help you find what you're looking for and they have a healthy mail-order business. The store is located at 117 West 26th Street, New York, N.Y. 10001; 212-352-3110; fax: -1477; www.ediclouet.com.

~*Entrez: Signs of France,* photographs by Steven Rothfeld, text by André Aciman, Artisan, a division of Workman Publishing Company, 2001. Open the "doors" of this book, and you enter the world of France itself, "the France the French know best and love best, their private France, the one they grow up with and have pictures of and instantly turn the clock to when no one's looking, the France they'd like nothing better than to hand over to their children in the twenty-first century, the way it was just barely handed over to them after two world wars from those who inherited it from the nineteenth century—a France that, for all its turmoil at home and elsewhere, and for all the changes brought on by the Information Age and the Age of Anxiety, has managed to safeguard the daily rhythm and precious rituals of its day-to-day life, a France that always seems to trust it will be there tomorrow, a France that is always open for business and infallibly closes at very set hours." A number of the signs featured here are to be found in the Southwest—in Bordeaux, Nîmes, Sarlat, Perpignan, Figeac, and elsewhere.

~*French Dreams,* photographs by Steven Rothfeld, introduction by Richard Reeves, Workman Publishing Company, 1993. With writings by the likes of Wharton, Balzac, Nerval, Baudelaire, James, Colette, and Stein to accompany the dreamy photos by Rothfeld, this book is a special treat and makes a nice gift for your favorite Francophile. The images—handmade Polaroid transfers—are not the predictable pictures one sees in so many other books on France. (Many seem to have been taken in the Midi.)

~Mediterraneo (On the Backroads) is a line of truly unique and beautiful desk calendars, notecards, and postcards that evoke aspects and images of the Mediterranean that I've never seen elsewhere. I absolutely *love* these goods, and if you are passionate about the Mediterranean (I presume you are, or you wouldn't be reading this book), you will, too. In addition to the pan-Mediterraneo line, there are individual lines featuring Tuscany and Provence as well as gorgeous travel documentaries and a compact disc entitled *Mosaic,* featuring solo guitarist Cole McBride. (McBride's music combines classical, Spanish, and original compositions; he absorbed the music of Asia, Africa, and the Middle East and studied flamenco guitar in Seville.) The founders of Mediterraneo, Kate Ryan and James O'Mara, have traveled extensively around the Mediterranean, and I feel we are kindred spirits, even though we've never met (yet). I hope the O'Mara and Ryan team never tire of sharing their views and sensibilities with us. Contact information: www. onthebackroads.com, 800-711-3224; 604-925-8330.

~Scarf of the Bordeaux or Southwest vineyards of France. If you like maps and scarves, you'll fall for this nifty line of silk scarves as hard as I did. Silk Road Marketing has created a variety of scarves—in three sizes, 11 by 11 inches, 17 by 17, and 21 by 21—that reproduce maps of cities, regions, and countries around the world, many of them Mediterranean destinations. According to Silk Road, maps reproduced on silk were originally used by the Allies during World War II. They were easy to hide, lightweight, and water-resistant, all qualities that are equally good for travelers. I discovered the line at a store in New York's SoHo neighborhood, Cité, located at 100 Wooster Street, between Prince and Spring, 212-431-7272, but scarf fans may contact the company directly in Montreal at 514-272-9516; www.microsoie.com.

~*Traveler's Journal* (Peter Pauper Press) and *Voyages* (Chronicle Books) are my two current favorite journals. They're spiral-bound, which I like because the pages lie flat. *Traveler's Journal* features five clear plastic sleeves at the back for ticket stubs, photos, receipts, and the like (brilliant). *Voyages*—a bigger journal measuring about 8½ by 11 inches—features an elastic band that wraps around the book from top to bottom (not quite as good as plastic sleeves, but the band helps to keep loose stuff inside).

~*Traveller's Literary Companion: France,* John Edmondson, Passport Books, 1997. This is one book in a series that explores the relationship between writers and places, and it includes extracts from literary works; maps; biographies of the writers; a town-by-town guide to each *département* highlighting writers' houses and museums and anything of literary interest; and a list of recommended novels, plays, and poetry. Each chapter represents a region of France, so readers are led all around the country and introduced to French writers and other writers who wrote in France. With numerous black-and-white photos of writers, there is no other book like this for literary enthusiasts.

~*Travels With Alice,* Calvin Trillin, Avon, 1989. Not all of the fifteen essays in this witty and entertaining collection are about the Southwest or even France, but I couldn't resist including it here because Trillin is on my short list of favorite writers. "Hanging Around in Uzès," "Full Basket," and—my favorite—"Damp in the Afternoon" are the only three pieces with the South of France (broadly defined) as backdrop, but it doesn't matter: Trillin is irresistible and a traveling companion *par excellence.*

additional credits

Practical Information: Polly Platt, *Savoir Flair! 211 Tips for Enjoying France and the French,* Distribooks International, 2000.

The Kiosk—Points of View: A. J. Liebling, *The Road Back to Paris,* Modern Library, 1997; Paragon House, 1988.

Bordeaux and Aquitaine: Freda White, *Ways of Aquitaine,* Faber and Faber, 1968.

Basque Country: Mark Kurlansky, *The Basque History of the World,* Walker & Co., 1999; Penguin, 2001.

The Dordogne and the Lot: Henry Miller, *The Colossus of Maroussi,* New Directions, 1988.

Corners of the Midi-Pyrenees: Alexis Lichine, *The Wines and Vineyards of France,* Alfred A. Knopf, 1979.

Languedoc-Roussillon: Brian Catlos, *The Rough Guide to Languedoc and Roussillon,* Rough Guides, 2001.

Flavors and Tables of the Southwest: Vicky Jones, *Dordogne Gastronomique,* Abbeville, 1994, and Waverly Root, *The Food of France,* Alfred A. Knopf, 1970; Vintage, 1992.

Good Things, Favorite Places: Betty Lou Phillips, *French by Design,* Gibbs Smith Publishers, 2000.

With the exception of six photographs that appear on pages 118, 244, 330, and 494, which were taken by the author, all other photographs in this book were kindly provided by the Aquitaine and

THE JOURNEY HAS JUST BEGUN

Don't miss the other books in Barrie Kerper's Collected Traveler series. Each is a rich source of literary delight and practical travel advice.

Paris: The Collected Traveler
0-609-80444-8
$16.00 ($25.00 Can)

Central Italy: The Collected Traveler
0-609-80443-X
$16.00 ($25.00 Can)

Provence: The Collected Traveler
0-609-80678-5
$16.00 ($24.00 Can)

Morocco: The Collected Traveler
0-609-80859-1
$16.00 ($24.00 Can)

Northern Spain: The Collected Traveler
0-609-80978-4
$17.00 ($26.00 Can)

Venice: The Collected Traveler
0-609-80858-3
$17.00 ($26.00 Can)